The Wild Flower Key

THE
WILD FLOWER
KEY

*A guide to plant identification in
the field, with and without flowers*

*Over 1400 species
compiled and described by*
Francis Rose

Illustrated by
**R.B. Davis, Lura Mason, Norman Barber
and Judith Derrick**

FREDERICK WARNE

Published by
FREDERICK WARNE (PUBLISHERS) LTD : LONDON
1981

To
PAULINE

While all the information in this book is believed to be true and
accurate, neither the author nor the publisher can accept any legal
responsibility for any errors or omissions that may have occurred.

Cased Edition: ISBN 0 7232 2418 8
Limp Edition: ISBN 0 7232 2419 6

Text filmset by Tradespools Ltd, Frome.
Colour reproduction and printing by
L. Van Leer & Co Ltd, Holland.
1522·1280

CONTENTS

INTRODUCTION

It has been a tremendous task single-handed to compile a popular flora in simple language of the British Isles and Western Europe, in which about 1450 species are mentioned, over 1400 fully described in the main text, and about 1000 illustrated. The degree of coverage that I have provided, for the British Isles and for Western Europe respectively, is set out on pp 9–10. Whereas I aimed to cover all native and long-established introduced flowering plants of the British Isles (except for highly critical groups, and the Grasses, Sedges and Rushes), it was not possible to include all the very rare natives of Western Europe that are absent this side of the Channel. I decided to use as criteria for inclusion (i) all species that I have seen *in situ* in northwest Europe, within the defined area; (ii) other species which, although I have not seen them in the field, are, according to national European floras, sufficiently frequent locally, or conspicuous, to be likely to be found by users of this book on field excursions or on holiday in northwest Europe. For example, several very rare plants that occur just across the Loire into Brittany, or very rarely in West Germany, are **not** included. For reasons of space it unfortunately proved impossible to deal **comprehensively** in this book with the Grasses, Sedges and Rushes.

With a few exceptions, dictated mainly by considerations of space, I have followed the sequence of families adopted in *Flora of the British Isles*, by A.R. Clapham, T.G. Tutin, and E.F. Warburg, Cambridge University Press, 2nd edition, 1962 (hereafter cited as CTW). Because this remains the most recent and readily available standard British flora, I have, on the advice of the Botanical Society of the British Isles, also in the main followed its usage for scientific names. The authorities of scientific names are not given in my book – they are as in CTW. Where names in *Flora Europaea*, by T.G. Tutin and others, Cambridge University Press, 5 vols, 1964–80, differ, these are given in my text in brackets, as alternatives, either in the form *Galeobdolon luteum* (*Lamiastrum galeobdolon*) if both generic and specific names differ, or, eg, *Scrophularia aquatica* (*S. auriculata*) if only the specific name differs. In a very few cases, following advice, there has seemed to be good reason for adopting *Flora Europaea* names; eg, *Hieracium pilosella* of CTW is cited as *Pilosella officinarum* because it is quite clear that this plant should not be regarded as a member of the genus *Hieracium*.

English names given in the main text (and added for species mentioned in the Vegetative Keys to plants not in flower but not elsewhere in the book) mainly follow *English Names of Wild Flowers* by J.G. Dony, C.M. Rob, and F.H. Perring, Butterworth's, for the BSBI, 1974. Any deviations from it either follow CTW or reflect my personal judgement.

Finally I would like to acknowledge the ideas and inspiration I have obtained from studying the keys, descriptions and illustrations in a number of works, particularly: CTW; *The Concise British Flora in Colour*, by W. Keble Martin, Ebury Press and Michael Joseph, 1968; 'Water Plants' by S.M. Haslam, C.A. Sinker, and P.A. Wolseley, in *Field Studies*, vol 4, 1975; *The Wild Flowers of Britain and Northern Europe*, by Richard and Alastair Fitter, illustrated by Marjorie Blamey, Collins, 3rd edition, 1978; *Den danske flora*, by E. Rostrup and C.A. Jørgensen, Gyldendal, Copenhagen, 1973; *Manuel de la Flore de Belgique*, by François Crépin, H. Desoer, Liège, 1928; *Collins' Pocket Guide to Wild Flowers*, by D. McClintock and R.S.R. Fitter, Collins 1956; *Flore complète portative de la France*, by G. Bonner and G. de Layens, Paris, c. 1910; *Further Illustrations of British Plants* by R.G. Butcher and M. Strudwick, Reeve, Ashford, 1930.

The keys are my own, but I could never have produced them without the background inspiration and ideas of many other people. Any errors are my own, however, and I hope that readers will inform me of them so that they can be corrected in any future reprints.

I would like to acknowledge the contribution of all those botanical colleagues and friends who have helped by the discussion of ideas on layout and contents, and by helping me check typescripts, proofs, etc; also in particular Bridget O'Donnell and Louise Nettleton for typing my manuscript – not always very easy to read; the editorial staff at Warne's for their excellent co-operation; and above all my wife Pauline, who has provided constant help and support in every way, and without whose encouragement the book would never have been written.

Francis Rose

THE SCOPE OF THIS BOOK

I THE AREA COVERED

The whole of the British Isles

Western Europe from the line of the Loire Valley northwards to include northern France and the Channel Islands; the whole of Belgium, Luxembourg, The Netherlands and Denmark; in West Germany the Rhine Valley from about Mainz to the Ruhr, Westphalia, Schleswig-Holstein and Lower Saxony, as far east as the border with East Germany. (The mountain areas of the Jura and the Vosges are excluded, although **most** of their species, except some non-British alpine plants, are in fact given.)

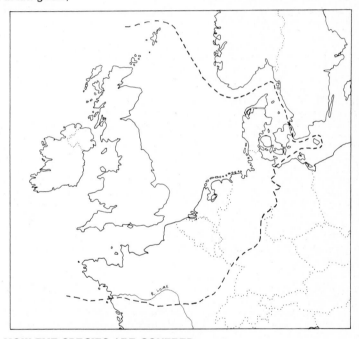

II HOW THE SPECIES ARE COVERED

Plants may be

(1) fully described and illustrated in the main text (in entries labelled both in text and on illustration A, B, C, D, etc)

(2) described in the main text by comparison with a similar fully described and illustrated species (labelled in the text Ai, Aii, Bi, Bii, etc)

(3) briefly described in the Keys to Genera, or in the Key to Commoner Grasses

(4) briefly described in the Vegetative Keys (to plants not in flower)

9

Note: every plant in the book appears in the index, under both its scientific and its English name (if the latter exists). Index references are normally to **main text** entries, but for a plant without such coverage, the reference is to the key to its genus, in which it features. Plants not strictly within the scope of this book (see below) may occur in the Vegetative Keys, to which their entries in the index will refer the reader.

III WHICH SPECIES ARE COVERED

In the British Isles ('Br Isles' in the text)

A Completely covered
   All the native and long-established introduced species of flowering plants (except for many Grasses, Sedges and Rushes, and for a very few 'critical' groups of species, see B below)
B Partially covered
   Well-established garden escapes
   The so-called 'critical' species among flowering plants, ie, very difficult similar species of the genera *Alchemilla* (Lady's-mantles), *Rubus* (Brambles) and *Sorbus* (Whitebeams) in the Rosaceae; the *Saxifraga hypnoides* agg in the Saxifragaceae; *Euphrasia* (Eyebrights) in the Scrophulariaceae; *Taraxacum* (Dandelions) and *Hieracium* (Hawkweeds) in the Compositae. In these groups either one 'aggregate' species is described, or a few examples are given (as for Hawkweeds, p 398) as some indication of the range of forms. Detailed treatment of these groups is beyond the scope of this book.
   Rushes, Sedges and Grasses. A full description is given of the characters of each of these families; a few representative species of them are illustrated; several others are described by comparison with those illustrated. In addition there is a Key to all the commoner British Grasses in flower; and a number of other commoner Rushes (Juncaceae), Sedges (Cyperaceae) and Grasses (Gramineae) are also covered in the Vegetative Keys, because they are sure to be found in the course of field studies.
   Ferns, Horsetails, Clubmosses, Quillworts (the vascular cryptogams or Pteridophyta). A few of these are included in the Vegetative Keys because they, like the Rushes etc, will be found during field studies and, if not 'keyed out', may cause confusion with flowering plants.
   Yew, Scots Pine and Juniper. These, the three native conifers (*Taxus baccata*, *Pinus sylvestris*, and *Juniperus communis*), occur in the Vegetative Keys, illustrated with small black and white drawings.

In 'Western Europe' ('Eur' in the text)

A Completely covered
   All common species also occurring in the British Isles
   All common species not occurring in the British Isles (all marked with an asterisk, they are either fully described and illustrated, or compared with a similar species that is illustrated)
B Partially covered
   Most of the rarer species (either described in the text or included in keys).

SPECIES TOTALLY EXCLUDED

   Garden plants, not well-naturalized in the wild
   Non-native (but widely introduced) conifers
   Mosses, Liverworts, Lichens, Algae and Fungi – the so-called 'lower plants'.

CONTENT OF THE BOOK

I THE ESSENTIAL FEATURES OF FLOWER STRUCTURE

The identification of plants is based upon variations in the shape and arrangement of their essential features. It is thus necessary for the reader to be familiar not only with the basic features of flower structure but also with some of the botanical terms used to name and describe the parts of stems, leaves, flowers and fruits. Although the book has been written in language as non-technical as possible, for brevity and precision it has been found necessary to use **some** botanical terms. Some of these terms are made clear in the section on the **Essential Features of Flower Structure**; all are explained in the **glossary** on p 22.

II THE GENERAL KEYS TO FAMILIES OF PLANTS IN FLOWER

These begin with a master key outlining (and illustrating by small black and white drawings) major, readily observed characters. A decision based on these will take the reader to one of a number of sub-keys, and hence ultimately to an entry that gives the name of the family (and very often of the genus) to which the plant belongs, and also the page number where text description of the family starts or where there is a key to the genera of the family.

III THE VEGETATIVE KEYS TO PLANTS NOT IN FLOWER

Nothing quite like these keys has been published before; arranged by habitats, they provide for the identification of plants on features other than flower structure and are for use at seasons when plants are not in flower (or have, perhaps, had their flowers grazed off by animals). The keys are prefaced with a comprehensive introduction and specific instructions for their use; and there is a short explanatory description of each of the habitats on which the keys are based. They should prove invaluable, not least for students obliged to work on ecological projects at a time of year when many plants are not in flower.

These keys (and all the other keys in this book) work basically on the so-called 'dichotomous' principle, by which at each numbered step the user is confronted with a choice between two clearly contrasting alternatives. Sometimes, to save space, at some particular stage in a key a choice has to be made from among 3, 4 (or, exceptionally, 5) different sets of contrasted descriptions. For detailed instructions on the use of the keys, see **How to Use This Book** below.

Normally only scientific names are used in the keys, but a plant's English name forms part of the main entry description of it. In the Vegetative Keys English as well as scientific names are given for those species **not** covered elsewhere. In these and in any other key, reference to a species with **no** page number added means that the plant is not described anywhere else in the book. For this reason, especially in some keys to the species within a genus, brief information about such a plant's distribution, habitat and frequency are supplied in the key concerned.

IV THE MAIN TEXT (pp 95–462)

In this part of the book are to be found full descriptions of the species, arranged according to their families. The English and scientific names of each family are given at the place where description of a family and/or of its members starts, and continue thereafter at the head of every main text page so long as descriptions of species in that family continue. Over 1400 species are here described; of these, about 1000 are illustrated, and are distinguished both in the text and on the illustration pages by capital letters, A, B, C, D, etc. The species **not** illustrated are described **by comparison** with the illustrated ones they most closely resemble, with reference either to diagnostic features of shape or parts, or to their size; they are labelled Ai, Aii, Bi, etc, the letter concerned denoting the described and illustrated species with which they are compared.

Features of a plant specially illustrated, such as the details of flowers, fruits, seeds, hairs on leaves, etc, are labelled Aa, Ab, Ba, etc. Most of the illustrations and details have a scale line beside them; those scale lines with no measurement indicated represent 1 cm length of the actual size of the plant concerned.

Normally illustration of a species occurs **opposite** the text description, on the same double-page spread; thus, for example, entry A on p 96 is illustrated by picture A on p 97. The reader may assume, therefore, that **normally** text on a left hand side page refers to illustrations opposite, on the right hand page. But occasionally text descriptions refer to an illustration on the previous page; eg, entry J on left hand p 128 refers to picture J on right hand p 127. Where this occurs, the reader is alerted by a **backward-pointing** arrow (◄) in the top left hand margin, as a reminder that the relevant illustration is **one page back**. A little further down such a page a new side-heading will introduce a fresh set of entries A, B, C, which refer, in the more normal way, to illustrations on the right hand page opposite. Where these begin, a **forward-pointing** arrow (►) has been placed to remind the reader that he or she no longer has to look back for the relevant illustration. These forward-pointing arrows also sometimes occur with A, B, C entries on a **right hand** (odd-numbered) page, and direct the reader to illustrations overleaf, on the **next** odd-numbered page. An example is the arrow on p 133, referring to illustrations on p 135.

In about three cases, near the bottom of a left hand page, A, B, C text begins that refers **not** to the illustration opposite, but to the one **overleaf, forwards**. This text (as on p 194) is marked with **double forward-pointing** arrows (▶).

The Form of the entries

Each entry in the main text follows a standard form:

    Code letter (and number, if the plant is not illustrated)

    English name

    Scientific name (in some cases alternative scientific names are also given, in brackets; the reasons for which this is done, and the authorities whose nomenclature is followed, are explained and cited in the Introduction).

    Description of the habit of the plant, with height and other measurements in metric units. There is a measure on the back cover of the book.

    Description of specific parts, ie, stem, leaves, inflorescence, flower structure, and fruits. **Measurements denote length** unless otherwise stated. They may indicate (a) the range of normal variation, eg '5–8 mm'; (b) an average, eg '5 mm', in which case some variation must be expected in plants studied; (c) the normal upper limit of size, eg 'to 10 cm'.

    Distribution and frequency of occurrence. These are given separately for the British Isles and for 'Europe' if they differ, and variations at more local levels, eg in counties or regions, are also often given. Distribution data are those of the plant **as a native**; if known to be introduced over part or all of its range, this is indicated by the abbreviation 'introd'. A region given in brackets following mention of introduction, is that of the plant's native place of origin, eg, 'NW France, Belgium, introd (S Eur)'.

    The plant's normal habitat

The time of flowering (and, with certain trees or shrubs, of fruiting). Months are cited 1–12; thus 'fl 4–6' shows that a plant flowers from April to June.

For **non-illustrated species** (Ai, Aii, etc) certain details of a plant's description, distribution, habitat and flowering times are sometimes **not** given. In such cases the reader should assume that they are the same as for the preceding and illustrated species (A) with which they are compared.

The illustrations

It was not the aim always to illustrate the **whole** of every plant. Where several plants are superficially very much alike (eg, especially, in the Umbelliferae), to have filled a page with complete illustrations of similar-looking plants would only have confused the reader. In these cases it was decided to illustrate **one** plant fairly fully, and merely to show the details (often enlarged) in which the other illustrated species **differ** from it. Sometimes it has been considered enough to show that a stem is square instead of round, or a fruit narrowed to its tip instead of rounded. By following this plan of illustration it has been possible to leave some space between the individual drawings, so that they are easier to distinguish and study. Illustrations are labelled A, B, C, etc, to link them with the relevant text descriptions. Drawings labelled Aa, Ba, etc are features of plants A or B respectively.

The Keys to genera and species

Interspersed with the text entries are keys that closely relate to them. These are of two kinds, keys to genera within a family, and to species within a genus. The former are always given for the larger families (ie, those with five or six genera or more); but for smaller families the features of the different genera are adequately distinguished in the general introductory description of the family. Keys to species are, again, given only for the larger genera.

Family keys normally occur at the beginning of the section of pages devoted to the family concerned; keys to species of the larger genera sometimes precede (or sometimes follow by a few pages) the text entries to which they refer (but a page reference to them is always given with the main entries). There is an indexed list (p 463) of all keys within the main text.

HOW TO USE THIS BOOK

I USE OF A LENS

Before setting out to look for plants or to examine a specific plant, equip yourself with a **good quality** × 10 pocket lens, preferably one with a field of view at least 12 mm across. Such lenses can be bought at most opticians' or optical shops. Do not be satisfied with a weaker magnification or with a plastic lens, with which you will be able to see very much less detail. Practise using the lens – you will find that in order to see properly, you need to hold it **very close** both to your eye and to the object you are examining. Keep the lens clean, inside and out (all good lenses can easily be unscrewed for this purpose). Clean the lens with a **soft** tissue only, and breathe on the glass first, or you may scratch it. When out of doors **always** carry the lens hanging round your neck on a string, or you will inevitably lose it!

II UNDERSTANDING BOTANICAL TERMS AND FLOWER STRUCTURE

Although the language in this book has been kept as simple as possible, **some** technical terms have had to be used, and are explained in the glossary on p 22. Also, identification of plants in flower depends very largely on their flower structure, and it is **essential** to understand it. If you are not already familiar with these features, read first the section, **Essential Features of Flower Structure**, on p 16.

III UNDERSTANDING AND USING THE KEYS

All the keys in this book work basically on the dichotomous principle, by which at each numbered step you are confronted with a choice between two contrasting alternatives (or sometimes between 3, 4, or even 5 different sets of descriptions). A key may start

1 Petals 4 .... **2**
  Petals 5 .... **6**

this means that if your plant has four petals, you proceed to figure **2** on the left hand side of the key, and then make a further choice between the alternatives given there. But if your plant has five petals, you go instead to figure **6** on the left, lower down the key, and study its alternatives. After further choices you will eventually reach an entry which, together with the features established at earlier stages in the key (eg, 'petals 4') seems finally to describe your plant and which will give its name (or that of its family and perhaps genus if you are using the General Keys).

The example 'Petals 4' was very simple. In many cases, because plants may vary in so many features, more than one character (sometimes three or four) may be given, eg

1 Petals 4 – lvs opp – stem hairy.. **2**
  Petals 5 – lvs alt – stem hairless **6**

if a **majority** of the characters agrees with your plant, then proceed to the number indicated.

Because some plants are so variable, and also because some features can be misinterpreted, some plants may 'key out' twice or even three times in the same key. If you, in effect, 'miss' a species at first (perhaps because your specimen is atypical) you thus have a chance of reaching it again further on in the key.

If you have had no experience of using keys, and they perhaps at first appear too complicated to tackle, practise using them as indicated above, but at first on plants whose names you already know, such as a Daisy, Dandelion, or Buttercup, or with a large simple flower whose parts are easy to see, such as a Daffodil or Dog Rose. If you are really stuck, try looking for an illustration that seems to match your species and then work backwards – read the text description and, if it seems to fit, try using the key to reach it. In this way you will gain confidence and experience in the use of the keys.

IV   PROCEDURE FOR IDENTIFICATION OF PLANTS IN FLOWER

If you have no idea to what family (or, still less, genus) your plant belongs (or only a very hazy idea), **(1)** go **first** to the General Keys to the families for plants in flower (p 30). **(2)** Start with the Master Key, which outlines major, readily observed characters and provides small black and white illustrations of them. **(3)** Choosing the major character that agrees with your plant, turn then to the sub-key indicated, and work through it (see **Understanding and using the keys**, above). The sub-key should take you eventually to the right family (or, very often, because some families are more difficult to define in a phrase or by only one or two characters than are genera, to a **genus** within a family). **(4)** Turn then to the page number given in the key (which is that where description of family or genus in the main text **begins**). **(5) First** read carefully the general description of the family; **(6)** if it agrees with your plant, **then** work through the family key (if there is one) to find (or to confirm) the correct genus; **(7) then** go through the genus key (if there is one) to find the correct species. **(8)** If the family (or genus) is a small one of only one or a few species, go straight to the description of the genus, and then to those of the one or more species that follow.

(9) Read the description **very** carefully, paying attention to the details of stem and leaves, as well as those of flowers and fruit (although the dimensions of the former are **much more** variable than those of the latter, and are therefore of less use in identification). If necessary, look up any technical terms in the glossary (p 22) and any abbreviations or symbols in the list on p 20 (they will soon all become familiar). **(10)** If the description seems to agree with your plant, then (and **only** then) turn to the illustration to **confirm** that you have identified your plant correctly. Should the plant concerned be a non-illustrated Ai or Bii species, look at illustration A or B respectively.

(11) If the description and illustration do **not** match your plant, work backwards to find where you may have gone wrong. Provided you have observed your plant accurately, you are unlikely to be very far away, and you will probably find the correct species among adjacent text descriptions and illustrations. Always pay more attention to **shape** and **size** of flower parts than to their **colour** – colours of flowers can often vary, and thus be misleading.

If you already have some knowledge of plants, and you think you know the family (or genus) of your plant, use the index to find the main text entries on that family or genus. Then first read carefully the general **description of the family or genus**. If your plant seems certainly to belong there, use the keys to the family and its genera (if there are any large enough to have needed keys) to find the specific description of your plant. If the family or genus is a small one, go straight to the description of the genus and then to that of the species.

Now continue from stage **9** outlined above.

V   PROCEDURE FOR IDENTIFICATION OF PLANTS NOT IN FLOWER

If the plant you wish to name is not in flower, turn to p 48 for the introduction and instructions for use of the Vegetative Keys to plants not in flower.

THE ESSENTIAL FEATURES OF FLOWER STRUCTURE

The accompanying drawing illustrates in simple form the structure of an imaginary flower of no particular species, with its parts clearly labelled. Flowers are very varied in form, and it should be remembered that some of the parts shown in the drawing may be missing in some species, or even in some of the flowers of a species; such points are covered in the text where they apply. However, in most cases all the parts illustrated are present, though of varied form; so this illustration serves to show in a general way the relative position and sequence of the parts normally present.

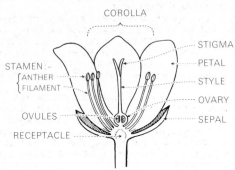

It is important to remember at the outset that flowers are the sexual reproductive organs of plants, and contain male and female organs; reproduction is the real *raison d'être* of flowers. The amazing variation that exists in flower form and structure is in fact connected with the diverse ways in which evolution has achieved cross-pollination mechanisms, either by various insects, or by the wind.

The flower-stalk normally has at its apex a swelling known as the **receptacle**, to which the parts of the flower are attached. This may be convex, or a concave cup.

The outermost whorl of flower parts, known as the **calyx**, is composed of a number of usually leaf-like structures, individually called the **sepals**, whose normal function is to protect the inner parts of the flower in the bud stage. (In some species the calyx is absent, or, as in some members of the Daisy family, represented only by a ring of hairs, the **pappus**, which later becomes a parachute for seed dispersal.)

Within the calyx, the next whorl, the **corolla**, is composed of leaf-like parts, normally coloured, called the **petals**. Their function in most flowers is to make the flower visually attractive to pollinating insects. They may secrete nectar at their bases or in special spurs, and also may have scent-producing glands, usually at their bases. In wind-pollinated flowers the corolla may be inconspicuous or absent.

Sometimes the sepals are joined together into a **calyx-tube**, and the petals may be joined together into a **corolla-tube**. In such cases the number of the parts can, however, usually be counted from the number of lobes or teeth on the tip of the tube.

The numbers of sepals and petals, and, indeed, of the inner parts, are of great importance in identification; also very significant is the point whether they are free or conjoined. For example, in the Buttercup family (Ranunculaceae) all the parts of the flower are free and separate, while in the Bellflower family (Campanulaceae) the calyx and corolla are both in tubular form; in the Daisy family (Compositae) even the stamens (see below) are joined into a tube. Sometimes the sepals and petals are identical in form and colour; then they are termed collectively a **perianth**, as in the Lily family (Liliaceae).

In some families, eg, those of Dead-Nettles (Labiatae), Peaflowers (Leguminosae) and Orchids (Orchidaceae) the sepals and petals are not in regular symmetrical whorls, but are modified to form flowers of **irregular** form, symmetrical only about one axis from front to back. Such flowers usually have one, or more, petals enlarged to form a **lip** at the front and a **hood** or arched structure at the back. These flowers are highly adapted to visits by special kinds of insects; the lip forms a landing platform for the insects, while the hood at the rear forms a roof that protects the sexual organs of the flower from rain. The form of such flowers may even be such as to permit only certain kinds of insects to enter. Peaflowers can be seen to have a **keel** of two lower petals in front, partially joined together, two **wings**, one on either side, and a **standard** at the back.

Within the flower are its reproductive organs. Working from the outside towards the flower's centre, there are first the **stamens**, called collectively the **androecium**. These vary in number, but each stamen consists of a stalk or **filament** and a head or **anther**. The anther contains two or more pollen sacs. The **pollen** consists of microscopic grains – copious and dust-like in wind-pollinated flowers, less plentiful and sticky in insect-pollinated flowers – which contain the male sexual nuclei or **gametes**.

Next there is the female organ of the flower, the **gynaecium**. This comprises a number of parts called **carpels**, which are quite separate in Buttercups but fused together in most families. In a normal fused gynaecium three parts can usually be distinguished. First, at the base, the **ovary**, a little case of one or more **cells**, which contains tiny **ovules**, each holding a single egg. Above the ovary is the stalk-like **style**, which may be single or multiple, and at the tip of each style is a **stigma**, the receptive surface for the pollen.

When pollen is transferred by insects, or wind, to a stigma at the right stage to receive it, each pollen-grain germinates, forming a microscopic tube which grows down inside the style to reach the ovules and their eggs. The male nucleus travels down the tube and fuses with the female nucleus in the egg, and the fertilized egg can then grow into an **embryo**, which, with its coverings, becomes a seed. In time the ovary becomes a seed-box, or fruit.

For purposes of identification the number of carpels is important, and also whether or not they are fused together. In the Buttercup family the carpels are all quite separate, each with its tiny ovary, single short style and stigma on top; in this family they are easy to count, but usually of a large, indefinite number. In most families, where the carpels are fused, their number can be determined either by counting the number of stigmas, or of styles, if these are separate, or else the number of cells in the ovary. The simplest way to see these is to cut (with thumbnail or penknife) a cross-section of the ovary and examine it with a good hand lens. In some plants, however, it is difficult to count the carpels; in such cases this feature is not used in this book.

Finally, the ovary (in those families where the carpels are fused) may be **superior** or **inferior**. A superior ovary is attached to the receptacle above the corolla-whorl and stamens; an inferior ovary has the calyx and the corolla arising from its top, so that it can be seen below the flower in side view. This character is important, for example, in distinguishing the Campanulaceae, with inferior ovaries, from the Gentianaceae (Gentian family), with superior ovaries. Similarly, the Liliaceae have superior ovaries, and the Iridaceae (Iris family), inferior ones.

In general the families described in the earlier part of the main text have free, regular parts and superior ovaries; families next described have the corollas in the form of tubes; later still are irregular two-lipped flowers; then flowers with inferior ovaries; finally, among the Dicotyledons, the Compositae, with tiny flowers with tubular corollas and inferior ovaries massed into heads. The last part of the book covers the Monocotyledons, which usually have their flower parts in threes, rather than in fives or fours as in the Dicotyledons, and usually have parallel-veined leaves.

Inflorescences   Flowers may be borne singly, that is, they are **solitary**, as in the Primrose and Daffodil, or they may be grouped together in various ways into an **inflorescence**. The various forms of inflorescence mentioned in the text (**cyme**, **raceme**, **spike**, **umbel**, **panicle**, **corymb**) are defined in the glossary, as are the leaves found in an inflorescence (**bracts** and **bracteoles**). A final word may, however, be said about the peculiar inflorescences of the Compositae and the Dipsaceae (Teasel family), in which the flowers are grouped into a head (**capitulum**) of unstalked tiny **florets** on a common receptacle. The whole may be mistaken for a single flower, especially if, as in the Daisy, there are symmetrical **ray-florets** at its outer edge which look like petals. Examination with a lens will, however, show the structure of the numerous tiny florets, each with a corolla and tube of stamens, with a corolla and a style, or with both stamens and style.

COLLECTION AND CONSERVATION

All users of this book are most strongly urged **never to dig up wild plants.** It is in any case illegal to do so without the landowner's permission (see note on the Conservation of Wild Creatures and Wild Plants Act, 1975, at the front of the book). For this reason no attempt has been made here to describe underground features of plants as aids towards identification. You are also asked **never** to pick any plant that might possibly be a rare species, even if it is locally abundant in a particular spot. Whenever possible, take this book to the plant in the field instead of taking the plant home to the book. Sometimes a single flower or floret may need to be picked to check internal structures; but please do this with great care and discretion. However, in order to study the structure of any plant growing floating or submerged in water, it will be necessary to collect a small piece of it; provided the specimen is returned to the water within a few minutes, it will usually continue to grow.

There is no objection to making a small reference collection of really common plants. Even so, the essential parts should be collected only sparingly. Normally one good basal leaf, one or two stem-leaves, a flower or inflorescence, and perhaps a fruit should be enough. These can be carefully pressed in absorbent paper – most ordinary newspaper is suitable – and when dry the specimens of each species can be glued onto stiff paper and labelled.

To help conserve our native flora, all readers are urged to join their local Conservation or Naturalists' Trust; there are now such organizations covering nearly every part of the British Isles and several parts of Western Europe. These bodies will be able to help you with information, lectures and field excursions. It may also be useful to join a local Natural History Society (details are usually available from a public library or local museum). If you are really keen, you may wish to join the Botanical Society of the British Isles, which welcomes membership from all those, whether beginners or experts, who are really interested in wild plants. To do this, contact the Hon General Secretary, Botanical Society of the British Isles, c/o Botany Department, British Museum (Natural History), Cromwell Road, London SW7 5BD.

ABBREVIATIONS, SYMBOLS AND CONVENTIONS

Scientific descriptions
agg   aggregate: a group of 2 or more very similar species, not separated in this book
sp   species (singular)
spp   species (plural)
ssp   subspecies (singular)
sspp   subspecies (plural)

Life of the plant
ann   annual
bi   biennial
per   perennial

Features of the plant and adjectives descriptive of them
alt   alternate, alternating
fl (s)   flower (s)
fr (s)   fruit (s)
infl (s)   inflorescence (s)
lf (lvs)   leaf, leaves
lft (s)   leaflet (s)
±   more or less
opp   opposite (of branches, or of leaves)
-   to (eg, oval-obovate denotes oval to obovate; Devon-Hants denotes Devon to Hants)
v   very

Measurements
cm   centimetre (s)
m   metre (s)
mm   millimetre (s)

Distribution
Br Isles   British Isles
E   East, Eastern
Eng   England
Eur   Europe (used restrictively, to denote to NW parts of Europe specifically covered
      by this book; this includes the Channel Islands, always regarded botanically as
      part of NW France)
Ire   Ireland (without political division)
N   North, Northern
S   South, Southern
W   West, Western
(Note: whereas, eg, 'NE' denotes Northeast, 'N, E' denotes North **and** East). Standard
abbreviations of English counties are used. It is botanical convention to follow the
names, divisions and boundaries of the counties as they were in about the mid-19th
century, before any modern changes.

Frequency
abs   absent
c   common
f   frequent
la   locally abundant
lc   locally common
lf   locally frequent

20

o occasional
r rare
rl rare locally
va very abundant
vc very common
vl very local
vla very locally abundant
vlc very locally common
vr very rare

Habitats and adjectives descriptive of them
ar arable
calc calcareous (ie, soil rich in lime, over chalk or limestone rock)
chk chalk
gd ground
gdns gardens
gslds grasslands
hbs hedgebanks
hds hedges
mds meadows
mt (s) mountain (s)
rds roads, roadsides
wa wasteland
wds woods or woodlands

Works of reference, and societies
BSBI Botanical Society of the British Isles
CTW *Flora of the British Isles* by A.R. Clapham, T.G. Tutin and E.F. Warburg, Cambridge University Press, 2nd edition, 1962.

ILLUSTRATED GLOSSARY

Alternate leaves

Arrow-shaped leaf

Awl-shaped leaf

Bract

Achene a little, one-seeded nutlet formed from a single carpel, shed in fruit **without** opening to release the seed.

Agg(regate) species a group of v closely related species, in this book treated as one.

Alt(ernate) leaves leaves alternating up a stem, occurring first on one side, then on the other.

Annual a plant completing its life cycle in one year, germinating in autumn or spring, flowering, fruiting and dying by the following autumn.

Anther the little sac, usually two (or more) -celled, containing the pollen at the top of a stamen.

Arrow-shaped leaf a wide-based leaf, tapering to a point above, with two backward-directed pointed basal lobes.

Auricle a lobe or pair of lobes at the base of a leaf, clasping the stem.

Awl-shaped leaf a leaf tapering from a cylindrical base to a fine point.

Awn a bristle on the tip or back of a lemma or a glume (qqv) in grasses.

Axil the upper angle between a leaf and the stem from which it grows.

Axis the main stem running up through an inflorescence.

Base-rich of soils, rich in alkaline nutrients (especially calcium salts).

Berry a fleshy fruit containing one or more seeds, which do **not** have a stony inner coat around each seed (see also **Drupe**).

Biennial a plant living for two seasons, normally germinating in the first spring and that year only forming leaves; it flowers and fruits in the second season, and then dies.

Bifid forked or cleft in two.

Bog an area of waterlogged **acid** peat, usually with vegetation composed of *Sphagnum* moss species (which form the bulk of the peat) and of sedges, low shrubs of the Heath family etc.

Bract (1) a leaf with a flower in its axil.
(2) in Umbellifers, used for the whorl of small leaves at the base of a **main** umbel.

Bracteole (1) a tiny leaf on a flower-stalk without any flower in its axil. (2) in Umbellifers, the whorls of small leaves or bracts at the bases of the **secondary** or partial umbels.

Bulb an underground swelling at the base of a plant, eg, in a Daffodil, made up of overlapping layers of scales (which are actually fleshy leaf-bases).

Bulbil a small bulb, usually developed above ground in a leaf-axil or on a leaf edge, which can fall off and grow into a new plant.

Calyx the whorl of sepals in a flower (used collectively).

Calyx-tube the tube formed when the lower parts of the sepals are fused together.

Capitulum a dense head of **tiny** flowers **without** individual stalks (as in the Daisy and Teasel families), surrounded by an **involucre** (qv) of bracts.

Cladode

Clasping leaf

Corymb

Cyme

Dichasium

Capsule　a dry fruit that opens into two or more parts (valves), or by holes or a lid, to release the seeds.

Carpel　one of the units in the gynaecium (female organs) of a flower; carpels are either **free** from one another (as in a Buttercup), or **joined** together into an **ovary** (as in Poppy or Flax). Each carpel has a **style** (qv) at its tip.

Catkin　a spike of tiny flowers, usually all of one sex, ie, with either stamen- or carpel-bearing flowers, found mostly on trees and shrubs.

Cell　(1) a cavity, or cavities, within an ovary, in which are attached the **ovules** (qv).

(2) cavities in an anther, containing the pollen.

(3) the microscopic units of which all plants (and animals) are built up.

Cladode　a **leaf**-like structure which is really a flattened **stem** (shown by the fact that it may bear a flower, or flowers, on its surface in the axil of a bract – eg, Butcher's-broom).

Clasping leaf　a (usually stalkless) leaf with basal lobes that project backwards and appear to clasp the plant's stem.

Compound leaf　a leaf divided into **separate** leaflets, **without** any flange joining them together along their common stalk (see also **Pinnate** and **Palmate**).

Cordate leaf　a heart-shaped leaf (broad below, pointed above, with two rounded basal lobes).

Corm　a swollen rounded underground mass of solid tissue at the base of a stem, eg, in a Crocus, **not** (as in a bulb, qv) composed of layers of scales; each corm is of one year's formation, the next year's growth arising separately on top of it.

Corolla　the petals of a flower (used collectively).

Corolla-tube　the tube formed when the petals are fused together below.

Corymb　a raceme (qv) in which the outer flower-stalks are much longer than the inner ones, so that the flowers are all more or less at the same level in a flat-topped cluster (as in an umbel, qv, but in the latter all flower-stalks arise from a single point on the top of the stem).

Cotyledon　(1) one of the **pair** of first leaves of a seedling in Dicotyledons.

(2) the **single** first leaf of a seedling in Monocotyledons.

Cyme　an inflorescence in which the **terminal** flower opens **first**, followed in succession by lateral flowers growing from bract-axils lower down the inflorescence-stalk. Cymes may be **simple**, with the flowers along the side of a **single** stem, or **double** (a **dichasium**, qv).

Deciduous　a woody plant that drops its leaves in autumn (in Europe, at least), and which produces new leaves from buds the next spring.

Decumbent　a stem that lies on the ground but tends to turn upwards at its tip.

Dichasium　a **forked** cyme, with the **oldest** flower in the first fork (at the stem-head) and the **next** oldest flowers terminating the **opposite** side-branches; successive opposite pairs of branches arise below each terminal flower, and the process is repeated.

Dicotyledons　one of the two great sub-divisions of the flowering plants, with **two** first-leaves (cotyledons) on the germinating seedling. Dicotyledon leaves are usually net-veined.

23

Digitate leaf

Digitate leaf   a palmate (qv) leaf, the leaflets of which are narrow and finger-like.

Dioecious plants   those plants with male and female flowers on **separate** individual plants (only male flowers on some, only female on others).

Disc-floret   one of the **tubular** florets (qv) in a flower-head in the Daisy and Teasel families etc.

Distant   widely spaced-out.

Drupe   a fleshy fruit, resembling a berry, but with the seed inside enclosed in a **hard stony** case (like a plum or cherry).

Ellipsoid   the three-dimensional equivalent of elliptical (applied to solid objects such as fruits).

Elliptical   shaped like an ellipse (applied to flat objects such as leaves).

Entire leaf   a leaf **without** any teeth along its edge.

Epicalyx   an extra **calyx** (qv) of small bract-like leaflets below the true calyx.

Epichile   in the Helleborines (part of the Orchid family), the **outer** segment of the lip of a flower.

Entire leaf

Epiphyte   a plant sitting upon another (usually woody) plant, and ± attached to it but, unlike a parasite, obtaining no nourishment from its host.

Falls   the drooping outer perianth segments in an Iris flower.

Family   a natural group of genera, with certain important features of flower, fruit, and/or vegetative structure in common.

Fen   a plant community on base-rich, often alkaline and calcareous, peat, dominated, **not** by *Sphagnum* mosses and Heath family members (as in a bog), but by Dicotyledonous herbs, Sedges and Grasses, etc.

Fen carr   boggy woodland developed over fen by invasion of shrubs and trees.

Filament   the **stalk** of an anther, which with it comprises a **stamen**.

Floret   a small flower, especially in the flower-head of members of the Daisy and related families; or the individual tiny flower in Grasses, Sedges and Rushes.

Epicalyx

Flush   an area where water (usually ± base-rich) flows or seeps through the ground, making its vegetation often very different and much greener than that of the more acid, stagnant or drier surroundings (mostly found in mountains or moorlands).

Follicle   a dry fruit formed from a **single carpel**, splitting open across the top and then a little down one side.

Fruit   the dry or fleshy case, surrounding a plant's seeds, that is formed from the **ovary** (qv) wall.

Genus (pl genera)   a grouping of species with important features of flower, fruit, and sometimes vegetative characters in common.

Gland   (1) a sticky tip to a hair, or a sticky spot or small knob on a leaf, petal etc, that secretes viscous juice.

(2) the fleshy yellow bracts, oval or crescent-shaped, that alternate with the leafy bracts around the flower-clusters in Spurges.

Glume   (1) the **single** chaffy scale, or bract, at the base of an individual floret of a Sedge.

(2) the **pair** of chaffy scales at the base of a Grass spikelet.

Halberd-shaped leaf

Halberd-shaped leaf   a leaf (in Sheep's Sorrel and Halberd-leaved Orache) shaped like a late medieval pike-head.

Heath   an area of vegetation covered with dwarf shrubs of the

24

Heath family, Dwarf Gorse etc, on poor, acid, usually sandy and well-drained soil, or it may be damp (**wet-heath**).

Herb   a non-woody plant dying back each winter to an underground tuber, rhizome etc, **or** to a basal leaf-rosette, **or** (if an annual) lasting only one season.

Hypochile   in the Helleborines (part of the Orchid family), the (often cup-shaped) **inner** segment of the lip of the flower.

Inferior ovary   an ovary **below** the calyx and/or corolla (ie, the rest of the flower sits **on top** of it).

Involucre

Inflorescence   any **grouping** of flowers on a stem or in a leaf-axil etc.

Internode   the length of stem **between** the points where two leaves (or pairs of opposite leaves, or leaf-whorls) arise.

Introduced   a plant brought to a site or region by human agency, not necessarily intentionally (in distinction from a 'native' plant that has arrived by natural means).

Involucre   a whorl, collar or ruff of bracts at the base of a flower-head, or (less often) of a single flower.

Irregular flower   one which is **not** radially symmetrical, with all petals equal, but **only** symmetrical on either side of **one vertical plane**; usually with **either** one or more petals enlarged as a lip, **or** with both a top and a bottom lip.

Kidney-shaped leaf

Keel   (1) of a **flower**, in the Pea family, the two lower, partly-joined petals which form a shape like the keel of a boat.

(2) a keel-like flange running along the length of one side of a leaf; **or** the edge of a leaf folded lengthwise.

Kidney-shaped leaf   a leaf of rounded outline with the stalk in a notch between two rounded basal lobes.

Labellum   the lip of an Orchid flower.

Lanceolate leaf   a long narrow leaf, slightly wider below, gradually tapering to its tip (lance-shaped).

Latex   an opaque milky (or coloured) juice found in canals in certain plants.

Leaflets

Leaflets   the separate leaf-blades of a **compound** pinnate, palmate or trifoliate leaf.

Lemma   the **lower** of the two scales that surround or enclose the stamens and ovary of a Grass floret.

Ligule   the little flap present where the leaf-blade joins its sheathing base in Grasses and Sedges.

Linear leaf   a long, narrow, parallel-sided leaf, as in most Grasses.

Lip   the lower (and sometimes also the upper) lobe of the corolla (or sometimes calyx) of an **irregular** (qv) flower.

Marsh   an area of wet ground on mineral soil (**not** on peat).

Midrib   the main, central vein of a leaf.

Mucronate leaf-tip

Monocotyledons   one of the two great subdivisions of the flowering plants, with only **one** first-leaf (cotyledon) on the germinating seedling. Monocotyledon leaves are usually parallel-veined.

Mucronate   a leaf (or, possibly, a fruit), otherwise blunt or rounded, with a small, often **sharp point** at its tip.

Nectary   a structure (knob-like, pouch-like, or tubular) within a flower (sometimes on a petal-base) that secretes the nectar collected by insects.

Node   the point (swollen in grasses) on a stem where a leaf, a pair of leaves, or a whorl of leaves is attached.

Oblong leaf

Oblong leaf   a leaf about twice or three times as long as broad, and parallel-sided at least in the **central** part of the blade.

Obovate leaf

Ochrea

Oval leaves

Panicle

Perfoliate leaves

Pinnatifid leaf

Obovate leaf a leaf with its broadest part **above** the middle, tapering suddenly to its ± blunt tip, and more gradually to its base.

Ochrea (pl ochreae) the membranous, chaffy, translucent tubular **stipules** (qv), often with a fringed tip, in the Dock family.

Opposite leaves leaves arising in pairs, one opposite the other on either side of the stem.

Oval leaf a leaf ± egg-shaped in outline, about twice as long as broad.

Ovary the carpels of a flower collectively, especially when they are fused together forming a little case of one or several cells in which are attached the ovules. After pollination and fertilization the ovary develops into the **fruit**, and the ovules into **seeds**.

Ovoid (of solid objects) ± egg-shaped.

Ovules the tiny bodies attached inside a carpel or ovary, which each contain an egg; when fertilized, the ovules develop into seeds.

Palea the upper and thinner (usually transparent and membranous) of the two scales that surround or enclose the stamens and ovary of a Grass floret.

Palmate leaf a compound leaf (qv) with more than three leaflets arising together from the top of the leaf-stalk.

Palmately-lobed leaf a lobed leaf with the main veins all radiating from the top of the stalk.

Panicle a branched **raceme** (qv).

Pappus a crown of hairs or bristles, sometimes branched like feathers, that sit on top of the tiny fruits of some members of the Daisy and Valerian families; formed from the calyx, they may act as parachutes for wind-dispersal of the fruits.

Parasite a plant that derives all, or part of, its nourishment from another plant (the **host**), by means of suckers attached to the host's roots or stems. **Total** parasites usually have scale-like tiny leaves and no green chlorophyll; **partial** parasites have at least some green leaves.

Pedicel a stalk of an individual flower.

Peduncle a stalk of an inflorescence.

Perennial a plant that lives for more than two years at least.

Perfoliate leaf a leaf (or a pair of conjoined opposite leaves) forming a **ring** around a stem.

Perianth the collective term for the calyx and/or corolla segments or lobes, especially when calyx and corolla are indistinguishable in form and colour, or when there is only one whorl of segments.

Perianth segments the sepals and/or petals that make up the **perianth** (qv) of a flower (used mostly either when they are indistinguishable, or there is only one whorl).

Petal one of the **inner** whorl of floral leaves (usually white or coloured) that surround the stamens and/or carpels of a flower.

pH in simple terms, a measurement of the alkalinity or acidity of soil or water. pH7 is neutral; values above it are alkaline, below it (particularly **below** pH5 for **plants**) are acid. pH can be measured roughly with soil-testing kits available at some garden and chemist's shops.

Pinnate leaf a compound leaf with the separate leaflets arranged along the leaf-stalk, usually in opposite pairs, and often with a terminal leaflet as well.

Pinnatifid leaf a leaf ± deeply cut into pinnately-arranged lobes, but not cut right to its midrib, the lobes remaining connected

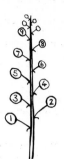

Raceme

Recurved sepals

Reflexed sepals

Simple leaf

by **at least** a narrow flange of leaf-blade bordering the midrib.

Pollen   minute yellow dust-like granules, containing the male sexual cells, that are produced inside the anthers of stamens. When pollen grains fall on a stigma (qv), they germinate to produce long but microscopic pollen-tubes which carry the male nuclei (the equivalent of sperms in animals) to the eggs to fertilize them.

Pollinium (pl pollinia)   a sticky mass of pollen grains cohering together within the anther of an Orchid (or a member of the Milkweed family); the entire pollinium can be transferred by insects to another flower.

Pome   the fleshy but firm fruit of an Apple or Pear, etc, its outer fleshy part, formed from the swollen cup-shaped receptacle of the flower, surrounding the gristly carpels in each of which are one or more seeds (pips).

Prickle   a sharp spine arising from the surface of a shoot or leaf.

Procumbent   lying loosely on the surface of the ground.

Raceme   a ± elongated inflorescence, in which the **lowest** flower opens first, and then the others **in sequence** towards the tip, which can continue to form new buds.

Ray-florets   the (usually) strap-shaped (qv) spreading florets found in some Compositae, occurring either around the **edge** of the flower-head (as in a Daisy) or forming the **whole** of the flower-head (as in a Dandelion).

Rays   the branches of an umbel.

Receptacle   the tip of the flower-stalk, to which all the floral parts (sepals, petals, stamens, carpels) are attached; it may be dome-shaped or conical (as in Buttercups); cup-shaped and hollowed out, with the carpels **within** the cup (as in many members of the Rose family); or a flat disc.

Recurved   **arched** backwards or downwards in a curve.

Reflexed   **sharply** (**not** in a gradual curve) bent backwards or downwards.

Regular flower   one which is **radially** symmetrical, with all petals equal.

Rhizome   a creeping underground stem, sometimes fleshy.

Root-leaves   basal leaves, ie, leaves arising from the **base** of the plant or of its ± erect stem; they sometimes (but not always) form a spreading **rosette**.

Runner   a stem creeping **above** ground, which can root at its tip, forming a new plant.

Salt-marsh   a marsh where the water is salt, usually from sea water flooding or seeping into it at high tide, but also (though rarely) beside salt springs inland.

Saprophyte   a plant, usually without green chlorophyll, which is **not** parasitic but nourishes itself on decomposing vegetable humus, usually through partnership with a fungus whose filaments are attached to its roots and spread out through the humus.

Sepal   one of the **outer** whorl of floral leaves (usually green) that surround the petals (corolla) of a flower; collectively, the term perianth (qv) may be used for either whorl, or for both whorls together.

Sessile   stalkless.

Shrub   a **woody** perennial branched from the base (**without one** main trunk, as in a tree), and usually not more than about 6 m tall.

Simple leaf   a leaf that is **not compound**, ie, not divided into leaflets; it may, however, be lobed or toothed.

Spadix a dense erect spike of florets found in the Arum family, usually with a **spathe** (qv). Its tip may be club-shaped, without florets (as in Lords-and-Ladies), or bearing florets to the tip (as in Sweet-flag).

Spathe a large bract (or pair of bracts) at the base of, wrapping round, or surrounding the inflorescences (especially in bud) of the Arum family, and of some members of the Lily, Daffodil and Iris families.

Spike

Species a population of individual plants, all of which closely resemble one another in **all important** features of structure, and are normally capable of cross-breeding **within** the population (though not always outside it). When breeding occurs with related plants **outside** the population of the species, the results are called **hybrids**, and are usually sterile.

Spike an unbranched raceme **without** stalks to the individual flowers.

Spikelet (1) in Sedges, the individual, often catkin-like spikes or racemes of florets, sometimes (but not always) all of one sex.

(2) in Grasses, the small ovoid or cylindrical spike-like stalked **units**, each comprising one or more florets, which collectively form the whole grass inflorescence.

Spoon-shaped leaf

Spoon-shaped leaf a leaf with a long narrow stalk-like lower part, suddenly widening into an oval, blunt tip (resembling a spoon or paddle).

Spur a cylindrical or conical, sometimes curved, hollow projection from the back or base of a petal or sepal, usually containing nectar.

Stamen one of the individual male organs of a flower, comprising the filament and anther (qqv).

Staminode a sterile or rudimentary stamen **without** a pollen-containing anther.

Standard (1) the rear petal in a flower of members of the Pea family.

(2) one of the erect inner perianth segments in an Iris flower.

Stem-leaves leaves (either alternate or opposite) arising from a plant's stem (as distinct from basal or root-leaves).

Stigma the (usually sticky) surface at the tip of a style, which receives the **pollen** (qv) and where the pollen grains are stimulated to germinate. A style may have one or several stigmas.

Stipules

Stipule a leaf-like or scale-like appendage at the **base** of a leaf-stalk; often a **pair** of them is present.

Stolon a runner, not necessarily forming a new plant at its tip.

Strap-shaped (of a leaf, petal, etc) flat, parallel-sided and blunt-ended.

Style the stalk-like structure at the tip of a carpel or on top of an ovary of several joined carpels, that bears on its tip the **stigma** (qv) or stigmas.

Superior ovary an ovary sitting **above** and **within** the whorls of stamens, petals and sepals, and which is **not** fused to them at all.

Thallus a plant body **not** separated into a distinct **stem** and **leaves**, as in Duckweeds (Lemnaceae), and in many lower plants such as Algae, some Liverworts and Lichens, etc.

Thorn a sharp-pointed woody structure, strictly speaking the tip of a modified branch or stem.

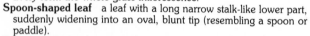

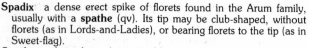

Trifoliate leaf

Trifoliate leaf a compound leaf with **three** leaflets only (as in Clovers).

Tuber   a **swollen** part of a root or underground stem, storing food.

Umbel   a ± flat-topped inflorescence, with several branches all arising from **one** point at the top of the main stem; it may be **simple** (composed of one whorl of unbranched branches only), or **compound** (when each branch **in turn** bears a similar 'secondary' or 'partial' umbel).

Vein   one of the thickened strands or lines visible in a leaf (or petal, etc), which contains the vessels or tubes that conduct water and food (as in the arteries and veins of the human body). Veins may be all ± parallel (as in most Monocotyledons) or in a branched network joining up again towards the leaf edges (as in most Dicotyledons).

Waste ground   disturbed, but unused or uncultivated ground (as alongside a new road, around an industrial area, on a heap of mine waste or in a quarry).

Whorled leaves   leaves arising three or more from a stem at the **same** level or point on it.

Wing   one of the two **side-petals** in members of the Pea family.

Winged stem   a stem with one or more broad **flanges** along its length.

Compound umbel

THE GENERAL KEY TO THE FAMILIES

MASTER KEY TO PLANTS IN FLOWER

1 Plants without fls, or submerged aquatic plants with minute, inconspicuous fls..................................
see Vegetative Key, p 48

Plants with fls present.. **2**

2 Plants with the individual fls, or florets, **v small** (3 mm wide or less, or if larger with a strap-shaped corolla like a Dandelion floret), grouped together in **v dense** heads, catkins, spikes, or clusters, with the individual stalks to each floret either abs or scarcely visible.. **3**

Plants with the individual fls of varied size, but each fl possessing a separate and clearly visible (but sometimes v short) fl-stalk of its own **5**

3 **Submerged** or **floating aquatic** plants with inconspicuous greenish or brownish fls .... **A**

Plants **neither** submerged **nor** floating in water (though they may be in marshy or boggy ground).. **4**

4 Individual fls, or florets, massed together into close **heads**, which may be either rounded, button-, disc-, or shaving-brush-shaped – all the florets stalkless and seated on a common **disc** or receptacle, which has a **collar** or **ruff** of lf-like **bracts** around it at its base – each **fl-head** with a definite stalk, and itself often superficially resembling a single fl... **B**

Individual tiny fls, or florets, massed into dense, simple, unbranched, cylindrical or ovoid **spikes** or **catkins**, these possessing a central **stalk** through its **length** to which the fls are attached .... **C**

Individual tiny fls or florets, grouped into dense, branched, often irregular, globular or rounded **clusters**, but **without** any collar or ruff of lf-like bracts around the base of the fl-cluster (though sometimes with one or two lf-like bracts) .... **D**

5 Individual fls **small** (5 mm or less across), grouped into **umbels**, in which the several fl-stalks **all** radiate from **one** point, like the ribs of an umbrella, on the tip of a stem – the umbels may be simple, or compound (an umbel of umbels) .... **E**

Individual fls of varied size, either solitary on the tip of a stem, or grouped into branched **infls** of various forms and shapes, but **never** with all fl-stalks radiating from **one** point as in an umbel **6**

6 Herbs without any green chlorophyll in lvs or stem – lvs reduced to **scales** .... **F**

Plants submerged or floating in water with inconspicuous greenish or brownish fls and lvs with green chlorophyll .... **A**

Green-lvd plants, **either** on dry **or** marshy ground, **or** water plants with **conspicuous** yellow or white fls.. **7**

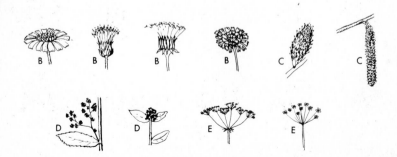

7 Fls **regular**, with the perianth segments or petals spreading out equally from the centre in a star, cup, or bell, and all of equal (or ± equal) length..**8**

Fls **irregular**, with obvious 'upper' and 'lower' sides to the fl, usually with an obvious lower lip and sometimes an upper lip as well – perianth segments or petals not all of equal length............**16**

Apparent fl like an Arum lily, with one v large 'petal' and a club-shaped 'style', the whole 15–30 cm long, in fact a bract (spathe) enclosing a spike-like infl within its base – lvs triangular to arrow-shaped, stalked, net-veined, 10–20 cm long............................**ARACEAE**, p 418 (*Arum*)

8 Lvs simple, in successive whorls of 4 or more along the stems – fls with 4–5-lobed corolla, **inferior** two-celled ovary, and calyx inconspicuous..**RUBIACEAE**, p 348

Lvs simple, in successive whorls of 3–6 – fls with a single six-lobed perianth and superior ovary
LILIACEAE, p 404 (*Polygonatum*)

Lvs alt, **or** in opp pairs (**or**, rarely, in whorls of 3), **or** all in a basal rosette, **or** in **one** whorl only some distance up stem **9**

9 Fls with a perianth comprising a distinct **calyx** and **corolla**, these differing markedly from each other in shape, colour and/or size...**10**

Fls with perianth of **one whorl** only, **or** of 2 or more whorls **similar** in shape, colour and size, **or** perianth **abs**...**14**

10 Fls with the petals **joined**, at least in their lowest part, to form a **corolla-tube**, which is usually lobed above..**13**

Fls with the petals **separate** from one another to their bases..**11**

11 Fls with the ovary **superior**...**12**

Fls with the ovary **inferior** ....**G**

12 Carpels and styles **free** and **separate** from one another, or almost so...**H**

Carpels or styles, or both, all **joined together** into a single ovary, or ovary apparently of one carpel only ....**I**

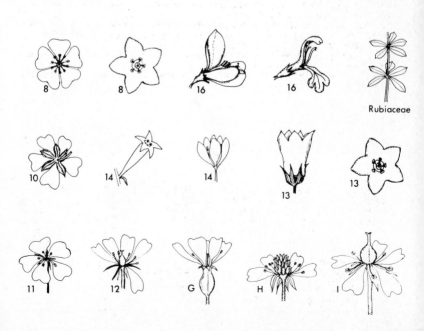

Rubiaceae

13 Fls with the ovary **superior**..J
    Fls with the ovary **inferior** ....K
14 Perianth coloured or white, of petal-like segments or lobes ....**L**
    Perianth either green, of sepal-like segments, or chaffy, or membranous, or scale-like, or abs..... **15**
15 Trees and **shrubs**.. **M**
    Herbs .... **N**
16 Petals **free**... **O**
    Petals **joined** below into a corolla-tube, with several lobes at its mouth ....**P**

A **Submerged or floating aquatic plants with inconspicuous, greenish to brownish fls** (in case of difficulty use also keys to aquatic plants not in flower, pp 80–81. If fls conspicuous, 5 mm or more wide, and coloured or white, continue from 7 in Master Key above)
  1 Plants consisting **either** of small, round or oval green discs, 3–10 mm across; **or** of pointed elliptical translucent green scales, 5–12 mm long, joined together by stalks, without distinction into stems and lvs, with one or more unbranched **roots** hanging from their undersides – fls in each case minute, in tiny pockets on edge of plant, hard to see and often abs – the whole plant free-floating... **LEMNACEAE**, p 443 (*Lemna*)
    Plants consisting of tiny (0.5–1.0 mm wide) green globular granules, **without** any roots or fls – free-floating..**LEMNACEAE**, p 443 (*Wolffia*)
    Plants with distinct **stems** and **lvs** present... **2**
  2 Plants composed of **rosettes** or **crowns** of narrow, linear lvs, 5–10 cm long, attached to a **v short stout stem**, rooted on bottom of ponds or lakes.. **3**
    Plants with long **stems**, bearing lvs along their length, floating or submerged **4**
  3 Fls solitary – male fls erect and emerging from water on a stalk 2–10 cm long, each with 4 tiny green sepals, and 4 stamens on stalks 1–2 cm long – female fls ± stalkless, 4–5 mm long, each with 3–4 tiny green sepals 4–5 mm long and an ovary with a style 1 cm long – in shallow water or on exposed sandy pond edges............................**PLANTAGINACEAE**, p 336 (*Littorella*)
    Fls grouped in a stalked infl, or abs .... see Vegetative Key V D, p 81
  4 Lvs **undivided**, linear to oval, toothed or not.. **5**
    Lvs much **divided** into narrow, linear segments, in whorls along the stems.................................... **9**
  5 Lvs (at least some of them) in **whorls** of 3 or more **6**
    Lvs **never** in whorls, but either in **opp** pairs or **alt** and borne singly along the stems....................... **7**
  6 Lvs strap-like, in whorls of **8 or more**, along stout stems (0.5–1.0 cm across) that are spongy inside – some stems erect and emergent from water, others submerged and trailing below water surface – fls in lf-axils, each fl with one reddish stamen and tiny green ovary with one long style only on emergent stems ....**HIPPURIDACEAE** (p 106)
    Lvs short and scale-like, in whorls of 4–30, on erect ridged rough-pointed stems arising from water – sometimes with branches in whorls, sometimes with oval **cones**, 1–2 cm long and containing powdery spores on tips of stems... **EQUISETACEAE** (**Horsetails**, not flowering plants)
    Lvs linear, translucent, strap-shaped, in **whorls of 3–5**, along slender submerged flaccid stems – female fls on long (to 20 cm) stalks, 5–10 mm across, green-purple or whitish, with 3 sepals, 3 petals and **inferior** ovary – male fls vr in Eur..
      HYDROCHARITACEAE, p 444 (*Elodea* and relatives) – see also Vegetative Key IV, p 76
    Lvs ± linear, fine-toothed, along slender submerged flaccid stems, mostly in **whorls of 3** (some only in **opp** pairs) – fls 1–3 together in lf-axils – male fls enclosed each in a little sheath, with minute two-lipped perianth and one stamen – female fls without sheath or perianth, with one carpel bearing 2–4 stigmas – fr ovoid, 3 mm long....................**NAJADACEAE**, p 449 (*Najas*)

7 Infls of dense, stalked leafless **spikes** of fls, borne in lf-axils, or on ends of stems – spikes 2–8 cm long, their stalks 2–25 cm long, sometimes stout – fls in these spikes in opp pairs, small (to 4 mm wide), each with 4 green to brown perianth segments, 4 stamens and 4 (or fewer) separate carpels that form nutlets 2–5 mm long – lvs either narrow-linear and stalkless, or ± oval and stalked and up to 20 cm long × 7 cm wide, floating or submerged, translucent or opaque, with translucent narrow stipules in lf-axils – in fresh or brackish water ....
POTAMOGETONACEAE, p 446 (see also Key, p 451)
Infl of narrow **flattened spikes enclosed** within basal sheaths of lvs – lvs linear, alt – in **sea** or estuaries..ZOSTERACEAE, p 449
Lower lvs long (to 60 cm) ribbon-like, floating, with a keel beneath – infl-stalk emerging from water, bearing usually some erect grass-like lvs and fls in **globular clusters** alt up the infl-stem, which may be branched or not – **upper** heads of **male** fls only, each with 3 or more stamens, **lower** ones of **female** fls only, each with a one-celled ovary, all fls with a perianth of 3–6 spoon-shaped membranous scales – females fl-heads form **spiky** globes to 3 cm across in fr......................
SPARGANIACEAE, p 420
Infls **not** of spikes or globose clusters of fls, but either of v **short racemes, ± stalkless clusters,** or of **solitary** fls in lf-axils – lvs **untoothed** **8**
8 Lvs linear to oval, in most spp opaque, green and partly floating in terminal rosettes, in some all submerged and translucent, **always** opp, ± stalkless 0.6–2.0 cm long – fls ± stalkless in lf-axils in **pairs**, one pair male with one yellow stamen, the other female with a four-lobed **oval** to globular ovary with 2 styles – in fresh water or mud........................CALLITRICHACEAE, p 443
Lvs **linear**, alt **or** opp, **always** translucent and submerged, **3–5 cm** long – infls short and **umbel-like** on **long** stalks (up to 10 cm in fr), in lf-axils – all fls with perianth abs, 2 short stamens, and an ovary producing a single short-beaked nut in fr – in brackish water near sea................................
RUPPIACEAE, p 449
Lvs linear, nearly all opp, **always** translucent and submerged, 2–3 cm long – infls in lf-axils, each of 2–6 tiny fls in **stalkless** or v short clusters in a tiny cup – male fls of one stamen, female of one carpel with **beak**-like style, forming a nutlet 2–3 mm long with ± wavy edge and a **beak** 0.5–1.5 mm long – in fresh or brackish water..ZANNICHELLIACEAE, p 449
Lvs linear to spoon-shaped, opp, 3–10 mm long × 2 mm wide, thin, untoothed, ± submerged, short-stalked – fls 2–3 mm across, stalked or not, **solitary** in lf-axils, each fl with 3 or 4 sepals, 3 or 4 pinkish-white petals, 6 or 8 stamens, and a tiny 3–4-celled globular superior ovary forming a capsule in fr – in fresh water or mud.................................ELATINACEAE, p 106
Lvs linear and opp, rather like the last, but slightly **fleshy, joined** at the base **in pairs round the stem,** 3–10 mm long – fls solitary and short-stalked in lf-axils, 1–2 mm across, with 4 free sepals and 4 larger white petals, 4 stamens and 4 separate carpels – in fresh water ....
CRASSULACEAE, p 219 (*Crassula aquatica,* and *C. helmsii,* latter not in text)
9 Lvs repeatedly **forked,** 1–3 times – fls **solitary** in lf-axils, with tiny perianth of many narrow lobes – male fls with 10–20 stamens – female with one carpel – fr an ovoid nut with long 4 mm beak – in fresh water...CERATOPHYLLACEAE, p 106
Lvs **pinnately** divided into narrow segments – infl ± lfy **terminal whorled spike** – fls with 4 tiny sepals, 4 tiny petals, 8 stamens in male fl, four-celled ovary in female fl forming 4 separate nutlets in fr – in fresh water...HALORAGACEAE, p 106 (*Myriophyllum*)

B Plants with individual fls, or florets, massed together into close heads, which may be either rounded, button-, disc-, or shaving-brush shaped – all florets stalkless and seated on a common disc or receptacle, which usually has a collar or ruff of lf-like bracts around it at its base – fl-heads stalked, often superficially resembling a single fl
1 Fls mixed with, or ± replaced by, ovoid bulbils – plant garlic-scented when bruised – lvs narrow-linear ....LILIACEAE, p 404 (*Allium,* key p 413)
Fls neither mixed with, nor replaced by, bulbils – no garlic scent **2**
2 Ovaries of florets **inferior**.. **3**
Ovaries of florets **superior**... **9**
3 Petals 5, **free,** not joined into a corolla-tube – stamens 5, free – lvs lobed, spiny-edged..................
UMBELLIFERAE, p 248 (*Eryngium*)
Petals **joined** into a corolla-tube.. **4**
4 Florets only 5 per head, each 6 mm wide, yellow-green, 4 facing **outwards** like the four faces of a public clock, one facing **upwards** – lvs yellow-green, slightly fleshy, twice-trifoliate.........................
ADOXACEAE, p 346
Florets few to many, all **side by side** in a flat or rounded head.. **5**

5 Climbing shrubs with **opp** lvs – **no** distinct whorl of bracts at base of head – florets trumpet-like, 4 cm or more long, two-lipped, with 5 long free stamens .... **CAPRIFOLIACEAE**, p 342 (*Lonicera*)
   Herbs, with distinct **whorl** of bracts at base of head **6**

6 Stamens 5, **joined** into a tube round the style, scarcely or not projecting from corolla-tubes.......... **7**
   Stamens **free**, **projecting** from corolla-tubes on obvious stalks **8**

7 **Calyx abs**, or represented by **hairs** (forming a **pappus** in fr) or by scales – florets **all** tubular; or **all** strap-shaped; **or** tubular in centre and strap-shaped around margin of head (as in a Daisy).........
   .... **COMPOSITAE**, p 356
   Calyx of 5 conspicuous, narrow **green** teeth – fls sky-blue – lvs alt, strap-shaped............................
   .... **CAMPANULACEAE**, p 338 (*Jasione*)

8 Lvs **opp** – stamens 3 – infl-stem repeatedly **forked** – plant to 20 cm – fls v small (2 mm wide), lilac-mauve .... **VALERIANACEAE**, p 345 (*Valerianella*)
   Lvs **opp** – stamens 5, long-projecting – corolla-lobes shorter than tube – long bristles between the florets – stem **not** forked – plants erect, usually 30 cm or more tall – calyx cup-like......................
   .... **DIPSACEAE**, p 354
   Lvs **alt** – stamens 5 – corolla-lobes much **longer** than tube, their tips at first cohering into a tube over stamens – calyx of 5 long narrow green teeth .... **CAMPANULACEAE**, p 338 (*Phyteuma*)

9 Lvs linear, all in basal rosette – infl-stem lfless – fl-heads pink or white – florets with **stalks equalling calyces** – petals free almost to base – stamens 5 – ovary superior, styles 5.......................
   .... **PLUMBAGINACEAE**, p 281 (*Armeria*)
   Lvs obovate, in basal rosette – infl-stem with lanceolate lvs – fl-heads blue – florets **unstalked**, corolla two-lipped, stamens 4 – ovary superior (within corolla-tube) – style 1 – in Br Isles..........
   .... **GLOBULARIACEAE**, p 352
   Lvs linear, all in a basal rosette, **deeply submerged in fresh** water – infl-stem leafless – fls in a greyish-white head 0.5–2.0 cm across – r – Scot, Ire............................**ERIOCAULACEAE**, p 444

C **Plants with individual tiny fls massed into dense, unbranched, cylindrical or ovoid spikes or catkins, these possessing a central stalk through their length to which fls are attached**

1 Trees or shrubs with alt lvs.. **2**
   Herbs.. **11**

2 Male catkins (with stamens) and female catkins (with styles) or frs on **separate** plants.................. **3**
   Male and female catkins separate, but on the **same** plant – male catkins always ± pendulous, female often shorter and erect... **6**
   Tiny pink fls in catkin-like spikes, but fls have 5 petals, 5 sepals, 5 stamens, and 3 styles **all** together in one fl – fls 3 mm wide – lvs tiny, scale- or needle-like – shrub or tree nearly always by the sea... **TAMARICACEAE**, p 230 (*Tamarix*)

3 Lvs narrow lanceolate, covered in silvery-grey scales – stems thorny – fls tiny in short catkins, male with 2 sepals and 4 stamens, female with 2 sepals and one style – frs orange globular berries 6–8 mm wide – on dunes etc by sea.................................. **ELAEAGNACEAE**, p 232 (*Hippophaë*)
   Lvs narrow-linear, evergreen, arranged pinnately along thornless stems – male catkins tiny (3–5 mm long), yellow – female fls solitary, green – fr a naked oval green seed seated in a fleshy, pinkish-red cup, to 1 cm long..
   .... **CONIFERALES** (*Taxus*, **Yew**; no text entry, see illustration p 51, in Vegetative Key
   Lvs **not** silvery-scaly, deciduous – no thorns on stems – frs dry... **4**

4 Lvs strongly **resinous-aromatic**, no stipules – male catkins 7–15 mm long, fls each with about 4 red stamens – female catkins 5–10 mm long, oval, green, fls each with 2 red stigmas – fr a dry nutlet.. **MYRICACEAE**, p 234
   Lvs not aromatic, with stipules – stamens 2 to many, stigmas 2 – fr a tiny capsule opening into 2 halves to release seeds plumed with long silky hairs.................................. **5** (**SALICACEAE**, p 239)

5 Catkin scales **toothed** into narrow segments – catkins long, **pendulous**, always **before** the lvs – fl-bases **cup-like** – stamens 4 to many, red – no nectaries – wind-pollinated ....*Populus*, p 242
   Catkin scales untoothed – catkins shorter (5 cm or less) erect, before or with lvs – no cuplike base to each fl – stamens 2, rarely 3 or 5, golden nectaries present – insect-pollinated ....*Salix*, p 240

6 Lvs narrow-linear, needle-like, mostly evergreen – male fls in oval yellow catkins – female infls form woody cones, which when ripe bear **naked** seeds on their scales
   .... **CONIFERALES** (not described in text nor illustrated, see *The Tree Key* for further details)
   Lvs broad-bladed, mostly deciduous – male fls in oval to cylindrical, pendulous yellow catkins – female infls erect catkins or few-fld clusters, sometimes superficially cone-like (*Alnus*) but seeds **always enclosed** inside large (or tiny) nut-like frs.. **7**

7 Frs large and nutlike (beechnuts, acorns, chestnuts), seated in a **hard woody**, often deeply lobed cup – female fls with 3 (or more) styles each..**FAGACEAE**, p 233
Frs either large and nutlike (hazelnuts) or else tiny, often winged nutlets, seated either in a **lfy** cup (*Corylus*), a papery cup (*Carpinus*) or naked – female fls with 2 styles each **8**

8 Female fls in **erect**, ovoid or cylindrical, **catkins** – frs **tiny flattened**, **winged nutlets**, **2 or 3** on each **scale** of the fruiting catkin ....**9 (BETULACEAE**, p 234)
Female fls either in short erect **bud**-like spikes, or in **drooping**, lfy catkins – frs ± **rounded nuts**, each with a **lfy lobed cup** or **bract** surrounding, or to one side of each ....
10 (CORYLACEAE, p 234)

9 Catkins appearing **with** the lvs – stamens **2** per male fl, but each two-lobed – female catkin **cylindrical**, its scales three-lobed, **falling** as frs fall... *Betula*, p 238
Catkins appearing **before** the lvs – stamens **4** per male fl – female catkin **ovoid** and cone-like, its scales five-lobed, **persistent** and **woody** (like a tiny pine cone) after frs have fallen from it ....
Alnus, p 234

10 Female fls **many** in each 2-cm-long **drooping** catkin, styles **greenish** – ripe fr with a three-lobed papery **bract** 2.5–4.0 cm long, to **one side** of the 5–10-mm long ± flattened oval nut ....
Carpinus, p 234
Female fls **few** in each 5-mm-long **erect bud-like** catkin, styles **crimson** and protruding from tip of bud – ripe fr with a much-lobed lfy **cup**, surrounding base of the globose 1.5–2.0-cm-long woody hazel nut... *Corylus*, p 234

11 Plants with broad, ribbon-like parallel-veined lvs and stout terminal or lateral fl-spikes................ **12**
Plants grass-like, with narrow parallel-veined lvs with sheathing bases, and slender, often branched infls.. **Grasses, Sedges** and **Rushes** – see p 452 for full details
Plants with net-veined lvs, not parallel-sided but ovate, lanceolate or lobed **13**
Plants v fleshy, with no obvious lvs, and with cylindrical jointed branches in opp pairs – fls minute (with 1 stamen only), protruding from pores in branch segments.
CHENOPODIACEAE, p 161 (*Salicornia*)

12 Lvs ribbon-like, **linear**, to 1 m long, ± erect, **parallel-veined**, **grey**-green – spike or catkin of fls **terminal** on an erect **unbranched** stem 1–2 m tall – **lower** part of spike **brown, sausage-shaped**, velvety, of many tiny female fls – **upper** part of spike golden, conical, furry, of many tiny male fls – growing in water or swamps.. **TYPHACEAE**, p 420
Lvs ribbon-like, **linear**, to 60 cm long, ± erect, parallel-veined, **fresh** green with **wavy edges** – dense spike or catkin of fls to 8 cm long, borne **on the side** of flattened lf-like stem **below** its tip – fls **each** with 6 perianth segments, 6 stamens, and three-celled ovary – plant with odour of dried oranges when bruised – growing in shallow water .... **ARACEAE**, p 418 (*Acorus*)

13 Climbing herb with opp, cordate-based ± deeply palmately lobed lvs – male and female fls on separate plants – female catkins cone-like, 15–20 mm long in fl, 5 cm long in fr (**hop cones**) – male infls much branched panicles of small (5 mm wide) fls with five-lobed perianth and 5 stamens – female fls with 2 stigmas...................................... **CANNABIACEAE**, p 228 (*Humulus*)
Erect, non-climbing herbs **14**

14 Lvs opp – plants dioecious – stipules small, green, spreading... **15**
Lvs alt – tubular, membranous, chaffy stipules surrounding stems above lf-bases **16**
Lvs **all** in a basal rosette – infl an erect long-stalked leafless spike – calyx and corolla each four-lobed, 2–3 mm wide ....**PLANTAGINACEAE**, p 336

15 Herbs 10–130 cm tall, with coarse-toothed oval to triangular lvs bristly with **stinging hairs** – male and female infls similar, spike-like, fls with 4 sepals, male with 4 stamens, female with one-celled ovary and one style .... **URTICACEAE**, p 226 (*Urtica*)
Herbs 10–40 cm tall, with fine-toothed oval to lanceolate downy or hairless lvs **without** stinging hairs – male catkins stalked, 3–5 cm long, erect in lf-axils, fls with 3 green sepals and 8–15 stamens – female fls either solitary in lf-axils or 1–3 on long stalks, with 3 sepals and a two-celled ovary with 2 styles... **EUPHORBIACEAE**, p 226 (*Mercurialis*)

16 Infls of dense unbranched cylindrical spikes, **each** with 5 pink or white ± equal sepals, 4–8 stamens and 2–3 styles – fr a hard three-sided or two-faced nutlet, enclosed in the sepals – lvs oval, lanceolate or arrow-shaped – stems smooth .... **POLYGONACEAE**, p 268 (*Polygonum*)
Infls of **interrupted** ± whorled, branched spikes, fls each with 6 perianth segments, the 3 outer small, narrow, greenish, the 3 inner larger, triangular, enlarging round the fr – fr a hard three-sided nutlet – lvs oval, lanceolate or arrow-shaped – stems with ridges lengthwise.................
POLYGONACEAE, p 268 (*Rumex*)

THE GENERAL KEY

D **Plants with individual tiny fls or florets grouped into dense rounded clusters, which are often branched or irregular in shape, but without any collar or whorl of narrow bracts at base of cluster as in key B (though sometimes with one or a pair of lf-like bracts at the base) – ovary always superior**

1 Shrubs or trees..**2**

Climbing herbs..**3**

Non-climbing herbs..**4**

2 Parasitic shrub on branches of trees with strap-shaped lvs 3–5 cm long – branches forked – fls in tiny yellow clusters – frs white berries..**LORANTHACEAE**, p 228

Shrub or tree with evergreen, leathery, oval-oblong, untoothed lvs – male fls with 4 sepals and 4 stamens – female fls with three-celled ovary producing a dry capsule...............**BUXACEAE**, p 228

Low shrubs of salt-marshes with fleshy, cylindrical lvs – 5 sepals, 5 stamens, 2–3 stigmas...............
CHENOPODIACEAE, p 161 (*Suaeda*)

Low shrub of salt-marshes with fleshy, flat, grey-mealy lvs – 5 sepals, 5 stamens (in male fls), stigmas 2..**CHENOPODIACEAE**, p 161 (*Halimione*)

Trees with deciduous, toothed, flat lvs, oval to diamond-shaped – lf-blade extending further down stalk on one side than on other – fls in tiny stalkless clusters appearing before lvs – fls with bell-shaped perianth 4–5-lobed and 2 mm long with 4–5 reddish stamens and 2 styles producing an oval winged fr to 2 cm long..**ULMACEAE**, p 238

3 Lvs palmately three-lobed, bristly – female infls like cones (hops), male fls in branched panicles......
CANNABIACEAE, p 228 (*Humulus*)

Lvs cordate-triangular, hairless but ± mealy below – fls in elongated clusters with both stamens and ovary – frs three-sided nuts enclosed by 3 enlarged sepals 3–4 mm long.....................
POLYGONACEAE, p 268 (*Polygonum*)

4 Plants with narrow-linear grass-like, or narrow-cylindrical lvs......**Rushes, Grasses, Sedges,** p 452

Plants with broad (1 cm wide or more) linear lvs, alt on stems arising from water.............................
SPARGANIACEAE, p 420

Plants with fleshy, jointed stems but apparently without lvs – tiny fls 1 or 3 together in pits in stem-joints – in salt-marshes..**CHENOPODIACEAE**, p 161 (*Salicornia*)

Plants not grass-like – lvs, if narrow-linear, v short (otherwise lvs broad) **5**

5 Lvs palmately lobed, with lobed lfy stipules at their bases – fls in clusters, with 4 green sepals, epicalyx of 4 extra outer sepals, but no petals............**ROSACEAE**, p 200 (*Aphanes* or *Alchemilla*)

Lvs **pinnate**-compound, with toothed **lfy** stipules at their bases – plants 15–40 cm tall – fls in terminal globular heads on long stalks – perianth four-lobed – male fls (lower on head) with many long stamens – female fls with purple feathery stigmas...................**ROSACEAE**, p 200 (*Poterium*)

Lvs not compound, and **without lfy** stipules..**6**

6 Lvs alt, with tubular, ± translucent, brown or silvery, membranous stipules, often fringed, enclosing stem above each lf-base..**POLYGONACEAE**, p 268

Lvs without tubular membranous stipules, though sometimes with small free ones **7**

7 Plants with milky **latex** (with burning taste, **poisonous**, do not taste!) – lvs untoothed – stipules abs – infl with **forking** branches, ending in fl-like clusters of tiny fls with a pair of lf-like bracts at base of each cluster – each cluster with one stalked female fl with a three-celled ovary, surrounded by several male fls each of one stamen..........**EUPHORBIACEAE**, p 243 (*Euphorbia*)

Plants **without** milky latex, infl-branches **not** forked...**8**

8 Lvs **alt**, at least in upper part of stem, toothed or not **9**

Lvs all **opp**, untoothed **12**

9 Fls with **2–3** styles each, stigmas **short, undivided** – fls with **5** tiny sepals and **5** stamens (sometimes female fls separate, then with 2 triangular sepal-like bracts only)..............................**10**

Fls with **1 style** each, stigma **tufted, pinkish, feathery** – fls with tiny **four-lobed** calyx and 4 **stamens** – lvs oval-lanceolate, untoothed – plant of old walls and rocks..
URTICACEAE, p 226 (*Parietaria*)

10 Small prostrate plant of shingly lake shores (vr) – sepals 5, green or red in centre, with **broad white margins** – petals 5, white or red-tipped, equalling petals – lvs strap-shaped, 1–2 cm long × 2–3 mm wide – fls in dense terminal clusters..
CARYOPHYLLACEAE, key p 142 (*Corrigiola*)

Taller or larger plants, with lvs oblong to triangular, or fleshy and cylindrical **11**

11 Sepals green, normally 5 – lvs and stems hairless, but often mealy or fleshy.....................................
CHENOPODIACEAE, p 161

Sepals chaffy, 3 or 5 – lvs and stems ± downy, never mealy or fleshy...
AMARANTHACEAE, p 160

12 Calyx six-lobed, reddish – style 1 – small creeping plant of wet muddy or sandy bare ground with obovate lvs.. **LYTHRACEAE**, p 226 (*Peplis*)

Calyx 4–5-lobed, whitish, green or greyish – styles 2 or more..
13 (small members of **CARYOPHYLLACEAE**)

13 Lvs grey-green, awl-shaped, joined in pairs at base – stipules abs – fls in terminal clusters – sepals 5, grey-green with **white** edges, no petals – tiny prostrate plants of dry, open ground ....
Scleranthus, p 158

Lvs green, oval – fls in whorled clusters in lf-axils **14**

14 Fls with 5 fleshy hooded white sepals 2 mm long with long pointed tips – in moist places, r................
Illecebrum, p 158

Fls with 5 thin flattish, greenish sepals 2 mm long, with blunt tips – in dry places, r...........................
Herniaria, p 158

E **Plants with individual fls small (5 mm or less across), grouped into umbels, with individual fl-stalks all radiating from one point on tip of infl-stem like the ribs of an umbrella – umbels either simple, or compound (umbels of umbels)**

1 Shrubs or woody climbers – ovary inferior – fr berry-like... **2**

Herbs... **3**

2 Shrub ± erect, with **opp**, oval, untoothed lvs, their side-veins turning up ± parallel to midrib – 4 sepals, 4 petals, 4 stamens, ovary two-celled, with one style – fls cream............................
CORNACEAE, p 230 (*Cornus*)

Woody climber with **alt**, oval or palmately lobed leathery evergreen lvs – 5 sepals, 5 petals, 5 stamens, ovary five-celled, with one style – fls yellowish-green .... **ARALIACEAE**, p 230 (*Hedera*)

3 Lvs **parallel-veined**, linear, ± cylindrical, or elliptical – ovary superior – perianth segments 6, all similar and petal-like – stamens 6 – one or two large, often papery, bracts at base of umbels ....**LILIACEAE**, p 404 (*Allium* and *Gagea*)

Lvs **net-veined**, oval, **oblong**, or ± **pinnately divided** – petals 5 (or 4).. **4**

4 Lvs **all** in a **basal** rosette, elliptical to spoon-shaped – sepals and petals respectively **fused** to form a calyx-tube and a corolla-tube below – ovary superior – 5 stamens attached to inside of corolla-tube – 1 style – fls pink or yellow (usually **more** than 5 mm wide)..
PRIMULACEAE, p 284 (*Primula*)

Lvs not all in a basal rosette, but at least **some** lvs **up the stem**.. **5**

5 Lvs **alt** (or, rarely, opp), undivided, ± unstalked – umbels simple, but bearing **forked clusters** of tiny green-yellow fls on tips of umbel-rays – each ultimate fl-cluster **looking like a little fl**, with one stalked central female fl with superior three-celled ovary and 3 styles, surrounded by several one-stamened male fls – the fl-cluster seated in a **calyx-like** toothed cup which bears fleshy yellowish petal-like bracts (**glands**) alternating with its teeth – **milky latex present** in plants ....**EUPHORBIACEAE**, p 243 (*Euphorbia*)

Lvs **alt**, stalked, often pinnate or twice-pinnate – umbels often compound, often with tiny bracts at base of main umbel and of secondary umbels – fls with 5 tiny sepals (or sepals abs), 5 petals (often notched), 5 stamens, and inferior ovary of 2 joined carpels and 2 styles – fr of 2 dry separating nutlets – no milky latex..**UMBELLIFERAE**, p 248

Lvs **opp**, undivided, ± unstalked, untoothed – no milky latex.. **6**

6 Lvs narrow-oblong, 10–25 mm long – umbels **tassel**-like – fls with 5 sepals, 5 white irregularly-toothed petals, 3–5 stamens and superior ovary with 3 styles – fr a dry capsule – r – not in Br Isles... **CARYOPHYLLACEAE**, p 142 (*Holosteum*)

Lvs oval, 1–3 cm long – umbels **dense**, **blackish-purple**, to 1 cm across, each surrounded at base by a whorl of 4 oval white bracts each 5–8 mm long, the whole resembling a single white four-petalled fl – each fl with 4 sepals, 4 petals, 4 stamens and an inferior ovary with one style – fr a red berry 5 mm long – r .... **CORNACEAE**, p 230 (*Chamaepericlymenum*)

F **Herbs without green colour (chlorophyll) in lvs and stem – lvs reduced to small scales**

1 Climbing parasitic plants, with ± reddish leafless thread-like stems twining over and attaching themselves to other plants by means of suckers – fls small (3–5 mm long) in globular clusters, with five-lobed calyx and five-lobed corolla .... **CONVOLVULACEAE**, p 294 (*Cuscuta*)

Erect (not climbing) herbs, with fls in spikes or racemes.. **2**

2 Ovary **inferior** – perianth segments 6, **free**, with one petal different from others and enlarged into a lip (either at bottom or top of fl), and sometimes spurred .... **ORCHIDACEAE**, p 422

Ovary **superior** **3**

THE GENERAL KEY

3 Fls **regular**, pale yellow or cream – calyx of 5 sepals, corolla of 4 or 5 **separate** and **equal** petals converging into a narrow bell or tube – stamens 8 or 10, free .... **MONOTROPACEAE**, p 281
Fls **irregular**, two-lipped, of various colours – stamens 4, attached to five-lobed corolla-tube – parasitic on various plants .... **OROBANCHACEAE**, p 331

G **Plants with regular fls with ovary inferior (or apparently so), petals free from one another, calyx distinct from corolla (or sometimes calyx abs) – lvs not in whorls of 4 or more along stems**
1 Shrubs or trees **2**
  Herbs **5**
2 Lvs **evergreen**, leathery, palmately lobed or oval, **alt – woody climber** – fls each with 5 sepals, 5 petals, 5 stamens – ovary five-celled with 1 style – fls yellow-green, in umbels ....
  ARALIACEAE, p 230 (*Hedera*)
  Lvs **deciduous** – plants not climbing **3**
3 Lvs **opp**, oval, **untoothed**, with side-veins curving round and ± parallel to midrib – fls each with 4 sepals, 4 petals, 4 stamens, ovary two-celled with 1 style – fls cream, in umbel-like heads ......
  CORNACEAE, p 230 (*Cornus*)
  Lvs **alt**, ± toothed **4**
4 Petals 5, **shorter** than the 5 sepals – stamens 5 – styles 2 – fr a berry, **soft** inside – lvs ± palmately lobed .... **GROSSULARIACEAE**, p 222
  Petals 5, as **long** as or much **longer** than the 5 sepals – stamens 10 or v many – styles 1 to many – fr fleshy and coloured, but **firm** (when opened, carpels may sometimes be found to be **free** of fr-wall, but ovary appears to be inferior) .... **ROSACEAE**, p 200
5 Lvs **fleshy**, **opp**, narrow-linear, triangular in cross-section, 7–10 cm long, joined in pairs at their bases – calyx-teeth lf-like, 5 – petals **numerous**, v narrow – stamens many – fr fleshy – fls 5 cm or more across, yellow or mauve, ± resembling large daisy fl-heads – on sea cliffs ....
  AIZOACEAE, p 400 (*Carpobrotus*)
  Lvs **not** fleshy, not triangular in cross-section – petals few, only 2, 3, 4 or 5 per fl **6**
6 Petals either 2 and notched, or 4 (rarely abs) – sepals 2 or 4 – stamens 2, 4 or 8 – ovary four-celled – stigma simple or four-lobed – lvs opp (or alt), unlobed .... **ONAGRACEAE**, p 222
  Petals 3 – sepals 3 .... **7**
  Petals 5 – sepals 5 (or abs) **10**
7 Plants **floating** in water – sepals green, distinct from the white petals **8**
  Plants **not** floating in water (though sometimes growing erect out of water) – sepals never wholly green – sepals and petals either **both** coloured or **both** white, often v alike – lvs linear, grass- or sword-like, untoothed, with veins all parallel **9**
8 Lvs **kidney-shaped**, **untoothed**, 3 cm wide, floating on water on long stalks (like tiny Water-lily lvs) .... **HYDROCHARITACEAE**, p 402 (*Hydrocharis*)
  Lvs **sword-shaped**, **sharp-toothed**, to 20 cm long, in a floating crown or rosette ....
  HYDROCHARITACEAE, p 402 (*Stratiotes*)
9 Stamens 6 – petals and sepals alike – (fl sometimes with a central trumpet as in Daffodil) ....
  AMARYLLIDACEAE, p 416
  Stamens 3 – petals and sepals alike, or of different shape .... **IRIDACEAE**, p 416
10 Creeping marsh or bog plants with circular, **parasol**-shaped lvs 1–5 cm across, held aloft and horizontal on 2–10-cm stalks attached to their centres – infls 3–5 cm tall, with fls in a head or a whorled spike – 5 sepals, 5 petals, 5 stamens – ovary two-celled, with 2 styles ....
  UMBELLIFERAE, p 248 (*Hydrocotyle*)
  Plants with lvs **not** circular, not parasol-shaped **11**
11 Fls in long **spikes** or **racemes** – stamens 10–20 – receptacle-cup below sepals with many **hooked spines** – carpels 2, **free** within oval or bell-shaped receptacle-cup (so technically ovary is not inferior though superficially so) – lvs alt, pinnate, with tiny lfts alternating with larger ones – fls yellow .... **ROSACEAE**, p 200 (*Agrimonia*)
  Fls in loose **panicles**, or solitary – stamens 10 – ovary of 2 carpels, **fused** in their lower parts to calyx-tube and to each other, but **free** above, each carpel with a style – fr a **many**-seeded capsule .... **SAXIFRAGACEAE**, p 216
  Fls in **heads** or **umbels** (simple or compound) – sepals small, or abs – stamens 5 – ovary of 2 completely fused carpels, with 2 styles – fr of 2 dry, separating, one-seeded nutlets – lvs alt, often compound .... **UMBELLIFERAE**, p 248

H **Plants with regular fls with free petals and sepals, and superior ovary of 2 to several carpels that are free and separate one from another (or nearly so) and not joined into an ovary – lvs not in whorls or 4 or more along stems**

1 Plants with **v fleshy**, oval, ovoid or cylindrical **undivided** lvs – petals 3, 4, or most often 5 – stamens as many as (or twice as many as) petals – carpels as many as petals, each carpel forming a 2- to many-seeded **follicle** in fr, opening to release seeds ....**CRASSULACEAE**, p 219
Plants with lvs **not** fleshy **2**

2 Lvs **parallel**-veined – 3 sepals, 3 petals, stamens and carpels 6 to many – plant always in wet places or in water **3**
Lvs with **net-veining**, often lobed or compound – 4–5 sepals, 4–5 petals, stamens and carpels v many... **4**
Lvs with net-veining, rounded-triangular – 3 green sepals, 8–9 yellow petals, stamens and carpels v many, carpels one-seeded achenes........ **RANUNCULACEAE**, p 95 (*Ranunculus ficaria*)

3 Fr-head of numerous one-seeded **achenes** – sepals **green**, petals white or pink – lvs with blade and stalk usually **distinct**...**ALISMATACEAE**, p 401
Fr-head of 6–9 several-seeded **follicles**, each opening to release seeds – sepals and petals **both** pink, but sepals shorter and narrower than petals – fls in an umbel – lvs **linear**, 1 m or more long, triangular in cross-section .... **BUTOMACEAE**, p 402

4 **Epicalyx** of extra green sepals **present** below calyx – fr-head of many **dry** achenes (in Strawberries embedded in a red fleshy mass) ....
....**ROSACEAE**, p 200 (*Potentilla, Fragaria, Geum, Sibbaldia*)
Epicalyx **abs**... **5**

5 Fr-head of many separate **fleshy globules** (like tiny berries cohering together, as in a Blackberry) ....**ROSACEAE**, p 200 (*Rubus*)
Fr-head of many **dry achenes** (or of **follicles**, each of which opens to release several seeds) **6**

6 Lfy **stipules** present at base of lf-stalks – receptacle concave..
....**ROSACEAE**, p 200 (*Filipendula, Dryas*)
Stipules **abs** – receptacle convex..**RANUNCULACEAE**, p 95

I **Plants with regular fls with calyx and corolla distinct, the petals separate from one another to their bases and not forming a corolla-tube – the carpels (or their styles, or both) either several but all joined together into a single, superior ovary, or else ovary apparently of one superior carpel only**

1 Aquatic plants with **large, rounded**, ± cordate-based **floating** lvs, and **solitary**, long-stalked, usually floating fls 5–20 cm across – sepals 4–6, green – petals 3 to about 25, yellow or white, the innermost often grading into stamens – stamens many – carpels 8 to many, forming a rounded or flask-shaped capsule 1.5–4.0 cm wide in fr ....**NYMPHAEACEAE**, p 106
Plants **without** large, rounded floating lvs, not truly aquatic **2**

2 Trees, shrubs, and woody climbing plants **3**
Herbs, sometimes woody at the (usually creeping) base... **14**

3 Stamens **many** (**more** than twice number of petals) **4**
Stamens **equalling**, or **up to** twice number of petals only.. **7**

4 Calyx-tube forming a globular **cup** round the single carpel (but **not** attached to it) with 5 calyx-teeth – the 5 petals and many stamens attached to top of calyx-cup – fr a cherry, or plum-like, with a 'stone' inside the fleshy part containing a single seed – petals white...............................
....**ROSACEAE**, p 200 (*Prunus*)
Calyx of **free** sepals, or sepals ± joined into a tube, but petals attached to base of fl **below** ovary, and not to calyx-tube or to sepals **5**

5 Trees – lvs **alt**, rounded, cordate-based, hairless above, with long-pointed tips and **long (2–5 cm) stalks** – infl with a conspicuous **oblong bract partly fused** to its stalk – fls with 5 sepals, 5 petals, many stamens, and five-celled ovary with five-lobed stigma, fragrant – fr a small nut ....
....**TILIACEAE**, p 236
Low shrubs, 10–40 cm tall – lvs **opp**, oblong to oval, short-stalked or stalkless – **no** bract fused to infl-stalk **6**

6 Stalks of stamens **joined** into **5 bundles** at their bases, free above – styles **3 or 5** – sepals 5, ± **equal** – lvs oval, **stalkless, no stipules** – fls yellow...
....**HYPERICACEAE**, p 136 (*Hypericum*)
Stamens **all free** to base – style **1** – **2** of the sepals far **smaller** than the other 3 – lvs narrow-oblong, **short-stalked**, often with stipules............................**CISTACEAE**, p 133 (*Helianthemum*)

7 **Evergreen** shrubs – lvs leathery, spiny, or heath-like **8**
    Deciduous shrubs – lvs broad, oval or lobed... **11**
    Deciduous shrub, or small tree (2–6 m) with **tiny** (to 2 mm) **scale-like**, **overlapping**, grey- or
    fresh-green lvs – fls in **catkin-like spikes**, **pink** or **white**, each fl 3 mm across, with 5 sepals, 5
    petals, 5 stamens and 3 styles – fr a capsule – plant near sea .... **TAMARICACEAE**, p 230
8 Low (to 80 cm) much-branched shrub with oval, dark green, spine-tipped apparent lvs 1–4 cm
    long, that are in reality flattened stems (**cladodes**) and bear on their surfaces 1 or 2 greenish fls
    3 mm across in the axils of the true lvs, which are chaffy scales under 5 mm long – fls with 3
    sepals, 3 greenish petals and **either** 3 stamens, **or** a three-celled ovary, forming a red round berry
    1 cm wide in fr .... **LILIACEAE**, p 404 (*Ruscus*)
    Shrubs with fls **not** apparently growing from spine-tipped lvs, but on **stalks** from normal stems,
    singly or in clusters **9**
9 Low (to 40 cm) **heath-like** shrubs with **linear**, **alt** lvs 4–6 mm long × 2 mm wide, their edges
    rolled under – fls 1–2 mm across, with 3 sepals, 3 pinkish petals, and **either** 3 stamens, **or** an
    ovary forming a black berry 5 mm wide in fr (rarely fls with stamens and ovary together) ....
    .... **EMPETRACEAE**, p 280
    Taller (to 100 cm) Rhododendron-like shrubs with linear to oblong **alt** lvs 1–5 cm long × 0.5–
    1.0 cm wide, dark green above, rusty-hairy below – fls 1.0–1.5 cm across in umbel-like heads
    with 5 green sepals, 5 cream petals, 10 stamens and five-celled ovary – fr a capsule – in bogs, r.......
    .... **ERICACEAE**, p 275 (*Ledum*)
    Lvs holly-like, with spines round the margins.. **10**
10 **Lvs pinnate**, **lfts** like thin holly lvs – fls yellow, 6–8 mm across, in clusters, each fl with usually 5
    whorls of perianth segments of 3 each, yellow, not all of same size – frs blue-black, like clusters of
    tiny grapes .... **BERBERIDACEAE**, p 104 (*Mahonia*)
    Lvs undivided, oval – fls white, in clusters, with 4 sepals, 4 petals (joined together at extreme
    base) and either 4 stamens or a four-celled ovary .... **AQUIFOLIACEAE**, p 230 (*Ilex*)
11 Lvs opp.. **12**
    Lvs alt **13**
12 Lvs **oval-elliptical**, fine-toothed – fls in clusters – 4 sepals, 4 greenish petals, 4 stamens, four-
    celled ovary, forming a salmon-coloured four-lobed capsule in fr, with orange seeds inside ....
    .... **CELASTRACEAE**, p 232 (*Euonymus*)
    Lvs **palmately lobed** – fls in pendulous racemes – sepals and petals 5, stamens 8, ovary two-
    celled – fr dry, with 2 propeller-blade-like wings... **ACERACEAE**, p 236
13 Lvs oval, toothed around edges (or not) – fls in loose clusters – sepals 4–5 – petals 4–5 –
    stamens 4–5 – ovary 2–4-celled – fr an oval dark red or black berry – stems sometimes thorny.......
    .... **RHAMNACEAE**, p 232
    Lvs obovate – spines present in threes on shoots – fls clustered, perianth segments yellow, in up
    to 5 whorls of 3, of different sizes – stamens 6 – style 1, v short – fr an oblong red berry, 8–12 mm
    long...**BERBERIDACEAE**, p 104 (*Berberis*)
14 Sepals **fused** into a **long calyx-tube**, with toothed tip – lvs opp **15**
    Sepals **separate** (or fused only at base into a v short cup) **17**
15 Calyx-tube six-toothed – petals 6 (or sometimes fewer), pink or purple – fls in spike-like racemes,
    or solitary in lf-axils.. **LYTHRACEAE**, p 226
    Calyx-tube five-toothed – petals 5, long-stalked, arising from within base of calyx-tube.............. **16**
16 **Prostrate** salt-marsh plant – stems ± **woody** – lvs heath-like, linear, 2–4 mm long, margins
    rolled under – fls stalkless, 5 mm wide, **solitary** along stems and in forks – petals **pink**, **crinkly** –
    stamens 6 – style 1, long, with 3 stigmas at tip – fr a capsule .... **FRANKENIACEAE**, p 134
    Plants ± erect, not heath-like, **not** woody – petals **flat** – stamens (when present) twice
    number of petals – styles 2–5, free to base – ovary one-celled – fr a capsule (rarely a berry) with
    many seeds – infl a dichasium, with a fl in each fork.................. **CARYOPHYLLACEAE**, key p 142
17 Lvs oval-elliptical, in a **single whorl** of 4 (3, 5 or 6) at top of stem just below solitary terminal fl –
    fl with 4 narrow green sepals and 4 similar petals, 8 stamens, four-celled ovary – fr a black
    berry... **TRILLIACEAE**, p 405
    Lvs **opp**, undivided **18**
    Lvs alt **21**
18 Infl a dichasium – 4–5 petals, 4–5 sepals **19**
    Fls solitary – 5 petals, 5 sepals **20**
    Fls in a loose raceme – lvs in a basal rosette and also in pairs up stem, stalkless, elliptical-
    lanceolate, downy – fls pale yellow with a **red spot** on each of the 5 petals – sepals 5, v unequal –
    stamens many – stigma ± stalkless, on globular ovary .... **CISTACEAE**, p 133 (*Tuberaria*)

19 Sepals, petals and stamens 5 – ovary five-celled – fr a five-celled capsule – petals white – lvs stalkless..**LINACEAE**, p 134 (*Linum*)

Sepals, petals and stamens 4 – ovary four-celled, fr a four-celled capsule – tiny bushy plant to 5 cm tall...**LINACEAE**, p 134 (*Radiola*)

Sepals 2 only, petals 5 – ovary one-celled, capsule 1–3-seeded.......... **PORTULACACEAE**, p 158

Sepals, petals 4–5 – stamens usually **twice number** of petals – white or pink – ovary one-celled, capsule many-seeded...**CARYOPHYLLACEAE**, key p 142

Sepals, petals 5 – stamens many, in 3 or 5 **bundles** – petals yellow – ovary 3- or 5-celled – lvs **stalkless** – fr a capsule...**HYPERICACEAE**, p 136

20 Lvs all in basal rosette, oval, long-stalked, untoothed, hairless, 1–2 cm long, glossy – fl on a long erect stalk, drooping, 15 mm wide, cream – 10 stamens with pores at tips – ovary five-celled, with one style...**PYROLACEAE**, p 280 (*Moneses*)

Lvs stalkless, close-set on cushion-forming and creeping stems – lvs 2–6 mm long, oval, with chalky white pit on blunt tip of each – fls 12–20 mm across, rose-purple – stamens 10 – carpels 2, free above, fused to each other and to calyx-cup below – in mts..
SAXIFRAGACEAE, p 216 (*Saxifraga oppositifolia*)

21 Stamens as many as, or up to twice number of petals..**22**

Stamens far more numerous than petals **28**

22 Sepals 3, narrow – petals 3, 2–8 mm long, oval-triangular, erect, greenish or reddish, sometimes with a large wart on each – stamens 6 – fr a three-angled nut 0.8–4.0 mm long – infl a panicle of erect, whorled, dense spikes or racemes – lvs simple, oval, lanceolate or arrow-shaped – chaffy tubular stipules round stem ....**POLYGONACEAE**, p 268 (*Rumex*)

Sepals 4 – petals 4, white or coloured (rarely abs, or with 2 petals rather longer than the other 2) – stamens 6 or 4 – ovary of 2 joined carpels – fr a capsule dividing into 2 parts vertically, **or** cross-wise, **or** else a nutlet – no stipules present ....**CRUCIFERAE**, p 113

Sepals 4 – petals abs, but **epicalyx** of 4 bracts below sepals (so sepals could be mistaken for petals) – stamens 1–4 – carpel 1, in a little receptacle-cup – lvs palmately lobed or veined – stipules lfy ....**ROSACEAE**, p 200 (*Alchemilla, Aphanes*)

Sepals and petals 5 of each, rarely more..**23**

23 Lvs **trifoliate**, long-stalked, **clover-like** – stamens 10 – ovary five-celled – fr a capsule without a beak...**OXALIDACEAE**, p 176

Lvs **not** clover-like..**24**

24 Lvs **all** in a basal rosette, infl-stalk leafless, erect..**25**

Lvs **both** basal **and** alt up stem...**27**

Lvs narrow, linear, stalkless, **all** alt up stem – no basal lf-rosette – infl a dichasium – stamens 5 – ovary five-celled – fr a globose capsule..**LINACEAE**, p 134 (*Linum*)

25 Lvs with many **long-stalked**, **sticky**, **red-tipped hairs**, insect-trapping – fls white, 5 mm wide – stamens same number as petals (5 or 6) – infl erect, forked ....**DROSERACEAE**, p 214

Lvs **without** sticky red-tipped hairs **26**

26 Lvs linear, 2 mm wide – infl a rounded head of pink or white fls, button-shaped, 2–3 cm across ......
PLUMBAGINACEAE, p 281 (*Armeria*)

Lvs oval or round, long-stalked, hairless, ± glossy, 2–4 cm long × 2–3 cm wide – infl a raceme of white or greenish fls, each with 10 stamens (with pores at their tips) and a five-celled ovary with a single stout style ....**PYROLACEAE**, p 280 (*Pyrola*)

27 Lvs palmately or pinnately lobed or divided – lower lvs long-stalked – stamens 10, 5 of them sometimes without anthers – ovary five-celled, with a long (1–3 cm) central beak bearing 5 stigmas at its tip – fr dry ....**GERANIACEAE**, p 171

Lvs varied in shape, from wedge-, kidney- or strap-shaped to deeply palmately lobed into narrow segments – stamens 10 – carpels 2, joined below, separate above – fr a capsule dividing into 2 parts..**SAXIFRAGACEAE**, p 216 (*Saxifraga*)

Lvs undivided – root-lvs cordate-oval, long-stalked – stem-lf one only, cordate-oval, stalkless, clasping – fl solitary, erect on stem 10–30 cm tall, 2 cm across, white – 5 normal stamens alt with 5 sterile palmately-branched ones – ovary with 4 stigmas......................**PARNASSIACEAE**, p 218

28 Lvs twice-pinnate, with glossy, oval, sharp-toothed lfts – fls in **spikes** – sepals 5 – 5 tiny cream petals – 1 carpel – fr an ovoid black berry...............................**RANUNCULACEAE**, p 95 (*Actaea*)

Lvs toothed, or pinnate, with narrow segments – sepals 2 – petals 4 – stamens many, free – carpels 2 to many, joined ....**PAPAVERACEAE**, p 108

Lvs palmately veined or lobed – sepals 5 – petals 5 – stamens all joined into a tube below – carpels many, joined into a flattened disc-like ovary separating into many one-seeded nutlets in fruit ....**MALVACEAE**, p 168

THE GENERAL KEY

J   **Plants with regular fls with petals joined into a corolla-tube, and ovary superior**

1 Petals joined into a v short tube only at extreme base, so at first sight petals appear free................ **2**
    Petals joined into an obvious corolla-tube, ⅓ or more length of free corolla-lobes......................... **3**

2 Shrub or tree with evergreen, spiny lvs – fls white – petals 4.................. **AQUIFOLIACEAE**, p 230
    Herbs with **either** 2 ± fleshy round lvs, joined and encircling stem, and white fls, **or** with a pair of lvs, rounded but not encircling stem, and pink fls – either variant with sepals 2, petals 5 ....
                          PORTULACACEAE, p 158

3 Stamens 8 or 10, twice number of corolla-lobes.. **4**
    Stamens as many as, or fewer than, corolla-lobes.. **5**

4 Shrubs or trees with linear, elliptical or oval lvs – carpels 4 or 5, joined together into an ovary..........
                          ERICACEAE, p 275
    Succulent herb with circular fleshy lvs attached by a central stalk – fls greenish, in a spike – carpels separate from one another – on rocks or walls......... **CRASSULACEAE**, p 220 (*Umbilicus*)

5 Ovary of 4 almost separate lobes from between which arises a style, forked at tip – fr of 4 nutlets – lvs and stems usually bristly, lvs alt .... **BORAGINACEAE**, p 324
    Ovary not divided into 4 lobes.. **6**

6 Stamens 2 – corolla-lobes 4 – lvs opp...**OLEACEAE**, p 294 (*Ligustrum*)
    Stamens **same** number as corolla-lobes.. **7**

7 Stamens **opp** the corolla-lobes... **8**
    Stamens **alternating** with the corolla-lobes.. **9**

8 Style 1 – lvs all in a basal rosette, **or** opp on stem **or** on stem in a single whorl below fl – fr a globose capsule with many seeds – calyx green.. **PRIMULACEAE**, p 284
    Styles 5 – fr a one-seeded capsule – lvs all in basal rosette – calyx chaffy.................................
                         PLUMBAGINACEAE, p 281

9 Shrub to 2.5 m tall, with lanceolate grey-green lvs and ± spiny stems – fls 1 cm across, rose-purple, five-lobed, funnel-shaped .... **SOLANACEAE**, p 296 (*Lycium*)
    Low creeping or cushion-forming **alpine** shrubs, with small narrow leathery lvs – calyx and corolla each five-lobed – stamens 5.. **10**
    Herbs.. **11**

10 Creeping shrub with tiny **oval** opp lvs, and pink fls 4–5 mm wide – ovary 2–3-celled – stigma undivided... **ERICACEAE**, p 275 (*Loiseleuria*)
    Cushion-forming shrub with **spoon-shaped** alt lvs in rosettes, and white fls 8–15 mm wide – ovary three-celled – stigma three-lobed .... **DIAPENSIACEAE**, p 275

11 Bog or swamp plant with erect, long-stalked **trifoliate** lvs – lfts 3–7 cm long, untoothed – fls in erect racemes – each fl 15 mm wide, with 5 white corolla-lobes fringed with long white hairs ....
                          MENYANTHACEAE, p 292 (*Menyanthes*)
    Floating aquatic plant with rounded, cordate-based, long-stalked floating lvs 3–10 cm across (like small Water-lily lvs) – fls floating, in few-fld long-stalked clusters – each fl 3 cm wide, with 5 yellow corolla-lobes fringed with long yellow hairs ..... **MENYANTHACEAE**, p 292 (*Nymphoides*)
    Plants of dry (or merely damp) ground, with stalkless or short-stalked mostly simple lvs (sometimes with 2 small lobes at lf-base) **12**

12 Lvs **opp**, always **simple**, without stipules – carpels 2 .... **13**
    Lvs **alt** – calyx and corolla each five-lobed... **15**
    Lvs **all** in a **basal** rosette – fls v small, in **spikes** – calyx and corolla each four-lobed, 2–3 mm wide.. **PLANTAGINACEAE**, p 336

13 Plants creeping – lvs glossy, short-stalked, oval-elliptical – fls solitary in lf-axils, violet – corolla five-lobed, **twisted** in bud, saucer-shaped when open – carpels **free** below, **joined** above into a common style surrounded by a **ring** above .... **APOCYNACEAE**, p 292
    Plants **erect** (rarely with stem creeping **at base only**) – carpels **fused** together below – **no** ring round style **14**

14 Lvs cordate-based, pointed, **short-stalked** – infls **long-stalked clusters in lf-axils** – fls cream, under 1 cm across, corolla five-lobed, star-shaped – stamens v short, each covered by a **fleshy scale** – style a short, **stout**, **five**-angled column – fr a pointed, cigar-shaped capsule 5 cm long, the seeds inside it with silky plumes – **not in Br Isles**............................... **ASCLEPIADACEAE**, p 294
    Lvs **stalkless** – infl a **dichasium**, or else of a solitary terminal fl – stamens **not** covered each by a fleshy scale – style **slender**, single or forked into two – calyx and corolla four- or five-lobed – seeds tiny, **not** plumed .... **GENTIANACEAE**, p 289

15 Ovary **three**-celled, with **3** stigmas – lvs pinnate................................... **POLEMONIACEAE**, p 294
    Ovary two-celled, with 1 or 2 stigmas – lvs **not** pinnate, but simple (or with 2 lobes at base only) **16**

16 **Twining** herbs with cordate-triangular lvs – corolla funnel-shaped, scarcely lobed..........................
$\qquad$ **CONVOLVULACEAE**, p 294
$\quad$ Herbs **not** twining their stems around other plants – lvs oval-elliptical – corolla **deeply** five-lobed.. **17**

17 Fls in terminal spikes or racemes, one corolla-lobe slightly larger than others – corolla-tube short
$\quad$ – stamens spreading... **SCROPHULARIACEAE**, p 297 (*Verbascum*)
$\quad$ Fls solitary, or in curved cymes – **either** anthers converging into a column, **or else** corolla-tube v
$\quad$ long... **SOLANACEAE**, p 296

K **Plants with regular fls with calyx and corolla distinct – petals joined into a corolla-tube – ovary inferior**

1 Small (to 10 cm) herb with twice-trifoliate, yellow-green, slightly fleshy lvs, from base and also in
$\quad$ a pair on stem – fls yellow-green, to 6 mm wide, in a **close, four-angled head of 5 fls only** – 4 of
$\quad$ the fls facing **outwards** like the **four faces of a clock tower**, each with 3 calyx-teeth, a five-lobed
$\quad$ corolla, and 10 stamens – 1 fl terminal, facing **upwards**, with 2 calyx-teeth, a four-lobed corolla,
$\quad$ and 8 stamens – ovary 3–5-celled – fr a green berry – woods in spring .... **ADOXACEAE**, p 346
$\quad$ Fls **not** in close four-angled heads of 5 fls only, but in (a) many-fld heads, or (b) loose infls, or (c)
$\quad$ solitary **2**

2 Stamens **8 or 10**, with **obvious pores** (use lens) on anther-tips – low shrubs (under 1 m) either
$\quad$ erect in drier ground, or prostrate and creeping over *Sphagnum* in bogs – lvs simple, **alt** – corolla
$\quad$ 4–5-lobed, either bell-shaped or with corolla-lobes arched back – frs berries...................................
$\qquad$ **ERICACEAE**, p 275 (*Vaccinium*)
$\quad$ Stamens 1 to 5 only, **without** pores on anther-tips **3**

3 Fls in **close heads**, with **many** unstalked florets in each – heads each surrounded below by a
$\quad$ collar or ruff (involucre) of **many** bracts – herbs **4**
$\quad$ Fls **neither** in close heads, **nor** with an involucre of many bracts – herbs or shrubs........................ **7**

4 Anthers of each floret **joined into a tube** round the style – lvs alt.................................... **5**
$\quad$ Anthers **free, long-stalked**.. **6**

5 Calyx of 5 conspicuous **long green teeth** – fl-heads sky-blue – fr a capsule with **several seeds** ....
$\qquad$ **CAMPANULACEAE**, p 338 (*Jasione*)
$\quad$ Calyx represented by a **pappus** of hairs or scales, or **abs** – fls rarely blue – frs tiny **nutlets**................
$\qquad$ **COMPOSITAE**, p 356

6 Corolla-lobes **long, narrow, joined** at tips in bud – calyx of 5 **long teeth** – lvs alt – fr a **capsule**
$\quad$ with **several** seeds...**CAMPANULACEAE**, p 338 (*Phyteuma*)
$\quad$ Corolla-lobes **shorter** than tube – calyx cup-like – lvs **opp** – frs tiny **nutlets** ....**DIPSACEAE**, p 354

7 Lvs simple, in successive **whorls** of 4 or more up stems – corolla 4–5-lobed, wheel- or funnel-shaped .... **RUBIACEAE**, p 348
$\quad$ Lvs **not** in whorls up stems – corolla five-lobed.. **8**

8 Herbs climbing by means of **coiled tendrils** – lvs palmately-lobed – frs red berries – plants
$\quad$ dioecious..**CUCURBITACEAE**, p 228
$\quad$ Tendrils **abs** **9**

9 Lvs **opp** – herbs or shrubs **10**
$\quad$ Lvs **alt** – all herbs **11**

10 Stamens 4 or 5 – calyx of 5 **teeth** – **either** erect, creeping or twining shrubs **without** stipules to
$\quad$ lvs, or herbs **with** stipules and pinnate lvs.. **CAPRIFOLIACEAE**, p 342
$\quad$ Stamens 1–3 – calyx **either** a ± **untoothed** tiny ring **or else** forming a **hairy pappus** –
$\quad$ herbs **without** stipules to lvs... **VALERIANACEAE**, p 345

11 Stamens 5, **opp** corolla-lobes – stigma 1, pinhead-shaped – fls small, white, cup-like, 3 mm
$\quad$ wide × 3 mm long .... **PRIMULACEAE**, p 284 (*Samolus*)
$\quad$ Stamens 5, **alternating** with corolla-lobes – stigmas 2–5 – fls blue, purple or white, bell- or
$\quad$ wheel-shaped, conspicuous, from 8 mm wide and from 6 mm long.... **CAMPANULACEAE**, p 338

L **Plants with regular fls with perianth (a) of one whorl only, or (b) of 2 or more whorls similar in shape, colour and size, coloured or white, of petal-like segments or lobes**

1 Ovary inferior.. **2**
$\quad$ Ovary superior.. **9**

2 Perianth tubular below.. **3**
$\quad$ Perianth segments 6, free, ascending **8**
$\quad$ Perianth segments 5, free, spreading – fls in simple or compound umbels – lvs often pinnate, alt –
$\quad$ stamens 5, styles 2 – fr of 2 segments, separating when ripe .... **UMBELLIFERAE**, p 248

3 Perianth unlobed, forming a single erect oval dull yellow flap, pointed at tip, 1–2 cm long –
   perianth-tube with a swelling at base above ovary – stamens 6, styles 6 – erect herbs with oval
   cordate, blunt, alt, stalked lvs – fls 4–8 in lf-axils ......**ARISTOLOCHIACEAE**, p 170 (*Aristolochia*)
   Perianth-tube symmetrically lobed into 3–6 segments or teeth in upper part................................. **4**
4 Fls with 6 ± equal petal-like perianth-lobes – ovary three-celled.. **5**
   Fls with 3 v short triangular perianth segments – fls bell-shaped, solitary, brownish, downy,
   15 mm long – plant creeping, with long-stalked, kidney-shaped, thick, glossy dark green lvs – r
   ....**ARISTOLOCHIACEAE**, p 170 (*Asarum*)
   Fls with 4 or 5 petal-like perianth-lobes **7**
5 Stamens 3..**IRIDACEAE**, p 416
   Stamens 6... **6**
6 **Twining**, **climbing** herb with glossy, **cordate**, **stalked** lvs and small (4–5 mm wide) fls in
   racemes in lf-axils – plants dioecious – fr a red berry.............. **DIOSCOREACEAE**, p 405 (*Tamus*)
   Non-climbing erect herbs with linear, parallel-veined lvs – fls solitary in loose umbels, all with
   stamens and ovary ....**AMARYLLIDACEAE**, p 416
7 Lvs simple, in **whorls** of 4 or more up the stem – stamens 4–5, ovary two-celled............................
   ....**RUBIACEAE**, p 348
   Lvs in **opp** pairs, simple or pinnate – stamens 1–3 .... **VALERIANACEAE**, p 345
   Lvs **alt**, strap-shaped to lanceolate, or linear, slightly fleshy, yellow-green, 1–2 cm long – plant
   prostrate – fls star-like, 3 mm across, perianth-lobes 4 or 5, white, star-like – stamens 5 ....
   ....**SANTALACEAE**, p 170
8 Stamens 3..**IRIDACEAE**, p 416
   Stamens 6..**AMARYLLIDACEAE**, p 416
9 Stamens v many in each fl – carpels many, in a head, all free from one another **10**
   Stamens equal in number to, or up to twice as many as, perianth segments............................. **11**
10 Woody climber with opp trifoliate or pinnate lvs – perianth segments 4, cream-coloured, free ....
   ....**RANUNCULACEAE**, p 95 (*Clematis*)
   Herbs with alt, simple, or ± trifoliate or pinnate lvs – perianth segments 5 or more, white or
   coloured, free – sepal-like bracts sometimes present below fl, but separated from it by a shorter or
   longer length of fl-stalk.. **RANUNCULACEAE**, p 95
11 Shrubs with red or black berries **12**
   Herbs.. **13**
12 Heath-like shrubs to 30 cm tall with narrow, alt lvs 4–6 mm long – fls with 6 free pinkish perianth
   segments, each fl 1–2 mm across, in lf-axils – fr a black berry 5 mm .... **EMPETRACEAE**, p 280
   Shrubs to 2 m tall, with alt, obovate, or pinnate lvs – **either** stems (or lf-margins) with **spines** –
   perianth 6–8 mm across, yellow, of **several** whorls, each of 3 **free** petal-like segments – stamens
   6...**BERBERIDACEAE**, p 104
   Shrubs to 1 m tall, with alt elliptical to obovate lvs 5 to 10 cm long – **no** spines on stem – perianth
   tubular, of one whorl, four-lobed at tip, pink or greenish-yellow, 8–12 mm long – stamens 8..........
   ....**THYMELAEACEAE**, p 228
13 Perianth segments 6, petal-like, **either** forming a tube below, **or** free to base, when usually in 2
   similar whorls of 3 each – stamens 6 – lvs **parallel-veined**, **linear** or **elliptical**, either all from
   base of plant or alt up the stem as well.. **14**
   Perianth segments 4 – fls in oblong terminal heads or spikes – stamens 4 – lvs ± stalked,
   either pinnate or cordate-oval **15**
   Perianth segments 5, joined into a tube at base, pink or white **16**
14 Carpels **free from one another** at least above, follicles pink-red – lvs linear, to 1 m, keeled – fls
   pink, in umbels – erect plant growing in water...**BUTOMACEAE**, p 402
   Carpels joined into a three-celled ovary ....**LILIACEAE**, p 404
15 Lvs **pinnate**, with oval toothed lfts – plant to 1 m tall – fls **red**, in oblong heads 1–2 cm
   long × 1 cm wide – perianth four-lobed – fr a one-seeded nutlet ....
   ....**ROSACEAE**, p 200 (*Sanguisorba*)
   Lvs cordate-oval, 1 long-stalked lf from base, stem-lf often stalkless – plant 10–15 cm tall – fls
   white, in oblong racemes to 5 cm long – 4 free perianth segments – fr a two-celled red berry ....
   ....**LILIACEAE**, p 404 (*Maianthemum*)
16 Creeping plant of salt-marshes – lvs **opp**, strap-shaped to obovate, no stipules – fls in lf-axils, pink
   or white, 5 mm across – stamens 5 – fr a **capsule** .... **PRIMULACEAE**, p 284 (*Glaux*)
   Erect or procumbent plants – lvs **alt**, linear to elliptical-lanceolate, with **chaffy**, **translucent**
   tubular stipules sheathing stem above each lf – fls pink, in lf-axils or in spikes, whitish or greenish
   – stamens 5–8 – fr a three-angled or lens-shaped brown **nutlet**..
   ....**POLYGONACEAE**, p 268 (*Polygonum*)

M Trees or shrubs with fls not two-lipped, with perianth (a) of one whorl of sepal-like green segments, or (b) of chaffy, membranous or scale-like segments, or (c) perianth abs

1 Fls in ovoid or cylindrical **catkins** .... see Key C, p 34
  Fls not in catkins, but in small clusters, panicles, or solitary in lf-axils.............. **2** (or see Key D, p 36)

2 Small bushy shrub, parasitic on branches of trees, with forked green branches and opp, untoothed, pale green, evergreen oblong or obovate lvs – fls in tiny clusters – berries white............
  LORANTHACEAE, p 228
  Trees or shrubs **not** parasitic on branches of trees.. **3**

3 Erect much-branched evergreen shrub to 1 m tall, with dark green, oval, spine-tipped lf-like blades 1–4 cm long (**cladodes**), some of which bear 1 or 2 tiny (3–5 mm wide) greenish six-petalled fls **on their surfaces**, in the axil of a tiny chaffy bract – stamens 6 – fr a red berry 1 cm wide .... **LILIACEAE, p 404** (*Ruscus*)
  Fls **not** borne on the surfaces of lf-like blades.. **4**

4 Shrub 1–2 m tall, with strap-shaped, silvery-grey deciduous lvs and orange berries – mostly on sand dunes.. **ELAEAGNACEAE, p 232**
  Shrub or small tree 1–5 m tall, with opp, oval, glossy, untoothed dark green, **evergreen** lvs 1.0–2.5 cm long – clusters of tiny 2 mm-wide yellow-green fls in lf-axils – perianth segments 4, male fls with 4 stamens, female with three-celled ovary – fr a three-horned capsule 8 mm long.................
  BUXACEAE, p 228
  Heath-like shrub to 30 cm tall, with linear-oblong, blunt evergreen lvs 4–6 mm long × 2 mm wide with rolled-under edges – fls 1–2 mm across, pinkish or purplish, with 6 free perianth segments – male fls with 3 stamens, female with a green superior ovary – fr a black berry 5 mm wide .... **EMPETRACEAE, p 280**
  Salt-marsh shrub to 1 m tall, with fleshy, **alt**, **cylindrical**, grey-green lvs and tiny green fls, 2–3 together in lf-axils – each fl 2 mm wide with 5 sepals and 5 stamens ....
  CHENOPODIACEAE, p 161 (*Suaeda*)
  Salt-marsh shrub to 50 cm tall, with fleshy **opp**, **flat** elliptical grey-mealy lvs, and tiny yellow fls in spikes – male fls with 5 sepals and 5 stamens, female with 2 broad sepal-like bracts and a tiny ovary.. **CHENOPODIACEAE, p 161** (*Halimione*)
  Tree with **opp** deciduous **pinnate** lvs, black buds, and tiny purplish fls in branched clusters, each with 2 stamens, no perianth, and a two-celled ovary – frs oblong, winged, 3 cm long ....
  OLEACEAE, p 238 (*Fraxinus*)
  Little-branched shrub, to 1 m tall, with obovate or elliptical evergreen glossy lvs – fls borne in short racemes in lf-axils, green, 8–12 mm long – long perianth-tube, with 4 spreading teeth at mouth, 8 stamens and an ovary – fr an ovoid black berry 12 mm .... **THYMELAEACEAE, p 228**

N Herbs with fls not two-lipped, but with (a) perianth of green, sepal-like segments, or (b) of chaffy, membranous or scale-like segments, or (c) perianth abs

1 Plants with individual fls v small (3 mm wide or less), and in either dense, catkin-like spikes or dense irregular clusters.. return to stage 4 in Master Key
  Plants with grass-like lvs (lvs linear, non-fleshy, long and narrow, flat, folded or bristle-like) with blade and sheathing base – florets, perianth abs, in axils of scales.......... **Sedges** and **Grasses** p 452
  Plants **not** as either of above.. **2**

2 Lvs **long** and **narrow**, **linear**, **cylindrical** (or **half-cylindrical**) – fls under 6 mm wide.................. **3**
  Lvs **neither** long and narrow, **nor** cylindrical (nor half so) **5**

3 Lvs ± fleshy – infl an **erect spike** or **raceme** – each fl with 6 tiny (to 3 mm long) **green** perianth segments.. **4 (JUNCAGINACEAE)**
  Lvs **not** fleshy, but firm, and **either** spongy, **or** hollow with cross-partitions, within – infl a branched panicle or cluster of fls, either terminal or from the **side** of a stem – each fl with 6 tiny brownish or purplish perianth segments, 6 or 3 stamens, and 3 stigmas........ **JUNCACEAE, p 455**

4 Lvs each with a **pore** at the tip, alt along stem – infl loose, 3–10-fld, 5 cm long, overtopped by lvs – fls 5 mm wide with 3 ovoid spreading carpels, only joined at the base – in bog pools, vr ....
  JUNCAGINACEAE, p 446 (*Scheuchzeria*)
  Lvs with **no** pore at tip, mostly from base – infl dense, many-fld, 10–20 cm long, longer than lvs – fls 3 mm wide, with 6 carpels all **fused** together – in salt and fresh water marshes ....
  JUNCAGINACEAE, p 446 (*Triglochin*)

5 Stamens **numerous** and **conspicuous** in each fl, **many more** than the number of perianth segments – carpels **free** from each other, either **achenes** or **follicles** – lvs without stipules, compound, pinnate or palmate .... **RANUNCULACEAE, p 95** (*Helleborus*, *Thalictrum*)
  Stamens **not** numerous in each fl, at most twice number of perianth segments.............................. **6**

THE GENERAL KEY

6 Fls **solitary, terminal**, 6–8 mm wide, erect on stalks of 5–10 cm – petals and sepals 5 each, greenish – stamens 5 to 10 – fr of many free nutlets in a long (to 7 cm) **cylindrical spike** rather like a Plantain infl – lvs linear, to 5 cm, all basal ....**RANUNCULACEAE**, p 95 (*Myosurus*)

Fls **grouped** in umbels, in spikes, or in axils of stem-lvs.. **7**

7 Fls in **loose, umbel-like heads**, with spreading, sepal-like green bracts round edges of infl or fl-clusters – lvs simple **8**

Fls in tall, often branched **spikes** or **racemes** – lvs simple, mostly alt................................. **9**

Fls in erect racemes – lvs pinnate, alt, with pointed clasping bases – sepals 4, stamens 6 ....

                                        CRUCIFERAE, p 113 (*Cardamine impatiens*)

Fls in loose or dense **panicle-like cymes** – lvs **palmately-veined** or lobed with conspicuous lfy stipules at base of each lf-stalk – perianth of 4 triangular green sepals and epicalyx of 4 similar green bracts outside the sepals, all attached to a calyx-cup – stamens 4, carpel 1 ....

                                            ROSACEAE, p 200 (*Alchemilla*)

Fls in loose **forked** cymes (dichasia) – lvs **simple, opp, untoothed**, no stipules – sepals 4–5 – **no** epicalyx – fr a one-celled capsule .... **CARYOPHYLLACEAE**, p 142 (*Sagina, Stellaria*)

Fls **solitary**, or in **small** close clusters, in **axils** of opp, **simple** lvs along **prostrate**, rooting stems – in damp places **10**

8 Plants with **milky** latex – infl a **true** umbel with several branches radiating from **one point** – fl-clusters, with opp bracts beneath each, fl-like, no perianths, but with several tiny yellow stamens surrounding a three-celled ovary in each fl-cluster – lvs alt (v rarely opp)...

                                            EUPHORBIACEAE, p 243 (*Euphorbia*)

Plants **without** latex – infl a repeatedly forked cyme with a fl in each fork – fls with 4 green sepals, 8 stamens, 2 styles – lvs opp or alt .... **SAXIFRAGACEAE**, p 216 (*Chrysosplenium*)

9 Fls in ± whorled spikes or racemes – tubular **membranous stipules** surrounding stem above each lf – lvs not fleshy – each fl with perianth of 3 tiny spreading outer segments, 3 larger (2–8 mm long) erect, ± triangular inner segments, often with a wart on outside, surrounding fr of a three-sided nutlet.....................................**POLYGONACEAE**, p 268 (*Rumex*)

Fls in ± irregular spikes, racemes or axillary clusters – **no** stipules – lvs often fleshy – perianth of 5 small greenish ± fleshy segments .... **CHENOPODIACEAE**, p 161

10 Ovary **inferior** – perianth 3 mm wide, of 4 spreading triangular teeth – stamens 8 – lvs **oval, pointed**, 2–5 cm long – whole plant ± red-flushed – vr............... **ONAGRACEAE**, p 222 (*Ludwigia*)

Ovary **superior**, in perianth-cup – perianth 2 mm wide, with 6 erect short pointed teeth – stamens 6 or 12 – lvs **obovate**, green, 1–2 cm long – stem and fls ± reddish ....

                                            LYTHRACEAE, p 226 (*Peplis*)

O Plants with irregular fls, with petals ± **free** from one another, not forming a corolla-tube

1 **Large trees** – fls showy, in **erect** spike-like panicles – lvs opp, palmate into 5–7 obovate lfts 10–20 cm long – sepals joined into a five-toothed calyx-tube – petals 4, white or pink, spotted – fr a large prickly green globe (to 6 cm) with shiny nut-like seeds inside ....

                                              HIPPOCASTANACEAE, p 236

Herbs, shrubs, or trees – if trees, infls **pendulous** racemes... **2**

2 Ovary inferior – lvs **parallel-veined** – perianth segments 6, in 2 whorls, the 3 outer ± alike, 2 of inner ones similar to each other, the third forming a lip, often lobed or spurred, either at top or at bottom of fl – anther 1 (or 2), stalkless – fls in spikes or racemes .... **ORCHIDACEAE**, p 422

Ovary **superior** – lvs **not** parallel-veined **3**

3 Fls shaped like those of **Peas** (see illustration at step 16 of Master Key, p 31), with a five-lobed calyx – 5 petals, one ± ascending at **rear** of fl (the **standard**), 2 at sides (the **wings**), and 2 ± joined together below in a boat-shape (the **keel**) – stamens 10, ± joined into a tube round the single carpel, which usually ripens into a fr like a little pea-pod with several seeds (but may be jointed, one-seeded, or not opening) .... **LEGUMINOSAE**, p 176

Fls **not** pea-flower like **4**

4 Fls with either a **spur**, or a swollen **sac**, below each one, formed from a petal or a sepal.............. **5**

Fls **without** a spur or sac below them **7**

5 Lvs much divided ± pinnately into narrow lfts – fls elongated and narrow with ± parallel petals, **flattened** on left and right of centre line in a vertical plane – sepals 2, small, coloured, lateral – petals 4, long and narrow, the uppermost one with a spur, or a blunt sac, at its rear end – stamens 2, each three-lobed..**FUMARIACEAE**, p 110

Lvs simple – fls not flattened to left and right, but with **spreading** petals – stamens 5, in a close ring round the style.. **6**

6 Plants with erect lfy translucent stems – lvs alt or opp, without stipules – infls short racemes or clusters in axils of upper, oval-oblong lvs – fls with 3 **petal-like** sepals (the lowest one with a curved pointed spur, the other 2 much smaller) and 5 petals (the upper largest, the lower 4 joined in pairs on either side, so total number apparently only 3) – frs oblong capsules that explode when ripe to release seeds...**BALSAMINACEAE**, p 134

Plants with decumbent, or v short erect, opaque, stems – lvs alt, long-stalked, cordate-triangular to elliptical, with a pair of long narrow ± toothed stipules at base of each – fls solitary, long-stalked, in lf-axils – sepals 5, short, green, ± equal, each with a **backward-pointing** as well as a forward-pointing lobe – petals 5, spreading outwards, lowest petal with a back-pointing **spur** – fr an ovoid three-sided capsule with a single style ....**VIOLACEAE**, p 139

7 Small low herbs, sometimes ± woody at base, with narrow untoothed alt or opp **lanceolate** or **obovate** lvs and no stipules – fls in racemes – 3 tiny sepals, plus 2 **large** 3–7-mm oval white or coloured **petal-like sepals** – **true** petals 3, tiny, fringed, joined to tube of 8 stamens ± hidden inside fl – fr a flat oval, two-celled capsule ....**POLYGALACEAE**, p 132

Erect herbs with lfy stems terminating in long erect racemes of fls.. **8**

8 Lvs **deeply palmately** lobed – fls with 5 petal-like blue-purple sepals, the rear sepal forming a **hood** 18–20 mm high over rest of fl – petals small and hidden in hood – stamens many – carpels 3–5, free, forming follicles in fr...**RANUNCULACEAE**, p 95 (*Aconitum*)

Lvs **undivided**, or **pinnately** lobed – no hood at rear of fl – fls ± flat, under 10 mm across – fr a capsule... **9**

9 Sepals 4, equal – petals 4, undivided and similar in shape, but the 2 lower **longer** than the 2 upper – stamens 6 – fr a two-celled capsule....................**CRUCIFERAE**, p 113 (*Iberis, Teesdalia*)

Sepals 4 or 6 – petals 4 or 6, spreading, repeatedly **lobed** or **divided** into narrow segments – stamens **free, many,** crowded to lower side of fl – ovary of one cell but with 3 or 4 stigma-bearing **lobes** at tip, **open** between the lobes even before fr is ripe..........................**RESEDACEAE**, p 130

P **Plants with irregular fls, with the petals joined into a corolla-tube below, either two-lipped, one-lipped, or with several unequal corolla-lobes**

1 Ovary inferior.. **2**

Ovary superior... **3**

2 Lvs long, linear to sword-shaped, ± erect, **parallel-veined** – fls in long spikes – perianth segments 6, unequal, the 3 upper ones each rather broader than the 3 lower ones which form a lower lip – all joined at base into a short tube – stamens 3 ....**IRIDACEAE**, p 416 (*Gladiolus*)

Lvs **either** elliptical and net-veined, alt up stem (on dry ground) **or** all in a basal rosette and strap-shaped (in shallow water) – fls in a loose raceme, sepals 5, corolla-tube five-lobed, the 3 lower lobes forming a lower lip, the 2 upper an upper lip – stamens 5 ....**LOBELIACEAE**, p 338

Erect or climbing shrubs with oval to elliptical opp lvs – corolla trumpet-shaped, two-lipped, five-lobed...**CAPRIFOLIACEAE**, p 342 (*Lonicera*)

3 Lvs all in a **basal rosette**, oval to oblong, simple, covered with **sticky, insect-trapping** glands – fls **solitary**, on long leafless stem stalks, each with 5 sepals and two-lipped corolla bearing a spur beneath the lower lip – in wet places.....**LENTIBULARIACEAE**, p 334 (*Pinguicula*)

Lvs floating or submerged in water, much divided into narrow linear segments, some of which bear tiny (1–4 mm long) insect-trapping **bladders** – fls in an erect, few-fld, leafless **raceme** emerging from water, with two-lipped calyx and five-lobed, two-lipped corolla with a spur below lower lip, yellow like small Snapdragon fls....................**LENTIBULARIACEAE**, p 334 (*Utricularia*)

Lvs alt or opp on **erect**, or sometimes creeping, **lfy stems** – corollas 4–5-lobed............................. **4**

4 Ovary of 4 small, **separate, rounded** lobes, with a long style, forked at tip, arising from **between** the 4 lobes – fr of 4, one-seeded nutlets (open corolla-tube to see this) **5**

Ovary globular, ovoid, conical, or lens-shaped and flattened on each side, with a long style, often forked at tip, arising from the **top of the ovary** **6**

5 Lvs in **opp** pairs – fls in densely branched clusters or whorls in the lf-axils – fls usually strongly two-lipped, with 4 or 2 stamens – stems four-angled – plants ± hairy (but not usually with stiff bristles all over stem and lvs)..**LABIATAE**, p 310

Lvs **alt** – infls one-sided clusters (cymes) **drooping** from lf-axils – fls with lowest of the 5 corolla lobes rather larger than the others, forming an indistinct lip – stamens 5, of **unequal** lengths – plants with ± **stiff bristles** on **round** stems and lvs ....**BORAGINACEAE**, p 324 (*Echium*)

6 Lvs **always** opp – ovary four-celled – fr of 4 nutlets – fls in long spikes in lf-axils, their bracts v short (half length of calyx only)..**VERBENACEAE**, p 294

Lvs alt, or sometimes opp – ovary two-celled – fr a globular or ovoid **capsule**, producing **many** seeds – infl varied, but if fls in spikes, bracts **longer** than calyx......**SCROPHULARIACEAE**, p 297

THE VEGETATIVE KEYS, TO PLANTS NOT IN FLOWER

These keys are designed to enable their user to identify at least the commoner and more widespread plants, at times when no flowers are available for practice of the more usual form of plant identification, by flower structure. Except for the admirable key "British Water Plants", by S.M. Haslam, C.A. Sinker and P.A. Wolseley, *Field Studies*, vol 4 (1975), there seem to be no vegetative keys available in this country for the majority of flowering herbs (as opposed to trees and shrubs, or grasses).

The keys will be useful not only to the amateur who wishes to know the name of a plant that he or she finds without flowers, but more specifically to the professional ecologist, or to the student doing a field project who has perforce to work in a particular habitat and at a season when few, if any, of the plants are in flower. The plants are grouped by **habitats** rather than by families because it is in their habitats that they are naturally grouped in the countryside. Some of the keys, particularly those to **woodlands** (I), **chalk grasslands** (II) and **heaths** (III), will be useful even in winter, as many plants of these habitats remain visible above ground at that time. Other keys will be more useful from spring to autumn, at times when, although some species are in flower, many others are only in leaf. Because some aquatic plants are shy flowering, the flowers of many others inconspicuous and their structure difficult to interpret, the key to **aquatic plants** (IV) should be useful throughout summer and early autumn (many water plants are not visible in winter and spring).

It proved impossible to include in these keys all the species described in the main, illustrated text (pp 95–462) of this book. Exclusions comprise some annuals that normally have flowers present nearly all the time they are above ground and may not be visible at all for the rest of the year. Critical (difficult), rare, or garden plants have also been omitted. In some cases firm identification beyond genus to distinct species cannot be achieved without flowers; with these the user is taken as far as possible, with an indication of further likely separation. However, many plants of grazed grassland, where animals have eaten all the flowers, should be identifiable with these keys. More detailed tips on the vegetative differences between plants in flower that look much alike are given in the main text, on the pages to which the key will have directed the user.

The keys work on the same principles as those to plants in flower in the rest of the book. Where the number of species to separate is large, a master key, based on the most immediately obvious and clear-cut characters is given first, and this takes the user direct to the relevant one of a number of sub-keys (distinguished by lettered headings). The keys work on the dichotomous principle, normally offering two choices at each step; however, in these vegetative keys three, four, or up to six choices may sometimes be presented when the distinctions they offer are sufficiently clear.

It is important to find the best leaves, shoots or fruits of each plant studied – tattered or broken leaves may be misleading. In many steps in the keys more than one character is given, in order to make identification more certain. Plants are very variable (it is man, not nature, that categorizes them), and sometimes two out of three (or three out of four) characters suggest one genus or species, but a fourth (or fifth) character another. In such cases the 'majority verdict' is to be preferred, and it must be accepted that identification must sometimes be tentative rather than conclusive.

Procedure

1 First identify the habitat – if necessary read the descriptive introduction at the beginning of the key.
2 Always use a pocket lens for studying fine details.
3 Work carefully through the master key to find the sub-key that clearly describes the salient features of the plant concerned.
4 Work through the sub-key until a reasonable correspondence of characters denotes a particular species. Some species 'key out' in more than one place; this has been done to allow for plant variation, or for possible different interpretations of the features.
5 In many places in the keys there are small drawings of the plant concerned, or of a particular feature of it; these should help in identification. But if there is no illustration in the key, look at the description and illustration in the main text, using the page references usually given. The absence of a page reference means that the species concerned is not mentioned elsewhere in this book; in these cases, the English plant names are given as well as the scientific, if the former exist.
6 If nothing in a key agrees with the plant being studied, try the key to an adjacent and possibly overlapping habitat.
7 If there is some, but not complete, agreement between plant and key, weigh up the balance of characters for and against the plant being the species described, on the majority principle referred to above. If a decision cannot be reached, go through the key again, to ensure that a wrong choice was not made at an earlier stage, if need be using a fresh section of the plant.
Note: The keys will become much easier to use with experience!

VEGETATIVE KEYS

I PLANTS OF WOODLANDS, SHADY HEDGEBANKS AND SUNKEN LANES

Woodland of some kind is the natural ('stable' and 'climax') vegetation of most of Western Europe below the tree line on mountains, so very many of our native plants are forest species. Woodlands vary in flora according to the type of geological parent rock and hence of soil, according to the degree of drainage, and, of course, according to the type of human management exercised over the centuries. Today, much forest is composed of planted evergreen conifers; such woodlands, unless of some age and partially thinned out, are of very little botanical interest except along the open rides or paths where more light penetrates. Deciduous woodlands, formerly often managed by coppicing (cutting the shrub layer every 8–15 years), more closely reproduce the light and shade conditions of primeval forests, and tend to have retained a continuity of flora from prehistoric times. Coppicing, when practised, lets in the light, and the plants respond by a burst of flowering one or two years later. But many old coppices have now not been cut for years, this form of management being no longer considered economic, and in such woods many plants do not flower at all. In less dense woodlands, with a less closed shrub layer and tall mature trees (and hence woodlands of a more natural structure) there is a 'light phase' in spring when most plants tend to flower before the leaves of the trees unfold and reduce the light, but when it is nevertheless warm and sunny enough for herb growth. In many such woods comparatively few plants are still in flower during mid to late summer, but many woodland herbs, most of them perennials, remain growing and visible as leaf-rosettes, leafy runners or non-flowering shoots, in the autumn and even throughout milder winters. Most of the commoner of these species can thus be identified with this key throughout much of the year.

Woodland soil variations greatly affect the flora. On heavy clay soils waterlogging is common in winter, and many marsh species may occur that can tolerate some shade (so see also Key IV). Light sandy or gravelly soils, or those on gritstones, granites or other ancient rocks, are often very poor in nutrients, particularly in lime, and are consequently very acid (with a pH often below 5). On such soils, where oak, birch or pine predominate, the woodland ground flora is often very limited and composed of heathland-type plants, especially where there is enough light (see Key III). On calcareous (lime-rich) soils, the pH is high (often above 7) and the soils are thus alkaline. Here ash, elm or hazel are often dominant, with beech in SE England or France, in drier areas; the ground flora is rich and may contain many species also found on chalk scrub or grassland, especially by rides and in glades where the light is good. It is not usual to find plants of acid and of alkaline soils side by side, but if there is a geological change they may occur in the same wood; in such cases it should be possible to see a change in the soil, eg, from sand to loam, or where pieces of chalk become noticeable.

Shady hedgebanks and hollow sunken lanes have been included in this key because they tend to have shade-loving (or shade-tolerant) woodland-type floras; indeed, ancient hollow lanes and hedges may preserve actual relics of former woodlands from the time when old forests bordered them.

MASTER KEY

3 Lvs once-pinnate ....D

Lvs twice or more times pinnate ....E

Lvs trifoliate ....F

Lvs palmately divided or lobed...G

Lvs simple, undivided (toothed or untoothed)...4

4 Lvs linear, grass-like ....H

Lvs untoothed, with many parallel veins, and no cross-veined network – but not grass-like – lvs either in a basal rosette, at or near base of stem, or along stem I

Lvs not grass-like, nor with many parallel veins, usually net-veined, though sometimes apparently one-veined 5

5 Lvs in **whorls** of 4 or more along the stems ....J

Lvs in **opp** pairs along the stems ....K

Lvs in a rosette raised 10–20 cm or more above ground, at tip of stem.........L

Lvs **alt** along, or at base of, the stems...M

Lvs entirely from base of stem, in a spreading or ± erect rosette (not in opp pairs) ....N

A Trees and taller shrubs (see also Key II F)

1 Lvs (or buds) in opp pairs **2**

Lvs (or buds) alt along stems......... **5**

2 Lvs pinnate...................................... **3**

Lvs palmately-lobed **4**

Lvs palmately compound – lfts large (10–20 cm long), obovate......
Aesculus hippocastanum (p 236 C)

3 Lfts oval to elliptical, 5 (or, rarely, 7), hairy on veins beneath – buds small (3–5 mm long) – twigs fluted, brown – frs black berries..................
Sambucus nigra (p 342 A)

Lfts oval, 9–13, hairless when mature – buds large (5–10 mm long), black – twigs smooth, round, grey – frs bunches of dry 'keys', with flat oblong tips..........................
Fraxinus excelsior (p 238 K)

4 Lvs 3–5-lobed, 3–5 cm wide, usually broader than long, lobes blunt, with few blunt teeth ....
Acer campestre (p 236 A)

Lvs five-lobed, 7–15 cm wide, as long as broad, lobes pointed, with many pointed teeth..........................
Acer pseudoplatanus (p 236 B)

5 Lvs evergreen, tough or thick **6**

Lvs ± thin, deciduous.................. **7**

6 Lvs glossy dark green, oval, ± edged with spinous teeth ....
Ilex aquifolium (p 230 E)

Lvs dull dark green, palmate to elliptical, untoothed – plant either climbing or creeping on the ground.........*Hedera helix* (p 230 F)

Lvs linear, needle-like, 3–8 cm long × 1–2 mm wide, borne in pairs on short side-shoots ....
Pinus sylvestris (**Scots Pine**)

Lvs linear, tapered to sharp points, 1.0–1.5 cm long, grey-green, borne in whorls of 3 on twigs ....
Juniperus communis (**Juniper**)

Lvs linear, strap-shaped, 1.0–2.5 cm long × 2–3 mm wide, in two spreading rows along twigs........
Taxus baccata (**Yew**)

7 Lvs pinnate, downy below – no prickles on stem – frs red berries ......
Sorbus aucuparia (p 202 A)

Lvs pinnate – stems with prickles – frs rose-hips...........................
Rosa canina (p 206 D)

Lvs simple **8**

8 Lvs unlobed, toothed or not **9**

Lvs ± deeply lobed **21**

9 Lvs rounded-obovate, and as if cut across at tip.................................
Alnus glutinosa (p 234 G)

Lvs ± pointed at tip **10**

10 Lvs rounded in outline............... **11**

Lvs oval to elliptical-lanceolate in outline **13**

11 Lvs with broad shallow blunt wavy teeth, tip not drawn-out................... (*Populus*) **12**

Lvs with small fine teeth and drawn-out tip, base cordate – lvs v **downy** both sides, also twigs............ *Corylus avellana* (p 234 F)

Lvs with fine teeth and pointed tip, base cordate – lvs **hairless** above, but with hair tufts in vein axils below – mature twigs hairless .... *Tilia* spp, especially *T. cordata* (p 236 F)

12 Lvs grey-felted below, dark glossy green above – stalk 1.5–4.0 cm....... *Populus canescens* (p 242 K)

Lvs green below, but downy when young – stalk v long, flexible and flattened (2.5–6.0 cm long) .... *Populus tremula* (p 242 J)

13 Lvs with blade extending further down stalk on one side than on other.............................. (*Ulmus*) **14**

Lvs symmetrical, blade extending ± equally down each side of stalk... **15**

14 Lvs large, obovate or elliptical to diamond-shaped, 8–16 cm long on short shoots...................................... *Ulmus glabra* (p 238 H)

Lvs small, oval-elliptical, 4–6 cm long on short shoots .... *Ulmus procera* (p 238 G)

15 Lvs oval, ± untoothed................ **16**

Lvs oval, toothed........................ **17**

Lvs elliptical-lanceolate............... **18**

16 Lvs smooth, hairless except on edges and on veins below – buds pointed, cigar-shaped, brown – twigs grey – tree to 30 m tall............. *Fagus sylvatica* (p 233 D)

Lvs ± wrinkled, downy (especially below) – buds blunt .... *Salix caprea* (p 242 F)

Lvs smooth, hairless, glossy green – buds without scales – twigs green and downy when young – shrub to 4–5 m – frs berries, red then black.........*Frangula alnus* (p 232 E)

17 Lvs smooth and glossy above, elliptical, hairless below, with 2 small red warts on stalk just below lf-blade – fr a cherry........................... *Prunus avium* (p 202 D)

Lvs ± wrinkled and deep green above, and **white-felted** below, no red warts on lf-stalk – fr a hard red berry................................... *Sorbus aria* (p 202 C)

Lvs oval, smooth, green both sides, with blunt teeth, some borne on short spur-shoots in clusters – thorns often present on twigs........... *Malus sylvestris* (p 204 I)

Lvs triangular-oval, to 5 cm long, flat .... (*Betula*) **20**

Lvs oval, to 10 cm long, with pleated side-veins and strongly doubly-toothed .... *Carpinus betulus* (p 234 E)

18 Twigs ending in strong straight thorns – lvs elliptical, 1–4 cm long, toothed – fr black with blue bloom like a small round plum.................... *Prunus spinosa* (p 202 E)

Twigs without thorns **19**

19 Lvs elliptical-lanceolate, sharply-toothed, 10–20 cm long, hairless when mature.... *Castanea sativa* (p 233 C)

Lvs elliptical-obovate, scarcely toothed, 3–7 cm long, v downy below (and also above when young) – twigs downy...................... *Salix cinerea* (p 242 G)

20 Lvs with ± truncate base, teeth themselves toothed, hairless – twigs hairless, warted...................... *Betula pendula* (p 238 J)

Lvs with rounded base, simple teeth, downy – twigs downy, no warts......*Betula pubescens* (p 238 I)

21 Lvs 5–12 cm long, margin with deep, wavy but rounded lobes – no thorns – frs acorns ...... (*Quercus*) **22**

Lvs 1.5–5.0 cm long, margins deeply lobed – thorns present on twigs – frs hard red berries............... (*Crataegus*) **23**

Lvs 7–10 cm long, margin pinnatifid or almost palmately-lobed, with few, deep, pointed, toothed lobes – no thorns present – fr a brown, spotted hard berry............... *Sorbus torminalis* (p 202 B)

22 Lvs hairless below, with **rounded basal lobes**, and stalks 1 cm long or less ....*Quercus robur* (p 233 A)

Lvs, with tufts of hairs in vein-axils underneath, **tapered** into stalks 2 cm or more long............................
Quercus petraea (p 233 B)

23 Lvs on short shoots **oval** in outline, with **deep, sharp-pointed** triangular lobes longer than broad – style one per fr..
Crataegus monogyna (p 204 J)

Lvs on short shoots **obovate** in outline, with **shallow rounded** lobes broader than long – styles 2– 3 per fr ....
Crataegus laevigata
(p 204 K)

B Low erect shrubs (under 1 m tall), or climbing or creeping plants with woody stems

1 Lvs **compound**, stems sometimes with prickles.................................. **2**

Lvs **simple**, at most lobed only, **stems** not prickly **3**

Much-branched lfless shrub (Nov– April), with younger stems green, four-angled......................................
Vaccinium myrtillus (p 276 A)

2 Lvs alt, **pinnate**, with stipules at bases of stalks – stems with prickles along them – frs red hips.... (*Rosa*) **4**

Lvs alt, **palmate**, with **3–7 lfts**, with stipules at bases – stems and lvs prickly – frs blackberries ....
Rubus fruticosus (p 206 E)

Lvs **opp**, **pinnate**, with 3–5 lfts – woody climber – frs with white feathery styles................................
Clematis vitalba (p 104 A)

3 Lvs **palmately-lobed**, leathery, evergreen – no stipules – plant creeping on (and carpeting) ground in shade, or climbing trees by means of sucker roots – frs purple-black berries ....*Hedera helix* (p 230 F)

Lvs **oval**, with **spines** on edges, leathery, evergreen, glossy – erect shrub (or tree) – frs red berries.........
Ilex aquifolium (p 230 E)

Lvs unlobed, spineless.................. **5**

4 Lvs with **blunt**, feebly-toothed, grey-green lfts – prickles on stem weak, without broad bases, hooked at tips......... *Rosa arvensis* (p 206 A)

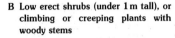

Lvs with pointed, strongly-toothed, bright green lfts – prickles on stem strong, broad-based, arched............
Rosa canina (p 206 D)

5 Lvs **opp**, dull grey-green, ± downy, oval-elliptical, untoothed, 3–6 cm long – plant carpeting ground in dry wds or climbing trees or hedges – frs red berries................
Lonicera periclymenum (p 344 F)

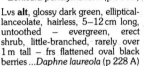

Lvs **alt**, glossy dark green, elliptical-lanceolate, hairless, 5–12 cm long, untoothed – evergreen, erect shrub, little-branched, rarely over 1 m tall – frs flattened oval black berries ...*Daphne laureola* (p 228 A)

Lvs **alt**, fresh green, oval, pointed, 1–3 cm long, finely-toothed all round, with net veins conspicuous, – stems much-branched, plant bushy, younger stems green, four-angled – frs globular black berries with grey-blue bloom and flattened tips – in hthy wds on acid soils ....
Vaccinium myrtillus (p 276 A)

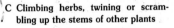

C Climbing herbs, twining or scrambling up the stems of other plants

1 Lvs in **opp** pairs, trilobed or palmately-lobed, rough – stems twining clockwise (as viewed from above) – in moist wds, hbs..............
Humulus lupulus (p 228 H)

Lvs **alt** along stems...................... **2**

2 Stems climbing by **coiled tendrils** in axils of **palmately 3–5-lobed** lvs – stems bristly – frs clusters of red berries .... *Bryonia dioica* (p 228 I)

Stems **without** coiled tendrils, but **twining** up stems of other plants – lvs cordate to arrow-shaped, untoothed.. **3**

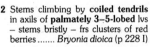

Stems **scrambling**, **not** twining up stems of other plants – lvs **oval**, sometimes with 2 pinnate basal lobes, not glossy – frs clusters of red berries ....
Solanum dulcamara (p 296 H)

3 Lvs **v glossy**, **oval**, with pointed tips and deeply **cordate** bases, twining anti-clockwise – frs clusters of **red berries** ....
Tamus communis (p 405 A)

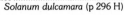

Lvs **not** glossy, arrow-shaped, bases cordate to square-cut – frs **dry**.. 4

4 Lvs mealy below, smooth above, with fringed chaffy stipules at bases – stem twining clockwise – frs three-angled....................................
Polygonum convolvulus or *P. dumetorum* (p 274 L, M)

Lvs **not** mealy on either side, no stipules present – stem twining anti-clockwise – frs dry globular capsules ... *Calystegia sepium* (p 294 B)

Herbs with once-pinnate lvs

1 Lvs pinnately-lobed but with **at least** a narrow flange of lf-blade along stalk connecting lf-lobes – milky latex present............................
Mycelis muralis (p 390 E)

Lvs pinnate compound, lfts quite **separate** from each other along a narrow stalk – no milky latex......... 2

2 Lvs with a **terminal** lft as well as side lfts – lfts all ± **toothed**............ 3

Lvs with **no** terminal lft, but sometimes with a branched **tendril** instead – stipules present at lf-base – lfts **never** toothed.......................... 8

3 Side lfts of **different** sizes, **small** ones alt with **larger** ones down lf-stalk – stipules **always** present at lf-base.. 4

Side lfts all ± of **same size** – stipules **abs**.................................... 6

4 Terminal lft much broader and longer than side ones..................... 5

Terminal lft not, or hardly, broader or larger than side ones – in damp or marshy places.............................
Filipendula ulmaria (p 214 A)

5 Terminal lft of (at least) root-lvs broadly orbicular to kidney-shaped, much broader than rest of lf, unlobed – in wetter places............
Geum rivale (p 214 D)

Terminal lft, even of root-lvs, ± triangular and ± trilobed, little or no broader than rest of lf – in drier places .... *Geum urbanum* (p 214 C)

6 Terminal lft of root-lvs (**a**) as broad as long, orbicular, **much** broader than side lfts – **upper** lvs (**b**) with all lfts **narrow**-oblong to linear ....
Cardamine pratensis (p 122 G)

Terminal lft of root-lvs longer than broad, little or no broader than side lfts – **upper** lvs with all lfts **oval**...... 7

7 Terminal lft scarcely-toothed – **all** lfts of similar size and shape ....
Cardamine amara (p 124 B)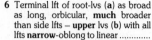

Terminal lft with large coarse blunt teeth, side lfts narrower but also coarsely-toothed...............................
Cardamine flexuosa (p 122 F)

8 Lfts 5–12 pairs per lf – stems **round** 9

Lfts 1–3 pairs per lf – stems **winged** 11

9 Lfts **oval**, widest near **base**, 5–6 pairs per lf, ± hairless ....
Vicia sepium (p 190 B)

Lfts **elliptical**, widest near **middle**, 6–12 pairs per lf 10

10 Lfts thinly **downy** – stipules half-arrow-shaped ....
Vicia cracca (p 190 A)

Lfts **hairless** – stipules long-toothed and **rounded** at base...................
Vicia sylvatica (p 192 J)

11 Lfts **one** pair only, narrow-lanceolate, 7–15 cm long – lf ending in branched **tendril** – climbing plant... *Lathyrus sylvestris* (p 192 F)

Lfts **2–3** pairs, elliptical-lanceolate, 1–4 cm long – **no** tendrils – erect plant................. *Lathyrus montanus* (p 192 B)

E Herbs with lvs twice, or more times pinnate

1 Lvs **fern-like**, with lfts deeply lobed... 2

Lvs **not** fern-like, lfts rounded, oval or coarsely-toothed....................... 5

2 Lf-stalk with **papery brown scales** – **no** erect stem present....................
Dryopteris (**Buckler ferns**)

Lf-stalk **without** papery brown scales – **erect stem** (or last year's dead one) present.......................... 3

3 Lfts **hairless**, 1–3 cm long, with bases **wedge**-shaped, tips **bluntly** 2–4-lobed – in wet places...............
Oenanthe crocata (p 262 A)

Lfts **hairy**, bases **rounded**, tips finely **cut** **4**

4 Lf-stalks **purple**-spotted – lfts v downy, **grey**-green, **blunt**...............
Chaerophyllum temulentum (p 252 E)

Lf-stalks **not** purple-spotted – lfts v sparsely and shortly downy, **fresh** green, **sharp**-toothed ....
Anthriscus sylvestris (p 251 A)

5 Lfts irregularly lobed, **coarsely**-toothed, **roughly hairy** – secondary lfts **webbed** together, not oval ....
Heracleum spondylium (p 256 D)

Lfts **rounded**, **finely** and regularly toothed, **smooth**, scarcely hairy – secondary lfts mostly **separate**, oval-elliptical **6**

6 Lfts **elliptical**, the side veins 4–5 mm apart – lvs and stalks uniformly fresh green – lf-stalk triangular, hardly inflated at base – lvs twice-**trifoliate** rather than twice-pinnate..
Aegopodium podagraria (p 256 A)

Lfts **oval**, side veins 2–3 mm apart... **7**

7 Lfts v **sharply**-toothed, sometimes lobed, **dark glossy** green above – stalks all **uniform** green, **not** inflated below – vl in calc wds ....
Actaea spicata (p 104 E)

Lfts v finely-toothed, fresh green, **not** glossy above – stalks **purple**-stained below, **purple**-spotted where lfts are attached – lf-stalk **inflated** at base – in moist wds.........
Angelica sylvestris (p 256 B)

F Herbs with trifoliate lvs

1 Lfts simple, toothed or not............ **2**

Lfts deeply palmately-lobed or divided **4**

2 Lfts untoothed, obovate, notched at tips, green on uppersides, purplish on lower sides, drooping from tips of long stalks – only a few scattered adpressed hairs present ....
Oxalis acetosella (p 176 I)

Lfts shallow-toothed, v hairy, oval-obovate, 1–4 cm long, lvs all from base... **3**

Lfts deeply-toothed, diamond-shaped, hairy, 5–7 cm long, their bases wedge-shaped – lvs alt along stem – **lower** lvs pinnate – stipules lf-like ..... *Geum urbanum* (p 214 C)

3 Lfts pointed, bright green, end tooth of each lft longer than its neighbours on each side ....
Fragaria vesca (p 210 J)

Lfts blunt, blue-green, end tooth of each lft not longer (often shorter) than its neighbours on each side ......
Potentilla sterilis (p 210 I)

4 Lvs v hairy – lfts oval, deeply and sharply palmately-lobed – no stipules – lfy rooting runners extend from lf-rosettes ....
Ranunculus repens (p 96 A)

Lvs hairless – lfts ± fleshy, yellowish-green, deeply palmately-lobed – lobes blunt, but tipped with tiny spines.....................................
Adoxa moschatellina (p 346 H)

Lvs hairless – lfts thin, dark green, lobed ± to base into narrow-oblong sharp-toothed segments which are not spine-tipped...............
Anemone nemorosa (p 102 D)

G Herbs with lvs palmately divided or lobed, ie, with 5 or more lfts or lobes radiating from tip of lf-stalk (on larger lvs at least)

1 Lvs **hairless** **2**

Lvs ± **hairy**.................................. **5**

2 Lvs **divided to base** of blade into **separate**, toothed lfts **3**

Lvs **lobed**, but **not** divided to base.. **4**

3 Lfts **dark blue**-green, narrow-lanceolate (to 1.5 cm wide), never forked, arising from **2 'arches'** at tip of lf-stalk, and **not** radiating from one central point – in open calc wds...
Helleborus foetidus (p 98 F)

Lfts **bright** green, broad-lanceolate (to 3 cm wide), lobed or forked, radiating from **one** central point at tip of lf-stalk – in ash and hazel wds.........*Helleborus viridis* (p 98 E)

I WOODLANDS

4 Lf-lobes **rounded**, untoothed, veins **pale** – lvs arising from **creeping stems** – older stems **woody** ....
Hedera helix (p 230 F)

Lf-lobes **pointed**, separated ¾ way to lf-base, themselves pinnately-lobed and toothed, veins not v pale – lvs in basal **rosette**, and alt up **erect non-woody** stems...................
Sanicula europaea (p 258 E)

5 Plants with ± creeping stems, lvs **alt** along them **6**

Plants with lvs in **basal rosette** on long stalks, and also **alt** along erect stems... **7**

6 Lvs **long-stalked** (5–8 cm), lvs 4–6 cm wide, divided **to base** into 5 (or 7) obovate, toothed lfts – **stipules** present where stalk joins stem .....*Potentilla reptans* (p 210 E)

Lvs **short-stalked** (0.5–1.0 cm), lvs 1.0–1.5 cm wide, **shallow-lobed** (like ivy lvs) – **no** stipules present ....
Veronica hederifolia (p 306 F)

7 Root-lvs (**a**) with palmate veins, but outline varying from round, through kidney-shaped to palmately-lobed – hairs sparse – stem-lvs (**b**) ± stalkless, divided to base into narrow segments – lvs all pale green..
Ranunculus auricomus (p 96 F)

Root- (and stem-) lvs palmately **divided to base** into triangular shiny lfts, themselves deeply twice-pinnate, stalks and lf margins ± reddish-flushed..........................
Geranium robertianum (p 172 A)

Root-lvs deeply **palmately-lobed**, **nearly** to base, into elliptical-obovate lobes, themselves deeply pinnately-lobed – lvs and stalks green, not shiny – in N of Br Isles................
Geranium sylvaticum (p 174 F)

Root-lvs (**a**) long-stalked, divided to **base** into 3 toothed lfts – stem-lvs (**b**) stalkless, with apparently 5 obovate toothed lfts (actually the 2 outer shorter lfts are stipules resembling lfts) – in hthy wds ....
Potentilla erecta (p 209 A)

H Herbs with linear, grass-like lvs

(Note: on calc soils other grasses, sedges or orchids may occur in woods; if plants fail to key out here, consult Key II)

1 Lvs brittle, fleshy-textured, bright glossy green, without distinction into blade and basal sheath – lvs in an erect rosette **2**

Lvs firm, thin-textured, clearly divided into blade and ± cylindrical or angled sheathing base – lvs usually many together in a dense tuft....................................... **3**

2 Lvs oblong-lanceolate, 1.5–4.0 cm wide × 12–30 cm long, with obovoid **seed-pod** 3–5 cm long arising from centre of a group of lvs on a short stalk in April–May ....
Colchicum autumnale (p 408 G)

Lvs linear, ± hooded at tip, 7–15 mm wide × 20–45 cm long, appearing Feb–March – fl-spike arising from centre of lvs in April–May – only dry spike of fr capsules (20–40 cm tall) present Aug–Feb....
Endymion non-scriptus (p 410 A)

3 Lvs alt, but in **2 opp** vertical ranks on **round, hollow**, pointed stem ...... (**Grasses**) **4**

Lvs in **3 vertical** ranks on stem – stem **solid**, ± **triangular** in cross-section................ (**Sedges**) **12**

4 Lvs **bristle-like**, dark green, not more than 1.5 mm wide, rough-edged – lf-sheath pinkish – in hthy wds...
Deschampsia flexuosa (**Wavy Hair-grass**)

Lvs **flat** or **furrowed**, over 1.5 mm wide **5**

5 Lvs to 3 mm wide.......................... **6**

Lvs over 3 mm wide....................... **7**

6 Lvs dark green, smooth, keeled, 1–2 mm wide, ligule v **short** or abs – sheaths **smooth** – infl drooping – in dry wds..
Poa nemoralis (**Wood Meadow-grass**)

Lvs yellow-green, 2–3 mm wide, flat, ligule **long**, pointed – sheaths **rough** – infl erect – in damp wds......
Poa trivialis (p 458 Ci)

7 Lvs flat, rigid, 3–5 mm wide, hairless, grey-green, with deep parallel **furrows** on upperside, **v rough** when rubbed downwards – plant forms dense tussocks in damper wds...
  Deschampsia caespitosa (**Tufted Hair-grass**)

Lvs without deep parallel furrows on upperside **8**

8 Lvs **bright deep** green, 10–20 cm long × 3–5 mm wide, soft, drooping at tips, with only a few hairs – sheaths downy with pointed flap at tip on side of stem opp to lf-blade – infl loose, fls purple-brown – in dry wds..*Melica uniflora* (**Wood Melick**)

Lvs **yellow**-green, **light** green, or **grey**-green.. **9**

9 Lvs **hairy** **10**

Lvs ± **hairless**............................... **11**

10 Lvs 6–13 mm wide, yellow-green, **soft**, **drooping**, downy – sheaths downy...
  Brachypodium sylvaticum (**False Brome**)

Lvs 5–10 mm wide, light green, **rough**-hairy, **not** drooping – sheaths with many long downward-pointing bristles ....
  Bromus ramosus (**Hairy Brome**)

11 Lvs to 18 mm wide, rough, **shining bright** green, with a pair of **pincer**-shaped purplish lobes (**auricles**) where lf-blade joins sheath ....
  Festuca gigantea (**Giant Fescue**)

Lvs 5–10 mm wide, rough, **whitish-grey**-green, with **no** auricles – infl (50–100 cm), persisting in winter, is loose, of whorled, egg-shaped spikelets, 2–3 mm long........
  Milium effusum (**Wood Millet**)

12 Plants forming large (50–100 cm wide) **tussocks** of lvs, often **raised** on a shaggy column 30–100 cm off ground – lvs 3–7 mm wide, deeply grooved above, with v **rough** edges – in v wet swampy wds ....
  Carex paniculata (**Greater Tussock-sedge**)

Plants forming **smaller** tufts or tussocks, **not** raised off ground – lvs ± **smooth**-edged **13**

13 Lvs 2 mm wide, **grooved** above, bright green – ligules 1–2 mm long, triangular – in wet places ....
  Carex remota (**Remote Sedge**)

Lvs 3–6 mm wide, ± **flat**, bright green – ligules 2 mm long, triangular – in drier places................
  Carex sylvatica (p 456 F)

Lvs 6–10 mm wide, ± flat, yellow-green, tips turning **orange-brown** in winter – ligules 10 mm long, triangular – in damp places .....
  Carex strigosa (**Thin-spiked Wood-sedge**)

Lvs 15–20 mm wide, ± flat, **dark green** on upperside, **paler** beneath – ligules 3–6 mm long, lanceolate – on heavy soils ....
  Carex pendula (**Pendulous Sedge**)

I **Herbs with lvs untoothed, with many parallel-veins, and no cross-veined network, but not grass-like – lvs in a basal rosette, or at or near base of stem, or along stem**

1 Lvs ± linear, grass-shaped but brittle and rather fleshy, arising at an angle of 50°–80° from ground, appearing in spring only .. **2**

Lvs not linear or grass-shaped ......, **3**

2 Lvs oblong-lanceolate, 1.5–4.0 cm wide × 12–30 cm long, with obovoid fleshy seed pod 3–5 cm long arising in April–May from centre of lf-group on a short stalk – local only......................................
  Colchichum autumnale (p 408 G)

Lvs linear, ± hooded at tips, 7–15 mm wide × 20–45 cm long, arise Feb–March – fl-spike arises April–May from centre of lf-group – only fr-spike visible July–Feb – capsules dry papery brown in autumn, winter ....
  Endymion non-scriptus (p 410 A)

3 Lvs elliptical, stalked, 1 or several, arising ± **vertically** from base of plant or on a short erect stem **4**

Lvs in an **opp pair** only, blunt, oval-elliptical, **spreading** at a **wide angle**, arising either directly from ground, or from a short stem a few cm above it.................................. **5**

Lvs elliptical, **alt** along a stem 20–60 cm tall that is erect below, arching above.............. (*Polygonatum*) **6**

Lvs several, in a basal **rosette** arising from ground, some lvs lying flat, some ascending at an angle **7**

4 Lvs ± fleshy, **garlic**-scented when bruised, **bright** green, arising direct from bulb – lf-stalks twisted through 180° – in moist wds ....
Allium ursinum (p 414 A)

Lvs **not** fleshy, **not** garlic-scented, **grey**-green, arising in a pair on a short erect stem – in dry wds............
Convallaria majalis (p 406 F)

5 Lvs elliptical to elliptical-lanceolate, in **one opp** pair arising **directly** from ground, and **spreading** ....
Platanthera chlorantha (p 436 B)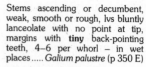

Lvs oval, in one opp pair a few cm **above** ground, on a fleshy **stem** – fl-spike (or bud of one) may be present above lvs....................
Listera ovata (p 432 E)

6 Stem **round** ....
Polygonatum multiflorum (p 405 C)

Stem **angled** – local, on limestone ....
Polygonatum odoratum (p 406 D)

7 Lvs **unspotted**...............................
Orchis spp (see Key II)

Lvs **purple**-spotted **8**

8 Rosette-lvs ± in 2 vertical **ranks**, **grey**-green – spots **transverse** across lvs ....
Dactylorhiza fuchsii (p 442 E)

Rosette-lvs radiating ± **equally** from base, glossy **deep** green – spots elongated **lengthwise** along lvs............*Orchis mascula* (p 433 A)

J Herbs with lvs in successive whorls of 4 or more along the stems

Stems erect smooth – lvs 6–8 per whorl, dark green, firm, hairless, with tiny **forward**-pointing prickles, lanceolate or elliptical, pointed........
Galium odoratum (p 352 B)

Stems erect at first, then scrambling, **v rough** with down-pointing prickles – lvs 6–8 per whorl, light green, hairy, with **v strong** backward-pointing prickles, obovate to lanceolate..
Galium aparine (p 350 H)

Stems ascending or decumbent, weak, smooth or rough, lvs bluntly lanceolate with no point at tip, margins with **tiny** back-pointing teeth, 4–6 per whorl – in wet places .....*Galium palustre* (p 350 E)

K Herbs with lvs in opp pairs along the stems – lvs simple, not with many parallel veins

1 Lvs quite untoothed **2**

Lvs with (at least) some shallow blunt teeth, or deeply-toothed **7**

2 Lvs linear-lanceolate, 4–6 cm long × 0.5 mm wide, fine-pointed, rough-edged, hairless, stalkless – stems square in cross-section...........
Stellaria holostea (p 150 C)

Lvs elliptical-lanceolate and stalkless on stem, obovate and broadly-stalked at base of stem, all **hairy**, smooth-edged, 5–20 cm long × 2–4 cm wide – stem rounded...............
Silene dioica (p 144 H)

Lvs all elliptical-lanceolate, stalkless, hairless, soft, smooth-edged – stem rounded, branched below ....
Melampyrum pratense (p 306 G)

Lvs ± oval....................................**3**

3 Lvs with **2 strong side-veins** ± **parallel to midrib**, lvs 1–2 cm long, v sparsely hairy – stem round ....
Moehringia trinervia (p 152 A)

Lvs with pinnate veins **4**

4 Lvs 1–3 cm long, thin and flaccid, hairless, on stalks 2–5 cm long – stem weak, straggling, ± hairy, round....................................
Stellaria neglecta (or large form of *S. media*) (p 150 E, A)

Lvs with stalks under 1 cm long – stem round – stem and lvs ± hairless – creeping plants.............. **5**

5 Lvs oval-elliptical, 3–7 cm long, grey-green, often slightly downy – stem somewhat woody below and far-creeping on ground....................
Lonicera periclymenum (p 344 F)

Lvs oval-elliptical, 0.5–2.0 cm long, hairless, glossy green – stem not woody but tough ....
Veronica serpyllifolia (p 304 C)

Lvs oval-orbicular, glossy bright green – stem weak and brittle, never woody, shortly **creeping** **6**

6 Lvs blunt, orbicular, 1.5–3.0 cm long ....
Lysimachia nummularia (p 288 C)

Lvs pointed, oval, 2–4 cm long ....
Lysimachia nemorum (p 286 B)

7 Stems round **8**

Stems square (or four-winged) in section **14**

8 Stems erect **9**

Stems creeping or ascending **10**

9 Lvs oval-triangular, 3–6 cm long, feebly wavy-toothed, hairless above, stalk 2–10 cm long – stem green, swollen at nodes, ± hairless .. *Circaea lutetiana* (p 224 J)

Lvs oval-elliptical, 3–8 cm long, finely and sharply-toothed, downy, stalk 3–10 mm long – stem green, not swollen at nodes, hairy ....
Mercurialis perennis (p 226 C)

Lvs oval-lanceolate, fine-toothed, hairless, stalk 3–6 mm only – stem reddish, ± hairless ....
Epilobium spp, especially *E. montanum* (p 223 A)

10 Lvs oval-elliptical **11**

Lvs ivy-shaped, 1–2 cm wide, long-stalked – lower lvs opp, but upper lvs alt ....
Veronica hederifolia (p 306 F)

11 Lvs with v shallow teeth, stalks 2 mm long or less **12**

Lvs with coarse blunt teeth **13**

12 Lvs 1–2 cm long, ± untoothed, hairless – stem downy.......................
Veronica serpyllifolia (p 304 C)

Lvs 2–3 cm long, shallow-toothed all round, hairy (as is stem) ....
Veronica officinalis (p 304 D)

13 Lvs with stalks 5–15 mm long – stem hairy all round ....
Veronica montana (p 304 B)

Lvs with stalks to 5 mm, or none – stem hairy only in 2 lines on opp sides ....
Veronica chamaedrys (p 304 A)

14 Lvs 1–2 cm long, pale green, fleshy, brittle, stalked, orbicular, with wedge-shaped base and blunt rounded tips, sparsely bristly – in creeping mats in boggy ground ....
Chrysosplenium oppositifolium (p 218 F)

Lvs various, over 2 cm, not brittle **15**

15 Lvs hairless **16**

Lvs hairy **18**

16 Lvs obovate-oblong, blunt, glossy dark green – teeth few, blunt wavy – rosette lvs long-stalked – plant with creeping lfy runners...................
Ajuga reptans (p 322 C)

Lvs oval-triangular – stems all erect **17**

Lvs with blunt rounded teeth and tips – stem four-winged ....
Scrophularia aquatica (p 298 G)

Lvs with pointed teeth and tips – stem square, unwinged.....................
Scrophularia nodosa (p 298 F)

18 Lvs kidney-shaped, glossy, with large blunt teeth all round edges – long lfy runners present, with long-stalked lvs held erect........................
Glechoma hederacea (p 318 I)

Lvs oval, oblong, or oval-triangular, (not kidney-shaped) **19**

19 Lvs bluntly oval, with sparse short bristles, teeth v few and shallow – runners with spreading lvs present ....*Prunella vulgaris* (p 322 A)

Lvs oblong, long-stalked in basal rosette, shiny dark green with coarse rounded teeth and blunt tip, ± hairless above, hairy underneath...
Betonica officinalis (p 320 D)

Lvs oval-triangular, tips pointed, teeth pointed, ± hairy above...... **20**

20 Lvs with sharp teeth all round, and covered with stinging hairs – stipules present................................
Urtica dioica (p 226 E)

Lvs without stinging hairs – no stipules **21**

21 Lvs cordate-based, v hairy, **long**-pointed, **sharp**-toothed, **un-pleasant smell – no lfy runners** ......
Stachys sylvatica (p 320 A)

I WOODLANDS

Lvs cordate-based, downy, wrinkled, grey-green, point rather **blunt**, **blunt**-toothed, no smell – **no** lfy runners......................................
Teucrium scorodonia (p 322 E)

Lvs **rounded** at base, ± wrinkled, shiny dark green, sparsely hairy, **teeth** and **tip pointed** – no smell – lfy runners present...............
Galeobdolon luteum (p 314 E)

L Herbs with lvs in a rosette raised 10–20 cm or more above ground, at tip of stem

Lvs **obovate**, hairless, 5–10 cm long, with 3–5 main veins and a network of veins between these – lvs are 3–8 (most commonly 4) in a whorl on tip of a **fleshy** stem – in wds on calc or richer soils...............
Paris quadrifolia (p 405 B)

Lvs oblong-**lanceolate**, downy, 3–8 cm long – lvs **many** in a rosette-like cluster on tip of a ± **reddish**, ± **woody** stem 20–30 cm tall, persisting through winter (infl appears from rosette in spring)..
Euphorbia amygdaloides (p 244 A)

Lvs obovate-lanceolate, **hairless**, ± untoothed, shiny grey-green, with one main vein and pinnate side-veins – lvs in a whorl of 5–6 on top of v slender stem – mostly in pinewoods in N of GB and N Eur.............................
Trientalis europaea (p 288 I)

M Herbs with lvs alt along, or at base of, the stems – lvs simple, not with many parallel veins

1 Lvs elliptical to oblong-lanceolate, broadest near or above middle **2**

Lvs kidney-shaped to oval-triangular in outline, broadest near base .. **7**

2 Lvs hairless (or nearly so) **3**

Lvs obviously downy, woolly, or bristly...**4**

3 Lvs all oval-lanceolate, 10–15 cm long, scarcely toothed, **stalked**, with bases rounded, tips pointed, and with chaffy tubular **stipules** around lf-bases.............................
Rumex sanguineus (p 270 A)

Lvs obovate in basal rosette, elliptical-lanceolate up stem, upper lvs pointed – all lvs 2–10 cm long, sparsely-toothed, narrowed to base – no stipules ....
Solidago virgaurea (p 366 G)

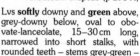

4 Lvs 10–40 cm long, **shallow**-toothed, mainly in a dense **spreading** basal winter rosette – in **open** glades etc.......................................**5**

Lvs 5–20 cm long, **untoothed**, in a sparse **ascending** winter rosette, or ± erect **6**

5 Lvs densely **whitish**-woolly, obovate-lanceolate to oblong, 15–40 cm long, short-stalked, sparsely-toothed – on ± calc soils.................
Verbascum thapsus (p 298 A)

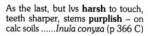

Lvs **softly** downy and **green** above, grey-downy below, oval to obovate-lanceolate, 15–30 cm long, narrowed into short stalks, with rounded teeth – stems grey-green – on acid soils..
Digitalis purpurea (p 300 I)

As the last, but lvs **harsh** to touch, teeth sharper, stems **purplish** – on calc soils ......*Inula conyza* (p 366 C)

6 Lvs roundish-oval and stalked in rosette, oblong-lanceolate, pointed and stalkless on stem – all lvs with dense spreading hairs on both sides, unspotted, all 5–10 cm long...
Myosotis sylvatica (per) and *M. arvensis* (ann; spp only distinguishable by fls; (p 325 C, D)

Lvs lanceolate, bristly-hairy, with pale **spots**, all 5–10 cm long (root-lvs may be up to 60 cm in autumn) ....*Pulmonaria longifolia* (p 330 F)

7 Lvs ± hairless (except lf-stalks sometimes hairy)................. **8**

Lvs obviously hairy or bristly **14**

8 Lvs **garlic-scented** when bruised, 3–8 cm long and wide – lower lvs kidney-shaped, upper rounded-triangular, all cordate-based, with wavy margins ....
Alliaria petiolata (p 124 H)

Lvs **not** garlic-scented................. **9**

9 Lvs cordate-based, thin, with **fringed stipules** at base of each lf-stalk...............................(**Violets**) **10**

Lvs **without stipules** at base of lf-
stalk.. **11**

10 Lf-stalks downy – lvs oval-round-
ed, blunt or ± pointed, dark
glossy green – stipules oval, fringes
short – plants with thick rhizomes
and rooting runners.........................
  Viola odorata (p 140 D)

Lf-stalks ± hairless – lvs oval-
triangular, pointed, not glossy dark
green – stipules narrow-lanceolate,
fringes long – plants with central lf-
rosette, without central stem or
rooting runners, but with fl-bearing
lfy side branches..............................
  Viola riviniana and *V. reichenbachiana* (indistinguishable except
by fls; p 140 A, B)

11 Root-lvs thin, long-stalked (8–
12 cm), 3–4 cm long, pale green,
varying from rounded **kidney-
shaped** to **trifoliate** with deep-
toothed lobes – stem-lvs stalkless,
divided to base into narrow, **linear**
lobes..
  Ranunculus auricomus (p 96 F)

Lvs **all** similar, dark green, glossy **12**

12 All lvs on long (10–20 cm) stout
stalks, triangular **arrow**-shaped,
untoothed, blades 10–20 cm long,
often purple-spotted........................
  Arum maculatum (p 418 E)

All lvs rather fleshy, cordate-based,
rounded to **oval**-triangular, bluntly-angled or -toothed, lower long-
stalked, upper ± stalkless **13**

13 Lvs 2–4 cm long and wide, rounded-triangular – stems **slender** (2–
3 mm wide) – Jan–April.................
  Ranunculus ficaria (p 96 I)

Lvs 5–10 cm long and wide,
kidney-shaped to blunt-triangular,
lower lvs broader than long – stems
stout (6–12 mm wide) hollow – in
wet places – all year.......................
  Caltha palustris (p 98 C)

14 Low creeping plant of **wet** springy
ground under alders – lvs long-
stalked (4–8 cm), kidney-shaped,
round, v bluntly-toothed, 2–3 cm
across, ± fleshy, with scattered bristles on upper surface – lvs
arise from creeping stems all year

(and are alt on erect fl-stems in
spring)...
  Chrysosplenium alternifolium
  (p 218 G)

Erect plants of **dry** ground with
cordate-triangular lvs, long-stalked
at base of stems, short-stalked
along stems **15**

15 Lvs v **large** (15–30 cm long and
10–20 cm wide), rough, **downy**
and green above, ± grey-
downy beneath, on stout (1 cm or
more wide) stalks............................
  Arctium minus (lf-stalk hollow) and
  A. lappa (lf-stalk solid; p 386 E, Ei)

Lvs **smaller** (5–10 cm long × 3–
5 cm wide), bristly, on slender
stalks – on ± calc soils ....
  Campanula trachelium (p 339 A)

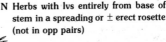

N **Herbs with lvs entirely from base of
stem in a spreading or ± erect rosette
(not in opp pairs)**

1 Basal rosette with central lfy bud,
producing erect lfy stem in following year...(**see key M, section 5**)

Basal rosette producing **only** fl-
buds, and not a lfy stem – lvs blunt,
fine-toothed, oval to obovate..........
  (*Primula*) **2**

2 Lvs narrowed **gradually** to base,
dark green and **hairless** above,
grey-downy underneath, **v wrinkled**, fine-toothed all round, stalk
short or **abs** – all side-veins in lf at
acute angle to midrib ....
  Primula vulgaris (p 284 A)

Lvs narrowed ± **suddenly**
into a winged **stalk** as long as the
blade – side-veins in lower part of lf
at 90° to midrib **3**

3 Lvs **wrinkled**, downy with sticky
hairs on **both** sides, 5–15 cm long,
narrowed v suddenly into stalk,
bright green ....
  Primula veris (p 284 C)

Lvs almost **smooth**, crisped-downy
beneath, almost **hairless** above,
10–20 cm long, narrowed more
gradually into stalk, **yellow**-green
– plant v local ....
  Primula elatior (p 284 B)

VEGETATIVE KEYS

II PLANTS OF CHALK AND LIMESTONE GRASSLAND AND SCRUB

Most chalk and limestone grasslands are semi-natural areas of vegetation, originally forested, cleared long ago by man, and eventually used as pasture, normally for sheep. They occur especially on steeper slopes difficult to plough, wherever chalk or limestone rocks are close to the surface. If ungrazed or unmown, as is often the case nowadays, they soon revert to scrub, and eventually to a more or less stable woodland 'climax' of beech or ash; in these areas will also be found many shrubs and the more light-demanding woodland herbs. The shallow, well-drained soils, alkaline from excess of lime (calcium carbonate), and with a pH often as high as 8 or more, favour the spread of many low-growing species that can well tolerate these conditions, while excluding the competition of other, often taller plants, that require either a lower pH or a better balance of nutrients, or cannot survive grazing, when it still occurs. But most chalk grassland plants are highly adapted to being constantly grazed, many having either well-developed basal leaf-rosettes or being grasses that readily produce new shoots. This key concentrates very much on the leaf-rosettes.

The flora of chalk grassland is not only rich in species, but most (like those of woodlands) are perennials and usually have leaves above ground through much of the year, and not only when in flower or fruit. The flowering season is a long one, beginning in April, with peaks in late May to early June for some plants and in late July to August for others. Thus it is rare for all the species to be in flower concurrently, and this key should be useful in summer as well as at other times of year.

MASTER KEY

Herbs with grass-like lvs .... A
Herbs with lvs not grass-like, but with strong parallel main veins – all lvs untoothed, and in a basal rosette .... B
Herbs with compound, pinnate or trifoliate lvs C
Herbs with simple, oval, oblong or cordate lvs, toothed or not, with one main vein only (not several parallel main veins) .... D
Herbs with lvs in whorls of 4–8 along stems .... E
Trees or shrubs, erect, usually 60 cm tall or much more .... F
Dwarf creeping shrubs, woody below, not over 20 cm tall, with lvs in opp pairs, untoothed .... G
Herbs with lvs deeply pinnatifid, but with their side-lobes joined by at least a narrow flange of lf-blade and themselves ± pinnatifid .... H

A Herbs with grass-like lvs

1 Lvs in 2 opp ranks – stems hollow, round .... **(Grasses) 2**

   Lvs in 3 vertical ranks – stems solid................................ **(Sedges) 8**

2 Basal lvs bristle-like, not easily flattened... 3

   Basal lvs flat or folded lengthwise, not bristle-like (except perhaps when dead) 4

3 Stem-lvs (**a**) flat (when fresh) – lf-sheaths forming a closed tube

round stem – basal lvs (**b**) 10–30 cm long – plant with runners.......
Festuca rubra (p 458 A)

Stem-lvs all bristle-like – lf sheaths forming a tube round stem, split at least half way down – basal lvs 3–8 cm long – no runners...................
Festuca ovina (p 458 Ai)

4 Basal lvs short (to 5 cm), lanceolate, ± flat on gd, hairless ... *Briza media* (**Quaking-grass**)

   Basal lvs longer, not flat on gd, ± erect 5

62

5 Basal lvs ± inrolled at edges, upper lvs flat *c.* 5 mm wide, hairless except for stiff bristles held at 45° from lf-blade along edges ....
Bromus erectus (**Upright Brome**)

Lvs all with inrolled edges, narrow, **many-grooved** above – lvs and stems **all v downy**...........................
Koeleria gracilis (**Crested Hair-grass**)

Lvs keeled, pointed, with folded blunt ligule and flattened sheath ......
Dactylis glomerata (**Cock's-foot**)

Lvs strongly keeled, blunt-tipped, grey-green, ligule flat, not folded .. **6**

Lvs flat, ribbon-like, broad, yellow-green.. **7**

6 Lvs waxy, hairless, with white dots on underside ....
Helictotrichon pratense (**Meadow Oat-grass**)

Lvs hairy, especially on sheaths, no white dots ....
Helictotrichon pubescens (**Downy Oat-grass**)

7 Lvs downy above, hairless below, to 10 cm long × 2–4 mm wide ....
Trisetum flavescens (p 458 D)

Lvs stiff, edges slightly inrolled, rough, hairless, to 8 mm wide ....
Brachypodium pinnatum (**Tor-grass**)

Lvs drooping, quite flat, downy, soft, to 13 mm wide ....
Brachypodium sylvaticum (**False Brome**)

8 Lvs waxy grey, carnation-like ....
Carex flacca (**Glaucous Sedge**)

Lvs bright green, flat, 2 mm wide, spreading...
Carex caryophyllea (**Spring-sedge**)

Lvs yellow-green, channelled, rough, 1.0–1.5 mm wide, erect – vlc......*Carex humilis* (**Dwarf Sedge**)

B Herbs with lvs not grass-like, but with strong parallel main veins; all lvs untoothed, and in a basal rosette

1 Lvs strongly corrugated lengthwise, stalked, ± hairy .... (*Plantago*) **2**

Lvs smooth, stalkless, hairless..........
(Orchids and *Centaurium*) **3**

(Note: Orchids and *Centaurium* have lvs up the stem in summer, as well as a basal rosette; this key is for identification when infl-stem is abs)

2 Lvs lanceolate (length 4–5 times breadth), scarcely hairy ....
Plantago lanceolata (p 336 A)

Lvs oval (length 2–3 times breadth), v downy ....
Plantago media (p 336 C)

3 Lvs spotted **4**

Lvs unspotted............................... **5**

4 Lvs grey-green, spots transverse......
Dactylorhiza fuchsii (p 442 E)

Lvs bright glossy green, spots lengthwise ....
Orchis mascula (p 433 A)

5 Lvs **alt**, but in two opp ranks, keeled, narrow-lanceolate, dark glossy green....................................
Gymnadenia conopsea (p 436 J)

Lvs in **opp pairs**, oblong-obovate, blunt, unkeeled, all in a flat rosette
Centaurium erythraea (p 290 F)

Lvs in a ± flat spreading rosette, oblong, not in opp pairs or opp ranks **6**

6 Lvs grey-green, unwrinkled.............
Ophrys apifera (p 440 A)

Lvs bright green, unwrinkled ....
Orchis spp, probably *O. morio* (p 434 G)

Lvs bright green, with transverse wrinkles near base ....
Aceras anthropophorum (p 434 H)

C Herbs with compound, pinnate or trifoliate lvs

1 Lvs trifoliate................................... **2**

Lvs pinnate................................... **8**

2 The 3 lfts of each lf deeply lobed, lobes toothed, hairy – no stipules at lf-base..
Ranunculus bulbosus (p 96 C)

The 3 lfts ± toothed, but not lobed – stipules present at lf-base . **3**

3 Lvs all from base of plant, lfts sharply-toothed, hairy ....
Fragaria vesca (p 210 J)

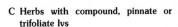

II CHALK GRASSLANDS

Lvs borne along erect or creeping stems **4**

4 Stipules lfy – lfts pointed, toothed, sticky-hairy ....
Ononis repens (p 180 A)

Stipules small, membranous – lfts blunt, not sticky-hairy **5**

5 Lfts with whitish band or spot across each **6**

Lfts without whitish band **7**

6 Plant erect – lf-stalks to 6 cm long at most – lfts untoothed, hairs on margins only ....
Trifolium pratense (p 184 A)

Plant with creeping and rooting runners – lf-stalks to 10 cm long – lfts fine-toothed, hairless ....
Trifolium repens (p 184 D)

7 Stem and lfts v downy – lfts mucronate, toothed ....
Medicago lupulina (p 196 C)

Stem and lfts usually hairless – lfts blunt, with an extra pair of lfts at lf-base (resembling stipules) untoothed ...... *Lotus corniculatus* (p 196 A)

8 Lvs once-pinnate **9**

Lvs twice or more pinnate or with lfts cut more than halfway to their midribs, hairy or downy **15**

9 Lfts quite untoothed **10**

Lfts toothed **12**

10 Lfts blunt – side lfts in 3 or more pairs, end lft of similar size to side ones **11**

Lfts pointed – end lft of lower lvs much larger than side ones ....
Anthyllis vulneraria (p 198 G)

Lfts ± blunt – side lfts in 2 pairs only, lower pair arising from junction of lf-stalk and stem – upper pair same size as end lft..................
Lotus corniculatus (p 196 A)

11 Lfts quite hairless.............................
Hippocrepis comosa (p 198 F)

Lfts downy ....
Astragalus danicus (p 182 H)

12 Lvs with pairs of tiny lfts alt with larger ones along midrib **13**

Lvs with all side-lfts of similar size, no smaller intermediate ones **14**

13 Lvs hairy – lfts oval-lanceolate, coarse-toothed ....
Agrimonia eupatoria (p 212 E)

Lvs hairless – lfts oblong-lanceolate, v deeply pinnatifid..................
Filipendula vulgaris (p 214 B)

14 Lfts of **all** lvs **hairless**, round to oval, deeply toothed, 0.3–2.0 cm long – lf-stalks **purplish** – lvs **cucumber**-scented when crushed ....
Poterium sanguisorba (p 212 G)

Lfts of basal lvs **downy**, oval, ± deeply toothed, 1.0–2.5 cm long – lfts of **stem-lvs narrow-linear**, themselves **pinnate** again – lf-stalks green – no cucumber scent...................................
Pimpinella saxifraga (p 254 E)

Lfts of **all** lvs **rough-hairy**, oval, coarse-toothed to **pinnatifid**, 3–**6 cm long**..
Pastinaca sativa (p 258 A)

15 Lvs triangular in outline, lobes oval to lanceolate, 5–10 mm long ....
Daucus carota (p 266 D)

Lvs triangular in outline, lfts oval, 3–4 × 1–2 cm ....
Pastinaca sativa (p 258 A)

Lvs oblong in outline, to 4 cm wide, lobes of twice-pinnate stem-lvs linear, to 1 cm long × 2 mm wide ....
Pimpinella saxifraga (p 254 E)

Lvs narrow-oblong in outline, to 2 cm wide, **repeatedly** lobed into **narrow linear** segments 2–3 mm long × **1 mm wide** ....
Achillea millefolium (p 372 D)

D Herbs with simple, oval, oblong or cordate lvs, toothed or not, with one main vein only (not several parallel main veins)

1 Lvs in **opp** pairs along stems **2**

Lvs **alt** along stems **11**

Lvs **only** in a basal rosette (so that not evident if alt or opp).............. **20**

Lvs in a **distinct** basal **rosette** and **also alt** along stems (in spring, no stem may be present so see also 20)... **16**

2 Plant quite **hairless** – lvs untoothed, unstalked **3**

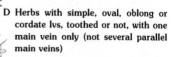

Plant **hairy**, at least on stem and lf-stalks **6**

3 Lvs **joined** in pairs, forming rings round stem, waxy grey-green, oval-triangular, pointed ....
Blackstonia perfoliata (p 292 J)

Lvs **not** joined in pairs round stem **4**

4 Lvs ± oval, **blunt**.......................... **5**

Lvs oval-lanceolate, 1–2 cm long, tapered to sharp **points**...................
Gentianella amarella or *G. germanica* (p 290 C, D)

5 Lvs **under** 1 cm long – stems thread-like ....
Linum catharticum (p 134 F)

Lvs **1–2 cm long, with** translucent **dots**, grey-green, oval-oblong.........
Hypericum perforatum (p 136 A)

Lvs 1–3 cm long, **without** translucent dots, **glossy** green with 3–7 strong veins, oval-obovate (often with basal rosette)..............................
Centaurium erythraea (p 290 F)

6 Lvs oblong, 2–5 cm long, blunt, hairy, ± **stalkless, untoothed** ....
Hypericum hirsutum (p 136 D)

Lvs oblong, 3–7 cm long, blunt, **long-stalked**, with few hairs and coarse blunt **teeth** (with basal rosette) ....
Betonica officinalis (p 320 D)

Lvs with **cordate** base, oblong, pointed, wrinkled, **sage**-scented, 7–15 cm long, blunt-toothed ....
Salvia pratensis (p 316 J)

Lvs oval-triangular, to 1 cm long, with sharp **bristle**-pointed teeth.......
Euphrasia nemorosa (p 308 A)

Lvs oval, 2–4 cm long, base round-ed, teeth v blunt or abs **7**

Lvs elliptical-lanceolate, 5–10 cm long, tapered into stalk.................. **9**

7 Lvs **long** (2–3 cm)-stalked, **blunt**, oval, downy, **unscented** ....
Prunella vulgaris (p 322 A)

Lvs **short** (to 1 cm)-stalked, **pointed**, oval, **scented**, hairy........ **8**

8 Lvs ± smooth, side-veins **faint**, sweetly aromatic, ± purple underneath, teeth almost abs.......*Origanum vulgare* (p 318 F)

Lvs ± wrinkled (with side-veins **impressed**), weakly aromatic, green underneath, teeth small but distinct..
Clinopodium vulgare (p 316 A)

9 Lvs quite **untoothed**, sparsely hairy, blunt or pointed ....
Succisa pratensis (p 354 E)

Lvs with shallow blunt **teeth**, some-times with side-lobes at base **10**

10 Basal lvs short-stalked, **hairy, pointed**, rough, to 12 cm long ....
Knautia arvensis (p 354 D)

Basal lvs long-stalked, ± **downy, blunt**, smooth, to 8 cm long..
Scabiosa columbaria (p 354 C)

11 Lower lvs (and perhaps others) with distinct narrow stalks over 2 cm long and with broad (1 cm or more) expanded blades.............. **12**

All lvs elliptical-lanceolate, 5 cm long or more, usually untoothed, 1–2 cm wide, tapering to base to form indistinct stalk, green, rough, with short bristly hairs ....
Centaurea nigra (p 385 A)

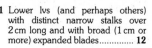

Lvs narrow-linear (3 mm wide or less) one-veined, ± fleshy, yellow-green, with stalks 1–2 mm long or abs......................................
Thesium humifusum (p 170 H)

12 Lvs cordate-based, triangular-rounded, with toothed stipules at base of stalk **13**

Lvs rounded-oblong, cordate-based or not, without stipules at base.. **14**

13 Lvs with ± **hairless** stalks and blades, **oval-triangular** – stipules narrow, their teeth long and hair-like ....
Viola riviniana (p 140 A)

Lvs with v **hairy** stalks and blades, blades **narrow-triangular**, pale green – stipules oval, their teeth not much longer than width of stipule ....
Viola hirta (p 140 C)

Lvs with **sparsely hairy** stalks and blades, blades oval to **rounded, dark green** – stipules and their teeth as in *Viola hirta*........................
Viola odorata (p 140 D)

II CHALK GRASSLANDS

14 Lvs **downy**, cordate-based, oblong-triangular, root-lvs and stem-lvs similar..
    Campanula glomerata (p 339 D)

Lvs **hairless** – root-lvs and stem-lvs different – root-lvs long-stalked .. **15**

15 Root-lvs spoon-shaped, wedge-shaped at base, with small pointed teeth – stem-lvs oblong, deeply-toothed, ± stalkless ....
    Chrysanthemum leucanthemum (p 369 A)

Root-lvs almost round, rounded at base, with few blunt teeth – stem-lvs narrow-linear...........................
    Campanula rotundifolia (p 339 C)

Root-lvs oval-oblong, with shallow rounded teeth, rounded or cordate at base – stem-lvs linear-lanceolate...
    Phyteuma tenerum (p 340 J)

16 Lvs hairless, untoothed.............. **17**

Lvs hairy or woolly **19**

17 Rosette-lvs 3–5 in number, under 20 mm long, elliptical or obovate, stalked, smooth **18**

Rosette-lvs many, to 15 cm long × 1.0–1.5 cm wide, linear-oblong, stalkless, wavy-edged and crinkled transversely.......................
    Reseda luteola (p 130 D)

18 Rosette-lvs **pointed**, **oval**, **shorter** than the pointed, elliptical-lanceolate stem-lvs..................................
    Polygala vulgaris (p 132 F)

Rosette-lvs **blunt**, **obovate**, **longer** than the blunt, obovate stem-lvs......
    Polygala calcarea (p 132 G)

19 Rosette-lvs v **bristly**, oblong, untoothed, short-stalked – stem-lvs stalkless, to 15 cm long × to 2 cm wide .... *Echium vulgare* (p 326 L)

Rosette-lvs v **woolly**, elliptical-lanceolate, to 20 cm long × 3–6 cm wide, pointed, bluntly-toothed, some ascending.............................
    Verbascum thapsus (p 298 A)

Rosette-lvs **cottony** below and above, especially when young, 3–5 cm long × 2 cm wide, broad-**oval**, blunt, untoothed, **flat** on gd.... *Senecio integrifolius* (p 364 C)

20 Lvs spoon-shaped, blunt, smooth, sparsely hairy, shallow-toothed, short-stalked, 2–4 cm long, mostly flat on gd ... *Bellis perennis* (p 370 I)

Lvs oval, blunt, wrinkled, with impressed veins, downy, 5–15 cm long, blunt-toothed, narrowed into long (5–6 cm) winged stalk..............
    Primula veris (p 284 C)

Lvs untoothed, elliptical-lanceolate, 3–8 cm long, white-woolly on underside, green on upperside with long scattered white hairs – short-lvd runners present................
    Pilosella officinarum (p 398 D)

Lvs blunt-toothed, oblong-lanceolate, 10–20 cm long, green and v hairy both sides – no runners present .... *Leontodon hispidus* (p 394 D)

Lvs untoothed, hairless, shiny, 1–3 cm long, glossy green, oval-obovate, with 3–7 strong veins..............
    Centaurium erythraea (p 290 F)

E Herbs with lvs in whorls of 4–8 along the stems

1 Lvs oval-elliptical, three-veined, hairy both sides, 4 per whorl, to 25 mm long × 6–10 mm wide.........
    Galium cruciata (p 350 I)

Lvs linear-obovate, one-veined, hairless or downy.......................... **2**

2 Lvs linear, 8–12 per whorl, hairless, 0.5–2.0 mm wide – stems erect .... *Galium verum* (p 350 J)

Lvs obovate below and 4 per whorl, linear above and 4–6 per whorl, 1–2 mm wide, all mucronate, hairless – stems ± prostrate..
    Asperula cynanchica (p 352 D)

Lvs obovate, 6–8 per whorl, mucronate, 2–4 mm wide, with forward-pointing prickles on edges, hairless or downy.............................
    Galium mollugo (p 349 A)

F Trees or shrubs, erect, usually 60 cm tall or much more

1 Lvs narrow-**linear**, tough, evergreen... **2**

Lvs broad, lvs (or their lfts) oval or lanceolate..................................... **3**

2 Lvs parallel-sided, blunt-tipped, dark glossy green, spreading on either side of younger branches (like barbs of a feather) – frs red, fleshy – male fls like tiny cones......... *Taxus baccata* (**Yew**)

Lvs tapered to v sharp points, grey-green, in whorls of 3 along stem....... *Juniperus communis* (**Juniper**)

3 Lvs (or buds in winter) in **opp** pairs **4**

Lvs (or buds in winter) **alt** along twigs... **11**

4 Lvs evergreen, leathery, oval-elliptical, edges curved back, untoothed, blunt, dark shiny green...................... *Buxus sempervirens* (p 228 D)

Lvs semi-evergreen, elliptical, pointed, untoothed, not leathery – edges flat – frs black berries .... *Ligustrum vulgare* (p 294 F)

Lvs deciduous **5**

5 Lvs pinnate (or, in winter, with stout black pointed buds).............. **6**

Lvs palmately-lobed **7**

Lvs simple, unlobed, toothed or not... **8**

6 Shrub climbing (by means of coiling lf-stalks or scrambling stems) – lfts tapered to pointed tips – bark fibrous, peeling in strips – frs clusters of nutlets with long white feathery-plumed styles .... *Clematis vitalba* (p 104 A)

Erect, non-climbing shrub or tree with smooth grey bark and large (5–10mm long) pointed black buds – lfts oval, fine-toothed – frs like a single propeller blade.............. *Fraxinus excelsior* (p 238 K)

7 Lvs usually five-lobed, broader than long, 3–5 cm wide, lobes blunt – twigs downy – frs like a complete, two-bladed propeller....... *Acer campestre* (p 236 A)

Lvs usually five-lobed, as long as broad, 7–16 cm wide, lobes pointed, toothed – twigs hairless – fr as above..................................... *Acer pseudoplatanus* (p 236 B)

Lvs three-lobed, as long as or longer than broad – lobes sharp-toothed – frs red berries in umbels... *Viburnum opulus* (p 342 D)

8 Lvs elliptical to oval-lanceolate, fine-toothed, 5–10 cm long – twigs hairless – frs four-lobed, salmon-coloured, seeds orange................... *Euonymus europaeus* (p 232 F)

Lvs narrowly oval-lanceolate, untoothed, 3–5 cm long – twigs downy when young – frs black berries .... *Ligustrum vulgare* (p 294 F)

Lvs oval....................................... **9**

9 Lvs wrinkled, v downy, fine-toothed, 5–10 cm long – side-veins spreading at wide angle to midrib – buds without protective scales in winter – frs red (then black) berries, flattened oval, in umbels................. *Viburnum lantana* (p 342 E)

Lvs smooth, hairless – side-veins turning up towards apex – frs globular black berries................. **10**

10 Lvs untoothed – twigs purple in winter.. *Thelycrania sanguinea* (p 230 A)

Lvs fine-toothed all round – twigs grey-brown in winter .... *Rhamnus catharticus* (p 232 D)

11 Lvs compound – stems prickly.... **12**

Lvs simple – stems smooth or with thorns... **14**

12 Lvs compound palmate, with 3–7 oval lfts – prickles on lfts as well as on stems.. *Rubus fruticosus* (p 206 E)

Lvs pinnate – thorns or prickles on stems............................... (*Rosa*) **13**

13 Lvs **sticky**-hairy, apple-scented – arched thorns along stems – fr **red**, oval. *Rosa rubiginosa* agg (p 206 C)

Lvs hairy or not, but **not** sticky-hairy – arched thorns along stems – fr **red**, oval............. *Rosa canina* agg (p 206 D)

Lvs hairless above – **numerous** stiff but **slender** bristles and prickles clothing stems – fr **black**, globose ...*Rosa pimpinellifolia* (p 206 B)

14 Lvs oval, toothed, green above, **white-felted** below – twigs without thorns, downy when young .... *Sorbus aria* agg (p 202 C)

Lvs green **both** sides.................. **15**

II CHALK GRASSLANDS

15 Twigs thorny................................ **16**

Twigs without thorns **17**

16 Lvs elliptical, toothed but not lobed – frs black with bluish bloom, globular...*Prunus spinosa* (p 202 E)

Lvs oval, deeply pinnately-lobed – frs red, oval......................................
Crateagus monogyna (p 204 J)

17 Lvs oval, smooth, quite untoothed, hairless except for silky hairs on margins and on veins below – twigs hairless – buds cigar-shaped............
Fagus sylvatica (p 233 D)

Lvs toothed **18**

18 Lvs rounded, but with toothed edges and long point at tip – twigs and lvs downy...........................
Corylus avellana (p 234 F)

Lvs oval in outline...................... **19**

19 Lvs oval-triangular, hairless, their teeth themselves toothed – twigs hairless, with warts...........................
Betula pendula (p 238 J)

Lvs rounded-oval, ± downy, teeth untoothed – twigs downy, without warts...................................
Betula pubescens (p 238 I)

G Dwarf creeping shrubs, woody below, not over 20 cm tall, with lvs in opp pairs, untoothed

1 Young stems hairy – lvs under 1 cm long, oval-elliptical, green underneath, edges flat............................ **2**

Young stems hairless – lvs to 2 cm long, oblong, white-downy beneath, green and ± hairless above, edges ± turned down ....
Helianthemum chamaecistus (p 133 A)

2 Erect infl-stems v hairy on the 4 corners, hairless on the 2 wider faces..
Thymus pulegioides (p 312 H)

Erect infl-stems hairy on two opp faces, hairless on other two..............
Thymus drucei (p 312 I)

Erect infl-stems ± round, equally hairy all round ....
Thymus serpyllum (p 312 J)

H Herbs with lvs deeply pinnatifid, but with their side-lobes joined by at least a narrow flange of lf-blade and themselves ± pinnatifid

1 Lvs with **spines** along margins **2**

Lvs **not** spiny **3**

2 Lvs hairless and shiny above, **all** in a close spreading rosette.................
Cirsium acaulon (p 382 F)

Lvs rough, grey-hairy above, in a basal rosette and also up erect stem .... *Cirsium vulgare* (p 381 A)

Lvs whitish-cottony both sides.........
Carlina vulgaris (p 388 D)

3 Lvs (at least those of basal rosette) with small pinnately arranged lobes at base only – upper part of lf formed by one large undivided terminal lobe...................................... **4**

Lvs with terminal lobe not obviously larger than side-lobes................ **7**

4 Lvs alt, smooth, hairless – terminal lobe of lf lanceolate, all lobes v finely toothed ....
Serratula tinctoria (p 388 B)

Lvs downy, or rough-hairy, or cottony, at least below....................... **5**

5 Lvs **alt** – side-lobes of winter rosette-lvs oblong, pointed, 3–8 mm long, shiny bright green above, cottony below – end-lobes of lvs large (to 3 cm long), oval, blunt...............
Senecio jacobaea (p 362 A)

Lvs **opp** – side-lobes of rosette-lvs v short, broad – end-lobes elliptical-lanceolate to obovate, 3–6 cm long, hairy **6**

6 Lvs rough, hairy – upper lvs with broad side-lobes..............................
Knautia arvensis (p 354 D)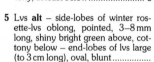

Lvs smooth, ± downy – upper lvs with v narrow side-lobes..
Scabiosa columbaria (p 354 C)

7 Side-lobes of lvs oblong, blunt, sparsely hairy, shiny dark green, often themselves pinnatifid into blunt lobes – rosette-lvs 10–25 cm long.. *Centaurea scabiosa* (p 385 B)

Side-lobes of lvs oblong, 1–2 cm long × 2–3 mm wide, blunt, hairless, themselves ± pinnatifid, – rosette-lvs 5–10 cm long...............
Reseda lutea (p 130 C)

Side-lobes of lvs repeatedly cut into narrow linear segments 2–3 mm long × **1 mm** wide, downy..............
Achillea millefolium (p 372 D)

Side-lobes of lvs cut again into short triangular pointed segments 2–10 mm long × 3–4 mm wide, ± hairless above, cottony below ...... *Senecio jacobaea* (p 362 A)

VEGETATIVE KEY

III PLANTS OF HEATHLANDS (DRY AND WET), MOORS, ACID *SPHAGNUM* BOGS AND HEATHY GLADES IN WOODLANDS

These plant habitats are combined in one key because their vegetation and flora have much in common. All these habitats are acidic, and very poor in plant nutrients, so the flora is restricted to species able to tolerate these inhospitable environments.

Dry **lowland heaths** occur on sandy and gravelly geological strata in several parts of England, especially on the Lower Greensand and Bagshot Sands of the South and on Glacial Sands, washed out from former ice-sheets, further north and east, and in western Europe. Most are semi-natural habitats, resulting from clearance of former natural forests, mostly by prehistoric man. Although subsequently often cultivated, their very porous soils allowed most of the plant nutrients to be quickly washed down into lower levels, beyond the reach of plant roots, once the forest oaks were no longer present to recycle these with their deep root systems. Indeed, apart from the surface black humus, the upper layers of heathland soils are often bleached a whitish grey by the acid percolating rain (though the **deeper** subsoil is usually red-brown from the presence of washed-down iron and other minerals). The pH of the surface soil is often very low (3.5 or less), and hence there is great acidity.

Heathland vegetation is very limited in species; mostly low evergreen shrubs of the Ericaceae and some low evergreen spiny shrubs of the Leguminosae predominate. Most of these can be identified without flowers at any season. More open areas beside paths often have a greater variety of herbs.

Wetter areas of heathland have some of the same plants, but the better water supply brings in a greater variety of species. In areas permanently wet, even in summer, such as some valleys and hollows on lowland heathland, the waterlogging prevents decay of vegetable litter and peat is formed, leading to the development of acid bog. This is built up and becomes dominated by *Sphagnum* mosses of various species; the yellow or green *Sphagna* tend to colonize the water-filled hollows first, followed by the red species. The latter build up hummocks, on which various heath-type shrubs tolerant of wet conditions, such as Cross-leaved Heath and Cranberry, will grow. Various sedges and insect-catching plants also occur, but these are not easy to identify in winter.

In wetter upland areas **heather moors** occur with a similar flora. In wet lowland basins extensive **raised** or **domed** bogs (so-called from their convex form) or concave **valley** bogs develop, and blanket peat bogs on the flat tops of the wetter hill and mountain areas, and at low levels in parts of western Ireland. Where, however, nutrient-rich water enters a bog or moorland, or there is a more rapid movement of water as on a slope, a **flush** area may develop, often much greener (because less acid) and more species-rich than the surrounding areas, that are dull brown from the prevailing heath-type vegetation. For some flush species see Key IV.

MASTER KEY

(Plants confined to bogs, or wetter heaths, are indicated in key)

1 Trees, and large shrubs over 2 m tall..**(see Key IA, p 51)**
   Low shrubs, under 2 m tall, with **woody stems**, erect or creeping along the ground.........................A
   Herbs **without** woody stems 2
2 Lvs ± linear, narrow, **grass-like**, in tussocks, tufts, rosettes, or along stems ....B
   Lvs **not** grass-like, but with broader blades...C
   Ferns with pinnately-divided fronds...D

A Low shrubs, under 2 m tall, with woody stems, erect or creeping along the ground

1 Evergreen shrubs with **spiny shoots**.. **2**

Shrubs (evergreen or not) **without spines** **5**

2 Without obvious lvs – stems bearing **pinnately-branched green spines** along their length – frs like tiny **hairy** pea-pods ....**(Gorses) 3**

With oval, pointed, hairless lvs 2–8 mm long – stems bearing **unbranched, yellowish-brownish** spines, 1–2 cm long, along their length – frs like tiny **hairless** pea-pods ....*Genista anglica* (p 178 A)

3 Spines **deeply furrowed**, v rigid, 1.5–3.0 cm long – main branches with **few** hairs – shrub 60–200 cm tall – fls mostly in **spring** ....
Ulex europaeus (p 178 E)

Spines **faintly** furrowed, 1.0–2.5 cm long – main branches **v hairy** – shrubs 10–100 cm tall – fls in **late summer**............................. **4**

4 Spines **stout, v rigid**, 1.0–2.5 cm long – main branches ± erect, to 1 m tall.............*Ulex gallii* (p 178 G)

Spines **weak, flexible, thin**, to 1 cm long – main branches creeping or straggling, usually under 50 cm tall ....*Ulex minor* (p 178 F)

(Note: certain identification of *Ulex gallii* and *U. minor* is impossible without fls; but the former is c in W of GB and Ire, whilst the latter ± replaces it in SE Eng)

5 Erect shrub to 2 m, with masses of long, green, five-ridged, hairless little-branched twigs – lvs on young shoots trifoliate or undivided, lfts elliptical – frs like tiny (4 cm long) black, ± hairy pea-pods ....
Sarothamnus scoparius (p 178 H)

Tiny **prostrate** shrub, creeping over mosses in **sphagnum** bogs, with leathery, oval-oblong lvs 4–8 mm long, dark green above, waxy-grey green below, edges rolled under, alt along thin woody stems – frs red berries 6–8 mm long, on 2–3 cm slender stalks – local..
Vaccinium oxycoccus (p 276 D)

Bushy shrubs, ± erect, but with creeping rhizomes at base, 10–60 cm tall, with oval or linear, **unlobed** lvs 1–30 mm long........... **6**

6 Lvs **narrow-linear** to oval, evergreen, **stalked**, edges sharply rolled under, lvs **2–7 mm long, spreading**, in whorls of 3–4 (or 5) – frs dry .... (*Erica*) **7**

Lvs **narrow-linear**, evergreen, **stalked**, edges strongly rolled under, **4–6 mm long, spreading**, dense-set, and **alt** along stems, **not** whorled – frs black berries – N of Br Isles and Eur ....
Empetrum nigrum (p 280 I)

Lvs v narrow **triangular**, evergreen, ± **stalkless**, edges strongly rolled under, 1–2 mm long, **adpressed** to stem in **opp pairs**, resembling tiny hat-pegs – frs dry – in dry hths and bogs ....
Calluna vulgaris (p 278 A)

Lvs **oval** to linear-**lanceolate**, **alt**, **3–30 mm long**, edges flat or slightly rolled under, evergreen or not **8**

7 Lvs in **whorls of 4, 2–4 mm long, linear, grey-downy**, with long white sticky-tipped hairs – dead fls in terminal **heads** – in wet hths and bogs ....*Erica tetralix* (p 278 B)

Lvs in **whorls of 3, 5–7 mm long**, **linear, hairless, dark green** or **purplish, shiny** – dead fls in **short racemes** – on dry hths only, W Eur only ....*Erica cinerea* (p 278 C)

Lvs in **whorls of 3, 2–3 mm long, oval**, ± **hairless** above, with long sticky-tipped hairs on **edges, white** beneath, margins only slightly rolled under – dead fls in **long racemes** – in damp hths in SW Eng, W France......*Erica ciliaris* (p 278 D)

8 Lvs **deciduous, thin**-textured, toothed or not............................... **9**

Lvs **evergreen, leathery**, untoothed, hairless **11**

9 Young twigs and buds silky-downy – lvs oval to elliptical-lanceolate, greyish and ± silky-hairy below, ± hairless on upper-sides, 1–4 cm long – grey-green (female) or golden (male) catkins in spring – frs **dry capsules** with white plumed seeds in summer..................
Salix repens (p 242 I)

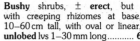

Young twigs and buds downy – lvs oval, blunt, **downy** below, hairless on uppersides, 3–5 mm long – frs like tiny **downy** pea-pods – GB vr, Eur f-lc.......*Genista pilosa* (p 178 B)

Young twigs and buds hairless or ± so – lvs hairless, 10–30 mm long – fls globular – frs **blue-black berries**.. **10**

10 Lvs **oval**, **pointed**, **toothed all round**, **light green** – younger twigs conspicuous when lfless in winter, **bright green**, with **4 angles** or **flanges** along their length – c in dry wds, hths, moors ....
Vaccinium myrtillus (p 276 A)

Lvs oval-**obovate**, blunt, untoothed, blue-green – twigs **brownish**, **cylindrical** – on moors, bogs – N of GB r, N Eur f....................................
Vaccinium uliginosum (p 276 C)

11 Lvs **flat**, **obovate**, blunt, fresh green, 1–2 cm long, with net-veining conspicuously pale – frs red berries – on hths, moors – N of Brit Isles, N Eur, lc..................................
Arctostaphylos uva-ursi (p 278 G)

Lvs with **rolled-under edges**, 1–3 cm long, **obovate**, blunt, **dark glossy** green above, **paler** green and dotted below, net-veining **inconspicuous** – frs red berries – on moors – N of Br Isles, N Eur, lc ....
Vaccinium vitis-idaea (p 276 B)

Lvs with **strongly** rolled-under edges, linear-lanceolate to elliptical, ± pointed, ± glossy green above, **waxy-white** below, 1.5–3.5 cm long – frs dry capsules – lf in *sphagnum* bogs ....
Andromeda polifolia (p 280 H)

B Herbs with lvs ± linear, narrow, grass-like, in tussocks, tufts, rosettes or along stems

1 Lvs (or narrow lf-like stems, if no lvs visible) all v narrow (1–2 mm wide), and **bristle-like**, not hollow, but cylindrical or three-edged, in a ± erect dense basal **tussock** or **tuft** **2**

Lvs **not** bristle-like, each with an obvious **blade**, either flat or folded along its length.............................. **5**

Lvs cylindrical, 1–4 mm wide, hollow, with **cross-partitions** inside, borne from base or **alt** along stems – in bogs.................. **12**

Lf-like stems cylindrical, 1.5–3.0 mm wide, **spongy** inside, in tuft from base of plant, bearing lateral infls near tip – in bogs **13**

2 Tussock composed of **dark green**, **three-angled lvs**, 1 mm wide and to 20 cm long, with **pale inflated** sheathing bases – stems (if present) bear shorter lvs with v inflated sheathing bases – in bogs and wet hths – r to S, c to N and W of Br Isles ....
Eriophorum vaginatum (p 456 D)

Tussock composed of **cylindrical**, **ridged stems**, 1–2 mm wide and to 30 cm long, each stem´ with tiny narrow basal **lf-sheaths**, with blades only 2–3 mm long, the whole tussock conspicuously **orange-brown** from Oct to March – remains of infls (ovoid, 3–5 mm long) sometimes visible on stem-tips – in bogs, wet hths.....................
Scirpus caespitosus (**Deergrass**)

Tussock composed of shorter (10–15 cm long) ± **cylindrical lvs** 0.2–0.4 mm wide, grooved or not on upper side – in dry hths............ **3**

3 Plant with a dense crowded basal tuft of erect, **pale**, tough, **stout shining lf-sheaths**, from which spread the grey-green ascending **bristle**-like lf-blades ± at 90°, in a rosette – infls one-sided spikes – on hths, moors...............................
Nardus stricta (**Mat-grass**)

Plant with the bristle-like lf-blades rising at an **acute** angle to their **slender** sheaths, which are **neither** tough nor shiny – in dry hths......... **4**

4 Lvs grooved above, **grey-green** and rough beneath – ligule (**a**) at tip of sheath (**b**) **narrow**, **pointed**, 2–4 mm long – florets of infl with projecting **bristles** – in dry hths in SW of GB, W France only................
Agrostis setacea (**Bristle Bent**)

Lvs grooved above, bright green and smooth – ligule (**a**) **blunt**, **less than 0.5 mm** long, scarcely visible – florets **without** bristles ....
Festuca tenuifolia (**Fine-leaved Sheep's-fescue**)

Lvs **dark** green, shiny, rough-edged, **not** grooved above – ligule c. **1 mm long**, with **square-cut** tip – florets **silvery**, with bristles............... *Deschampsia flexuosa* (**Wavy Hairgrass**)

5 Lvs like those of a **tiny iris, flattened in one plane**, all edge-on to stem, orange in autumn – erect dead straw coloured fr-spikes persistent in winter, with frs conical – in *Sphagnum* bogs .... *Narthecium ossifragum* (p 412 D)

Lvs **not** iris-like, **not** flattened in one plane **6**

6 Lvs **tough**, glossy dark green, wiry, grooved above, 3–5 mm wide at base, **spreading at 90°** to their erect basal sheaths in a **flat** rosette like a sweep's brush – on bare or trampled places on hths.................... *Juncus squarrosus* (p 455 Aiii)

Lvs **not** spreading at 90° to their sheaths, not in a **flat** rosette **7**

7 Lvs in an ascending rosette, with channelled blades, to 6 mm wide, and to 12 cm long, bright or grey-green, with **long white hairs** thinly clothing the blades – no ligule to lvs... *Luzula multiflora* (**Heath Woodrush**)

Lvs with ± **hairless** blades **8**

8 Lvs arranged in 3 vertical ranks, on solid stem that is triangular in section below.................................... **9**

Lvs in 2 opp vertical ranks on hollow round stem...................... **10**

9 Lvs with purplish-red three-angled tips – fr-heads 2–5 per infl, cottony – in bogs... *Eriophorum angustifolium* (p 456 Di)

Lvs with tips neither purplish-red nor three-angled.............................. (**Sedges**, *Carex* spp) **14**

10 Lvs flat, **ribbon**-like, to 10 mm wide × 50 cm long, grey-green, almost hairless, in **large, dense tussocks** to 80 cm across – ligules of lvs composed of a fringe of hairs only – dead lvs in winter (Nov–

May) **straw**-coloured, curled – in wet hths, bogs................................... *Molinia caerulea* (**Purple Moorgrass**)

Lvs **not** ribbon-like, **not** in dense tussocks – lf-blades **linear-lanceolate**, to 15 cm long × 1–5 mm wide – **ligules membranous** – creeping lfy stems present........... **11**

11 Ligules 2–5 mm long, pointed – infl-branches ascending.................. *Agrostis canina* (**Brown Bent**)

Ligules 0.5–2.0 mm long, blunt – infl-branches spreading .... *Agrostis tenuis* (**Common Bent**)

12 Erect plant, 30–100 cm tall – lvs 2–4 mm wide, stiff, ascending, each of one tube, with internal cross-partitions v distinct – in bogs.................. *Juncus acutiflorus* (p 455 B)

Creeping plant with ± erect tufted stems, 10–20 cm tall – lvs 1–2 mm wide, flaccid, each of **two** tubes, with many indistinct cross-partitions – in bog pools, wet hollows.. *Juncus bulbosus* (**Bulbous Rush**)

13 Stems ± smooth.............................. *Juncus effusus* (p 455 Ai)

Stems with many lengthwise ridges .... *Juncus conglomeratus* (p 455 A)

14 Lfy shoots many, in a dense tussock – lvs 2–3 mm wide, deeply channelled, bright green, arched outwards – on dry hths .... *Carex pilulifera* (**Pill Sedge**)

Lfy shoots few, in a loose tussock – lvs 5–10 mm wide, slightly channelled, glossy green but orange-brown tipped in winter – on dry hths .... *Carex binervis* (**Green-ribbed Sedge**)

Lfy shoots ± separate, hardly in tussocks – lvs 3–5 mm wide, waxy grey-green – on wet hths and bogs .... *Carex panicea* (**Carnation Sedge**)

Not as any of above 3 alternatives... *Carex* spp, unidentifiable without frs

III HEATHLANDS

C Herbs with lvs not grass-like, but with broader blades

1 Lvs ± circular, green, hairless, 2–3 cm wide, held aloft on stalks, like tiny, flat umbrellas – in **bogs**...................................
    Hydrocotyle vulgaris (p 264 E)

Lvs **all** in a **basal rosette**............... **2**

Lvs along the stems in **whorls** of 4 or more... **6**

Lvs **alt** along the stems, **not** in whorls, **not** all in a basal rosette – on dry hths **8**

Lvs in opp pairs **along** stems – lvs orbicular-oval, 3–8 mm long – plant creeping in **bogs** ....
    Anagallis tenella (p 288 F)

2 Lvs **without** stalks, tapering from broad base to narrow tip, untoothed...**3**

Lvs with **distinct** stalks – lf-blades undivided, untoothed, broader than their stalks, clothed with bright **red sticky hairs** like tentacles – in wet hths or **bogs** ..... (*Drosera* spp) **5**

Lvs **pinnatifid** or **pinnately-compound**, without red sticky hairs – on open dry sandy hths **7**

3 Lvs **greasy-looking**, spreading **star-wise** on ground, unspotted – in bogs.......................(*Pinguicula*) **4**

Lvs glossy, but **not** greasy-looking, in 2 ± opp vertical ranks, with transverse purple spots ....
    Dactylorhiza maculata (p 442 F)

4 Lvs yellow-green, **pointed**, in a starfish-like rosette – in **basic** bogs .. *Pinguicula vulgaris* (p 334 A)

Lvs **olive**-green, **blunt**, purplish-tinged – in **acid** bogs.........................
    Pinguicula lusitanica (p 334 C)

5 Lf-blades almost **circular**, 1–2 cm wide, on stalks 2–4 cm long – lc.......
    Drosera rotundifolia (p 214 E)

Lf-blades **obovate** to spoonshaped, **0.5–1.0 cm long**, **quickly narrowed** into stalk – l ....
    Drosera intermedia (p 214 F)

Lf-blades **linear-obovate** to **linear-oblong, 2–5 cm long**, **gradually narrowed** into stalk – vl ....
    Drosera anglica (p 214 G)

6 Lvs 6–8 per whorl, obovate, tips **mucronate**, prickles on edges pointing **forwards** – on dry grassy hths ....*Galium saxatile* (p 349 B)

Lvs 4–6 per whorl, linear-oblong to obovate, tips **blunt**, prickles on edges pointing **backwards** – in **bogs** .... *Galium palustre* (p 350 E)

7 Lvs pinnatifid, 2–6 cm long, with lobes **linear**, downy, often lobed themselves, in outline like deers' antlers – on dry sandy gd ....
    Plantago coronopus (p 336 E)

Lvs **pinnate**, 2–10 cm long, with lfts **oval**, **pinnatifid**, **hairy** – on dry sandy gd..
    Erodium cicutarium (p 174 G)

Lvs **pinnate**, 1.5–4.0 cm long, with lfts **elliptical**, **untoothed**, **downy** – on dry sandy gd..............................
    Ornithopus perpusillus (p 182 I)

Lvs **pinnatifid**, 2–5 cm long, with lobes **themselves deeply pinnatifid**, ± **hairless** – on damp hths . *Pedicularis sylvatica* (p 308 D)

8 Lvs **stalkless** on stem, **palmately divided** into 5 obovate, sharply-toothed lfts (actually 3 lfts + 2 lf-like stipules) – basal lvs long-stalked, trifoliate ....
    Potentilla erecta (p 209 A)

Lvs **stalked** in **rosette and on stem, halberd-shaped** triangular, with 2 narrow side-lobes spreading at 90° and turning forward at tips...............
    Rumex acetosella (p 272 J)

D Ferns with pinnately-divided fronds

Tall (1–2 m) fern with v broad 3-times pinnate fronds – fronds arising separately from ground – plant forming brownish litter on ground Nov–May – in dry places.................
    Pteridium aquilinum (**Bracken**)

Shorter (0.5–1.0 m) ferns with oblong-lanceolate twice-pinnate fronds – fronds arising in crowns or rosettes together – in damp places..
Dryopteris etc (**Buckler Ferns**)

Short (20–50 cm) fern with narrow lanceolate once-pinnate fronds arising in crowns – in damper places, ditches...................................
Blechnum spicant (**Hard Fern**)

(For further details consult H.A. Hyde and A.E. Wade, *Welsh Ferns, Clubmosses, Quillworts and Horsetails*, HMSO, 1969. The species described in the book are found in all parts of the British Isles)

VEGETATIVE KEYS

IV PLANTS OF FENS AND MARSHY MEADOWS

This key covers the vegetation of nutrient-rich, often alkaline, waterlogged areas. Where such waterlogging has been prolonged, preventing the decay of plant remains, peat will develop (though less rapidly than in an acid bog), and a fen results.

Fens tend to have very different floras from those of acid bogs. Instead of *Sphagnum* moss with various heath-type shrubs and a few sedges, many different kinds of sedges, grasses and broad-leaved herbs occur, so that the flora may be almost as rich as in a chalk grassland. Unfortunately, however, most of the herbs die right back in autumn, while the grasses and sedges leave only very similar-looking leaves, so that identification without flowers in winter (and, indeed, until early summer) is difficult. But this key should enable the user to name at least some of the commoner or more distinctive species on leaf characters.

Fens are unstable, and if not mown regularly are soon invaded by shrubs and become wet woodland. Meadows are often partly drained areas of former fen, mown for hay, or else used for summer grazing; they (like mountain flush areas, *see* Key III) have some of the same plants as fens. For acid bogs, see also Key III.

---

1 Lvs **circular**, 2–4 cm across, held ± horizontal on erect stalks, margin bluntly-toothed – stem creeping ....
  Hydrocotyle vulgaris (p 264 E)

Lvs **trifoliate** – lfts 5–10 cm long, oval-elliptical, untoothed, borne alt and ± erect on **long** fleshy stalks from base of plant..................
  Menyanthes trifoliata (p 292 A)

Lvs trifoliate – lfts 5–10 cm long, elliptical-lanceolate, toothed, borne opp on **short** stalks on erect stem to 1 m tall......................................
  Eupatorium cannabinum (p 372 F)

Lvs **linear**, 30–60 cm long × 3–4 cm wide, erect, **folded** lengthwise, and all **flattened** in one plane ..... *Iris pseudacorus* (p 417 A)

Lvs **once-pinnate** 2

Lvs **twice-pinnate** 7

Lvs **palmately-lobed**..................... 8

Lvs in **whorls** of **4 or more** lvs, up stems... 9

Lvs simple, oval-lanceolate, **alt** up stems.. 10

Lvs **simple**, oval-lanceolate in outline, either lobed, toothed or untoothed, in **opp** pairs (or **whorls** of 3) up stems................................. 11

Lvs **linear**, with **grass-like blades** 14

Lvs either **abs**, plant with cylindrical stems only, or with the lvs **linear, cylindrical** 17

2 Lfy **stipules** present at base of lf-stalks – lfts 5–7 in number, 3–6 cm long, obovate, deeply-toothed, dark green above, grey below..........
  Potentilla palustris (p 212 A)

Lfy stipules **abs**............................. 3

3 **All** lvs pinnate............................... 4

Upper lvs pinnate or pinnatifid, with terminal lft wider and longer than side ones, all lfts untoothed – **basal** lvs oval-elliptical, simple, untoothed, long-stalked......................
  Valeriana dioica (p 346 B)

4 Lfts blunt, oval-elliptical, **scarcely-toothed** – terminal lft larger than side ones ....
  Rorippa nasturtium-aquaticum (p 124 C)

Lfts pointed, oval-elliptical, teeth prominent – terminal lft not obviously larger than side-lfts 5

Lfts linear, untoothed, stems and lf-stalks hollow, inflated, ridged...........
  Oenanthe fistulosa (p 262 D)

5 Lfts smooth, veins **pinnate**, **not** impressed – stem hairless **6**

Lfts with veins prominent but **pinnate**, side veins **not parallel** – lfts ± **white downy** below – terminal lft three-lobed – pairs of tiny lfts alt with pairs of larger ones along lf-stalk – stem ± hairless ....
Filipendula ulmaria (p 214 A)

No pairs of tiny lfts between larger ones – lfts with midrib and side veins prominent and **deeply impressed**, side veins running almost **parallel** with midrib – stem **hairy** below ....
Valeriana officinalis (p 346 A)

6 **Dark line** visible (against the light) across lf-stalk below lowest pair of lfts – lfts v sharp-toothed, **dull** green, in 7–10 pairs.........................
Berula erecta (p 264 B)

No dark line visible across lf-stalk – lfts with blunt teeth, **shiny** bright green, in 4–6 pairs..........................
Apium nodiflorum (p 264 C)

7 Lfts **oval**, **pointed**, fine-toothed, 2–8 cm long × 2–3 cm wide..............
Angelica sylvestris (p 256 B)

Lfts **linear-lanceolate**, sharp-toothed, 2–10 cm long × 1 cm wide .... *Cicuta virosa* (p 256 C)

Lfts **pinnatifid**, their lobes lanceolate, bluntish, 1–2 cm long × 0.2–0.5 cm wide, mucronate, with **rough** edges.............................
Peucedanum palustre (p 266 E)

Lfts linear, untoothed, ± blunt, with **smooth** edges.........................
Oenanthe lachenalii and other *Oenanthe* spp (p 262 G)

Lfts **obovate**, 3–4-lobed, to 1 cm wide, bases **wedge-shaped**, dark green above, pale beneath – upper lvs only once-pinnate – lf-stalks without inflated basal sheath present in Umbellifers ....
Thalictrum flavum (p 104 B)

8 Lvs fleshy, hairless, glossy, lobes blunt...
Ranunculus sceleratus (p 96 G)

Lvs firm, downy, dull green, lobes v pointed and narrow ....
Ranunculus acris (p 96 B)

9 Lvs **obovate**-lanceolate, **mucronate** – backward-pointing prickles (v tiny) on lf-edges..........................
Galium uliginosum (p 349 D)

Lvs **elliptical**-lanceolate, **blunt** – prickles as above ....
Galium palustre (p 350 E)

10 Stem-lvs to 25 cm long × 2.5 cm wide, lanceolate – root-lvs oval, blunt, cordate-based, long-stalked, to 20 cm long × 8 cm wide (autumn to spring only) ....
Ranunculus lingua (p 98 B)

Stem-lvs to 10 cm long × 1.5 cm wide, lanceolate – root-lvs as above in shape, but to 4 cm long × 3 cm wide only, persisting in summer.......
Ranunculus flammula (p 98 A)

11 Lvs oval, with **blunt teeth, stalked, mint-scented** – stems four-angled ..
Mentha aquatica, and other Mints (p 311 A)

Lvs elliptical in outline, **deeply-toothed** in upper part, to **pinnatifid** especially in lower part of lf, **stalked, unscented** – stems four-angled ....
Lycopus europaeus (p 312 G)

Lvs untoothed, stalkless **12**

12 Tiny creeping plant, rooting at intervals – lvs oval, under 1 cm long, in opp pairs.....................................
Anagallis tenella (p 288 F)

Tall erect (30–100 cm) plants – lvs in opp pairs or whorls of 3, pointed and downy **13**

13 Lvs 5–12 cm long, **oval**-lanceolate, light green, sticky-hairy, with orange or black glands present – side-veins pinnate – fr-head **pyramidal** – stem **round**........................
Lysimachia vulgaris (p 286 A)

Lvs 4–7 cm long, lanceolate, not sticky-hairy, dark green – main side-veins turning up **parallel with midrib** – fr-head **cylindrical** – stem **four-angled**, at least when young....
Lythrum salicaria (p 226 A)

14 Lvs with only shortly sheathing bases, flat, **grey-green**, 1 cm wide or more, × 60–130 cm long, not keeled, all from base of plant ....
Typha latifolia (p 422 E)

IV FENS

Lvs alt with sheathing bases, up stem in two vertical rows – stems hollow .... **Grasses** (pp 458–462)

Lvs with sheathing bases, in 3 vertical ranks on stem – stems solid .... **(Sedges) 15**

15 Shoots forming large **tussocks** raised 30–60 cm above ground, on a cylindrical fibrous pillar **16**

Shoots not in large tussocks............. **other Sedges**

16 Lvs 5–7 mm wide, fresh green......... *Carex paniculata* (**Greater Tussock-sedge**)

Lvs 3–6 mm wide, grey- or blue-green.... *Carex elata* (**Tufted-sedge**)

17 Stems tall (1–3 m), stout (over 1 cm thick), interior spongy............. *Scirpus lacustris* (p 456 Ei)

Stems less than 0.5 cm thick **18**

18 Lvs abs – stems spongy inside – infl on side of stem below tip **19**

Cylindrical hollow lvs present, with cross-partitions inside **20**

19 Stems ribbed lengthwise, brightish green, 3–5 mm thick....................... *Juncus conglomeratus* (p 455 A)

Stems not noticeably ribbed lengthwise, bright green, 3–5 mm thick .... *Juncus effusus* (p 455 Ai)

Stems ribbed, grey-green, 2–3 mm thick ...... *Juncus inflexus* (p 455 Aii)

20 Vertical as well as cross-partitions inside hollow lvs .... *Juncus subnodulosus* (p 456 Bii)

Cross partitions only, inside hollow lvs.......... (*Juncus articulatus* agg) **21**

21 Lvs flattened strongly – frs oval, pointed abruptly............................... *Juncus articulatus* (p 455 B)

Lvs scarcely flattened – frs conical, tapered to a long point..................... *Juncus acutiflorus* (p 455 Bi)

V FLOATING AND SUBMERGED AQUATIC PLANTS

Open water is a very interesting and important plant habitat, but it is a specialized one, and gives its flora a very different appearance from that of land habitats. The vegetation varies according to a number of factors: (1) the depth of the water (there is more light near the surface, and it is warmer); (2) the amount of current (plants adapted to grow in fast-running rivers, where there is much more oxygen, are often very different species from those of stagnant ponds); (3) the nature of the bottom (the species growing on the bottoms of stony or sandy-bedded lakes or rivers are different from those growing on muddy ones); (4) the turbidity or clarity of the water (upland streams or lakes over hard rocks are much clearer and hence let more light through to plants than lowland ones over clays or loams – though lowland chalk streams are often very clear); (5) the nutrient content, or the pH of the water. Some of these factors are also affected by environmental pollution; where this is severe, almost no plants except some algae (and a few Water-lilies) will grow, as in parts of the Norfolk Broads, and in some midland and northern English rivers.

Aquatic plants tend to be either submerged, with narrow translucent leaves, or floating, when their leaves may be broad and opaque; both types of leaf may occur on one plant. Most aquatic plants pass the winter as buds at the bottom of the water, so this key is unlikely to be very useful then. However, many water plants have such tiny inconspicuous flowers or even inflorescences, extremely difficult to interpret or even to dissect, that vegetative identification is often easier than that based on flower structure. Thus, this key will be most useful in high summer.

In general, the user of this book is asked not to collect plants at all, but to bring the book (and the hand lens) to the plant *in situ*. With water plants, however, this rule must be modified. In most cases it is necessary to collect bits of plants in order to see their details; a grapnel (three hooks fastened together on the end of a long string) is most effective for this purpose. The plant should be thrown back into the water after study. It will almost certainly grow again if it has not been allowed to dry out.

A very few flowering plants (species of Eelgrass, *Zostera*) are confined to salt water, either on the shallow offshore sandbanks or mudbanks that exist on more sheltered coastlines, or else in shallow estuaries. Quite a number of aquatics, however, occur in slightly salt (brackish) water in estuarine areas behind sea walls out of direct reach of the tides.

MASTER KEY

Rounded, flat, long-stalked floating lvs like those of Water-lilies .... A

Lvs grass-like to oval, opp or alt, undivided and unlobed, normally **over** 5 cm long, borne along **branched** stems, but **not** in close whorls .... B

Lvs translucent, **strap**-shaped, **under** 3 cm long and less than 10 times as long as wide, in **whorls** of 3 or more along the stems C

Lvs linear, strap- or quill-like, undivided, in ± erect or spreading crowns, tufts or rosettes, growing on the bottom of lakes or ponds .... D

Lvs **much divided** into narrow segments, normally submerged (flat, shallow-lobed lvs with broad blunt divisions may also be present) .... E

Lvs like long (50–100 cm) green ribbons to 2 cm wide, floating on surface, but attached to submerged stem .... *Sparganium* spp (p 420)

Plants **either** small, round or oval discs 3–10 mm across, **or** of pointed elliptical translucent green scales 5–12 mm long, jointed together by stalks, **without** distinction into stem and lvs – one or more unbranched slender roots hanging from undersides – free-floating .... *Lemna* spp (p 444)

Plants like tiny (0.5–1.0 mm) green grains of sand, without roots, floating on water .... *Wolffia* (p 444)

V AQUATIC HABITATS

A **Plants with lvs rounded, flat, floating, like those of Water-lilies**

Lvs 3–10 cm across, orbicular, cordate-based – lvs of floating stems opp.. *Nymphoides peltata* (p 292 B)

Plants without floating stems – lvs normally over 10 cm across, all from a rhizome deep in water or mud..
Water-lily family, *Nymphaeaceae* (p 106)

Lvs 2–3 cm across, round kidney-shaped, borne in tufts from floating stems, with large chaffy stipules at their bases ....
Hydrocharis morsus-ranae (p 402 F)

B **Plants with lvs grass-like to oval, opp or alt, undivided and unlobed, over 1.5 cm long, borne along branched stems, but not in close whorls**

1 **In the sea** – lvs ribbon-like, 6–50 cm long, 1–10 mm wide – fls in **flattened spikes** ± **enclosed** within **lf-sheaths** .... *Zostera* (p 449)

In **fresh** or **brackish water** – lvs **not** ribbon-like, mostly (if narrow) under 10 cm long – fls **not** in flattened spikes enclosed within lf-sheaths **2**

2 Frs and fls in stalked **spikes** in axils of upper lvs, each fl with 4 perianth segments or, if **without** fls or frs, lvs elliptical to oval.................................
Potamogetonaceae (see key p 451)

Frs and fls in **stalked umbels** – lvs narrow, grass-like ....*Ruppia* (p 449)

Frs and fls in small **clusters** in lf-axils – lvs narrow **3**

Frs and fls **abs**................................ **4**

3 Lvs in **opp** pairs, **untoothed** – frs stalked, with beaks 0.5–2.0 mm long................*Zannichellia* (p 449)

Lvs **opp**, or in **whorls** of 2–3, **toothed** – frs unstalked, ovoid, with 3 styles....................... *Najas* (p 449)

4 Lvs opp **5**

Lvs **alt** (but may be in an opp pair when infls present in their axils), linear to oval, with membraneous **stipules** ....
Potamogeton (see key p 451)

Lvs 3 per whorl, or in opp pairs, toothed, linear to oblong, with no stipules but with sheathing bases .....
Najas (p 449)

5 Lvs **oval-triangular**, **without** stipules, **finely-toothed**, 1.5–4.0 cm long × **5–15 mm wide** ....
Groenlandia densa (p 448)

Lvs **linear**, **flat**, with **sheathing stipules**, **untoothed**, 1.5–6.0 cm long **0.5–2.0 mm wide**....................
Zannichellia (p 449)

Lvs **linear**, or **thread-like**, with **sheathing bases** but **no** stipules, untoothed, 5–10 cm long × **0.5–1.0 mm wide** ....*Ruppia* (p 449)

C **Submerged waterweeds with lvs translucent, strap-shaped, under 5 cm long and less than 10 times as long as wide, in whorls of 3 or more along the stems, resembling Canadian Pondweed (p 444 H)**

1 Lvs strongly arched or curled back, bluntly-toothed, in close whorls of 4 – S, mid Eng, o-lf – in still water ....
Lagarosiphon major (**Curly Water Thyme**)

Lvs ± wavy, but not strongly arched or curled back **2**

2 Lvs 20 mm or more long.............. **3**

Lvs 15 mm or less long................. **4**

3 Lvs light green, narrow lanceolate, tapered to a point, 25 mm long, in distant whorls of 3 (**rarely** 2) – stems **weak, slender** – S Eng r – in still to slow fresh water ....
Elodea callitrichoides

Lvs light green, **strap**-shaped, to 5 cm long × to 3 mm wide, **6–12** per whorl – stems **stout** (to 6 mm wide), **spongy**...................................
Hippuris vulgaris (p 106 C)

Lvs dark green, narrow-oblong, abruptly pointed, to 30 mm long × 5 mm wide, in crowded whorls of 4 – stems weak, slender – long-stalked white fls to 1 cm across – S Lancs r – in still fresh water ....
Egeria densa (**Large-flowered Water Thyme**)

4 Lvs dark green, 10 mm long × 3–4 mm wide, 3 (rarely 4) per whorl, oblong, blunt or abruptly pointed, edges minutely-toothed – tiny scales on upper side of lf near base, green, untoothed – c......................
Elodea canadensis (p 444 H)

Lvs light green, 10 mm long × 1–2 mm wide, 3–5 per whorl, linear-lanceolate, tapered to a point, edges with tiny projecting teeth – tiny scales on upper side of lf near base, brown, fringed – Cumbria, W Ire, r – France to Netherlands c – in deep fresh water...............................
Elodea nuttallii (**Esthwaite Waterweed**)

D Aquatic plants with lvs linear, strap- or quill-like, undivided, most in ± erect crowns, tufts or rosettes, growing on the bottom of lakes or ponds

1 Plants with tufts of lvs **connected** by creeping runners or rhizomes... **2**

Plants with tufts of lvs in **separate** crowns or rosettes, **not** connected to other tufts by runners or rhizomes....................................... **5**

2 Lvs firm, opaque, v narrow (1.5 mm wide or less) either borne singly or in tufts............................. **3**

Lvs either fleshy, or translucent, 2.0 mm wide or more in erect crowns or rosettes........................ **4**

3 Lvs **solid**, arising **singly** from creeping rhizome, tips of young lvs coiled in a spiral – (small fern, with hard pill-like swellings on rhizome – in ponds on hths ....
Pilularia globulifera (**Pillwort**)

Lvs **hollow**, each composed of **two** tubes within, arising in **tufts**, tips **not** coiled ....
Juncus bulbosus (**Bulbous Rush**)

4 Lvs fleshy, **opaque**, **cylindrical**, **parallel**-sided to **blunt** tip, **spongy** inside.... *Littorella uniflora* (p 336 F)

Lvs **translucent**, flattened, **tapered** to pointed tip, with the **hollow** inside divided by **cross-partitions**

– W Ire, NW Scot only, vl.................
Eriocaulon septangulare (p 444 I)

5 Lvs ± **cylindrical** above, **tapered** to **pointed** tips, composed of **4 tubes** (a) internally, **with** cross-partitions – spore-capsules (b) usually present sunken in expanded lf-bases – (mostly in mt lakes lf – non-flowering plants).......................
Isoetes spp (**Quillworts**)

Lvs **flattened**, with **blunt**, rounded tips, composed of **2 tubes** internally, **without** cross-partitions – no spore-capsules but sometimes with tall (30–40 cm) fl- or fr-spike – N of Br Isles and N Eur, lf ....
Lobelia dortmanna (p 338 H)

Lvs **flattened**, **tapered** to pointed tips, **triangular** in cross-section, **solid** – short erect racemes of white four-petalled fls 2.5 mm wide, producing egg-shaped flattened frs 2.5 mm long, sometimes present – a Crucifer of mt lakes, lf ....
Subularia aquatica (**Awlwort**)

E Aquatic plants with lvs much divided into narrow segments, normally submerged (flat, shallow-lobed lvs with broad blunt divisions may also be present)

1 Lvs alt along stems........................ **2**

Lvs opp or whorled........................ **3**

2 Tiny bladders present on some or all lf-segments..... *Utricularia* (p 334)

Bladders abs, lvs palmately divided ....
Ranunculus subgenus *Batrachium* (p 100)

Bladders abs, lvs pinnately lobed or divided ....
Oenanthe (p 262), or *Apium inundatum* (p 264 D)

3 Lvs pinnate................................... **4**

Lvs forked 1–3 times......................
Ceratophyllum (p 106)

4 Lvs in rosettes, with flat linear segments .... *Hottonia* (p 286)

Lvs in whorls spaced out along stems, with hairlike segments..........
Myriophyllum (p 106)

VEGETATIVE KEYS

VI HERBS OF ROADSIDES, WASTE GROUND, WELL LIT HEDGEBANKS, ARABLE AND DRY MEADOWS

In all these habitats a great many species of plants occur. In some very cultivated or suburbanized areas these may be almost the only habitats available for study. Well lit hedgebanks are best grouped here (for shady hedgebanks see Key I).

It was difficult to decide which species of the roadside and waste ground habitats to include and which to omit from this key, because their incidence is so varied, many plants being present in one place and many others in another but similar habitat. The choice ultimately made is of plants most likely to be found and, of these, those easiest to identify. All sorts of introduced or garden plants can turn up in such places, but these are not included, for reasons of space.

With arable weeds the problem is that most of them are annuals; when present they may quite likely be at least partially in flower, while in winter many of them completely disappear. Hence the key contains few plants that are strictly weeds of arable land. The key concentrates very much on leaf-rosette form; but it is worth remembering that many plants whose leaves are confined to a basal rosette occur in trampled places, and that some other plants which only show a rosette in winter may in summer bear a tall leafy stem.

MASTER KEY

(For roadsides in calc areas use also Key II; for shady lanes or dense tall roadside hedges use Key I)

1 Lvs grass-like, linear, with sheathing bases .... A
  Lvs not grass-like 2
2 Lvs compound with separate lfts, or deeply divided into lobes more than halfway to the midrib or base of lf 3
  Lvs simple, and, if toothed or lobed, not divided into lobes more than ⅓ way to midrib, or to base, of lf 4
3 Lvs **palmately** divided or lobed, into **5 or more** lfts or main lobes all radiating from tip of lf-stalk .... B
  Lvs **trifoliately** divided or lobed, with 3 main lfts or lobes only C
  Lvs **pinnately** divided or lobed, with the lfts or lobes in one to many **pairs** along central midrib of lf, with sometimes a terminal lft at lf-tip .... D
4 Lvs simple, in opp pairs along stems .... E
  Lvs in **whorls** of 4 or more along stems .... F
  Lvs simple, alt along stems .... G
  Lvs all in a spreading **basal rosette** (so impossible to see whether alt or opp) .... H

A **Herbs with lvs grass-like, linear, with sheathing bases**

  1 Lvs in 3 vertical ranks, stems solid, ± triangular .... (**Sedges**) 2

    Lvs in 2 vertical ranks, stems hollow, round .... (**Grasses**) 3

  2 Lvs hairy ....
        Carex hirta (**Hairy Sedge**)

    Lvs hairless, with grey waxy bloom on upperside ....
        Carex flacca (**Glaucous Sedge**)

    Lvs hairless, bright green on upper-side ....
    other *Carex* spp (fls or frs needed to name these)

  3 Root-lvs bristle-like, 1mm wide or less 4

    Root-lvs not bristle-like, over 2mm wide, either flat or folded lengthwise 5

  4 Root-lvs (**b**) grooved on upperside, stem-lvs (**a**) flat – ligule v short, blunt .... *Festuca rubra* (p 458 A)

    Root-lvs not grooved on upperside, stem-lvs also bristle-like – ligule pointed – on sandy or hthy rdside banks...
    Deschampsia flexuosa (**Wavy Hair-grass**)

  5 Root-lvs flat 6

82

Root-lvs strongly folded and keeled, rough – sheath flattened – ligule blunt, folded...........................
Dactylis glomerata (**Cock's-foot**)

6 Lvs linear-lanceolate – ligules long, pointed – stems creeping................
Agrostis stolonifera (p 458 G)

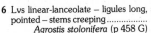

Lvs parallel-sided most of their length – stems tufted.....................**7**

7 Lvs with several deep parallel grooves above, v rough when rubbed downwards – lvs 20–30 cm long in large tussocks – ligules long, pointed..
Deschampsia caespitosa (**Tufted Hair-grass**)

Lvs without deep grooves above .. **8**

8 Lvs grey-green, v downy, sheaths pinkish – ligules long, blunt..............
Holcus lanatus (**Yorkshire-fog**)

Lvs fresh green, flaccid, not downy, sheaths green – ligules long, blunt..
Arrhenatherum elatius (**False Oat-grass**)

Lvs as last, but rigid, rough, hairless – long underground runners............
Agropyron repens (p 458 Fi)

B **Herbs with lvs palmately divided or lobed into 5 or more lfts or main lobes, all radiating from tip of lf-stalk**

1 Lvs palmately **divided** into 5 (or 7) **separate** lfts – lfts obovate, deeply toothed .... – lvs long-stalked – stem creeping.................................
Potentilla reptans (p 210 E)

Lvs ± deeply palmately **lobed**, but **not** divided to base into separate lfts **2**

2 Lvs hairless, shiny, ± red-tinged – lobes v blunt – local, in hbs .... *Geranium lucidum* (p 172 D)

Lvs hairy, main lobes divided again into pointed narrow segments.......**3**

3 Root-lvs **five-angled** in outline – lf-stalks **green** – lvs with 3 larger twice-pinnately cut lobes, and 2 **smaller** basal lobes cut into few sharp teeth......................................
Ranunculus acris (p 96 B)

Root-lvs seven-angled in outline – lf-stalks red-flushed below – lvs with 5–7 main lobes, all twice-pinnately cut – calc soils..................
Geranium pratense (p 174 B; also other Geraniums, pp 172–174)

C **Herbs with lvs trifoliately divided or lobed, with 3 main lfts or lobes only, which may (or may not) themselves be lobed again**

1 Lfts simple, unlobed, with small teeth or none.................................**2**

Lfts deeply divided into lobed segments..**4**

2 Stems **creeping** – lfts oval-obovate, **finely-toothed**, ± hairless, each often with a whitish crescent across it – lf-stalks 5–14 cm long...............
Trifolium repens (p 184 D)

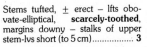

Stems tufted, ± erect – lfts obovate-elliptical, **scarcely-toothed**, margins downy – stalks of upper stem-lvs short (to 5 cm)................**3**

3 Lfts usually with a whitish crescentic band across each, oval-obovate, blunt, dull green – upper parts of stipules **broad**-triangular with fine brown **erect bristle**-points...............
Trifolium pratense (p 184 A)

Lfts usually without a whitish band across each, narrow-elliptical, pointed, **bright** green – upper parts of stipules **narrow-oblong**, with green **awl-shaped spreading** points .... *Trifolium medium* (p 184 B)

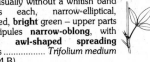

4 Plant with **creeping** and **rooting runners** – the 3 lfts v hairy, mid lft **stalked**, **three-lobed**, the lobes divided into deeply but **bluntly** lobed segments................................
Ranunculus repens (p 96 A)

Plant erect, **without** runners – the 3 lfts ± hairy, mid lft **un-stalked**, each lft **twice-pinnately** divided into **narrow**-lanceolate, **pointed** segments..........................
Ranunculus acris (p 96 B)

Plant **erect**, **without** runners, but with corm at stem-base – the 3 lfts ± hairy, mid lft **stalked**, three-lobed, the lobes divided into rather narrow, **pointed** segments.....
Ranunculus bulbosus (p 96 C)

VI ROADSIDES, WASTE GROUND

D Herbs with lvs **pinnately divided or lobed**, with the lfts or lobes **in two to many pairs** along central midrib of lf, with sometimes a terminal lft at lf-tip

(Note: if lobes only shallow and divided less than halfway to midrib of lf, like coarse teeth, return to **4** in Master Key VI above)

1 Lvs **pinnatifid** (ie, with the lobes on each side of main lf midrib joined together by a **continuous**, though sometimes v narrow, **flange** of lf-blade) **2**

Lvs **pinnately compound** (ie, with **separate lfts**, the pairs of lfts along the main lf midrib **separated** from each other, at least **in lower part** of lf, by a length of stalk **without** any flange of lf-blade) **14**

2 Lvs **spine**-edged and/or -tipped **11**

Lvs **without** spines (though sometimes bristly-hairy) **3**

3 Lvs with **terminal lobe much larger** than side-lobes **4**

Lvs with terminal lobe **not** conspicuously larger than side-lobes .. **5**

4 Lvs soft, not glossy, with v large (4–6cm long × 3–5cm wide), **oval**, often cordate, wavy-toothed terminal lobe – and few, much smaller, undivided side-lobes along the flanged lf midrib ....
Lapsana communis (p 394 G)

Lvs of **basal rosette** (a) with terminal lobe **oval**, firm, glossy, 2–3cm long – side-lobes themselves ± pinnately lobed – lvs (b) **above** rosette have terminal lobe no larger than side-lobes ....
Senecio jacobaea (p 362 A)

Lvs of basal rosette with terminal lobe **triangular, pointed**, 1–2cm long – side-lobes undivided ....
Crepis spp (pp 395–396)

5 Lvs **white-felted** below, green and ± hairless on upperside, aromatic when bruised, twice-pinnatifid into **flat**, pointed lobes ....
Artemisia vulgaris (p 376 E)

Lvs **not** white-felted below **6**

6 Lvs **twice-pinnatifid, not** aromatic when bruised – lf outline oval-oblong, 3cm or more wide – segments **blunt**, furrowed, dull green, ± sparsely downy above and below, not cottony above ....
Senecio jacobaea (p 362 A)

Lvs **twice-pinnatifid**, but aromatic, with **pointed, fine-toothed, ± hairless** segments ....
Chrysanthemum vulgare (p 369 C)

Lvs once-pinnatifid only **7**

7 Lvs **deeply** pinnatifid into **narrow, ± linear** lobes **8**

Lvs **shallowly** pinnatifid into **broad**, ± triangular lobes – lvs all in a basal rosette **10**

Lvs **deeply** pinnatifid (a) into **broad**, oblong, pointed side-lobes – lvs **waxy grey-green** – stem-lvs (b) with pointed basal lobes – latex **milky** *Sonchus oleraceus* (p 400 H)

8 Lvs **aromatic** when bruised – segments flat, linear, finely-toothed, ± hairless – lvs 3cm wide or more, **broad**-oblong in outline ....
Chrysanthemum vulgare (p 369 C)

Lvs **not** aromatic when bruised – lvs to 2cm. wide only, **narrow**-oblong to lanceolate in outline **9**

9 Lvs ± **cottony** above, especially near their base – lf-lobes all blunt, **crisped, wavy**, coarse-toothed – end lobe **no longer than** side-lobes – lvs 3–6cm long × 1–2cm wide, mostly clasping and alt up stem – basal rosette usually abs – ann plant, often with erect infl in winter .....*Senecio vulgaris* (p 362 F)

Lvs **not** cottony, but with ± **sparse stiff** hairs above – lf-lobes all **narrow**, pointed, flat, ± untoothed – end lobe **much longer than** side-lobes – lvs 10cm or more long × 1–2cm wide, **all** in a basal rosette – per plant ....
Leontodon autumnalis (p 394 E)

Lvs ± **hairless** above, v **variable** from broad-lanceolate and shallow-toothed, to deeply pinnatifid into narrow, toothed lobes – terminal lf-lobe **oval**, toothed – alt stem-lvs like root-lvs but with clasping bases – ann plant ....
Capsella bursa-pastoris (p 128 D)

10 Lvs ± **hairless**, **glossy**, **bright** green – side-lobes broad-triangular, sharp-toothed, teeth of upper lobes **backward-pointing** – much milky latex in lvs......................
Taraxacum officinale (p 388 A)

Lvs hairless, waxy **grey-green** – side-lobes irregularly-toothed, end-lobes triangular and often wider than side-lobes – much **milky latex** in lvs.. *Sonchus oleraceus* (p 400 H)

Lvs roughly **hairy**, **dull** green – side-lobes blunt, rounded, wavy-edged, shallow, untoothed, side-ways-pointing – little or no milky latex in lvs...
Hypochoeris radicata (p 392 A)

11 Lvs **waxy grey-green** with **milky latex** – all in basal rosette in winter.............. *Sonchus asper* (p 400 I)

Lvs **not** waxy grey-green, juice **watery**.. **12**

12 Lvs **prickly** and **rough**-hairy on upperside, hence dull grey-green above ..... *Cirsium vulgare* (p 381 A)

Lvs **not** prickly on upperside, only sparsely (or not at all) hairy there, hence ± glossy above................. **13**

13 Lvs **dark green** and ± **purple-flushed**, all in a basal rosette in winter – stem, when present, has continuous spiny wings up it and alt lvs – bi plant ....
Cirsium palustre (p 381 D)

Lvs **grey-green**, **never** purplish – stem **unwinged** – per plant ....
Cirsium arvense (p 381 E)

14 Lvs **once**-pinnate – lfts lobed or toothed or not so, but not divided again into lfts **15**

Lvs **twice or more times pinnate** into separate lfts.......................... **25**

15 Lfts quite untoothed – tip of lf with a branched tendril instead of a lft **16**

Lfts toothed or lobed – tip of lf with a lft.. **18**

16 Lvs hairless, with 1 pair of lfts only – stem **square**, **angled** – large triangular lfy stipules at lf-base ....
Lathyrus spp, especially *L. pratensis* (p 192 A)

Lvs ± hairy, with 3–12 pairs of lfts – stem **round**...................... **17**

17 Lfts 3–8 pairs, obovate – low plant (to 30 cm) ...... *Vicia sativa* (p 190 C)

Lfts 6–12 pairs, oblong-lanceolate – climbing plant (to 200 cm) ....
Vicia spp, especially *V. cracca* (p 190 A)

18 Side-lfts all ± **equal** in size.......... **19**

Tiny side-lfts alt with **larger** ones along lf-stalk **24**

19 Lfts strongly lobed and toothed, 2 cm wide (or much more).......... **20**

Lfts not lobed or only weakly so, teeth blunt or shallow – side-lfts under 2 cm wide **21**

20 Lvs hairless, glossy dark green.........
Pimpinella major (p 254 F)

Lvs roughly hairy, dull greyish-green..
Heracleum sphondylium (p 256 D)

21 Terminal lft of root-lvs **pointed**-oval, blunt-toothed, similar in shape to side-lfts – lvs **grey**-green – crushed lf-stalks produce **orange** liquid ....
Chelidonium majus (p 108 H)

Terminal lft of root-lvs **rounded** to kidney-shaped, **much** wider than side-lfts – lvs fresh to dark green – crushed lf-stalk produces watery liquid **22**

22 Stem-lvs (**b**) with all lfts v **narrow**-lanceolate – root-lvs (**a**) with terminal lft kidney-shaped, dark glossy green, to 2 cm wide – per plant of damp places........................
Cardamine pratensis (p 122 G)

Stem-lvs with all lfts **oval**-elliptical, bluntly-toothed – root-lvs with terminal lft kidney-shaped, but pale green, to 1 cm wide..................... **23**

23 Root-lvs many in a rosette – ann plant of dry open ground ....
Cardamine hirsuta (p 122 Fi)

Root-lvs few, in sparse rosette – per plant of damp ground ....
Cardamine flexuosa (p 122 F)

24 Lfts **silvery**, silky-hairy – stems **creeping**..
Potentilla anserina (p 210 H)

Lfts **green**- or purple-flushed, downy – stems **erect** ....
Agrimonia eupatoria (p 212 E)

85

25 Lvs with lfts narrow-linear, almost bristle-like – lf-outline oblong **26**

Lvs with lfts broad and flat – lf-outline **triangular**...................... **27**

26 Lvs narrow-oblong in outline, end-lfts grey-green, downy, dense-set, only 1–2 mm long ....
Achillea millefolium (p 372 D)

Lvs broad-oblong in outline, end-lfts dark green, ± fleshy, hairless, loosely-set, 5–15 mm long.......
Tripleurospermum maritimum (p 374 A)

27 Secondary lfts **oval**, 3–6 cm long × 3–4 cm wide, **finely-toothed**.................................... **28**

Secondary lfts **deeply** cut, 0.5–2.0 cm long × 0.5 mm wide – whole lf fern-like.................................... **29**

28 Lfts oval-elliptical, 4–8 cm long, borne mostly in **threes** on side-branches of lf – lfts and stalks **wholly** fresh green – sheathing lf-bases **not** inflated ....
Aegopodium podagraria (p 256 A)

Lfts **oval**, 2–8 cm long, **pinnately** arranged on side branches of lf – **purple** blotches where side branches of lf join main stalk – sheathing lf-bases **inflated** ....
Angelica sylvestris (p 256 B)

29 Lf-stalks with **papery brown scales** numerous below ....
(Ferns) *Dryopteris* spp

Lf-stalks **without** papery brown scales below................................. **30**

30 Lfts and lf-stalks hairy **31**

Lfts and lf-stalks hairless.............. **32**

31 Lfts grey-green, **downy**, blunt – lf-stalks and stems **purple**-spotted, softly downy ....
Chaerophyllum temulentum (p 252 E)

Lfts grey-green, **rough**, v pointed – lf-stalks and stems **unspotted**, rough........*Torilis japonica* (p 251 B)

Lfts fresh green, smooth, ± hairless on uppersides, with pointed teeth – lf-stalks and stems unspotted.... *Anthriscus sylvestris* (p 251 A)

32 Lfts with narrow, flat lobes – lf-stalks and stems **unspotted** – ann plant.......
Aethusa cynapium (p 252 G)

Lfts with many fine-cut lobes – lf-stalks and stems **purple**-spotted – bi plant.. *Conium maculatum* (p 252 F)

E Herbs with lvs simple, in opp pairs along stems

1 Lvs fleshy, linear, 2 mm wide, or less **2**

Lvs not fleshy, but flat, over 4 mm wide **3**

2 Lvs blunt, 1–3 cm long, half-cylindrical – papery stipules at lf-bases – clusters of lvs in lf-axils (thus lvs appearing ± whorled) – plant to 20 cm tall – on dry open sandy wa and ar...
Spergula arvensis (p 156 E)

Lvs pointed, under 1 cm long – no stipules – tiny creeping plant (to 5 cm tall) of paths etc ....
Sagina procumbens (p 156 G)

3 Basal rosette-lvs 10–20 cm long, oblong-lanceolate, untoothed, with strong swollen-based **prickles** on **uppersides** – stem-lvs sometimes toothed, with prickles only on **underside** of midrib – stem angled, prickly...
Dipsacus fullonum (p 354 A)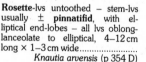

All lvs **without** spines or prickles ... **4**

4 Lvs v **hairy**, **downy**, or **rough** on upper and on lower surfaces......... **5**

All lvs ± **hairless** and **smooth** on upper and lower surfaces (but **edges** may be rough) **11**

5 **Rosette**-lvs untoothed – stem-lvs usually ± **pinnatifid**, with elliptical end-lobes – all lvs oblong-lanceolate to elliptical, 4–12 cm long × 1–3 cm wide......................
Knautia arvensis (p 354 D)

All lvs **untoothed** – stems round ... **6**

All lvs toothed – **stems round** – lvs **not** cordate-based **7**

All lvs toothed – **stems four-angled** – lvs **cordate**-based..................... **9**

6 Lvs narrow-oblong, 1.0–2.5 cm long × 0.3–0.5 cm wide, short-stalked at base, stalkless above, all ± blunt – stems creeping and ascending ....
Cerastium holosteioides (p 152 A)

Lvs oval-oblong, 2–5 cm long × 1–2 cm wide, all blunt and un-stalked – stems all erect, **not** swollen at joints ....
Hypericum hirsutum (p 136 D)

Lvs oblong-lanceolate to elliptical, 5–10 cm long × 2–3 cm wide, lower lvs narrowed to short stalks, upper stalkless – stems **swollen** at joints, erect .... *Silene alba* (p 144 G)

7 Rosette-lvs with **coarse**, blunt, often **backward**-pointing teeth – upper lvs ± coarsely pin-natifid – **all** lvs opp ....
Knautia arvensis (p 354 D)

All lvs with sparse, tiny, pointed, forward-pointing teeth – upper lvs often alt, lower always opp **8**

8 Lvs 6–12 cm long, v hairy, their bases **clasping** stem – plant to 150 cm tall......................................
Epilobium hirsutum (p 223 E)

Lvs 3–7 cm long, **softly** hairy, **not** clasping stem – plant to 60 cm tall ....
Epilobium parviflorum (p 223 F)

9 Lvs bluntly oval, with coarse, blunt teeth – ann plants ....
Lamium purpureum (p 314 A)

Lvs oval-triangular, pointed, teeth sharp – per plants **10**

10 Lvs and stem with long rigid stinging hairs – stem ± purplish, with more than 4 ridges ....
Urtica dioica (p 226 E)

Lvs and stem with soft, non-stinging hairs – stem green, with 4 angles only ....
Lamium album (p 314 D)

11 Lvs untoothed **12**

Lvs finely-toothed, oval-lanceolate to oblong – stems ± red-flushed below **15**

12 Lvs **oblong**, **blunt**, with **transparent** pellucid **dots** (hold up to light), all stalkless, 1–2 cm long × 0.5–1.0 cm wide – stems round with 2 raised ridges, often **reddish** below ....
Hypericum perforatum (p 136 A)

Lvs **oval**, **pointed**, the lower **stalked**, the upper **stalkless** – no pellucid dots – stems round, green.. **13**

VI ROADSIDES, WASTE GROUND

Lvs **linear-lanceolate**, **pointed**, **all** stalkless – no pellucid dots – stems **square** in cross-section, green **14**

13 Lvs yellowish to bright green, **flat**, **soft**, 0.3–2.5 cm long × 0.5–1.5 cm wide – plant **spreading**, much-branched, floppy ....
Stellaria media (p 150 A)

Lvs greyish-green, lower ± **folded** lengthwise, **firm**, 4–5 cm long × 1.0–1.5 cm wide – plant **erect**.........*Silene vulgaris* (p 146 A)

14 Lvs rigid, sharp-pointed, edges rough, broadest at base ....
Stellaria holostea (p 150 C)

Lvs less rigid, short-pointed, edges smooth, lvs broadest near middle ....
Stellaria graminea (p 150 B)

15 Stems **cylindrical**, ± **hairless** – lvs **oval-lanceolate**, short-stalked..
Epilobium montanum (p 223 A)

Stems with **4 raised**, lengthwise **ridges** above, with **many curly** and **sticky hairs** above – lvs oblong-lanceolate, short-stalked..................
Epilobium spp, probably *E. adenocaulon* (p 223 C)

F Herbs with lvs in whorls of 4 or more along stems

1 Lvs **fleshy**, **cylindrical**, **linear**, **blunt** – **clusters** of lvs in lf-axils can **appear** like whorls of lvs............
Spergula arvensis (p 156 E)

Lvs **not** fleshy or cylindrical........... **2**

2 Lvs with 3 main veins, **oval**-elliptical, 4 per whorl, hairy ....
Galium cruciata (p 350 I)

Lvs one-veined, **lanceolate** to **linear**, 6 or more per whorl, never oval **3**

3 Lvs **linear**, 0.5–2.0 mm wide, **8–12** per whorl, hairless ....
Galium verum (p 350 J)

Lvs obovate to linear-lanceolate, **mucronate**, **6–8** per whorl, ± hairy or prickly.......................... **4**

4 Lvs obovate – lvs and stem not prickly, ± hairy but scarcely rough..... *Galium mollugo* (p 349 A)

Lvs linear-lanceolate – lvs and stem with large downward-pointed prickles ... *Galium aparine* (p 350 H)

G Lvs simple, alt along the stems – if toothed or lobed, not divided into lobes more than ⅓ of way to midrib, or to base, of lf

1 Lvs with veins **palmately** arranged, lower always with obvious stalks ... **2**

Lvs with veins **pinnately** arranged, or with only one vein visible **4**

2 Stipules at base of lvs tiny, 2–3 mm long × 1–2 mm wide, oval-lanceolate – lvs not pleated along veins, ± glossy **3**

Stipules at base of lvs conspicuous, 5–10 mm long × 5–10 mm wide, lf-like, toothed – upper lvs short-stalked, lower long-stalked – lvs pleated along veins, not glossy.........
Alchemilla vulgaris agg (p 212 C)

3 Basal lvs 5–10 cm across, sparsely hairy, outlines ± angled, lobed ⅓ way to base........................
Malva sylvestris (p 168 A)

Basal lvs 4–7 across, ± downy, rounded, kidney-shaped, lobed ¼ way to base or less ....
Malva spp, especially *M. neglecta* (p 168 B)

Basal lvs 2–3 cm across, ± deeply lobed....................................
Geranium spp (pp 172–174)

4 Stems erect – lvs over 5 cm long and over 1 cm wide........................ **5**

Stems ± **prostrate**, or **climbing. 14**

5 Lvs **hairy**... **6**

Lvs **hairless** **10**

6 Lvs cordate-based, oval-triangular, 10–30 cm long × 10–20 cm wide, the lower lvs on long ± erect stalks, upper lvs short-stalked – all lvs green on uppersides, grey-cottony on undersides – stout erect plants to 1 m tall................................
Arctium spp (p 386 E, Ei)

Lvs not cordate-based but elliptical-lanceolate, or oblong, or linear **7**

7 Basal lvs ± erect, **not** in a spreading rosette (or no basal lvs present).. **8**

Basal lvs in a **large spreading rosette** – lvs 10–30 cm long, elliptical-lanceolate to oblong, narrowed into a v short stalk........................ **9**

8 Basal lvs 5–15 cm long, elliptical-lanceolate to oblong, narrowed into long stalks – stem-lvs stalkless – all lvs ± roughly hairy, untoothed to ± pinnatifid, dark green........................
Centaurea nigra (p 385 A)

Basal lvs 5–8 cm long, obovate-lanceolate, soon withering – stem-lvs **numerous**, **linear**-lanceolate, pointed – all lvs pale green, short-stalked, ± hairy, with few or no teeth ....
Conyza canadensis (p 368 H)

9 Lvs clothed with dense soft white wool .... *Verbascum thapsus* (p 298 A)

Lvs dark green and thinly downy on upperside, hairier underneath.....
Verbascum spp, probably *V. nigrum* (p 298 B)

10 Lvs numerous, in spiral up **un-branched** stem, **without** stipules – lvs 5–15 cm long, oblong-lanceolate, ± untoothed, narrowed to each end, uppersides dark green, lower grey-green....................
Chamaenerion angustifolium (p 224 I)

Lvs well spaced-out up **branched** stem, with papery sheathing **stipules** at base of each **11**

11 Lvs **arrowhead-shaped**, with **down**-pointing basal lobes – **stipules** fringed with bristles – infls branched – stems weakly ribbed lengthwise ....*Rumex acetosa* (p 272 I)

As the last, but basal lobes of lvs arching **forwards** or **outwards**.........
Rumex acetosella (p 272 J)

Lvs **not** arrowhead-shaped......... **12**

12 Lvs **lanceolate** – stipules **fringed** with bristles – lvs **not over 2 cm** wide × 10 cm long, v **short**-stalked, often **black-blotched** – stems slender (2–4 mm wide at base), **smooth** and round................
Polygonum spp, especially *P. persicaria* (p 274 F)

Lvs oval-oblong to lanceolate, the lowest **over 3 cm wide × 15 cm long**, **long**-stalked – lvs **never** blotched – stipules **without** fringes – stems **stout** (5 mm or more wide at base), **ridged** length-wise........ **13**

13 Lower lvs **oval-oblong**, cordate-based, **blunt**-tipped, to 25 cm long – edges wavy but not crisped – stems and infls erect ....
Rumex obtusifolius (p 270 C)

Lower lvs **oblong-lanceolate**, with **crisped wavy** edges, blunt-tipped, to 30 cm long, **narrowed** to or **rounded** at base – stems and infls **erect**........ *Rumex crispus* (p 270 D)

Lower lvs **oblong**, with wavy edges and **pointed** tip, 15–20 cm long, rounded at base – stems ± **wavy** – infls ± **spreading** from vertical ....
Rumex conglomeratus (p 270 B)

14 Lvs elliptical-lanceolate, not over 3 cm long × 1 cm wide, untoothed, v short-stalked, with papery sheathing stipules at lf-bases ....
Polygonum aviculare (p 272 A)

Lvs arrow-shaped to cordate-triangular, 2–6 cm long × 2–3 cm wide, long-stalked, with pointed basal lobes – plants both creeping and climbing.............................. **15**

15 Papery sheathing stipules at lf-bases – lvs ± mealy on undersides, pointed.........................
Polygonum convolvulus (p 274 L)

No stipules at lf-bases – lvs not mealy on either side...................... **16**

16 Basal lobes pointed, spreading, lvs 2–3 cm long ....
Convolulus arvensis (p 294 A)

Basal lobes blunt, backward-pointing, lvs 5–8 cm long.........................
Calystegia sepium (p 294 B)

H Herbs with lvs simple, all in a spreading basal rosette – no lvs on stems (or no stems present, so impossible to see whether lvs alt or opp)

Note: this section of the key covers some plants that **may** have lfy stems in summer, but in winter have lvs only in a basal rosette.

Some of the spp appearing below occur also in other sections of the Roadsides Key (VI), but are repeated here because (a) some spp included in section D may occur with scarcely pinnatifid lvs, and (b) because some spp in sections G and E may be without stems **in winter**. Species with **compound** or **deeply-lobed** lvs should be sought in sections B, C and D.

1 Lvs with **broad** (8 cm or more wide), **rounded** blades, and **cordate** bases, borne **erect** on **long stout** stalks that are **grooved** above **2**

Lvs with several ± **parallel main veins**, with inconspicuous cross-veins – lvs 10–15 cm long ... **4**

Lvs with **spiny** margins **5**

Lvs with **swollen-based** prickles on upperside **8**

Lvs ± **hairless**............................. **9**

Lvs **hairy**.................................... **10**

2 Lvs up to 90 cm wide in summer (only about 10–12 cm wide at fl-time in spring), rounded-triangular, grey-downy below, green above (but not glossy), with few, sharp, distant teeth and stout grooved stalks .. *Petasites hybridus* (p 372 B)

Lvs 10–20 cm wide in summer **3**

3 Lvs kidney-shaped, equally fine-toothed, **blunt**, **glossy** green above, persistent through winter......
Petasites fragrans (p 372 C)

Lvs rounded-**polygonal**, with 5–12 shallow, **pointed** lobes, white-felted on both sides in spring, then light green above, grey beneath ....
Tussilago farfara (p 372 A)

4 Lvs elliptical-lanceolate to **linear**, shiny and scarcely hairy above, scarcely toothed, **gradually** narrowed to a **short** stalk ....
Plantago lanceolata (p 336 A)

Lvs **oval** or elliptical, not shiny, downy or not downy, feebly-toothed, **abruptly** narrowed to a stalk **equalling** lf.....................................
Plantago major (p 336 B)

5 Lvs waxy grey-green, with milky latex .... *Sonchus asper* (p 400 I)

Lvs not waxy grey-green, with watery juice **6**

89

6 Lvs **prickly-hairy** on upper surface, **not shiny**......................................
Cirsium vulgare (p 381 A)

Lvs **not** prickly above, though ± hairy, ± glossy.......................... **7**

7 Lvs cottony above, ± **purple-flushed** – bi plant ....
Cirsium palustre (p 381 D)

Lvs scarcely cottony above, wholly **grey**-green, **without** purple flush – per plant with **creeping** rhizome ......
Cirsium arvense (p 381 E)

8 Lvs hairless and shiny, ± pointed, with **few** scattered swollen-based prickles – lvs **15–30** cm long....Dipsacus fullonum (p 354 A)

Lvs **v bristly**, with each bristle arising from a whitish wart – blunt lvs 5–10 cm long ....
.... Picris echioides (p 396 H)

9 Lvs tapered to base, stalkless, fresh glossy green, with triangular teeth, the upper ones ± arched backwards – milky latex in lvs
Taraxacum officinale (p 388 A)

Root-lvs with **long** narrow stalks, roundish **spoon-shaped**, few-toothed, 1–2 cm long × 1.5 cm

wide, green, ± ascending – no milky latex in lvs .... Chrysanthemum leucanthemum (p 369 A)

10 Lvs **spoon**-shaped, tapered below into a **broad stalk**, with **sparse** hairs and few blunt teeth – lf-blade 1–2 cm long × 1.0–1.5 cm wide.....
Bellis perennis (p 370 I)

Lvs ± **unstalked**, **oblong** to **lanceolate**................................... **11**

11 Lvs elliptical-lanceolate, 10–30 cm long, only **feebly**-toothed ....
(Verbascum) **12**

Lvs oblong, 5–10 cm long, ± **deeply**-toothed............................ **13**

12 Lvs clothed with **soft white** woolly fur .... Verbascum thapsus (p 298 A)

Lvs **dark** green, **thinly** downy on upperside, hairier underneath..........
Verbascum nigrum (p 298 B)

13 Lvs with **scattered** white bristles – side and terminal lobes **narrow-linear**, flat, untoothed.....................
Leontodon autumnalis (p 394 E)

Lvs **rough-hairy** – side-lobes **blunt**, rounded, wavy-edged, shallow, untoothed................................
Hypochoeris radicata (p 392 A)

VII PLANTS OF SALT-MARSHES

Salt-marsh vegetation is that of the zone between low and high tide marks on flat, muddy or sandy substrates in sheltered places, along estuaries or behind beaches that protect it from the wave action of the sea. In fact, most of the flowering plants of salt-marshes only occur in the uppermost part of the intertidal zone; lower down, where the mud or sand flats are covered for more than about a fifth of the time, only seaweeds (algae, non-flowering plants) occur. There is also, within the salt-marsh community, a clear zonation of plant species, according to the length of time per day (or per month) each zone is inundated with salt water. Many more species only occur at the very uppermost edge of the marshes, by sea walls, or on banks which are dry nearly all the time but are percolated by salt water from below (thus excluding from the habitat most ordinary land or fresh water plants).

Salt-marsh plants have several devices that enable them to exist in such a habitat. Some are very fleshy and swollen, often with reduced or modified leaves; others have very mealy leaves. Some have creeping rhizomes that help to bind the sand, or mud, thereby gradually raising the level of the marsh until it becomes dry land. Most have in their cell-sap very high concentrations of salt (much higher than that of the sea water). This enables them, by the process known as osmosis, to absorb water through their roots, even when the external salt concentration is high.

Most salt-marsh plants flower in late summer, or even autumn. This key will therefore be useful in spring or early summer, at least for those plants with vegetative parts above ground at that time.

1 Low bushy shrubs, to ± 1 m tall, evergreen.............................. **2**

Herbs **3**

2 Erect much-branched shrub to 1 m, with alt, sausage-shaped to **cylindrical** fleshy, hairless, green lvs 5–18 mm long × 2 mm wide, **blunt at both ends** (if tips **pointed**, see stage **10** below) ....
Suaeda fruticosa (p 164 E)

More spreading shrub to 40 cm, with opp, **oval-elliptical, mealy-grey, flat**, short-stalked lvs 3–5 cm long × 1–2 cm wide......................
Halimione portulacoides (p 166 G)

3 Plant **without** obvious lvs, composed only of opp-branched, fleshy stems, jointed into cylindrical or ovoid, swollen segments – (in spring only **shrivelled** last year's plants of ann spp will be visible).......
Salicornia spp (p 164 A–C)

Plants with **obvious lvs** **4**

4 Lvs **grass-like** (flat, grooved, folded or rolled, narrow-linear, **non-fleshy** and **thin-bladed** **5**

Lvs narrow-linear but **fleshy**, either flattish or half cylindrical, all in a **basal** tuft or rosette, 10 cm long or more... **8**

Lvs ± **cylindrical** or strap-shaped, stalks v short or abs, **fleshy, 1–5 cm long only**, borne either alt, or in opp pairs, or in clusters, **along** the stems............. **10**

Lvs with definite **blade** and **stalk**, blade oval, triangular, or elliptical-lanceolate.................................... **11**

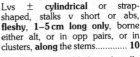

Lvs and stems **cylindrical, not** fleshy but tough and rigid, sharp-tipped, in erect tufts 20–60 cm tall – lvs both basal and alt up stem ....
Juncus maritimus (**Sea Rush**)

Lvs twice-**pinnately** divided into linear 1 mm-wide **white-woolly** segments *Artemisia maritima* (p 376 H)

5 Plant with **creeping lfy** rooting runners forming a compact **turf** – lvs grey-green, hairless, ± folded or inrolled, 1–3 mm wide × to 20 cm long, with hooded tips ....
Puccinellia maritima (**Salt-marsh Grass**)

Plant **erect**, with underground rhizomes....................................... **6**

6 Lfy stems arising separately from mud, **stout** (1 cm or more thick), 40–80 cm tall – lvs tough, **ascending**, 7–15 mm wide, with sharp rigid points, flat or inrolled, smooth,

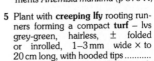

VII SALT-MARSHES

ribbed above – ligule a fringe of hairs – infl of several spreading spikes like fingers of a spread hand...
Spartina townsendii (**Townsend's Cord-grass**)

Lvs and lfy stems densely **tufted**, erect, stems thin (3 mm or less thick) **7**

7 Lvs **rigid**, **grey**-green, rough-edged, **ribbed** on upperside, sharp-pointed, erect, 2–6 mm wide ....
Agropyron pungens (p 458 F)

Lvs **flexible**, **bristle**-like, 0.5 to 1.0 mm wide, dark green, mostly from base .. *Festuca rubra* (p 458 A)

Lvs narrow-linear, 1–2 mm wide, flattened above, dark green, mostly on infl-stem which is three-angled above and bears branched cluster of brown capsules each 1.5–2.0 mm long ....
Juncus gerardii (**Salt-marsh Rush**)

8 Lvs **spreading** in a dense basal rosette or cushion, ± fleshy, ± hairless, 2–10 cm long × 1–2 mm wide – infls button-shaped heads 2–3 cm wide on stems 5–20 cm tall ....*Armeria maritima* (p 281 E)

Lvs ± **erect** in a rosette or tuft, hairless, 5–20 cm long........... **9**

9 Lvs **flattened**, v fleshy, 3–5-veined, 5–15 cm long × 5–10 mm wide ...*Plantago maritima* (p 336 D)

Lvs **half-cylindrical**, fleshy, grooved on upperside, vein not obvious, lvs 10–20 cm long × 2–3 mm wide.....................................
Triglochin maritima (p 446 K)

10 Bushy, **much**-branched plant often red-tinged, with stout stems and **alt**, half-cylindrical **pointed** lvs 5–25 mm long × 1–2 mm wide (if lvs **blunt**, see **2** above) – stipules abs ....
Suaeda maritima (p 164 D)

Sprawling or creeping **little**-branched plant with weak stems and **opp** lvs 1.0–2.5 cm long × 1–2 mm wide, ± half-cylindrical,

pointed, with membranous trans-lucent **stipules** at bases...................
Spergularia spp (p 156 A, B)

Erect ± bushy plant, 20–80 cm tall, branched above only, with lvs **alt**, hairless, fleshy, strap-shaped, to 4 mm wide and 2.5–5.0 cm long, sometimes three-lobed at tip, cross-section elliptical – fls in yellow daisy-like heads in umbel-like clusters at stem-tips in July–Sept.......................................
Inula crithmoides (p 366 D)

11 Lvs **alt**, oval or obovate to oblong or elliptical-lanceolate – stems erect **12**

Lvs **mostly alt** (some lower lvs may be opp), diamond-shaped to tri-angular or strap-shaped.............. **13**

Lvs in **opp** pairs on prostrate stems, **small**, oval-oblong, 0.5–2.0 cm long, flat, fleshy ....
Glaux maritima (p 288 G)

12 Lvs firm, but **not** fleshy, elliptical-lanceolate, with **mucronate** tips, 4–12 cm long × 2–4 cm wide, stalked, **all in a basal rosette** ....
Limonium spp, mostly *L. vulgare* (p 281 F)

Lvs **fleshy**, hairless, basal lvs stalked, obovate, to 2 cm wide, **not mucronate**, upper **stem**-lvs nar-rower, oblong – fls or frs in daisy-like heads ....*Aster tripolium* (p 368 F)

Root-lvs in rosette, oval to oblong-ovate, shiny dark green, **fleshy**, bases **tapered** into long stalks – stem-lvs oval-elliptical, stalkless, clasping – white four-petalled fls in racemes in spring.............................
Cochlearia anglica (p 130 I)

As above, but root-lvs **cordate**-based...
Cochlearia officinalis (p 128 G)

13 Lvs alt, **glossy dark** green, to 10 cm long...*Beta vulgaris* (p 166 F)

Lvs alt or opp, **grey-mealy** ....
Atriplex spp (p 166 A–D)

VIII PLANTS OF SHINGLE BEACHES AND SAND DUNES

These maritime habitats have a specialized flora. The action of the sea often makes them unstable, and their plants have to be able to recolonize disturbed ground. Because of the instability, plant communities are often open, with much ground totally bare; hence competition between those plants that can grow there is often less intense than in closed, inland plant communities. Modifications to withstand drought (a common feature of such maritime, well-drained habitats), exposure to wind, and to salt spray, are frequent. Leaves are often fleshy, wax-covered (hence greyish or bluish), tough, or fleshy, many plants present a 'low profile' to the wind, and have either thick protective layers of hairs or wax to check water loss, or very deep roots to tap underground fresh water supplies.

Further from the sea, these habitats become with age more stable (and more closed), and the vegetation may become more heath- or scrub-like. Or, if there is much lime in the dunes from incorporated shells of shellfish, the vegetation may resemble that of chalk grassland (so for sand dunes see also Key II). Many plants of open waste ground, including many introduced species, sometimes colonize sand-dunes, particularly near ports, or in areas where there are gardens nearby.

Successive dune ridges may be built up, and fixed over time by the agency of Marram (*Ammophila*), with its creeping rhizomes and fibrous roots. This plant can grow up through new layers of sand that may cover it when onshore winds bring in sand from a beach dried out at low tide, forming a new layer of rhizomes and roots on top of the old ones. Thus Marram-dominated dunes may grow to a considerable height.

In between dune ridges there are often fresh water marshes with fen vegetation, because the dunes and ridges act as natural spongy reservoirs of rain water, which may seep out into the intervening hollows. For such places, Key IV may be useful.

In winter, most dune plants, except the grasses and shrubs such as Sea-buckthorn, tend to die back; but the key should be useful especially in autumn or late summer, when many dune plants are visible but not in flower.

For this habitat also consult Key VI.

1 Creeping tufted plant with small **opp** fleshy oval pointed lvs, 6–20 mm long – on dunes ....
Honkenya peploides (p 154 B)

Lvs over 2 cm long, not in opp pairs **2**

2 Lvs pinnately lobed or divided...... **3**

Lvs palmately lobed or veined, waxy bluish-grey, edged with **spines** – on dunes ....
Eryngium maritimum (p 264 F)

Lvs oval-oblong, fleshy, waxy grey-green, not spine-edged, 1–2 cm long, alt and closely set up reddish stems – on dunes...........................
Euphorbia paralias (p 244 B)

Lvs elliptical-oblong, bright green, edges wavy and crisped, 10–15 cm long, in erect crowns from root and up stems – on shingle......................
Rumex crispus (p 270 D)

Lvs grass-like **4**

3 Root-lvs v thick and fleshy, 20–40 cm long, oval, **hairless**, waxy grey-green, often purplish-flushed when young, with shallow pinnate lobes – each fr size and shape of garden pea, borne in large open much-branched rounded heads – on shingle......................................
Crambe maritima (p 130 A)

Root-lvs **v** hairy, 10–20 cm long, waxy-grey, deeply pinnately-lobed – frs 15–30 cm long, rough, hair-less, sickle-shaped – on shingle........
Glaucium flavum (p 108 F)

Root-lvs hairless, 3–10 cm long, **shiny dark** green, twice-pinnate into **hair**-like segments – on dunes, beaches..
Tripleurospermum maritimum (p 374 A)

VIII BEACHES AND DUNES

Root-lvs hairless, 10–15 cm long, **grey**-green, twice-pinnate into v **fleshy** blunt segments – on shingle and rocks...
Crithmum maritimum (p 258 D)

Root-lvs hairy, to 10 cm long, once-pinnate into thin, flat, rounded, toothed segments – on grassy dunes..
Erodium cicutarium (p 174 G)

Root-lvs hairy, with sharp spines on edges and upper surface..................
Cirsium vulgare (p 381 A)

4 Lvs in 3 vertical ranks, on shoots in rows along rhizomes – on dunes.
Carex arenaria

Lvs in 2 vertical ranks on stem **5**

5 Lvs in dense tufts 50–100 cm tall, grey-green, strongly inrolled, cylindrical, rigid, sharp-tipped – on dunes ....*Ammophila arenaria*

Lvs in small tufts on shoots arising from rhizomes creeping in sand, flat when moist, to **1 cm wide**, **grey-green**, strongly ribbed above – on open dunes......................................
Agropyron junceiforme (**Sand Couch**)

Lvs **blue-grey**, to 2 cm wide, flat, rigid, ribbed, pointed – on dunes.....
Elymus arenarius

Lvs grey-green, bristle-like, to 2 mm wide – on dunes....................
Festuca rubra var *arenaria* (p 458 A var)

DICOTYLEDONS

BUTTERCUP FAMILY   *Ranunculaceae*

This is a group of primitive flowering plants not easy to define from the evolutionary point of view. They are herbs (except the woody climber *Clematis*) with alt lvs (except *Clematis* with opp lvs), and with no stipules. Lvs mostly palmately-lobed or divided (linear in *Myosurus*). Fls usually have 5 sepals (4 in *Clematis*) and often 5 petals. The features common to ± all are the many stamens and the many carpels, free from each other and superior. Some herbs in the Rose family have similar-looking fls with many separate stamens and carpels, but these have an epicalyx, at least a slight cup to the fl below the sepals, and lfy stipules, all features abs in the Buttercup Family.

KEY TO THE BUTTERCUP FAMILY

1 Woody climber with opp lvs and 4 petal-like sepals .... *Clematis* (p 104)
   Herbs with spirally-arranged alt lvs – not climbers **2**
2 Fls with 1 carpel only **3**
   Fls with 2 or many carpels **4**
3 Fr a black oval berry – fls small, white, without spurs .... *Actaea* (p 104)
   Fr a dry follicle – fls blue, with long spurs .... *Delphinium*
4 Carpels ripening into one-seeded achenes **5**
   Carpels ripening into many-seeded follicles that open at top when ripe **10**
5 Fls with both petals and sepals **6**
   Fls with one perianth-whorl only **8**
6 Fls solitary and terminal on a lfless stem – lvs all basal and linear – fr-head a long slender spike covered with achenes .... *Myosurus* (p 104)
   Fls in branched lfy infls – lvs variously lobed or lanceolate **7**
7 Lvs bi- or tri-pinnate, with linear, ± hair-like segments – petals red with no nectary – achenes wrinkled .... *Adonis* (p 98)
   Lvs palmately-lobed or divided, or undivided – petals yellow or white with a nectary at base ....
                                                                                            Ranunculus (p 96, 100)
8 Fls small (1 cm or less across) – stamens conspicuous – fls many together in a loose infl – lvs 2–4 times pinnate, with small toothed lfts .... *Thalictrum* (p 104)
   Fls large (2 cm or more across), solitary, or 2 together only – sepals white or coloured, resembling petals – a whorl of 3 lvs below the fl (or pair of fls). **9**
9 3 stem-lvs some way below fl, each lf with 3 broad spreading lobes – achenes unplumed ....
                                                                              Anemone (p 102)
   3 stem-lvs, oval, undivided, close below fl (as if sepals) – achenes unplumed .... *Hepatica* (p 102)
   3 stem-lvs close below fl, erect, deeply-cut into narrow lobes – achenes with long feathery styles .... *Pulsatilla* (p 102)
10 Fls two-lipped, with a hood and a lip (but petals not joined) .... *Aconitum* (p 102)
   Fls radially symmetrical **11**
11 All 5 petals with long spurs – sepals coloured like petals .... *Aquilegia* (p 102)
   No spurs on perianth segments **12**
12 One whorl of (yellow) perianth segments only .... *Caltha* (p 98)
   Sepals petal-like – petals represented by narrow nectaries within fl **13**
13 Nectaries narrow, strap-shaped, yellow – sepals many (about 10), yellow, forming a globe-shaped fl .... *Trollius* (p 98)
   Nectaries tubular, two-lipped **14**
14 Fls solitary, with a ruff of deeply-cut lvs below fl – sepals and nectaries yellow .... *Eranthis* (p 102)
   Fls in branched infls, no ruff of lvs below fls – lvs lobed like fingers of a hand – sepals and nectaries greenish .... *Helleborus* (p 98)

95

BUTTERCUP FAMILY

Buttercups (*Ranunculus*) are herbs with alt lvs and yellow fls (white in **Water Crowfoots**, subgenus *Batrachium*, p 100). They have 5 (or 3) free green sepals, 5 free petals (except **Lesser Celandine** with different numbers of sepals and petals), many free stamens, and many tiny carpels in a head, which each develop into one-seeded achenes.

A   Creeping Buttercup, *Ranunculus repens*, per herb with creeping runners; lvs (**Aa**) hairy, three-lobed; fl-stalk **grooved**; sepals (**A**) **spreading**; fls deep yellow. Br Isles, Eur; vc in wds, mds, wa. Fl 5–8.

B   Meadow Buttercup, *R. acris*, erect hairy per herb, 20–60 cm tall; stems branched, no runners; lvs deeply three-lobed, lobes deeply-toothed; fl-stalks **not** grooved; sepals spreading; fls bright yellow. Br Isles, Eur; vc in mds, gsld. Fl 5–8.

C   Bulbous Buttercup, *R. bulbosus*, erect hairy per, 15–40 cm tall, with basal tuber, no runners; lvs three-lobed; fl-stalk **grooved**; sepals **reflexed**; fls bright yellow. Br Isles, Eur; vc on dry gsld, especially on calc soils. Fl 4–6.

D   Corn Buttercup, *R. arvensis*, ann, erect; stem-lvs deeply-cut; fls 9–12 mm across, yellow; achenes (**Da**) with strong **border** and **long spines**. Br Isles, Eur; now r-lf on ar, especially on calc soil. Fl 6–7.

E   Small-flowered Buttercup, *R. parviflorus*, spreading hairy ann, to 20 cm; lvs lobed; fls 3–4 mm across, pale yellow; achenes (**Ea**) 2.5–3.0 mm, narrowly-bordered, with hooked spines, especially on their edges. Br Isles: Eng, Wales, o; Ire r; Eur o; on dry banks, open gsld on calc soil. Fl 6–7.

F   Goldilocks Buttercup, *R. auricomus*, erect ± hairy per; root-lvs kidney-shaped to three-lobed, stem-lvs with narrow divisions. Fls few, 1.5–2.5 cm across, with smooth stalks, the golden-yellow petals often partly missing; achenes smooth, downy. Br Isles, Eur; f-lc in wds on basic soils. Fl 4–6.

G   Celery-leaved Buttercup, *R. sceleratus*, ann, with stout short stem (20–60 cm); root-lvs palmately three-lobed, long-stalked, shiny; stem-lvs short-stalked, more divided. Fls in much-branched infl; fls 5–10 mm across, petals shiny pale yellow; achenes many in a long head. Br Isles: Eng c; Wales, Ire, S Scot, o-lc; N Scot r; Eur c; on mud by ditches, ponds, streams. Fl 5–9.

H   Hairy Buttercup, *R. sardous*, is like **C**, with sepals bent back and fl-stalks grooved, but has no tubers, spreads more, is hairier, has **pale** yellow fls, and **warts** in a ring on achenes (**Ha**) inside the thick border. Br Isles: GB N to mid-Scot; W Eur; c on damp gsld near sea, inland on ar on clay. Fl 6–9.

I   Lesser Celandine, *R. ficaria*, per herb to 20 cm, with stems creeping and rooting, then ascending; lvs long-stalked, cordate, fleshy, blunt, hairless, glossy green, 1–4 cm long and wide, in rosettes. Fls 2–3 cm across, solitary, long-stalked; 3 oval sepals; 8–12 narrow oval petals, glossy yellow, 1.0–1.5 cm long; achenes smooth, round. Sometimes with bulbils in lf-axils. Br Isles, Eur; vc in wds, mds, hbs. Fl 3–5.

KEY TO YELLOW BUTTERCUPS

cont

97

 7 Lvs hairless **8**
   Lvs hairy **9**
 8 Fls less than 1 cm across – fr-head oblong ....*R. sceleratus* (p 96 G)
   Fls more than 1 cm across – fr-head round ....*R. auricomus* (p 96 F)
 9 Fl-stalks smooth **10**
   Fl-stalks grooved **11**
10 Lvs woolly-hairy – lf-lobes 3, v blunt-toothed – lf in wds in Germany, Denmark – **Br Isles abs**........
   R. lanuginosus
   Lvs adpressed, hairy – lf-lobes 3–5, sharp-toothed................................*R. acris* (p 96 B)
11 Plant with runners – lf-lobes 3, stalked, shallow-toothed ....*R. repens* (p 96 A)
   Plant without runners – lf-lobes 5, stalkless, deeply-toothed – r in wds, E France to Denmark – **Br**
   Isles abs ....*R. polyanthemos*

Spearworts, Hellebores etc

A   Lesser Spearwort, *Ranunculus flammula*, hairless erect per, with hollow stem, lanceolate stem-lvs, and oblong, stalked root-lvs. Fls few, 8–20 mm across, with **furrowed** stalks; achenes in globose heads; sepals yellowish. Br Isles, Eur; c in marshes, wet places. Fl 5–9.   **Ai   Adder's-tongue Spearwort**, *R. ophioglossifolius*, of low habit, has broadly oval, cordate-based lvs on long stalks. Br Isles: S Eng vvr; Eur: W France r; in wet mud by ponds. Fl 6–7.   **Aii   Creeping Spearwort**, *R. reptans*, has runners and roots at every node; vr by lakes in N GB and mts of Eur. Fl 6–8.

B   Greater Spearwort, *R. lingua*, resembles a taller (50–120 cm) and stouter A, with lanceolate stem-lvs to 25 cm long; fls brighter yellow, 2–5 cm across; **unfurrowed** fl-stalks. Br Isles, Eur; o-lc in fens. Fl 6–9.

C   Marsh-marigold, *Caltha palustris*, hairless stout buttercup-like per herb, with hollow stems and cordate or kidney-shaped lvs to 10 cm across, long-stalked below; fls, 15–50 mm across, have 5 yellow petal-like sepals, **no** true petals and many yellow stamens. Carpels form into green sac-like **follicles** to 1 cm long, each opening to release several seeds. Br Isles, Eur; c in wet mds, fens, wet wds, by rivers etc. Fl 3–5.

D   Globeflower, *Trollius europaeus*, resembles C, but is more erect, with lvs palmately-lobed, ± deeply-toothed. The numerous (5–15) petal-like sepals form a **globe**, enclosing the small strap-shaped nectar-secreting **petals** and the many stamens; frs as in C. Br Isles: Wales to N Scot lc; N W Ire lc; r lowland Eur except to the N; on upland wet mds, mt cliffs and mt woods. Fl 6–8.

E   Green Hellebore, *Helleborus viridis*, bushy, ± hairless per herb; lvs long-stalked, with 7–11 digitate lfts, arising from a central point; lvs are 15 cm across, deciduous, deep green; fls like those of C in structure, but with 5 green spreading sepals, 9–12 nectaries. Br Isles: S Eng lf; Wales r; **Ire abs**; Eur o-lf; in wds on basic soils. Fl 3–4.

F   Stinking Hellebore, *H. foetidus*, is more erect than E, with long-stalked **dark blue-green** evergreen lower lvs, each with 3–9 **narrower** (0.5–2.0 cm) segments that rise from two 'arches' on tip of lf-stalks and **not** from a single point at stalk-tip. Fls more **cup-like** than in E and with **purple** edges to green sepals. Br Isles: S Eng, Wales; **Scot, Ire abs**; Eur N to Belgium; vlf in open wds on shallow chk and limestone soils. Fl 1–4.

G   Pheasant's-eye, *Adonis annua*, erect hairless ann herb, with 2–3-times pinnate lvs with hair-like segments and scarlet fls with dark stamens. Br Isles: S Eng, S Eur; r on ar on chk. Fl 7. All Pheasant's-eyes have pinnate lvs with narrow segments and wrinkled achenes (**Ga**).   ***Gi**   *A. aestivalis* has sepals adpressed to the red petals (in *A. annua* petals are erect, not touching sepals). Eur: France; lf on ar.

2mm
Ga

99

BUTTERCUP FAMILY

Ranunculaceae

Water-crowfoots (*Ranunculus*, subgenus *Batrachium*)

All these have **white** fls, with yellow base to petals, and grow in water or on mud. Some have finely-divided underwater lvs only, some palmately-lobed floating or exposed lvs only, some both sorts of lvs. All are f in Br Isles and Eur unless stated, and fl 5–9. All the species illustrated opposite are adequately described in the following key. Hi (not illustrated) is closest to H. In the case of this subgenus English names are not given.

KEY TO WATER-CROWFOOTS

1 **Both** divided submerged and palmate floating lvs present.. 2
  Only divided lvs present.. 3
  Only palmate lvs present, usually on mud.. 4
2 Petals over 6 mm long – stamens more than 12 5
  Petals less than 6 mm – stamens fewer than 12 – r in S Eng and Wales, lf in W France ....
                                                                     Ranunculus tripartitus
3 Submerged lvs circular, with **rigid** segments in one plane, like spokes of a bicycle wheel with no rim (**D**) – lf in ditches (not N Scot) ....*R. circinatus* (p 101 D)
  Submerged lvs three-dimensional, not in one plane 7
4 Fls 3–6 mm (**Ia**) – lvs ivy-shaped – f-lc on mud..*R. hederaceus* (p 101 I)
  Fls 6–12 mm across – lvs rounded, with lobes almost touching – lf on mud in S and W of GB, S Ire, Eur N to Netherlands..*R. omiophyllus* (p 101 H)
  Fls 6–12 mm – lvs with lobes well-spaced apart – in ponds, on mud – r in S Eng and Wales, lf in W France.. *R. tripartitus*
5 Achenes (**Ca**) 40–100, each 1.0–1.4 mm long, **hairless** – lvs deeply three-lobed – f-lc in ditches, ponds near coasts of Br Isles and Eur..*R. baudotii* (p 101 C)
  Achenes less than 40, each more than 1.5 mm long, **hairy** – lvs not deeply three-lobed 6
6 Petals **more** than 10 mm – fr-stalks **more** than 5 cm – floating lvs **kidney-shaped** (**Ba**) – f, ponds, ditches ....*R. peltatus* (p 101 B)
  Petals **less** than 10 mm – fr-stalks **less** than 4 cm – floating lvs (**Aa**) ± circular – f in ponds and ditches..*R. aquatilis* (p 101 A)
7 Lvs with short (1–2 cm) rigid segments – petals less than 6 mm long – achenes (**Ea**) hairy – f in ponds..*R. trichophyllus* (p 101 E)
  Lvs with longer (more than 4 cm) segments 8
8 Lvs not more than 8 cm long, light green – receptacle of fls downy – la in chky rivers........................
                                                                R. penicillatus (p 101 F)
  Lvs 10–30 cm, dark green – fl receptacle hairless – o-lf in southern non-chky rivers ....
                                                               R. fluitans (p 101 G)

These plants may vary in form with the level of the water, but the Key should make it possible to name most well-developed specimens.

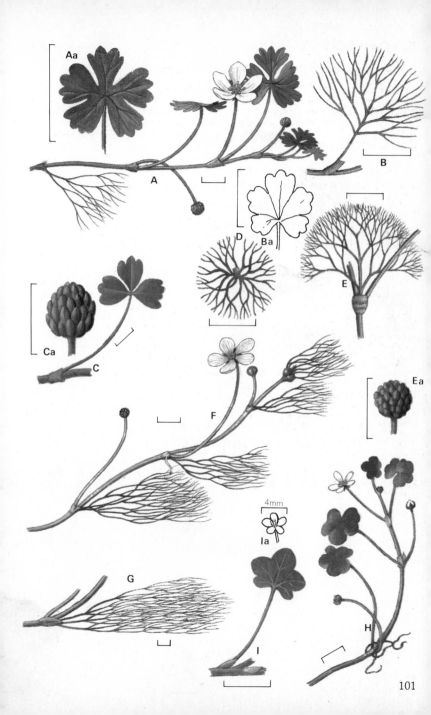

101

BUTTERCUP FAMILY

Ranunculaceae

Anemones, Monk's-hood, Columbine

Anemones (A–E below) have coloured petal-like sepals, but no petals, and many stamens; also a whorl of 3 lvs on fl-stalk, sometimes resembling a calyx.

*A Hepatica, *Hepatica nobilis*, per hairless herb with thick fleshy three-lobed lvs, evergreen and purplish underneath; solitary fls (15–25 mm) have 3 green oval sepal-like bracts, 6–9 blue-purple (sometimes pink or white) petal-like sepals, and many white stamens. NW Eur f-la (f on mts only to S in Eur); in wds on calc soils. Fl 3–5.

B Pasqueflower, *Pulsatilla vulgaris*, hairy per herb with feathery lvs twice-pinnate, from base; large, solitary, rich purple fls, 5–8 cm across, first erect, then drooping and bell-like; 6 sepals, silky outside; no petals, many golden anthers; a whorl of bracts with many narrow hairy lobes, 2–5 cm, below fl. The head of achenes develops silky plumes 3.5–5.0 cm long. Br Isles: S, mid, E Eng vlf; Eur o-la; in chk gslds especially on S slopes. Fl 4–5. ***Bi Small Pasqueflower**, *P. pratensis*, is like a small version of B with fls always bell-shaped, drooping, 4 cm across and dark purple outside. NW Eur; on sandy gslds. Fl 4–6.

*C Pale Pasqueflower, *P. vernalis*, has less-divided lvs; fls white inside, pink outside, first drooping then erect. NW Eur r; on sandy gslds. Fl 4–6.

D Wood Anemone, *Anemone nemorosa*, per hairless herb with creeping rhizome and star-like white fls with 6 (or more) spreading sepals. Halfway up stem is a whorl of 3 palmately-lobed lvs; other long-stalked similar lvs arise from root. Fls often pink-purple-flushed, especially outside. Br Isles, W Eur; c in dry deciduous wds, old hbs, upland mds. Fl 3–4. ***Di** *A. sylvestris* has lvs with narrower, lanceolate lfts and fls 50–70 mm wide with 5 white sepals. E France, Germany, o. Fl 4–6.

E Yellow Anemone, *A. ranunculoides*, is similar to D, but is slightly hairy, has yellow fls like buttercups, often 2 or 3 together; 5 or more sepals. Br Isles, only introd; W Eur lf-la, commoner to N; in dry deciduous wds especially on basic soils. Fl 3–5. **Ei Winter Aconite**, *Eranthis hyemalis*, has a ruff of 3 deeply-cut lvs below fls; fls 20–30 mm across, with yellow sepals only (no petals); carpels are many-seeded follicles. Br Isles, Eur; introd, o in wds, parks. Fl 1–3.

F Monk's-hood, *Aconitum napellus*, hairless per to 1 m or more, with deeply-cut palmate lvs; hooded-tipped, blue or violet fls, 3–4 cm across. Br Isles: SW GB r by streams and in wds; Eur r and S, commonest in mt wds. Fl 5–9.

G Columbine, *Aquilegia vulgaris*, tall hairless per with large twice-trifoliate lvs; rounded, stalked, lobed lfts; large blue fls with 5 spurred sepals and 5 petals, all blue or violet-blue, sometimes pink or white. Br Isles: Eng, Wales, S Scot lf; Ire r; Eur f; in calc scrub, wds, fens. Fl 5–6.

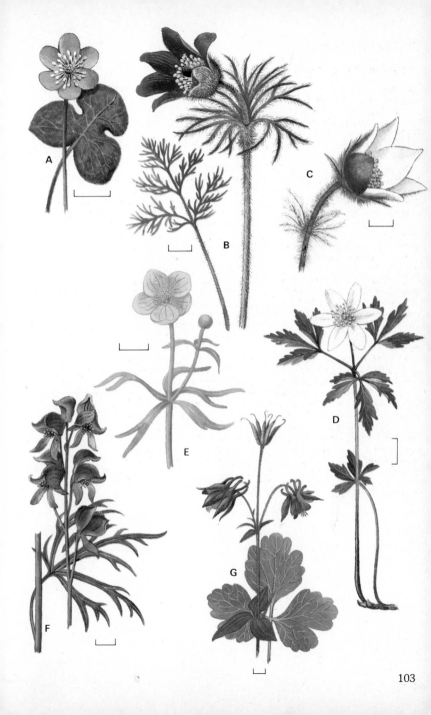

BUTTERCUP FAMILY

Clematis, Meadow-rues, Mousetail, Baneberry

Clematis is characterized in the Buttercup family by woody stems, opp lvs and four-sepalled fls.

A   Traveller's-joy, *Clematis vitalba,* woody climber with peeling fibrous bark, and opp, pinnate compound lvs with narrow oval pointed, usually toothed lfts. Fls 2 cm across, fragrant, terminal and in panicles, in lf-axils, with 4 greenish-creamy sepals, hairy outside, and many stamens. Achenes each develop long white plumed styles in fr. Br Isles: Eng, Wales, N to Morecambe Bay, c on chk and limestone; Ire introd; Eur N to Netherlands c. Fl 7–8.

B   Common Meadow-rue, *Thalictrum flavum,* erect, nearly hairless per herb, 50–100 cm tall; lvs 2–3-times pinnately compound with wedge-shaped lfts longer than broad above, 1–2 cm long; dense panicles of erect small fls (**Bb**) with 4 narrow whitish sepals and many conspicuous erect yellow stamens; achenes (**Ba**) 1.5–2.5 mm long. Br Isles: GB N to Inverness lf; Eur f; in fens, streamsides, mds. Fl 7–8.

C   Lesser Meadow-rue, *T. minus,* more branched, spreading plant than B, with more divided (3–4-times pinnate) lvs, and smaller lfts as broad as long. Fls (**Ca**) in more diffuse spreading panicles, with drooping stamens; achenes (**Cb**) larger (3–6 mm). Br Isles, especially in Breckland and in N and W vlf; Eur lf; on dry gsld on chk or dunes, rocky river banks. Fl 6–8.   **Ci   Alpine Meadow-rue,** *T. alpinum,* small hairy per herb, 8–15 cm tall, with lvs 2–5 cm long and twice-trifoliate; fls in simple racemes. Mts of GB and Eur; vl on rocks and in flushes. Fl 6–7.

D   Mousetail, *Myosurus minimus,* small hairless ann herb, with basal rosette of linear fleshy lvs and erect stems, 5–12 cm long, bearing solitary erect greenish-yellow fls (**Da**); 5 sepals, 5 petals, 5–10 stamens and a cylindrical, mouse-tail-like receptacle which elongates to 3–7 cm in fr, bearing many tiny achenes. Br Isles: Eng, Wales; Eur, N to Denmark; once f, now becoming r on damp sandy ar, open ground. Fl 5–7.

E   Baneberry, *Actaea spicata,* per, almost hairless herb, 30–60 cm tall; glossy, long-stalked root-lvs, twice-trifoliate or twice-pinnate, with toothed lfts; stem-lvs smaller. Fls creamy-white in dense stalked spikes, with 3–6 sepals, 4–6 petals, many stamens, and a single carpel which ripens to a black berry (**Ea**) 1 cm long. Br Isles: N Eng, vl on limestone pavements and calc wds; Eur f-la in chk wds. Fl 5–6.

BARBERRY FAMILY

F   Oregon Grape, *Mahonia aquifolium,* shrub with holly-like lvs, yellow fls in dense spikes, and frs in racemes like tiny blue-black grapes. Br Isles, Eur, introd from NW of N America; in hbs, scrub. Fl 1–5, fr 9.   **Fi   Barberry,** *Berberis vulgaris,* native to Eur, shrub with oval toothed lvs, and three-pointed spines; fls in drooping spikes, usually with 5 whorls of yellow perianth segments, 6–8 mm across, and 10 mm-long red berries. GB and Eur; now r because it is secondary host of wheat rust, and has been much destroyed; in hds, scrub. Fl 5–6.

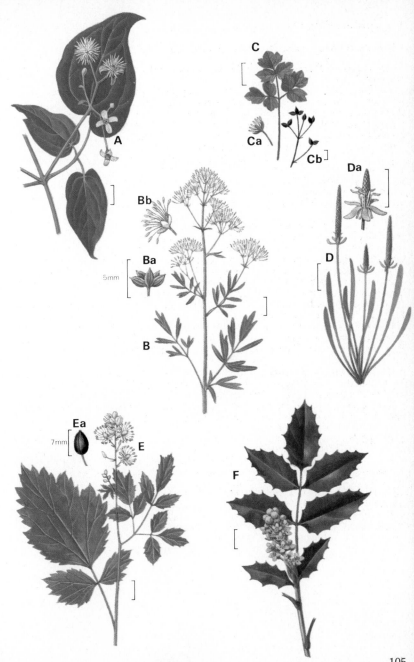

A

Bb

Ba

5mm

B

C

Ca

Cb

Da

D

Ea

7mm

E

F

105

Some Aquatic plants (see also Vegetative Key V)

WATER-LILY FAMILY   *Nymphaeaceae*

   A Yellow Water-lily, *Nuphar lutea*, has a massive fleshy rootstock which creeps in underwater mud, and bears leathery cordate floating lvs (**Aa**) on long elastic stalks, and some thinner submerged lvs. Fls (4–6 cm across) have 5–6 yellow concave sepals, about 20 smaller, narrower yellow petals, and many large stamens in a dense whorl; flask-shaped ovary has a flat cap with 10–25 **radiating stigmas**. Br Isles, Eur; c in ponds, canals, slow rivers. Fl 6–8.   **Ai Least Water-lily**, *N. pumila*, is smaller in all parts than A, with 7–12 stigma-rays and fls 1.5–3.5 cm across; stigma-disc deeply-lobed. Hybridizes with A. N GB; NW Eur; r in mostly acid lakes. Fl 7–8.
   B White Water-lily, *Nymphaea alba*, has almost circular lvs (**Ba**), much larger fls (10–20 cm across), with 4 green sepals and 20–25 petals, white in the usual wild form. Br Isles, Eur; c in ponds and lakes. Fl 7–8.

MARE'S-TAIL FAMILY   *Hippuridaceae*

   C Mare's-tail, *Hippuris vulgaris*, aquatic unbranched per herb, with stout spongy round stems bearing strap-like blunt lvs in **whorls**; stems both erect emergent, and trailing submerged. Fls tiny, petalless, green; male and female fls separate at base of lvs on emergent stems, male with one reddish anther. Br Isles, Eur; lf in base-rich waters of lakes and slow streams. Fl 6–7.

WATER-MILFOIL FAMILY   *Haloragaceae*

   D Alternate-flowered Water-milfoil, *Myriophyllum alterniflorum*, is slenderer than E (below); smaller lvs, usually 3 or 4 to a whorl; upper fls alt (not whorled) in short spikes in axils of tiny bracts; petals yellow, red-streaked. Br Isles, Eur; vlf in peaty water. Fl 5–8.
   E Spiked Water-milfoil, *M. spicatum*, submerged aquatic herb; lvs (usually in whorls of 4), finely **pinnate** into bristle-like segments. Fls tiny, whorled, in spikes in **tiny** bract-axils, emerge from water; lowest female, middle bisexual, uppermost male. Tiny petals are reddish; stamens yellow, 4 carpels per fl. Br Isles, Eur; c in still or slow, fresh or brackish water. Fl 6–8.
   F Whorled Water-milfoil, *M. verticillatum*, is like E but with larger lvs, usually 5 in a whorl; fls in whorls in axils of **pinnate lf-like** bracts. Br Isles, Eur; lf in basic fresh water. Fl 7–8.

HORNWORT FAMILY   *Ceratophyllaceae*

   G Rigid Hornwort, *Ceratophyllum demersum*, resembles a Water-milfoil, but the whorled lvs (**Ga**) are twice-forked, and **toothed** (not pinnately-divided); fls solitary in lf-axils; female fls produce frs (**Gb**) with 2 spines at base. Br Isles: Eng, Ire lf; Wales, Scot r; Eur f; in still fresh and brackish water. Fl 7–9.   **Gi Soft Hornwort**, *C. submersum*, has softer, thrice-forked lvs and frs without spines. SE Eng r-o; Eur N to Denmark r; in still fresh and brackish water. Fl 7–9.

WATERWORT FAMILY   *Elatinaceae*

   H Six-stamened Waterwort, *Elatine hexandra*, has short-stalked undivided strap-shaped lvs, widened above, in whorls of 4 or in opp pairs; tiny stalked three-petalled and three-sepalled pinkish fls (**Ha**) in lf-axils. Br Isles v scattered and r (lf in S Eng); Eur r-lf; in ponds with acid peaty water. Fl 7–9.   **Hi Eight-stamened Waterwort**, *E. hydropiper*, is v like H, but fls are stalkless with 4 sepals and petals. Similar places and distribution, but vr.

A

Aa

20cm

B

Ba

20cm

C

D

E

F

Ga

G

5mm

Gb

Ha

2mm

H

107

POPPY FAMILY

Papaveraceae

This family has fls with 2 sepals that soon fall, four petals, many stamens, and milky or yellow juice called *latex* in canals in stem and lvs. **Poppies** (*Papaver*) have crinkly petals to the large bright fls, and a fr of 4–20 carpels forming a capsule that opens by pores below the stigma-disc; and white latex.

KEY TO POPPIES (*PAPAVER*)

Poppies, Greater Celandine

A Common Poppy, *Papaver rhoeas*, bristly erect ann, 20–60 cm tall, with pinnate lvs and large fls, 7–10 cm across; scarlet petals, often with a dark basal blotch; fr globular, hairless. Br Isles, Eur; c on ar, wa, rds. Fl 6–8.

B Rough Poppy, *P. hybridum*, similar, but has smaller crimson fls, 2–5 cm across; oval frs (**B**) covered in stiff bristles. S Br Isles, S Eur; on ar. Fl 6–7.

C Prickly Poppy, *P. argemone*, resembles B, but has **long** narrow bristly pods (**C**) and smaller paler red fls with narrower petals. S Br Isles, S Eur; f on ar. Fl 6–7.

D Long-headed Poppy, *P. dubium*, has frs smooth as in A, but elongated (**D**) as in C. Br Isles, Eur; f-lc on ar. Fl 6–7. **Di** *P. lecoqii*, has latex yellow (on exposure to air) and petals not overlapping at bases. SE Eng; Eur; rarer than D.

E Opium Poppy, *P. somniferum*, stouter, taller (to 80 cm), almost hairless Poppy with oblong wavy waxy-grey coarsely-toothed lvs (not pinnate and bristly as in A and D). Fls, 8–18 cm wide and white, pale lilac (or pink in cultivated forms), with purple-black centres. Capsule (**E**) oval, smooth, with disc at top 2 cm long. Opium and its derivatives are produced from its latex. Eng, W Eur introd (native of Asia); o-lf on ar, wa. Fl 6–8.

F Yellow Horned-poppy, *Glaucium flavum*, tall (30–90 cm) branched per herb, with a waxy bloom. Root-lvs pinnately-lobed, waxy, hairy, in a rosette, over-wintering; stem-lvs less divided; fls yellow, 6–9 cm; sepals hairy. Capsule is two-celled, sickle-shaped, to 30 cm long, rough; latex yellow. Br Isles (not N Scot); W Eur; f-la on coastal shingles. Fl 6–9.

G Welsh Poppy, *Meconopsis cambrica*, almost hairless per herb, 30–60 cm tall, with pinnate lvs, the lower long-stalked; yellow poppy fls; frs rather like those of D, 2.5–3.0 cm long, elliptical, with 4–6 stigmas, but with a distinct style and opening by **slits** about ¼ of fr's length. Br Isles: SW, N Eng; Wales: W Ire; Eur; W France; lc in damp shady rocky places, also introd. Fl 6–8.

H Greater Celandine, *Chelidonium majus*, branched slightly hairy per herb, 39–90 cm tall, with grey-green pinnately-lobed lvs and orange latex. Fls are like tiny Poppies, four-petalled, yellow and 20–25 mm across, in groups; fr a narrow capsule, 3–5 cm long, opening into 2 parts from **below**. Br Isles (especially S), Eur; f-lc on hbs, walls, wa. Fl 5–8. **Poisonous**.

FUMITORY FAMILY

Fumariaceae

Fumitory, Corydalis

This family consists of delicate, usually sprawling, hairless, often waxy-lvd plants with repeatedly pinnate lvs; racemes of tubular two-lipped fls with 2 tiny sepals, 2 outer petals (with 1 or both spurred, or with basal sacs), 2 narrower inner petals (often partly joined), and 2 stamens, each three-lobed. Fr of Fumitory (*Fumaria*) is an achene; that of *Corydalis* is a two-valved many-seeded oblong capsule. Related to Poppies, but with watery latex and v different fls. See also key, p. 112.

A   Common Fumitory, *Fumaria officinalis*, the commonest sp, is a weak scrambling ann, rarely over 20 cm tall; 2–4 pinnate lvs, with flat lanceolate narrow grey-green lfts; fls 6–8 mm long; sepals 2 mm long, 1 mm wide; lowest of the **pink** petals **spoon-shaped** at **deep-red** tip; bracts **shorter** than the straight fl-stalks; fr rounded, 2.0–2.5 mm wide, with a flat or hollowed tip. Br Isles vc (rarer to W); Eur vc; on ar, especially on chk and sand, wa. Fl 5–10.

B   White Ramping-fumitory, *F. capreolata*, is more robust (to 1 m) than A; larger denser infls of more and **larger** (10–12 mm-long) fls (**Ba**), which are **white** with deep **red** tips and have strongly **recurved** or **arched** fr-stalks (**Bb**); lowest petal is narrow. Br Isles (mostly S and W) lf; Eur (mostly SW) f-c; on wa, ar, hbs, old walls. Fl 5–9.

C   Fine-leaved Fumitory, *F. parviflora*, differs from A in its smaller (5–6 mm long) white or merely pink-**tinged** fls (**Ca**), sepals not over 1.5 mm long and 1.0 mm wide, and narrow, channelled lf-segments. S Eng o-lf; Eur N to Belgium f; on ar on chk. Fl 6–9.

D   Tall Ramping-fumitory, *F. bastardii*, has large fls (**Da**) 9–12 mm long, toothed sepals, upper petal laterally compressed, lower part with spreading edges; compressed rough frs and robust habit, but fr-stalks not arched as in B. W of Br Isles widespread and lc; Eur: W France o; on ar, wa. Fl 4–10.

E   Few-flowered Fumitory, *F. vaillantii*, has small fls (**Ea**) like C, but **wholly** pink, and lfts flat. S Eng vl; Eur lf; on ar on chk. Fl 6–9.

F   *F. micrantha* resembles A, with 6–7 mm fls (**F**), pink, but in **dense** racemes with **broad, rounded** sepals 20–30 mm wide and bracts longer than fl-stalks. Br Isles: S Eng, Scot, Ire; Eur: N to Netherlands; lc on ar on chk. Fl 6–10.

G   Common Ramping-fumitory, *F. muralis* ssp *boraei*, resembles D, but the pink fls (**G**) are fewer (10–15) per raceme, and 10–20 mm long; lowest petal has **turned-up edges**; frs smooth. Br Isles, Eur; lf on ar, wa. Fl 5–10.

H   Climbing Corydalis, *Corydalis claviculata*, delicate climbing ann with bipinnate lvs ending in tendrils, and short spikes of creamy fls (**Ha**) each 5–6 mm; pods (**Hb**) 6 mm and three-seeded. Br Isles lc (more c in W); Eur: N to Denmark lf; in dry wds, hths, on shady rocks on more acid soils. Fl 5–9.

I   Yellow Corydalis, *C. lutea*, stouter per plant with no tendrils and bright yellow fls (**I**) 12–18 mm long. Br Isles, W Eur; f, introd on old walls (native S Eur). Fl 5–8.

J   *C. solida* is like I, but with purple fls (**J**) 15–22 mm long, with **long** straight spurs, toothed bracts to fls, fleshy scales on stem below lvs; solid globular tuberous root. Eng (introd) r; Eur lf; in dry wds. Fl 4–5.   **Ji**   *C. cava* (*C. bulbosa*) is close to J, with purple fls, but with hollow tubers; no stem-scales; untoothed bracts to fls and curved spurs. Eng r (only introd); Eur N to Sweden lf; in wds.

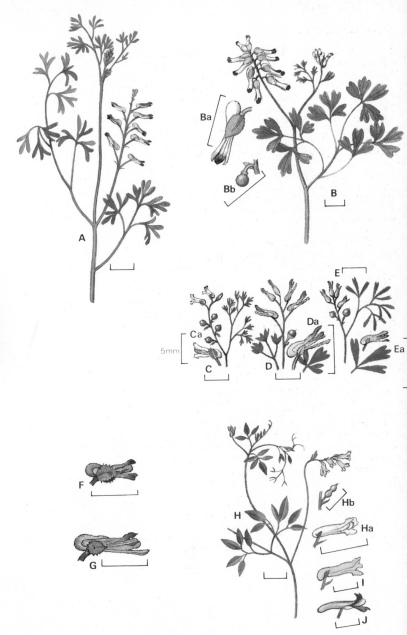

5mm

111

FUMITORY FAMILY

Fumariaceae

KEY TO FUMITORIES (*FUMARIA*)

(Spp named, but without page reference, are not described elsewhere)

1 Fl 9 mm or more long – lower petal not spoon-like at tip **2**
  Fl 5–8 mm long – lower petal spoon-like at tip – lf-lobes always narrow.......................... **6**
2 Lower petal with broad edges – fr 3 mm wide – v large plant – Cornwall only ....*Fumaria occidentalis*
  Lower petal with narrow edges – fr less than 2.5 mm wide................................. **3**
3 Pedicel bent back in fr – infl-stalks longer than raceme – 20 fls per spike **4**
  Pedicels ± straight – infl-stalk not longer than raceme – 15 fls per spike **5**
4 Fls white in dense spikes – upper petal folded lengthwise ....*F. capreolata* (p 110 B)
  Fls purple in looser spikes – upper petal not folded lengthwise – western, r .... *F. purpurea*
5 Lower petal with erect edges – fr smooth – fls to 15 per spike.............*F. muralis* ssp *boraei* (p 110 G)
  Lower petal with spreading edges – fr rough – sepals toothed – fls about 20 per spike – upper petal
  folded lengthwise ....*F. bastardii* (p 110 D)
  As *F. bastardii*, but fr smooth, upper petal not folded, sepals untoothed – r in Cornwall, W
  France...*F. martinii*
6 Sepals at least 2 mm long – fls 6 mm or more.. **7**
  Sepals not over 1.5 mm long – fls 5 mm or less... **8**
7 Bracts longer than fl-stalks – fr rounded – lf-segments channelled ....*F. micrantha* (p 110 F)
  Bracts shorter than fl-stalks – fr truncate – lf-segments flat .... *F. officinalis* (p 110 A)
8 Bracts equal to fr-stalks – lf-segments channelled – fls white – spikes unstalked..................................
                                        F. parviflora (p 110 C)
  Bracts shorter than fr-stalks – lf-segments flat – fls pink – spikes clearly stalked..................................
                                        F. vaillantii (p 110 E)

CRUCIFER (OR CABBAGE) FAMILY   *Cruciferae*

A large and distinctive family of herbs; none is poisonous, and many (eg, Cabbage, Turnip, Mustard, Cress, Water-cress etc) are useful vegetables. Lvs alt, without stipules; fls in a racemose infl. Fls have 4 free sepals, 4 free (usually equal) petals, arranged in a cross, usually 6 (sometimes fewer) stamens, and 2 carpels joined along their inner sides to form a superior ovary. Ovary normally ripens to a two-celled fr, which opens from the bottom upwards by 2 valves (strips of tissue on outside of carpels). Fr either long and narrow (a siliqua), or less than 3 times as long as wide (a silicula); seeds remain attached to central framework of fr for a time. Some Crucifers have a specialized beak on top of the two-valved part of the fr; beak may contain 1 or more seeds. In a few (eg, Radish), seeds are confined to the beak, which either breaks transversely into one-seeded joints or remains in one piece (as in Sea-kale or Bastard Cabbage). Frs are vital in identification of many spp. **Do not confuse with**: members of Poppy Family (p 108), which also have 4 free petals and superior ovary, but many stamens; some Potentillas (p 208) with 4 free petals but many stamens; Willowherbs (p 222) with 4 free petals, but inferior ovary.

KEYS TO CRUCIFER (OR CABBAGE) FAMILY

(Consult first the main headings A,B,C,D,E, and F)

A Crucifers with white or pink fls, and either with frs lacking 2 obvious, parallel, valve-opening carpels or not developing frs at all

1 Plants not producing ripe frs – lvs once-pinnate, with violet-brown **bulbils** in lf-axils – erect wdland herb – rose-pink fls in spring – vl in SE Eng .... *Dentaria bulbifera* (p 122 E)
Plant not producing ripe frs – lvs **v large** (to 60 cm long), glossy, oblong, wavy, sometimes pinnatifid – fls white, in large panicles in May–June – frs obovoid, never ripen in Br Isles ....
Armoracia rusticana (p 130 B)
Plant producing frs – not in wdlands **2**

2 Large cabbage-like seashore plant – broad rounded **heads** of white fls – frs shape and size of garden peas, 10–12 mm across, on stalk-like lower joints .... *Crambe maritima* (p 130 A)
Frs not pea-like **3**

3 Fr with upper part 8–20 mm long, shaped like bishop's mitre, on a stalk-like stout lower joint – lvs fleshy, pinnatifid – fls pink (or white) in racemes .... *Cakile maritima* (p 122 D)
Fr cylindrical, tapered to a long point **4**

4 Fr constricted into bead-like joints that separate when ripe – on ar, wa ....
Raphanus raphanistrum (p 118 A)
Fr sausage-shaped (except for tapered point), not constricted .... *Raphanus sativus* (p 118 Ai)

B Crucifers with white or pink fls, fr of 2 obvious parallel carpels opening into valves, and less than 3 times as long as wide

1 Plants small, **prostrate** – fls tiny (2.0–2.5 mm across) – frs of 2, almost distinct, round carpels, covered with network of pits or ridges – carpels finally separate into 2 one-seeded achenes ....
Coronopus (p 128)
Plants ± erect – 2 carpels joined along their length **2**

2 Petals deeply bilobed – stems lfless – rosettes of undivided root-lvs – tiny (5–10 cm) plant of early spring .... *Erophila verna* (p 128 F)
Petals not bilobed **3**

3 Petals unequal-sized (2 outer of each fl much larger than inner) **4**
Petals equal-sized (or abs) **5**

4 Lvs up stem – shorter petals twice length of sepals – on chk .... *Iberis amara* (p 128 E)
Lvs ± confined to basal rosette, pinnatifid – shorter petals ± same length as sepals – on sandy or stony gd .... *Teesdalia nudicaulis* (p 128 C)

5 Fr egg-shaped, round in cross-section, not flattened – lvs fleshy – at seaside and in N hill country .... *Cochlearia* (p 128)
Fr distinctly flattened in cross-section **6**

6 Fr two-celled, each cell with only 1 seed **7**
Fr two-celled, each cell with 2 or more seeds **9**

7 Lvs all unlobed, untoothed, linear – partition of fr-cells across widest diameter – mostly seaside ......
Lobularia maritima (p 130 J)
Lvs (some at least) lobed or toothed – partition of fr-cells across narrowest diameter..................... 8
8 Fls in a much-branched umbel-like head – lvs grey – fr without wings or flanges, cordate at base, tapering into style above ....*Cardaria draba* (p 128 I)
Fls in spike-like infls – fr without cordate base, but with wings or flanges at edges, or downy ....
Lepidium (p 126)
9 Fr with winged edges...*Thlaspi* (p 126)
Fr without winged edges... 10
10 Fr shaped like triangle standing on its point ....*Capsella bursa-pastoris* (p 128 D)
Fr oval to elliptical 11
11 Lvs unlobed – fr elliptical, flat or twisted – partition of fr-cells parallel with flat sides (ie, across widest diameter)...*Draba* (p 126)
Lvs pinnately-lobed – fr oval, short – partition of fr-cells at right angles to broader sides (ie, across narrowest diameter).. *Hornungia petraea* (p 130 K)

C **Crucifers with white (or pink or purple) fls, fr of 2 obvious carpels, long and narrow, at least 3 times as long as wide**
1 Style of fl deeply lobed into 2 stigmas.. 2
Style of fl with a single disc-shaped stigma... 3
2 Stigmas with a horn-like swelling on back of each – seaside plant.........................*Matthiola* (p 122)
Stigmas with no swelling on backs – tall inland plant of wa and riversides...............*Hesperis* (p 122)
3 Fr strongly flattened, cross-section elliptical.. 4
Fr either four-angled, or cross-section cylindrical... 6
4 Fr's 2 valves with no obvious veins, rolling up on opening – lvs compound, pinnate ....
Cardamine (p 122–124)
Fr's 2 valves with a strong central vein – lvs untoothed to pinnatifid only.................................. 5
5 Basal lvs long-stalked, pinnatifid – pods held at an angle...............................*Cardaminopsis* (p 124)
Basal lvs elliptical, short-stalked, only slightly toothed – pods adpressed to stem .... *Arabis* (p 124)
6 Lvs pinnate ....*Rorippa nasturtium-aquaticum* (p 124 C)
Lvs all undivided, toothed only 7
7 Lvs heart- to kidney-shaped, ± hairless, long-stalked – tall (50–100 cm) plant with garlic smell when bruised... *Alliaria petiolata* (p 124 H)
Lvs elliptical, ± hairy, short-stalked, mostly in basal rosette – shorter (5–30 cm) plant with no garlic smell ....*Arabidopsis thaliana* (p 124 F)

D **Crucifers with yellow fls, and fr not obviously composed of 2 parallel carpels, and not opening into 2 valves**
1 Fr elongated, composed of bead-like rounded joints with constrictions between, when ripe breaking into one-seeded segments .... *Raphanus* (p 118)
Fr with 2 joints: the upper globular, 4 mm long, with a long beak like an old Chianti bottle; lower joint like a stout stalk ....*Rapistrum rugosum* (p 120 G)

E **Crucifers with yellow fls, and frs in 2 parts: lower part of 2 obvious parallel carpels that separate from below and open into 2 valves; upper part (the beak), between top of valves and stigma, does not split open vertically, but may contain 0–6 seeds**
1 Fr-valves one-veined – beak short, usually seedless .... (*Brassica*) 2
Fr-valves 3–7-veined.. 3
2 Fr-valves rounded (so fr cylindrical), with faint veins – beak only $\frac{1}{10}$ of whole fr's length, seedless – lvs fleshy – on sea cliffs...*Brassica oleracea* (p 116 A)
Fr as above, but beak $\frac{1}{5}$–$\frac{1}{3}$ of whole fr's length, containing seeds – fls over-topping buds...............
Brassica rapa (p 116 C)
Fr-valves keeled, with strong central vein (so fr four-angled in cross-section) – fr stiffly erect, adpressed to stem .... *Brassica nigra* (p 116 B)
3 Beak short, swollen below, to $\frac{1}{2}$ length of valves – fr erect, adpressed to stem – plant v hairy below, ± hairless above – introd in wa – lf...*Hirschfeldia incana*
Beak long, not swollen below – fr not adpressed to stem 4
4 Sepals erect... *Rhynchosinapis* (p 116)
Sepals spreading ....(*Sinapis*) 5
5 Beak conical, $\frac{1}{2}$ length of valves ....*Sinapis arvensis* (p 116 F)
Beak sabre-shaped, as long or longer than valves...*Sinapis alba* (p 116 E)

CRUCIFER (CABBAGE) FAMILY   *Cruciferae*

F **Crucifers with yellow fls, and fr of 2 obvious valves, without an upper joint or beak between top of valves and stigma**
1 Fr only 4 times as long as wide (or less) **2**
  Fr 6 or more times as long as wide... **6**
2 Fr flattened... **3**
  Fr rounded in cross-section, ± veinless **4**
3 Fr elliptical, erect – small tufted plant – lvs in basal rosette – r .... *Draba aizoides* (p 126 Aii)
  Fr oblong, winged, pendulous, like an Ash 'key' – tall robust plant – r .... *Isatis tinctoria* (p 120 F)
4 Fr 9–18 mm, oblong..*Rorippa sylvestris* (p 120 A)
  Fr less than 9 mm long.. **5**
5 Fr 4–9 mm, shortly oblong, stalk ± of equal length with fr .... *Rorippa islandica* (p 120 B)
  Fr 3–6 mm, oval, stalks twice as long as fr...*Rorippa amphibia* (p 120 C)
6 Style deeply divided into 2 spreading stigmas – lvs oblong, untoothed – bushy plant of old walls..*Cheiranthus cheiri* (p 120 E)
  Style with a single, ± disc-shaped stigma **7**
7 Fr strongly flattened, elliptical in cross-section – fls v pale yellow – on rocks near Bristol – r..............
                                                                                 Arabis stricta (p 124 E)
  Fr ± cylindrical or four-angled in cross-section... **8**
8 Lvs unlobed, ± toothed – plant hairy throughout ....*Erysimum* (p 118 D)
  At least root-lvs pinnatifid... **9**
9 Lvs twice pinnate into fine, almost hairlike, hairy segments ....*Descurainia sophia* (p 118 F)
  Lvs no more than once pinnate.. **10**
10 Valves of fr one-veined... **11**
   Valves of fr 3–7-veined – lvs all ± pinnatifid to pinnate..........................*Sisymbrium* (p 116–118)
11 Seeds in 2 vertical rows in each cell of fr **12**
   Seeds in 1 vertical row in each cell of fr... **13**
12 Upper stem-lvs clasping stem, hairless, waxy grey-green, with half-arrow-shaped bases – root-lvs hairy, pinnatifid – frs adpressed to stem – fls v pale yellow.......................... *Turritis glabra* (p 120 D)
   Upper stem-lvs not clasping stem – frs spreading – fls bright yellow.....................*Diplotaxis* (p 116)
13 Fr with convex rounded valves.. *Brassica oleracea, B. rapa* (p 116 A,C)
   Fr four-angled in cross-section **14**
14 Stem and lvs all ± hairless – all lvs bright glossy green – rosette-lvs stalked – upper lvs stalkless and clasping..*Barbarea* (p 118)
   Lower stem and lvs bristly, grass-green – upper stem and lvs hairless, grey-green – all lvs stalked .... *Brassica nigra* (p 116 B)

CRUCIFER (CABBAGE) FAMILY   *Cruciferae*

Yellow Crucifers with jointed pods

A Wild Cabbage, *Brassica oleracea*, the ancestor of cabbage, kale, etc, is a robust hairless herb, with stout stem bearing lf-scars on its woody base; lvs waxygrey green, oblong, thick and fleshy, pinnately-lobed in lower part. Fls in long spikes, lemon-yellow, 25–50 mm across; fr 5–10 cm, cylindrical, lower part comprising two cells, each with several seeds, and a seedless beak 5–10 mm. Br Isles: S Eng, S Wales; Eur: W France; vla on sea cliffs. Fl 5–8.

B Black Mustard, *Brassica nigra*, tall ann (to 1 m); lyre-shaped, pinnatelylobed, bristly bright green lvs; upper lvs undivided, elliptical, **narrowed below**, hairless, glaucous. Racemes of yellow fls, 10–15 mm across. Pods (**B, Ba**) **erect**, **adpressed, four-angled**, hairless, 12–20 mm long, **beaded**, with a seedless slender beak. Br Isles: Eng, Wales f-lc; Scot, Ire vr; Eur f-lc; on riverbanks, cliffs, wa. Fl 6–9.

C Wild Turnip, *Brassica rapa*, tall ann or bi like B, but with upper stems-lvs **clasping**, with cordate bases; fl-spike flat-topped, fls overtopping the buds above them. Br Isles, W Eur; c on riverbanks, cliffs, wa. Fl 6–8.   **Ci Rape**, *B. napus*, is an escape, similar to C, with all lvs waxy-grey-green and buds overtopping the pale yellow fls above.

D Isle of Man Cabbage, *Rhynchosinapis monensis*, **hairless** bi, 15–30 cm; lvs nearly confined to a basal rosette, glaucous, deeply pinnately-lobed; petals pale yellow; pods spreading, 4–7 cm, on stalks 6–10 mm; beak (⅓ of pod) with up to 5 seeds. Br Isles: W coasts of GB (Devon–Argyll); **not Eur**; lc on cliffs, beaches. Fl 6–8.   **Di** *R. cheiranthos* is a similar casual, with stem and lf undersides hairy; fr hairless.   **Dii** *R. wrightii*, confined to Lundy Island, Devon, has lvs v hairy on both sides, and **hairy** fr.

E White Mustard, *Sinapis alba*, is often confused with F, but is an escape. **All** lvs pinnately-lobed; beak of fr is **winged** and sabre-like, and as **long** or **longer** than lower two-valved part. Br Isles, W Eur; c on ar, wa. Fl 6–8.

F Charlock, *S. arvensis*, roughly hairy ann, 30–60 cm, with stalked lyreshaped lower lvs, bristly and strongly-toothed; upper lvs simple. Fls yellow, 15–20 mm across; frs hairy, 25–40 mm long, **spreading**; beak of fr not much more than ½ as long as lower two-valved part. Br Isles, Eur; vc on ar. Fl 5–8.

G Annual Wall-rocket, *Diplotaxis muralis*, erect to spreading branched ann or bi; root-lvs to 10 cm, elliptical, stalked, deeply pinnate. Fls (**Gb**) lemon-yellow, about 10 mm across; frs (**Ga**) narrowed at both ends, **longer** than **stalk**, ascending at an angle to stalk; **not stalked** above sepal-scars. Br Isles, W Eur; southern, widely introd on ar, wa, walls, rocks. Fl 6–9.

H Perennial Wall-rocket, *D. tenuifolia*, similar, but taller more erect per, quite hairless, with larger fleshier lvs. Petals to 15 mm long; fr stalked above sepal-scars, stalk ± same length as fr (**Ha**). S Eng; Eur, SW (casual to N); lc on old walls, wa. Fl 5–9.

I Hedge Mustard, *Sisymbrium officinale*, stiffly erect ann to bi herb, 30–90 cm, branched above, bristly. Basal lvs deeply pinnately-lobed, with round terminal lobe; fls 3 mm across, short-stalked, in dense long racemes; frs (**Ia**) pale yellow, cylindrical, with v short beak, two-valved, stiffly erect, adpressed to stems. Br Isles, W Eur; a on hbs, wa, rds, etc. Fl 6–7.

116

117

Cruciferae

Crucifers with elongated frs and yellow fls (but A is often white-fld)

A Wild Radish, *Raphanus raphanistrum*, bristly ann with lyre-shaped pin-natifid lvs, rather like Charlock (p 116 F) in build, but has long-beaked frs, with 3–8 **weakly-ribbed**, **bead-like** joints which easily break apart when ripe: beak to 5 times length of top fr-joints. Fls may be yellow, white or lilac, usually veined with deeper lilac. Br Isles, Eur, possibly originally introd; vc on ar, wa. Fl 5–9. **Ai Garden Radish**, *R. sativus*, often occurs as an escape; fls white or violet; tuberous radish root present; fr inflated, like small sausages tapered to a long beak, hardly constricted and not easily breaking into separate joints.

B Winter-cress, *Barbarea vulgaris*, erect bi or per herb, with strong tap-root and upright parallel branches, is like Hedge Mustard (p 116 I) in habit, but stouter and hairless, with pinnately-lobed, deep green, shiny, lower lvs, in which terminal lobe is oval and larger than others, but shorter than rest of lf; upper lvs simple, oval. Dense racemes of small (7–9 mm) yellow fls produce erect, four-angled narrow frs (**Ba**), 15–25 mm long, on stalks of 4–5 mm. Br Isles, Eur; vc on streamsides, hbs, damp wa. Fl 5–8.

C American Winter-cress, *B. verna*, has all lvs pinnately-lobed; basal lvs with terminal lobes much **smaller** and narrower, 6–10 pairs of side lobes; frs **curved upwards**, 30–60 mm long. Other spp occur with different lf forms, as casuals. Br Isles: Eng, Wales o-lf; Scot, Ire r; Eur f; escape, on ar, wd. Fl 5–7.

D Treacle Mustard, *Erysimum cheiranthoides*, resembles B and Hedge Mustard (p 116 I) in its erect spikes of small yellow fls and narrow erect pods (**Da**), but has a **square** stem with adpressed hairs, and all lvs lanceolate and **undivided**, though shallowly-toothed. Lowland and S in Br Isles, Eur; f-lc in ar and wa. Fl 6–8.

E Sea Radish, *Raphanus maritimus*, differs from A in having fls (**E**) normally always yellow; frs (**Ea**) with **fewer** (1–5) bead-like joints, which are **strongly ribbed**, but do not readily break apart when ripe; beak of fr v short, only to twice length of top joint. Br Isles, Eur (N to Netherlands); f on beaches, cliffs. Fl 6–8.

F Flixweed, *Descurainia sophia*, another erect ann yellow Crucifer (to 60 cm), with elongated frs; lvs and lower stem **grey** with star-shaped adpressed hairs; lvs 2 or 3 times **pinnately** cut, with **linear** segments; fls (**Fa**) **pale** yellow, pods (**Fb**) rounded, 15–25 mm by 1 mm, curving upwards, erect, from long slender stalks. Br Isles (not N Scot), Eur; lf on sandy wa, rds etc (perhaps introd originally). Fl 6–8.

G Tall Rocket, *Sisymbrium altissimum*, resembles F in its finely-cut lvs and long frs; but taller (to 100 cm), stem-lvs stalkless, only **once pinnate**, and **hairless**, with longer narrower segments; hairless frs (**Ga**) far longer, 50–100 mm (root-lvs pinnately-lobed and hairy, but soon wither). Introd to Br Isles and W Eur; o in wa (especially sandy) gd. Fl 6–8.

H Eastern Rocket, *S. orientale*, resembles G, but its **stalked**, pinnate stem-lvs have broader, **halberd-shaped** terminal lobes and short side-lfts; uppermost stem-lvs merely lanceolate, undivided; frs (**Ha**) like those of G, 40–100 mm long, but hairy at first. Introd Br Isles, Eur; o on wa. Fl 6–8.

119

Crucifers with yellow flowers, continued (**Yellow-cresses**, *Rorippa*)

Yellow-cresses (*Rorippa*) are yellow-fld per Crucifers with fls in erect racemes, and oblong to cylindrical frs, with two convex valves and no obvious midrib. Found in wet or waste places.

A **Creeping Yellow-cress**, *Rorippa sylvestris*, 20–30 cm, straggling and hairless, with pinnately-lobed lvs, the lobes toothed; frs (**Aa**) cylindrical-oblong, 9–18 mm long, equalling their fr-stalks. Br Isles, Eur; f-lc on wa, gdns, wet places. Fl 6–8.

B **Marsh Yellow-cress**, *R. islandica* (*R. palustris*), is taller (to 60 cm), stronger and more erect than A; lvs (**B**) auricled and less deeply divided; fls 3 mm across; frs (**Ba**) **shorter** (4.9 × 1.5–2.0 mm), more **oblong**, swollen and **curved**, contracted into short style above. Fr-stalks 4–10 mm. Br Isles, Eur; f in wet places. Fl 6–9.

C **Great Yellow-cress**, *R. amphibia*, erect hairless per with stout stem 40–120 cm; lvs (**C**) lanceolate, erect, mostly toothed only, sometimes pinnately-lobed below. Fls larger than in B (6 mm across); fr (**Ca**) 3.6 × 1.3 mm, oval, straight, with style (1–2 mm) longer than in B; fr-stalks 16 mm long. Br Isles, Eur; lc by streams, ponds etc. Fl 6–8.

D **Tower Mustard**, *Turritis* (*Arabis*) *glabra*, stiffly erect bi with a basal rosette of hairy, deeply-toothed root-lvs, and glaucous-waxy, hairless, grey-green, arrow-shaped stem-lvs that clasp the hairless stem. Fls in a long raceme, creamy yellow, about 6 mm; pods (**Da**) stiffly erect, stalked, 30–60 mm × 1.0 mm, cylindrical. Eng, especially E, vl and decreasing; Eur o-lf; in dry sandy hbs, rds, dry wds. Fl 5–7.

E **Wallflower**, *Cheiranthus cheiri*, per herb 20–60 cm tall, with stem woody below, lfy and angled above; lvs 5–10 cm, oblong lance-shaped, untoothed, sessile above; adpressed forked hairs on lvs and upper stems; fls in short racemes, bright orange-yellow, 2.5 cm across; sepals ½ length of petals. Pods (**Ea**) 2.5–7.0 cm long, narrow, flattened, hairy, valves one-veined. (Not to be confused with Garden Wallflowers, hybrids of *Erysimum* genus, having much larger fls of various colours.) Introd Br Isles and W Eur (native SE Eur); f-lc on old walls. Fl 4–6.

F **Woad**, *Isatis tinctoria*, source of the blue dye, is a tall, branched, ± hairless, usually bi herb, with basal rosettes of stalked, wavy-edged, lanceolate downy lvs; upper lvs (**Fa**), arrow-shaped, hairless, grey-green, clasp the stem. Branched infl (**F**) bears yellow fls, 4 mm across; frs (**Fb**) pendulous, obovate, (8–20 × 3.6 mm) and purplish-brown. Eng r, introd on cliffs (Tewkesbury, Guildford) and in W Eur (native of S and Central Eur). Fl 7–8.

G **Bastard Cabbage**, *Rapistrum rugosum*, in habit like Hedge Mustard (p 116 I), is a hairy branched ann with pinnately-lobed lvs and pale yellow fls, 5 mm across. The erect frs (**G**) are distinctive (shaped like old Chianti bottles), each with an upper **globular** (about 3 mm wide) segment having strong wavy vertical ribs, abruptly narrowed to the shorter style above; and a narrow cylindrical lower segment ½–⅓ length of stalk. S Eng, Eur; introd, la on wa. Fl 5–9.

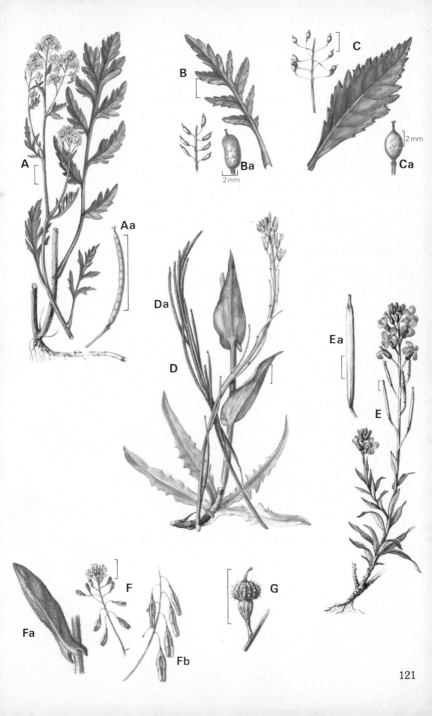

A

Aa

B

Ba

2 mm

C

Ca

2 mm

Da

D

Ea

E

F

Fa

Fb

G

Pink and/or white-fld Crucifers with long frs

A   Hoary Stock, *Matthiola incana*, showy ann or per of erect, bushy habit, woody and lfless below like Wallflower; lvs narrow, lanceolate, the lower in rosettes, the upper sessile, all ± **untoothed**, grey-downy. Fls 2.5–5.0 cm across, in loose racemes, with hairy sepals and purple, red or white petals. Frs (**Aa**) 4.5–13.0 cm long, ± erect, narrow, compressed, downy, **not glandular**. Br Isles: probably native on S coast Eng and S Wales; S Eur to W France; on sea cliffs. Fl 4–7. Fragrant.

B   Sea Stock, *M. sinuata*, bi with non-woody stem; lvs **wavy-edged** to **lobed**, grey-woolly, not bushy; looser infl of purple-pink fls (**Ba**); frs 7–12 cm, downy, and with **sticky glands**. SW Eng vr; S Eur to W France; on sea cliffs and dunes. Fl 6–8.

C   Dame's-violet, *Hesperis matronalis*, tall bi or per herb, with lfy stems, 40–90 cm tall, branched, ± hairy. Lvs lanceolate, toothed, pointed, stalked, and hairy. Fls 18–20 mm across, stalked, v fragrant, violet or white, in racemes. Frs 9 cm across, curving upwards, hairless. GB introd; on riverbanks and wa. Fl 5–7.

D   Sea Rocket, *Cakile maritima*, ann herb with stems that sprawl, then rise to bear succulent, shiny, hairless, simple or pinnate-toothed, linear to oblong lvs; and lilac-pink or white fls, 6–12 mm across, in racemes: frs (**Da**) 10–25 mm, on thick stalks, lower joint shorter, top-shaped, upper joint longer and mitre-shaped. Br Isles, W Eur; f-lc on sandy seashores. Fl 6–9.

E   Coralroot Bitter-cress, *Dentaria (Cardamine) bulbifera*, graceful per herb with slender erect hairless unbranched stems, 30–70 cm, rising from a fleshy rhizome. Lower lvs stalked, pinnate, upper three-lobed or simple; lfts **dark** green, stiffly spreading, lanceolate, acute, ± toothed, v sparsely hairy, with strong veins. Axils of upper lvs bear purple-brown **bulbils** (**Ea**) by which plant normally reproduces. Fls in a short raceme, almost like an umbel, are rose-pink, 12–18 mm across. Frs elongated, but rarely ripening in GB. SE Eng (almost confined to the Weald and the Chiltern Hills) r to vla; Eur: Central France N to Denmark (and Sweden), more c; in dry sandy or chky wds. Fl 4–5, v briefly only.

F   Wavy Bitter-cress, *Cardamine flexuosa*, slender hairy bi to per herb, with erect but **v wavy stem**. Lvs pinnately compound; lfts oval or rounded below, narrower on upper lvs, all sparsely hairy, especially terminal lft. Raceme short at first, then elongates; fls white; small narrow petals, 2–4 mm long, are twice length of sepals. Stamens 6, pale; frs narrow, 12–25 mm, ascending at an angle. Br Isles, Eur; vc in damp places, streamsides, wa, gdns. Fl 3–9.   **Fi   Hairy Bitter-cress**, *C. hirsuta*, is smaller, ann, straight-stemmed, with 4 pale stamens; otherwise like F. Br Isles, Eur; vc on wa, gdns, walls, rocks. Fl 3–9.

G   Cuckooflower (or **Lady's-smock**), *C. pratensis*, per, is a taller herb than F, with runners. Lower lvs (**Ga**) have large round lfts, terminal lft much larger than side ones, and kidney-shaped; upper lvs with narrow lfts; all sparsely hairy. Fls rose-pink to white, 12–18 mm across; fr 24–40 mm, long narrow and straight. Br Isles, Eur; vc on mds, streamsides, moist wds. Fl 4–6.

White-flowered Crucifers with long frs

A   Narrow-leaved Bitter-cress, *Cardamine impatiens*, is like a tall version of *C. flexuosa* (p 122 F), with a stouter, ridged stem to 60 cm, but lvs have ± **strongly-toothed** lfts, in up to 6–9 pairs per lf; conspicuous **stipule-like** pointed **auricles** (Ac) clasp stem at lf-base. Fls (**Aa**) like *C. flexuosa*, but usually **without** petals (Ab); 6 yellow stamens. Frs, 18–30 mm × 1 mm, ascend stiffly at 45°. Pods burst explosively to scatter seeds. GB to Mid Scot; Eur; lf in rocky (limestone) wds, especially on scree, and on riverbanks in SE Eng. Fl 5–8.

B   Large Bitter-cress, *C. amara*, also resembles *C. flexuosa* (p 122 F) but is per, ± hairless, taller, and all its pale green lvs have **oval** side and terminal lfts. Fls (**Ba**) **large**, 12 mm across, white, with conspicuous **violet** anthers; frs 20–40 mm long, spreading at 45°. Br Isles: Eng, Wales, NE Ire; Eur; la in springy wds, fens, streamsides, often with Golden-saxifrages (p 218). Fl 4–6.

C   Water-cress, *Rorippa nasturtium-aquaticum*, hairless per with creeping stems and erect flowering shoots; lvs, rather like those of B, but darker green, and with broader lflts below, persist in winter. White fls (Ca) much smaller (4–6 mm across) than B's; stamens **pale**. Frs (Cb) only 13–18 cm, stouter (2–4 mm wide), curved, and with seeds visible in **2 rows** inside pod. Br Isles, Eur; vc in streams, ditches etc, in running water. Fl 5–10. **Ci   One-rowed Water-cress**, *R. microphylla*, differs in having longer pods with only **one row** of seeds, and lvs turning purple-brown in autumn; hybridizes with C.

D   Hairy Rock-cress, *Arabis hirsuta*, short to medium hairy bi or per herb, 10–60 cm; basal rosette of hairy oval-oblong lvs, scarcely toothed, narrowed to base; narrower oblong **stalkless**, **clasping** lvs up stem. Fls many, white, 3–4 mm across, in a long erect raceme; frs narrow, stiffly erect, ± flattened, 15–50 mm × 1.3 mm. Br Isles, Eur; lc on calc gslds, rocks, dunes (a characteristic sp of chk downs: W dune forms look different, with non-clasping stem-lvs). Fl 5–8. **Di   Alpine Rock-cress**, *A. alpina*, has oval, toothed, basal lvs; fls 6–10 mm across. Scot: mt rocks in Skye r; (S and Central Eur mts r). Fl 6–8.

E   Bristol Rock-cress, *A. stricta* (*A. scabra*), lower (8–25 cm) per herb, with one or **more** stems less erect than in D, stem hairless above, hairy like the lvs below. Rosette-lvs oblong-lanceolate and wavily-lobed, darker green than in D; stem-lvs hairy, few, clasping as in D. Infl of only 3–6 fls, each 5–6 mm across; petals creamy-yellow; frs (**Ea**) 25–40 mm long. Eng: **about Bristol only**, vr (Eur: S France and Jura vl); on open limestone rocks. Fl 3–5.

F   Thale Cress, *Arabidopsis thaliana*, resembles a smaller ann to bi slender version of D, 5–50 cm tall, with a similar lf-rosette of stalked elliptical hairy lvs, but is hairless on upper stems and lvs. Fls 3 mm across, white; frs 10–18 × 0.8 mm, slenderer than in D, and **curved**, borne **obliquely** on **slenderer spreading** stalks, **cylindrical** with convex **strong-veined** valves. Br Isles, Eur; fc on walls, dry sandy open gd, not on chk. Fl 4–5.

*G   Tall Rock-cress, *Cardaminopsis arenosa*, ann or per herb with basal rosette of pinnately-lobed, ± hairy lvs and usually several stems 10–20 cm tall; fls about 8 mm, white or lilac; frs elongated, curved, flattened, spreading, beakless, 12–30 mm, on long slender stalks 6–10 mm. Eur, eastern, N to Denmark; l on limestone rocks and chk. Fl 5–6. **Gi   Northern Rock-cress**, *C. petraea*, per; hairy below, not above; lvs only shallowly-lobed; fls white, smaller (about 6 mm across) than in G. **Br Isles**: N Wales, Scot, W Ire; lf mt rocks. Fl 6–8.

H   Garlic Mustard, *Alliaria petiolata*, distinctive ± hairless, erect per herb, 20–120 cm; cordate, toothed, glossy, thin lvs, long-stalked below, **smell of garlic** when bruised. Fls in a raceme, white, 6 mm across; frs (**Ha**) diverging from stem, curving up erect, 35–60 mm, and angled. Br Isles, Eur; vc in hbs, open wds (especially on chk). Fl 4–7.

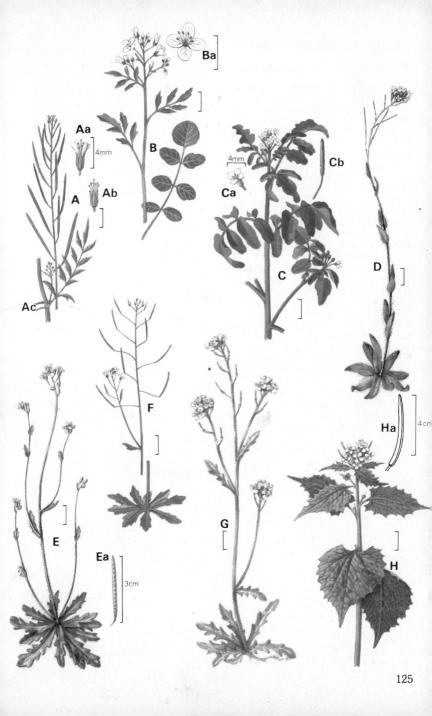

Aa

4mm

Ab

A

Ac

Ba

B

Ca

Cb

C

4mm

D

F

E

Ea

3cm

G

Ha

4cm

H

125

White-flowered Crucifers with short frs

A Hoary Whitlowgrass, *Draba incana*, bi to per herb with short creeping stock, bearing erect hairy stems 7–50 cm tall. Basal lvs in rosettes, v hairy (hairs star-shaped), oblong, narrowed to a stalk below, entire or with a few teeth. Stems with **narrow**-elliptical, hairy, erect lvs, stalkless and slightly clasping at base, usually toothed. Infl at first dense, elongating as frs ripen, with white fls, 3–5 mm, with slightly notched petals (**Aa**); frs (**Ab**) 7–9 × 2.0–2.5 mm, erect, elliptical, **twisted** when ripe. Br Isles: N Wales and N Eng to Scot; **not lowlands** of W Eur; vl on screes, cliffs, rocks, dunes, especially on limestone. Fl 6–7. **Ai Rock Whitlow-grass**, *D. norvegica*, smaller plant with ± leafless fl-stems and pods **not twisted**, 5–6 mm long. Scot, vr on a few high mt rocks. Fl 7–8. **Aii Yellow Whitlow-grass**, *D. aizoides*, has narrow lvs, all basal, heads of **yellow** fls, 8 mm wide, and flat elliptical frs 6–12 mm. S Wales; vr limestone (Central Eur). Fl 3–5.

B Wall Whitlowgrass, *D. muralis*, is ann, shorter (8–20 cm) than A, much less hairy above; **broadly oval**, clasping, **toothed stem-lvs**; petals (**Ba**) unnotched; frs (**Bb**) 3–6 × 1.5–2.0 mm, flat, not twisted. Eng vl on limestone walls and rocks; Eur o-lf. Fl 4–5.

C Perfoliate Penny-cress, *Thlaspi perfoliatum*, ann, 5–25 cm, smaller than E; fl (**Ca**); lvs **waxy** grey-green, root-lvs obovate, stalked, stem-lvs with **deeply clasping rounded bases**; cordate winged frs (**Cb**) only 4–6 mm long × 3.5 mm wide, narrowed to stalk; style shorter than fr-notch. S midland Eng r and vl; Eur widespread but l; on limestone scree. Fl 4–5.

D Alpine Penny-cress, *T. alpestre*, per of varied height (10–40 cm) with fls and fr (**Da**) similar to those in C, except that the style is as long as or longer than the notch, anthers are usually violet, not yellow, and the basal rosette lvs **spoon-shaped** and **long-stalked**, while auricles of the green stem-lvs are pointed. GB, vl on limestone and other basic rocks from Somerset to Scot (mts of Eur). Fl 4–8.

E Field Penny-cress, *T. arvense*, branched erect hairless ann, 10–60 cm, with broad-lanceolate, toothed clasping stem-lvs; no basal rosette; fls white, 4–6 mm, with yellow anthers; frs almost circular and coin-shaped, flattened, with v broad wings, 12–22 mm across, deeply-notched above, with style shorter than notch, on stalks curved upwards. Br Isles, Eur; c in ar and wa. Fl 5–7.

Pepperworts (*Lepidium*) resemble **Penny-cresses** (*Thlaspi*), but have frs shaped like tiny coal-shovels, with **one** seed per cell (2–5 in *Thlaspi*).

F Field Pepperwort, *Lepidium campestre*, is the commonest *Lepidium*. Ann or bi herb 20–60 cm; basal lvs entire or lyre-shaped, soon withering; stem-lvs triangular, stalkless, clasping with pointed basal lobes; all softly hairy and toothed. Inconspicuous white fls 2.0–2.5 mm, in long racemes; 6 stamens, anthers yellow. Frs (**Fa**) 5 × 4 mm, covered with small **white bladder-like** hairs (use lens), style short, not projecting beyond notch of shovel-shaped fr. Br Isles, Eur, generally f in lowlands, except to N; on dry gslds, ar, wa, hbs, rds. Fl 5–8.

G Smith's Pepperwort, *L. heterophyllum*, differs from F in being less erect; many-stemmed; frs with few or no bladder-like hairs; style projecting well beyond apical notch of fr (**G**). Br Isles, Eur; f in similar habitats. Fl 5–8. **Gi Garden Cress**, *L. sativum*, is the salad plant: a single erect stemmed hairless ann with Cress smell; upper stem-lvs pinnate, not clasping; style not projecting on capsule; garden escape.

H Narrow-leaved Pepperwort, *L. ruderale*, is hairless, strongly cress-smelling, slenderer than F and G; lower lvs pinnate, upper lvs simple, not clasping. Usually 2 or 4 stamens (not 6); frs (**Ha**), unlike those of F and G, shorter than their stalks, **less than 2 mm wide**; style v short, **within** fr-notch. Br Isles: Eng, Wales f in SE, r elsewhere; Scot vr; Eur f-lc; on grassy banks near sea, wa. Fl 5–7.

Aa 3mm

A

b mm

Bb 5mm

Ba 3mm

B

Cb 5mm

Ca 2mm

C

Da 6mm

D

E

Fa 4mm

F

G 4mm

H

Ha 2.5mm

Ia 4mm

Ib

I

Jb 2mm

Ja 2.5mm

J

127

◄ **I** **Hoary Cress**, *Cardaria draba*, bushy per herb, 30–90 cm, with runners; branched stems; oblong auricled clasping wavy-toothed hairy grey-green lvs (**Ib**); fls 5–6 mm, white; fr (**Ia**) 4 × 4 mm, cordate, tapering into the style above. Racemes in dense umbel-like heads. Native of S Eur, introd W Eur lc; and introd GB with bedding of sick troops from 1809 Walcheren expedition; most c in SE Eng especially Kent; on ar, wa. Fl 5–6.

J **Dittander**, *L. latifolium*, much the tallest, stoutest *Lepidium*; a per, 50–130 cm, with long-stalked oval simple basal lvs to 30 cm × 5 cm, sometimes with side-lobes below, all grey-green, but **hairless**. Infl a large branched pyramidal panicle; fls (**Ja**) 2.5 mm across, white; sepals **white-margined**; frs (**Jb**) elliptical to rounded with no notch, downy, hardly winged, style v short. Br Isles: Eng, Wales o in SE; S Ire vl; Eur lc; on saltmarsh edges and wa near sea. Fl 6–7.

Low-growing Crucifers with small white flowers

A **Swine-cress**, *Coronopus squamatus*, prostrate ann or bi, with spreading stems 5–30 cm long; stalked, deeply pinnate, scarcely hairy lvs with ± toothed segments; stalkless heads of fls on stem-tip and in lf-axils; fls 2.5 mm across, white; stamens 6; frs (**Aa**) 2.5 × 4 mm, notched below, tapered into short style above, with **strong ridges and pits** on the carpels, not opening when ripe. Br Isles vc in S; Eur c; on wa, ar, especially on trampled places near gates. Fl 6–9.

B **Lesser Swine-cress**, *C. didymus*, a smaller version of A, with a strong **cress smell** when bruised; stamens usually 2, petals often none; frs (**B**) only 1.5 × 2.5 mm, shorter than stalks, notched above as well as below; carpels rounded, pitted but **not ridged**. Introd from S America in Br Isles, Eur, now f-lc; on ar, wa. Fl 7–9.

C **Shepherd's Cress**, *Teesdalia nudicaulis*, neat ann or bi, hairless to ± downy, 8–20 cm tall; basal rosette of pinnate-lobed lvs with broader end-lobes and few stem-lvs (none on erect flowering central stem). Fls 2 mm, white, in short racemes, outer petals **longer** than inner; frs widely cordate, concave above, narrowed to base, 3–4 mm long; style v short. Br Isles: lc to S, r Scot, Ire; Eur lc; on open sandy gd, dry gsld, shingle, avoids chk. Fl 4–6.

D **Shepherd's-purse**, *Capsella bursa-pastoris*, variable ann or bi herb with erect main stem, 3–40 cm, hairy or not; rosette of pinnately-lobed to undivided lvs; clasping stem-lvs with basal pointed auricles. Fls in erect racemes; fls white, 2.5 mm across; frs erect, cordate, narrowed to base, notched above, **flat**, 6–9 mm long, on long stalks. Br Isles, W Eur; va weed of wa, rds, ar. Fl ± 1–12.

E **Wild Candytuft**, *Iberis amara*, ann, with toothed glossy green hairless lvs on ± erect stems. Fls (**Ea**), 6–8 mm across, white or lilac, with two outer petals **much longer** than two inner; in flat-topped heads elongating in fr. Frs 4–5 mm, almost round, with wings and a deep notch above, in which is set the short style, convex when ripe. S and mid Eng vlc; Eur lf; on bare chky gd on downs and ar, especially where rabbits are c. Fl 7–8.

F **Common Whitlowgrass**, *Erophila verna*, is a complex of closely similar spp. Ann, 2–10 cm (rarely more) with a basal rosette of broad lanceolate lvs narrowed into wide stalks, minutely hairy. Fl-stems lfless; fls (**Fa**) in short racemes, petals white, 2.5 mm, **deeply notched**; frs oval to elliptical, flattened, 3.9 × 15.3 mm, long-stalked. Br Isles, Eur; c-la on walls, rocks, open dry sandy gd. Fl 3–5, then soon disappearing.

Scurvygrasses (*Cochlearia*) are seaside or mt rock plants with fleshy lvs, white fls, and ± oval **swollen** frs. The spp are not all v easy to distinguish.

G **Common Scurvygrass**, *Cochlearia officinalis*, is a bi or per hairless herb, with 1 or more ascending stems, 5–50 cm. Basal lvs in a loose rosette, long-stalked, kidney-to heart-shaped; stem-lvs triangular-ovate, fleshy, clasping, the

Aa

4mm

A

B

3mm

C

D

Ea

6mm

E

Fa

2.5mm

F

Ga

G

Ha

H

I

Ja

6mm

J

Jb

Jc

2.5mm

K

Ka

3m

129

◀ upper lvs stalkless. Fls (**Ga**) 8–10 mm, white, rarely lilac; frs 3–7 × 2.5–6.0 mm, globose, rounded below, **swollen**, narrowed into style. Br Isles, Eur; lc on salt-marshes and cliffs (not SE Eng), also inland on basic rocks on hills. Fl 5–8.

H   Danish Scurvygrass, *C. danica*, low-growing plant, with stems 2–20 cm long; long-stalked cordate basal lvs (**H**), stem-lvs **stalked**, the lower ivy-shaped. Fls 4–5 mm. Frs (**Ha**) oval, **swollen**, **narrowed at both ends**. Br Isles, Eur; lc on sandy, shingly and rocky shores, banks near sea (also in railway ballast inland). Fl 2–6.

I   English Scurvygrass, *C. anglica*, like G, but basal lvs (**I**) have bases **wedge-shaped**, **tapering** into stalks; fls 5–7 mm across; frs **flattened**. Br Isles (including SE Eng), W Eur; lc on coasts, salt-marshes. Fl 4–7.

J   Sweet Alison, *Lobularia maritima*, short tufted grey-hairy per with narrow-lanceolate, untoothed lvs. Fls (**Ja**) 6 mm across, white, fragrant, in dense racemes which elongate (**Jb**); frs (**Jc**) obovate, 2.5 mm, with convex sides, on spreading stalks. Introd from Mediterranean on coasts of Eng (especially S), also in Eur. Fl 4–9.

K   Hutchinsia, *Hornungia petraea*, small ann herb rather like C; stalked rosette-lvs pinnately cut into small elliptical segments, but with similar stalkless lvs **up stem**. Fls 1.3 mm across, greenish-white; frs (**Ka**) 2–4 mm, narrow, **elliptical** to oval, hardly notched, compressed, held spreading on the stem. Br Isles: W, N Eng, Wales r-lf; Eur lf; on limestone rocks and calc dunes. Fl 3–5.

▶ **White Crucifers with v large lvs**

A   Sea-kale, *Crambe maritima*, large, cabbagy per herb, 40–60 cm tall and to 100 cm across lvs; basal lvs oval, long-stalked, waxy-grey, hairless, v fleshy, up to 30 cm long, with lobed, wavy margins; upper lvs smaller and narrower. Fls (**Aa**), white, 10–16 mm across, borne in large, rather flat-topped, much-branched heads to 30 cm across. Frs are 12–14 × 8 mm, with a stalk-like lower joint, and a spherical one-seeded non-opening pea-shaped upper joint. Br Isles (not N Scot), Eur (on Atlantic and Baltic coasts); o but la on shingle beaches and sand by sea. Fl 6–8.

B   Horse-radish, *Armoracia rusticana*, tall hairless per with tap-roots, used as a condiment; erect root-lvs 30–50 cm, oval or oblong, shiny dark green, long-stalked, toothed or sometimes pinnately-cut. The erect lfy branched stems (to 125 cm), less often produced, bear branched panicles of white fls 8–9 mm across, and oval frs later. Introd (from SE Eur) in Br Isles and W Eur; f-lc on wa, rds. Fl 5–6.

MIGNONETTE FAMILY   *Resedaceae*

C   Wild Mignonette, *Reseda lutea*, a bi to per hairless herb, with ± erect or sprawling branched **ribbed** stems, 30–75 cm. Basal lvs in a rosette; stem-lvs many; all lvs deeply once or twice pinnately cut; fls 6 mm across, greenish-yellow, in conical racemes, not scented; 6 sepals; 6 petals, upper petals two- or three-lobed, the 2 lower undivided; stamens 12–20, bent down. Fr an oblong warty capsule open at top even in fl; 3 stigmas. Br Isles: Eng c; Wales, Ire, E Scot o-lf; Eur c; on wa, gsld, disturbed gd, especially on chk. Fl 6–9.

D   Weld, *R. luteola*, a bi rather similar to C, but 50–150 cm, stiffly erect, hardly branched, with all lvs lanceolate, **untoothed**, **wavy-edged**. Fls (**Da**) in **long narrow** racemes, shorter-stalked, with **4 sepals** and **4 petals**; fr (**Db**) globular. Br Isles (r Scot); Eur; f-lc on disturbed gd, especially on chk. Fl 6–9.

E   Corn Mignonette, *R. phyteuma*, is like C, but shorter, downy, and ann; lvs often unlobed, cream petals to fls; pods drooping. SE Eng; r on ar on chk. Fl 6–8.

Aa
1.5cm

A

2cm

B

C

Db
5mm

D

Da
5mm

E
8mm

G

I

F

H

◀ **Milkworts** (*Polygala*) are low hairless pers with narrow-lanceolate lvs without stipules; small irregular fls have 3 tiny outer sepals and 2 large, coloured, lateral, petal-like ones; 3 true petals, v small, joined together into a little whitish fringed tube. 8 small stamens are joined into a tube with petals. Fls are blue, purple, mauve, pink or white, borne in spikes. Fr a notched two-celled compressed capsule with winged edges.

F Common Milkwort, *Polygala vulgaris*, has **alt** pointed lvs widest at or below middle, lower lvs shorter; fls 6–8 mm long, with **pointed** inner enlarged sepals. Br Isles, Eur; c in gsld on basic soils. Fl 5–9. ***Fi** *P. comosa* has fls half length and width of F, but conspicuous **bracts** (tiny in F) twice length of fl-stalks, in longer racemes. Eur: N, E France, S Belgium; r-lf on calc gsld. Fl 5–6.

G Chalk Milkwort, *P. calcarea*, resembles F, but the alt stem-lvs are **widest above middle**; **blunt** basal lvs are **larger**, forming a **stalked rosette**. Fls 6–7 mm long; inner sepals blunt. Blue forms have bright **gentian-blue** fls, much brighter than blue forms of F. Br Isles: S, SE Eng N to Lincs only, la; Eur N to Belgium o-la; on short calc gsld. Fl 5–6 only.

H Dwarf Milkwort, name for 2 closely related spp. *P. austriaca* (illustrated) has basal lf-rosettes like G and all lvs broadest above middle, but tiny fls, 2–5 mm across, white, lilac, pink or pale (never bright) blue; inner sepals only ½ width of and shorter than capsule. Kent vr; N France, Denmark, r-lf; on chk gsld. Fl 5–7. **Hi** *P. amara* is taller; stem-lvs pointed; sepals ⅔ width of and longer than capsule. Yorks, on damp mt limestone gsld, vr; Germany, in fens, lf.

I Heath Milkwort, *P. serpyllifolia*, is close to F, but has **opp** lower lvs, more diffuse growth, and fls more **deeply** (but not so brightly) coloured. Br Isles, Eur; vc on acid gslds, hths. Fl 5–9.

The **Rock-rose Family** (*Cistaceae*), comprises low downy shrubs (but *Tuberaria* is ▶ an ann herb) with undivided elliptical lvs in opp pairs, and fls with 5 strong-veined sepals (3 large, 2 tiny) and 5 spreading petals; many stamens, and egg-shaped capsules splitting into 3 lobes.

A **Common Rock-rose**, *Helianthemum chamaecistus* (*H. nummularium*), a ± prostrate undershrub, 5–30 cm, with many branches from thick woody stem. Lvs 0.5–2.0 cm, oblong (or oval), green, scarcely hairy above, white-woolly below, with untoothed, slightly inrolled margins, and long stipules at bases. Fls (in 1–12-fld lax infls), 2.0–2.5 cm across, bright yellow, with crinkly petals in bud, stalks downy. Br Isles: GB f-lc, abs some parts; Ire vvr; Eur c; on gsld, scrub on chk, and on acid soils in Scot. Fl 5–9.

B **White Rock-rose**, *H. apenninum*, resembles A, but has lvs **grey-downy** above with margins strongly inrolled; stipules no longer than lf-stalks; petals **white**. Eng vr, but la Somerset, Devon; Eur N to Belgium vl; on limestone rocks. Fl 4–7.

C **Hoary Rock-rose**, *H. canum*, has yellow fls as in A, but only 1.0–1.5 cm across; strongly bent (instead of straight) styles (**Ca**); and narrower lvs (less than 2 mm wide), without stipules. Br Isles: Eng (Yorks, Westmorland), Wales, Ire vl; Eur: France, W Germany o-vla; on limestone rocks, gsld. Fl 5–7. ***Ci** **Fumana**, *Fumana procumbens*, a prostrate shrub like C, but with linear **alt lvs**, **without stipules**; smaller yellow fls, with petals squared off at ends. Eur: France, Belgium; o-vlc on sunny limestone rocks and gsld. Fl 5–6.

D **Spotted Rock-rose**, *Tuberaria guttata*, ann, 6–20 cm tall, with three-veined, elliptical, hairy lvs; yellow fls 10–20 mm across, often with red spot at petal bases. Stipules usually long. Channel Is r; Eur: W and Central France f-lc. Var *breweri* (without stipules) N Wales, W Ire; on rocky cliffs. Fl 4–8.

cont

SEA-HEATH FAMILY   *Frankeniaceae*

E Sea-heath, *Frankenia laevis*, prostrate mat-forming shrub resembling a Heather; opp linear lvs, 2–4 mm long, with inrolled edges; crinkly five-petalled open pink fls (**Ea**), 5 mm across; 6 stamens; three-celled capsules. Br Isles: Eng, Hants to Norfolk; France N to Normandy; r but lf on dry stony or sandy salt-marshes. Fl 7–8.

FLAX FAMILY   *Linaceae*

Flaxes are hairless erect herbs with narrow, unstalked lvs; fls in loose, repeatedly forked (dichasial) cymes, with 5 sepals, 5 stamens; five-celled ovaries forming dry globose capsules.

F Fairy Flax, *Linum catharticum*, erect ann herb, 5–25 cm; oblong, **blunt**, **opp** lvs; open, forked infl of white fls (**Fa**), only 4–6 mm across. Br Isles, Eur; vc in calc gsld, dunes, flushes, rock ledges, fens. Fl 6–9.

G Pale Flax, *L. bienne*, ann or per, 20–30 cm, with alt three-veined **narrow pointed** lvs, **pointed** sepals, and pale lilac-blue fls, 12–14 mm across. Br Isles: Eng; Ire; Eur: France; lf dry gsld, especially near sea. Fl 5–9.

H Perennial Flax, *L. perenne*, resembles G, but is always per, usually taller (30–60 cm), with **one-veined** lvs; blunt, shorter, **inner** sepals, and sky-blue fls (**H**), 25 mm across. Eng vl on calc gsld in E only; Eur: central and E France r. Fl 6–7. **Hi Common Flax**, *L. usitatissimum*, resembles H in stature and fl size, but is ann, with three-veined lvs, sepals all pointed, and pale blue fls. Br Isles, Eur, o-lf (escape). Fl 6–9.

*I *L. tenuifolium*, shorter than G, has v narrow lvs, pointed sepals and rosy-pink fls (**I**) 1 cm wide. Eur: central France to W Germany o-lf; on calc gslds. Fl 6–7.

J Allseed, *Radiola linoides*, tiny ann, 2–8 cm tall, with bushy forked stems; opp eliptical lvs 2–3 mm long; numerous tiny fls 1 mm across, each with 4 tiny white petals equalling the 4 sepals, and 1 mm-wide globose capsules. Br Isles: widespread, r (but lf in S and W Eng, W Ire); Eur r-lf in W; on damp bare acid sandy gd on hths and on paths in wds. Fl 7–8.

BALSAM FAMILY   *Balsaminaceae*

Balsams are hairless ann herbs, with fleshy stems, and oval stalked toothed lvs. Fls in spikes, irregular, five-petalled, with wide lip, smaller hood and spur; frs explosive oblong capsules.

K Indian Balsam, *Impatiens glandulifera*, tall (1–2 m); reddish stem; lvs in **whorls** of 3, red-toothed; fls 2.5–4.0 cm long, with short curved spurs, purple-pink (or white). N Eng, Eur vl (introd from Himalayas); on river banks, wa. Fl 7–10.

L Touch-me-not Balsam, *I. noli-tangere*, 20–60 cm tall; stem nodes swollen, lvs **alt**, with 10–15 teeth (2–3 mm deep) on each side; fls (**L**) bright yellow, 3.5 cm long, including gradually curved and tapered spur. Br Isles: N Wales, NW Eng, vlf; N and E Eur lc (native, often introd); in wet wds, riversides. Fl 7–9.

M Small Balsam, *I. parviflora*, has alt lvs with more than 20 teeth each side, and small (5–15 mm) pale yellow fls (**Ma**). GB, Eur (widely introd from E Asia); lf in wds, etc. Fl 7–10.

N Orange Balsam, *I. capensis*, like L, but has less than 10 (shallower, 1–2 mm deep) teeth on each side of lf; **orange, red-spotted** fls (**N**) with spur suddenly narrowed and bent into a hook. Br Isles: Eng, Wales; Eur: France; by rivers o-la (introd N America). Fl 6–8.

5mm

135

Per herbs (or shrubs, F,G); lvs opp, untoothed, stalkless, simple, with translucent veins; fls in branched cymes (or solitary, G); fls yellow, 5 sepals and 5 petals, many stamens; frs capsules (except F, a berry) with 3 or 5 cells. See key, p 138.

A Perforate St John's-wort, *Hypericum perforatum*, erect per herb, 30–90 cm; round stems with **two** opp raised ridges; lvs (**Aa**) hairless, elliptic to oblong, blunt, 1–2 cm, with many translucent dots (use lens). Golden-yellow fls, 20 mm across, with black dots on petal edges; **pointed sepals**. Br Isles, Eur; vc in scrub, hbs, rds, gsld, especially on chk and sand. Fl 6–9.

B Imperforate St John's-wort, *H. maculatum*, is like A, but has **square** but **unwinged** stems (**Bb**), **no leaf dots** (**B**), **blunt sepals** (**Bc**) and fls (**Ba**) with black dots on petal surfaces. Hybridizes with A. Br Isles o-lf; Eur lf; in wd-borders, hbs, rds, usually on damp or heavier soils. Fl 6–8.

C Square-stalked St John's-wort, *H. tetrapterum*, resembles B, but has **square, four-winged** stems (**Ca**), oval lvs with **translucent dots**, paler fls (**C**), 10 mm across, narrow **pointed sepals** (**Cb**) without black dots. Br Isles, Eur; c in damp mds, marshes, by water. Fl 6–9. **Ci Wavy St John's-wort**, *H. undulatum*, has four-winged stems like C, but differs in red-flushed fls, **wavy-edged** lvs, pointed oval sepals **with black dots**. Br Isles: SW Eng, Wales; Eur: W France; r and vl in marshes. **Cii Irish St John's-wort**, *H. canadense*, has four-angled stems like C, but has slender erect habit of I; narrow, linear, three-veined lvs; petals, 3–4 mm across, have crimson lines on backs, and spread like stars. **Br Isles Ire only**; W France; vr on wet peaty gd. Fl 7–9.

D Hairy St John's-wort, *H. hirsutum*, resembles A in build and round stem, but is **downy** on lvs (**Db**) and stem; lvs oblong, much longer (2–5 cm), and **strongly veined**, with translucent dots; petals (**Da**) **pale yellow**; pointed sepals have **stalked black dots** on edges. N Scot r; Eur o – vc to S; on gsld on chk and clay, scrub, open wds. Fl 7–8.

E Pale St John's-wort, *H. montanum*, has the stiff erect habit, pale yellow fls, longer lvs and round stem of D, but its oval-oblong lvs are **hairless** on upper sides, and **lack translucent dots**; black dots on lf-edges beneath; sepals have stalked black dots on edges as in D. Br Isles: Eng, Wales, r-lf; **not Scot or Ire**; Eur o-lf; on scrub, wds, hbs, on calc soil, especially where sand or gravel overlies thinly. Fl 6–8.

F Tutsan, *H. androsaemum*, hairless low shrub, 40–100 cm, with two-edged, usually red, stems; oval lvs, 5–10 cm long, aromatic when bruised; fls few together, 20 mm across, sepals blunt, unequal, oval. Fr (**Fa**) a red berry turning black, 5–8 mm wide. Br Isles c in S, W, and Ire; o to E, N (N Scot vr); Eur N to Belgium o-lf; in wds, and hbs, cliffs (avoids v acid soils only). Fl 6–8.

G Rose-of-Sharon, *H. calycinum*, creeping low evergreen shrub up to 60 cm, with four-angled stems and elliptical lvs 5–10 cm; fls solitary, v large, 7–8 cm across. Br Isles, Eur (introd from SE Eur); in wds, banks, by gdns. Fl 7–9.

H Marsh St John's-wort, *H. elodes*, creeping grey-hairy per herb; almost circular to oval lvs, and upright fl-stems bearing groups of yellow fls, 15 mm across, **less open** than in other spp; sepals have red marginal dots. Br Isles (not N Scot) o-lc; Eur N to Netherlands r-lf; by acid bog pools and hollows, wet hths. Fl 6–9.

I Slender St John's-wort, *H. pulchrum*, hairless, strictly erect, slender, 20–40 cm; round reddish stems and blunt oval lvs with **cordate** bases and translucent dots; fls 15 mm; petals, orange-yellow, red-dotted, reddish below, have black dots on edges, as do sepals. Br Isles f-c; Eur f; on gsld, scrub, dry wds, usually on non-calc soils. Fl 6–8.

J Trailing St John's-wort, *H. humifusum*, creeping hairless per, with two-ridged stems and elliptic-oval, gland-dotted lvs 0.5–1.5 cm long. Fls few, 10 mm across, petals scarcely longer than sepals. Br Isles, Eur; c on hths, open acid wds. Fl 6–9. **Ji Flax-leaved St John's-wort**, *H. linarifolium*, resembles J, but flowering

A

Aa

Ba

Bc

4mm

B

Bb

3mm

C

Cb

Ca

3mm

D

D

Db

5mm

F

Fa

H

E

I

G

J

137

stems ascend more, and lvs longer (1.0–2.5 cm), linear, almost without translucent dots; petals twice length of sepals, which have fringes of stalked black dots. Br Isles: SW Eng, Wales vr; Eur: W France vr; on acid rocks. Fl 6–7.

KEY TO ST JOHN'S-WORTS (*HYPERICUM*)

1 Low shrubby plants – petals soon falling – stamens in 5 bundles **2**
  Herbs, rarely woody and at base only – petals persisting – stamens in 3 bundles **3**
2 Erect, without creeping woody stems – freely branched – fls 2 cm across – stamens same length as petals – fr a berry... *Hypericum androsaemum* (p 136 F)
  Creeping woody stems, hardly branched – fls 7–8 cm across – stamens shorter than petals – fr a dry capsule...*H. calycinum* (p 136 G)
3 Plant downy, at least on undersides of lvs... **4**
  Plant hairless.. **6**
4 Lvs hairless above, ± downy below .... *H. montanum* (p 136 E)
  Lvs hairy on both sides.. **5**
5 Bog plant with runners and short erect stems to 20 cm tall – lvs round to oval, woolly – fls only 4–5 together ....*H. elodes* (p 136 H)
  Dry-gd plant with erect stems only to 60 cm tall – lvs oblong to elliptical, only downy – fls many together .... *H. hirsutum* (p 136 D)
6 Stems with 4 angles or 4 wings.. **7**
  Stems round, or with 2 raised ridges only **10**
7 Petals shorter than, or equalling sepals – stem four-winged **8**
  Petals 2–3 times length of sepals – stem four-winged or only four-angled **9**
8 Stems to 20 cm, v slender – lvs to 8 mm long, narrow-elliptical – petals golden yellow....................
                                                     H. canadense (p 136 Cii)
  Stems 30–60 cm, stout – lvs 1–2 cm long, broad oval – petals pale yellow........................
                                                   H. tetrapterum (p 136 C)
9 Sepals blunt – stem four-angled, not winged – lvs narrowed to base – translucent lf-dots few or none ....*H. maculatum* (p 136 B)
  Sepals pointed – stem four-winged – lvs wavy-edged, clasping stem – translucent lf-dots many.......
                                                 H. undulatum (p 136 Ci)
10 Stems creeping to ascending – petals not much longer than sepals............. *H. humifusum* (p 136 J)
  Stems erect – petals at least twice length of sepals **11**
11 Lvs of main stem with cordate bases – sepals oval, blunt...............................*H. pulchrum* (p 136 I)
  Lvs of main stem narrowed to base – sepals narrow, pointed **12**
12 Sepals without fringe of black glands – many translucent lf-dots – oval lvs ....
                                               H. perforatum (p 136 A)
  Sepals with fringe of black glands, no or v few translucent lf-dots on linear lvs................................
                                               H. linarifolium (p 136 Ji)

VIOLET FAMILY

Violaceae

Of this family, there is only one genus, *Viola*, in Br Isles and W Eur. They are herbs (**Violets** per, some **Pansies** ann) with alt, stalked lvs with stipules in pairs at lf-bases. Fls solitary, irregular; 5 sepals, all with back-pointing appendages; 5 petals, the lower lip-petal with a spur; frs three-valved capsules. Many Violets form hybrids which are hard to name. Pansies have conspicuous divided lf-like stipules, side petals directed upwards, often forming a flat 'face'; Violets have narrow unlobed stipules, and side petals horizontally spreading.

KEY TO VIOLETS AND PANSIES (*VIOLA*)

1 Stipules undivided to merely fringed, not pinnately- or palmately-lobed – side petals spreading outwards..**(Violets) 2**
  Stipules lfy, pinnately- or palmately-lobed – side petals arching up to top of fl, often forming a 'face' to fl ....**(Pansies) 9**
2 Bog or marsh plant with no stems above gd – undergd rhizome from which arise long-stalked, blunt, kidney-shaped lvs and lilac, dark-veined fls..*V. palustris* (p 140 G)
  Stems above gd – plants with tufts of lvs, or lfy shoots – all lvs ± pointed at tips **3**
3 Lf-stalks, frs, and (usually) lvs downy **4**
  Lf-stalks, frs and lvs hairless.. **6**
4 Lvs and their stalks with spreading hairs – no runners – fls unscented.. **5**
  Lvs often ± hairless, but stalks with close down – creeping runners present – fls sweet-scented ....*V. odorata* (p 140 D)
5 Sepals pointed – central lf-rosette without fls – fls on side-branches only – (vr, Teesdale)..............
                                                                                                              V. rupestris (p 140 Ai)
  Sepals blunt – fls and lvs all direct from rootstock..*V. hirta* (p 140 C)
6 Central lf-rosette without fls – fls on side-branches – lvs little longer than wide, oval-cordate – stipule-teeth hair-like.. **7**
  Main stem from root grows directly into a fl-stem – lvs at least twice as long as wide, oval-lanceolate – stipule-teeth triangular.. **8**
7 Fls deep violet-blue – spur paler, blunt, curved, notched – sepals with back-appendages 2–4 mm long.. *V. riviniana* (p 140 A)
  Fls pale lilac-blue – spur darker, pointed, straight, unnotched – sepals with back-appendages tiny, about 1 mm long..*V. reichenbachiana* (p 140 B)
8 Lvs oval-lanceolate, base rounded – stipules to only ⅓ length of lf-stalk ....*V. canina* (p 140 F)
  Lvs lanceolate, base tapered into stalk – stipules to ½ length of lf-stalk................*V. lactea* (p 140 E)
9 Per plants of hths, dunes, moors, gsld **10**
  Ann plants of ar and open gd.. **11**
10 Flowering shoots arising singly (from undergd creeping rhizome), bearing only 1 or 2 fls on long (5–9-cm) stalks – fls 2.0–3.5 cm across from top to bottom, yellow (or purple) ....*V. lutea* (p 142 J)
  Flowering shoots arising in branched tufts, with many fls on each – fls on shorter (2–5 cm) stalks – fls 1.5–2.5 cm across from top to bottom, yellow, or yellow and purple ....
                                                                                                V. tricolor spp *curtisii* (p 142 I)
11 Petals longer than sepals, violet-blue and yellow...............................*V. tricolor* spp *tricolor* (p 142 I)
  Petals shorter than sepals, yellow ....*V. arvensis* (p 140 H)

VIOLET FAMILY

Violaceae

Violets, Pansies

A Common Dog-violet, *Viola riviniana*, our commonest Violet, is an un-scented per, ± hairless herb, 2–20 cm, with lfy shoots bearing fls, arising round a central flless lf-rosette. Lvs long-stalked with cordate blades, 0.5–4.0 cm long, and 2 narrow stipules with **wavy fringes** at stalk-base. Fls 14–25 mm across, on stalks 5–10 cm. Sepals pointed, with large **square-cut** appendages. Petals blue-violet, but variable. Spur **curved up**, **blunt**, **notched**, **paler** than petals. Strong purple veins especially on lower petal. Capsule **hairless**, three-angled, pointed. Br Isles, Eur; vc in wds, hbs, gslds, rocks. Fl 3–5; often again 8–10, often without petals. **Ai Teesdale Violet**, *V. rupestris*, resembles A in having fls on lfy side-shoots (not direct from flless central rosette), and C below in closely **downy lvs**, **lf-stalks** and **frs**. Lvs 5–10 mm, blunt to **kidney-shaped**; spurs thick, pale, furrowed. N Eng; vr on limestone rocks in Teesdale. Fl 5.

B Early Dog-violet, *V. reichenbachiana*, is close to A but lvs and stipules narrower; sepal appendages v short (less than ¼ sepals); fls (**Ba**) **pale lilac**, **spur straight**, **pointed**, **unnotched**, **violet**, **darker** than petals (petals narrower than in A). Br Isles: S Eng, Wales lc; N Eng, Ire vl; Scot vr; Eur c; in dry, especially chky wds and hbs. Fl 3–5.

C Hairy Violet, *V. hirta*, differs from A and B in its **spreading** hairs on lvs, stalks and capsules; **blunt** sepals; all lvs and fls arise directly from **rootstock** of plant, no lfy stems or runners. Petals pale-violet blue, unscented; lvs **narrow**, cordate. Br Isles; GB N to mid Scot f-la; Ire vr; Eur f; on calc gsld, scrub, rocks. Fl 3–5.

D Sweet Violet, *V. odorata*, our only fragrant Violet, like C is hairy, has blunt sepals, and lvs and fls all arise from rootstock; but it is **closely downy** – (**not spreading** –) hairy, has broader, glossier lvs, (becoming bigger in summer) and rooting runners; fls (**D**) **dark** violet or white (sometimes other tints). Scot vr-o in N, f-lc in S; Eur c: in hbs, wds, scrub, usually on calc soils (often an escape). Fl 3–5.

E Pale Dog-violet, *V. lactea*, resembles F, but has still narrower lanceolate lvs with rounded to **wedge-shaped** bases, **not cordate** below. Fls all pale milky-violet to **greyish-pink**, with **short greenish** spurs, upper stipules **as long as** lf-stalks. Br Isles: Eng, Wales vl on hths, c in SW only; W Ire vl in damp gsld; W France lc. Fl 5–6. **Ei Fen Violet**, *V. stagnina*, has narrow lanceolate lvs, long stipules, and pale fls like E, but lvs have **truncate** to **cordate** (**not** wedge-shaped) bases; petals round, blunt, **bluish-white**; spurs v short, **no longer than** calyx-appendages (twice calyx-appendages in F). E, central Eng, vr; Ire, E France to Denmark, r; in fens. Fl 5–6.

F Heath Dog-violet, *V. canina*, is ± hairless like A, with creeping stems, but without a basal lf-rosette. Lvs narrowed, **oval-lance-shaped**, with rounded bases; stipules ⅓ to ½ length of lf-stalk, teeth broader, not fringe-like. Fls deep slate-blue (not violet); spur straight, blunt, yellowish. Br Isles, Eur; lf only on hths, acid gsld, fens. Fl 4–6.

G Marsh Violet, *V. palustris*, low per herb; long creeping runners bear long-stalked hairless **kidney-shaped** lvs 1–4 cm wide. Fls 10–15 mm wide, with **pale lilac**, **blunt** petals with **dark** purple veins, and blunt spurs. Br Isles, Eur; o-lc in acid marshes and bogs (decreased through drainage). Fl 4–7.

H Field Pansy, *V. arvensis*, ann with oval, deeply- but bluntly-toothed lvs; pinnate stipules with large, toothed, lf-like end-lobes. Fls creamy-yellow, 8–20 mm across from top to bottom of fl, petals not longer than sepals. Br Isles, Eur; c on ar, wa. Fl 4–10. **Hi Dwarf Pansy**, *V. kitaibeliana*, tiny downy ann with concave fls 5 mm across vertically. Cornwall, vr on dunes; France N to Calais r on coast. Fl 4–7.

140

cont

141

VIOLET FAMILY

Violaceae

◀ **I Wild Pansy,** *V. tricolor*, is variable: either ann weed of wa and ar (ssp *tricolor*) or tufted per (ssp *curtisii*) of dry gsld and dunes. Pinnate stipules have end-lobes narrow, untoothed, not lf-like; fl 1.5–2.5 cm across from top to bottom, yellow, blue-violet or partly both; petals longer than sepals, flat. Br Isles, W Eur f-lc. Fl 4–9.

J Mountain Pansy, *V. lutea*, **low creeping** per with fls large (2.0–2.5 cm across from top to bottom), on **long** stalks, bright yellow or sometimes blue-violet; stipules with palmate lobes. N and W Br Isles, f on upland and mt gslds, moors on less acid soils; Eur: France, Germany vl in uplands. Fl 5–8.

CAMPION FAMILY

Caryophyllaceae

Herbs with lvs nearly always in opp equal pairs, unlobed and untoothed, mostly without stipules (but see Key and pp 156–158). Fls in forked cymes, rarely solitary or in lf-axils. Petals and sepals 5 (sometimes 4), petals sometimes abs; stamens normally twice number of sepals. Ovary superior, styles 2, 3 or 5; fr a one-celled capsule (berry in *Cucubalus*), opening by teeth at top, equal (or twice) number of styles. Larger members of the family are easily recognized; v small ones are more difficult, because fl-details are so hard to see.

KEY TO CAMPION FAMILY

1 Lvs alt – tiny prostrate plant of lake shores (S Devon, Eur r) .... *Corrigiola litoralis* (p 158 F)
  Lvs opp **2**
2 Lvs without stipules **3**
  Lvs with stipules **21**
3 Fls with a receptacle-cup – fr a one-seeded nut, enclosed in the cup – small prostrate herbs with awl-shaped lvs, joined in pairs .... *Scleranthus* (p 158)
  Fls with no receptacle-cup – ovary free from sepals **4**
4 Fr a berry – climbing herb with joined sepals, 3 styles .... *Cucubalus* (p 152)
  Fr a capsule **5**
5 Sepals joined into a calyx-tube **6**
  Sepals all free **11**
6 Styles 2 .... **7**
  Styles 3 to 5 (or male plants with stamens only) **9**
7 Calyx-tube with white seams alternating with the teeth – fl-head surrounded by a sheath of chaffy scales .... *Kohlrauschia* (p 144)
  Calyx-tube without white seams – no sheath of chaffy scales to fl-heads **8**
8 Base of calyx enclosed tightly by epicalyx of 1–3 bracts .... *Dianthus* (p 144)
  No epicalyx around base of calyx .... *Saponaria* (p 144)
9 Calyx with long narrow teeth longer than petals – fls large, 2–4 cm across, purple ....
                                                                                                        Agrostemma (p 144)
  Calyx-teeth not longer than petals **10**
10 Styles 3 or 5 (normally) – capsule opening has twice as many teeth as there are styles ....
                                                                                                        Silene (key p 148)
  Styles 5 – capsule opening with 5 teeth .... *Lychnis* (p 146)
11 Petals present **12**
  No petals present **20**
12 Petals deeply bifid **13**
  Petals not bifid, sometimes toothed **15**
13 Styles 3, lvs almost hairless .... *Stellaria* (p 150)
  Styles 5 .... **14**
14 Lvs, almost hairless, 2–5 cm, cordate at base – petals bifid more than ½ their length ....
                                                                                                        Myosoton (p 150)
  Lvs v hairy, 0.5–2.5 cm, rounded at base – petals bifid to less than ½ their length ....
                                                                                                        Cerastium (key p 149)

15 Petals jaggedly toothed – fls in umbel-like head...*Holosteum* (p 150)
   Petals not jagged – fls in forked cymes.. **16**
16 4–5 sepals – 4–5 styles.. **17**
   5 sepals – but 2–3 styles only.. **18**
17 Small erect (3–10-cm tall) herb – narrow strap-shaped grey-green lvs – sepals with white margins
   – fls erect, not often opening – capsule with 8 teeth..*Moenchia* (p 152)
   Low (2–5 cm tall) creeping to ascending herb – linear lvs less than 2 mm wide, bright green –
   capsule splitting to base into 4 or 5 parts... *Sagina* (key p 160)
18 Lvs broad fleshy close-set – greenish petals – spherical frs – seashore plant ....*Honkenya* (p 154)
   Lvs not fleshy.. **19**
19 Lvs oval, to 2.5 cm, with 3 strong veins in each – in shady places......................*Moehringia* (p 152)
   Lvs oval, less than 1 cm, one strong vein in each – in open places.........................*Arenaria* (p 154)
   Lvs linear ....*Minuartia* (p 154)
20 Lvs linear, rounded on back..*Sagina* (key p 160)
   Lvs oval, 5–7 mm long × 4–5 mm wide ....*Stellaria pallida* (p 150 D)
21 Small sprawling herb, 5–10 cm tall, much-branched, with forking stems – tiny obovate lvs in
   whorls of 4 – fls 3 mm across...*Polycarpon tetraphyllum* (p 158 C)
   At least the lower lvs in opp pairs... **22**
22 Fls in open forked, or one-sided cymes – conspicuous petals, at least as long as sepals – lvs
   almost cylindrical, fleshy... **23**
   Fls minute in dense, clusters in lf-axils – petals and sepals, 5, minute – lvs oval – low creeping
   plants.. **24**
23 Styles 5 ....*Spergula* (p 156)
   Styles 3 ....*Spergularia* (p 156)
24 Fls white, in apparent whorls in lf-axils – sepals hooded with a little white point on tip of each –
   upper lvs in equal pairs..*Illecebrum* (p 158)
   Fls green, in axillary clusters, not whorled – sepals not white, not hooded – upper lvs alt.................
   Herniaria (p 158)

CAMPION FAMILY *Caryophyllaceae*

Pinks, Campions, Catchflies

Pinks (*Dianthus*) have stiff, linear opp lvs, often waxy-grey; fls pink to red, or white, sometimes fragrant, with petals toothed or fringed, often spotted. Sepals fused into a cylindrical tube; epicalyx of scales below the calyx. **Campions** and **Catchflies** (*Lychnis* and *Silene*) are usually taller than Pinks, with 5 petals, cleft ± deeply into 2 lobes; ribbed, often inflated calyx-tubes with **no** epicalyx; styles 5 or 3.

KEY TO PINKS (*DIANTHUS*)

1 Fls in heads with bracts around head.. **2**
   Fls solitary or few, not in heads... **4**
2 Bracts and epicalyx hairy – fls 8–13 mm across.. *D. armeria* (p 144 A)
   Bracts and epicalyx hairless – fls 20 mm or more across **3**
3 Lvs linear – epicalyx of tough brown scales ½ length of calyx...............*D. carthusianorum* (p 144 C)
   Lvs broadly lanceolate – epicalyx of green scales as long or longer than calyx.......................................
   D. barbatus (p 144 Ci)
4 Petals cut ⅓–½ way down.. **5**
   Petals undivided or only toothed to ⅓ length or less.. **6**
5 Stem downy below – petals cut ⅓ way down .... *D. gallicus* (p 144 Diii)
   Stem hairless below – petals cut to middle...*D. plumarius* (p 144 Dii)
6 Stem downy below – each petal with a dark bar across base, and pale dots..... *D. deltoides* (p 144 B)
   Stem hairless – petals without bars or dots **7**
7 Plant 10–20 cm – lvs rough-edged – petals bearded above .... *D. gratianopolitanus* (p 144 D)
   Plant 20–50 cm – lvs smooth – petals smooth ....*D. caryophyllus* (p 144 Di)

Pinks, Soapwort, Corncockle, Campions, Catchflies etc

A   Deptford Pink, *Dianthus armeria*, rigidly erect ann, 30–60 cm, with linear, pointed, keeled stem-lvs, and a basal rosette of lanceolate lvs, all dark **green** (**not grey**). Fls stalkless, rose-red, 8–13 mm, in close terminal heads with erect green hairy calyx, bracts and epicalyx scales. Br Isles: Eng, Wales, r and l; Scot vr; Eur o-lc to S; on hbs, rds, dry sandy gslds. Fl 7–8.   **Ai   Childling Pink**, *Kohlrauschia* (*Petrorhagia*) *nanteulii*, resembles a slender ± hairless A; linear lvs fused into short sheath below, and the small (6–9 mm) pink fls in dense oval heads (opening one at a time), with white **seams** on the calyx-tube, surrounded by a group of broad, papery, shiny-brown bracts; petals notched. S Eng vr on coast; Eur: W France r on shingly or sandy gd usually near sea. Fl 7–8.   ***Aii**   *K. prolifera* differs only in downy stem and lf-sheaths longer. Eur; o on chk gsld. Fl 7–8.

B   Maiden Pink, *D. deltoides*, per herb with both creeping stems and erect fl-shoots 10–20 cm. Lvs 10–25 mm, linear, pointed, grey-green, edges **hairy**. Fls larger than in A, 18 mm, **solitary** or **2–3** in terminal groups; rose-red, toothed petals (**Ba**) with a dark stripe across base and pale dots above. Epicalyx of 2–4 oval hairy scales ½ length of calyx-tube. GB (not N Scot) r – vlf; Eur lf; on dry sandy fields, hbs. Fl 6–9.

*C   Carthusian Pink, *D. carthusianorum*, is like a much taller (20–60 cm) per version of A; lvs linear, **hairless**, with basal sheaths 4 times as long as wide; fls 20 mm across, red, crimson-spotted, in dense heads; bracts and epicalyx of leathery **brown** scales; calyx-tubes **purple**. Eur f to E and S; on dry gsld, hbs, open wds. Fl 5–8.   **Ci   Sweet-William**, *D. barbatus*, sometimes introd (from S Eur) o, has dense flat-topped fl-heads and (unlike C) epicalyx-scales longer than calyx. Fl 7–8.

D   Cheddar Pink, *D. gratianopolitanus*, **hairless tufted** per herb, 10–20 cm; creeping runners and erect fl-stems with **rough**-edged grey linear lvs, 2–6 cm. Fls usually **solitary**, about 25 mm across, fragrant; petals toothed to ⅙ of length, rose-pink, bearded; epicalyx of 4–6 blunt grey-green scales, ¼ length of calyx. **Eng** (**Cheddar only**) vr; Eur vl on limestone rocks. Fl 6–7.   **Di   Clove Pink**, *D. caryophyllus*, taller (20–50 cm) than D; lvs **smooth**-edged; fls **larger** (35–40 mm), fragrant, with **unbearded** narrower petals. Introd from S Eur in GB, Eur; r on old walls. Fl 7–8.   **Dii   Wild Pink**, *D. plumarius*, resembles D in its rough-edged lvs, but has petals cut ½ **way** into slender teeth; fls 25–35 mm; epicalyx of 2–4 pointed lobes to ⅓ length of calyx. Introd from S Eur in GB, Eur; r on old walls. Fl 7–8.   ***Diii   Jersey Pink**, *D. gallicus*, also resembles D, but has deeply cut petals (to ⅓ length), stiff short lvs and downy stems. Jersey, W France; vr on dunes. Fl 6–8.

E   Soapwort, *Saponaria officinalis*, robust hairless erect per herb (30–90 cm) with runners. Branched fl-stems bear pink fls, about 2.5 cm across, in forked cymes. Sepals joined into a cylindrical tube with 5 teeth; no epicalyx. Petals long-stalked, unnotched. Stamens 10. Br Isles (probably an ancient introd) o-lf on hbs, rds, wa; Eur o in damp wds. Fl 7–9.

F   Corncockle, *Agrostemma githago*, tall hairy ann with narrow lanceolate lvs; pale reddish-purple fls, 3–5 cm across; calyx-tube v hairy, ribbed; sepals hairy, linear, much longer than the broad, notched petals. GB now r; Eur la but decreasing; on ar. Fl 6–8.

G   White Campion, *Silene alba*, sticky-hairy ann to per herb, 30–100 cm, with elliptical – lanceolate opp lvs, 3–10 cm. Infl forks repeatedly, with a fl in each fork. Fls white, 25–30 mm; petals deeply-forked with a scale on each petal where it narrows to its stalk. Plants dioecious, male fls with 10 stamens, female with 5 styles. Capsules with 10 **erect** teeth at top. Br Isles, Eur: c in ar, wa, hbs. Fl 5–10.

H   Red Campion, *S. dioica*, v like G, but usually per, with creeping rhizomes;

A

B

Ba

5mm

C

D

E

F

G

H

I

J

145

narrower blunt calyx-teeth; bright rose-pink petals; capsule-teeth on female plants are **arched back**. Br Isles, Eur; vc (but vlr, eg, Cambridge area); in hbs, wds, on base-rich soils. Fl 3–10. Hybrids (pinkish-white petals) between G and H are c where they meet.

I Ragged-Robin, *Lychnis flos-cuculi*, resembles H in coloured fls 30–40 mm, but petals **deep** rose-red, usually divided each into **4 v narrow lobes**. Lvs narrow-lanceolate, rough but **hairless**, broader from root. Both stamens and styles are present in each fl (unlike G and H). Br Isles, Eur; c in moist mds, fens, wet wds. Fl 5–8.

J Sticky Catchfly, *L viscaria*, differs from I in having stems **sticky** below the lf-pairs; infls more whorled, denser; petals **red**, only slightly notched into 2 lobes; fls 18–20 mm. Br Isles: Wales, Scot vr; W Eur N to Denmark, lf; on dry volcanic rocks in GB, sandy gslds in Eur. Fl 6–8. **Ji Alpine Catchfly**, *L. alpina*, much smaller (5–15 cm) than J, fls 6–12 mm in rounded heads; stems not sticky; Br Isles: vr on mts Cumbria, E Scot on metalliferous rocks; **not Eur** (outside mt areas or Arctic). Fl 6–7.

Campions, Catchflies, continued

A Bladder Campion, *Silene vulgaris*, waxy ± hairless per herb, 25–90 cm, with erect shoots bearing branched forking infls. Lvs oval, pointed, greyish; fls white, 18–20 mm across, with cleft petals; calyx-tubes strongly ribbed and inflated, 10–12 mm long, like oval bladders; 3 styles, 10 stamens. Br Isles, Eur, c in S, rarer to N; on ar, rds, hbs, open gd, especially on chk and sand. Fl 6–8.

B Sea Campion, *S. maritima*, resembles a lower-growing (8–25 cm) version of A, with cushions or mats of non-flowering shoots of smaller, fleshier, more **waxy** lvs. Infls few (1–4); fls larger (20–25 mm), **erect**, (not drooping); calyx-tubes **cylindrical**-oblong, not oval, 17–20 mm long. Br Isles, Eur, c on coasts, shingle, cliffs; also on mts inland. Fl 6–8. **Bi Moss Campion**, *S. acaulis*, forms dense green mossy cushions, dotted with pink, solitary, 9–12-mm fls on v short stalks. N Wales to N Scot f-la on mt cliffs and screes. Fl 7–8.

C Spanish Catchfly, *S. otites*, erect per herb, 20–90 cm, with **much smaller** fls than in A or B, and **sticky** stems below; basal rosette-lvs **narrow spoon-shaped**, **stalked**; upper lvs linear-lanceolate, stalkless, with close short hairs. Infl branched, with open apparent whorls of fls 3–4 mm across, greenish-yellow; calyx shortly bell-shaped and ten-veined; petals undivided, lack scales above; plants usually dioecious, but sometimes bisexual fls occur on otherwise male plant. **Eng vl and r** **(Breckland only)** on dry sandy chk gsld; Eur o-lf; on dunes (a 'steppe' plant). Fl 6–8.

D Night-flowering Catchfly, *S. noctiflora*, hairy erect ann, 15–60 cm, rather like a much smaller less branched rosy-fld sticky *S. alba*, (p 144 G), but fls open at night, with petals rolled inwards by day to show yellow undersides; 10 stamens, 3 styles in each fl. Br Isles, lf in S, vr to N; Eur f: on ar on sand and chk. Fl 7–9. **Di Small-flowered Catchfly**, *S. gallica*, stickily-hairy ann, 15–40 cm; narrow lanceolate sessile upper lvs, spoon-shaped lower ones; elongated spike-like infl of white fls 10–12 mm across, often red-spotted, with shallow notched petals. Br Isles o; Eur lf; on sandy ar, wa. Fl 6–10. **Dii Forked Catchfly**, *Silene dichotoma*, has infls that are forked below (with fls in forks), elongated like one-sided spikes above; fls white, 15 mm, petals cleft. Introd GB and W Eur; on wa. Fl 7–8.

E Nottingham Catchfly, *S. nutans*, erect per herb ± downy below and sticky in upper parts, 25–80 cm; root-lvs **(Eb)** spoon-shaped, stalked; upper lvs narrow-lanceolate, sessile, pointed, all hairy. Fls **(Ea)** 18 mm, creamy-white, drooping, opening fragrantly at night with rolled back deeply-cleft narrow petals in

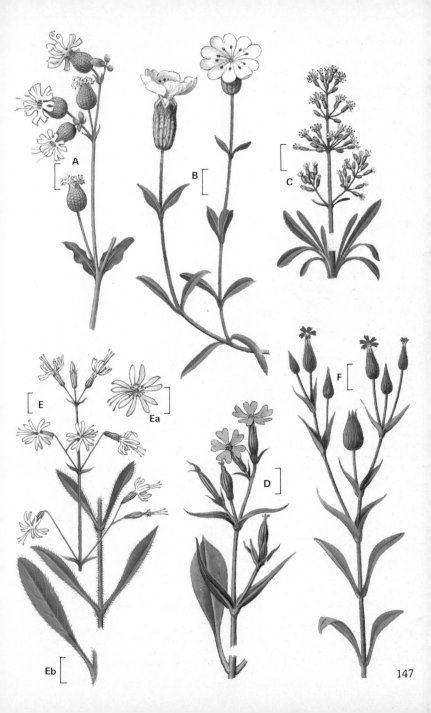

147

◄ loose apparently whorled infls; some populations have yellow or pink-tipped fls. Fr **short-stalked** within calyx. Br Isles: E and Central GB N to Aberdeen vla; Eur o-f; on shingle beaches, chk gsld, limestone cliffs, etc. Fl 5–8. **Ei Italian Catchfly,** *S. italica,* is v like E; per herb, but with erect, more open fls; capsule-stalk (within calyx-tube) at least as long as fr. Introd **SE Eng vr** (SE Eur on calc rocks). Fl 5–6.

F Sand Catchfly, *S. conica,* short erect few-fld sticky-hairy grey-green ann; narrow lanceolate lvs; fls 4–5 mm across; petals rose-coloured, bifid, with scales; long, stickily-hairy, oval-conical calyx-tube with about 30 green ribs on a grey background, enlarged in fr. Styles 3. GB N to E Scot o-lf; Eur widespread o-la; on dunes, sandy gsld, especially near coast. Fl 5–6.

KEY TO CAMPIONS AND CATCHFLIES (*SILENE* AND *LYCHNIS*)

1 Styles 5 .... **2**
  Styles 3 .... **6**
2 Plants dioecious **3**
  Plants hermaphrodite (fls with both stamens and styles) **4**
3 Fls white – capsule-teeth upright .... *Silene alba* (p 144 G)
  Fls red – capsule-teeth bent back .... *S. dioica* (p 144 H)
4 Stems less than 15 cm tall – fls pink, 6–12 mm across, in a dense head – on mts, vr ....
  .... *Lychnis alpina* (p 146 Ji)
  Stems over 30 cm – fls in a loose infl **5**
5 Stems v sticky below fl-pairs – fls in a spike-like panicle – petals slightly notched ....
  .... *L. viscaria* (p 146 J)
  Stems not sticky below lf-pairs – fls in loose forking cymes – petals deeply four-times-cleft ....
  .... *L. flos-cuculi* (p 146 I)
6 Calyx with 20–30 veins, inflated **7**
  Calyx with 10 veins, not inflated **9**
7 Ann plant – calyx downy, swollen below, conical, strongly ribbed, not net veined, teeth narrow
  .... *S. conica* (p 148 F)
  Per plant – calyx hairless, bladder-like, net-veined, teeth broad, triangular **8**
8 Plants forming patches of prostrate non-flowering shoots – fl-stems erect, to 20 cm, one-four-fld
  – calyx cylindrical .... *S. maritima* (p 146 B)
  Plants without prostrate non-flowering shoots – erect fl-stems 25–80 cm, many-fld – calyx egg-
  shaped .... *S. vulgaris* (p 146 A)
9 Calyx hairless **10**
  Calyx hairy or sticky **11**
10 Mt plant, forming cushions with linear lvs 6–12 mm long – fls solitary, pink, 9–12 mm across, on
  short (2 cm) stalks .... *S. acaulis* (p 146 Bi)
  Lowland plant of sandy soils, r – basal lvs narrow, spoon-shaped – stem sticky below – fls yellow-
  green, 3–4 mm across, in an erect panicle 20–30 cm tall .... *S. otites* (p 146 C)
11 Per plant – non-flowering shoots – infl an erect loose panicle of pairs of forked cymes, 25–60 cm
  tall – fls drooping, cream-coloured, 18 mm across .... *S. nutans* (p 146 E)
  Ann plant – no non-flowering shoots – erect infl, few-fld, 15–30 cm tall – petals rosy above,
  rolled up during day, spreading at night .... *S. noctiflora* (p 146 D)

Chickweeds, Stitchworts, etc (*Stellaria, Myosoton, Holosteum,* see key p 149)

Mostly ± hairless slender brittle-stemmed herbs; small white fls in forked cymes, with a fl in each fork (*dichasia*); petals forked; sepals not forming a calyx-tube, but spreading; capsules oval. Styles 3, capsule-teeth 6 (*Stellaria*); styles 5, capsule with 5 split teeth (*Myosoton*).

CAMPION FAMILY
Caryophyllaceae

KEY TO CHICKWEEDS AND STITCHWORTS (*STELLARIA*)

1 Lvs oval or cordate, lower stalked – stems round.. **2**
  Lvs narrow, linear to narrow-oblong, stalkless – stems four-angled **5**
2 Erect plant – petals twice length of sepals .... *Stellaria nemorum* (p 150 I)
  Sprawling plant – petals none, or equalling, or scarcely longer than sepals........................ **3**
3 Stamens 10 – fls 12 mm – sepals 5.0–6.5 mm – seeds have pointed warts .... *S. neglecta* (p 150 E)
  Stamens 1–8 – fls 4–8 mm – sepals 2–5 mm – seeds with blunt warts........................... **4**
4 Petals present – sepals 4–5 mm – stamens 3–7 – anthers reddish – seeds 0.9–1.3 mm ....
                                                                           S. media (p 150 A)
  No petals – sepals 2.0–3.5 mm – stamens 1–3 – anthers grey-violet – seeds 0.6–0.8 mm ....
                                                                           S. pallida (p 150 D)
5 Petals shorter than sepals – calyx funnel-shaped below..*S. alsine* (p 150 J)
  Petals equal to or longer than sepals – calyx rounded below... **6**
6 Bracts wholly green, without chaffy margins – lvs rough-edged – fls 20–30 mm, petals bifid less
  than ½ their length.. *S. holostea* (p 150 C)
  Bracts with white chaffy margins – lvs smooth-edged – fls 5–18 mm – petals bifid more than ½
  length... **7**
7 Bracts with hairs on edges – lvs green – fls 5–12 mm .... *S. graminea* (p 150 B)
  Bracts hairless – lvs ± grey – fls 12–18 mm .... *S. palustris* (p 150 F)

Mouse-ears (*Cerastium*) resemble **Chickweeds** and **Stitchworts** (*Stellaria*), but
mostly have roughly hairy blunt, oblong, stalkless lvs, 5 styles (except for *C.
cerastoides*, which has 3) and **cylindrical** (**not oval**) capsules; 5 free sepals, 5 free
bifid petals. Sandworts (*Arenaria, Minuartia*) are similar, but have undivided petals,
see p 154.

KEY TO MOUSE-EARS (*CERASTIUM*)

1 Styles usually 3, capsule-teeth 6 – vr in high mts in N Eng, Scot ....*C. cerastoides*
  Styles 5, rarely 4 – capsule-teeth twice number of styles... **2**
2 Fls 12 mm across or more – petals usually twice length of sepals – pers with many creeping, non-
  flowering shoots.. **3**
  Fls less than 12 mm across – petals not more than 1½ times length of sepals – mostly ann plants.... **6**
3 Lvs linear-lanceolate to narrow-oblong, with close down .... *C. arvense* (p 152 E)
  Lvs oblong to almost circular, with spreading hairs – r in mts of N GB and N Wales.......................... **4**
4 Stem and young lvs woolly, with long soft white hairs – lvs oval to eliptical – sepals narrow – fr
  curved..*C. alpinum* (p 152 Ei)
  Stem and young lvs with short white hairs – sepals oval-lanceolate – fr straight.............................. **5**
5 Lvs almost round, dark purple-tinged, with many short sticky hairs – vr in Shetland......*C. nigrescens*
  Lvs narrow or wide-elliptical – few sticky hairs – on high mts of N GB ....*C. arcticum*
6 Per, with some non-flowering shoots – no sticky hairs anywhere – fr curved, 9–12 mm long.............
                                                                           C. holosteoides (p 152 A)
  Ann, all shoots have fls – sticky hairs on lvs and sepals – fr less than 10 mm long **7**
7 Fls in compact heads – fr 7–10 mm, curved, with stalk no longer than sepals.................................
                                                                           C. glomeratum (p 152 C)
  Fls in loose infls – fr 4.5–7.0 mm, ± straight, with stalk much longer than sepals and fr................... **8**
8 Bracts of fls wholly green – fl-stalks erect – fls usually four-petalled (rarely five-petalled) ....
                                                                           C. atrovirens (p 152 D)
  Bracts of fls with silvery margins – fl-stalks bent down – 5 petals.. **9**
9 Upper half of bracts silvery – petals ⅔ length of sepals – fr-stalk bent down, but not curved – lvs all
  green..*C. semidecandrum* (p 152 B)
  Bracts with only a narrow silvery edge – petals equalling sepals – fr-stalk curved down – lower lvs
  reddish...*C. pumilum* (p 152 Bi)

Chickweeds, **Stitchworts** etc (see also key to Mouse-ears p 149)

A Common Chickweed, *Stellaria media*, ± hairless ann of sprawling habit, with round stems, cordate lvs; fls 5–38 mm, with deeply bifid white petals, no longer than the spreading, oval, usually hairy sepals; 3–8 red-violet stamens; 3 styles. Seeds round, 0.9–1.3 mm across, red-brown, with rounded warts on surface. Br Isles, Eur; vc in ar, wa everywhere. Fl 1–12. One of the world's most successful weeds.

B Lesser Stitchwort, *S. graminea*, is similar to C below, but has lvs 1.5–4.0 cm long, smooth-edged; bracts hairy with chaffy margins; fls only 5–18 mm across, petals split more than halfway, equalling sepals. Br Isles, Eur; c on acid gslds, hths, open wds. Fl 5–8.

C Greater Stitchwort, *S. holostea*, per herb with weak brittle ± erect stems 15–60 cm long, square, rough-angled; lvs narrow-lanceolate, rigid, 1.5–5.0 cm long, stalkless, ± hairless, but rough-edged (**Ca**); bracts all green. Fls 20–30 mm across, petals divided halfway or less. Br Isles, Eur; vc in hbs, wds, except on v acid soils. Fl 4–6.

D Lesser Chickweed, *S. pallida*, is like small version of A, with no petals (**D**), 1–3 grey-violet stamens; seeds 0.6–0.8 mm across, pale yellow brown, with blunt warts. Br Isles: Eng, Wales (mainly S and E) lf; Scot, Ire vr; Eur lf; on dunes, sandy wa. Fl 3–5, then dries up.

E Greater Chickweed, *S. neglecta*, is like large version of A; fls (**E**) 10–12 mm across; 10 reddish stamens; seeds 1.3–1.7 mm across, dark red-brown, with narrow conical warts. Br Isles: Eng, Wales lf; Scot, Ire vr; Eur lf; on hbs, damp wds, shady riversides. Fl 4–7.

F Marsh Stitchwort, *S. palustris*, resembles C in general habit, with square weak stems and narrow lanceolate lvs; but differs in the wide, chaffy, smooth, hairless bract-edges (**Fa**); lvs smooth-edged, usually waxy grey-green. Fls 12–20 mm across, in few-fld cymes; petals split to base. Br Isles: GB (not N Scot) r-vlf; Ire o; Eur o-vlc (decreasing); on fens, basic marshes. Fl 5–8.

G Water Chickweed, *Myosoton aquaticum*, resembles a large (20–100 cm), more erect version of E; larger, ± hairy, oval, cordate lvs; fls 12–15 mm across, with sticky-hairy stalks, petals far longer than sepals; 10 stamens, **5 styles**; oval capsules open by **5 split teeth**. Br Isles: Eng, Wales; Eur; lc in marshes, streamsides, wet wds on basic soils. Fl 6–10.

*H Umbellate Chickweed, *Holosteum umbellatum*, erect Chickweed-like ann, 3–20 cm tall; easily recognized by tassel-like fl-heads with long, radiating, ± equal fl-stalks; hairless grey lanceolate lvs. Fls 4–5 mm across; white, irregularly jagged petals exceed sepals. Eur N to Denmark now r; on sandy gd, old walls, roofs. Fl 4–6.

I Wood Stitchwort, *Stellaria nemorum*, per of 15–60 cm, resembling tall erect version of E, but with stems hairy all round; lvs (**I**) long-stalked, cordate; fls 13–18 mm across, petals twice length of sepals. Br Isles: W and N of GB lf (**abs SE Eng**); **abs Ire**; Eur vl; in damp wds, especially by streams. Fl 5–6.

J Bog Stitchwort, *S. alsine*, resembles B, but lvs shorter (5–20 mm), smooth, ± grey-green; petals (**Ja**) shorter than sepals; calyx-base funnel-shaped. Stem square (**Jb**). Br Isles, Eur; lc in marshes, wet wds, especially on acid soils. Fl 5–6.

A

B

C
Ca

D 3mm

E

F
Fa

I

H

Ja 3mm

J

G

Jb 5mm

Mouse-ears, etc (see also key, p 149)

A Common Mouse-ear, *Cerastium holosteoides* (*C. fontanum*), is the commonest sp; a low per herb usually less than 20 cm, with runners and erect fl-shoots; stems and lvs all densely **hairy** (but without gland-tipped hairs). Fls in loose cymes, 3–12 mm across; petals white, bifid, equal to or slightly longer than sepals; upper bracts and sepals hairy, with narrow chaffy edges. Stamens usually 10; capsule 9–12 mm long, curved. Br Isles, Eur; vc in gsld, beaches, dunes, rds, wa, mds, etc (grows much taller in wet mds). Fl 4–9.

B Little Mouse-ear, *C. semidecandrum*, much smaller than A, 1–10 cm, ann and **glandular-hairy**. Fls 5–7 mm across; petals only slightly notched; upper bracts (**Bb**) and sepals with **broad** silvery margins, central green part v narrow; 5 stamens; capsule (**Ba**) 4.5–6.5 mm long, scarcely curved; fr-stalks shortly bent down. Br Isles, Eur; f-lc on dry open sandy gd. Fl 4–6. **Bi** *C. pumilum* is close to B in size and habit, but bracts with only a narrow silvery margin, and petals equal sepals; fr-stalk curved. S Eng, r on calc gslds; Eur lc.

C Sticky Mouse-ear, *C. glomeratum*, similar size to A, but like B erect, **ann**, **glandular-hairy**. Fls 8–10 mm, in rather **dense** terminal heads, lvs yellowish; 10 stamens; bracts **without** silvery margins; capsule (**Ca**) 7–10 mm long, curved. Br Isles, Eur; vc on ar, wa, walls, hbs, dunes. Fl 4–9.

D Sea Mouse-ear, *C. atrovirens* (*C. diffusum*), another low glandular-hairy ann resembling B, but of much more open branching, and with all bracts wholly green (no silvery margins); fls 3–6 mm across; capsule (**Da**) 5.0–7.5 mm long, straight. Br Isles, Eur; lc on open sandy gd, usually by sea. Fl 4–7.

E Field Mouse-ear, *C. arvense*, low creeping per, readily distinguished among lowland Mouse-ears by its large fls (12–20 mm across), petals twice length of sepals, and narrow lvs downy with no long hairs. Br Isles: E Eng lf-lc, r-o elsewhere; Ire vr; Eur f; on dry gslds, hbs, rds, especially on chk and sand. Fl 4–8. **Ei** *C. alpinum* also has large fls (18–25 mm across) and v hairy, **rounded** lvs. On basic rock ledges of mts of Scot, N Wales, Eng Lakeland, and of Eur. Fl 6–8.

F Upright Chickweed, *Moenchia erecta*, is not much like a Chickweed; it is a short stiffly erect hairless ann, 3–12 cm; lvs strap-shaped below, acute above, v rigid and waxy. Fls about 8 mm long, usually with 4 petals, 4 sepals, erect on long stalks, only opening briefly in fine weather; sepals pointed with conspicuous white edges. Stamens and styles usually 4. Br Isles: S Eng, S Wales o-lf; **Scot, Ire abs**; Eur: N to Netherlands r-lf; on dry gslds, cliffs, dunes. Fl 4–6.

G Berry Catchfly, *Cucubalus baccifer*, straggling hairy per herb, 60–100 cm, scrambling over other plants; it resembles a large Water-chickweed (*Myosoton aquaticum*, p 150 G) with hairy oval lvs, but fls are 18–20 mm across, sepals joined into a short calyx-tube as in the Campions, and the greenish-cream petals are deeply bifid with scales above their spreading narrow lobes. Frs (**Ga**) – unique in European Caryophyllaceae – are round black berries, 6–8 mm. Br Isles: **Norfolk only**, vr; Eur lc to E and S; in damp wds, riversides. Fl 6–8.

Sandworts, etc (illustrated p 155)

A Three-veined Sandwort, *Moehringia trinervia*, a small, slightly downy ann, 10–30 cm; rather like Chickweed (p 150), but with 3 strong veins in each lf, narrow sepals longer than petals, and petals undivided. Br Isles, Eur; f-lc in wds on richer soils. Fl 5–6.

cont

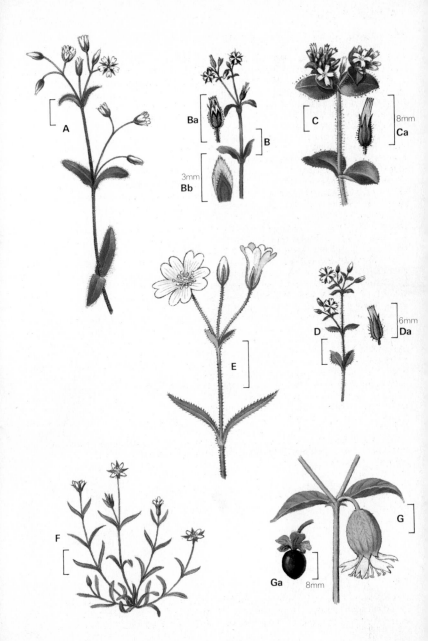

A

Ba

B

Bb 3mm

C

Ca 8mm

E

D

Da 6mm

F

G

Ga 8mm

B Sea Sandwort, *Honkenya peploides*, creeping per, with fleshy lvs (oval-pointed) and stems; fls, among lvs, 6–10 mm across; 5 petals, not notched, greenish-cream, blunt, undivided, not longer than sepals. Br Isles, Eur; lc on beaches and open sand dunes by the sea. Fl 5–8.

C Spring Sandwort, *Minuartia verna*, low cushion-forming per herb, either hairless or sticky-hairy, with many dark green rigid 3-veined linear lvs, 6–15 mm long; fls (**Ca**) with petals white, oval, not notched, a little longer than narrow chaffy-edged sepals. Br Isles: W and N of GB, scattered and vl; Ire vr; Eur: N to Belgium, r; on basic open rocks and screes, especially on old lead workings. Fl 5–9. **Ci** *M. rubella* is a low per, forming cushions 2–8 cm across, with few-fld stems 2–6 cm tall; lvs only 4–8 mm; petals ⅔ sepals; vr on mts of Scot. Fl 6–8. **Cii Mossy Cyphel**, *Cherleria sedoides*, is a cushion-forming alpine herb rather like C, but with tiny green almost stalkless fls of sepals only, 4–5 mm across. Mts of Scot lf. Fl 6–8.

D Fine-leaved Sandwort, *M. hybrida*, slender erect hairless branched ann, 5–20 cm tall, with acute linear lvs and no sterile shoots; fls 6 mm across, white, petals much shorter than white-bordered sepals. Br Isles: Eng, Wales, r-lf; Eur o-lf; on walls, dry stony gsld, sandy ar etc. Fl 5–6. **Di Teesdale Sandwort**, *M. stricta*, also erect tufted per herb, 5–10 cm, with v narrow one-veined lvs 6–12 mm, in remote pairs on fl-stems; fls 5–8 mm across, white, in few-fld cymes, petals equalling sepals. Teesdale only, in calc flushes; Eur, mts only. Fl 6–7.

E Thyme-leaved Sandwort, *Arenaria serpyllifolia*, low, spreading to bushy-branched hairy ann, 2.5–20 cm tall, with many tiny hairy oval pointed lvs. White fls 5–6 mm across, petals undivided, shorter than sepals; fr (**Eb**) flask-shaped, thick-walled. Seeds (**Ea**) 0.6 mm wide, black. Br Isles, Eur; c on bare gd, chk gsld, ar, walls, wa etc. Fl 6–8.

F *A. leptoclados* differs in having slenderer habit, smaller fls, and narrow-conical, straight-sided capsules (**F**) with thin walls. Distribution and frequency as for E. Fl 5–6.   Other, vr *Arenaria* spp, with petals longer than sepals, occur in mt areas of GB and Ire.   **Fi** *A. ciliata* is a hairy creeping per with lvs oblong to 5 cm tall; fls 12–16 mm across; sepals hairy. **W Ire only**; vr on limestone cliffs near Sligo. Fl 6–7.   **Fii** *A. norvegica* is similar to Fi, but with sepals hairless, lvs almost so; fls 9–12 mm across. Br Isles: N Eng, Scot; r on basic rocks. Fl 6–7.

KEY TO SANDWORTS (*ARENARIA, MINUARTIA*)

1 Lvs **oval-triangular, pointed**, 3–5 mm long – fls 3–6 mm across, petals shorter than sepals......... **2**
   Lvs **obovate** to **spoon-shaped**, 4–6 mm long – fls 9–16 mm across, petals longer than sepals...... **3**
   Lvs **linear**, under 2 mm wide.. **4**
2 Capsule flask-shaped, sides curved, thick-walled – fls 5–8 mm across.......................................
                                  Arenaria serpyllifolia (p 154)
   Capsule conical, straight-sided, thin-walled – fls 3–5 mm across .... *Arenaria leptoclados* (p 154)
3 Lvs and sepals with hairy edges – fls 12–16 mm across – W Ire only, r .... *Arenaria ciliata* (p 154)
   Lvs hairless or hairy only at base – sepals ± hairless – fls 9–12 mm across – N Eng, Scot, r... *Arenaria norvegica* (p 154)
4 All stems erect and with fls, not tufted – fls 6 mm across – petals much shorter than sepals – ann plant... *Minuartia hybrida* (p 154)
   Plant with tufts or cushions of non-flowering shoots as well as erect fl-shoots – petals ⅔ length of sepals, or more – per plant **5**
5 Lvs 4–8 mm long – petals only ⅔ length of sepals – fls 5–9 mm across – Scot mts, vr ....
                                   Minuartia rubella (p 154)
   Lvs 6–15 mm long – petals as long or longer than sepals.. **6**
6 Lvs three-veined – fl-stalks sticky-hairy – fls 8–12 mm across, infls ascending from dense cushion of lfy shoots – lf-pairs ± own length apart on fl-stems................................. *Minuartia verna* (p 154)
   Lvs one-veined – fl-stalks hairless – fls 5–8 mm across – infls strictly erect from small tuft of lfy shoots – lf-pairs much more than own length apart – Teesdale, vr.............. *Minuartia stricta* (p 154)

155

Spurreys, Pearlworts

Spurreys (*Spergula* and *Spergularia*) are low herbs with cylindrical, ± fleshy lvs, **chaffy stipules** and small fls, with 5 white or pink uncleft petals and 5 spreading sepals; either 3 styles (*Spergularia*) or 5 (*Spergula*). **Pearlworts** (*Sagina*, see key p 160), v small plants of Campion family, per or ann, tufted; linear fleshy lvs fused at base in pairs, and **no stipules**; creeping or ascending fl-stems. Fls globular in bud, with 4–5 sepals; petals white, not notched, 4, 5, or none; capsules v tiny.

A   Greater Sea-spurrey, *Spergularia media*, almost hairless, creeping to ascending per herb, to 30 cm long, with v fleshy pointed lvs; fls (**Aa**) white or pink, 8–12 mm across; capsule 7–10 mm long, equalling or longer than stalk; seeds (**Ab**) with a clear **winged** border. Br Isles, Eur; c in salt-marshes. Fl 6–9.

B   Lesser Sea-spurrey, *S. marina*, only to 20 cm long, ann; fls (**B**) always **deep pink**, 6–8 mm across; capsule 4–6 mm long, shorter than stalk; seeds (**Ba**) **without winged** border. Br Isles, Eur; c salt-marshes, r salt springs inland. Fl 6–9.

C   Sand Spurrey, *S. rubra*, is ann, 5–25 cm long, sticky-hairy above, with grey-green, non-fleshy stiff-pointed lvs; stipules silvery (not pale brown as in A and B), narrow; fls (**Ca**) 3–5 mm across, pink; seeds **unwinged**. Br Isles: GB f-lc; Ire r; Eur f-lc; on open sandy or stony acid gslds, hths, wa. Fl 5–9.   **Ci   Greek Sea-spurrey**, *S. bocconii*, like C in lvs and seeds, but stipules broad-triangular, dull, fl-stalks shorter than sepals, and fls 2 mm across in curved, one-sided, unforked racemes. Cornwall, Guernsey; vr on sandy rocky gd by sea. Fl 5–9.

D   Rocky Sea-spurrey, *S. rupicola*, per resembling A, but is 5–15 cm long, with densely stickily-hairy stems and lvs (**D**), and **unwinged** seeds. Br Isles: c on W coasts, vr to S and E; Eur: c W coast France only; sea cliffs. Fl 6–9.

E   Corn Spurrey, *Spergula arvensis*, sticky-hairy ann, 10–30 cm, looking taller than A and C, with weak ascending stems; lvs in conspicuous whorled clusters, **furrowed** below, blunt, with **tiny** stipules that soon fall; fls (**Ea**) 4–7 mm across, white, in forked cymes; seeds with **v narrow wing** or none. Br Isles, Eur; vc on sandy ar and wa. Fl 6–8.

F   *S. morisonii*, v similar to E, but with stiffly erect fl-stem; lvs **unfurrowed** below; seeds with broad wings. Eng vr (introd Sussex); Eur; lf on ar, wa. Fl 4–6.

G   Procumbent Pearlwort, *Sagina procumbens*, low per tufted herb, with a **central non-flowering rosette**, from which arise rooting **runners** that turn up and bear the infls; lvs linear, bristle-tipped; fls on long stalks, 4 sepals, usually no petals (but **Ga** with petals). Br Isles, Eur; vc everywhere, especially on paths, lawns, wall tops, wa, hbs. Fl 5–9.   **Gi   Alpine Pearlwort**, *S. saginoides*, is like G, but larger, mat-forming, with lfy flowering shoots from basal rosette as well as from runners; fls about 4 mm, borne singly on stalks 1–25 cm; 5 sepals, usually 5 petals; 10 stamens. Scot on high mt ledges; Eur: only on mts of centre and N. Fl 6–8.

H   Annual Pearlwort, *S. apetala*, is close to G, but is ann, 3–10 cm tall, and the main stem from the central rosette (which withers early) produces fls (**Ha**); the side branches do not root; lvs have small hairs on edges (**Hb**); 4 blunt sepals, no petals. Br Isles, Eur; c on walls, paths, bare gd. Fl 5–8.   **Hi   *S. ciliata*** is ann v similar to H, but with outer sepals **pointed** (not all blunt as in H) and **adpressed**, also not spreading in fr (as in G and H). Br Isles, o, lc to S; Eur o-lf; dry sandy gd. Fl 5–7.

I   Sea Pearlwort, *S. maritima*, resembles H, but has dark green **fleshy**, **blunt** lvs (**I**); fls (**Ia**) with 4 sepals adpressed in fr as in Hi. Br Isles, Eur; widespread but only lc on bare saline gd on sea coasts. Fl 5–9.

J   Knotted Pearlwort, *S. nodosa*, low tufted per, 5–15 cm, with narrow cylindrical pointed lvs in stiff lateral groups or knots along the stems; fls few, 0.5–1.0 cm across, with 5 white unnotched **petals** twice length of sepals; 10 stamens, 5 styles. Br Isles: l mostly to W and N; Eur widespread but lf; on bare damp sandy or peaty gd on dunes, hths, mts, etc. Fl 7–9.

cont

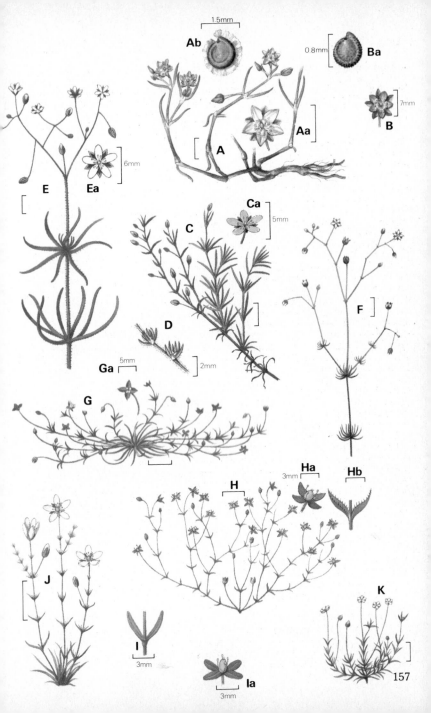

157

◀ **K Heath Pearlwort**, *S. subulata*, forms low cushions of dark green sticky-hairy bristle-tipped lvs, from which arise long, 2–4 cm, erect, ± leafless fl-stalks, bearing erect white fls 4–5 mm across; 5 petals and glandular sepals of equal length. Br Isles: widespread but vl, except in N of GB and NW Ire; Eur o; on dry sandy hths. Fl 6–8.

▶ **Smaller ± prostrate plants of open ground**

A Coral Necklace, *Illecebrum verticellatum*, prostrate hairless ann of v distinctive form: tiny stipulate oval grey-green lvs (2–6 mm long) in pairs subtend conspicuous shining whorl-like clusters of tiny fls, 8–12 per whorl. Each fl, about 2–3 mm long, has 5 thick corky white sepals, hood-shaped with bristle-tips; 5 v tiny petals; 5 stamens. **SW Eng only**; W Eur: N to Denmark, western; vlf on damp acid sandy gd by ponds, or in trackways on hths or wds. Fl 7–9.

B Annual Knawel, *Scleranthus annuus*, low spreading **ann**, with linear-pointed lvs (no stipules), joined in pairs at base around stem. Clusters of minute fls, 4 mm across, with 5 sepals and no petals, occur in lf-axils and terminally. Sepals, straight, grey-green, pointed, with narrow white margins, arise from a short hairless calyx-tube (**Ba**) that encloses the 10 or fewer stamens and tiny ovary. Br Isles widespread but only lf; Eur f-lc; on dry sandy and gravelly wa, ar, gsld. Fl 6–8. **Bi Perennial Knawel**, *S. perennis*, much rarer **per**, woody below; sepals **blunt** with broad white margins, incurved in fr; basal cup hairy. Br Isles: E Anglia, central Wales vr; Eur r; on basic rocks or chk gsld. Fl 6–8.

C Four-leaved Allseed, *Polycarpon tetraphyllum*, is another small ann plant, with branched erect stem, 5–15 cm tall, hairless, with blunt oval lvs apparently in whorls of 4 (really 2 pairs, close-set), 8–13 mm long. Fls tiny, 2–3 mm across, in much-forked cymes (*dichasia*); 5 white-margined, hooded sepals, 5 narrow tiny petals. SW Eng; Eur: W France; r and l in open sandy wa near sea. Fl 6–7.

D Smooth Rupturewort, *Herniaria glabra*, prostrate mat-forming ann or bi herb, ± hairless, with clusters of tiny (2 mm) green fls in axils of oval lvs 3–7 mm long. 5 sepals, green, hairless; 5 petals, white, minute; ovary in a cup; frs acute, longer than sepals. E Eng r and l; Eur o-lf; on bare chalky gd. Fl 7.

E Fringed Rupturewort, *H. ciliolata*, differs from D in being a per, woody at base, with **hairy** lvs (**E**), and **blunt** frs no longer than calyx. Br Isles: Cornwall, Channel Is; Eur: W France; vr and l on sandy gd and rocks. Fl 6–8.

F Strapwort, *Corrigiola litoralis*, is another small, branched prostrate ann. Stems often reddish; lvs linear-lanceolate, all alt, fleshy glaucous-grey, with blunt apices, widest near tips, tiny stipules. Fls minute, 1–2 mm across, in crowded terminal and axillary clusters; 5 blunt green-red sepals with **white** edges; 5 white or **red**-tipped petals about equal length. **Eng, only now in S Devon**, vr but la; Eur: W France to Denmark r in damp sandy or gravelly open places, usually on lakeshores flooded in winter. Fl 7–8.

PURSLANE FAMILY *Portulacaceae*

Portulacaceae resemble Caryophyllaceae except for their calyx of 2 sepals and their three-seeded (not many-seeded) capsules.

G Pink Purslane, *Montia sibirica*, erect hairless fleshy ann to per herb, 15–40 cm; long-stalked oval basal lvs, tapered at both ends, stem-lvs in a single, opp, stalkless, but **separate** pair. Fls in raceme-like cymes, 15–20 mm across; 5 notched petals, **pink** with darker veins; 5 sepals, 5 stamens to each fl. Br Isles: GB lf in S, r to N; Ire r; W Eur lf; introd in damp wds (native of N America). Fl 4–7.

cont

5mm

Ba

5mm

Ia 3mm

159

PURSLANE FAMILY

Portulacaceae

H Spring Beauty, *M. perfoliata*, though of similar floral structure, looks v little like G; it is a hairless ann, 10–20 cm, with long-stalked root-lvs rather like those of G, but with its fleshy stem-lvs (**H**) **joined in a pair**, forming a ring round the stem; tiny (5–8 mm) white fls have scarcely-notched petals. GB, W Eur; introd on light sandy open gd, ar, wa (native of western N America). Fl 5–7.

I Blinks, *M. fontana*, also looks rather unlike G and H, but more like a Water-starwort (*Callitriche*, p. 443) or Canadian Pondweed (*Elodea*, p. 444). Straggling plant, 2–50 cm long, with narrow spoon-shaped lvs in opp pairs, 2–20 mm long; tiny fls, 2–3 mm across, 2 or 3 together; each fl (**Ia**) has 2 sepals and 5 white petals joined below; 3 seeds to each fr, dark brown or black. Br Isles, W Eur; f-lc on non-chalky springs, bare, usually damp gd, wds or moist ar. Fl 5–10.

CAMPION FAMILY

Caryophyllaceae

KEY TO PEARLWORTS (*SAGINA*)

1   Fls with 4 sepals, 4 stamens – petals usually abs (or else 4, v tiny)... **2**
    Fls with 5 sepals, 8 or 10 stamens – 5 obvious petals **5**
2   Per plant – creeping, rooting runners bearing fl-stems – basal central lf-rosette **without** fl-stems
    from it .... *Sagina procumbens* (p 156 G)
    Ann plant – erect or ascending branches – fls on central stem **from** basal rosette........................... **3**
3   Lvs blunt-tipped – plant only present near sea .... *S. maritima* (p 156 I)
    Lvs bristle-pointed – in dry places – c.. **4**
4   Sepals spreading in fr, all blunt... *S. apetala* (p 156 H)
    Sepals adpressed to fr, 2 outer sepals pointed ....*S. ciliata* (p 156 Hi)
5   Petals twice length of sepals – fls short-stalked – upper lvs in tight clusters on stems ....
    .... *S. nodosa* (p 156 J)
    Petals no longer than sepals **6**
6   Calyx sticky-hairy – fls long-stalked, erect – on dry hths. ....*S. subulata* (p 158 K)
    Calyx neither sticky nor hairy – in mts only... **7**
7   Tiny tufted plant, 1–3 cm tall – lvs 3–6 mm long – ripe fr 2.5 mm long, greenish, dull – on Ben
    Lawers (Scot) only – vr ....*S. intermedia*
    Spreading plants, over 3 cm tall – basal lvs 1.5–3.0 cm long – ripe fr 3–4 mm long, yellowish,
    shiny **8**
8   Rosette-lvs to 2 cm long – stems ascending, not creeping, 2–7 cm tall – fr 3.5–4.0 mm long (with
    seeds).. *S. saginoides* (p 156 Gi)
    Rosette-lvs to 3 cm long – stems creeping, rooting, 2.5–10.0 cm long – fr 3.0–3.5 mm long,
    usually seedless – Scot mts, r... *S. normaniana*

AMARANTH FAMILY

Amaranthaceae

(*Not illustrated*) **Common Amaranth**, *Amaranthus retroflexus*, somewhat resembles a downy Goosefoot; erect downy branched grey-green ann, 20–80 cm tall; rough stem; oval, blunt but mucronate, long-stalked lvs; infls dense, stout, branched, of many-fld spikes, lfless above. Fls small, green, with calyx of spoon-shaped sepals 2 mm long; 5 stamens; fr a rounded flattened nut with 2–3 persistent stigmas. Eng, Eur; introd from N America, o in wa, ar. Fl 7–9. Other similar spp sometimes occur on ar or wa.

GOOSEFOOT FAMILY
Chenopodiaceae

KEY TO THE GOOSEFOOT FAMILY

1 Plant **without** obvious lvs, composed of opp-branched, cylindrical, jointed, fleshy stems with swollen segments – lvs in fact adpressed to and fused with stem, only their short tips free – fls minute, not obvious – stamens or styles emerging from pores in segments in Sept ....
Salicornia (p 164)

   Plant **with** obvious **lvs**.. **2**

2 Lvs cylindrical or half-cylindrical, alt... **3**

   Lvs **flat**, though often thick and fleshy... **4**

3 Lvs spine-tipped – on sandy shores..*Salsola* (p 164)

   Lvs not spine-tipped – in salt-marshes...*Suaeda* (p 164)

4 Fls with both stamens and style – sepals 5, ± equal.. **5**

   Fls **either** male **or** female – male fls with 5 sepals and 5 stamens, female with 2 triangular sepal-like bracts only and a tiny ovary.. **6**

5 Calyx-lobes much **thickened** at base and adhering in clusters in fr – lower lvs untoothed...............
Beta (p 166)

   Calyx-lobes **not** thickened at base, **not** adhering in clusters in fr – all lvs ± lobed or toothed ....*Chenopodium* (below)

6 Small shrubs with untoothed elliptical, mealy-grey lvs, lower lvs opp – 2 bracts of the female fls joined into a **cup** well over half way up – in salt-marshes (or a vr herb)............*Halimione* (p 166)

   Herbs with lvs triangular, diamond- or strap-shaped, ± toothed and alt, sometimes opp below – 2 bracts of female fls either free or only joined less than half way up............*Atriplex* (p 166)

KEY TO GOOSEFOOTS (*CHENOPODIUM*)

1 Tufted per, 30–50 cm – lvs sharply triangular – long stigmas projecting from fls...............................
C. bonus-henricus (p 162 F)

   Ann – lvs never sharply triangular – stigmas short... **2**

2 Larger stem – lvs cordate, or truncate-based, with few large wavy teeth ......*C. hybridum* (p 162 G)

   Lvs never cordate, tapered to base.. **3**

3 Stem of infl and fls hairless **4**

   Stem of infl and fls mealy... **8**

4 Lvs oval, untoothed, to 5 cm long, green or purple both sides – stems four-angled – seeds black...*C. polyspermum* (p 162 E)

   Lvs toothed (except uppermost) – stems ridged but not four-angled **5**

5 All fls with 5 sepals, 5 stamens – seeds black – plant tall (40–70 cm)..............................*C. urbicum*

   All fls (except at stem-tip) with 2–4 sepals and stamens – seeds red-brown **6**

6 Lvs mealy-white below, green above, oval, wavy-edged, 1–5 cm long – plant ± creeping...*C. glaucum* (p 162 Bi)

   Lvs not mealy-white, ± red on underside.. **7**

7 Lvs diamond-shaped, much-toothed, thick, fleshy, ± reddish – sepals green with a red flush, not joined above middle – plant tall, ± erect..*C. rubrum* (p 162 D)

   Lvs triangular, scarcely-toothed, thin, purple below – infl dense – fls small – sepals bright red, joined almost to tips, forming a little bag round fr.......................................*C. botryodes* (p 162 H)

8 Lvs oval, grey – sepals rounded on back – plant stinking of rotten fish, ± prostrate.........................
C. vulvaria (p 162 Ei)

   Lvs narrow to linear – sepals keeled on back – plant not stinking, ± erect **9**

9 Lvs toothed, but not clearly three-lobed... **10**

   Some lvs clearly three-lobed ....*C. ficifolium* (p 162 B)

10 Infl lfy to top, with short spreading branches – lvs triangular with many small sharp teeth ....
C. murale (p 162 C)

   Infl lfless above, branches long, erect – lvs diamond-shaped with few shallow teeth ....
C. album (p 162 A)

Goosefoot (*Chenopodium*) is a genus of often robust and erect, sometimes sprawling ann herbs (*C. bonus-henricus* is per), with grooved, often striped stems, often mealy lvs, and clusters of tiny inconspicuous fls in branched cymes; 5 sepals, sometimes partly fused; no petals; stamens usually 2–5; fr a tiny nutlet with one seed. Some of the spp are not v easy to identify; lvs can be significant, but seeds (although they can only be studied with a microscope) are the best guides. **Oraches** (*Atriplex*) are v close, but have **separate** male and female fls, the latter enclosed by conspicuous **triangular bracts**. See also Key, p 161.

A   **Fat-hen**, *Chenopodium album*, v common ann weed, 30–100 cm; lvs grey-green, ± covered with whitish-grey meal, lanceolate to diamond-shaped, bluntly-toothed; infls erect, dense, greyish, not spreading, lfless above. Fls 2 mm wide, five-sepalled (**Aa**). Br Isles, Eur; vf in ar, wa etc. Fl 7–10.

B   **Fig-leaved Goosefoot**, *C. ficifolium*, differs from A in its three-lobed lower lvs (**B**) deeply three-lobed, mid-lobes largest. Eng; Eur; less f than A in ar, wa etc. Fl 7–9.   **Bi Oak-leaved Goosefoot**, *C. glaucum*, smaller, often prostrate plant, with wavy-edged narrow oblong lvs 1–5 cm long, mealy below, green above. Infl dense, spike-like, to 3 cm long. Eng; Eur; r on wa, seashores. Fl 6–9.

C   **Nettle-leaved Goosefoot**, *C. murale*, has slightly mealy, diamond-shaped, sharp-toothed lvs (**C**); infl more **spreading** than in A, and lfy above. Br Isles: Eng, Wales; Eur; lf on rich ar, wa, dunes. Fl 7–10.

D   **Red Goosefoot**, *C. rubrum*, glossy (**not mealy**) ann, often red-tinged (especially on stem and underside of lvs); lvs (**Db**) diamond-shaped, irregular-sharp-toothed; infl reddish, dense; fls (**Da**) have 2–4 sepals, not joined above middle. Br Isles, Eur c to S, r to N; on wa, manure heaps, especially near sea. Fl 7–9.

E   **Many-seeded Goosefoot**, *C. polyspermum*, spreading or erect ann, usually not at all mealy, except perhaps below, with square, ± red stems; lvs undivided, elliptical, ± untoothed, 3–5 cm long; loose, hairless, infls of tiny green fls. Br Isles: Eng, f-la, r elsewhere; on wa, ar. Fl 7–10.   **Ei Stinking Goosefoot**, *C. vulvaria*, similar plant, but with no red colouring, often prostrate, smelling of rotten fish; oval mealy-grey lvs, ± untoothed. **S** Eng vr; Eur r; drier salt-marshes and shingly or sandy beaches. Fl 7–9.

F   **Good King Henry**, *C. bonus-henricus*, per herb, 30–50 cm, with broadly triangular, wavy-edged, scarcely-toothed lvs to 10 cm long and 8 cm wide at base; lvs mealy at first, later becoming smooth and green. Fls in erect terminal pyramidal lfless spikes, all with 5 sepals, 5 stamens, and 2–3 stigmas. Br Isles, Eur; introd, o-lf on rds, wa. Fl 5–7.

G   **Maple-leaved Goosefoot**, *C. hybridum*, tall ann like C and D, not mealy; lvs (**G**) hairless, cordate to **triangular**, with few but large acute triangular teeth; infls spreading, lfless. Br Isles; Eur; introd on rich wa. Fl 8–10.

H   **Small Red Goosefoot**, *C. botryodes*, is related to D, but is a smaller, usually prostrate plant, ± always **red** in fr on stem and **lf-undersides**; lvs triangular, hardly-toothed, 2–4 cm long; dense **red clusters** of v numerous fls, **smaller** than in D; the sepals joined, persisting, and forming a cup around the frs; each sepal keeled on back. SE Eng, vlf, especially on Thames Estuary; W Eur; vlc in brackish and saline hollows and creeks near the sea. Fl 8–10.

Aa 3mm

Da 3mm

163

Some salt-marsh plants: Glassworts, Sea-blites, Saltwort

Glasswort (*Salicornia*) is a strange-looking herb, erect or prostrate, usually v branched and bushy. The main stem and the branches (in opp pairs) are succulent and jointed into swollen segments. Each segment has on its upper margins a pair of opp triangular lobes that represent the lvs. Fls are borne on the upper stems and are in opp groups of 1–3 in the axils of the lobes representing the lvs. Each fl consists of a small fleshy disc or segment with a central pore, from which emerges in Aug or Sept a single tiny anther; the bifid stigma usually remains hidden. The frs are small nutlets, released as the stems break up in winter. There are many spp of *Salicornia*, and they are not easy to distinguish.

A *Salicornia ramosissima*, is ann, dark shining green, or ± red- or purple-tinged, with each segment v convex; contractions between segments give the stems a beaded effect (**Aa**). Fls always in threes, the disc of the central one of the triad much enlarged. Br Isles: S and E Eng, S Wales; f-lc in the middle consolidated parts of salt-marshes. Fl 8–9.

B *S. dolichostachya* is sprawling, bushy, pale grey-green to yellow, with many, hardly beaded, long, cylindrical branches (**Ba**) from the base; the three fls in each triad equal in size. Br Isles: S coasts of GB, Ire lc; Eur l; on lower unconsolidated salt-marshes, on mud. Fl 8–9. **Bi** *S. europaea* is similar to B in branch shape, but erect, with short opp branches, not bushy. Eng; Eur; lc on lower muddy parts of salt-marshes. **Bii** *S. pusilla* is like a small A in its beaded branches, but its fls are borne singly in lf-axils (not in threes). Br Isles: SE Eng, S Ire; Eur: NW France; lf on drier uppermost parts of salt-marshes.

C *S. perennis* is a per with creeping woody stems to 1 m long that produces low bushy tussocks of ascending green to orange-yellow shoots to 20 cm tall. Fls in threes in each lf-axil. Br Isles: SE Eng o-la; Wales, N Eng vr; Eur: France o-la; on upper, firmer often gravelly parts of salt-marshes. Fl 8–9.

D **Annual Sea-blite**, *Suaeda maritima*, another fleshy ann salt-marsh plant, but its lvs and fls are distinct, not fused into a cylindrical mass with the stem. The branched stems, prostrate to erect, glaucous-green to red-flushed, are up to 60 cm tall, and bear **half**-cylindrical fleshy alt lvs, 3–25 mm, **pointed** at tip and **tapered** to base. Fls (**Da**), 1–2 mm across, are in small clusters; 5 unkeeled succulent sepals; 5 stamens; 2 stigmas. Br Isles, Eur; c in salt-marshes generally (but r N Scot), also on beaches. Fl 7–10.

E **Shrubby Sea-blite**, *S. fruticosa* (*S. vera*), similar but larger per shrub, 40–120 cm, with ± **cylindrical** evergreen lvs (**Ea**), 5–18 mm long, **rounded** at tip and at base; fls (**Eb**) with 3 stigmas. Br Isles: SE Eng from Dorset to S Lincs; Eur: coast of France from Normandy SW; o but vlc on shingle above high-water mark. Fl 7–10.

F **Saltwort**, *Salsola kali*, distinctive, ± prostrate prickly ann; stems 20–40 cm long, striped pale green or reddish, branched; lvs 1–4 cm long, succulent, rounded, tapered into a spine at the tip; tiny fls (**Fa**) in lf-axils, each with a pair of bracts and 5 sepals; fr (**Fb**) 3–5 mm across, winged on back, top-shaped. Coasts of Br Isles, W Eur; f-lc on sandy shores along drift line. Fl 7–9.

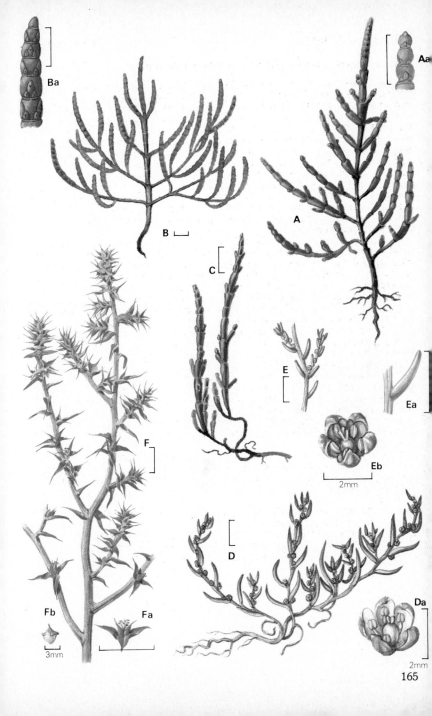

165

GOOSEFOOT FAMILY

Chenopodiaceae

Oraches, Beet, Sea-purslane

Oraches (*Atriplex*) are ann, rather fleshy, often mealy herbs, prostrate to erect, 10–60 cm, resembling Goosefoots, with alt lvs and spikes of inconspicuous fls, but with male and female fls separate; female fls sepal-less, within a pair of triangular bracts that enlarge in fr. They are plants of wa or ar, usually on rich soil, or on the coastline.

A   Halberd-leaved Orache, *A. hastata*, has **triangular** lower lvs, 3–6 cm long, the base of the lf making a right-angle with its stalk; bracts (with fr, **Aa**) fused only at the base. Br Isles, Eur; vc on wa and ar, salt-marshes, sea walls, beaches. Fl 7–10.

B   Common Orache, *A. patula*, similar to A, but lower lvs (**B**) **diamond-shaped**, with the lf-base tapering **gradually** into the stalk, and more toothed than in A; upper lvs oblong-linear, narrower than in A. Fr-bracts (**Ba**) close to A. Br Isles, Eur; c in similar places. Fl 7–10.

C   Grass-leaved Orache, *A. littoralis*, differs from both A and B in that the lvs (**C**) are **all linear** to oblong-linear, and the plants are consistently erect, 50–100 cm (whereas in A and B they tend to sprawl). Br Isles, Eur; c on coasts only (shores and sea walls, upper salt-marsh edges). Fl 7–10.

D   Babington's Orache, *A. glabriuscula*, is not perhaps always fully distinct from A; its bracts (**D**) are joined together to halfway up, and are more diamond-shaped than triangular. Br Isles, Eur; f on coastal beaches. Fl 7–10.

E   Frosted Orache, *A. sabulosa*, is distinct in its thick, silvery-mealy, frosted-looking, whitish-grey diamond-shaped lvs with wavy edges, and its usually reddish stems. The plants are sprawling, and up to 30 cm; bracts silvery-mealy, joined halfway up. Male fls (**Ea**) with 5 stamens. Br Isles, Eur; lc on sandy beaches. Fl 7–10.

F   Sea Beet, *Beta vulgaris*, tap-rooted sprawling hairless per herb with lfy shoots to 100 cm; fleshy stems usually red-striped; lvs from cordate (below) to diamond-shaped or oblong (above), **untoothed**, dark **glossy** green; fls (**Fa**) resemble those of Goosefoots (p 162) in having 5 equal sepals, but fleshy, conspicuous, and thickened in fr; frs adhere in groups by their swollen sepal-bases. Br Isles, Eur; c on seashores, sea walls, etc. Fl 7–9.

G   Sea-purslane, *Halimione portulacoides*, low shrub to 80 cm, with elliptical, untoothed, stalked, opp, whitish-mealy lower lvs; upper lvs narrower. Infls of dense spikes of tiny greyish fls, each with 5 sepals like an Orache; fls stalkless; stamens (**Ga**) in separate fls; paired bracts enclosing frs (**Gb**), fused nearly to top, are reversed triangular (broadest at three-lobed tip). Br Isles: GB to S Scot la; Ire r and S; Eur: from Denmark S; f on drier salt-marshes, especially forming fringes to channels and pools. Fl 7–9. ***Gi**   *H. pedunculata* is a small erect or spreading ann with similar but alt lvs; long-stalked frs. Eur: Denmark to N France; r on sandy salt-marshes. Fl 8–9.

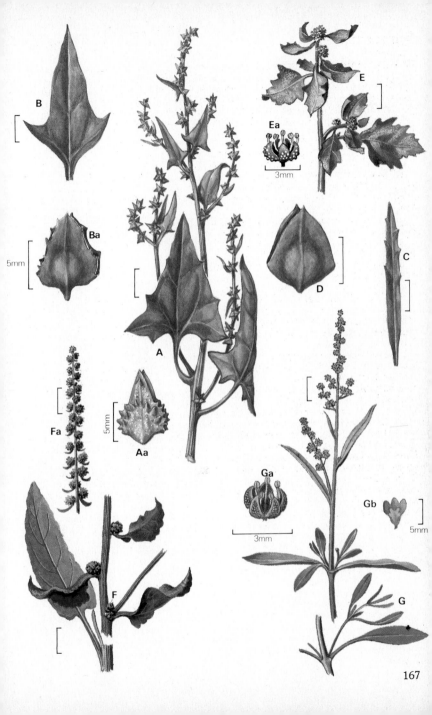

B

5mm

Ba

Ea

3mm

E

A

Aa

5mm

D

5mm

C

Fa

F

Ga

3mm

Gb

5mm

G

MALLOW FAMILY

Malvaceae

Softly hairy or downy plants with palmate, lobed, stalked, alt lvs, with stipules at bases. Fls are 1–6 together in lf-axils, usually showy and open, with 5 sepals, 5 notched petals, and many stamens joined into a tube below; a superior ovary of many carpels joined into a flattened ring ripens into a fr that divides into many one-seeded segments. An epicalyx is present below the true calyx. In *Malva* the epicalyx is of 3 free segments; in *Lavatera* the 3 epicalyx segments are joined together; in *Althaea* there are 6–9 epicalyx segments.

KEY TO MALLOW FAMILY

1 Epicalyx of 3 lobes 2
  Epicalyx of 6–9 lobes 3
2 Epicalyx of free parts 4
  Epicalyx a cup of lobes joined below 6
3 Tall per herb – lvs velvety-downy .... *Althaea officinalis* (p 170 E)
  Shorter (to 40 cm) ann or bi herb – stems bristly .... *A. hirsuta* (p 170 Ei)
4 Stem-lvs deeply-cut, with pinnately-cut lobes – fls rose-pink .... *Malva moschata* (p 168 C)
  Stem-lvs bluntly-lobed 6
5 Per, ± erect – fls 2.5–4.0 cm .... *M. sylvestris* (p 168 A)
  Ann, ± prostrate – fls 1.8–2.5 cm .... *M. neglecta* (p 168 B)
6 Bushy plant, 60–300 cm, woody below – epicalyx enlarged in fr – lvs velvety – nutlets wrinkled ....
                                             Lavatera arborea (p 168 D)
  Plant 50–150 cm, bristly not woody below – epicalyx not enlarged in fr – nutlets smooth ....
                                             L. cretica (p 168 Di)

A Common Mallow, *Malva sylvestris*, robust per herb, 45–90 cm, erect or spreading; lvs sparsely hairy, palmately-lobed, the lobes shallowly-toothed. Fls 2.5–4.0 cm, stalked, in axillary clusters up the stem; petals, 20–45 mm, rose-purple with darker veins, are 3–4 times length of sepals; fr (**Aa**) has segments sharp-angled, netted. Br Isles: c in S, rarer in N (especially r N Scot); Eur c; on rds, wa, hbs. Fl 6–9.

B Dwarf Mallow, *M. neglecta*, prostrate downy **ann**; kidney-shaped to roundish lvs, v shallowly-lobed, 5–7 times. Fls (**Ba**) 10–20 mm in clusters along stems; petals 8–13 mm, whitish with lilac veins, are only 2–3 times length of calyx; fr (**Bb**) with segments blunt-angled, smooth. Br Isles: SE Eng c, rarer N and W; Eur f-lc; on wa, rds, hbs, beaches. Fl 6–9. Several other ann or bi *Malva* spp, casual aliens, have petals only 3–9 mm, with ridged or netted segments. **Bi** *M. verticillata*, erect bi; fls 1.0–1.5 cm across, in dense clusters; fl-stalks less than twice length of sepals. **Bii** *M. pusilla*, with fls 0.5 cm across, in loose clusters; fl-stalks 4–5 times length of sepals; green calyx; netted untoothed nutlets. **Biii** *M. parviflora*, similar to Bii, but with a **chaffy** calyx enlarging in fr; toothed, netted, winged nutlets.

C Musk Mallow, *M. moschata*, erect per herb with sparse simple hairs; stem-lvs deeply palmately-cut into narrow pinnately-cut segments; root-lvs kidney-shaped with 3 shallow lobes, long-stalked. Fls, 3–6 cm, rose-pink, solitary in lf-axils and in a terminal cluster; epicalyx-segments v narrow. Br Isles: GB f-c (NW Scot r); Ire o-f; Eur f-c; on rds, hbs, gslds, especially on sand and clay. Fl 7–8.

D Tree Mallow, *Lavatera arborea*, erect shrub-like bi, to 3 m, woody below, downy with star-shaped hairs above. Lvs rounded, 5–7-lobed, velvety; fls 3–5 cm, purplish-pink and purple-veined, in terminal racemes; epicalyx a three-lobed cup of broadly oval segments wider than calyx, especially in fr; nutlets wrinkled. Br Isles: S and W coasts of GB, N to Ayr; S coast of Ire; Eur: W coast of France N to Normandy (c to W, o to E); on rocks and wa by sea. Fl 7–9. **Di** *L. cretica*, ann or bi herb to 150 cm, resembles A in appearance, but has the cup-like epicalyx of D, though with lobes shorter than the calyx and not enlarged in fr; nutlets smooth. Fl 6–7.

cont

Ha
3mm

MALLOW FAMILY

Malvaceae

◀ **E Marsh Mallow**, *Althaea officinalis*, erect velvety-downy per herb, 60–120 cm, with a slightly-branched stem bearing stalked, roundish to oval, slightly 3–5-lobed velvety-downy lvs, folded like fans above. Fls 2.5–4.0 cm across, 1–3 together in lf-axils; epicalyx a cup of 8–9 narrow triangular lobes; sepals velvety; petals pale pink; fr downy. Br Isles: coasts of S half of Eng and Wales o-lf; S Ire r; W Eur; upper parts of salt- and brackish-marshes, and ditches, banks near salt water. Fl 8–9. **Ei Rough Mallow**, *A. hirsuta*, ascending bristly ann or bi herb, 8–60 cm, bristles have swollen bases; lower lvs stalked, kidney-shaped, bluntly five-lobed; upper lvs deeply palmately-cut. Fls cup-shaped, 2.5 cm across, their stalks long; sepals and epicalyx-lobes lanceolate; petals longer than sepals, broadest at tips, rose-pink. **S Eng vr**; Eur: N to Belgium o-lf; on chky ar, wa, gsld. Fl 6–7.

BIRTHWORT FAMILY

Aristolochiaceae

F Asarabacca, *Asarum europaeum*, creeping evergreen herb with fleshy downy stems; lvs glossy, dark green, kidney-shaped, untoothed, 4–8 cm across, on stalks to 10 cm long, in habit reminiscent of Ivy. Fls solitary, bell-shaped, 15 mm long, on short stalks with a three-lobed downy brownish single perianth, 12 short stamens, and six-celled ovary inferior to calyx. Eng (probably introd in a few wds); W Eur, native but r-o (c in beechwds of central Eur). Fl 5–8.
G Birthwort, *Aristolochia clematitis*, v different from F, is a hairless erect per herb, 20–80 cm, with simple stems bearing alt bluntly cordate, stalked lvs; yellow fls in clusters of 4–8 in lf-axils; trumpet-shaped calyx-tubes, 2–3 cm long, with an oval blunt lip on top, and a basal swelling. Eng, W Eur; introd but r (native E and central Eur); on wa, hbs. Fl 6–9.

SANDALWOOD FAMILY

Santalaceae

H Bastard Toadflax, *Thesium humifusum*, prostrate semi-parasitic hairless per herb, 10–20 cm long, with yellow-green fleshy-looking stems and lvs. Lvs linear, alt, one-veined; infl terminal, loose, spike-like; fls, each with 3 bracts, like tiny white stars, 3–4 mm; a five-lobed calyx of spreading triangular sepals, white within, green-yellow outside, and a short tube; ovary inferior, oval, ribbed, in fr (**Ha**) twice length of calyx-lobes. Br Isles: SE Eng, N to Lincs o-lf; Eur, N to Belgium lf; on dry calc gsld, dunes. Fl 6–8. ***Hi** *T. pyrenaicum* has fr equalling length of calyx-lobes. Eur: Germany, Denmark, Belgium; r on calc gsld. ***Hii** *T. ebraceatum* has only **one** bract per fl. Eur: Germany, Denmark; r on calc gsld.

GERANIUM FAMILY

Geraniaceae

This family, in the Br Isles and W Eur, is composed of herbs with alt lobed or compound lvs with stipules; fls solitary or in cymes; bisexual; with 5 separate sepals and 5 petals; 10 stamens, 5 of which lack anthers in **Stork's-bill** (*Erodium*). Ovary of 5 one-seeded cells, and a **long beak** topped with 5 stigmas; fr a five-lobed capsule. **Crane's-bills** (*Geranium*) have palmately-lobed lvs and 10 fertile stamens (except *G. pusillum*), and carpels whose beaks roll up to release seeds; **Stork's-bills** (*Erodium*) have pinnate lvs, only 5 of the stamens with anthers, and carpel beaks twisting spirally when ripe, the seeds remaining inside the carpel cells.

KEY TO CRANE'S-BILLS (*GERANIUM*) AND STORK'S-BILLS (*ERODIUM*)

1 Lvs with **pinnate** veins – only 5 of 10 stamens have anthers................................*Erodium* (p 174)
  Lvs with **palmate** veins ....*Geranium* **2**
2 Petals usually 10 mm or more long (per) **3**
  Petals (without their stalks) less than 10 mm (ann) **9**
3 Lvs kidney-shaped to round, lobes widened to tips – petals 10 mm or less, deeply-notched ....
                                                   G. pyrenaicum (p 172 G) **4**
  Lvs with pointed lobes narrowed to tips – petals more than 10 mm **4**
4 Fls borne singly, 25–30 mm, purple-crimson (rarely white or pink) – petals rounded – lf-lobes not widened in middle..*G. sanguineum* (p 174 C)
  Fls in pairs – not purple-crimson – lf-lobes widened in middle **5**
5 Petals blackish-purple, bent back, pointed ....*G. phaeum* (p 174 D)
  Petals not blackish-purple, forming a cup, round or notched **6**
6 Petals notched, veins darker than petal ....*G. versicolor* (p 174 E)
  Petals rounded – veins not darker **7**
7 Fls pink – no sticky hairs ....*G. endressii* (p 174 A)
  Fls blue to violet – sticky hairs above **8**
8 Fls pale violet-blue, saucer-shaped – petals 15–18 mm – lf-lobes with pointed teeth 3–4 times as long as wide ....*G. pratense* (p 174 B)
  Fls reddish-violet, cup-shaped – petals 10–15 mm – lf-lobes with blunt teeth 1½ times to twice as long as wide .... *G. sylvaticum* (p 174 F)
9 Petals notched **10**
  Petals unnotched **12**
10 Lvs divided at least ⅚ of length into linear lobes that are pinnately lobed again – frs and lvs hairy... *G. dissectum* (p 172 Fi)
  Lvs divided to ¾ or less of length into lobes widened above... **11**
11 Stems with hairs 1–2 mm – petals 3–7 mm, pink – fr hairless, wrinkled.............. *G. molle* (p 172 F)
  Stems closely downy – petals 2–4 mm, mauve – fr hairy, unwrinkled............ *G. pusillum* (p 172 E)
12 Lvs dull green, downy – sepals spreading... **13**
  Lvs shiny bright green – sepals erect **14**
13 Lvs divided to ⅚ of length into linear lobes – fl-stalks 2 cm or more – frs hairless................................
                                                  G. columbinum (p 172 B)
  Lvs divided to ½ of length or less into broad lobes – fl-stalks 0.5–1.5 cm – frs hairy........................
                                              G. rotundifolium (p 172 C)
14 Lvs rounded, 5–7-lobed to ½ of length or less – sepals ± hairless, keeled, forming a five-angled calyx... *G. lucidum* (p 172 D)
  Lvs triangular, lobed to base – sepals hairy, unkeeled, forming a rounded calyx ....
                                                G. robertianum (p 172 A)

GERANIUM FAMILY

Geraniaceae

Crane's-bills

A **Herb-Robert**, *Geranium robertianum*, ann, 10–40 cm high, often over-wintering, with a strong smell; lvs palmate to base, sparsely hairy, shining bright green, the lfts pinnately-cut; stem and lvs often reddish-flushed. Petals 9–12 mm with stalk, blade 4–6 mm, pink (or white), unnotched; anthers orange or purple; frs netted. Br Isles, Eur; vc in wds, hbs, rocks, shingle. Fl 4–9. **Ai** **Little Robin**, *G. purpureum*, has smaller lvs, petals **only 6–9 mm**, **yellow** anthers, and more wrinkled frs. SW Eng, W France; r on shingle and rocks near sea.

B **Long-stalked Crane's-bill**, *G. columbinum*, slender, spreading to erect ann, 10–40 cm, with adpressed hairs; lvs (**Ba**) long-stalked below, **five-angled** in outline, divided to ⅚ of length into 5–7 pinnate lobes with narrow segments. Fls on long, 2–6-cm, stalks; a few together on common stalks to 12 cm. Sepals bristle-tipped; **petals unnotched**, pink, 7–9 mm; frs (**Bb**) ± **hairless**, unwrinkled. Br Isles: Eng, Wales lf-lc; Scot r and E; Ire lf; Eur lc; on gsld, scrub on calc soil. Fl 6–7.

C **Round-leaved Crane's-bill**, *G. rotundifolium*, branched v hairy ann, 10–30 cm, with long-stalked, kidney-shaped downy lvs, cut for ½ of length or less into 5–7 two- to three-toothed blunt lobes, wider above; fls numerous in open cymes, fl-stalks 0.5–1.5 cm; sepals pointed (no bristle); petals **unnotched**, pink, 5–7 mm; frs **downy**, unwrinkled. Br Isles: S Eng, S Wales o-lf; **Scot abs**; Ire vr; Eur o-lf; on dry hbs, walls, gsld on limy sand. Fl 6–7.

D **Shining Crane's-bill**, *G. lucidum*, branched, ascending, ± hairless ann, 10–40 cm, with brittle fleshy stems, and shining green lvs, often red-tinged. Lvs long-stalked, 5–7-lobed for ½ of length or less, with ± hairless lobes widened above, each with 2–3 blunt teeth; sepals ± hairless, keeled, netted, forming a five-angled calyx; petals 8–9 mm including stalk, pink, **unnotched**. Br Isles: GB o-lf (N Scot vr); Ire o-lf; Eur o-lf; on calc rocks, walls, hbs. Fl 5–8.

E **Small-flowered Crane's-bill**, *G. pusillum*, branched spreading ann, with closely downy (not hairy) stems and lvs. Lvs round, with 7–9 lobes, widened above; sepals **hairy**; petals 2–4 mm, notched, dingy mauve; 5 of 10 stamens lack anthers; frs downy, smooth. Br Isles: Eng, Wales, c to E, r to W; Scot vlc in E; Ire vr; Eur f-lc; on dry gsld, wa ar, especially on sand. Fl 6–9.

F **Dove's-foot Crane's-bill**, *G. molle*, resembles E, but has long 1–2-mm hairs on stems; petals 3–7 mm, **pink**, notched; 10 rosy-pink anthers; frs **hairless**, **wrinkled**. Br Isles, Eur; c on dry gsld, ar, wa, dunes. Fl 4–9. **Fi** **Cut-leaved Crane's-bill**, *G. dissectum*, is close to F, but lvs divided more than halfway into linear lobes that are lobed again; frs and lvs hairy. Br Isles, Eur; c on ar, wa, hbs. Fl 5–8.

G **Hedgerow Crane's-bill**, *G. pyrenaicum*, rather like an erect, larger (25–60-cm) version of F, but has a per rootstock; stems and lvs hairy; lvs more rounded than in F, root-lvs long-stalked, and 5–8 cm across; petals 7–10 mm, pink-purple, notched; frs downy, smooth. Br Isles (probably introd): Eng c, especially in SE; rest of GB rarer W and N; Ire o; Eur f-lc; on hbs, wa, scrub. Fl 6–8.

173

GERANIUM FAMILY

Geraniaceae

Crane's-bills, Stork's-bills

A   French Crane's-bill, *Geranium endressii*, erect hairy per herb, 30–80 cm; palmately-lobed lvs cut more than ½ of their length; fls in pairs on long peduncles; petals about 16 mm, unnotched, deep pink, veins **not darker**; frs downy, unwrinkled. GB and France introd, mostly hybrids with E, o (native to W French Pyrenees); on rds, hbs. Fl 6–7.

B   Meadow Crane's-bill, *G. pratense*, erect hairy per herb, 30–80 cm; sticky-hairy above (including fl-stalks and calyx); basal lvs deeply 5–7-times palmately lobed, lobes pinnately-cut into narrow sharp teeth 3–4 times as long as wide; fls in pairs, saucer-shaped; petals 15–18 mm, violet-blue to sky-blue, unnotched, veins paler; fr hairy, unwrinkled, stalk bent down. Br Isles: GB (except N Scot) f but l (c mid Eng to S Scot); Ire vr; Eur f-lc; on mds, rds, gsld, especially on calc soils. Fl 6–9.

C   Bloody Crane's-bill, *G. sanguineum*, bushy per herb, 10–40 cm; deeply 5–7-lobed lvs, with white adpressed hairs and long stalks below, the lobes trilobed and with almost parallel-sided segments; fls solitary on long stalks; petals usually purple-crimson, 12–18 mm, not notched. Br Isles lf on rocks, gsld, open wds, fixed dunes or calc or basic soils (**SE Eng, abs**); Eur v local and scattered in lowlands (more f in Denmark). Fl 7–8.

D   Dusky Crane's-bill, *G. phaeum*, has habit of F (below) and is a per herb, 30–60 cm; lvs far less narrowly divided than in F; fls (**D**) with blackish-purple pointed petals that are bent backwards. Br Isles: GB introd l, especially Eng, S Scot; Ire vr; Eur introd vl (native Central Eur); on hbs, scrub, rds. Fl 5–6.

E   Pencilled Crane's-bill, *G. versicolor*, hairy per of habit like F, but with pale pink or white notched petals, 15–18 mm, with darker, violet veins, and cup-shaped fls (**E**). Br Isles: introd, especially in S Eng (c Cornwall); Eur introd (native S, SE Eur); in hbs etc. Fl 5–9.   **Ei   Knotted Crane's-bill**, *G. nodosum*, has fls as E, but, unlike it, has its stems swollen at the nodes and stem-hairs abs or adpressed; the 3–5 main lf-lobes merely toothed (not secondarily lobed). Also native S Eur, it is locally introd in GB and Eur. Fl 5–9.

F   Wood Crane's-bill, *G. sylvaticum*, is rather close to B (above), but differs in having broader lf-lobes with blunt teeth only 1½–2 times as long as wide; fls **reddish** or **pinkish-violet**, more cup-shaped; petals smaller, 10–15 mm; frs held erect. Br Isles: N Eng, Scot f-lc (Worcs vr); Ire vr; Eur vl and r in lowlands (Denmark f-lc); on mds, hbs, damp wds, rocks. Fl 6–7.

G   Common Stork's-bill, *Erodium cicutarium*, resembles a Crane's-bill with pinnate lvs. Spreading ann to 30 cm, usually v hairy, often sticky, with lvs pinnate, the lflts pinnately-cut; stipules whitish, conspicuous, pointed. Fls in loose umbels of 1–9; petals 6–8 mm, often **unequal**, rose-purple to white, often with black spots at bases of the 2 upper ones; only 5 of the stamens have anthers. Fr (**Ga**) 5.0–6.5 mm, carpels hairy with beaks 15–40 mm, that twist spirally when ripe and remain attached to the separating carpels (which retain their seeds inside). Br Isles: GB, c to S, f to N; Ire f; Eur lf; all along coasts on dunes, cliffs; inland on sandy wa, ar. Fl 6–9.   **Gi**   *E. glutinosum*, a densely sticky-hairy plant, has equal pale pink petals, 3–4 mm, unspotted; fr, less than 5 mm, has a tiny pit at apex (in G pit is nearly as wide as fr). Br Isles: S and W coasts of GB and Ire; Eur: coasts of France to Netherlands; vlf on dunes.   **Gii   Musk Stork's-bill**, *E. moschatum*, smells of musk and is v sticky. Lfts of lvs only **shallowly** toothed, stipules broad and **blunt** (not pointed). Br Isles: SE Eng, Ire; Eur: W France; r near coast on wa. Fl 5–7.

H   Sea Stork's-bill, *E. maritimum*, has **simple lobed** (not pinnately-cut) lvs (**H**), and the petals either none or falling v soon. Br Isles: S and W coasts of GB, Ire; Eur: coasts of W France; lc on dunes and gsld near sea. Fl 5–9.

cont

WOOD-SORREL FAMILY

Oxalidaceae

◄ **I Wood-sorrel**, *Oxalis acetosella*, creeping per herb, 5–10 cm, with long-stalked trefoil lvs like those of White Clover (p 184), but more delicate, with lfts drooping, purplish below, yellow-green above. Fls, 10–25 mm across, solitary on delicate 5–10-cm stalks, with 5 equal broad white lilac-veined petals, 10 stamens and 5 styles; fr a hairless five-angled capsule, 3–4 mm. Br Isles, Eur; c-la in shady dry oakwds, beechwds, and among rocks (avoids wet or v chky soils). Fl 4–5.

J Yellow Oxalis, *O. corniculata*, has fl (**Ja**) with narrower yellow petals, 8–10 mm, and creeping rooting stems with alt trefoil lvs, tiny stipules and fr-stalks reflexed. Br Isles, Eur; introd, l in gdns, wa etc. Fl 6–9. **Ji** *O. europaea*, is erect, not rooting, with lvs in whorls, and no stipules; yellow petals 4–10 mm; fr-stalks erect. Eng, Eur; o in wa and gdns (introd from N America). Fl 6–9. **Jii Bermuda Buttercup**, *O. pes-caprae*, has lvs all rising from the base, yellow fls in umbels, and petals 20–25 mm. SW Eng (introd from S Africa); vl in ar. Fl 3–6.

K Pink Oxalis, *O. articulata*, has lfts ± downy with orange spots below; pink fls (**K**) in umbels; petals 10–15 mm. SW Eng, Eur; o in wa and gdns (introd from S America). Fl 5–10.

PEA FAMILY

Leguminosae

A v distinctive family, easily recognized by its pea-like five-petalled fls, with wide, often erect **standard** at top, the two **wing** petals at the sides, and the two lower petals forming a ± boat-shaped **keel**. Stamens 10, often joined into a tube below; 1 style, 1 carpel; fr an elongated pod, often splitting into two **valves** when ripe to release several seeds, but sometimes not opening (then usually one-seeded). Sepals 5, forming a calyx-tube below. Ovary superior. Stipules usually conspicuous and lfy. Lvs various, usually trifoliate or pinnate in herb spp, sometimes reduced to spines, or one lft, in wdy shrub spp.

KEY TO PEA FAMILY

1 Trees – or shrubs, sometimes small and creeping.. 2
  Herbs (some may be wdy at extreme base) 9
2 Trees with pendulous racemes 3
  Shrubs with erect infls 4
3 Fls white – lvs pinnate .... *Robinia pseudoacacia* (p 180 F)
  Fls yellow – lvs trifoliate...*Laburnum anagyroides* (p 180 E)
4 Fls solitary in lf-axils (but often close together)... 5
  Fls in erect leafless racemes 8
5 Spines branched (see also *Genista germanica*, p 178 Ai)...*Ulex* (p 178)
  Spines unbranched or none 6
6 Fls pink – low shrub-like herbs .... *Ononis* (p 180)
  Fls yellow – wdy shrubs... 7
7 Twigs rounded, with or without spines – style curved (see also *Spartium*, p 178)..... *Genista* (p 178)
  Twigs winged, spineless – style curved .... *Chamaespartium sagittale* (p 178 D)
  Twigs angled, no spines – plant usually over 1 m tall – style coiled in a spiral.....................................
    Sarothamnus scoparius (p 178 H)
8 Lvs palmate – pod hairy, narrow, hard..*Lupinus arboreus* (p 180 I)
  Lvs pinnate – pod hairless, inflated, bladder-like .... *Colutea arborescens* (p 180 Ei)
9 Some lvs trifoliate.. 10
  None of the lvs trifoliate... 15
10 Fls solitary.. 11
   Fls 2 to many, in heads, racemes or spikes 12
11 Fls yellow, on long stalks, with a lf below fl – pod 25–50 mm, four-angled....................................
    Tetragonolobus maritimus (p 198 E)
   Fls pink or yellow, on short stalks in lf-axils – pod 1 cm long or less ....*Ononis* (p 180)

176

12 Pods spirally-coiled or sickle-shaped ....*Medicago* (p 196)
Pods straight **13**
13 Lvs apparently trifoliate, but with 2 extra lfts at base of lf-stalk as well as a pair of narrow stipules
– fls in heads, yellow – pods to 3 cm long...*Lotus* (p 196–198)
Lvs truly trifoliate – stipules different shape from lvs – pods 7 mm or less **14**
14 Infl a loose elongated raceme with many fls.. *Melilotus* (p 194)
Infl a dense head, or with few fls arranged like spread-out fingers....................*Trifolium* (key p 182)
15 Lvs palmate, lfts 6 or more – fls in spikes...*Lupinus* (p 180)
Lvs pinnate, simple, or none **16**
16 Lvs simple, like grass blades...*Lathyrus nissolia* (p 192 C)
Lvs composed of a tendril only, with pair of lfy stipules at base....................... *L. aphaca* (p 192 D)
Lvs pinnate **17**
17 Lvs pinnate – lfts one to many pairs, but with no terminal lft, ending with or without a tendril...........
Vicia and *Lathyrus* (see Key, p 189)
Lvs pinnate, with terminal lft **18**
18 Fls in heads or umbels... **19**
Fls in racemes.. **24**
19 Heads usually in pairs, each pair with lfy bract below – calyx inflated, white-woolly – fls yellow
(sometimes other colours)..*Anthyllis vulneraria* (p 198 G)
Heads solitary – calyx hairless or only sparsely hairy, not inflated, not woolly............................... **20**
20 Heads 10–20-fld – fls pink to purplish – calyx-teeth equal .... *Coronilla varia* (p 198 I)
Heads 2–10-fld – fls yellow or white with red veins... **21**
21 Fls white with red veins, 3–4 mm long – pods pointed, hairy .... *Ornithopus perpusillus* (p 182 I)
Fls yellow, over 6 mm long... **22**
22 Lvs appearing trifoliate, but with lfts at base of lf-stalk resembling stipules – actual stipules v
narrow – pod straight, without joints ....*Lotus* (p 196–198)
Lvs with more than 5 lfts – pods curved, and jointed into segments – plant ± hairless................ **23**
23 Plant hairless – fls 10 mm long – fl-head stalks longer than lvs – pod segments shaped like tiny
horseshoes...*Hippocrepis comosa* (p 198 F)
Plant almost hairless – fls 6–8 mm long – fl-head stalks not longer than lvs – pod-segments
barrel-shaped – SW Eng, vr .... *Ornithopus pinnatus* (p 182 Ii)
24 Stipules chaffy, brown – fls bright pink or red ....*Onobrychis viciifolia* (p 198 H)
Stipules green – fls blue, purple, or yellow.. **25**
25 Plant hairless, robust... **26**
Plant hairy... **27**
26 Plant creeping and ascending – fls greenish-yellow – infl-stalk much shorter than lf...........................
Astragalus glycyphyllos (p 180 G)
Plant erect – fls white or mauve – infl-stalk at least as long as lf.................................*Galega* (p 198)
27 Keel of fl blunt – fls blue or purple ....*Astragalus danicus* (p 182 H)
Keel of fl pointed – fls purple or yellow – Scot, r .... *Oxytropis* (p 182)

PEA FAMILY

Leguminosae

Whins, Gorses, Broom etc

Whins (*Genista*), **Gorses** (*Ulex*), **Broom** (*Sarothamnus*) are ± evergreen shrubs with yellow fls that explode when insects (bees) alight on the lip, breaking the join between keel petals and thus releasing the coiled spring-like stamens that shoot out a cloud of pollen onto the insect. **Gorses** (*Ulex*) have no normal flat lvs on mature plants, and they are always spiny with branched spines. The calyx is yellow, divided into 2 lips to the base; upper lip has 2 tiny teeth at the top. **Whins** and **Greenweeds** (*Genista*) have simple, oval or oblong lvs; spines, if present, simple (except in *G. germanica*); the green or brown calyx is five-toothed, with 2 teeth on upper lip, 3 on lower; but the 2 lips not divided more than ½ way down.

A Needle Whin, *Genista anglica*, low straggling shrub with sparse spreading spines, lfy when young, with also oval pointed **hairless** waxy-green lvs, 2–8 mm long. Fls in short terminal racemes, yellow, 8 mm long; pods **swollen, pointed, hairless**. Br Isles: GB f-lc; **Ire abs**; Eur lf (abs central Eur); on dry hths. Fl 5–6. ***Ai German Greenweed**, *G. germanica*, has **branched** spines and hairy yellow fls with a five-toothed calyx. Eur: N France to Denmark; r on gsld, hths. Fl 5–6.

B Hairy Greenweed, *G. pilosa*, spineless straggling shrub with oval lvs, 3–5 mm long, v **downy** below (**Bb**); fls (**Ba**) in short racemes, yellow, 10 mm long; calyx, corolla, stalk all downy; pods **flat, downy, pointed** at tips. Br Isles: S, SW Eng and Wales vl and r; Eur: N to Denmark lf; on hths, sea cliffs. Fl 4–6.

C Dyer's Greenweed, *G. tinctoria*, shrub of 20–50 cm, ± erect; oblong lanceolate pointed lvs, with hairs on margins only. Infls of long racemes, mostly terminal; fls hairless, about 15 mm long; pods **flat, blunt, hairless**. Br Isles: Eng, Wales, S Scot f-lc; **Ire abs**; Eur f-lc; in gsld, scrub on heavy soils. Fl 6–8.

*D Winged Broom, *Chamaespartium sagittale* (*Genista sagittalis*), is rather like C, but with 2–4 broad wings to its stems, and short blunt terminal infls. Eur: N to Belgium and Germany; f in calc gsld. Fl 5–6.

E Common Gorse, *Ulex europaeus*, spiny evergreen shrub to 2 m; has trifoliate lvs only when a v young plant. Fls, 2 cm across, coconut-scented, have 3–5-mm-long bracteoles at bases; spines, 1.5–2.5 cm long, deeply furrowed. Br Isles c (except high mts and the Fens); W Eur: N to Belgium, but never more than about 50 km inland as native; introd Denmark; on rough gslds, hths, mostly on acid soils. Fl 1–12, peak 4.

F Dwarf Gorse, *U. minor*, usually much smaller than E, but up to 1 m; its weaker, often ± prostrate stems have spines about 1 cm long, with only faint furrows; fls, 10–12 mm long, deeper yellow, have bracteoles 0.5 mm only, **diverging** calyx teeth, and **straight** wing petals **shorter** than the keel. Br Isles: SE, S Eng; **SW Eng, Scot, Ire abs** (distribution in Eng overlaps v little with that of G); Eur: W France; f-la on acid hths. Fl 7–9.

G Western Gorse, *U. gallii*, in habit is intermediate between E and F, but not a hybrid; spines more rigid than in F, 1.0–2.5 cm long, and faintly furrowed (as in F). Fls 10–12 mm, deep yellow, bracteoles about 0.6 mm; plant differs from F in that calyx-teeth **converge** together, and wing petals are **curved** and when straightened longer than keel of fl. Br Isles: W of a line Dorchester–Nottingham–Edinburgh, and near coast of E Anglia, vc on hths, hill gslds; SE Eng vr; Eur: W France c. Fl 7–9.

H Broom, *Sarothamnus scoparius*, spineless shrub with long green straight hairless five-angled stems, borne ± in fascicles. Stalked lvs, with 1–3 lfts each, occur on younger stems. Fls golden yellow, 20 mm long, on stalks to 10 mm; calyx (**Ha**), fl-stalks hairless; pods black, hairy. Br Isles, Eur; c on scrub on dry acid soils. Fl 5–6. **Hi Spanish Broom**, *Spartium junceum*, resembles H, but has cylindrical, smooth stems and simple lanceolate lvs; fls yellow. Now introd S Eng, W France. Fl 4–6.

178

cont

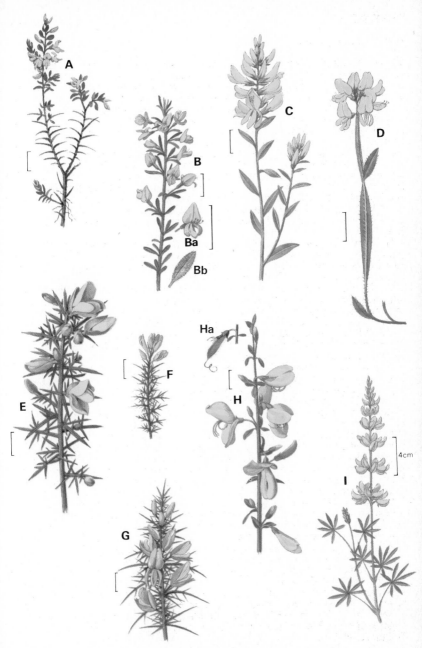

4cm

179

◀ **I Tree Lupin**, *Lupinus arboreus*, erect shrub to 3 m, with palmate compound lvs with 7–11 radiating lfts to 3 cm long, silky below, hairless above. Fls in long racemes, yellow or white, 1.5–2.0 cm long. Br Isles, Eur (introd from California); o-la, especially on rds, dunes. Fl 6–9. **Ii Wild Lupin**, *L. nootkatensis*, per herb with blue fls and 6–8 lfts. Scot (introd from N America); vl by rivers. Fl 5–7. **Iii Garden Lupin**, *L. polyphyllus*, garden escape; per herb with 9–16 radiating lfts, up to 10 cm long; long spikes with fls of various colours. Originally from N America. Fl 5–7.

Restharrows, Laburnum, Robinia, Milk-vetches, Bird's-foots

Restharrows (*Ononis*) are low shrubs or herbs with trifoliate lvs or with 1 lft; fls solitary in lf-axils, pink or yellow; plants ± sticky-hairy; all 10 stamens joined into a tube round the ovary. **Milk-vetches** (*Astragalus*) have pinnate lvs with terminal lfts, no tendrils, blunt keeled fls in heads or short spikes.

A Restharrow, *Ononis repens*, creeping to ascending rhizomatous per herb; stems 30–60 cm long to 30 cm tall, usually spineless, rooting at the base; stems **hairy all round**. Lvs with downy stalks 3–5 mm long, large stipules, and blunt-toothed lfts 10–20 mm long, all sticky-hairy with a harsh odour. Fls 10–15 mm long, pink, short-stalked, wings equalling keel; pods erect, shorter than calyx. Br Isles: Eng, Wales, S Scot, S Ire f-c especially on calc gsld, scrub, dunes; NW Scot, N Ire r on mts; Eur c. Fl 6–9.

B Spiny Restharrow, *O. spinosa*, erect per shrub without rhizomes, 30–40 cm tall, but usually with straw-coloured **spines** on stem, which is hairy in two opp vertical lines: lfts narrower and more pointed than in A, fls deeper purple-pink, wings shorter than keel. Pods erect, longer than calyx. Br Isles: Eng f-lc; Scot vr; **Ire abs**; Eur f-lc: on mds, gsld on heavy soils. Fl 6–9.

*C Large Yellow Restharrow, *O. natrix*, low sticky-hairy spineless shrub, to 20 cm; deep golden-yellow fls with reddish veins, about 15 mm long, in branched spikes. Pods shorter than in A and B. Eur: France N to Laon f-la; in calc gsld, dunes. Fl 6–7. ***Ci** *O. pusilla* is smaller (10–15 cm tall) than C, with **pure** yellow fls 6–8 mm long; calyx-teeth **as long as** corolla (corolla in C twice length of calyx); ripe pods **no longer than calyx** (much longer in C). Eur, central, E France; o-lf on calc gslds. Fl 6–7.

D Small Restharrow, *O. reclinata*, erect downy ann, only 4–8 cm tall, sticky, without spines; fls pink, 7 mm or less, pods (**Da**) **hanging downwards** when ripe, by bending of fr-stalks (only 6–7 mm long, enclosed in calyx). Lfts 3–5 mm, narrow, blunt. Br Isles: S Devon, S Wales, S Scot vr; Eur: W France r; on rocky turf on limestone by sea, dunes. Fl 6–7.

E Laburnum, *Laburnum anagyroides*, tree to 7 m with trifoliate lvs, oval lfts; fls yellow, 20 mm long, in pendulous racemes 10–20 cm long; pods downy, 3–5 cm, **seeds v poisonous**. Br Isles o; Eur c introd on wds, gslds, railway banks. Fl 5–6. **Ei Bladder-senna**, *Colutea arborescens*, shrub to 4 m; pinnate lvs with oval lfts, silky-hairy below; erect racemes of yellow fls with red veins; yellow-green **balloon-like** oval pods about 5 cm long. Introd in wa, on railway banks, especially in SE Eng; c in Eur (S Eur). Fl 5–7.

F False Acacia, *Robinia pseudoacacia*, tree to 25 m, with suckers; v furrowed bark; stipules on twigs, thorny; lvs pinnate, about 10 cm long; racemes pendulous, fls white, fragrant; pods flattened. Br Isles, Eur, introd (from E of N America); lc especially on railway banks. Fl 6.

G Wild Liquorice (**Milk-vetch**), *Astragalus glycyphyllos*, ± hairless robust sprawling per herb; stems 60–100 cm long, zig-zag; lvs 10–20 cm, pinnate, lfts elliptical, 15–40 mm; stipules arrow-shaped, 2 cm; infl 2–5 cm, on stalks shorter than lvs; racemes of greenish-cream fls (**Ga**) 10–15 mm long, with a greyish tinge;

181

◄ pods (**Gb**) 25–35 mm, banana-shaped, rounded, pointed. Br Isles: SE and central Eng o-la in calc gsld, scrub; N Eng, SE Scot vr; **Ire abs**; Eur f-la. Fl 7–8.

H Purple Milk-vetch, *A. danicus*, more like Horseshoe Vetch (p 198 F) in habit; low hairy per herb, 5–20 cm; hairy pinnate lvs 3–7 cm, lfts 5–12 mm; stipules joined below; racemes on stalks **much larger** than lvs, fls in heads, **bluish-purple**, erect, each about 15 mm long. Swollen pods (**Ha**) are dark brown, with crisp white hairs. Br Isles: E Eng, E Scot (N of Hants to Sutherland) lc on calc gslds to S, dunes to N (**not in SE Eng**); Ire (Aran Is only), W Scot vr; Eur: **France abs**; Denmark l on dunes and calc gslds. Fl 6–7. **Hi Alpine Milk-vetch**, *A. alpinus*, has free stipules, spreading, bluer fls, short infl-stalks. Scot vr on calc mt rocks. Fl 7. **Hii Mountain Milk-vetch**, *Oxytropis halleri*, has short heads of purple fls and hairy pinnate lvs as in H; but **silky-hairy** rather than downy; lfless infl-stalk stout, erect, from **base** of plant, **much longer** than lvs; fls 2 cm long; pod downy, 2.5 cm long, with a **pointed** keel (keel-tip blunt in *Astragalus*, G,H,Hi). N Scot; r but la on calc mt ledges, dunes. Fl 6–7. **Hiii Yellow Milk-vetch**, *O. campestris*, resembles Hii in pointed keel to pod and silky-hairy lvs; but fls **pale yellow** or ± purple-tinged, on infl-stalk **shorter** than lvs. Scot; vr on calc mt rocks. Fl 6–7.

I Bird's-foot, *Ornithopus perpusillus*, prostrate downy ann, stems 2–40 cm long. Fls in small heads, 3–6 together, with a pinnate bract below fl-head; fls (**Ia**) 3 mm or larger, short-stalked, creamy with red veins; pods (**Ib**) spreading like a bird's foot, curved, 10–20 mm, downy, constricted into many one-seeded joints. Br Isles: Eng, Wales f-la; S and E Scot lf; Ire, only E, vr; Eur f-la; on dry sandy and stony gd, gslds, dunes. Fl 5–8. **Ii Orange Bird's-foot**, *O. pinnatus*, similar to I, but fls wholly orange; no bracts; pods have only slight constriction. Scilly Is, W France; lr on sandy turf, especially near sea. Fl 4–8.

Clovers (*Trifolium*) form a large genus of ann or per herbs with small fls in heads; trefoil lvs with stipules; fls with five-toothed calyx; wing petals longer than keel, and straight short pods enclosed in the withered calyx.

KEY TO CLOVERS (*TRIFOLIUM*)

1 Fls yellow 2
   Fls white, pink or purple 6
2 Fl-heads 2–3 cm long, sulphur-yellow .... *Trifolium ochroleucon* (p 184 C)
   Fl-heads 1 cm long or less, bright yellow 3
3 Standard petal flat, bent forward – heads 30–40-fld, hop-like... 4
   Standard folded like a roof-ridge over pod – heads to 25-fls 5
4 Stipules oval – fls 4 mm long, pale yellow.. *T. campestre* (p 184 H)
   Stipules v narrow – fls 5 mm long, golden .... *T. aureum* (p 186 Hi)
5 Fl-stalks shorter than calyx-tube – standard not notched – 10–20 fls per head ....
                                                                                        T. dubium (p 184 G)
   Fl-stalks equal to calyx-tube – standard notched – 2–6 fls per head .... *T. micranthum* (p 186 I)
6 Creeping pers – rooting runners – fl-heads on long stalks, all in lf-axils 7
   Plants not creeping – no rooting runners 8
7 Calyx bladder-like, pink and hairy in fr – fls pink .... *T. fragiferum* (p 184 F)
   Calyx not bladder-like or hairy – fls white or pinkish.................................... *T. repens* (p 184 D)
8 Fls in lax heads, 6 or less together, spreading like fingers – plants ± prostrate, ann...................... 9
   Fls many, crowded in dense heads 10
9 Plant hairless – fls pink – pods longer than narrow calyx.................... *T. ornithopodioides* (p 186 G)
   Plant downy – fls creamy – pods enclosed in swollen calyx .... *T. subterraneum* (p 186 F)
10 All fl-heads terminal – plants ± erect.. 11
   Some fl-heads in lf-axils 14
11 Calyx with long silky adpressed brownish hairs – fls crimson (pink in ssp molinerii) ....
                                                                                        T. incarnatum (p 188 J)
   Calyx hairless, or with few long hairs.. 12

12 Ann plant – fls to 7 mm long – petals pale pink, scarcely longer than calyx, which has stiff spreading spine-like teeth – by sea, r...*T. squamosum* (p 186 A)
   Per plant – fls 10–15 mm long – petals rose to red, far longer than calyx.................................... **13**
13 Fl-heads obviously stalked – stipules v narrow, but not bristle-pointed............*T. medium* (p 184 B)
   Fl-heads scarcely stalked – stipules triangular, bristle-pointed .... *T. pratense* (p 184 A)
14 Fl-heads stalked – plants ± erect, 10–20 cm tall.. **15**
   Fl-heads stalkless – small ± prostrate plants of dry sandy gd **17**
15 Fl-heads cylindrical, v woolly – lvs downy .... *T. arvense* (p 188 H)
   Fl-heads globular, not woolly – plant hairless **16**
16 Fls 8–10 mm, white to pinkish – calyx scarcely ribbed – stipules untoothed.................................
   .... *T. hybridum* (p 184 E)
   Fls 4–5 mm, bright pink – calyx strongly ribbed and angled – stipules toothed – Cornwall, r
   ann .... *T. strictum* (p 188 K)
17 Plants downy, at least on lf-undersides – calyx-tube strongly ribbed, with spine-like teeth.......... **18**
   Plants hairless – fl-heads dense, rounded, 0.5–1.0 cm across.. **20**
18 Lfts hairless above, downy below – fl-heads paired – fls white – Cornwall, vr.................................
   .... *T. bocconei* (p 188 I)
   Lfts hairy both sides **19**
19 Calyx-tube inflated, veins reddish, teeth erect – fls pink..................................*T. striatum* (p 186 D)
   Calyx-tube not inflated, veins dark, teeth bent outwards in fr – fls white .... *T. scabrum* (p 186 C)
20 Lvs held erect on long, 2–3-cm stalks, above prostrate stems – corollas white but hidden in calyx ....*T. suffocatum* (p 186 E)
   Lvs spreading, on 1–3-cm stalks from slightly ascending stems – corollas pink, projecting from calyx ....*T. glomeratum* (p 186 B)

Melilots (*Melilotus*) are close to Clovers (*Trifolium*), and like them have trifoliate lvs; but infl is a loose, many-fld, erect raceme (in Clovers either a dense rounded head or v few-fld). Pods straight, short, oval, never spiny, rarely open. **Medicks** (*Medicago*) also resemble Clovers in trifoliate lvs and short fl-heads, but differ from both Clovers and Melilots in their **sickle-shaped** or **spirally-coiled** frs (bearing spines in some spp).

KEY TO MELILOTS (*MELILOTUS*)

1 Fls white, 4–5 mm ....*M. alba* (p 194 Bi)
   Fls yellow **2**
2 Fls about 2 mm – pod 2–3 mm, olive ....*M. indica* (p 194 Bii)
   Fls 4–6 mm – pod 3–6 mm **3**
3 Pods hairy, pointed, netted, black when ripe – petals all equal ....*M. altissima* (p 194 B)
   Pods hairless, blunt, ridged, brown when ripe – keel petal shorter.................. *M. officinalis* (p 194 A)

KEY TO MEDICKS (*MEDICAGO*)

1 Tall, ± erect plants (30–40 cm) – racemes 20–40 mm – fls 7–9 mm... **2**
   Low sprawling plants (less than 20 cm tall) – racemes 3–8 mm – fls 2–5 mm **3**
2 Fls yellow – fl-stalks longer than calyx-tube – pod smooth, sickle-shaped or only ± curved...............
   M. falcata (p 196 D)
   Fls purple – fl-stalks shorter than calyx-tube – pod smooth, spiral of 2–3 turns..... *M. sativa* (p 196 E)
3 Fl-heads 10–50-fld, compact – pod without spines, kidney-shaped, black when ripe.........................
   M. lupulina (p 196 C)
   Fl-heads 1–5-fld, loose – pod with spines, brown when ripe **4**
4 Pod hairy, 3–5 mm across..*M. minima* (p 196 H)
   Pod hairless, 4–6 mm across.. **5**
5 Lfts with dark spot – pod globular, dense spiral of 3–5 turns .... *M. arabica* (p 196 G)
   Lfts without dark spot – pod flat – open spiral of 1½–3 turns.................. *M. polymorpha* (p 196 F)

Clovers (see key p 182)

A   Red Clover, *Trifolium pratense*, hairy per, 10–40 cm tall, with grey-green elliptical to ovate lfts, 10–30 mm, often with a whitish crescent-shaped spot across them; stipules triangular, bristle-pointed, purple-veined. Fl-heads oval or globose, to 30 mm long, often paired, ± stalkless, with a pair of lvs close below. Fls (**Aa**) pink-purple, 12–18 mm across, stalkless; calyx-tube **hairy**. Cultivated forms are larger than wild ones, with untoothed lfts, hollow instead of solid stems, and pale pink fls. Br Isles, Eur; a in mds, rds, hbs, etc. Fl 5–9.

B   Zigzag Clover, *T. medium*, is v like A, but has ± **zigzag** (not straight) stems; lfts 15–40 mm, **narrower** than in A, **deep** green (not grey-green), with only a **faint** whitened spot; stipules **oblong**, **spreading** (not bristle-pointed); fl-heads clearly stalked; ± **hairless** calyx-tube; fls deep **purple-red**; lf-stalks shorter (to 8 cm only). Br Isles f but only lc; Eur f; on scrub, hbs, wd borders, mds. Fl 6–9.

C   Sulphur Clover, *T. ochroleucon*, a 'continental' sp, has habit of A, but fls **sulphur-yellow** to whitish-yellow, fading brown, and lfts **without** white spots; stipules oblong (not bristle-pointed); 2 lvs close below globose, sessile fr-heads (2–4 cm long). Eng, E Anglia to Lincs, vl – lf on rds, hbs, wd borders, gsld, mostly on calc clay or limestone; Eur: France vl, not near W coast. Fl 6–7. ***Ci Mountain Clover**, *C. montanum*, has yellowish-white **globular** fl-heads, 12–15 mm across, on **long** stalks (3 cm). Eur: E France, Belgium, Denmark; widespread but l and r on gslds, mds. Fl 5–7.

D   White (Dutch) Clover, *T. repens*, creeping rooting per herb, ± hairless; lfts oval, usually with a white spot, long-stalked (to 14 cm). Fl-heads globular on long (5–20 cm) stalks from lf-axils on creeping stems; fls white, 8–10 mm, sometimes ± pink- or purple-tinged, scented. Calyx-teeth narrow, about ½ length of tube. Br Isles, Eur; a in gslds on all soils except v acid ones. Fl 6–9. **Di Western Clover**, *T. occidentale*, is smaller, has tiny ± circular lfts without spots, red stipules and calyx, no scent. SW Eng, W France; vlf on dry gd near sea. Fl 3–5.

E   Alsike Clover, *T. hybridum*, has habit of A but is nearly **hairless**, has **white** fls (8–10 mm) flushed with **pink** below, in globular heads (close to D), on stalks to 15 cm, all in lf-axils (none terminal); oblong, untoothed, oval **long-pointed** stipules; calyx-teeth broad-based, triangular, about twice length of tube. Br Isles, Eur; f cultivated and as escape on ar, wa. Fl 6–9.

F   Strawberry Clover, *T. fragiferum*, creeping ± hairless per with habit of D, but fls always pink; calyx-tubes **hairy**, swell in fr to form **pinkish**, **netted**, **downy bladders**, 5–6 mm long × 3–4 mm wide, hence resemblance of the 15–20 mm globular fruiting-heads to pink strawberries. Br Isles: S, E Eng f-la; Wales, Ire, r; Scot vr; Eur o-lc; in damp mds, gsld near sea; rarer inland, on heavy soils. Fl 7–9. **Fi *T. resupinatum*** has calyx-tubes inflated in fr as in F, but is a slender **ann**, and the pink fls are twisted, upside-down, and bent down. W France, lc in dry gsld especially near sea (**r alien weed in Eng**). Fl 5–6.

G   Lesser Trefoil, *T. dubium*, close to H, but smaller, almost hairless, with fl-heads (5–7 mm across) of 10–20 yellow fls, each 3 mm long; fl-stalks shorter than calyx-tube; standard petals of fls **fold** down on **either side** of mid-line over the pods like a ridged roof, turning brown in fr (so that fl- and fr-heads **not** hop-like). Br Isles, Eur; vc on gslds, rds, hbs. Fl 5–9.

H   Hop Trefoil, *T. campestre*, sparsely hairy ann, 10–30 cm tall, ± erect; globular fl-heads, 10–15 mm across, of 20–30 fls, each 4–5 mm long; fl-stalks ½ length of calyx-tube; standard petals of fls broad and flat, bending **forwards** and **downwards** over the pods, turning pale brown in fr, so that fl- and fr-heads are like tiny **hop-cones** in form. Br Isles, Eur; c on dry gslds, rds, hbs. Fl 6–9. (Black Medick, *Medicago lupulina*, p 196 C, can be confused with G and H on this page,

Aa

A

B

C

D

E

F

G

6mm

H

I

Ia

2mm

185

but it is v downy, its lfts have minute points in centres of tips, and frs are black and curved, not straight.) **Hi Large Hop Trefoil**, *T. aureum*, taller version of H, with narrower lfts, **all unstalked**; larger (5–6 mm long), richer, golden-yellow fls without stalks; stipules **linear** (not oval); oblong two-seeded (not oval one-seeded) pods. GB (introd) r; Eur o-lf; on ar, wa, gslds. Fl 7–8.

I Slender Trefoil, *T. micranthum*, resembles G, but has tiny 2.0–2.5-mm-long fls, only 2–6 per fl-head, on **stalks** to 2 mm long. Fls (**Ia**) fold down mid-line as in G, but standard is **deeply notched** at top; lfts of lvs are almost stalkless. Br Isles: Eng, Wales o (SE Eng c); Ire (E and S) r; Scot vr; Eur f-c, especially to S; on grass on light soils. Fl 5–7.

Clovers continued

A Sea Clover, *Trifolium squamosum*, ± erect, ± downy ann, 10–30 cm, with lfts 10–25 mm × 3–4 mm, broader above; terminal, oval, short-stalked fl-heads subtended by a pair of lvs; many tiny pink fls; strongly-ribbed (5–7 mm-long) tough bell-shaped calyx-tubes, with rigid star-like spreading triangular green teeth, and spreading hairs. Br Isles: S Eng r and l, decreasing (still lf Thames Estuary); Eur NE to Netherlands lf, r to N; on dry banks near sea, especially on clay. Fl 6–7.

B Clustered Clover, *T. glomeratum*, hairless, ± prostrate or ascending ann, with stems 5–25 cm long. Lfts 5–7 mm long, widened above, toothed; stipules oval, long-pointed; lf-stalks 10–15 mm, **spreading**. Fl-heads, terminal and in lf-axils, 5–10 mm, unstalked, globular, each contain many dense-set fls (**Ba**); tiny pink corollas (length to three times calyx-tube); calyx-tubes, hairless, green, bell-shaped, with triangular, green sharp-pointed, spreading teeth. Br Isles: S Eng, Cornwall to Norfolk r; lf to E: formerly SE Ire vr; Eur: W France NE to Cherbourg vl; in dry open short turf on sand or gravel soils, especially near sea. Fl 6–8.

C Rough Clover, *T. scabrum*, downy all over, is close to D, but fls have calyx-tube **bell-shaped**, not inflated (**Ca**), with dark ribs, and rigid **outward-curving** teeth; petals white. Br Isles: Eng, Wales o-lc; E Ire, E Scot vr; Eur: coastal N to Holland lf; on dry open sandy or gravelly gsld, especially by the sea, r inland. Fl 5–7.

D Knotted Clover, *T. striatum*, ann of similar habit to B, but usually taller, and v **downy** throughout; fl-heads egg-shaped, unstalked, 10–15 mm; calyx-tube **downy, inflated (Da)**, with strong reddish ribs and sharp **erect** teeth; petals pink. Br Isles: Eng, Wales f-lc; E Scot, E Ire r; Eur f-lc; on dry open sandy and gravelly gsld, by sea and inland. Fl 5–7.

E Suffocated Clover, *T. suffocatum*, prostrate hairless ann, rather like B; dense globular heads of fls **unstalked** on prostrate stems, but set in axils of **long-stalked** (20–30 mm) trifoliate lvs which are held **erect** like tiny parasols. Corollas of fls tiny (2 mm long), and white, but soon fading, and almost hidden in calyx-tubes (cylindrical, ribbed, with pointed spreading teeth). Br Isles: Eng, coastal, Cornwall to Yorks r (but lf in SE) on dry sandy and gravelly gslds near sea, vr inland; Eur, coastal SW from Normandy. Fl 4–8.

F Subterranean Clover, *T. subterraneum*, also a prostrate ann, hairy like C and D; long (2–5 cm)-stalked dark green lvs, but fls are creamy, ± unstalked, only 4–6 together, with long (8–12 mm) narrow corollas (**Fa**) spreading **fan-wise** from their short common stalk; long curved bristle-like calyx-teeth. Some fls sterile, without corollas, but with rigid, palmate-lobed, enlarged calyx-teeth. Frs globular, 2.5 mm long, are forced downwards on elongating stalks when ripe. Br Isles: Eng (S and SE only) o-lf; Wales r; Ire vr; Eur N to Belgium near coast o-lf; in dry open sandy and gravelly places. Fl 5–6.

G Fenugreek, *T. ornithopodioides*, is close to F in habit; a prostrate ann, but

has **light** green and **hairless** lvs; fls 2–4, held fanwise on short-stalked heads, white or pale pink, 6–8 mm long; pods straight, much longer than calyx-tube: calyx-teeth narrow, straight. Br Isles: Eng, Wales o, lf to SE and E, elsewhere r; Ire (SE) vr; Eur N to Denmark lf to S; on dry open sandy and gravelly gd, especially near sea. Fl 5–9.

H   Hare's-foot Clover, *T. arvense*, tall usually erect ann, 5–20 cm, with spreading lvs; lfts 10–15 mm × 3–4 mm, stipules oval, bristle-pointed; fl-heads **terminal** and **axillary**, oval to cylindrical, to 25 mm long, v **downy** with **soft white hairs**, set on stalks to 20 mm; fls white or pink, ± hidden in the hairs; calyx bell-shaped, with long hairy teeth. Br Isles: Eng f-lc, especially E and SE, rarer to N and in Ire; Eur f-la; on sandy gsld, dunes etc, commonest near sea, but also inland. Fl 6–9.

The next three spp (I, J, K), plants of S Eur, are **confined to SW Cornwall in Br Isles** and to SW France in Eur.

I   Twin-flowered Clover, *T. bocconei*, ± erect, downy ann, 5–10 cm tall, most like a small D, with lfts 5–13 mm, **hairless** above, **downy** beneath; long bristle-like stipules; fl-heads oval, to 10 mm, unstalked and usually in pairs, with strongly **ribbed, dark** (not inflated) calyx with spine-like erect teeth; corolla (**Ia**) persistent, obvious, longer than calyx, white, then pink. Near Lizard, Cornwall, vr; W France, r; on short gsld on cliffs. Fl 5–6.

J   Long-headed Clover, *T. incarnatum* ssp *molinerii*, ± erect silky-hairy ann, 5–20 cm, with oval lfts; cylindrical fl-heads, all terminal, 10–20 mm long, of pale pink or cream fls, ± hidden among long, silky, buff-coloured hairs on calyx-tubes (cylindrical with long bristle-like teeth spreading starwise in fr). Lizard, Cornwall, vr; W France lf; on short gsld on cliffs. Fl 5–6.   **Ji   Crimson Clover**, *T. incarnatum* ssp *incarnatum*, is often cultivated, sometimes introd in S Eng; it is like J, but 20–50 cm tall, with fl-heads 15–40 mm; fls **deep crimson**, rarely paler colours.

K   Upright Clover, *T. strictum*, erect **hairless** ann, 3–15 cm, with narrow elliptical (5–15 mm) lfts; **oval, toothed**, whitish stipules; terminal and axillary globular heads of pale pink fls; calyx-tubes (**Ka**) strongly ribbed with spine-like teeth. Lizard, Cornwall vr; W France lf; on short gsld on cliffs. Fl 5–6.

Other clovers may occur sometimes as casual introductions, rarely persisting.

The two genera, **Vetches** (*Vicia*), p 190, and **Peas and Vetchlings** (*Lathyrus*), pp 192 – 194, are closely related, and best considered together. The technical differences are not easy to see. In practice, *Vicia* spp **usually** have 2 to many pairs of lfts, **round** stems and round styles. *Lathyrus* spp have either none, 1, or 2 pairs of lfts, **angled or winged stems**, and flattened styles. Both genera are non-spiny herbs with pinnate lfts in 1 to many pairs, or none; the **terminal** lft found in other Pea-flowers is either abs or replaced by a tendril or a little **point**. Pods are straight, not spiny, oblong, two-valved and pea-like.

KEY TO VETCHES, VETCHLINGS AND PEAS

1 Lfts none... **2**
  Lfts present **3**
2 Lvs of grass-like blades – stipules tiny – tendrils none – fls red...............*Lathyrus nissolia* (p 192 C)
  Lf-blades abs – stipules triangular, lf-like – tendrils long – fls yellow................. *L. aphaca* (p 192 D)
3 Lfts 1 pair only **4**
  Lfts 2 or more pairs **9**
4 Stem flattened and clearly winged... **8**
  Stem square, four-angled.. **5**
5 Fls 1–3, purple with cream-white keel – pod hairy **6**
  Fls 3–15, yellow, red or pink, keel same colour – pod hairless.................................. **7**
6 Fls 20 mm, standard lilac-purple, keel cream – stipules broad-triangular, toothed...........................
                                                                              Vicia bithynica (p 190 H)
  Fls 10–12 mm, standard red-purple, keel cream – stipules narrow, lanceolate, untoothed..............
                                                                              L. hirsutus (p 194 A)
7 Fls bright pink, 20–30 mm – lfts oval – stipules nearly as wide as stem........... *L. latifolius* (p 194 G)
  Fls a yellow-flushed pink, 15–17 mm – lfts lanceolate – stipules less than ½ width of stem ....
                                                                              L. sylvestris (p 192 F)
8 Lfts lanceolate – fls yellow – pod flattened..*L. pratensis* (p 192 A)
  Lfts oval – fls red – pod ± cylindrical..*L. tuberosus* (p 192 E)
9 Tendrils abs, but lf ending in short point... **13**
  Tendrils present **10**
10 Stem round – lfts 6–9 pairs – fls lilac-white with purple veins .... *Vicia orobus* (p 192 I)
   Stem winged, or four-angled – lfts 2–6 pairs – fls purple to red **11**
11 Stem winged – lfts elliptical ....*L. montanus* (p 192 B)
   Stem angled.. **12**
12 Lfts broad-based, oval-triangular, **long-pointed** – raceme-stalks hairless .... *L. vernus* (p 194 E)
   Lfts oval, blunt – raceme-stalks downy..*L. niger* (p 194 D)
13 Stem winged or angled.. **14**
   Stem round.. **16**
14 Stem winged – pod flattened – hairless erect fen plant .... *L. palustris* (p 194 B)
   Stem angled – not in fens **15**
15 Prostrate seashore plant – pod hairless, inflated ....*L. japonicus* (p 194 C)
   Erect plant of dry gsld or scrub – pod hairy, flattened – stipules broad-toothed, triangular..............
                                                                              Vicia bithynica (p 190 H)
16 Fls in stalked racemes.. **17**
   Fls borne singly or in stalkless clusters of 1–3 in upper lf-axils.. **21**
17 Fls showy, 10 mm long, or more **18**
   Fls small, 8 mm, or less.. **20**
18 Raceme-stalks 3 cm or more – lfts narrow-elliptical – racemes elongated.................................. **19**
   Raceme-stalks 1 cm or less – lfts oval – racemes short – fls pink-purple .... *V. sepium* (p 190 B)
19 Fls purplish-blue – lvs slightly hairy – pods brown..*V. cracca* (p 190 A)
   Fls white or lilac-flushed, purple-veined – lvs hairless – pods black.................. *V. sylvatica* (p 192 J)
20 Fls lilac-white, 4–5 mm, 2–9 per raceme – fr hairy ....*V. hirsuta* (p 190 E)
   Fls lilac-blue, 4–7 mm, 1–2 per raceme – fr hairless ....*V. tetrasperma* (p 190 G)
21 Fls 1–3, 10–30 mm long **22**
   Plant creeping – fls solitary, ± unstalked, 5–7 mm, lilac-pink.................... *V. lathyroides* (p 190 D)
22 Plant hairy, ± erect – fls pink-purple – pod sparsely hairy ....*V. sativa* (p 190 C)
   Plant almost hairless, ± creeping – fls yellow-white – pod densely hairy..............*V. lutea* (p 190 F)

Vetches

A Tufted Vetch, *Vicia cracca*, ± downy climbing per herb, 60–200 cm; lfts 10–25 mm long, in 8–12 pairs; **branched** tendrils; racemes 2–10 cm long on 2–10-cm stalks, 10–40-fld, dense; fls 10–12 mm, purplish-blue; calyx-teeth unequal, pod 10–20 mm, hairless, brown, two-six-seeded. Br Isles, Eur; c on hds, wd borders, scrub. Fl 6–8. **Ai** *V. cassubica* has lfts 8–12 mm; fls 4–15 per raceme, standard red-lilac, keel and wings whitish, pod shorter, two-three-seeded. S Eng introd, r; W Eur: Denmark, Germany, E France, o; in open wds. ***Aii** *V. tenuifolia* has narrower lfts, larger fls with white lilac wings. Eur: Denmark, Germany, o; in wds, scrub.

B Bush Vetch, *V. sepium*, climbing or spreading, ± hairless per, 20–50 cm; lfts 3–9 pairs, 10–30 mm long, oval, base cordate, tip blunt; tendrils branched, stipules half-arrow-shaped. Racemes short (1–2 cm), rounded, on short stalks, 2–6-fld; fls 12–15 mm long, pink-purple; pods 20–25 mm, black. Br Isles, Eur; vc in wds, hbs, scrub. Fl 6–8.

C Common Vetch, *V. sativa*, erect, trailing or scrambling downy ann, 15–40 cm; lfts 10–20 mm, 4–8 pairs, tendrils simple or branched; stipules half-arrow-shaped, toothed, usually with a dark spot. Fls 1–2, 10–30 mm long, in lf-axils, purple; pods (**Ca**) hairy or hairless, 4–12-seeded. Wild form (ssp *angustifolia*) slender with narrow lfts, fls 10–16 mm long, deep purple; native Br Isles, Eur; vc in hds, hbs, gsld, scrub. Fl 5–9. Cultivated form (spp *sativa*) v robust, with broader lfts 20–30 mm long, often with terminal bristles; fls paler, pods to 80 mm.

D Spring Vetch, *V. lathyroides*, slender prostrate downy ann; stems 5–20 cm long; lfts 2–3 pairs, 4–10 mm long, narrow, with bristle-points in notched tips; fls solitary, 5–7 mm, lilac-pink; pods hairless, black, 15–25 mm. Br Isles: GB o-lf in dry sandy gd, especially by sea, mostly to E; Ire vr to E; Eur f-lc. Fl 4–5.

E Hairy Tare, *V. hirsuta*, slender trailing ± hairless ann, 20–30 cm; lfts 4–10 pairs, linear-oblong; racemes 1–9-fld, on slender stalks 1–3 cm long; fls (**Ea**) mauve-whitish, 4–5 mm; calyx-teeth longer than tubes, ± equal; pod (**Eb**) 10 mm, oblong, **downy**, usually two-seeded. Br Isles generally c but rarer NW Scot, Ire; Eur c; on hbs, gslds on less acid soils. Fl 5–8.

F Yellow Vetch, *V. lutea*, prostrate, almost hairless ann; 3–10 pairs of lfts; tendrils on lf-tips; fls 1–3, pinky-white fading to pale greyish-yellow, 20–35 mm long; pod (**Fa**) v hairy. S Eng, vlc; Eur lc; mainly on shingle beaches near sea. Fl 6–9. (Other, clear **yellow-fld** Vetches, eg, *V. pannonica*, erect and with v hairy lvs, introd, are often confused with *V. lutea*.)

G Smooth Tare, *V. tetrasperma*, also hairless ann with lfts 10–20 mm long, in 3–6 pairs, a little wider than in F; racemes 1–2-fld; fls (**Ga**) deep lilac, 4–8 mm, calyx-teeth unequal, upper 2 shorter than tube; pod (**Gb**) 12–15 mm, oblong, **hairless**, four-seeded. Br Isles: Eng, Wales, f; Scot, Ire vr; Eur c; in gsld, hbs on heavier soils. Fl 5–8. **Gi Slender Tare**, *V. tenuissima*, is close to G, but fls larger (8–9 mm); lfts longer (to 25 mm), fewer; infl-stalks longer than lvs; pods 5–8-seeded. **S Eng r and l**; Eur (and S Eur) vl and S; on gslds on heavier soils. Fl 6–8.

H Bithynian Vetch, *V. bithynica*, climbing or trailing ± hairless per herb, 30–60 cm tall; stem angled, ± **winged**; lvs with 2–3 pairs (rarely 1 pair) of elliptical lfts, 20–50 mm long, lower blunt, upper narrower and pointed; **v large, oval-triangular**, spreading-toothed stipules, 1 cm or more long; branched tendrils. Fls 20 mm long, 1–3 on a common stalk; standard-petal lilac-purple, wings and keel cream. Pod 30–40 mm, beaked, hairy. Br Isles: S Eng, Cornwall to Essex, r and l; S Wales vr; Scot, Galloway; Eur: W coast France o-lf; on scrub, gsld, especially on heavy soils and near sea. Fl 5–6. (**Hairy Vetchling**, *Lathyrus hirsutus* (p 194 A) is rather similar, but has **v narrow, untoothed stipules**; smaller fls with **crimson-purple** standards.)

190

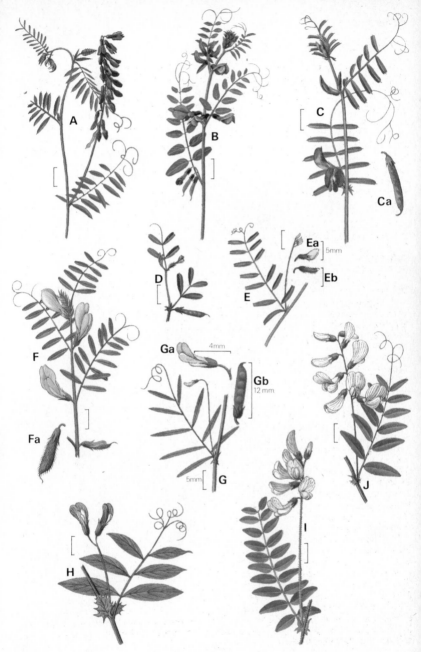

191

◀

I Upright Vetch, *V. orobus*, spreading to erect ± downy per, 30–60 cm; stem round; lvs have **no** tendrils, but a minute point at tip and 6–11 pairs of 10–15-mm, elliptical-mucronate lfts; stipules toothed, half-arrow-shaped; racemes stalked, 1–3 cm, 6–20-fld; fls with orange-pink-flushed calyx with short teeth; corolla, 12–15 mm, lilac-white, flushed with pink above, and with purple veins to standard and wings. Pod 20–30 mm, oblong, pointed, hairless. Br Isles: W of GB, Cornwall to Sutherland, r but vlf; W Ire r; Eur: Denmark, SW and Central France r-o; in mds, scrub, rocks in hilly districts. Fl 6–9.

J Wood Vetch, *V. sylvatica*, climbing hairless per, 60–200 cm; stems round. Lvs with 6–10 pairs of 5–20-mm elliptical mucronate lfts and much-branched tendrils; stipules lanceolate, with many narrow teeth. Racemes 1–7 cm long, on stalks to 10 cm, 6–20-fld, loose, one-sided; fls 15–20 mm, white with pencilled purple veins. Pods 30 mm, pointed, black when ripe, hairless. Br Isles, scattered, o-lf (Ire r); Eur: E France to Denmark lf; in old open wds and wood borders, cliffs by sea. Fl 6–8. ***Ji** *V. dumetorum*, climber, rather like J, but with winged, angled stems, 100–150 cm long; lvs with 4–5 pairs of smooth, oval, broad-pointed lfts and much-branched tendrils; stipules crescent-shaped, long-toothed; raceme long-stalked, with 3–8 purple red fls. Eur: SE France to Denmark; r in wds. Fl 7–8.

▶ **Vetchlings, Peas**

A Meadow Vetchling, *Lathyrus pratensis*, scrambling per herb, 30–120 cm long, with angled stems, each lf with 1 pair lanceolate grey-green lfts 1–3 cm long, with parallel veins, tendrils, and lf-like, arrow-shaped, 1.0–2.5-cm long stipules. Racemes on stalks longer than lvs, 5–12 fls, yellow, 15–18 mm; pod 25–35 mm, black when ripe. Br Isles, Eur; vc in hbs, gslds, scrub. Fl 5–8.

B Bitter Vetch, *L. montanus*, erect hairless per, 15–40 cm, with tuberous rhizome; lvs with 2–4 pairs of 1–4-cm long, narrow lanceolate to elliptical, pointed or blunt lfts; no tendrils; stipules toothed. Raceme stalked, with 2–6 fls, each 12 mm, crimson-red, turning blue or green; pod 3–4 cm, rounded, hairless, brown. Br Isles f-lc, but abs E Anglia and central Ire; Eur f-lc. On hilly wds, hbs, scrub, hths on more acid soils. Fl 4–7.

C Grass Vetchling, *L. nissolia*, resembles a grass superficially when not in fl. Erect, hairless ann, 20–30 cm, with lvs composed of **phyllodes** (broad, grasslike midribs only) with no lfts; stipules tiny at base, tendrils abs. Fls bright crimson-red, 15 cm, erect, 1–2 together on long stalks; pods (**Ca**) 30–50 × 2–3 mm, straight, hairless, pale brown when ripe. SE Eng: Devon to Lincs o-la especially near sea in SE; Eur, N to Belgium, Germany lc, r to N; gsld, scrub on ± basic soils. Fl 5–7.

D Yellow Vetchling, *L. aphaca*, hairless, waxy grey-green, scrambling hairless ann, to 40 cm; no lfts in mature plants, but long simple tendrils, that have 1–3-cm long, broad-triangular stipules paired at their bases and functioning as lvs. Fls on long stalks, yellow, erect, solitary, 10–12 mm long, with long calyx-teeth; pod 20–30 mm, ± curved. SE Eng: Devon to E Anglia r-lf. Eur from Germany S, c to S, r to N; in dry gslds. Fl 6–8.

E Tuberous Pea, *L. tuberosus*, scrambling ± hairless per herb, with tuberous roots and angled stem. Lvs with 1 pair of lfts, 1.5–3.0 cm long, elliptical; tendrils present; stipules narrow, 1.5 cm long, half-arrow-shaped. Long-stalked racemes with 2–7 fls, crimson, 12–20 mm long. Pod (**Ea**) 25 mm, hairless, rounded. Introd in Eng r-o; Eur, native to Denmark: c to S, o to N; in ar, wa. Fl 7.

F Narrow-leaved Everlasting-pea, *Lathyrus sylvestris*, tall climbing hairless per herb, to 3 m. Stem broadly-winged; only one pair lfts, 7–15 cm long, narrow-lanceolate; tendrils branched; stipules to 2 cm long, less than ½ width of stem, lanceolate. Racemes on stalks 10–20 cm long, with 3–8 fls; Fls 15–17 mm long, buff-yellow flushed with rose-pink above on each fl; calyx-teeth shorter than tube.

cont

A

B

C

Ca

D

Ea

E

F

G

193

◀ Br Isles: Eng, Wales o-lc; SW Scot r; Eur o-lc; in open wds, scrub, hds. Fl 6–8.

    G Broad-leaved Everlasting-pea, *L. latifolius*, is close to F in habit, but has lfts **oval** and **blunt**, stipules more than ½ width of winged stem, fls 20–30 mm long, of vivid **magenta**-pink, calyx-teeth longer than tube. Introd in S of GB, Eur; o-lc on railway banks, wa, scrub (S Eur). Fl 6–8.

▶ **Vetchlings, Peas,** continued

    A Hairy Vetchling, *Lathyrus hirsutus*, ± hairless, climbing ann, 30–100 cm, with winged stem; linear-oblong lfts in 1 pair per lf; tendrils branched; stipules 1.0–1.5 cm, v narrow, half-arrow-shaped, untoothed. Fls 7–12 mm long, 1–2 together on a long stalk. Standard red-purple, wings pale blue, keel cream. Pod (**Aa**) 30–50 × 6–8 mm, densely hairy, brown when ripe. **Eng vr**, introd; native on gsld on clay in Essex; Eur: E France (S and E Eur). Fl 6–8.

    B Marsh Pea, *L. palustris*, erect, climbing per herb, 60–120 cm, with winged stem; lvs with 2–5 pairs narrow-lanceolate lfts 3.5–7.0 cm long; branched tendrils; narrow half-arrow-shaped stipules. Racemes long-stalked, with 2–6 fls, clear light purple, 12–20 mm long. Pod 3–5 cm, flattened, hairless. Br Isles: Eng, Wales r-lf (mostly E Anglia to SE Yorks); also Somerset, S Wales, vr; central Ire r; Eur from Denmark S r-lf; in calc fens and marshes. Fl 5–7.

    C Sea Pea, *L. japonicus*, prostrate, grey-green ± hairless per herb, with angled stems to 100 cm long; lvs with 2–5 pairs lfts 2–4 cm long, oval, blunt, rather fleshy; tendrils sometimes abs; stipules broad-triangular, 2 cm. Racemes short-stalked, with 5–15 fls; fls 14–20 mm long, purple, fading blue with pale keel; pod (**Ca**) 3–5 cm, hairless, swollen and garden pea-like in form and flavour of seeds. Eng: S and E coasts Cornwall to Suffolk o-lva; rest of Br Isles vr and sporadic; Eur: Denmark c; Netherlands r; on shingle beaches by sea. Fl 6–8.

    *D Black Pea, *L. niger*, erect ± hairless per herb, 30–60 cm; stem angled; lvs with 3–6 pairs of elliptical lfts 1–3 cm long, with linear half-arrow-shaped stipules and **no tendrils**; racemes of 2–8 fls, with downy stalks; fls 12 mm long, bright purple, fading blue; calyx downy. Pods 5 cm, swollen, rough, **black. E Scot, now extinct**; Eur: Denmark to E (and S) France; o-lf in hilly wds. Fl 6–7.

    *E Spring Pea, *L. vernus*, erect hairless per herb, 15–30 cm; stem angled; lvs with 2–4 pairs of broad-based, oval-lanceolate lfts with finely tapered points; stipules lanceolate; no tendrils. Fls 3–10 per short-stalked raceme, 13–20 mm long, red-purple, then blue; pods brown. Eur: E France to Denmark; o-lc especially in calc and mt wds. Fl 4–6.

▶▶ **Melilots, Medicks** (see keys, p 183)

    A Ribbed Melilot, *Melilotus officinalis* (*M. arvensis*), ± erect hairless bi, 60–120 cm; lvs trifoliate, lfts 15–20 mm; racemes **elliptical**, 20–50 mm, loose; fls 5–6 mm, **yellow**, wing and standard petals **equal**, but **longer** than keel; pods (**Aa**) 3–5 mm, **hairless**, oval, with **transverse ridges**, blunt, brown when ripe, style soon falling. Br Isles: widely introd (native SE Eur), especially in S and E Eng, f; Ire r; Eur f; in wa, gslds, scrub, ar, dunes. Fl 6–9.

    B Tall Melilot, *M. altissima*, is v close to A, but has upper lfts ± parallel-sided; wing, standard and keel petals **all equal**; pods (**B**) **5–6 mm**, **hairy**, oval, pointed, with **netted** surface, **black** when ripe, style **persisting** in fr (frs are best distinction from A). Br Isles: GB (native) N to S Scot; central and SE Eng a-lf; Ire vr; Eur f; on hbs, gslds, scrub, especially on heavy soils. Fl 6–8. **Bi White Melilot**, *M. alba*, is close to A in **hairless** frs, brown when ripe, but frs netted as in B, and fls **white**, 4–5 mm. Br Isles: S and E of GB, introd (from SE Eur), f; Ire vr; Eur f; on wa, dunes. Fl 6–8. **Bii Small Melilot**, *M. indica*, has **yellow** fls, **only** 2 mm long, wings and standard equal, shorter than standard petal; pod 2–3 mm,

hairless, **netted**, **olive-green** when ripe. Br Isles: GB introd (native SE Eur to India), o-lf to SE, r to W; Ire vr: Eur o-lf; on wa. Fl 6–8.   ***Biii**   *M. dentata* has 3–4-mm long yellow fls, stipules with **long**, **pointed** teeth below; pods brown, hairless, net-veined. Denmark; vlf in meadows by sea.

   C   Black Medick, *Medicago lupulina*, is v like the small yellow Clovers, notably *Trifolium dubium* (p 184 G), but lvs closely **downy** (*T. dubium*, *T. campestre* have few, scattered hairs) and frs **curved**, **black** when ripe, not covered by remains of fl. Ascending, downy per, 5–25 cm; lfts 5–20 mm, toothed; fl-heads stalked, compact, 3–8 mm, 20–40-fld; pods (**Ca**) 2 mm across, kidney-shaped, coiled, netted, black when ripe. Br Isles, Eur; vc on gslds, rds, especially on base-rich soils. Fl 4–8.

   D   Sickle Medick, *M. falcata*, hairless ascending or erect per, 30–40 cm; lfts (**Da**) linear-lanceolate; fls in short racemes, 10–25 mm, clear yellow; fl-stalks longer than calyx-tube. Pod (**Db**) curved or sickle-shaped, smooth, ± hairless, 2–5-seeded, 1–2 cm long. Eng: native in E Anglian Breckland, lf; introd elsewhere, o; Eur; lf on calc gsld, rds. Fl 6–7.

   E   Lucerne, *M. sativa*, is close to D, but more erect, with longer racemes (to 40 mm) of **purple** or **lilac** fls, with fl-stalks shorter than calyx-tube; pod smooth, ± hairless, but a **spiral** with **2–3 twists**. Br Isles, Eur; introd (from S Eur), in wa. Fl 6–9. Hybrids between D and E occur where they meet: fls yellow-green to purple-black, pods from almost straight to spiral.

   F   Toothed Medick, *M. polymorpha*, similar to G, but has a few hairs on stem, no blotches on lvs; jagged stipules; fls 3–4 mm; hairless pods (**Fa**) 4–6 mm across, in a flat spiral of 1½–3 turns, **strongly** netted, with a double row of hooked spines. Fl-head stalks as long as lf-stalks. Eng, native S and SE coasts, o-lf, introd inland; Eur: W France lf, introd to NE; on dry sandy gd near sea. Fl 5–8.

   G   Spotted Medick, *M. arabica*, prostrate ann, ± hairless; toothed trifoliate lfts dark-blotched; short-toothed stipules. Fl-heads 5–7 mm, few-fld, stalks shorter than lf-stalks; fls (**Ga**) 4–7 mm. Hairless pods (**Gb**) 4–7 mm across, **globular**, densely spiral, with 3–5 turns, faintly netted, with hooked spines in a **double** row on edge of spiral. Br Isles: Eng, Wales, lc to SE; Scot only casual; **Ire abs**; Eur: N to Holland, lc to SW; on dry open sandy gd, especially near sea. Fl 4–9.

   H   Bur Medick, *M. minima*, v downy ann, smaller than F, with **untoothed** stipules; pods (**Ha**) like those of F in shape, with a double row of spines, but v **downy**, only 3–5 mm across. SE Eng: Sussex – Norfolk vlf on beaches, dunes, Breckland hths; Eur coast N to Denmark. Fl 5–7.

Bird's-foot-trefoils etc (illustrated p 199)

Bird's-foot-trefoils (*Lotus*) are low herbs with lvs that appear trifoliate, but have a lower pair of lfts arising from base of stalk, like stipules; the true stipules are brown, minute, hard to see. Fls few together in one-sided heads, on long stalks in lf-axils. Pods elongated, spreading stiffly from common stalk like the toes of a sparrow from its leg.

   A   Common   Bird's-foot-trefoil, *Lotus corniculatus*, low ± creeping, ± hairless per herb; stems solid, 10–40 cm long; lfts oval, in fl-stalks to 8 cm long; 2–8 fls per head; fls 15 mm long. Calyx-teeth (**Aa**) erect in bud, the two upper with an **obtuse** angle between them; buds flattened, deep red; open fls deep yellow or orange. Br Isles, Eur; vc in gslds, rds etc, except on v acid soils. Fl 6–9.

   B   Narrow-leaved Bird's-foot-trefoil, *L. tenuis*, is close to A, but slenderer, often more erect; **linear to lanceolate** lfts, usually 3 mm wide or less; **pale** yellow fls, 2–4 per head, about 10 mm long; 2 rear upper calyx teeth **converge together**. Br Isles: Eng o-lf, especially in SE and E; Wales vr; **Scot**, **Ire abs or casual**; Eur o-

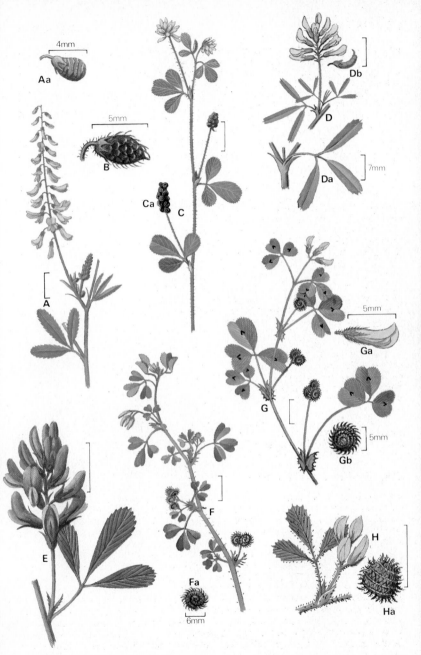

197

lf; in dry gslds, especially on heavy clay soils. Fl 6–8.

C Greater Bird's-foot-trefoil, *L. pedunculatus*, close to A, but taller (to 60 cm), ± erect, usually v **hairy**; stem **hollow**, stout; lfts (15–20 mm long) are **broadly oval**, **blunt**; infl-stalks to 15 cm long; 5–12 fls per head; calyx-teeth (**Cb**) **spread** in bud, the two upper ones separated by an **acute** angle. Fls (**Ca**) clear yellow, not normally with any orange or red tinge. Br Isles (except NW Scot r), Eur; f-la in damp mds, marshes, fens. Fl 6–8.

D Hairy Bird's-foot-trefoil, *L. hispidus* (*L. subbiflorus*), low ± spreading ann or sometimes per, with stems 3–30 cm long. Lfts to 20 mm, narrow-oval, **v hairy**; fl-heads, each of 2–4 small yellow fls only about 8 mm long, on stalks about 2 cm long, longer than lvs. Pods 6–12 mm long. Br Isles: Eng, Cornwall to Hants; Wales, Pembroke; W Eur: France; r but vlf in dry glsd close to sea. Fl 7–8. **Di Slender Bird's-foot-trefoil**, *L. angustissimus*, is close to C, but always **ann**, less hairy; fl-heads, one–two-fld, on stalks **shorter** than lvs; pods 20–30 mm. Br Isles: Eng, Cornwall to Kent r, vr to E; Eur: W France f; on dry gsld, usually near sea. Fl 7–8.

E Dragon's-teeth, *Tetragonolobus maritimus*, ± downy prostrate per, like a large *Lotus*, but lacks the lower pair of lfts on each lf, having large green triangular stipules instead; fls **solitary**, on stalks longer than subtending lf, with trefoil bract at base of calyx; fls pale yellow, 25–30 mm long, with brown veins in standard. Fr 30–50 mm (**Ea**), **four-angled**, dark brown when ripe, stout, parallel-sided. Br Isles: S Eng r but lf (introd, but possibly native in Kent); Eur o-la; on calc or clay gslds, also dunes in N France. Fl 6–8.

F Horseshoe Vetch, *Hippocrepis comosa*, spreading ± hairless per herb, 5–20 cm tall, with woody rootstock, bearing pinnate lvs with 4–5 pairs of side lfts and a terminal lft, all narrow-oblong, 5–8 cm long, with 2 narrow, pointed stipules at lf-base; no tendrils. Fl-heads have stalks 5–10 cm, bearing whorls of 5–8 fls (clear yellow, 8–10 mm long). Pods (**Fa**) arranged as in *Lotus*, but sinuous, about 30 mm long, breaking into horseshoe-shaped segments. Br Isles: N to Teesdale f-la; Wales r; Eur N to Belgium f-la; on old, short calc gsld and cliffs. Fl 5–7.

G Kidney Vetch, *Anthyllis vulneraria*, prostrate to erect silky-hairy per, up to 30 cm tall; pinnate lvs 3–6 cm long, silky-white below, green above; terminal lft much larger (elliptic on lower lvs); on upper lvs all lfts linear-oblong and equal (lowest lf sometimes one lft only). Fl-heads rounded, ± paired, 2–4 cm wide, of many fls (**Ga**) with **inflated white-woolly** calyx-tubes; petals usually yellow (white, pink, cream, purple or crimson in some coastal sites). Pod 3 mm long, rounded, flattened. Br Isles, Eur; f-va on calc gslds, sea cliffs, dunes. Fl 6–9.

H Sainfoin, *Onobrychis viciifolia*, downy, erect (sometimes prostrate) per herb, 20–40 cm; pinnate lvs, lfts 6–12 pairs, with oblong, pointed, **chaffy stipules**: fl-spikes many-fld, **conical**, on stalks longer than lvs; fls 10–12 mm, **bright pink** with **red veins**; calyx-teeth longer than hairy tube; pods (**Ha**) not opening, 6–8 mm, oval, netted and warted, one-seeded. Eng, Eur; introd, lf on rds, gslds on calc soils (smaller, more prostrate form probably native locally in old calc gsld in SE Eng, France). Fl 6–8.

I Crown Vetch, *Coronilla varia*, straggling hairless per herb, stems 30–60 cm; pinnate lvs 5–10 cm long, with terminal lfts; fl-heads globular, 10–20-fld, on stalks longer than lvs; fls 12 mm, particoloured with pink and lilac, purple tips to pointed keels; pods four-angled, 4–5 cm long, breaking into one-seeded segments. GB N to SE Scot o-lf; W Eur o; introd in wa, scrub, especially on calc soils (central Eur). Fl 6–8. **Ii Goat's-rue**, *Galega officinalis*, erect hairless per herb, 60–100 cm; pinnate lvs with lfts broader (to 1 cm wide) than in H; erect oblong·racemes (their stalks longer than lvs) of white or lilac-pink fls with bristle-like calyx-teeth; pods cylindrical, rounded, 2–3 cm. GB, W Eur; (introd) o-lf in wa (S and E Eur). Fl 6–7.

ROSE FAMILY

Rosaceae

The Rose family is a natural group, but for this reason difficult to define simply. Its members are trees, shrubs or herbs, always with alt lvs, often much lobed or divided (though sometimes not so), always with stipules. Fls regular, mostly with their parts in fives (but Ladies-mantles, Burnets, and some Cinquefoils have them in fours). Epicalyx present in many of the herb members. Petals not joined into a tube below. Stamens usually 2, 3 or 4 times number of the sepals, rarely fewer. Carpels usually numerous (though there may be only 1 or a few). Carpels and their styles usually free, though sometimes fused to the **receptacle-cup** of the fl. All, however, have a **receptacle-cup** which surrounds stamens and carpels and bears the calyx-teeth, petals and stamens; it may be fused to the carpels, making the fl either **perigynous** when unfused, or **epigynous** when fused to them. Frs either **achenes**, which sit on a fleshy receptacle (Strawberry) or on a non-fleshy one (Cinquefoils) or may be drupes (Plums and Cherries) or pomes (Apples, Pears, *Sorbus* etc) or in other forms (see glossary for meanings of these words).

KEY TO TREES AND SHRUBS OF THE ROSE FAMILY

1 Trees or upright shrubs **2**
  Herbs, sometimes with a slightly woody creeping stem..............................see Key to Herbs (p 201)
2 Fls bright yellow, with epicalyx – lvs pinnate – shrub without thorns – less than 1 m............
                                                                                      Potentilla fruticosa (p 209 C)
  Fls white or pink – no epicalyx.. **3**
3 No cup below sepals, carpels on a conical receptacle – fr blackberry- or raspberry-like, red or black – prickles on stem and lvs – lvs with 3–7 lfts.................................... *Rubus* (p 206)
  Receptacle forming a deep cup below sepals... **4**
4 Many styles and carpels within a fleshy cup – pinnately-lvd shrubs with broad-based prickles on sides of shoots..
                                                                                      Rosa (key p 205)
  Only 1–5 styles and carpels – trees or shrubs with no prickles along stems or lvs, but sometimes with woody thorns at tips of the short shoots – lvs usually undivided (if pinnate then not thorny)... **5**
5 Only one carpel, forming a cherry- or plum-like fr with receptacle-cup not fused to it – lvs undivided...*Prunus* (p 202)
  Carpels 1–5, fused to receptacle cup (so that ovary inferior) **6**
6 Infls in erect racemes-carpels free from cup above – introd r – lf........................ *Amelanchier laevis*
  Infls umbel-like, or fls only 1 or 2–3 together.. **7**
7 Fls 1–3 together, or in simple umbels.. **8**
  Fls in dense compound umbel-like heads... **11**
8 Fls less than 1 cm across – frs 1 cm or less, red, berry-like ....*Cotoneaster* (key p 205)
  Fls 3 cm across or more – frs 2 cm or more, green or brown, firm.................................. **9**
9 Fls borne singly – fr like small apple, but with the 5 carpels exposed on the top in a broad disc, which is surrounded by long (10–15 mm) sepals – twigs thorny – lvs downy elliptical – S Eng r, France lf – in wds ....*Mespilus germanica*
  Fls several together in an umbel – fr with the small (3–7 mm) sepals surrounding a tiny pore...... **10**
10 Petals pink-tinged – stamens yellow – fr like a small apple, fleshy not gritty ....*Malus* (p 204)
   Petals white – stamens purple – fr pear-shaped with gritty flesh.................................. *Pyrus* (p 204)
11 Woody thorns at ends of short shoots – lvs lobed or pinnatifid – stamens purple – carpels inside the fr stony (haw) ....
                                                                                      Crataegus (p 204)
   No thorns – lvs oval, lobed or pinnate – stamens cream to pink – carpels gristly (not stony) **12**
12 Lvs pinnate, green both sides, lfts toothed – fr scarlet........................... *Sorbus aucuparia* (p 202 A)
   Lvs oval, white underneath – frs scarlet...*S. aria* (p 202 C)
   Lvs deeply-lobed, green both sides – fr brown .... *S. torminalis* (p 202 B)

ROSE FAMILY

KEY TO HERBS OF THE ROSE FAMILY

1 Epicalyx present below calyx of fls... **2**
 No epicalyx present.. **8**
2 Styles long, zigzag in middle in fl, persisting in fr as hooked bristles – root-lvs pinnate – end lft
 much larger than side lfts...*Geum* (p 214)
 Styles short, not zigzag, not persisting in fr – if lvs pinnate, end lft hardly larger than side lfts.......... **3**
3 Petals conspicuous, yellow or white **6**
 Petals abs or tiny – fls v small.. **4**
4 Lvs palmate or pinnate – fls yellow or white ....*Potentilla* (key p 208)
 Lvs trifoliate – fls white **5**
5 Fr fleshy (like little Strawberry) – fr-receptacle hairless ....*Fragaria* (key p 208)
 Fr dry – fr-receptacle hairy ....*Potentilla sterilis* (p 210 I)
6 Lvs trifoliate – petals none or tiny – carpels 5–12 – on mts only..
 ....*Sibbaldia procumbens* (p 210 Iii)
 Lvs palmately-lobed – petals none – fls with 4 green sepals only.. **7**
7 Lvs normally over 2 cm wide, clearly stalked – fls in loose terminal heads – per plant over 10 cm
 tall...*Alchemilla* (p 212)
 Lvs less than 1 cm wide, scarcely stalked – fls in dense clusters in lf-axils – ann plant under 10 cm
 tall..*Aphanes arvensis* (p 212 D)
8 Lvs pinnate – plant ± erect **9**
 Lvs trifoliate or undivided – plant low, creeping – fls white **13**
9 Petals present – lvs with pairs of smaller lfts between larger lfts.. **10**
 Petals abs – lvs without smaller lfts between larger lfts – fls in dense heads or spikes.................... **11**
10 Fls white (or pink-tinged), in loose umbel-like panicles – receptacle-cup of fl and fr, spineless.........
 ....*Filipendula* (p 214)
 Fls yellow, in long loose spikes – receptacle-cup of fl and fr with a crown of conspicuous hooked
 spines...*Agrimonia* (p 212)
11 Plant creeping – erect fl-stems – fls in round heads – conspicuous hooked spines on fr-head –
 (introd from Australia) vl ....*Acaena anserinifolia*
 Plant erect – no spines on fr-head **12**
12 Fls in oblong spikes – each fl with 4 crimson sepals, 4 stamens, undivided stigma.............................
 ....*Sanguisorba officinalis* (p 212 H)
 Fls in globular heads – each fl with 4 green sepals – lower fls male with many stamens only –
 upper fls female with a red feathery stigma only ....*Poterium sanguisorba* (p 212 G)
13 Petals usually 8 – stems creeping, ± woody below – lvs oval, lobed like tiny oak-lvs, green
 above, white below – fr-head a group of achenes with long white feathery styles ....
 ....*Dryas octopetala* (p 212 B)
 Petals 4 or 5 – stems not woody – fr a head of red or orange fleshy berry-like drupes (rather
 resembling a raspberry)... **14**
14 Lvs simple, palmately-lobed, rounded (like mulberry lvs) from underground rhizomes – fls
 solitary, not always produced – fr red, then orange – mts in N of Br Isles.......................................
 ....*Rubus chamaemorus* (p 206 H)
 Lvs trifoliate – fls 2–8 in a loose head – plant with creeping runners above ground ....
 ....*Rubus saxatilis* (p 206 F)

ROSE FAMILY

Rosaceae

Trees and shrubs

Sorbus (Whitebeams, Service-trees, Rowan) is a genus of trees with white five-petalled fls in branched, umbel-like heads (technically compound corymbs) and pome-type fruits in which the gristly-walled carpels are enclosed in the fleshy receptacle-cup, as with apples and pears. The twigs have no spines and the lvs are toothed, lobed or pinnate.

A Rowan, *Sorbus aucuparia*, smooth-barked tree, ± 15 m; lvs **pinnate**, compound, 10–20 cm long, bearing strongly-toothed lfts 3–6 cm long, terminal lft **no longer** than side ones, hairless above, **whitish-grey** and **downy** below when young. Dense corymbs of fls resemble branched umbels; petals 5, creamy-white, 3–5 mm long; fl-stalks woolly; styles 3–4, stamens many. Frs (**Aa**) scarlet, globose, 6–9 mm long, like tiny apples in structure, a fleshy outer case enclosing gristle-like carpel walls, each containing 1 or 2 seeds. Br Isles, Eur; f-lc especially to N, in dry wds usually on acid soils, and on mt rocks. Fl 5–6; fr 9.

B Wild Service-tree, *S. torminalis*, has fls similar to A but is larger tree (to 25 m) with rough bark of a pear tree (not smooth as in A), and lvs v different, 7–10 cm long, oval-oblong, not divided into lfts, but with triangular-pointed, toothed lobes that diverge at ± 45°, resembling those of Maple (p 236), but narrower, with lowest 2 lobes not (or scarcely) wider than rest of lf; lvs downy **below** when young, ± hairless, dark green, leathery when mature. Frs (**Ba**) similar in form to A but 12–16 mm long, oblong, not globose, **brown** with **dark spots**. Eng, Wales, scattered and lf only; Eur: France, Denmark lo-lf; in old wds on either clay or calc soils, rarely many trees together. Fl 5–6.

C Whitebeam, *S. aria* (agg), a complex of closely related micro-spp, with simple, but always toothed, often ± pinnately-cut lvs, dark green, ± hairless above when mature, woolly-white below. White fls and reddish frs (**Ca**) as in A. Br Isles, Eur; f-lc in dry wds and usually on limestone rocks. Fl 5–6; fr 9. **Common Whitebeam**, *S. aria* in narrow sense, has lvs egg-shaped, small-toothed, but not lobed, pure white below; oval red frs. S Eng, c on chk, limestone, o on sandy soils, in wds and scrub; Eur: S from N France, r-o. (Illustrated, C.)

Prunus (Plums) have five-petalled fls with concave or cup-like receptacles; 1 carpel which in fr forms a **drupe** (with fleshy outerpart and a stony inner part, containing the seed or kernel).

D Wild Cherry (Gean), *Prunus avium*, tree, 25 m, with suckers and peeling bark with horizontal lines on it when young, rough when old. Lvs oval-elliptical, doubly-toothed, pointed, hairless above, downy below, **not shiny**, 6–15 cm, with two red knobs (**Db**), or glands, on stalk just below lf-blade. Fls 2–6, in umbels without a common stalk, white, cup-shaped; petals 8–15 mm, narrowed to base, arising from reddish cup which bears bent-back sepals and also the stamens, and is 'waisted' above. Fr (**Da**) 1 cm, globular, red, hairless, like a tiny garden cherry. Br Isles: Eng, Wales, Ire f-lc; Scot r to N; Eur f-lc; in wds, hbs on better soils. Fl 4–5. **Di Dwarf Cherry**, *P. cerasus*, is similar to D, but usually only a shrub; lvs **broader, shorter** (5–8 cm), **thicker**, dark green, **shiny**, ± hairless below; flat fls, receptacle with **no 'waist'**, petals rounded below. Br Isles: S Eng, Wales, Ire introd everywhere, o-f; N Eng, Scot r; Eur f; in hbs; wds. Fl 4–5.

E Blackthorn (Sloe), *P. spinosa*, spiny rigid shrub, 1–4 m, forming thickets; twigs downy when young, dark, with many straight side-shoots that become thorns; lvs elliptical-lanceolate, dull, tapered below, toothed; fls appear before lvs, 1 or 2 together, petals white, 5–8 mm; fr (**Ea**) 10–15 mm, globular, blue-black with a grey bloom, v astringent. Br Isles, Eur; c and la in scrub, wds, hbs. Fl 3–5 **Ei Wild Plum**, *P. domestica*, is similar to E, but usually more of a tree and not thorny; twigs soon hairless as are fl-stalks; fls 1–3, appear with lvs; petals 7 mm or

◀ more; fr 4–8 cm, oval-oblong, colour varied. Br Isles, Eur; escape, f in hbs, wds. Fl 4–5. **Eii Bullace**, *P. domestica* var *insititia*, often thorny, with downy twigs and fl-stalks; fr globular or shortly oval, 2–3 cm, blue-black with a bloom. S Eng, Eur; possibly native in scrub, but formerly introd. **Eiii Cherry Plum**, *P. cerasifera*, has **hairless** glossy (**usually spineless**) twigs and lf upper sides (only hairy on lf-stalks and lower midribs); lvs oval, glands small or abs; petals 7–11 mm, oval; fr 2.0–2.5 cm, globose, yellow or red. Br Isles, W Eur introd (native E Eur, Asia); o-f in hbs. Fl 3–4, earliest Plum to flower.

*F St Lucie's Cherry (Mahaleb), *P. mahaleb*, cherry-like shrub, 1–3 m; round-oval lvs, cordate at base, blunt above, with corky-tipped rounded teeth; no glands on stalk. Fls white, scented, in small erect simple corymbs; petals 4–5 mm; frs oval, black, 5–8 mm. From Belgium and Germany S; o-lc in scrub on chky soils, rocks. Fl 5.

G Bird Cherry, *P. padus*, tree, 3–15 m, with odorous peeling bark; lvs 5–10 cm, elliptical, toothed, thin, ± hairless, with red glands on stalk as in D. Fls in **long ± drooping racemes**, 10–40 together (unlike other deciduous *Prunus* spp); petals white, **toothed**, 4–6 mm; fr (**Ga**) black. Br Isles: N half of GB, Wales f-lc; E Anglia r and l; Eur: Denmark to E France f to N, r to S; in wds (especially moist) in mt areas. Fl 5. **Gi Cherry Laurel**, *P. laurocerasus*, evergreen, with shiny leathery lvs, 5–8 cm; fls in erect racemes, 5–12 cm long; petals white, 4 mm long. Introd from SE Eur.

H Wild Pear, *Pyrus communis*, deciduous tree, to 20 m; rough-fissured bark; spineless twigs; oval, scarcely-toothed lvs. Fls in umbel-like heads; 5 petals, white, 10–15 mm, styles free; stamens purple; fr familiar pear-shape. Br Isles, Eur; widely introd in hbs (native S and E Eur). Fl 4.

I Crab Apple, *Malus sylvestris*, thorny small rounded tree, to 10 m; irregularly **scaly** bark; toothed, oval pointed deciduous lvs, hairless when mature. Five-petalled fls in umbel-like heads as in H, but petals **pink-flushed on white**, 1.3–3.0 cm long, stamens **yellow**, styles joined below. Fr globular, 2 cm, apple-shaped, yellow to red-flushed, acrid. Eng, Wales, W Eur f; Ire, S Scot r; native in old oakwds, scrub. Fl 5. **Ii Cultivated apples**, *M. domestica* agg, have downy mature lvs, no thorns, and larger frs; often introd in hbs.

J Hawthorn, *Crataegus monogyna*, hairless, v thorny deciduous shrub or tree to 10 m; **deeply** 3–5-lobed lvs, cut more than halfway to midrib; lobes triangular, longer than broad; fls in flat corymbs, 10–16 together; 5 petals 4–6 mm long, white (rarely pink); one style. Fr of one stony carpel in a hollow, 8–10 mm-long crimson oval cup, forming the familiar 'haw'. Br Isles (except N Scot r), Eur; vc in hbs, scrub, wds; r on v acid or wet soils. Fl 5–6.

K Midland Hawthorn, *C. laevigata*, similar to J, but lvs (**K**) lobed less than halfway to midrib, lobes **rounded**, broader than long, lf oval, tapering to the base; 5 petals 5–8 mm, styles 2 or 3; carpels, 2 or 3, joined below, free above. SE, mid Eng f-lc; Eur lf; mostly in old wds on heavy soils; hybridizes with J. Fl 5–6.

L Wild Cotoneaster, *Cotoneaster integerrimus*, shrub rarely over 1 m, without spines; hairless twigs except when young; lvs deciduous, shortly oval, 15–40 mm, untoothed, grey-woolly below. Fls (**La**) 2–4 together in clusters, 5 petals, 3 mm, pink; fr (**Lb**) 6 mm, globular, red, like a small 'haw', but the 2–5 carpels are not (as in K) joined on their inner sides. Br Isles: on limestone rocks near Llandudno vr; N, central Eur, W to Belgium and E France, vl on calc rocks. Fl 4–6. Several other *Cotoneaster* spp are now c introd in GB (see Key, p 205).

ROSE FAMILY

KEY TO COTONEASTERS

1 Tall shrub to 6 m – hairless when mature, 6–12 cm long – (from Himalaya) ....*C. frigidus*
   Low shrubs to 4 m – lvs hairy at least below, 0.5–4.0 cm long **2**
2 Petals spreading, white – lvs 5–8 mm, obovate – on rocks (from Himalaya) ....*C. microphyllus*
   Petals erect – pink lvs 10 mm or more, oval...**3**
3 Lvs grey-woolly – lf-base rounded ....*C. integerrimus* (p 204)
   Lvs green, sparsely downy below, tapering to base **4**
4 Stems ± erect – lvs 1–3 cm long – on rocks (from India) ....*C. simonsii*
   Stems spreading horizontally, branched, flattened in one plane – lvs 0.5–2.0 cm long – on rocks
   (from W China)...*C. horizontalis*

Wild Roses (*Rosa*) are shrubs with prickly stems, pinnate lvs with obvious stipules; fls solitary or in clusters, 5 sepals and petals, many stamens, styles and carpels many, enclosed in, but not fused to, a deep receptacle-cup, ripening to a coloured 'hip'. Petals large, soon falling. Wild roses are numerous in spp and varieties; many are ancient hybrids in origin, hence 'critical' and not easy to name. Only the commoner are fully described here, but a key to more of the less rare British spp follows. However, not **all** specimens will be nameable with this key.

KEY TO COMMONER ROSES

1 Styles (joined into a column in both fl and fr) equal shorter stamens – trailing shrub..........................
                                                      Rosa arvensis (p 206 A)
   Styles free, or joined into a shorter column in fl, free in fr – erect or arching shrubs........................**2**
2 Fls solitary, bractless – lfts 3–5 pairs, rarely over 1.5 cm – stems with prickles and stiff bristles – fr
   not hairy, globose, purple-black...*R. pimpinellifolia* (p 206 B)
   Fls 1 or usually more together – bracts present – lfts 2–3 pairs – stems scarcely bristly but ±
   hairy – fr oval, red **3**
3 Styles joined into a column (shorter than stamens) in fl, but free in fr – disc below stamens conical
   – local only...*R. stylosa*
   Styles free – disc flat...**4**
4 Lvs v sticky below, with stalked scented glands – prickles strongly hooked...................................**5**
   Lvs not v sticky below, not scented (though sometimes with glands on main veins), ±
   hairy...**7**
5 Lfts wedge-shaped below – fl-stalks hairless – r...*R. agrestis*
   Lfts rounded below – fl-stalks sticky-hairy **6**
6 Stems erect – styles v hairy – sepals persistent till fr ripe ....*R. rubiginosa* (p 206 C)
   Stems arched – styles ± hairless – sepals falling before fr ripe – lc on calc soils..............*R. micrantha*
7 Prickles hooked – lvs hairless or ± downy...*R. canina* agg (p 206 D)
   Prickles ± straight or slightly curved – lvs v downy **8**
8 Stems arching – prickles curved, stout – lfts pointed – stipule-bases straight or outspread – fls
   many together, pink or white – sepals narrowed at base, falling before fr ripe – c in S Eng.................
                                                            R. tomentosa
   Stems erect, straight – prickles straight, slender – lfts blunt, rounded – stipule-bases in-curving –
   sepals not narrowed at base, persistent till fr ripe – fls deep pink-red – c N Eng, Scot...........*R. villosa*

ROSE FAMILY

Rosaceae

Roses and Brambles

A Field Rose, *Rosa arvensis*, low scrambling or trailing shrub to 1 m; weak green stems; narrow-based arching prickles; lvs hairless with 2–3 pairs 1.0–3.5-mm long, oval lfts. Fls white, 30–50 mm, 1–6 together, styles joined in a column above (**Aa**). Sepals usually hairless, less than 1 cm, almost unlobed, falling before oval fr ripens red. Br Isles: S Eng, Wales, Ire, vc in wds, scrub, especially on heavy soils; N Eng r; **Scot abs**; Eur c. Fl 6–7.

B Burnet Rose, *R. pimpinellifolia*, low, suckering patch-forming shrub, to 50 cm, sometimes ± creeping; stems with many long straight narrow prickles and long stiff bristles; lvs with 3–5 pairs small 0.5–1.5-cm long oval lfts; often flushed purple (as may be stems). Fls solitary, cream, 20–40 mm across, styles free, woolly; sepals unlobed, persisting on globose purple-black fr (**Ba**). Br Isles o-la, especially near coasts; Eur f-la; on dunes, hths, shingle, calc gsld, scrub. Fl 5–7.

C Sweet Briar, *R. rubiginosa*, not unlike D below, but less tall and vigorous (to 1.5 m); lfts and fl-stalks covered with brownish sticky gland-bearing apple-scented hairs. Prickles unequal, ± hooked; sepals pinnately-lobed, sticky-hairy, persistent in fr (**Ca**); styles hairy, free. Br Isles: Eng, Wales f-lc; Scot r; Ire o-lf; Eur f; on gsld, scrub, usually on calc soils. Fl 6–7.

D Dog Rose, *R. canina* agg, has strong arching stems to 3 m, broad-based strongly-hooked prickles; lvs with 2–3 pairs of toothed lfts, hairless or ± hairy; fls 1–4, 4–5 cm, pink (or white), styles free; sepals (**Da**) spreading, falling before fr; v variable. Most c rose in S Br Isles and W Eur. Fl 6–7.

Brambles are a genus of scrambling, erect, or creeping shrubs and herbs, mostly spiny; lvs undivided, or usually with 3–5 (or more) pinnately or palmately arranged lfts, with stipules; fls with no epicalyx, 5 sepals joined below in a cup, 5 separate petals, many stamens, many separate carpels on a conical receptacle; frs aggregates of many tiny fleshy drupes, each with a tiny stone or pip containing a seed.

E Bramble (Blackberry), *Rubus fruticosus*, is really an agg of v numerous microspecies, differing in types of stem armament, hair and gland distribution, lf shape, fl colour, and fr shape, colour and flavour. In general, a scrambling shrub, 1–3 m, with usually arching and angled stems bearing hooked spines, prickles, hairs (sometimes gland-tipped, sticky), and lvs with 3–5 (rarely 7) oval or oblong palmately arranged lfts, which also vary in hairiness and prickliness etc. Fls white or pink (**Eb**), in panicles on ends of last year's stems. Petals often crinkly. Frs (**Ea**) red at first, then usually **shiny** black or purple-red, rarely v dark red. Br Isles, Eur; va in scrub, wds, wa, hbs, etc. Fl 5–9.

F Stone Bramble, *R. saxatilis*, creeping per herb with long runners and erect ann fl-stems of 10–25 cm, both downy, scarcely prickly, bearing trifoliate lvs; end lft 2.5–8.0 cm, stalked, downy beneath. Fls only 8–10 mm across; petals narrow, white, 3–5 mm, no longer than sepals. Fr (**Fa**) scarlet, with fewer (2–6) and larger segments than in E and G. Br Isles: Wales, N Eng, Scot o-lc; Ire o-lf; S Eng vr; Eur vl, in mt areas mostly, but f-lc to N in Denmark; on wds, rocky gd, especially on basic soils. Fl 6–8.

G Raspberry, *R. idaeus*, has erect rounded stems with straight slender prickles; lvs **pinnate**, with 3–7 lfts, green above, **white-woolly** below; fls (**Ga**) in panicles, with **erect, narrow**, white petals; ripe frs (**Gb**) **red, downy**. Br Isles, Eur; f-lc in rocky or wet wds, hths. Fl 6–8.

H Cloudberry, *R. chamaemorus*, low per herb, 5–20 cm, with creeping rhizome; lvs few, simple, rounded, shallowly palmate, 5–7-lobed (resembling mulberry lvs), wrinkled, downy; fls solitary on ends of erect shoots, with 4–5 white petals 8–12 mm long and longer than sepals (a shy flowerer). Dioecious; fr (**Ha**)

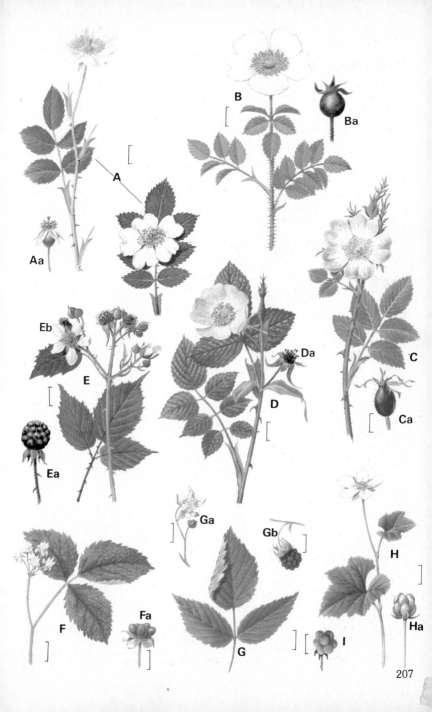

◄

orange when ripe, of few large segments. Br Isles: N Wales, r; N Eng, Scot, la on mt moors and upland bogs; **S Eng, Ire abs**; W Eur vr but la in Denmark in raised bogs at sea level, (Arctic sp of mts of central Eur and Scandinavia). Fl 6–8.

I Dewberry, *R. caesius*, the only easily named member of the agg sp E; stems few-prickled, rounded, weak, with a waxy bloom; only 3 lfts per lf; fls always white; frs (**I**) with **bluish waxy** bloom, and larger, fewer (to 20) segments per fr than in E. Br Isles: Eng, Wales, SE Scot, f-c; N Scot r-abs; Ire lf; Eur c; in damp wds, hths, etc. Fl 6–9.

Cinquefoils, Barren Strawberry (*Potentilla*) are herbs (rarely shrubs) with alt, lobed or compound lvs with lfy stipules; fls yellow, white or purple, with almost flat receptacle-cup bearing an epicalyx of 5 (less often 4) lobes and the same number of sepals and unjoined petals; many stamens; many separate tiny carpels, and a receptacle which does **not** swell up into a juicy fr. (Buttercups, in contrast, have **no** epicalyx, **no** cup below fl and **no** lfy stipules.) **Strawberries** (*Fragaria*) differ in lvs **always** trifoliate, fls **always** white, and in receptacle which **swells up** into a **juicy red** fr.

KEY TO CINQUEFOILS AND STRAWBERRIES

1 Ripe fr becoming red, fleshy, juicy, with tiny achenes embedded in it – lvs with 3 lfts only – fls always white...
Ripe fr remaining dry, scarcely fleshy, head of tiny achenes only – fls yellow (rarely white) – lvs trifoliate, palmate or pinnate.. **2**.. **5**

2 Lfts ± hairless above – terminal lfts rounded at base – fls 20–35 mm across – frs 3 cm or more wide, achenes sunk in flesh .... Garden Strawberry, *Fragaria* × *ananassa* (p 210 Kii)
Lfts hairy above – terminal lfts narrowed to base – fls 12–20 mm – frs less than 1.5 cm wide, achenes projecting **3**

3 Calyx adpressed to fr – fr not easily detached from calyx...*F. viridis* (p 210 Ki)
Calyx spreading – fr easily detached from it... **4**

4 Runners few or none – fl-stalk with spreading hairs – frs 15–25 mm – no achenes at base of fr........
.... *F. moschata* (p 210 K)
Runners many and long – fl-stalk with adpressed hairs – fls 12–18 mm – achenes all over fr...........
.... *F. vesca* (p 210 J)

5 Fls purple – fr purple-red, but dry – lvs palmate above, pinnate below – tall marsh plant to 45 cm...*Potentilla palustris* (p 212 A)
Fls white or yellow – fr green or yellow **6**

6 Fls white.. **7**
Fls yellow **8**

7 Lvs trifoliate – terminal tooth of end lft shorter than side ones – low plant, to 15 cm only ....
.... *P. sterilis* (p 210 I)
Lvs pinnate below – tall erect branched plant to 40 cm – vr............................. *P. rupestris* (p 210 G)

8 Lvs pinnate **9**
Lvs digitate (5–7 lfts) or trifoliate (3 lfts) **10**

9 Branched shrub to 100 cm – lfts narrow, untoothed, grey below.................. *P. fruticosa* (p 209 C)
Creeping herb with runners – lfts oval, toothed, silvery below .... *P. anserina* (p 210 H)

10 Lvs with undersides white-woolly.. *P. argentea* (p 209 B)
Lvs green on both sides.. **11**

11 Fl-stems stiffly erect – fls terminal – lfts often 7...*P. recta* (p 209 D)
Fl-stems creeping or ascending – lfts 3–5 .... **12**

12 Fls in groups or clusters, five-petalled... **13**
Fls borne singly, four–five-petalled (if in groups, four-petalled) **15**

13 Petals shorter than calyx – fls many, in terminal clusters – lvs trifoliate......... *P. norvegica* (p 209 Di)
Petals exceeding calyx – fls few, on branches from basal lf-rosette **14**

14 Stems creeping and rooting – stipules of rosette-lvs long, narrow – fls 10–15 mm wide ....
                                                                        P. tabernaemontani (p 210 F)
   Stems ascending, not rooting – stipules of rosette-lvs oval, blunt – fls 15–25 mm wide ....
                                                                                P. crantzii (p 210 Fi)
15 Stems creeping to erect, never rooting – lf-stalks less than 5 mm or abs – fls four-petalled, 7–
   11 mm wide...*P. erecta* (p 209 A)
   Stems creeping and rooting – lf-stalks 2.5 cm – fls five-petalled, 18–25 mm wide...........................
                                                                                P. reptans (p 210 E)
   (Plants intermediate between the last two are either *P. anglica* or, if with imperfect frs, hybrids of
   the two)

Cinquefoils, Strawberries   ▶

   A   Tormentil, *Potentilla erecta*, creeping and ascending per herb to 10 cm tall;
tufted branched stems, without the long rooting stolons of E below. Lvs shiny deep
green, almost hairless above, silky below, **without** stalks; all but basal lvs have 3 lfts
each but 2 stipules at lf-base make them appear digitate. Lfts deeply-toothed,
obovate. Fls on long stalks, 2–4 cm long, in lf-axils, loosely grouped, 7–11 mm
across, with usually only 4 yellow petals. Br Isles, Eur; vc on gslds, hths, moors
(avoids chk). Fl 6–9.
   B   Hoary Cinquefoil, *P. argentea*, similar to A, but more erect; stems **woolly**,
undersides of lfts (**Bb**) **silvery-white**, with dense down below; lfts 5, plus two small
untoothed stipules. Fls (**Ba**) yellow, 10–15 mm across, five-petalled. Br Isles: GB
from River Tay S, lf to E and SE, r to W; Wales vr; **Ire abs**; Eur o-lf; on dry sandy
gslds. Fl 6–9.
   C   Shrubby Cinquefoil, *P. fruticosa*, shrub to 1 m tall; downy stems and lvs; lvs
pinnate with 3–7 (usually 5) lfts, 1–2 cm long, **untoothed**, elliptical, pointed,
greyish-downy especially below; stipules chaffy. Fls in loose infls, yellow, five-
petalled, 20 mm across. Br Isles: N Eng (Teesdale, Lakeland), W Ire vla; lowland W
Eur S of Sweden abs; on damp rocky slopes and shingle by rivers and lakes. Fl 6–
7.
   D   Sulphur Cinquefoil, *P. recta*, erect hairy per herb, 30–70 cm tall; long-
stalked palmate lvs with 5–7 lfts, lfts to 7 cm long, deeply-toothed, hairy; fls pale
yellow, 20–25 mm across; 5 petals, longer than sepals. Introd S, E Eng, Eur (native
central Eur); on wa, gsld. Fl 6–7.   **Di   Ternate-leaved Cinquefoil**, *P. norvegica*,
is shorter (20–50 cm) with lvs all trifoliate; deeper yellow fls, 10–15 mm across;
sepals equalling petals. Introd S, E Eng, Eur (native E Eur) on wa. Fl 6–9.

                                                                                        cont

E   Creeping Cinquefoil, *P. reptans*, resembles A, but has wholly creeping stems rooting at nodes; **long-stalked** almost hairless lvs, with 5–7 lfts to 3 cm long, and untoothed stipules; fls five-petalled, 17–25 mm across, solitary on **long** stalks. Br Isles, Eur; vc in lowland hbs, gslds, wa. Fl 6–9.   **Ei   Trailing Tormentil**, *P. anglica*, appears intermediate between A and E, but is not a hybrid; stems trail and root as in E, but has ascending stems with mostly trifoliate lvs, hairy below; lower lvs with **short stalks** (1–2 cm), upper lvs with v short (0.5 cm) stalks, and ± untoothed stipules. Fls borne singly on long stalks in lf-axils, mostly four- (a few five-) petalled, 14–18 mm across, yellow. Br Isles (except N Scot), Eur f; on paths and wd borders on moderately acid soils, hths etc. Fl 6–9. (The hybrid between A and E, *P. × italica*, also occurs and resembles Ei, but with larger, longer-stalked lvs; it is obviously nearly sterile as frs do not develop properly.)

F   Spring Cinquefoil, *P. tabernaemontani*, resembles an early-flowering hairy A; but fls are in definite terminal infls, with 5 petals; stems mat-forming, prostrate, rooting at nodes, and arise from a thick branched stock covered with old lf-base fibres. Lvs palmate, the lower stalked, 0.5–2.0 cm long, with 5 lfts, upper lvs stalkless with 3 lfts; stipules narrow and long. Fl-stems, obviously downy and hairy, in axils of basal rosette-lvs; fls 10–15 mm across. Br Isles: N to central Scot, vl and scattered; **Ire abs**; Eur lf; on calc gslds and limestone rocks in sunny places. Fl 4–6.   **Fi   Alpine Cinquefoil**, *P. crantzii*, resembles F, but branches never root or form mats; stipules **oval**; fls **15–25 mm**, **orange-yellow**. Br Isles: N Wales, N Eng, Scot Highlands, vl; **Ire abs**; lowland Eur abs; on calc mt rocks. Fl 6–7.

G   Rock Cinquefoil, *P. rupestris*, tall erect per herb, 20–50 cm; hairy **pinnate** root-lvs (**Ga**) 7–15 cm, trifoliate upper stem-lvs. Fls in loose forked infls, white, five-petalled, 15–25 mm across. Br Isles: NE Scot, mid Wales vr; lowland Eur abs; on basic rocks. Fl 5–6.

H   Silverweed, *P. anserina*, creeping per herb with lvs **pinnate, silvery-silky** (especially below), in rosettes and on long rooting runners; lfts toothed; fls long-stalked in lf-axils, yellow; 5 petals, 15–20 mm across. Br Isles, Eur; vc on wa, rds, mds, hollows of sand dunes. Fl 6–8.

I   Barren Strawberry, *P. sterilis*, per herb 5–15 cm tall, with short runners; lvs, dull **bluish**-green, 0.5–2.5 cm long, trifoliate, with terminal tooth of lfts shorter than those on either side. Fls white, 10–15 mm across; petals 5, scarcely longer than sepals; ripe frs do not become fleshy and red. Br Isles (except N Scot) c; Eur: S Sweden to N Portugal, c; in scrub, wds. Fl 2–5.   ***Ii**   *P. montana* has fls 20–25 mm across, lfts untoothed except at tip. France; lf on hthy gslds. Fl 4–6.   **Iii**   *Sibbaldia procumbens*, low per herb, resembles I, but lfts wedge-shaped, three-toothed at tip only, purple-tinged below; petals yellow, v narrow, shorter than sepals or abs. N Eng to Scot; lf mt gslds, rocks. Fl 7–8.

J   Wild Strawberry, *Fragaria vesca*, per herb 5–30 cm tall, is v like I, but with long arching runners; lvs long-stalked, bright **glossy** green, hairy, ± unstalked; lfts 1–6 cm long, oblong, toothed, acute, terminal tooth longer than side-teeth; fls white, 12–18 mm across; petals 5, exceeding sepals in length; fl-stalks with adpressed lvs. Fr bright red, fleshy, 1–2 cm long, like tiny garden strawberry. Br Isles, Eur; c in woods, scrub, basic gslds. Fl 4–7.

K   Hautbois Strawberry, *F. moschata*, is taller than J, with **few** or **no** runners; **stalked** lfts; fl-stalks much exceeding lvs, with **spreading** hairs. Fls 15–25 mm; fr purplish-red, oblong, without achenes at base. Introd Br Isles r; native and introd Eur, N France to Germany; in wds, scrub. Fl 4–7.   ***Ki**   *F. viridis* is like K, but with **short** runners, lfts **downy** above, fls 15–25 mm, and sepals adpressed to fr, which is hard to detach from calyx. Eur, France to Denmark; o on calc gslds. Fl 5–7.   **Kii   Garden Strawberry**, *F. × ananassa*, has lfts ± hairless above, terminal lft rounded to base; fls 20–35 mm across; frs, 3 cm or more wide, have achenes embedded in flesh.

Cinquefoils, Avens etc

A Marsh Cinquefoil, *Potentilla palustris*, per herb to 45 cm, with woody creeping rhizome; lower lvs pinnate, with 5 or 7 lfts; lfts 3–6 cm, oblong, strongly-toothed; upper lvs palmate to trifoliate. Fls (**Aa**) in loose terminal cymes, with 5 narrow purple petals and 5 purplish sepals longer and wider than petals; frs purple, not fleshy. Br Isles, Eur; o-la in marshes and wet pools, avoids v limy water. Fl 6–7.

B Mountain Avens, *Dryas octopetala*, low creeping shrub to 8 cm tall; oblong lvs lobed like tiny oak-lvs, dark green above, white-woolly below; white fls 2.5–4.0 cm across, with usually 8 petals, many golden stamens. Sepals oblong with sticky hairs, no epicalyx. Styles form a feathery head (**Ba**) in fr. Br Isles: N Wales, N Eng r; Scot Highlands lf; N and W Ire la; lowland Eur abs; Arctic-alpine plant of limestone or basic rocks on mts, down to sea level in W Ire, N Scot. Fl 5–7.

C Lady's-mantle, *Alchemilla vulgaris* agg, complex of microspecies; spreading or erect per herbs with palmately-lobed lvs (**Ca**), hairy or not, with strong veins and terminal infls (cymes) of many small yellow-green fls with 4 sepals, no petals, 4–5 stamens, and 4 epicalyx lobes. Fls (**Cb**) usually 3–5 mm across; fr a tiny single achene. Br Isles, Eur, widespread but l in mds (most of the microspecies are upland plants). Fl 6–9.   **Ci Alpine Lady's-mantle**, *A. alpina*, has **compound palmate** lvs with **separate** elliptical lfts **silvery-silky** below; mts of NW Eng, Scot, la on acid rocks; Ire vr; lowland Eur abs. Fl 6–8.

D Parsley-piert, *Aphanes arvensis*, is like a miniature of C, ann, 2–20 cm; lvs fan-shaped, short-stalked, with 3 deeply-toothed main lobes; lvs only 2–10 mm long. Fls (**Da**) minute (less than 2 mm) in dense clusters in lf-axils, surrounded by cups formed by lf-stipules; 4 sepals, epicalyx, but no petals; stamens usually one. Br Isles, Eur; vc on ar, bare gd in gsld, on paths on dry or chalky soils. Fl 4–10.   **Di Slender Parsley-piert**, *A. microcarpa*, is even smaller, with **oblong** (**not triangular**) stipule-lobes, **inturned** (**not erect**) sepals. Br Isles; c acid soils.

E Agrimony, *Agrimonia eupatoria*, erect hairy per herb, to 60 cm; stems often reddish; lvs pinnate, with smaller lfts between the pairs of main ones, largest lfts to 6 cm long, strongly-toothed and acute, not scented or scarcely so. Fls many in long spikes, 5–8 mm across; 5 yellow petals, 5 sepals, no epicalyx. Receptacle (**Ea**) below fl enlarges in fr to form a **grooved top-shaped** cup covered with hooked spines, the outermost **horizontal**, not bent back. Br Isles f-c (except N Scot); Eur c; on hbs, rds, gslds, scrub, especially on chky soils. Fl 6–9.

F Fragrant Agrimony, *A. odorata* (*A. procera*), similar, but more robust (to 1 m), **never** reddish-tinged; lfts (**F**) more pointed, bearing strongly lemon-scented glands; fruiting cups (**Fa**) **ungrooved**, **bell-shaped**, with the outermost hooked spines **bent back**. Br Isles, more l than Agrimony, more c to S; Eur f-lc; always on acid soils, especially on wd borders, hbs. Fl 6–8.

G Salad Burnet, *Poterium sanguisorba* (*Sanguisorba minor*), ± hairless erect per herb, 15–40 cm tall; basal rosettes of pinnate lvs, with rounded but deeply toothed lfts, smell of cucumbers when crushed and can be used in a salad. Stem-lvs similar but smaller. Branched stem terminates in globular heads of tiny greenish fls 7–12 cm across; lower fls male with many long stamens, upper female with 2 purple feathery stigmas; all with 4 green or purplish sepals, no petals, no epicalyx; fruiting-cup 4 mm long, four-angled, ridged, oval, netted. Br Isles: Eng, Wales f-la; S Scot r; S Ire l; Eur vc; on calc gslds. Fl 5–8.   **Gi Fodder Burnet**, *P. polygamum*, more robust alien sp, with more deeply-toothed lfts and larger (6 mm long) fruit-cup, four-**winged**, with **pitted rough** surface.

H Great Burnet, *Sanguisorba officinalis*, similar but much larger (to 1 m tall); lfts to 4 cm long with cordate bases; fl-heads oblong, dull crimson, 1–2 cm long, each fl with 4 short stamens **and** a pale unlobed style. Br Isles: Eng, Wales f-lc (except S r); S Scot vr; Ire vr; Eur o-lc; in wet mds, fens. Fl 6–9.

213

ROSE FAMILY

Meadowsweets, Avens etc

A   Meadowsweet, *Filipendula ulmaria*, tall (to 120 cm) per herb; lower lvs stalked, pinnate, 30–60 cm long, with 2–5 pairs of main lfts (to 8 cm long) oval, pointed, sharp-toothed, dark green and hairless above, white-woolly or pale green and only downy below; pairs of tiny (1–4 mm) lfts alternate with larger ones; stipules lfy, rounded. Fls, in dense irregular umbel-like infls to 15 cm across, are fragrant, creamy, 4–10 mm across; usually 5 sepals, 5 petals, many stamens; fr of 6–10 green carpels twisted together, hairless. Br Isles, Eur; c in swamps, mds, fens, wet wds and by rivers on less acid soils. Fl 6–9.

B   Dropwort, *F. vulgaris*, per herb of similar habit to A, but usually **only 10–50 cm tall**; lvs (**Bb**) with 8–20 pairs of larger lfts, 5–15 mm long and 5 mm wide, oblong, deeply **pinnately**-cut into **narrow**, toothed lobes, green both sides, shiny, hairless. Fl-head more flattened, of **fewer**, **larger** (10–20 mm across) fls, cream, tinged **reddish** outside; carpels (**Ba**) **erect**, **downy**. Br Isles: Eng, Wales lc-la; E Scot vr; Ire vl to W; Eur o, only lc to E; on calc gslds. Fl 5–8.

C   Wood Avens, *Geum urbanum*, downy per herb to 60 cm tall; pinnate root-lvs (**Ca**) with large, usually three-lobed blunt-toothed terminal lft, and 2–3 pairs of smaller unequal side-lfts 5–10 mm long; large, lfy stipules at base; upper lvs trifoliate or undivided. Fls 1.0–1.5 cm across, long-stalked, erect, with 5 **spreading yellow** 5–9-mm unstalked, **rounded** petals. Fr-head (**Cb**) of many hairy achenes, with 5–10 mm-long zigzag-shaped hairless styles; in fr, lower part of style persists as a hook for animal dispersal. Br Isles, Eur; vc in wds, hbs, scrub on less acid soils. Fl 5–8.

D   Water Avens, *Geum rivale*, is close to C and hybridizes with it; its root-lvs (**Da**) have a normally **unlobed**, **rounded** terminal-lft (**Da**) up to 10 cm across, with small **sharp** teeth; **drooping** fls with **orange-pink**, **erect** petals, 10–15 mm long, with obvious stalks and **shallow-notched** tips, **purple** (not green) sepals and epicalyx. Fr-head stalked, styles hairy above. Br Isles: GB f-lc, but SW Eng r, **SE Eng abs**; Ire o-lf; Eur o-la (W France abs); in wet mds, marshes, moist wds, rock ledges on mts. Fl 5–9.

SUNDEW FAMILY

Sundews (*Drosera*) are small per herbs with undivided, long-stalked lvs, in basal rosettes, and covered with sticky, red-tipped, gland-bearing hairs. They trap, then digest the proteins in, small insects, probably to supplement their nitrate nutrition because their normal acid bog habitats are nutrient-deficient. Fls, 5 mm across, in erect sometimes forked infls, with 5–8 white petals, 5–8 sepals, 5–8 stamens, only open briefly in sunshine; frs tiny many-seeded capsules.

E   Round-leaved Sundew, *Drosera rotundifolia*, has almost circular lf-blades, to 1 cm across, on long horizontally-spreading hairy stalks; infl lfless, 10–15 cm tall, sometimes forked; fls usually six-petalled. Br Isles, Eur; lc in wet acid peat on hths or among Sphagnum in bogs, decreasing through habitat destruction. Fl 6–8.

F   Oblong-leaved Sundew, *D. intermedia*, has narrow **spoon-shaped** lvs (**Fa**) with blades to 1 cm long × 0.5 cm wide, narrowing **quickly** into long (1–3 cm) **erect**, **hairless** stalks; infl **barely longer** than lvs, arising from **below** rosette, upward-curving. Br Isles widespread but vl: W Scot, W Ire and hths of S Eng lc; Eur o-lf; on bare acid damp peat on hths or in bog pools also on Sphagnum. Fl 6–8.

G   Great Sundew, *D. anglica*, has v narrow obovate lvs (**G**) widest below tips, **gradually** narrowing into v long stalks; blades to 4 cm long, stalks up to 12 cm; infl, to **twice** length of lvs, springs from **centre** of rosette. Br Isles: W, N Scot, W Ire f-la; Wales, Eng r (but lf in Norfolk, New Forest–Dorset); Eur r, decreasing, but vlf to W and N; in Sphagnum in bog pools and open fen pools. Fl 6–8.

SAXIFRAGE FAMILY   *Saxifragaceae*

A family of mostly short (except the taller A, below), mostly per herbs, with simple but often lobed lvs, 2 stigmas, and capsular frs formed of 2 carpels joined only below; sepals joined below to form a shallow cup. Stamens twice number of sepals. **Saxifrages** proper (*Saxifraga*) have 5 sepals, 5 petals, 10 stamens; **Golden-saxifrages** (*Chrysosplenium*) have 4 sepals, 4 petals, no petals, 8 stamens. **Grass of Parnassus**, the only genus in the family Parnassiaceae, is close to the Saxifragaceae, but has white fls with green veins, 5 fan-shaped sterile stamens alternating with normal ones, and 4 stigmas. Except for A and B (below), Saxifrages are mostly mt plants only. See key, p 218.

Saxifrages, Golden-saxifrages

A   Meadow Saxifrage, *Saxifraga granulata*, per herb 10–50 cm tall, with bulbils in axils of lower lvs, and no runners. Basal rosette-lvs (**Ab**) kidney-shaped, long-stalked, bluntly-toothed, 2–3 cm across, with scattered hairs; smaller, shorter-stalked, narrower lvs up the erect stems. Fl-stems loosely-branched, sticky-hairy, with 2–12 white fls, 1–2 cm across. Receptacle-cup fused to ovary, which it encloses more than halfway up; two carpels (**Aa**), conspicuous both in fl and in the two-celled capsular fr. Br Isles: Eng (except SW, Sussex) f-lc; Scot o-lf in E and S, **NW and mts abs**; Ire vr (E coast only); Eur f-lc in lowlands; on dry, sandy gsld, mds by rivers, avoids v acid soils. Fl 4–6.   **Ai   Drooping Saxifrage**, *S. cernua*, vr Scot alpine, is close to A, but 3–15 cm tall, with lower lvs sharp-lobed; red bulbils in axils of upper lvs; 1 or no fls.

B   Rue-leaved Saxifrage, *S. tridactylites*, small erect sticky-hairy ann, 2–15 cm tall. Red-tinged lvs, lower with broad, stalked, 3–5-lobed or fingered blades 1 cm long or less, upper lvs simple, smaller. Fls solitary or in branched open cymes, 3–5 mm across, with bell-shaped reddish calyx; 5 white petals only 2–3 mm long. Br Isles: Eng, Wales f-lc; Scot r, mostly E; Ire f; Eur f-lc; on dry open sandy gd, wall-tops especially in lowlands. Fl 4–5.

C   Purple Saxifrage, *S. oppositifolia*, creeping, mat-forming per herb with densely-set, tiny, oval lvs (2–6 mm long) in opp pairs along stems, with **chalky pits** on tips and bristly margins; fls solitary, almost stalkless, **rosy-purple**, 10–20 mm across, five-petalled. Br Isles: from Brecon and Yorks N on basic mt rocks and cliffs, at sea level in N Scot, r-lf (Scot Highlands f-lc); NW Ire vr; lowlands of W Eur (S of Arctic) abs. Fl 3–5.

D   St Patrick's Cabbage, *S. spathularis*, has basal rosettes of ± erect, hairless, spoon-shaped lvs, sharp-toothed above, tapered into broad, long stalks only hairy at base, 3–5 cm long (with stalks); fl-stems lfless, branched above, sticky-hairy, with **many** fls 8–10 mm across; petals (**Da**) white, with 1–3 yellow spots at base, many red spots above. **GB abs**; W Ire lf-la; Eur, not N of Pyrenees; among acid rocks, usually where damp, in mt areas. Fl 6–8.   **Di   *S. umbrosa*** has blunt teeth on the spreading 1–6 cm long lvs; terminal tooth shorter than neighbours; lf-stalks **v hairy**. Introd W Yorks vr.   **Dii London Pride**, *S. spathularis* × *umbrosa*, has larger, more erect lvs than Di, with up to 12 teeth on each side. Garden escape, f.   **Diii Kidney Saxifrage**, *S. hirsuta*, differs from D in its hairy **kidney-shaped** lvs, cordate (not wedge-shaped) at base; lf-stalks narrow, 1 mm wide. Hybridizes in Ire with D; lc in SW Ire (and Pyrenees).

E   Mossy Saxifrage, *S. hypnoides*, mat-forming mossy-looking per herb, with both flowering rosettes and long trailing sterile lfy shoots; rosettes bear mostly three-lobed lvs, 1-cm long; lobes linear, pointed, hairy only on their long stalks; sterile-shoot-lvs ± undivided. Infls erect, **few**; fls white, five-petalled, 10–15 mm across. Br Isles: Wales, Derby, N Eng to N Scot lf-la; Mendips r; Ire vl in W and N; lowland Eur abs (native Norway, Vosges); on rock ledges and scree, mostly basic, in hills and mts. Fl 5–7.   **Ei   Yellow Saxifrage**, *S. aizoides*, has many

creeping sterile shoots and erect lfy fl-shoots, all with stalkless, pointed, undivided, narrow-oblong lvs, 10–20 mm long; fls in loose heads, 8–15 mm across, **yellow** with **red** spots on petals. Mts N Eng to N Scot lc; NW Ire r; lowland Eur abs. Fl 6–8.

F   Opposite-leaved Golden-saxifrage, *Chrysosplenium oppositifolium*, low per herb with mats of creeping shoots; opp pairs of stalked, rounded lvs with wedge-shaped bases; erect 5–15 cm-tall fl-stems bear repeatedly forked umbel-like cymes of tiny 3–5 mm-wide golden fls (**Fa**), surrounded by large green-yellow bracts; calyx four-toothed, no petals, 8 stamens, 2 carpels. Br Isles (except in E mid Eng) c-la; Eur lc mainly near W coasts; in springy areas and by streams in wds, mt rocks. Fl 4–5.

G   Alternate-leaved Golden-saxifrage, *C. alternifolium*, larger version of F, with creeping **lfless** stolons (no creeping lfy stems); **long-stalked**, **kidney-shaped** basal lvs, 1.0–2.5 cm across, with scattered bristles; stem-lvs usually only l, not opp; fl-heads slightly larger, with a more golden sheen on bracts. Br Isles: GB o-lf to E, **abs W**; **Ire abs**; Eur c, **away** from W coastal region; in boggy wds and mt rocks on more base-rich soils. Fl 4–5.

GRASS OF PARNASSUS FAMILY

Parnassiaceae

H   Grass of Parnassus, *Parnassia palustris*, erect hairless per herb, 10–30 cm tall; root-lvs oval-cordate, long-stalked; one stalkless cordate stem-lf low down; fl (**Ha**) **solitary**, 15–30 mm across; 5 white, oval, green-veined petals; 5 fertile stamens; 5 alt **fan-branched sterile stamens (Hb)** with **yellow glands on tips; 4 stigmas**; fr a capsule. Br Isles, widespread, but c only in Scot, **abs extreme S Eng**; Ire lf; Eur o-lc; in marshes, fens, especially where basic. Fl 7–10.

KEY TO SAXIFRAGE FAMILY

1 Petals abs – sepals 4 – stamens 8 – fls green...*Chrysosplenium* (p 218 F,G)
   Petals normally present – sepals 5 – stamens 10...*Saxifraga* 2
2 Lvs alt – fls white or yellow... 3
   Lvs opp – fls purple – stem creeping – mts only, r.............................*S. oppositifolia* (p 216 C)
3 Fls yellow... 4
   Fls white, sometimes spotted red or yellow.. 5
4 Ovary free from calyx – fls usually solitary – lower lvs stalked, 1–3 cm long – stem with red hairs
   – on mt bogs, vr – N Br Isles, Denmark...*S. hirculus*
   Ovary fused to calyx – fls several – all lvs stalkless, 1–2 cm – stem with no red hairs ....
                    S. aizoides (p 216 Ei)
5 Fl-stem naked 6
   Fl-stem lfy... 9
6 Lvs ± stalkless, teeth few – infl loose – in flushes on mts, o ....*S. stellaris*
   Lvs stalked, closely toothed... 7
7 Fls in a dense head, unspotted – mts of Scot, vr ....*S. nivalis*
   Fls spotted, in an open branched infl.. 8
8 Lvs kidney-shaped, bases cordate – lf-stalk hairy, to 1 mm wide – Ire, r......... *S. hirsuta* (p 216 Diii)
   Lvs wedge-shaped at base – lf-stalk hairless, 2 mm broad or more – W Ire, lf...................................
           S. spathularis, and hybrids with *S. umbrosa* (p 216 D,D)
9 Erect plants – no barren, creeping or rosette-forming shoots 10
   Creeping plants of mossy habit... 12
10 Lvs 3 or more fingered, tapered to stalk – ann – lowlands, f ....*S. tridactylites* (p 216 B)
   Lower lvs cordate at base, rounded at top – per 11
11 Tall (10–50 cm) lowland plant – lvs kidney-shaped, bluntly-lobed – fls many...................................
           S. granulata (p 216 A)
   Shorter (3–15 cm) alpine plant – lvs kidney-shaped, the lower sharp-toothed – fls one or none –
   red bulbils in upper lf-axils – vr ....*S. cernua* (p 261 Ai)
   Short (2–8 cm) alpine plant – lvs palmate, lobes blunt – fls 1–3 – mts of Scot, r .... *S. rivularis*

SAXIFRAGE FAMILY

12 Lf-lobes oblong, blunt – lvs only in dense compact rosettes at base of fl-stems – petals 5 mm, greenish-white – mts of Scot, vr .... *S. caespitosa*
Lf-lobes linear, pointed – lvs in loose rosettes and on trailing shoots – petals 5–10 mm, white – on limestone hills, lf .... *S. hypnoides* (p 216 E)

STONECROP FAMILY
Crassulaceae

A family of **succulents**, with undivided **fleshy** lvs, no stipules; fls mostly small, star-like, five-petalled, with 5 sepals, 5 or 10 stamens, and 5 separate carpels which develop into follicles. In **Stonecrops** (*Sedum* and *Crassula*) petals are free; in **Wall Pennywort** (*Umbilicus*) petals are joined into a cylindrical tube, and lvs peltate.

KEY TO STONECROPS (*SEDUM, CRASSULA*)

1 Tiny succulent plant, becoming blood-red when in fr – opp oval lvs only 1.2 mm long – fls inconspicuous, with 3 (or 4) petals – in bare sandy places .... *Crassula tillaea* (p 220 G)
Larger succulent-lvd plants – lvs over 3 mm long – conspicuous white, yellow or purplish fls ....
(*Sedum*) **2**
2 Lvs **broad, flat**, ± toothed – tall plants (15–60 cm) – dense umbel-like infls. **3**
Lvs **narrow**, either round in cross-section or flat above and rounded below, untoothed – fls five-petalled **4**
3 Fls **yellow** – petals 4 – obvious fleshy rhizome – on mts .... *S. rosea* (p 220 Ai)
Fls **pink-purple** – petals 5 – rhizome neither obvious nor fleshy .... *S. telephium* (p 220 A)
4 Petals **pink** – lvs alt, v sticky-hairy, reddish-flushed – on mts .... *S. villosum* (p 220 Fi)
Petals **yellow** **5**
Petals **white** **8**
5 Small plants (to 10 cm tall) – lvs **blunt**, ± oval or cylindrical, 7 mm long or less. **6**
Larger plants (15–30 cm tall) – lvs **pointed**, linear, parallel-sided, 8 mm long or more **7**
6 Lvs **oval** to blunt-triangular, adpressed to stem, taste peppery .... *S. acre* (p 220 D)
Lvs **cylindrical**, spreading, taste mild – r .... *S. sexangulare* (p 220 Di)
7 Lvs **round** in cross-section, spread **evenly** along fl-less shoots .... *S. reflexum* (p 220 C)
Lvs **flattened** on upper side, round below, **clustered** at tips of fl-less shoots. ....
S. forsterianum (p 220 Ci)
8 Lvs **opp**, ± downy, oval, round in cross-section .... *S. dasyphyllum* (p 220 F)
Lvs **alt**, hairless **9**
9 Lvs 6–12 mm long, green or reddish, elliptical – infl stalked, umbel-like, 7–15 cm tall. ....
S. album (p 220 B)
Lvs 3–5 mm long, grey-green, ± oval – infl little-branched, 2–5 cm tall .... *S. anglicum* (p 220 E)

STONECROP FAMILY

Crassulaceae

See also key to Stonecrops, p 219.

A Orpine, *Sedum telephium*, hairless, succulent, erect, rather waxy-lvd, per herb, 20–60 cm tall, often reddish below, with flat, toothed, alt oval-oblong lvs 2–8 cm long, up the stems; fls in dense umbel-like heads, red-purple, 9–12 mm across; stamens 10, 5 purple erect carpels. GB widespread but only lf (N Scot vr); Ire, probably introd; Eur o-lc; on dry wd borders, hbs, especially on sand or gravel, also among rocks. Fl 7–9. **Ai Roseroot**, *S. rosea*, similar to A, but with obvious fleshy rhizome above gd level; dioecious orange-yellow **four**-petalled fls. Br Isles: Wales, N Eng, S Scot, W and N Ire, vlf; Scot Highlands f-lc; lowland Eur abs. On mt rocks, sea cliffs. Fl 5–8.

B White Stonecrop, *S. album*, hairless evergreen per, 7–15 cm tall, with shiny, green to red-tinged, cylindrical-oblong, blunt lvs 6–12 mm long, alt along both creeping and erect stems. Fls 6–9 mm across, in branched umbel-like cymes; 5 petals, **white** or pink-tinged, spreading. Br Isles widely introd (probably native SW Eng); Eur, native in W and S France, introd elsewhere; on rocks, walls, sea cliffs. Fl 6–8.

C Reflexed Stonecrop, *S. reflexum*, taller than B (10–30 cm); lvs, on creeping stems, deeply-set, longer (8–20 mm), alt, cylindrical, pointed; spur-like projections on the lf-bases; dense umbel-like heads of **yellow** fls 15 mm across, usually with 7 petals. Br Isles, widely introd in Eng, Wales, Ire; W Eur (native in S Eur); on walls, rocks, dry banks. Fl 6–8. **Ci Rock Stonecrop**, *S. forsterianum*, similar, but native plant on rocks in **W Eng and Wales**; with lvs **flat** above, forming dense heads on tips of sterile shoots. Eur N to Netherlands introd (S and W Eur native). Fl 6–7.

D Biting Stonecrop, *S. acre*, low (2–10 cm) mat-forming plant; lvs adpressed, **egg-shaped**, fleshy, yellow-green, only 3–5 mm long, with peppery taste; infls branched, not forming dense heads, fls 12 mm across, yellow. Br Isles, Eur; f-c on dry gsld (often where chky), dunes, beaches, walls. Fl 6–7. **Di Tasteless Stonecrop**, *S. sexangulare*, has no peppery taste; lvs spreading, **cylindrical**; fls smaller (9 mm across), yellow. GB, Eur, introd on old walls (perhaps native on beaches in Denmark). Fl 7–8.

E English Stonecrop, *S. anglicum*, low (2–5 cm) mat-forming evergreen per; lvs alt, egg-shaped, waxy-grey, fleshy, usually red-tinged; little-branched infls of few white fls, 12 mm across, pink-tinged on back of petals. Br Isles vc W coast, lc S, E coasts; Ire f-lvc; Eur: W France lc; introd N to Denmark; on acid rocks, coastal shingles, dry gsld. Fl 6–9.

F Thick-leaved Stonecrop, *S. dasyphyllum*, is close to E, but has **sticky-downy** grey-green lvs in **opp** pairs on **erect** sterile shoots (F); fls white, 6 mm across. Br Isles: S Eng, S Ire introd; Eur: W France, S Germany native; on old walls. Fl 6–7. **Fi Hairy Stonecrop**, *S. villosum*, has erect stems 5–15 cm; lvs alt, **linear**, blunt, **reddish**, **hairy** with many **sticky** glands **flat** above; fls in open cymes, **pink**. N Eng to central Scot: lowland Eur abs; o-vlf in wet stony places on basic soils in mts. Fl 6–7.

G Mossy Stonecrop, *Crassula tillaea*, resembles a minute ann *Sedum*, with creeping and ascending lfy stems 1–5 cm long, that become **bright red**; dense-set fleshy lvs, 1–2 mm long, joined in opp pairs; fls (**Ga**) white, 1–2 mm across, stalkless, in axils of most lvs; usually 3 sepals, 3 petals. S Eng, E Anglia, vlf; Eur: France to NW Germany; on bare sandy, gravelly gd on hths. Fl 6–7. ***Gi** *C. aquatica*, related plant of pond margins, has distant, linear lvs 3–5 mm; four-petalled fls. Denmark, N Germany r.

cont

A

B

C

D

E

F

G   Ga   2mm

Ia   I

Ib   2mm   Ic

J

Ha   5mm   H

Ka   2mm

L

K

M   Ma

221

STONECROP FAMILY
Crassulaceae

H   Navelwort or **Wall Pennywort**, *Umbilicus rupestris*, erect hairless per herb, 10–40 cm tall; lvs, mostly from the base, on long fleshy stalks, peltate (resembling hollow-centred navels), are circular, fleshy, bright green with rounded teeth, 1–7 cm across. Infl a long spike of many greenish-white fls (**Ha**) with cylindrical or bell-shaped five-toothed corollas, 8–10 mm long. Br Isles: GB c to W, N to Argyll, rarer E to Kent; Ire f-c; Eur: W France c; in crevices of acid rocks and walls (oceanic sp). Fl 6–8.

CURRANT FAMILY
Grossulariaceae

Small shrubs with alt, palmately-lobed lvs; fls in racemes; 5 petals, 5 sepals, ovary **inferior**; 2 styles, joined below; fr a **berry**.

I   Red Currant, *Ribes sylvestre*, deciduous shrub 1–2 m tall; lvs 3–5-lobed, **downy**, **unscented**, cordate at base; spreading racemes of 6–20 greenish fls; receptacle-cup (on which sepals sit) **five-angled** (**Ia**), **saucer-shaped**, with a raised rim round base of styles (section **Ib**); berries (**Ic**) **red**, 6–10 mm across, globular. GB, Eur f-lc; Ire vr; in moist wds, probably native but often escape. Fl 4–5.

J   Black Currant, *R. nigrum*, looks like I, but lvs hairless above, with glands beneath that have a **tom-cat smell** when bruised; berries (**J**) **black**, 12–15 mm across. Br Isles: GB widespread and lc, Ire r; Eur f; in moist wds, fen carrs (native or introd as I). Fl 4–5.

K   Downy Currant, *Ribes spicatum*, close to I, with red fr, but lvs (**K**) usually **without** a cordate base; fl-receptacle **circular**, with **no raised rim** and **not saucer-shaped** above (section **Ka**). Br Isles: N Eng, Scot; Eur: Denmark, N Germany; lf wds on limestone, native but sometimes an escape. Fl 4–5.

L   Mountain Currant, *R. alpinum*, has red frs like I, but dioecious; racemes always **erect**, bracts of fls **exceed** fl-stalks. Br Isles: N Wales, N Eng; Eur: Denmark; native on limestone rocks (escape elsewhere in GB, lowland Eur), o-r. Fl 4–5.

M   Gooseberry, *R. uva-crispa*, shrub with **spines** at lf-bases, fls only 1–3 together, bent back petals; frs (**Ma**) oval, 10–20 mm long, bristly, yellow-green. GB, Eur f-lc; in wds, hbs (probably sometimes native in wet wds, also escape). Fl 3–5.

WILLOWHERB FAMILY
Onagraceae

Herbs with lvs in opp pairs, undivided; fl-parts in twos or fours (4 sepals, 4 petals, 8 stamens; 4 carpels in **Willowherbs**, *Epilobium*; parts in twos in **Enchanter's-nightshades**, *Circaea*). Ovary **inferior**.

KEY TO WILLOWHERB FAMILY

1 Petals present.. **2**
  Petals abs – stamens 4 – creeping aquatic plant...*Ludwigia* (p 224)
2 Petals 2, white, but each deeply cleft – stamens 2 – fr a bristly nut............................ *Circaea* (p 224)
  Petals 4 – stamens 8 – fr a capsule... **3**
3 Fls yellow, large – seeds not plumed.. *Oenothera* (p 224)
  Fls pink (or white) – seeds with plumes of hairs **4**
4 Lvs spirally arranged – petals not equal..*Chamaenerion* (p 224)
  Lvs opp, at least below – petals all equal .... *Epilobium* (key below)

KEY TO WILLOWHERBS (*EPILOBIUM*)

(**Willowherbs** (*Epilobium*) are sometimes difficult to separate; occurrence of hybrids makes matters even more difficult)

1 Stem wholly creeping, rooting at nodes – lvs circular – introd from New Zealand – in wet places in hills of Br Isles – lf.. *Epilobium neterioides*
  Stem at least partially erect.. **2**

2 Stem and lvs with long spreading hairs, many without glands – stigma four-lobed..........................**3**
Stem and lvs hairless, or with adpressed hairs and spreading gland-tipped hairs only (use lens) – stigma various...**4**
3 Petals over 1 cm long, purple-pink – lvs 6–12 cm, clasping stem ....*E. hirsutum* (p 223 E)
Petals less than 1 cm, pale pink – lvs 3–7 cm, not clasping stem................*E. parviflorum* (p 223 F)
4 Stigma with 4 lobes in a cross...**5**
Stigma undivided, club-shaped..**6**
5 All lvs in opp pairs, lf-stalks v short – lf-base rounded ....*E. montanum* (p 223 A)
Upper lvs alt – lf-stalks long – lf-base tapered into stalk............................*E. lanceolatum* (p 223 B)
6 Stem cylindrical, without ridges running down it – lvs usually less than 1 cm wide..........................
E. palustre (p 224 G)
Stem with 4 (sometimes only 2) ridges running down it – lvs wider than 1 cm across....................**7**
7 Lvs with stalks 0.5 cm or more..*E. roseum* (p 223 D)
Lvs with stalks less than 0.5 cm, or none **8**
8 Stems wholly erect – fl-buds erect **9**
Stems creeping, then ascending – upper fls drooping – alpine only **11**
9 Stem and ovary with short spreading gland-tipped hairs as well as crisped adpressed ones ....
E. adenocaulon (p 223 C)
Stem without glandular hairs...**10**
10 Lvs strap-shaped – no gland-tipped hairs anywhere – capsule over 7 cm – no runners ....
E. tetragonum (p 224 H)
Lvs oval-lanceolate – gland-tipped hairs on calyx-tube – capsule 4–6 cm – long runners..............
E. obscurum (p 224 Hi)
11 Stem 1–2 mm across – lvs lanceolate, 1–2 cm – obvious runners – fls 4–5 mm across – in mt
flushes in N of GB, vl...*E. anagallidifolium*
Stem 2–3 mm across – lvs oval, 1.5–4.0 cm long – stolons underground only – fls 8–9 mm
across – in mt flushes in N GB, vl...*E. alsinifolium*

Willowherbs etc

   A   Broad-leaved Willowherb, *Epilobium montanum*, erect per herb, 20–60 cm, nearly hairless, or with few curved hairs on **round** stem (**Ab**); lvs opp, oval-lanceolate (sometimes in whorls of 3), toothed, nearly hairless, with **rounded** bases and **v short** stalks. Fls 6–9 mm across, in terminal racemes; petals rosy-pink, notched; stigma (**Aa**) of 4 white lobes; capsule 4–8 cm, downy with curved hairs. Br Isles, Eur; vc in wds, hbs, walls, rocks etc. Fl 6–8.
   B   Spear-leaved Willowherb, *E. lanceolatum*, has the nearly hairless **round** stem (**Bb**) and **four-lobed** stigma (**Ba**) of A, but the nearly hairless lvs are **alt** above, **elliptical-**lanceolate, sparsely-toothed except at base, with stalks 4–8 mm long into which lvs **gradually narrow**. S Eng, S Wales lf; Eur, from Belgium S, lc; in open wds, walls, hbs, wa, rocks. Fl 7–9.
   C   American Willowherb, *E. adenocaulon*, per herb, with short-stalked hairless oval-lanceolate lvs (**C**) and habit of A, but with 4 **raised ridges** on the stem (**Cb**), which has many **crisped** and **short, spreading, gland-tipped hairs** above and on the ovaries (**Cc**). Stigma (**Ca**) **club-shaped**, undivided. Eng, Wales, much of Eur; introd since 1890 from N America, c in wds, hbs, wa. Fl 6–8.
   D   Pale Willowherb, *E. roseum*, has club-shaped stigmas (**Da**), capsule with sticky hairs, and four ridges on stem as in C, but the nearly hairless, elliptical pointed lvs (**D**) **taper gradually** into a **long stalk** up to 20 mm long, much as in B. Br Isles: Eng f-lc; Scot r; Ire vr; Eur lf; in wds, wa, hbs, gdns. Fl 7–8.
   E   Great Willowherb, *E. hirsutum*, tall per herb, 80–150 cm, with round stems; densely downy on stem and lvs, with **spreading** hairs, both gland-tipped and without glands; lvs opp, lanceolate, clasping, pointed, stalkless, 6–12 cm long; fls deep purple-pink, 15–23 mm across; stigma (**Ea**) with 4 stout creamy lobes that arch back. Br Isles (except NW Scot and some islands) vc; Eur vc; in fens, marshes, river banks. Fl 7–8.
   F   Hoary Willowherb, *E. parviflorum*, has round hairy stem, hairy lvs, and four-

lobed stigma (**Fa**), as in E, but less tall (30–60 cm), less stout; hairs throughout much shorter; lf-bases do not clasp or run down stem as in E; fls (**F**) only 6–9 mm across, with pale pink petals. Br Isles (except Scot Highlands), Eur vc; on streamsides, marshes, wa. Fl 7–8.

G   Marsh Willowherb, *E. palustre*, erect per herb, 15–60 cm, much slenderer than all the foregoing spp. Stem (**Gb**) cylindrical without ridges (though sometimes 2 rows of crisp hairs); lvs stalkless, strap-shaped, 0.4–1.0 cm wide, narrowed to apex and base. Small fls (4–6 mm across) have club-shaped stigmas (**Ga**). Br Isles, Eur; f-lc in **acid** marshes, bogs, ditches. Fl 7–8.

H   Square-stalked Willowherb, *E. tetragonum*, resembles C in its 4 v conspicuous raised stem-ridges (**Hb**) and club-shaped stigmas (**Ha**), but lvs (**H**) strap-shaped, blunt, narrow (2–7 cm long × 0.3–1.0 cm wide), almost parallel-sided, almost stalkless. Capsules 7–10 cm long; gland-tipped hairs quite abs everywhere, though plants downy above. Br Isles: Eng, Wales f-lc; Scot, Ire vr; Eur lc; in damp wd glades, hbs, streamsides, wa. Fl 7–8. **Hi   Short-fruited Willowherb**, *E. obscurum*, closely resembles H in its stems with 4 raised ridges, its stalkless, almost hairless lvs and club-shaped stigma; but has elongated summer runners, broader lanceolate lvs (3–7 × 0.8–1.7 cm), glandular hairs on the calyx, and shorter frs (4–6 cm long). Br Isles, Eur; vc moist wds, marshes, etc. Fl 7–8.

I   Rosebay Willowherb, *Chamaenerion angustifolium*, tall erect per herb to 120 cm, nearly hairless; lanceolate alt lvs (**Ia**) spirally arranged up stems. Fls rose-purple, 2–3 cm across, borne in spikes, spread out horizontally; 2 upper petals broader than the 2 lower. Stigma (four-lobed) and stamens bend down eventually. Br Isles: GB vc-lva; Ire o, in e; Eur c; wa, wds, gdns, railways etc. Fl 7–9.

J   Enchanter's-nightshade, *Circaea lutetiana*, per herb with creeping root-stock and **erect stems** 20–70 cm tall, v sparsely downy; lf-stalks round, lvs opp, oval, **rounded** at bases, tapering to tips, 4–10 cm long, with v small shallow teeth. Infl spike-like, elongated, held well above lvs; fls (**Ja**) each with 2 petals 2–4 mm long that are divided halfway, 2 long stamens, 2 stigma-lobes. Fr covered with hooked white bristles, not bursting open when ripe. Br Isles vc (N Scot and Scot islands r); Eur vc; in shady wds, hbs, on base rich soils. Fl 6–8.

K   Alpine Enchanter's-nightshade, *C. alpina*, smaller almost hairless per herb, 10–20 cm, with a **tuberous** rootstock; lvs 2–6 cm long, **cordate** at base, with **strong** but distant teeth, are v thin, shiny, almost translucent, with **winged** stalk. Fls in **tight cluster**, infl elongating after they have fallen. Frs with soft, less hooked bristles. Br Isles: SW Wales, N Eng, SW Scot, r and l in hilly rocky mt wds; Eur: Denmark S, lf, to E France r; in damp wds, (abs in lowlands to S and SW). Fl 7–8. **Ki   Upland Enchanter's-nightshade**, *C. × intermedia*, the hybrid of J and K, is ± intermediate between them, with J's elongated fl-spikes and K's cordate strongly-toothed lvs. More c than K in Wales, N Eng, Scot, N Ire; also N Eur.

L   Common Evening-primrose, *Oenothera biennis*, tall bi herb, with downy lfy stems with no red-based hairs; lvs lanceolate; petals yellow, 18–25 mm. Like other Evening Primroses, introd from N America; Br Isles, widespread in wa. Fl 6–9. **Li   Large-flowered Evening-primrose**, *Oe. erythrosepala*, has petals 35–50 mm long and red bulbous-based hairs on stem. **Lii   Small-flowered Evening-primrose**, *Oe. parviflora*, has petals 11–18 mm and red-based hairs on the stem. **Liii   Fragrant Evening-primrose**, *Oe. stricta*, has v narrow wavy-edged lvs, no red-based hairs; petals 30–40 mm, yellow, turning orange-red.

M   Hampshire-purslane, *Ludwigia palustris*, per **reddish**-suffused aquatic herb, creeping on mud or floating in water, with hairless stems rooting at nodes below; lvs 1.5–3.0 cm long × 0.5–2.0 cm wide, in opp pairs, oval to elliptical, short-stalked, blunt, hairless. Fls (**Ma**) 3 mm across, solitary in lf-axils; ovary inferior, 4 sepals, no petals, 4 stamens, and a four-lobed stigma. Eng vr (only in and around ponds, swamps in New Forest); Eur, W France r. Fl 6–8.

224

225

PURPLE-LOOSESTRIFE FAMILY   *Lythraceae*

Herbs (in Eur) with opp or whorled lvs; fls radially symmetrical, usually with parts in sixes; ovary superior, within calyx-tube; fr a capsule.

A   Purple-loosestrife, *Lythrum salicaria*, downy erect per herb, 60–120 cm; lvs sessile, oval-lanceolate, pointed, untoothed, in opp pairs or in whorls of 3 below, alt above. Infl dense, spike-like, 10–30 cm long; fls 10–15 mm across, in whorls in bract-axils, with downy calyx-tubes, 12 stamens, 6 red-purple petals. Br Isles f-la, (but **r to abs N Scot**); Eur f-la; by rivers, lakes, swamps, fens. Fl 6–8.   **Ai   Grass-poly**, *L. hyssopifolia*, ann, 10–20 cm, with narrow linear lvs and pale pink fls 4 mm across, solitary in lf-axils. Eng now vr (Cambridge only); Eur only to S, r; on bare gd flooded in winter. Fl 6–7.

B   Water-purslane, *Peplis portula*, hairless creeping ann; stems 5–20 cm long, rooting at nodes; oval lvs widest above, 1–2 cm long; fls 1 mm across, solitary in lf-axils, calyx-tube (**Ba**) with 6 pointed teeth, petals hardly visible; fr a globular capsule 2 mm across. Br Isles f-lc especially in S, **abs N Scot**; Eur f-lc; on damp bare gd on hths, wdland paths, by ponds, on acid soils flooded in winter. Fl 6–10.

SPURGE FAMILY (see also p 243)   *Euphorbiaceae*

C   Dog's Mercury, *Mercurialis perennis*, hairy per herb, 15–40 cm tall, with creeping rhizomes; unbranched stems bear pairs of short-stalked opp oval-elliptical lvs, 3–8 cm long, with small teeth. Sexes separate; male fls (**Cb**) in erect, catkin-like spikes in lf-axils, each fl with 3 green sepals 2 mm long, and 8–15 stamens; female fls (**Ca**) in groups of 1–3 on 3 cm-long stalks, each with 3 sepals, and rounded ovary that forms a two-celled **hairy** fr 6–8 mm broad. (Lvs on female plants wider than on males.) Br Isles: GB c-la (except N Scot vr); Ire native one spot in Clare; Eur vc; in wds on basic or calc soils, rocks on mts. Fl 2–4.

D   Annual Mercury, *M. annua*, of similar habit, but ann, almost hairless; stems branched; lvs only 2–5 cm long, fresh **shiny** green, with stalks 2–15 mm long; male fls in catkins (**Db**), female fls (**Da**) almost stalkless with **bristly** frs 3–4 mm broad. Br Isles: SE Eng lc, rarer to N and hardly into Scot; Ire r, SE only: Eur N to Denmark f-lc; in ar, gdns, wa, on good soils. Fl 7–10.

NETTLE FAMILY   *Urticaceae*

Herbs, often with stinging hairs and simple lvs. Fls small, of separate sexes, usually on the same plant; calyx four-lobed, green; petals none; stamens 4–5; ovary one-celled; fr a tiny nut.

E   Common Nettle, *Urtica dioica*, coarse, roughly hairy erect per herb with yellow fleshy far-creeping rhizomes. Lvs in opp pairs, oval-cordate, pointed, short-stalked, coarsely-toothed, covered (like stem) with stinging hairs that release irritant histamine-containing juice when broken. Plants dioecious; fls in drooping catkin-like infls, have 4 sepals; male have 4 or 5 stamens, female one carpel, enclosed by a larger sepal in fr. Br Isles, Eur; c in wa, wds, rds, hbs, fens especially on phosphate-enriched soils. Fl 6–8.

F   Small Nettle, *U. urens*, smaller (10–50 cm) ann plant; longer-stalked, more deeply-toothed lvs (**F**), 1.5–4.0 cm long; infls (**Fa**) short (1 cm), borne on leafy side-branches, male and female fls both on one plant. Br Isles: Eng, E Scot c; Wales, Ire o-lf; W Scot r; Eur c; in wa, ar, gdns, especially on light soils. Fl 6–9.

G   Pellitory-of-the-wall, *Parietaria diffusa* (*P. judaica*), softly hairy per herb, 30–60 cm, with cylindrical, much-branched, reddish stems and stalked, alt, oval-lanceolate untoothed lvs to 7 cm long. Fls in clusters, male (**Ga**) and female separate, with greenish-red-tinged, four-toothed calyx; female fls terminal, male to sides of infl. Br Isles: Eng, coastal Wales f-lc; Scot r, **abs to N**; Ire f in S; Eur f-lc; on rocks, old walls, hbs. Fl 6–10.

226

cont

3mm

227

HEMP FAMILY

Cannabiaceae

◀ **H Hop**, *Humulus lupulus*, roughly hairy, square-stemmed, herbaceous climbing per, twining clockwise; lvs deeply palmately-lobed, long-stalked, toothed, 10–15 cm; male fls in branched yellow-green clusters (**H**), female catkins (**Ha**) resembling yellow-green pine cones, 15–20 mm long in fl, enlarging to 5 cm long in fr. Br Isles: Eng c; Wales, Ire o; Scot r; Eur f-lc; in hbs, wds, fen carr (probably native in S Eng but often an escape). Fl 7–8.

GOURD FAMILY

Cucurbitaceae

I White Bryony, *Bryonia dioica*, climbing per herb up to 4 m, with angled bristly stems, climbing by unbranched spirally-coiled tendrils arising from side of lf-stalk; lvs palmately-lobed, dull green. Plant dioecious; fls in axillary cymes, pale green; male fls 12–18 mm across, with 5 sepals, 5 net-veined hairy petals, 5 stamens (one free, 2 joined in pairs); female fls smaller (10–12 mm across) with 3 downy bifid stigmas, ovary inferior, oval; fr a red berry 5–8 mm across. Br Isles: Eng N to Northumberland, mid, E, SE Eng c; Wales r; **SW Eng, Scot, Ire abs**; Eur c (r to N); on hbs, scrub, wd edges, especially on calc soils. Fl 5–9.

▶ **Flowering Shrubs**

SPURGE-LAUREL FAMILY

Thymelaeaceae

Small shrubs with alt undivided lvs without stipules; fls in short racemes or umbels, bisexual, with long calyx-tube bearing 4 spreading sepals; petals abs; stamens 8; ovary one-celled; fr a drupe.

A Spurge-laurel, *Daphne laureola*, erect hairless **evergreen** shrub to 1 m tall; little-branched stems bear leathery lanceolate lvs gathered towards tops of shoots, reminiscent of Rhododendron. Fls (**Aa**) **green**, 8–12 mm long, in clusters in lf-axils; calyx four-lobed, fragrant; fr (**Ab**) 12 mm long, oval, black, fleshy. Br Isles: Eng f-lc; Wales vl; Scot vvr (Argyll); **Ire abs**; Eur N to Belgium, W Germany f-lc (abs to E); in wds (especially beech) especially on calc soils. Fl 2–4.

B Mezereon, *D. mezereum*, deciduous shrub of similar habit; lvs (**Bb**) pale green, thinner than in A; fls rich **rosy-pink**, strongly-scented; fr (**Ba**) **red**. Eng now r; **abs rest of Br Isles**; Eur native, widespread and c (except W France); in wds on calc soils. Fl 2–4.

MISTLETOE FAMILY

Loranthaceae

C Mistletoe, *Viscum album*, woody parasitic shrub; repeatedly forked branching: narrow-elliptical lvs, blunt, leathery, widest near tip. Fls dioecious, in small tight clusters, with 4 tiny petals; fr a sticky white berry. Br Isles: Eng, E Wales, N to Yorkshire, lc in SE, and W Midlands; **Scot, Ire abs**; Eur; France c; N to Denmark r; parasitic on various trees, especially apple, lime. Fl 2–4; fr 11–12.

BOX FAMILY

Buxaceae

D Box, *Buxus sempervirens*, evergreen shrub or small tree, 2–5 m, rarely to 10 m, with green, angled, downy twigs; lvs 1.0–2.5 cm, oval, shiny, leathery, opp, blunt, short-stalked. Fls in clusters in lf-axils, each with a terminal female fl (**Da**) of 4 sepals and three-celled ovary, and several male fls (**Db**) of 4 sepals, 4 stamens. Fr a capsule. Br Isles: widely planted (native SE Eng, vr and I but la); Eur: native N to Belgium, c to S, vr to N; on steep hillsides on calc soils in scrub or wdland. Fl 4–5.

cont

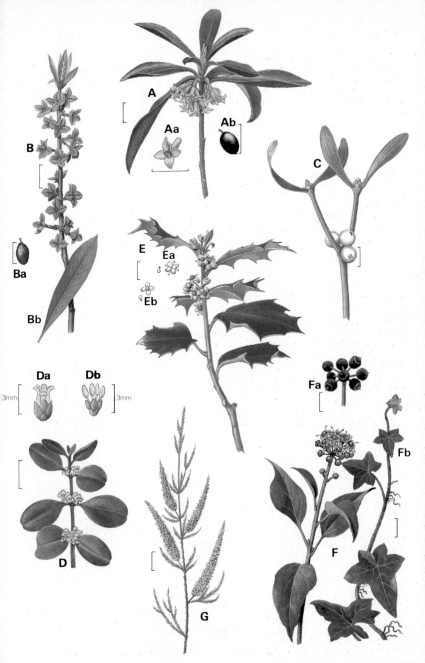

229

HOLLY FAMILY   *Aquifoliaceae*

◀ **E Holly**, *Ilex aquifolium*, small tree or shrub, usually 3–15 m, rarely to 20 m,
with smooth thin bark and green twigs. Lvs alt, dark glossy green, leathery, oval,
with wavy margins bearing large spine-pointed teeth; lvs at top of tree often
spineless. Fls with 4 white petals joined below, 6 mm across, dioecious; male fls
(**Ea**) have 4 stamens, female (**Eb**) 4 carpels; fr a scarlet berry, 7–12 mm across. Br
Isles c generally (except mid Eng), **abs Caithness**; Eur c along W coasts, rarer to E;
in wds, scrub, hbs, on drier soils. Fl 5–8; fr winter.

IVY FAMILY   *Araliaceae*

F Ivy, *Hedera helix*, evergreen woody climber, ascends to 30 m, and also
forms carpets on wdland floors; stem clothed with sucker-like adhesive roots,
young twigs downy. Lvs 4–10 cm long, hairless, glossy dark green with paler veins
above, paler below; lvs of non-fl stems (**Fb**) palmately 3–5-lobed, with triangular
untoothed lobes; lvs of fl-shoots (**F**) oval or elliptic, untoothed. Fls (only borne on
shoots in good light at top of tree or wall) in umbels, with 5 small sepals, 5 yellow-
green 3–4-mm petals, 5 yellow stamens. Fr (**Fa**) a black globular berry. Br Isles,
Eur; vc on gd in dry wds, and climbing trees, hbs, rocks, walls etc. Fl 9–11.

TAMARISK FAMILY   *Tamaricaceae*

G Tamarisk, *Tamarix gallica*, hairless evergreen shrub, to 3 m; reddish twigs;
lvs minute, scale-like, grey-green, overlap closely on the twigs; fls pink, 3 mm, in
dense spike-like racemes; 5 sepals, petals and stamens, 3 styles; fr a capsule. S, E
coasts of Eng and W Eur introd; native in Eur N to Brittany; by the sea. Fl 7–9.

▶ DOGWOOD FAMILY   *Cornaceae*

Shrubs with opp oval untoothed lvs; fls in umbels, with 4 petals; ovary inferior; fr a
berry.
   A Dogwood, *Thelycrania sanguinea* (*Cornus sanguinea*), deciduous shrub to
4 m tall; twigs purplish-red; lvs opp, 4–8 cm long, oval, pointed, rounded at base,
without stipules, untoothed, slightly downy on both sides; the 3–5 main veins on
each side curve round towards apex of lf as in D below (but D's lvs **toothed**); lf-
stalk 8–15 mm. Infl a flat-topped stalked umbel of many creamy-white fls, each 8–
10 mm wide with 4 tiny sepals, 4 petals, 4 stamens alt with petals; two-celled
inferior ovary forms a black globular drupe in fr (**Aa**). Eng, N to Morecambe Bay
and Tyne c-la; Wales r-lf; **Scot abs**; Ire r; Eur N to Denmark, more c to S; in wds,
scrub on calc soils. Fl 5–7.
   *B Cornelian Cherry, *Cornus mas*, shrub or small tree to 8 m tall; twigs
yellowish; oval lvs 4–10 cm long; umbels ± unstalked, with 4 yellow-green
bracts at base; fls **yellow**, 3–4 mm across, produced before lvs expand; fr (**Ba**)
scarlet, elliptical, 1.0–1.5 cm long. Br Isles introd; Eur: N to N France (Pas de
Calais), native, c to S; on scrub, wds, on calc soils. Fl 2–3.
   C Dwarf Cornel, *Chamaepericlymenum suecicum* (*Cornus suecica*), low
creeping per herb, with lf shape and fl structure as in A. Erect fl-stems 6–20 cm tall;
lvs opp, 1–3 cm; infls dense terminal heads, resembling fls, with 8–25 tiny (2–
4 mm) blackish-purple fls, each surrounded by 4 large (5–8 mm) oval, white,
petal-like bracts; frs (**Ca**) red, globular, 5 mm across. Br Isles: central Highlands
Scot (**not in islands**) f-lc; S Scot, Yorks, Lancs vr; **Ire abs**; Eur: only Denmark,
N Germany, in lowlands o-lf; on mt moors, and boggy pinewds in Denmark.
Fl 7–8.

230

cont

BUCKTHORN FAMILY

Trees and shrubs with simple lvs; fls small, in small clusters in lf-axils; 4 or 5 petals, sepals, stamens; calyx tubular, ovary superior; stamens **opp** petals; fr a berry.

D Buckthorn, *Rhamnus catharticus*, shrub or small tree to 6 m tall, usually with some thorns; lvs **opp**, deciduous, oval, 3–6 cm long, with side veins curving up towards tip (as in A, but D's lvs **toothed**, and twigs grey or brown, **not purple**); buds with scales. Fls in small clusters on short spurs below this year's lvs, green, four-petalled, 7 mm across; sexes in separate fls. Fr a berry (**Da**) 6–10 mm across, green then **black**. Br Isles: Eng, Wales f-lvc in S and SE, far N r, **SW abs**; Scot abs; Ire r-o; Eur f-lc; in scrub, wds on calc soil and on fen peat. Fl 5–6.

E Alder Buckthorn, *Frangula alnus*, shrub or small tree, with deciduous oval lvs, **alt, untoothed**, broadest near tips, 2–7 cm long, with veins **not curved towards tip**; buds **without scales**, v hairy; fls (**Ea**), 3 mm across, in small clusters in axils of upper lvs, have **5** greenish-white petals. Fr a berry 6–10 mm wide, green then **red**, finally black. Br Isles: Eng, Wales f-lc; **Scot abs as native**; Ire r; Eur f-lc; in fen carr, in damp wds, hths on acid soils (r on calc soils). Fl 5–6.

SPINDLE FAMILY

Celastraceae

Shrubs with simple, usually opp lvs; stamens **alt** with petals.

F Spindle, *Euonymus europaeus*, deciduous shrub or small tree, 2–6 m tall, hairless; twigs green, four-angled; lvs opp, **oval-lanceolate**, 3–13 cm long, only **finely** toothed, orange in autumn. Fls (**Fa**), in stalked forking cymes in lf-axils, 3–10 together, each fl 8–10 mm across, with 4 greenish-white petals, 4 short alt stamens; fr (**Fb**) four-lobed, 10–15 mm wide, bright **coral-pink**, opening by slits to expose the seeds, each with a bright orange sheath. Br Isles: GB N to Forth, vc to S, r to N; Ire f; Eur f-lc; in wds, scrub, hbs on calc soils. Fl 5–6; fr 9–10.

OLEASTER FAMILY

Elaeagnaceae

Trees and shrubs with simple untoothed lvs covered with silvery scales; sepals 2 or 4; fr a coloured drupe.

G Sea-buckthorn, *Hippophae rhamnoides*, thorny densely-branched shrub 1–3 m tall, spreading by suckers. Lvs 1–8 cm, alt, untoothed, linear-lanceolate, stalkless, covered with **silvery scales**. Fls v small, dioecious, borne in short spikes in lf-axils; 2 sepals, no petals; fr a bright **orange** berry. Eng, native and lva on E coastal dunes, SE Scotland to E Sussex, planted elsewhere on coasts and inland; Eur: North Sea and Channel coasts, a-lf on dunes; abs W, S France. Fl 3–4; fr 9.

BEECH FAMILY

Fagaceae ▶

Trees with alt undivided lvs, and male and female fls in separate catkins. Male catkins many-fld, mostly long; perianth 4–6-lobed, stamens twice number of lobes. Female fls in groups of 1 or 3, with involucre of **bracts**, that grows later to form a woody **cup** round fr; fr a one-seeded nut. Wind pollinated – hence fls have no petals or nectar to attract insects.

A Pedunculate Oak, *Quercus robur*, large, spreading deciduous tree, to 30 m or more, with rugged bark; hairless twigs; lvs hairless, oblong, pinnate-lobed with rounded side-lobes, basal lobes (**auricles**) rounded and exceeding the short lf-stalk; acorns (**Ab**) in cups, 1, 2 or 3 together on **long** common stalk; male catkins (**Aa**) pendulous. Br Isles (**except outer Scot is**), Eur; vc in wds, hbs, etc, except on v poor soils. Fl 4–5; fr 9–10.

B Sessile Oak, *Q. petraea*, differs from A in more ascending branches and narrower crown; lvs (**B**) long-stalked, lf-base tapering into stalks (without basal auricles), less deeply-lobed, broadest above middle, with star-shaped **hairs** in axils of side veins beneath (**Ba**); acorns (**Bb**) almost **stalkless** on twigs. GB, Eur lc, (dominant Oak of the poorer soils of N, W Britain, and of some sandy areas of SE Eng). Fl 4–5; fr 9–10. **Bi Evergreen Oak**, *Q. ilex*, evergreen tree with darker scaly bark; lvs elliptical, toothed or not, woolly-downy below; acorn-cup woolly. Introd GB, Eur (native Mediterranean and W France, N to Brittany); in dry wds, especially on calc soils. Fl 5; fr 9.

C Sweet Chestnut, *Castanea sativa*, large spreading deciduous tree with bark longitudinally fissured, fissures often in spiral curves round trunk. Lvs 10–25 cm, oblong-lanceolate, pointed, with large pointed teeth; catkins 12–20 cm long, erect; male fls (**Cb**) above, with many conspicuous yellowish stamens and a sickly scent, female fls (**Cc**) at base of catkins, 3 together in scaly cups; frs (**Ca**) large, shiny-brown, 1–3 together in a green cup 5–7 cm wide, with many long spines. Introd GB, W Eur, widespread S Eng, France (native S France, S Germany etc). Fl 7; fr 10.

D Beech, *Fagus sylvatica*, large deciduous tree to 30 m or more, with smooth, grey bark. Buds red-brown, cigar-shaped. Lvs 4–9 cm, stalked, oval, pointed, scarcely-toothed, veins prominent at edges; edges and veins beneath silky-hairy, rest of **mature lf** hairless; male catkins (**Db**) tassel-like on long stalks; female fls (**Da**) in **pairs** on a long stalk, surrounded by a scaly cup, which develops into the deeply-lobed woody cup that encloses the beech nut; frs 1–2 together, 12–18 mm long, with one flat and one curved face. Native S Eng, S Wales, widely introd rest of Br Isles; Eur native N to Denmark; c-la in wds on chk, limestone, also on sands, light loams. Fl 4–5; fr 9–10.

cont

HAZEL FAMILY

Differs from Beech family in lacking perianth to male fls, and in their **leafy**, lobed cup (not woody, scaly case) around nut.

E Hornbeam, *Carpinus betulus*, deciduous tree to 30 m (usually much less); smooth grey bark, as in D, but trunk fluted or angled (not rounded). Buds shorter, broader, less pointed than in D, pale brown, hairless; twigs **downy**. Lvs 3–10 cm long, oval, rather like those of D in shape, but more pointed and strongly, sharply **doubly-toothed**, pleated along veins, hairless above, hairy on veins below. Male catkins (**Eb**) 2.5–5.0 cm, with oval greenish bracts; female catkins (**Ea**) 2 cm in fl, 5–10 cm in fr; each fl with green three-lobed involucre, mid-lobe much the longest and enlarging in fr to a 4 cm trident-shaped lfy bract around the 5–10-mm, green, oval, ribbed nut. SE Eng, N to Norfolk, W to Hants (possibly further W) native and lc, widely introd elsewhere in Br Isles; Eur, native, f-lc; in wds, hbs, especially on loams, sandy clays. Fl 4–5.

F Hazel, *Corylus avellana*, many-stemmed deciduous shrub to 8 m; coppery-brown smooth bark tends to peel. Twigs v hairy, with reddish gland-tipped hairs; buds oval, blunt, hairy; lvs 5–12 cm, rounded-oval with drawn-out point, cordate at base, sharply doubly-toothed, downy; stalk hairy. Male catkins (**Fa**) appear before lvs, in groups 2–8 cm long, pendulous, with yellow stamens and oval yellowish bracts; female catkins (**Fb**), 5 mm long, resembling lf-buds, erect, with red styles protruding from tip. Frs (**Fc**) 1.5–2.0 cm, in clusters of 1–4, globular to oval, with brown woody shell, surrounded by involucre deeply divided into toothed lfy lobes. Br Isles, Eur; vc in wds, scrub, hbs, on less acid soils. Fl 1–3; fr 9–10.

BIRCH FAMILY (see also p 238)

Betulaceae

Fls of Alders and Birches are v like those of Hazels, but with 3 (not 1) male fls in each catkin-scale; no perianth; fr a **flattened, tiny nutlet** on surface of a fleshy or woody scale, so female catkins cone-like in fr; frs with rounded wing (for wind dispersal).

G Alder, *Alnus glutinosa*, deciduous tree to 20 m; v dark fissured bark, twigs hairless; buds blunt, purplish. Lvs 3–9 cm, rounded, tip usually truncate with no point, tapered into stalk, doubly-toothed, dark green, hairless except in vein-axils below, sticky when young; stalk to 3 cm. Male catkins (**Ga**), 2–6 cm, pendulous, yellow with dark tips to bracts, appear before lvs; female catkins (**Gb**) green, egg-shaped, 1 cm long, become in fr (**Gc**) woody (like small pine-cones) and to 2.5 cm long. Br Isles, Eur; c, general in wet wds, fen carr, streamsides etc. Fl 2–3.

BOG MYRTLE FAMILY

Myricaceae

H Bog Myrtle, *Myrica gale*, deciduous shrub to 2 m tall; red-brown twigs; buds oval, red-brown, blunt. Lvs 2–6 cm, narrow-oblong, tapered to base, wider above middle, scarcely stalked, ± toothed near apex, grey-green, hairless above, downy below, with many stalkless yellow glands producing resinous fragrance if lvs bruised or rubbed. Usually dioecious; male catkins (**Ha**) red-brown, 7–15 mm, with red stamens; female catkins (**Hb**) 4–5 mm in fl, dark green, oval with red styles, 5–10 mm in fr; nutlets small, winged. Br Isles, widespread and lc, but r-abs most of central Eng, SE Scot, S Wales; Eur: lc to W and N to Denmark; lowland France r inland; in bogs, wet hths, fens. Fl 4–5.

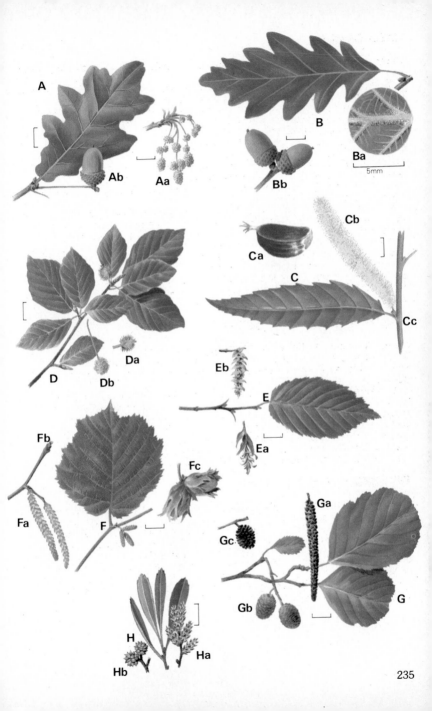

A

Ab

Aa

B

Bb

Ba

5mm

Ca

Cb

C

Cc

D

Da

Db

Eb

E

Ea

Fb

Fc

Fa

F

Ga

Gc

Gb

G

H

Ha

Hb

MAPLE FAMILY

Aceraceae

Trees and shrubs with opp, usually palmate lvs, without stipules; infl a raceme; 5 sepals, 5 petals, 8 stamens; fr dry, of two carpels, each with a propeller-like wing.

A   Field Maple, *Acer campestre*, deciduous tree up to 20 m or sometimes (in hds) a shrub. Bark fissured, flaking off. Twigs **downy**; lvs opp, palmate, bluntly 3–5-lobed, lobes ± untoothed, 4–7 cm long and almost as wide; lvs downy below, hairless above when mature; infl an **erect rounded panicle**; fls 6 mm across, cup-shaped, yellow-green; fr (**Aa**) usually **downy**, with two **horizontally-spreading** propeller-shaped wings. Br Isles: Eng, vc in S, r to N and W; Scot, Ire, planted only and r; Eur c; in wds on basic soils, scrub, hds, la on chk. Fl 5–6.

B   Sycamore, *A. pseudoplatanus*, deciduous tree up to 30 m, with a wide crown. Bark smooth when young, later in flakes; stalked opp palmate lvs, 7–16 cm long, five-lobed, hairless, blunt-toothed. Twigs **hairless**. Infl (**Ba**) a narrow drooping panicle, 5–20 cm long; fls as in A, but yellower, **not cup-shaped**. Fr (**Bb**) **hairless**, with two wings at an **acute angle**. Br Isles introd in 15th century, but now c in wds and hds on richer soil, as well as planted; native in mts of central Eur from NE France to S. Fl 4–6.   **Bi   Norway Maple**, *A. platanoides*, has sharp teeth to lf and erect infls. Mts of Eur, often planted in Br Isles.

HORSE-CHESTNUT FAMILY

Hippocastanaceae

C   Horse-chestnut, *Aesculus hippocastanum*, deciduous tree to 25 m, with broad, dense crown, and stout twigs curving up at ends. Bark dark grey-brown, finally flaking. Buds stout, to 3.5 × 1.5 cm, oval, red-brown, sticky. Twigs hairless. Lvs palmate, divided into 5–7 lfts, 8–20 cm long, obovate, tapered to base, pointed at tip, toothed, hairless and dark green above, downy below when young, long-stalked. Infls large erect panicles, terminal on twigs, 20–30 cm long; fls 2 cm across, with 4 white petals with pink spots below; stamens arching down. Fr (**Ca**) to 6 cm across, globular, green, prickly (then brown). Seeds glossy brown, 1–2, globular, 3–4 cm across. Br Isles, Eur; vc planted and self-sown (Greece). Fl 5–6.

LIME (LINDEN) FAMILY

Tiliaceae

Limes (*Tilia*) are trees with alt, long-stalked, cordate lvs; blunt buds; fragrant fls in small clusters whose common stalk is fused halfway to an oblong bract; globular nut-like frs 6–10 mm long.

D   Common Lime, *T. × europaea* (*T. × vulgaris*) is the hybrid of E and F. Large irregular bosses on trunk. Lvs 6–10 cm long, hairless below, except for tufts of white hairs in vein-axils. Fls 4–10 per infl; fr (**Da**) oval with a pointed tip. Br Isles, Eur; planted and vc, also as a natural hybrid. Fl 7.

E   Large-leaved Lime, *T. platyphyllos*, has smooth dark bark; lvs 6–12 cm long, grey-downy all over below, and sometimes above; side veins of lvs strong; infl drooping, with 2–5 fls; frs (**Ea**) strongly ribbed. Br Isles; Eng, SE Wales r but lf, N to Yorks, native but also planted; Eur o-lf; in old wds on base-rich soils, and on wooded cliffs. Fl 6.

F   Small-leaved Lime, *T. cordata*, has a smooth bark usually without swollen bosses; lvs only 3–6 cm long, rounded, cordate, with abrupt points, grey-green, **hairless** below (except for **tufts** of **rusty hairs** in vein-axils), side veins not prominent. Infl 4–10-fld, not drooping; frs (**Fa**) smooth, with pointed tips. Br Isles: Eng, Wales o, only lc; Eur f-lc; in old wds on fertile soils, wooded limestone cliffs. Fl 7.

cont

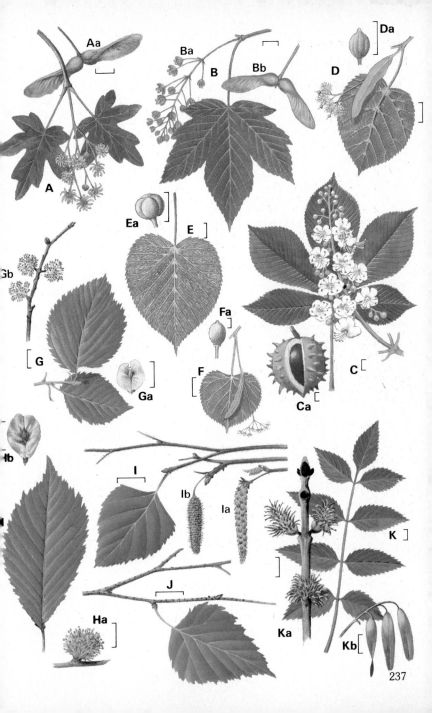

237

ELM FAMILY

Ulmaceae

◄ **Elms** (*Ulmus*) are deciduous trees with alt, unlobed, but toothed, ± hairy lvs, with blade often extending lower down stalk on one side than the other. Tiny fls in globular heads, with calyx 4–5-lobed and bell-shaped, no petals, and many purplish-red stamens in early spring; fr a tiny achene surrounded by a thin, oval, notched wing.

G   English Elm, *Ulmus procera*, tall tree (to 30 m) with erect trunk, rough bark, and oblong outline. Twigs short, hairy; lvs 4–9 cm, rounded-oval, rough-hairy, with v unequal bases. Suckers produced freely from base of trunk. Catkins (**Gb**) purplish, tassel-like; fr rarely produced; seeds (**Ga**) above middle of fr-wing. Br Isles: Eng, Wales, c in lowlands; Scot, Ire r; Eur abs; much reduced in recent years by Dutch Elm Disease, but suckers are surviving; in hds, parks, riverside wds. Fl 2–3.   **Gi   Smooth-leaved Elm**, *U. carpinifolia*, has hairless twigs; narrower elliptical shiny lvs, hairless below, often also above; includes several forms described as separate spp. Br Isles: SE, mid, SW Eng, lf; Eur c. Fl 2–3.

H   Wych Elm, *U. glabra*, tall tree, with broad, spreading outline; suckers abs or few. Twigs only hairy when young; lvs large (8–16 cm long), oval to diamond-shaped or elliptical, v rough, bases unequal, stalks v short. Catkins (**Ha**) larger than in G; fr (**Hb**) with seed in centre of fr-wing. Br Isles, Eur; o-la in hilly or rocky wds on calc soils, especially in N and W of GB, also planted. Fl 2–3.

BIRCH FAMILY

Betulaceae

Birches (*Betula*) are deciduous trees or shrubs with alt simple toothed lvs; separate male and female catkins, male drooping, female erect, catkin-scales three-lobed; frs with rounded papery wings.

I   Downy Birch, *Betula pubescens*, tree to 25 m, with **brownish** peeling papery bark; downy twigs; oval-triangular, simply-toothed lvs, downy below; male catkins (**Ia**) 3–6 cm long, female (**Ib**) shorter. Br Isles, Eur, c especially to N; in woods, hths, bogs. Fl 4–5.

J   Silver Birch, *B. pendula*, tree to 25 m, differs from I in white papery bark when young (dark and fissured when old); twigs **hairless**, but warted, more pointed; lvs triangular, doubly-toothed, hairless. Br Isles, Eur: c especially to S; in dry wds, downs, hths. Fl 4–5.   **Ji   Dwarf Birch**, *Betula nana*, tiny, ± prostrate shrub (to 30 cm tall) with downy twigs; almost circular, deeply but bluntly-toothed lvs, 5–15 mm long, hairless when mature; tiny male catkins 6–8 mm long. Br Isles: Scot Highlands o-vlf, N Eng (Teesdale) vr; Eur: N Germany vr, otherwise mts; on mt moors and Sphagnum bogs. Fl 5–6.

See also *Alnus*, p 234.

OLIVE FAMILY

Oleaceae

Trees and shrubs with opp lvs; fls with 4 sepals, usually four-lobed corolla, 2 stamens; superior ovary of 2 joined carpels.

K   Ash, *Fraxinus excelsior*, tall tree (to 30 m), deciduous, with pale grey bark, ridged with age; twigs **smooth**, **grey**; buds **black**, 5–10 mm long; lvs opp, 20–30 cm long, pinnate, with 3–6 pairs of oval, pointed, shallow-toothed lfts. Fls (**Ka**), in panicles, appear before lvs; no perianth; 2 purple stamens, and a narrow ovary that forms a flat, oblong fr (**Kb**), 3 cm long, winged at tip like a propeller-blade. Br Isles, Eur; c-la in wds, hds, on moister, base-rich soils. Fl 4–5.

See also *Ligustrum*, p 294.

WILLOW FAMILY

Salicaceae

A family of deciduous, dioecious trees and shrubs with (usually) alt simple lvs with stipules. Fls in catkins; no perianth; carpels 2; fr a one-celled **capsule**, which bursts to release the **many** silky-plumed seeds. **Willows** (*Salix*) have narrow, lanceolate-oval lvs; catkins usually erect, a single outer scale enclosing the bud; catkin-scales untoothed; 2–5 stamens; nectar glands present (insect pollination). **Poplars** (*Populus*) have broad, triangular, cordate or rounded lvs; catkins hanging, several toothed outer scales to the bud; fls cup-like, with many red stamens but no nectar (wind pollination). Only commoner lowland spp of Willow are illustrated here; for alpine and other rarer spp see the Keys to Willows below.

KEYS TO WILLOWS (*SALIX*)

A Key to lowland spp of Br Isles and Eur

Note: many willows form hybrids with one another. These are not included in the keys. Plants found with a mixture of characters of two spp, or intermediate, are probably hybrids; only specialists can normally name them accurately.

1 Shrubs ± prostrate (under 50 cm) with some creeping stems – lvs to only 25 mm long, silvery or silky below – on hths, moors .... *Salix repens* (p 242 I)
  Taller shrubs or trees – no creeping shoots **2**

2 Lvs mostly **opp**, oblong to linear-lanceolate, hairless, dull bluish-green – young twigs purplish ....
                                        S. purpurea (p 240 C)
  Lvs all **alt** **3**

3 Lvs ± hairless **4**
  Lvs clearly hairy, at least below – stamens always 2 per male fl **8**

4 Lvs 2–8 cm, oval, pointed but not long-tapering, waxy-grey below, only 2–3 times as long as wide – stamens 2 – only in N of GB and of Ire .... *S. phylicifolia*
  Lvs 5–15 cm long, elliptical-lanceolate, long-tapering **5**

5 Bark peeling off main stems in patches – 3 stamens per male fl .... *S. triandra* (p 240 E)
  Bark not peeling – male fls with 2, or 5 stamens **6**

6 Twigs v brittle, especially where they join stems – 2 stamens – lvs lanceolate, grey to pale green below – lf-apex not symmetrical – tall tree .... *S. fragilis* (p 240 B)
  Twigs pliant, not brittle – lvs green below – lf-apex symmetrical **7**

7 Lvs only 2–4 times as long as broad, **dark, polished, leathery green** above, paler below – stamens 5 per male fl – bush or low spreading tree .... *S. pentandra* (p 240 Ei)
  Lvs more than 4 times as long as broad, **blue-green** above – stamens 2 per male fl – erect tree ....
                                       S. alba var *coerulea* (p 240 Ai)

8 Lvs lanceolate or linear, over 5 times as long as wide, with adpressed silky hairs **9**
  Lvs oval or oblong, 4 times as long as wide (or less) **10**

9 Tall tree – lvs 5–10 cm long, 5–8 times as long as wide, with silky adpressed hairs on both sides .... *S. alba* (p 240 A)
  Shrub – lvs 10–25 cm long, 7–18 times as long as wide, dark green and hairless above, silky hairs below only .... *S. viminalis* (p 240 D)

10 Shrub under 150 cm – lvs 4 cm long or less, pointed, elliptical, with silky **adpressed** hairs both sides – on dunes, fens .... *S. repens* (p 242 Ia)
  Larger shrub or tree – lvs with **spreading** hairs, ± **woolly** below, tips ± rounded **11**

11 Lvs round to oval, **wrinkled**, 2–3 cm long, with large round stipules at lf-bases – shrub to 2.5 m with spreading branches .... *S. aurita* (p 242 H)
  Lvs oval to oblong, **not wrinkled**, 4–10 cm long, stipules less conspicuous – tall shrub (3–10 m) or tree, with erect branches **12**

12 Lvs oval or oval-oblong, 1–2 times as long as wide – mature twigs hairless, without raised ridges under bark .... *S. caprea* (p 242 F)
  Lvs obovate to oblong-lanceolate, 2–4 times as long as wide – mature twigs downy, with raised ridges under bark (peel off bark to see) .... *S. cinerea* agg (p 242 G)

cont

WILLOW FAMILY

B Key to Willows of mt rocks and moors over 600 m – r-o in Scot – all small shrubs

1 Low prostrate creeping shrub – lvs rounded at tips.. **2**
 Shrub not creeping – stems ± erect – lvs ± pointed at tips.. **4**

2 Lvs oval to elliptical, densely silky, with adpressed hairs at least below – catkins on sides of
 shoots, appear before lvs..*S. repens* (p 242 I)
 Lvs almost round, ± hairless – catkins on tips of shoots, appearing with lvs.................... **3**

3 Lvs shiny green both sides, 6–10 mm long, less than 1½ times as long as wide, veins not strongly
 imprinted above – lf-stalks 5 mm or less – branches 2–3 cm long....................*S. herbacea*
 Lvs green above, waxy-grey below, 10–30 mm long, less than twice as long as wide, veins
 strongly imprinted above, forming a **raised** network below – lf-stalks 5–15 mm long – branches
 to 10 cm long...*S. reticulata*

4 Lvs ± hairless **5**
 Lvs hairy, at least below **7**

5 Shrub 1 m or more, ± erect – lvs 2–8 cm, pointed, waxy grey-green below ....*S. phylicifolia*
 Low shrub, 60 cm or less – branches spreading, bushy **6**

6 Lvs equally green both sides, 1.5–3.0 cm long ....*S. myrsinites*
 Lvs pale or grey-green below, 0.5–2.0 cm long, sometimes with a few silky hairs below ....
 ....*S. arbuscula*

7 Lvs thinly downy below, especially on veins – shrub rarely to 4 m tall ....*S. nigricans*
 Lvs densely silky or woolly with white hairs both sides – twigs downy at first, hairless when 1 year
 old **8**

8 Lvs oval, 1½–2 times as long as wide – branches stout – buds stout, woolly ....*S. lanata*
 Lvs elliptical-oblong, 2–4 times as long as wide – branches slender – buds small, ± downy
 only..*S. lapponum*

Willows, Poplars

A **White Willow**, *Salix alba*, tree to 25 m with rugged bark; twigs not fragile.
Lvs hairy, silver-grey, toothed, narrow, lanceolate-acute; catkins (male, **Aa**) with
the lvs, slender, cylindric, 2.5–5.0 cm; 2 stamens per male fl. Br Isles, Eur, c to S, r
to N (probably native SE Eng, Eur; but much planted); on streamsides, wet wds,
fens on richer soils in lowlands. Fl 4–5. **Ai Cricket-bat Willow**, *S. alba* var
coerulea, has less hairy lvs, blue-green above. **Aii Weeping Willow**, *S.
babylonica*, from Asia, has branches drooping to gd and narrower lvs. Often
planted, only female in GB.

B **Crack Willow**, *S. fragilis*, more spreading tree, with **fragile** twigs; lvs
hairless at maturity; female catkin (**Bb**), male (**Ba**); 2 stamens per male fl. Br Isles,
Eur; distribution, habitat as A (but more c in Eng as native than A). Fl 4.

C **Purple Willow**, *S. purpurea*, shrub with long slender purplish twigs; upper
lvs ± **opp**, narrow-oblong, obovate, tapered to base, finely-toothed, hairless,
blue-green above, waxy below. Male catkins with purple-tipped scales and
stamens, female red-purple. Fls appear before lvs. Br Isles, Eur; f-la in fens and by
fresh water. Fl 3–4.

D **Osier**, *S. viminalis*, shrub with long straight flexible branches, downy young
twigs; lvs 10–25 cm long (7–18 times as long as wide), untoothed, linear-
lanceolate, with inrolled edges, dark green, hairless above, silvery-silky below.
Oblong catkins appear before lvs. Br Isles, lowlands c, hills r; Eur, by ponds,
streams, in fens, marshes. Fl 4–5.

E **Almond Willow**, *S. triandra*, shrub or small tree with brown smooth peeling
bark, hairless olive twigs; lvs, 5–10 cm long, oblong-obovate, shiny green above,
waxy green below. Catkins among lvs; male fls (**Ea**) with **3** stamens each. Br Isles:
S, E Eng, SE Scot f-lc; Ire r; Eur f-c; by water and in marshes. Fl 3–5. **Ei Bay
Willow**, *S. pentandra*, shrub or small tree with grey rugged bark, shiny hairless
twigs; lvs 5–12 cm long, broadly elliptical, dark shiny green (polished-looking)
above; lvs and buds sticky and fragrant when young. Catkins appear after lvs; male
fls with **5** stamens each. Br Isles: **S Eng abs**; N Eng to mid Scot f-lc; N Ire c; Eur c to
N, r to S in lowlands. Fl 5–6.

cont

241

◀

F   Goat Willow, *S. caprea*, shrub or (especially in W Scot, Ire) tree, to 15 m; twigs downy when young. Lvs **oval** with pointed tips, hairless above, grey-downy below, 5–10 cm long, 1.2 to two times as long as wide. Catkins ('Palm') appear before lvs, erect, stout, male 2–4 cm, female 3–7 cm when mature, unstalked, oval to oblong; scales dark brown with many silvery-white hairs, male with 2 golden stamens per fl, female with downy green-grey ovaries and 2 green stigmas. Br Isles, Eur; vc in wds, hds, scrub, wa. Fl 3–4.

G   Grey Willow, *S. cinerea* agg, is close to F, but twigs remain downy, with raised ridges on the wood under bark (peel to see this). Lvs obovate, narrower than in F, tapered to stalk, 2.5–7.0 cm long, 2–4 times as long as wide, downy above when young, persistently downy below. Catkins (male **Ga**, female **Gb**) as in F, but smaller. The most typical ssp, *cinerea*, with lvs softly woolly-grey below, no rusty hairs, is c in E Eng and Eur; ssp *atrocinerea*, with lvs only downy on veins below when mature, some hairs rusty, is c in most of Br Isles (not E Eng) and in W France; in wet wds, fen carr, fens, by fresh water. Fl 3–4.

H   Eared Willow, *S. aurita*, shrub to only 2 m, smaller than F or G; twigs slenderer, **angled**, **spreading**, with ridges as G. Lvs 1.5 to 2.5 times as long as wide, obovate, rounded, v wrinkled, woolly-grey below, with conspicuous large rounded stipules (the 'ears'). Catkins smaller (1–2 cm) versions of G. Br Isles, Eur; f but much more c to N and in uplands; on hths, moors, damp wds, especially on acid soils. Fl 4.

I   Creeping Willow, *S. repens*, low shrub with creeping and ascending stems to 2 m tall (variable; only 40 cm in hth form, **I**). Lvs 2.5–4.5 cm long, oval, usually with white silky hairs below (dune-slack forms, **Ia**, with larger lvs, silky both sides, ± toothed). Catkins short, 5–25 mm, appear before lvs; male (**I**) oblong with golden stamens, female globose; scales dark-tipped; seeds (**Ib**) 1.5 mm. Br Isles, Eur; lc especially to N, on hths, fens, dune-slacks. Fl 4–5.

J   Aspen, *Populus tremula*, tree to 20 m with suckers, sticky hairless buds, **hairless** mature twigs. Lvs on v long flattened stalks (2.5–6.0 cm), v flexible, trembling in any breeze. Lf-blades almost round, with large rounded teeth, hairless except when v young. Sucker-lvs downy below. Catkins 4–8 cm, pendulous with deeply jagged scales; red stamens in male, purple stigmas in female (**Ja**). Br Isles c in N and W, f-lc in S and E; Eur f; in damp wds on heavier poorer soils. Fl 2–3.

K   Grey Poplar, *P. canescens*, large tree (to 30 m) with smooth yellowish-grey bark with horizontal lines (like Birches) when young, roughly fissured below when older, and with suckers. Twigs and buds thinly downy; lvs of short shoots (**K**) 3–6 cm, wide, oval, rounded, coarsely-toothed, grey above, **grey-downy** below, then later ± hairless; lvs of suckers and summer lvs larger (to 10 cm long), oval-triangular, more coarsely toothed, remaining grey-woolly below. Lf-stalks to 4 cm, not flattened. Catkins to 10 cm, stout, stigmas yellow, scales jagged. Native in S and E Eng, planted in rest of Br Isles; Eur; f-lc in damp wds. Fl 2–3.   **Ki   White Poplar**, *P. alba*, has **thickly downy** buds and twigs, wider lvs to short shoots, **white** below, then ± hairless; lvs of suckers and summer lvs **palmately-lobed** and maple-like, remaining white-woolly below. Catkin scales only toothed, not jagged. Planted, especially in S Eng and Eur (central and S Eur). Fl 3.   **Kii   Black Poplar**, *P. nigra*, tall tree with rugged black bark and trunk-bosses; **no** suckers; branches arching down; twigs and sticky buds hairless; lvs green, triangular, hairless. E, mid Eng r; Eur: France, f to S; by streamsides in wet wds. Fl 4.   **Kiii   Lombardy Poplar**, *P. nigra* var *italica*, has a narrow column-like form with stiffly erect branches; often planted in Br Isles and Eur.   **Kiv   Italian Poplar**, *P.* × *canadensis* (*P. nigra* × *deltoides*), is like K, but has no trunk-bosses; ascending branches curve upwards; lvs hairless; glands at base of lf-blade; always male. Widely planted (from N America).

Spurges (*Euphorbia*) in Eur are all herbs, with alt simple lvs and acrid latex. Fls in open umbel-like terminal heads, with primary branches in an umbel, further branches forked. Bracts conspicuous, often wider than lvs. Infl of perianth-like cups of 4–5 small teeth, alt with 4–5 conspicuous rounded or crescent-shaped **glands**; each cup surrounding a group of several tiny one-stamened male fls and 1 central female fl comprising a stalked three-celled ovary with 3 stigmas.

KEY TO SPURGES (EUPHORBIA)

1 Lvs opp.. **2**
  Lvs alt **3**
2 Plant prostrate, purple-suffused – stipules present – lvs not different from umbel bracts, unequal-sided – vr – on seashore...*E. peplis* (p 246 E)
  Tall erect woodland plant – no stipules – lvs strap-shaped in 4 rows .... *E. lathyrus* (p 246 B)
3 Glands surrounding fl-clusters rounded both sides **4**
  Glands with crescent-shaped horns on outer side.. **9**
4 Plants per – oblong untoothed lvs, tapered to base – many stems **5**
  Plants ann – single stems – lvs toothed above... **7**
5 Frs with prominent warts – plant 30–50 cm tall.. **6**
  Frs with short warts – plant v branched, 50–100 cm – abs Br Isles .... *E. palustris* (p 246 Ci)
6 Upper bracts rounded below, yellow – glands yellowish – lvs hairy below .... *E. hyberna* (p 246 C)
  Upper bracts truncate below, green – glands soon purple – lvs ± hairless............... *E. dulcis* (p246Cii)
7 Bracts and lvs blunt, tapered to base – fr smooth...................................*E. helioscopia* (p 244 D)
  Bracts and lvs pointed – lvs cordate below – capsule with warts.......................... **8**
8 Plant v branched – capsule with hemispherical warts................................*E. platyphyllos* (p 246 Di)
  Plant taller, slender – capsule with cylindrical warts ....*E. stricta* (p 246 D)
9 Tall hairy plant – lf rosettes raised above gd..*E. amygdaloides* (p 244 A)
  Plant hairless.. **10**
10 Single-stemmed ann – few lvs – on ar, wa.. **11**
   Many-stemmed bi or per – many lvs – not on ar.. **12**
11 Lvs oval, stalked...*E. peplus* (p 244 E)
   Lvs linear, stalkless..*E. exigua* (p 244 F)
12 Plants grey-green, fleshy – lvs oval to obovate, less than 2 cm – seaside **13**
   Plants not fleshy – lvs linear to lanceolate, mostly more than 2 cm – inland................. **14**
13 Lvs v fleshy, no pointed tip, midrib obscure..*E. paralias* (p 244 B)
   Lvs leathery, pointed tip, midrib prominent below ....*E. portlandica* (p 244 C)
14 Lvs of fl-stems linear, 2 mm or less wide..*E. cyparissias* (p 246 A)
   Lvs of fl-stems linear–lanceolate, 4 mm or more wide **15**
15 Lvs tapering to tip, broadest near middle – umbel bracts 12–30 mm ....*E. uralensis* (p 244 G)
   Lvs tapering to narrow base, broadest at apex – umbel bracts 5–15 mm .... *E. esula* (p 244 Gi)

See also *Mercurialis*, p 226.

SPURGE FAMILY

Euphorbiaceae

Spurges

A Wood Spurge, *Euphorbia amygdaloides*, downy per herb, 30–80 cm tall; tufted over-wintering stems, 10–20 cm tall, bear terminal rosettes (**Ab**) of strap-shaped downy dark green short-stalked lvs, 3–8 cm long; fl-shoots arise from rosettes. Umbel 5–10-rayed, with oval bracts, upper bracts kidney-shaped, joined in pairs, yellow. Glands around fls crescent-shaped (**Aa**); capsule rough. Br Isles: Eng, Wales, c in S, **abs N of S Lincs**; S Ire vr (introd); **Scot abs**; Eur: France c, N to Belgium r; in woods on basic-neutral soils. Fl 4–5.

B Sea Spurge, *E. paralias*, hairless per, 20–40 cm tall, with several erect stems. Lvs 0.5–2.0 cm, alt, close-set on stems, v thick, fleshy, waxy-green, untoothed, oval, blunt, stalkless, midrib obscure. Umbel 3–6-rayed, bracts oval; glands crescent-shaped; seeds smooth. Br Isles: GB coasts N to Galloway and to Norfolk lf; Ire ± all round coasts; Eur N to Belgium f-lc; on dune sands, beaches. Fl 7–10.

C Portland Spurge, *E. portlandica*, is close to B, but slenderer; lvs rather thinner, obovate, with pointed tips (**Ca**), tapered to base, midribs prominent beneath; seeds pitted. Br Isles: GB on S and W coasts, Sussex to Galloway; Ire ± all round coasts vlc; Eur: W France lc; on dune sands, sea cliffs. Fl 5–9.

D Sun Spurge, *E. helioscopia*, hairless ann 10–30 cm tall; single erect stems; lvs 1.5–3.0 cm, obovate, v blunt, tapered to base, toothed above. Umbel five-rayed, with 5 large obovate **toothed**, yellow-green bracts; 4 infl-glands, **oval, untoothed**, green; fr (**Da**) smooth. Br Isles, Eur; vc on ar, wa. Fl 5–10.

E Petty Spurge, *E. peplus*, hairless ann, smaller version of D, but all lvs stalked, untoothed, green, oval, blunt; bracts shorter, narrower than in D, green; 4 glands of infl **crescent-shaped** (**Ea**) with long horns. Umbel usually three-rayed, main bracts in a whorl of 3, oval, pointed, untoothed; upper bracts triangular, pointed. Br Isles, Eur; vc on ar, wa. Fl 4–11.

F Dwarf Spurge, *E. exigua*, slender grey-green ann, 5–15 cm, lvs narrow, linear, unstalked, untoothed. Bracts triangular-lanceolate with cordate bases; glands crescent-shaped. Br Isles: S, E Eng c; Wales, S Scot, Ire r; Eur c; on ar, especially on calc soils. Fl 6–10.

G Twiggy Spurge, *E. uralensis*, hairless per, 30–50 cm, with creeping rhizomes and erect branched stems, patch-forming; lvs numerous, alt, strap-shaped, pointed, stalkless, tapering to tip, 3–8 cm long × 4–6 mm wide. Bracts of umbel lanceolate (**Ga**), 12–35 mm long; upper bracts (**Gb**) triangular, yellow-green; glands (**Gc**) crescent-shaped. GB, Eur, introd, lf (E Eur); on wa, gslds. Fl 5–7. **Gi Leafy Spurge**, *E. esula*, differs from G in lvs widest at apex, tapering to base; bracts of umbel 5–15 mm. GB introd, r; Eur f; in wds, wa. Fl 5–7.

Da
5mm

Ea
2mm

D

E

B

Aa
5mm

F

C

Ca

G

Ga

Gb

A

Ab

245

Spurges continued

A **Cypress Spurge**, _E. cyparissias_, patch-forming hairless per herb, 10–30 cm, with tufted stems; fl-stems often with side branches above, taller than infl. Lvs v many, alt, narrow-linear, 1.5–3.0 cm × 1.2 mm, stalkless, untoothed. Umbel 9–15-rayed, with oblong bracts; upper bracts 3–6 mm, triangular, yellow, turning red. Glands crescent-shaped. Eng (possibly native in S, r escape elsewhere); Eur f-lc; on calc gsld and scrub. Fl 5–7   ***Ai** _E. gerardiana_, hairless per, with many erect lfy stems 10–20 cm; lvs **broader**, linear-lanceolate, grey-green, pointed, 3–6 mm wide; bracts triangular, yellow-green; glands **rounded**. France; r on calc rocks, gslds. Fl 6–7.

B **Caper Spurge**, _E. lathyrus_, tall erect (30–120 cm) hairless bi, with lvs (**Ba**) 4–20 cm, **opp**, in **4 vertical rows**, **strap-shaped**, blunt, **waxy** grey-green. Umbel wide, 2–6-rayed, bracts triangular, lanceolate; upper bracts cordate; glands crescent-shaped. Fr (**Bb**) **v large**, 8–20 mm long, smooth. Eng: probably native in S, r; more c as garden escape; Eur: France o-f; in wds on basic soils. Fl 6–7.

C **Irish Spurge**, _E. hyberna_, per herb, with many erect simple stems 30–50 cm; lvs 5–10 cm, alt, oblong to elliptical, blunt, tapered to base, ± stalkless, untoothed, hairless above, downy on midrib below. Umbel 4–6-rayed, bracts 3–6 cm, elliptic, **yellow**; upper bracts 8–30 mm, oval, base ± **cordate**, **yellow**. Glands 5, yellow, kidney-shaped; fr 5–6 mm, hairless, with cylindrical warts. Eng: Cornwall to Somerset r; Ire lc in SW; Eur: W and central France lc; in open wds, scrub, gsld, not on calc soils. Fl 4–7.   ***Ci Marsh Spurge**, _E. palustris_, tall **much-branched** per herb, 80–120 cm, with a reddish stem; lvs lanceolate, hairless; umbels 5- (or more) rayed; bracts elliptical, blunt, narrowed to base; glands rounded, yellow; fr with short warts. Eur: France to Denmark r, especially to W; in fens and marshes. Fl 5–6.   **Cii Sweet Spurge**, _E. dulcis_, is near to C, but slenderer; lvs 3–5 cm, ± hairless; bracts to umbel 2–3 cm; upper bracts truncate at base, green; glands rounded, turning purple; frs with long warts. GB introd r; Eur: France to Belgium r.

D **Upright Spurge**, _E. stricta_ (_E. serrulata_), erect hairless ann, to 50 cm; stems red; lvs (**Da**) oval-oblong, fine-toothed; lower bracts with **clasping** bases, upper bracts (**Db**) **progressively** shorter and more cordate. Glands (**Db**) **rounded**; fr (**Dc**) three-angled, with **long, cylindrical** warts. Eng, round Forest of Dean, vr; Eur: France, S Belgium r; in open rocky wds on limestone. Fl 6–9.   **Di Broad-leaved Spurge**, _E. platyphyllos_, although more like Petty Spurge (p 244 E) in habit and habitat, differs from it in having warted frs like D, but warts hemispherical (not cylindrical) and frs rounded. Umbel bracts (like lvs) elliptic-oblong, but upper ones all shortly cordate, unlike the umbel bracts. S Eng r; Eur N to Netherlands r; on ar, wa, on heavy soils. Fl 6–9.

E **Purple Spurge**, _E. peplis_, prostrate hairless ann; stems crimson, branches forked; lvs 3–10 mm, opp, waxy-grey, stalked, oblong, blunt, with a large round lobe on **one** side of base of each lf; forked stipules, bracts like lvs (**Ea**); glands undivided; fr smooth. SW Eng, probably extinct; W France o; sandy beaches. Fl 7–9.

247

CARROT FAMILY (UMBELLIFERS) *Umbelliferae*

Herbs with alt lvs, no stipules (except in **Marsh Pennywort**); fls small, in umbels which may themselves also be in umbels (hence infls often umbrella-like). Fls with 5 **separate** petals (sepals 5, or **abs** in many *genera*), 5 stamens, 2 stigmas; ovary **inferior**, with 2 carpels or lobes that are variously ridged, winged or flattened in fr. Frs dry, dividing into 2 parts. Useful characters in identifying spp in this rather confusing family are (1) lf form (2) presence or absence of whorl of bracts (in Key called 'bracts') at base of **main** umbel (3) presence or absence of whorl of bracts (in Key called 'bracteoles') at base of **secondary** umbels (4) shape of frs. However, the spp are actually all quite distinct, v rarely forming hybrids.

KEY TO UMBELLIFERS
(Based mainly on lf and bract characters)

Lvs undivided, or palmately-lobed, or spiny.. **A**
Lvs (at least lower ones) pinnately-lobed, pinnate or trifoliate .... **B**

A Umbellifers with undivided, or palmately-lobed, or spiny lvs
  1 Lvs spiny – 'fls in dense rounded to oval heads (resembling Thistles, but petals separate, not joined in a tube as in Thistles and Teasels)....................................*Eryngium* (p 264)
    Lvs not spiny.. **2**
  2 Lvs undivided, linear or oval – fls yellow .... *Bupleurum* (p 260)
    Lvs undivided, circular, stalk attached to centre – fl in in whorled spikes..........*Hydrocotyle* (p 264)
    Lvs palmately-lobed – fls white or pink.. **3**
  3 Bracts tiny – fls in loose compound umbels – frs bristly......................*Sanicula europaea* (p 258 E)
    Bracts in a conspicuous toothed ruff below the dense, head-like simple umbel – frs smooth............
    ....*Astrantia major* (p 258 F)

B Umbellifers with at least lower lvs pinnately-lobed, pinnate or trifoliate
  1 Plants growing in water – submerged lvs finely divided **2**
    Plants without submerged fine-cut lvs **4**
  2 Plants large – lvs 15–30 cm long.. **4**
    Plants small, creeping – lvs 1–8 cm long .... *Apium inundatum* (p 264 D)
  3 Stout erect fl-stems present – submerged lvs with hairlike segments – aerial lvs with flat, deep-cut lfts – in still water ....*Oenanthe aquatica* (p 262 B)
    Slender ascending fl-stems sometimes present – submerged lvs with flattened, linear-segmented lfts – aerial lvs twice-pinnate with broad oval lfts – in rivers.................*Oenanthe fluviatilis* (p 262 C)
  4 Lower lvs only once pinnate, or pinnately-lobed.. **C**
    Lower lvs 2–4 times pinnate .... **D**

C Umbellifers with lower lvs once pinnate only
  1 Plants ± hairy, at least on lower lvs **2**
    Plants quite hairless... **5**
  2 Fls yellow – lfts oval, coarse-toothed .... *Pastinaca sativa* (p 258 A)
    Fls white or pink.. **3**
  3 Bracts, bracteoles abs – plant sparingly downy – on gsld ....*Pimpinella saxifraga* (p 254 E)
    Bracteoles present – plant roughly hairy.. **4**
  4 Stout plant with no bracts – calyx minute .... *Heracleum sphondylium* (p 256 D)
    Slender plant, with both bracts and bracteoles – calyx-teeth half as long as petals – r ....
    ....*Tordylium maximum* (p 252 L)
  5 Lf-stalks and stems tubular, swollen – umbels dense, globular – on marshy gd..............................
    ....*Oenanthe fistulosa* (p 262 D)
    Lf-stalks not swollen – secondary umbels loose, flat.. **6**
  6 Lf-segments thread-like, many, in dense whorls – vl..........................*Carum verticillatum* (p 254 C)
    Lf-segments lanceolate-oval, not whorled **7**
  7 Bracts abs.. **7**
    Bracts present **8**
  8 Umbels almost stalkless, lf-opposed – in wet places..*Apium* (p 264)
    Umbels terminal, on long stalks – in wds, hbs..................................*Pimpinella major* (p 254 C)
  9 Some bracts up to half length of shorter umbel-rays **10**
    All bracts much shorter than umbel-rays – stems much branched – lft-teeth shallow – gsld on clay soils.
    ....*Sison amomum* (p 254 D)

10 Bracts bristle-like – stem solid, wiry – lft-teeth deep – in dry places.............................
    Petroselinum segetum (p 254 A)

    Bracts wider, sometimes divided – stem hollow, brittle – in wet places...........................**11**

11 Lf segments 4–6 pairs – lfts finely-toothed – plants 1–2 m tall .... *Sium latifolium* (p 264 A)

    Lf segments 7–10 pairs – lfts coarsely-toothed – plants 30–100 cm tall ...... *Berula erecta* (p 264 B)

D Umbellifers with at least lower lvs 2 or more times pinnate

    Fls yellow or green-yellow ....**E**

    Fls white or pinkish...**F**

E Umbellifers with yellow fls and pinnate lvs

  1 Lf-segments fleshy, cylindrical – on seashores...............................*Crithmum maritimum* (p 258 D)

    Lf-segments not fleshy, but flat or thread-like..**2**

  2 Lf-segments linear or thread-like, over 10 times as long as wide.....................................**3**

    Lf-segments lobed or toothed, 2–6 times as long as wide..**4**

  3 Lfts long-narrow, linear, but flat and not thread-like – near sea – vr....................................

    Peucedanum officinale (p 260 F)

    Lfts pinnately-divided into cylindrical thread-like segments .... *Foeniculum vulgare* (p 258 E)

  4 Lvs mostly once pinnate only – lfts oval, coarse-toothed, v hairy............ *Pastinaca sativa* (p 258 A)

    Lvs all 2 or more times pinnate...**5**

  5 Lower lf-segments large (3 cm or more), oval-oblong, toothed, blunt..................................

    Smyrnium olusatrum (p 258 B)

    Lower lf-segments small, pinnatifid, with narrow pointed lobes.......................................**6**

  6 Lf-stalks with broad whitish margins – lfts crisped, edges not fine-toothed..........................

    Petroselinum crispum (p 254 G)

    Lf-stalks with only narrow margins – lfts flat, edges with fine teeth.............. *Silaum silaus* (p 258 C)

F Umbellifers with white (or pinkish) fls, and lvs 2 or more times pinnate

  1 Stems purple-spotted...**2**

    Stems green, without purple spots...**3**

  2 Stems and lvs hairy..*Chaerophyllum temulentum* (p 252 E)

    Stems and lvs hairless... *Conium maculatum* (p 252 F)

  3 Plants hairy, at least on lf edges or veins or on infl-stalks (use lens).................................**4**

    Plants quite hairless throughout ....**I**

  4 Fl-stems hollow..**G**

    Fl-stems solid (or almost so) ....**H**

G Umbellifers ± hairy, with hollow unspotted stems, lvs 2 or more times pinnate, and white or pinkish fls

  1 Plant hairless (except for infl-stalks) – lfts narrow-lanceolate-oblong, v finely-toothed (use lens) – in fens ....*Peucedanum palustre* (p 266 E)

    Plant downy, at least on **lower** stem or **lvs**...**2**

  2 Lower lf-segments broad (at least 1 cm wide × 3 cm long), only shallowly-toothed – v large robust plants **3**

    Lower lf-segments narrow (0.5 cm wide × 2.0 cm long), deeply cut.................................**4**

  3 Lvs with hairless, oval, evenly-toothed lfts – stems round, only downy below – infl downy ....

    Angelica sylvestris (p 256 B)

    Lvs with roughly hairy, irregularly-lobed lfts – stems ridged, roughly hairy ....

    Heracleum sphondylium (p 256 D)

  4 Plants smelling of aniseed – lvs fern-like – frs stout, 20–25 cm long – l in N of GB...........................

    Myrrhis odorata (p 252 J)

    Plants not smelling of aniseed..**5**

  5 Frs 30–70 mm, long, slender-beaked – umbel only 1 or 2 rays – stem only hollow when old – r on ar ....*Scandix pecten-veneris* (p 252 K)

    Frs short, 3–10 mm long – umbels 3–10-rayed **6**

  6 Stems hairless – frs prickly, 3 mm long... *Anthriscus caucalis* (p 252 D)

    Stems downy – frs smooth, 6 mm long...*Anthriscus sylvestris* (p 251 A)

H Hairy Umbellifers with white (or pinkish) fls, solid unspotted stems, and lvs 2 or more times pinnate

1 Stems with many straight and downward-adpressed hairs – frs oval, spiny........ *Torilis* (p 251–252)
   Stems hairy, but hairs not straight or downward-adpressed...**2**

2 Hairs on stem tiny, crisped **3**
   Hairs on stem spreading...**4**

3 Slender plant – bracts, bracteoles abs – calyx abs – umbel-rays ± hairless – no fibrous
   stock at base – fr smooth ....*Pimpinella saxifraga* (p 254 E)
   Stout plant – bracts and bracteoles present – calyx conspicuous – umbel-rays downy – many
   fibres crown rootstock at stem-base – fr hairy – r chk S, E Eng.................*Seseli libanotis* (p 266 B)

4 Bracts of umbel 7–13, large, pinnately-lobed, lfy – centre fl of umbel red – fr spiny ....
   ....*Daucus carota* (p 266 D)
   Bracts of umbel 0–5, tiny, undivided – but bracteoles conspicuous – fr not spiny but long-
   pointed ....*Scandix pecten-veneris* (p 252 K)

I Hairless Umbellifers with lvs 2 or more times pinnate, unspotted stems, and white (or pinkish) fls (check that plant really hairless)

1 Bracteoles abs (or 1 only)..**2**
   Bracteoles 2 or more...**3**

2 Lower lvs persistent, twice trifoliate – lfts oval, toothed, not pinnatifid, 3–6 cm long – many
   creeping fleshy rhizomes – c garden weed....................................*Aegopodium podagraria* (p 256 A)
   Lower lvs soon withering, 3 times pinnate – lfts deeply pinnatifid, small (to 1 cm long) – root a
   round tuber...*Conopodium majus* (p 252 H)

3 Lf-segments long, narrow (to 30 × 2 cm), strap-shaped, sharp-toothed, curved.............................
   ....*Falcaria vulgaris* (p 264 Gi)
   Lf-segments under 10 cm long, not strap-shaped...**4**

4 Bracteoles conspicuous, long, pointing downwards...........................*Aethusa cynapium* (p 252 G)
   Bracteoles small, spreading...**5**

5 Plant low (3–20 cm), erect – waxy-grey solid stem – rosette of waxy-grey fine-cut lvs – persistent
   fibrous lf-bases – dioecious – frs oval – vr on limestone turf........................*Trinia glauca* (p 266 C)
   Taller plant, not as above **6**

6 Tall plants of fen, marsh or meadow...**7**
   Plants of dry gslds, wds or rocks **11**

7 Lfts 3–10 cm long, 1 cm wide, narrow-lanceolate, toothed all along – no bracts – many
   bracteoles – r in swamps..*Cicuta virosa* (p 256 C)
   Lfts 1–2 cm long, pinnatifid...**8**

8 Lfts broad oval, 1 cm wide, with 2–3 blunt broad teeth, wedge-shaped at base – bracts,
   bracteoles many – in ditches, marshy wds – **poisonous**......................*Oenanthe crocata* (p 262 A)
   Lfts narrow, less than 1 cm wide, divisions narrow-lanceolate **9**

9 Secondary umbels dense – fl-stalks shorter than fr – fr oblong, with conspicuous calyx-teeth...........
   ....*Oenanthe* (p 262)
   Secondary umbels open – fl-stalks longer than frs – fr globular – no calyx....................................**10**

10 Bracts 4 or more – lfts 1–2 cm, pinnatifid – lobes blunt without cusps at tips – vl in fens..................
   ....*Peucedanum palustre* (p 266 E)
   Bracts none – lfts less than 1 cm, pinnatifid – lobes with tiny cusps at tips – vr in fens ....
   ....*Selinum carvifolia* (p 266 F)

11 Basal lvs 3–4 times pinnate, segments hairlike, whorled, v aromatic – rootstock bearing fibrous
   bases of old lvs – plants stout – l on upland mds, rds ....*Meum athamanticum* (p 254 Ci)
   Basal lvs with flat lfts (not whorled, hairlike or aromatic)...**12**

12 Stout plants – lower lvs 1–2 times trifoliate – lfts oval, ± unlobed, 3–5 cm long × 2 cm
   wide..**13**
   Slender plants – stems narrowed to base – lower lvs 2–3 times pinnate – lfts linear-lanceolate, 1–
   2 mm wide – root with rounded tuber...**14**

13 Lfts only toothed in upper half – umbel-rays 8–12 – on rocks by sea in N ....
   ....*Ligusticum scoticum* (p 254 B)
   Lfts toothed all round, downy below – umbel-rays 20–25 – on river banks, mds in N......................
   ....*Peucedanum ostruthium* (p 256 Ai)

14 Bracts, bracteoles abs (or, rarely, 1) – styles of fr erect – stem hollow when in fr – in acid gsld,
   wds ....*Conopodium majus* (p 252 H)
   Bracts and bracteoles many – styles of fr bent back – stem always solid – r on chk in Eng...............
   ....*Bunium bulbocastanum* (p 252 I)

250

White-fld Umbellifers with much-divided lvs ▶

A Cow Parsley, *Anthriscus sylvestris*, downy tall erect per herb, 60–100 cm; stems **hollow**, furrowed, **unspotted**, downy below; lvs 2–3 times pinnate, fern-like, scarcely downy, **fresh green**, lfts pointed; umbels to 6 cm across, 4–10-rayed, with no bracts, but with bracteoles; fls pure white, 3–4 mm across, fl-stalks thin. Fr (**Aa**) 6 mm long, smooth, oblong, short-beaked. Br Isles, Eur; vc in hbs, rds, wd borders (by nearly every Eng rdside in May except on v poor soils). Fl 4–6. **Ai Garden Chervil**, *A. cerefolium*, ann, garden escape; stems downy above nodes; umbels lf-opposed; frs smooth, 10 mm long.

B Upright Hedge-parsley, *Torilis japonica*, July–Aug successor to A on rds; ann, slenderer than A; stems **solid**, **unspotted**, **rough**, with **down-pressed** straight hairs; lvs narrower than in A, rough-hairy, dull green; umbels to 4 cm across, 5–12-rayed, bracts and bracteoles present; frs (**B**) oval, 3–4 mm, covered with **hooked** spines, styles bent back. Br Isles (except N Scot), Eur; vc on rds, hbs, wd borders. Fl 7–8. **Bi Spreading Hedge-parsley**, *T. arvensis*, short (10–20 cm) spreading ann; 3–5 umbel-rays, bracts none or 1; frs 4–5 mm, with spines curved but not hooked. SE Eng, Eur, now r-o; on ar. Fl 7–9.

cont

C Knotted Hedge-parsley, *T. nodosa*, prostrate or erect v slender ann, to 30 cm tall; stems solid; lvs under 10 cm long; umbels (**C**) small (0.5–1.0 cm), ± stalkless, lf-opposed; no bracts, but bracteoles; fls 1 mm across, pinkish; fr (**Ca**) 2–3 mm, covered with straight spines and warts. Br Isles: Eng, Wales, f-lc to E, o to W; SE Scot vr; Ire r; Eur lc; on dry grassy banks on sea coasts, ar inland in E Eng. Fl 5–7.

D Bur Chervil, *Anthriscus caucalis*, small version of A (to 50 cm), but ann; stems hollow, hairless; lvs with tiny (5 mm) lfts; fls only 2 mm across, pale green; frs (**D**) 3 mm long, oval, on stout stalks and covered with **hooked spines**. Br Isles lc in SE, r and scattered elsewhere; Eur f-lc; on sandy wa, hbs, mostly near sea. Fl 5–6.

E Rough Chervil, *Chaerophyllum temulentum*, resembles A and is its June–July successor on hbs and rds; stems (**Ec**) hairy, ridged, solid, **purple-spotted**; lvs **dull** dark **grey-green**, **v hairy**, with lfts **blunter** than in A; fl (**Ea**) as in A; frs (**Eb**) 5–7 mm, much as in A. Br Isles: GB (not N,W Scot) c; Ire r; Eur c; in hbs etc. Fl 6–7.

F Hemlock, *Conium maculatum*, resembles E in its **purple-spotted stems** (**Fb**), but is **hairless**; tall (to 2 m) erect unpleasant-smelling bi, with fine-cut fern-like lvs to 30 cm long; umbels 2–5 cm across, rays 10–20; bracts, bracteoles few; frs (**Fa**) 3 mm long, **globular**, with **wavy ridges**. Br Isles (except NW Scot), Eur; c by streams, on wa. Fl 6–7.

G Fool's Parsley, *Aethusa cynapium*, is another herb like A, but ann, to 50 cm tall, and hairless; bractless umbels have **conspicuous narrow bracteoles 1 cm long**, **hanging down** from the partial umbels; frs (**Ga**) 3–4 mm, **oval**, with broad ridges and no spines. Br Isles (except N,W Scot), Eur c; on ar, wa. Fl 7–8.

H Pignut, *Conopodium majus*, slender erect per; smooth stem, 30–50 cm tall, narrows downwards into gd to the brown-skinned, white-fleshed tuber-root (**Hc**), 1.5–3.5 cm across (stem becomes hollow after flowering). Basal lvs (**Hb**) soon wither; lvs twice pinnate, lfts deeply-cut, segments linear, 1–2 mm wide; umbel 3–7 cm across, 6–12 rays, bracts (usually) none, bracteoles few. Fr (**Ha**) 4 mm, narrow, oval, beaked, styles short, **erect**. Br Isles c; Eur: W France lc; in dry wds, old gsld on non-calc soils. Fl 5–6.

I Great Pignut, *Bunium bulbocastanum*, is v like H in habit and has similar tubers, but stems always solid; umbels (**Ib**) have many bracts and bracteoles; styles of fr (**Ia**) bent back. Eng: SE Midlands only, r and vl; Eur: Netherlands vr; SE Belgium r; W Germany o; N,E France lc; on chk gslds, rds. Fl 6–7.

J Sweet Cicely, *Myrrhis odorata*, has aspect of A, but is bushier; when bruised smells strongly of aniseed. Stem hollow, ± downy; lvs fern-like, ± downy, to 30 cm long, often white-blotched at base; frs (**J**) **linear-oblong**, **v long and stout** (25 mm long × 8–10 mm wide), sharply-ridged with **pointed beak**. Br Isles: most c early-flowering Umbellifer of upland N Eng and S Scot; **abs** (or escape only) **SE Eng**; N Scot, Ire r; Eur introd in lowlands o (probably native in mt areas); rds, mds. Fl 5–6.

K Shepherd's-needle, *Scandix pecten-veneris*, erect ann, 15–50 cm; stems ± downy, hollow (only) when old; lvs oblong, 2–3 times pinnate, with segments widened at tips. Umbels simple, or of only 2 short stout rays, spiny-edged bracteoles; fls small (1 mm across), white. Frs (**K**; **Ka**) opening), 30–70 mm long, with v distinctive **long slender beaks**. Eng: SE, E Eng N to Durham, formerly c weed of cornfields, now becoming r; Eur still lc; in ar, especially on calc soils. Fl 5–7.

L Hartwort, *Tordylium maximum*, erect branched ann to 1 m tall; appressed-hairy stem and roughly-hairy lvs give it resemblance to B, but lvs only simply pinnate, with lfts toothed, oval below, lanceolate above; umbels with bristly bracts, long bracteoles; fls (**La**) white to pinkish; fr (**Lb**) 5–8 mm, broadly oblong, bristly, with **thickened whitish hairless ridges**. Eng: Essex only, vr on gsld on clay; Eur: S,W France o, r to N of Loire. Fl 6–7.

Aa 5mm

A

B 3mm

Ec 3mm

Eb 6mm

Ea 2mm

E

C 3mm

Ca 3mm

Ga 3mm

F

Fa 3mm

Fb

D 3mm

H

Hb

Hc

Ha 4mm

G

Ga 3mm

La 2mm

L

L 6mm

Ia 3mm

I

Ib

J

K

Ka

253

Umbellifers with white fls, mostly broad-lobed root-lvs, or whorled lfts

A   Corn Parsley, *Petroselinum segetum*, slender hairless bi, 30–100 cm, parsley-scented; stem round, solid; lvs once-pinnate, linear-oblong; many pairs lfts, 0.5–1.0 cm long, oval, toothed or lobed; upper lvs with narrow lfts. Umbels irregular, few-rayed, 1–5 cm across, bracts and bracteoles bristle-like. Fls (**Aa**) white, 1 mm across, 3–5 only per partial umbel. Fr (**Ab**) egg-shaped, ridged, no calyx. S and E Eng, lf near coast, o inland; **abs rest Br Isles**; Eur: N to Belgium, f to S; on dry grassy banks, near sea and on hbs, rds inland. Fl 8–9.

B   Scots Lovage, *Ligusticum scoticum*, **stout-stemmed** celery-scented per, 20–90 cm; stems often **purplish**, lvs (**B**) twice trifoliate, **dark shiny green**; lfts **oval, toothed in upper half**, 3–5 cm long; lf-stalks **inflated**, sheathing stem. Fls greenish-white, 2 mm across, in dense umbels (**Ba**); bracts and bracteoles linear. Fr (**Bb**) 4 mm long, oblong, with calyx-teeth and sharp ridges. Br Isles: coasts of Scot, N Ire, o-lf; Eur: Denmark r; among rocks or shingle by sea. Fl 7.

C   Whorled Caraway, *Carum verticillatum*, erect slender hairless per, 30–60 cm, with solid, little-branched stem; erect once-pinnate lvs (**C**); lfts divided deeply into linear **bristle-like** green lobes, appearing as if **in whorls** up lf-stalks. Umbels 2–5 cm across, rays 8–12; bracts and bracteoles many, narrow; fls 1 mm across, white. Fr (**Ca**) 2 mm long, oval, with sharp ridges. Br Isles: S, SW Eng, Wales, r-lf; W Scot lc; Ire N, SW vl; Eur: W France c, to Holland r; in damp acid mds, gslds. Fl 7–8.   **Ci   Spignel**, *Meum athamanticum*, like C has **apparently-whorled** hair-like lobes to lfts of the three-four times pinnate lvs; but a stouter plant, with larger triangular lvs, with few or no bracts; frs **elliptical**, 6–10 mm long. Br Isles: N Wales, N Eng, Scot; Eur: Belgium (mts of France); ol-lf on gslds, rds in mts and hills. Fl 6–8.

D   Stone Parsley, *Sison amomum*, erect, **much-branched**, bushy, slender hairless bi, 50–100 cm, with unpleasant oily smell; stem solid; root-lvs once-pinnate, long-stalked, lfts 2–7 cm, **oval**, lobed and toothed; upper lvs trifoliate, lfts v narrow. Umbels both terminal and in lf-axils, 1–4 cm across, **few-rayed, few-fld**; bracts and bracteoles 2–4, bristle-like. Fls white, 1 mm across, petals notched; fr (**Da**) globular, 3 mm long, ridges thin. S, E Eng, f-lc; N Wales r; **abs rest of Br Isles**; Eur: W France lc; on gslds, rds, hbs on heavy clay soils. Fl 7–9.

E   Burnet-saxifrage, *Pimpinella saxifraga*, erect slender **downy** per, 30–100 cm, with rough round stem. Root-lvs (**Eb**) once-pinnate, with **oval**, toothed lfts; stem-lvs twice-pinnate, with **v narrow** lfts, no bracts or bracteoles. Fls 2 mm across, white, styles v short. Fr (**Ea**) 3 mm long, wide-oval. Br Isles vc (but **abs NW Scot**); Eur vc; on dry mostly calc gslds. Fl 7–9.   **Ei   Bladderseed**, *Physospermum cornubiense*, has lfts rather like those of E, but a **hairless woodland** herb to 75 cm; lvs **twice-trifoliate**, lfts deep-cut, dark green, with **wedge-shaped** bases, on long stalks; umbels of white fls have lanceolate bracts and bracteoles; frs **smooth**, 4–5 mm long, rounded, resembling tiny green **bladders**. S Eng: Bucks, Cornwall r (S Eur); in dry open wds. Fl 7–8.

F   Greater Burnet-saxifrage, *Pimpinella major*, erect hairless per, 50–120 cm tall, **not** v like E; stem (**Fa**) smooth, hollow, strongly ridged; **lvs all once-pinnate**, with **glossy**, dark green, **oval-elliptical** coarse-toothed lfts 2–8 cm long, lf-stalks sheathing. Umbels terminal, 3–6 cm across, flat, many-rayed; no bracts or bracteoles (**Fc**); fls 3 mm across, white (pinkish in N); styles long. Fr (**Fb**) 4 mm long, narrow-oval. Br Isles: Eng, lc in parts of Midlands, SE, abs in many parts; S Ire vlf; Eur c; on rds, wd-borders, hbs, on heavier usually base-rich soils. Fl 6–7.

G   Garden Parsley, *Petroselinum crispum*, stout erect hairless bi, 30–70 cm, has familiar parsley scent. Solid, ridged stem; lvs thrice-pinnate, triangular in outline; lfts 1–2 cm, bases wedge-shaped, toothed at tips, often much **crisped**. Umbels flat-topped, 2–5 cm across, many-rayed; bracts and bracteoles with **white**

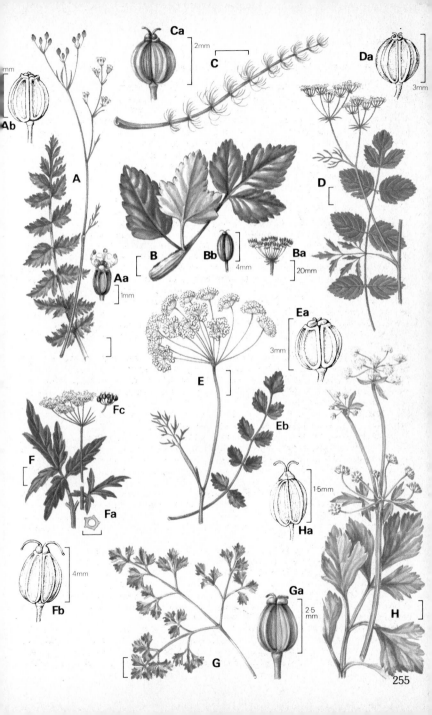

Ca

2mm

C

Da

3mm

Ab

mm

A

Aa

1mm

B

Bb

4mm

Ba

20mm

D

E

Ea

3mm

Eb

F

Fc

Fa

Ha

1·5mm

Fb

4mm

G

Ga

2·5
mm

H

255

◀ **edges** and **sheathing bases**. Fls 2 mm across, yellowish. Fr (**Ga**) 2.5 mm long, oval, finely-ridged. Br Isles o, especially in S (garden escape); Eur o (S Eur); on wa, rocks, old walls. Fl 6–8.

H **Wild Celery**, *Apium graveolens*, stout erect hairless bi, 30–60 cm, has familiar scent of celery. Stems hollow, grooved; root-lvs once-pinnate, with long sheathing stalks, lfts diamond-shaped to triangular, 0.5–3.0 cm long, dark shiny-green, lobed and toothed; upper lvs trifoliate, lfts narrower. Umbels both short-stalked, terminal, and stalkless in lf-axils; rays unequal, bracts, bracteoles abs. Fls greenish-white, 0.5 mm across; fr (**Ha**) oval, ridged, 1.5 mm long. Br Isles: Eng, Wales, S Ire, lc near coasts, r inland; **Scot abs**; Eur lf; in brackish mds, marshes, ditches, riversides by tidal water or near sea. Fl 6–8.

▶ **Umbellifers with white fls and broad lfts**

A **Ground-elder**, *Aegopodium podagraria*, erect hairless per, 40–100 cm tall, with stout hollow grooved stem (**Ab**); lvs 10–20 cm, triangular in outline, long-stalked, once or twice trifoliate; lfts oval to elliptical, 2–7 cm long, toothed, ± stalkless, fresh light green; umbels terminal, 2–6 cm across, many-rayed, no bracts or bracteoles; fls white, 1 mm across. Fr (**Aa**) 4 mm long, egg-shaped. Br Isles, Eur; vc (except in mts) on rds, wa, hbs, wd borders, and a serious garden weed because of far-creeping rhizomes. Fl 5–7. **Ai** **Masterwort**, *Peucedanum ostruthium*, tall per; twice-trifoliate lvs with broad, oval, toothed lfts as in A, but stems stouter with inflated sheathing lf-stalks, lfts downy below; umbels 5–10 cm across, bracteoles present; fls often pinkish; fr almost spherical. N Eng, Scot, N Ire, Eur, r-vl; introd (S Eur) mds, riversides, rds. Fl 7–8.

B **Wild Angelica**, *Angelica sylvestris*, ± hairless per to 200 cm tall, with v stout hollow **purplish** stems (**Bd**), downy only near base; lvs (**B**) 30–60 cm, triangular in outline, 2–3 times pinnate; lfts 2–8 cm, oblong-oval, sharp-toothed; lf-stalks (**Be**) broad, hollow, channelled on upperside, with broad, inflated, sheathing bases; upper lvs reduced to sheaths around umbels. Umbels terminal and in lf-axils, 3–15 cm across, many-rayed, no bracts, bracteoles few, narrow. Fls (**Bb**) 2 mm across, white or pink; no calyx, petals curved inwards; frs (**Ba**) 5 mm long, oval, v flattened (section **Bc**), with broad wings on edges. Br Isles, Eur; c in damp mds, fens, wds. Fl 6–9. **Bi** **Garden Angelica**, *A. archangelica*, larger than B; stems and fls green, fls with calyx, fr with corky wings. Native in Denmark; introd elsewhere in GB and Eur; in wa, riversides etc. ***Bii** **Sermountain**, *Laserpitium latifolium*, robust per, like B in habit and in its twice-pinnate lvs with inflated sheaths, but lvs and stem grey-green (never purplish), and lfts **blunt**, with cordate bases; fr oval, ridged, but not flattened as in B. Eur o to S, r to N; in calc scrub. Fl 6–8.

C **Cowbane**, *Cicuta virosa*, erect hairless per, 50–130 cm tall, with ridged hollow stem (**Cb**); lvs (**C**) triangular in outline, to 30 cm long, with long hollow stalks, 2–3 times pinnate, with linear-lanceolate, strongly and sharply-toothed lfts 2–10 cm long. Umbels 7–13 cm across, convex, many-rayed, bracteoles none, bracts many and strap-shaped; fls white, 3 mm across, with oval calyx-teeth; fr (**Ca**) 2 mm long, globular, wider than long, with blunt ridges. Br Isles, v scattered and l (lc in Norfolk and central Ire); Eur o-vlc; on fens, lake borders, ditches. Fl 7–8.

D **Hogweed**, *Heracleum sphondylium*, robust, roughly hairy bi to 200 cm; stems hollow (**Dc**), ridged, with downward-pointing hairs. Lvs 15–60 cm, once-pinnate, rough, grey-green, with clasping bases, and with oval- to oblong-lobed, pointed, coarse-toothed lfts to 15 cm long, lower ones stalked. Umbels 5–15 cm, stalked, many-rayed; bracts usually none, bracteoles bristle-like, down-turned. Fls (**Db**) white or pinkish, 5–10 mm across; petals notched, **unequal**. Fr (**Da**) 7–8 mm long, oval, whitish green, v flattened, smooth with club-shaped dark marks on

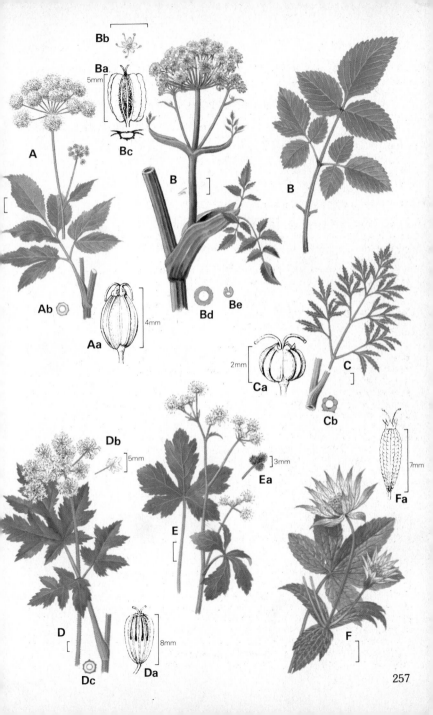

257

◄ sides. Br Isles, Eur; vc on rds, hbs, gslds, wds. Fl 6–9. **Di Giant Hogweed**, *H. mantegazzianum*, perhaps the largest herb wild in W Eur; like D, but to 5 m tall; stem red-spotted, to 10 cm across; lvs to 1 m long, with teeth sharper than in D. Umbels to 50 cm across; petals to 12 mm long. Introd (from Caucasus) in Br Isles, Eur; o-la on wa, riversides. Fl 6–7.

E Sanicle, *Sanicula europaea*, hairless per, 20–60 cm tall, with long-stalked root-lvs palmately-lobed (rather like ivy lvs, but more deeply-cut and with lobes toothed), to 6 cm wide below, upper lvs smaller. Umbels few-rayed, bracts 3–5 mm, pinnatifid; bracteoles undivided. Fls pink or white. Fr (**Ea**) 3 mm long, oval, covered with hooked bristles (animal-dispersed). Br Isles, Eur; vc in wds on richer soils, especially beechwoods on lime. Fl 5–8.

F Astrantia, *Astrantia major*, has simple umbels and is superficially more like a Scabious than an Umbellifer. Erect hairless per, 30–75 cm tall, with long-stalked palmately-lobed root-lvs, 8–10 mm across, with coarsely toothed lobes, veins stronger than in E. Umbels **simple**, dense, rounded, 1.5–2.0 cm across, with a ruff of long lanceolate bracts, green-purplish above. Fls white or pink, 2 mm across, fine-stalked; fr (**Fa**) 6–8 mm long, oval, with swollen wrinkled ridges. Eng, Shropshire vr; Eur o (probably introd from central Eur, where c in mt wds); in wds, mds. Fl 5–7.

► **Yellow-fld Umbellifers**

A Wild Parsnip, *Pastinaca sativa*, erect downy branched per, with hollow, furrowed, angled stems; rough once-pinnate lvs with oval-pinnatifid and toothed segments. Umbels 5–10 cm across, 5–15-rayed; fls (**Ab**) yellow, 1.5 mm across; fr (**Aa**) oval, flattened, with narrow winged edges (the ancestor of the vegetable). Br Isles: S, central, E Eng c; Wales r; Scot, Ire, escape only; Eur c; on rds, gsld, scrub, wa, especially on dry calc soils. Fl 6–8. (Handling plant in sunlight can cause blisters.)

B Alexanders, *Smyrnium olusatrum*, stout celery-scented bi with furrowed stem, solid until old, with branches often opp above; lvs dark green, shiny; root-lvs thrice trifoliate, to 30 cm long; lfts stalked, **oval** to diamond-shaped, lobed, toothed; upper lvs less divided; stalks with sheathing bases. Umbels terminal and in lf-axils, ± globular, many-rayed; few bracts and bracteoles. Fls 1–5 mm across, **yellow-green**; fr (**Ba**) 8 mm long, **oval**, **angled**, **black**. Br Isles: Eng, Wales, Ire, f-lc near coasts, r-o inland; Scot r; Eur, S from NW France f-lc; on cliffs, wa near sea, hbs. Fl 4–6.

C Pepper-saxifrage, *Silaum silaus*, slender branched erect per to 100 cm, with solid, ridged stems. Lower lvs triangular, 2–3-times pinnate, with linear, often pinnatifid, finely-toothed, pointed lfts 1–5 cm long; umbels 2–6 cm wide, on long stalks; 5–10 rays; usually no bracts, bracteoles linear; fls (**Cb**) 1.5 mm, **sulphur-yellow**; fr (**Ca**) oblong-oval, nearly smooth, shiny, brownish-purple. Br Isles: Eng f-lc; Scot SE only, Wales r; **Ire abs**; Eur, S from Belgium f-lc; on mds, gslds, rds on heavy clay soils. Fl 6–8.

D Rock Samphire, *Crithmum maritimum*, fleshy, spreading per to 30 cm tall; stems solid, ridged; lvs triangular, short-stalked, once-twice-trifoliate, with fleshy rounded segments; lf-stalks sheathing. Umbels 3–6 cm wide, many-rayed, with many narrow bracts and bracteoles. Fls 2 mm across, yellow-green. Fr (**Da**) 6 mm long, corky, purplish, oval, round, thick-ridged. Br Isles: coasts of GB round clockwise from Suffolk to Hebrides; SW of GB c, to N r; Ire lc; Eur: France SW from Calais lf; on sea cliffs, shingle. Fl 6–8.

E Fennel, *Foeniculum vulgare*, stout erect hairless per with solid stem; lvs repeatedly pinnate into long thread-like waxy-green lfts, not all in one plane. Umbels 4–8 cm wide, many-rayed, no bracts or bracteoles; fls 1–2 mm wide,

◀ **bright yellow**. Fr (**Ea**) **oval**, rounded, stout-ridged. Br Isles: Eng, Wales, c on coasts, o inland; S, E Ire r; Eur o (S Eur); on cliffs, wa near sea; gdn escape inland. Fl 7–10. **Ei Dill**, *Anethum graveolens*, similar gdn escape; frs **flattened**, with **winged** ridges.

F Hog's Fennel, *Peucedanum officinale*, robust, hairless, erect per to 150 cm tall; stems stout, ridged, solid; lvs 4–6-times trifoliate, with **flat**, narrow-linear, untoothed lfts 4–10 cm long (**not rounded** as in E). Umbels 8–20 cm wide, many-rayed, bracts few or none, bracteoles bristle-like; Fls (**Fb**) 2 mm across, **sulphur-yellow**. Frs (**Fa**) 5–10 mm long, **elliptical**, ridged. Eng: Kent, Essex only, r but la; Eur: central, W France o; on clayey banks near tidal water and sea, also inland in Eur. Fl 7–9.

G Sickle-leaved Hare's-ear, *Bupleurum falcatum*, erect hairless per, 50–100 cm, stem hollow; lvs **undivided**, untoothed (as in all genus *Bupleurum*), narrow-elliptical, curved; lower stalked, upper clasping, 3–8 cm long. Umbels stalked, 2–6 cm wide, 5–11 rays, bracts and bracteoles lanceolate; fls golden-yellow, 1 mm wide; fr (**Ga**) oblong, ridged, **red-tipped**. Eng: Essex vr; Eur: N, central France, Belgium, o-la; on calc gslds. Fl 7–9. **Gi Thorow-wax**, *B. rotundifolium*, has oval lvs, the upper forming rings round stem. Umbels simple or few-rayed; no bracts; bracteoles like upper lvs; fls yellow, 1.5 mm; fr smooth. S, E Eng, almost extinct; Eur, r; in ar, especially on calc soils. Fl 6–8.

H Slender Hare's-ear, *B. tenuissimum*, slenderer than G, has wiry stems and linear-lanceolate lvs 1–5 cm. Umbels only to 5 mm across, in lf-axils, ± stalkless; bracts, bracteoles bristle-like. Fls (**Hb**) 1 mm, yellow; fr (**Ha**), 2 mm long, globular, **black**, **rough**. S, E Eng from Severn to Yorks, f-lc; Eur lf; on grassy banks, saltmarsh edges near sea. Fl 7–9. **Hi Small Hare's-ear**, *B. baldense*, is tiny (2–10 cm), with sharp-pointed spoon-shaped lvs 1.0–1.5 cm; umbels 5–10 mm across, with few short rays, few fls, few bristle-like bracts. Oval, spine-tipped bracteoles hide yellow 2-mm fls; fr smooth, 2–3 mm. Eng: S Devon, Sussex vr; Eur: W France, Channel Is, lf; on dunes, banks, rocky places on coast. Fl 6–7.

Water-dropworts (*Oenanthe*) are hairless Umbellifers usually found in water or moist places; stems often ± swollen, ridged; lvs 2–4 times pinnate, of triangular outline, with lfts either linear, or wedge-shaped at bases, with sharp teeth above. Lf-stalks sheathing stem. Umbels many-rayed, mostly long-stalked, bracts and bracteoles many, v narrow. Fls white, 2 mm across, petals unequal. Frs strongly angled, oval, ridged, calyx-teeth prominent. **All are poisonous; A is deadly.**

KEY TO WATER-DROPWORTS (*OENANTHE*)

1 Most of plant submerged in **running** water – lvs often all submerged, twice-pinnate, lfts with wedge-shaped bases, cut into fine narrow segments – aerial lvs (if present) once-twice-pinnate, with oval, blunt, toothed lfts – fr 5–6 mm, oblong, 3 times length of styles ...... *O. fluviatilis* (p 262 C)
   Plant **not in running** water, but in mds, gsld or still water.. **2**

2 Plant in still water – stem 30–60 cm, **v swollen** (3–4 cm) below, thinner above, fine-ridged, with transverse joints – submerged lower lvs 3-times pinnate, with hairlike segments – upper, aerial lvs with oval, fine-toothed lfts 5 mm long – bushy-branched, short-stalked umbels in lf-axils and terminal – fr 3–4 mm, oval, twice length of styles.. *O. aquatica* (p 262 B)
   Plant in marshes or gsld – stem not swollen below.. **3**

3 Tall (50–150 cm) robust plant – stems strong, ridged, but not swollen, and evenly tapering above – upper lvs 3–4 times pinnate, lfts 2 × 1 cm, with wedge-shaped bases and coarse teeth at ends – umbels long-stalked – fr 5–6 mm, cylindrical.. *O. crocata* (p 262 A)
   Less robust, slenderer plants, rarely over 90 cm – upper lvs with **narrow linear** lfts......................... **4**

4 Stems **slender** but **hollow**, **inflated** between lf-junctions – lf-stalks hollow, **inflated**, **longer** than pinnate blades – partial umbels form dense balls of frs after flowering .... *O. fistulosa* (p 262 D)
   Stems solid, not inflated, but ridged – lf-stalks solid, not inflated, **shorter** than pinnate blades – partial umbels either open, or dense and flat in fr... **5**

5 Root-lvs with lfts **oval**, bases **wedge-shaped**, with **several pointed teeth** – umbels dense in fr, flat-topped, rays stout (0.5–1.0 mm) – on mds, gslds....................................*O. pimpinelloides* (p 262 E)
   Root-lvs with lfts narrow, spoon-shaped or **elliptical**, **blunt** – umbels open in fr, convex, rays slender (0.25 mm) – in fens, marshes near sea.. *O. lachenalii* (p 262 G)
   Root-lvs with lfts narrow, **linear-lanceolate**, **pointed**, like those of upper lvs – umbels rather open in fr, flat-topped, rays v stout (1–2 mm) – on inland mds .... *O. silaifolia* (p 262 F)

CARROT FAMILY

Umbelliferae

Water-dropworts

A Hemlock Water-dropwort, *Oenanthe crocata*, robust erect hairless per to 150 cm, **v poisonous**. Stems hollow, cylindrical, grooved, lvs triangular, 3–4 times pinnate; lfts oval, bases tapered to stalk, with several deep teeth above; lf-stalks sheathing stem. Umbels stalked, terminal, 5–10 cm across, many-rayed, bracts and bracteoles many, linear, deciduous. Fls (**Ab**) white, 2 mm wide, petals unequal. Fr (**Aa**) 4–6 mm long, cylindrical, styles 2 mm, erect. Br Isles: S, W of GB va; E, central Eng, N Scot r – abs; Ire f-lc; Eur: W, NW France, lc, abs to NE; in marshes, wet wds, ditches. Fl 6–7.

B Fine-leaved Water-dropwort, *O. aquatica*, rather bushy per, 30–100 cm tall, with runners; stem (**Ba**) **v swollen** in lower part, 3–4 cm thick, hollow, v finely-ridged, with **transverse** joints. Lvs 3 times pinnate, lfts hairlike on submerged lvs, lanceolate, finely-toothed, on aerial lvs (**Bc**). Umbels **short-stalked**, terminal and in lf-axils; 4–10 rays; bracts 0–1, bracteoles bristle-like. Fls white, 2 mm wide, petals ± equal. Fr (**Bb**) 3–4 mm long, oval, twice length of styles. Br Isles: Eng, f-lc in E, SE Midlands, r elsewhere in GB; Ire o; Eur f-lc; in ponds, ditches. Fl 6–9.

C River Water-dropwort, *O. fluviatilis*, related to B, but grows in ± fast-flowing, chky rivers; often lacks infls; submerged lvs (**C**) twice-pinnate, with narrow linear lfts; lvs on aerial fl-shoots once- or twice-pinnate, lfts broad oval, blunt-toothed, 1–2 cm long. Fls as in B; fr 5–6 mm, oblong, 3 times length of styles. S, E Eng vlc; Ire r; Eur: Denmark, W Germany only, r. Fl 6–9.

D Tubular Water-dropwort, *O. fistulosa*, erect slender hairless per, 30–60 cm, with slender but **hollow** stems, **inflated** between lf-junctions. Lvs (**Db**) once- (or twice-) pinnate; lfts of lower lvs oval-lobed, of upper lvs linear, untoothed. Lf-stalks longer than pinnate blades. Umbels few-rayed, rays stout, bracts none; partial umbels 1 cm, forming **dense balls** of frs after flowering; bracteoles many, fls white, 3 mm wide; fr (**Da**) 3–4 mm long, angled; styles spreading. Br Isles: Eng f-lc, r-o elsewhere; Eur f-lc; on marshes, pond edges. Fl 7–9.

E Corky-fruited Water-dropwort, *O. pimpinelloides*, erect hairless per, 30–80 cm; stems solid, cylindrical, ridged; root-lvs (**Ec**) twice-pinnate, with oval, deeply-toothed lfts as in A, but half size. Upper stems-lvs once-pinnate, lfts long, linear. Umbels (**Ed**) terminal, 2–6 cm wide, compact, **dense, flat-topped** with stout rays; **bracts**, bracteoles bristle-like; fls (**Eb**) 3–4 mm wide. Frs (**Ea**) 3 mm long, ribbed, **cylindrical**, with **swollen** corky bases; styles erect. Br Isles: Eng, lc S of Thames – Severn, **abs elsewhere**; Eur: N to Belgium o; on mds, gslds on clay, often near sea. Fl 6–8.

F Narrow-leaved Water-dropwort, *O. silaifolia*, v close to E, but with root- and stem-lvs twice-pinnate, all (**F**) with narrow-linear, pointed lfts; umbels flat-topped but ± open (not dense-topped) in fr; bracts usually abs; frs (**Fa**) cylindrical, corky-based, rounded at tops, narrowed suddenly at junction with stalks. SE, central Eng r; Eur: France, Belgium r; in mds by inland rivers. Fl 6.

G Parsley Water-dropwort, *O. lachenalii*, is close to both E and F: differs from both in that the twice-pinnate root-lvs (**Gc**) have narrow, but **bluntly elliptical** or **obovate** lfts without teeth; differs from E in umbels (**Gb**) **open, convex**, especially in fr; from F in having **bracts**, **oval** (not corky-based) frs (**Ga**), and **slender** umbel-rays. Br Isles: all round coast c (but **N Scot abs**), vlc inland; Eur f-lc; in brackish mds, coastal marshes, inland fens. Fl 6–9.

Umbellifers with white fls and once-pinnate lvs; also spiny-lvd spp

A **Greater Water-parsnip**, *Sium latifolium*, robust, erect, hairless per; stem thick, hollow, ridged, to 2 m tall; lvs to 30 cm long, **long-stalked**, once-pinnate, with 4–6 pairs **oval** to oblong, toothed lfts, 2–15 cm long, bright green; lf-stalks (**Ac**) hollow, sheathing stem. Umbels 6–10 cm wide, **terminal**, **flat-topped**, **long-stalked**, with many rays, 2–5 cm; bracts, bracteoles **large**, **lfy**. Fls (**Ab**) white, **4 mm wide**; **sepals present**. Fr (**Aa**) oval, **3 mm** long, ridges low. **Poisonous**. Br Isles: N to S Scot r, but lc in E Anglia; Ire vr; Eur o-lc; in fens, marsh ditches. Fl 7–8.

B **Lesser Water-parsnip**, *Berula erecta*, smaller version of A, 30–100 cm tall, but less erect and has **runners**; lvs, once-pinnate, have lfts (**B**) more **deeply toothed**, oval, 2–5 cm long, in 7–10 pairs, dull **bluish**-green; stem-lvs much smaller than in A. Umbels only 3–6 cm wide, **short-stalked**, in **lf-axils** and terminal (**Bb**), with fewer, **shorter** (1–3 cm) rays. Bracts (**Bc**), bracteoles as in A. Fr (**Ba**) almost **spherical**, 2 mm long. **Poisonous**. Br Isles, f (lc to S and E); Scot, N Ire vr; Eur f-lc; in fens, ditches, ponds. Fl 7–9.

C **Fool's Water-cress**, *Apium nodiflorum*, rather close to B, but ± creeping, with ascending fl-stems to 80 cm. Lvs (**Cb**) once-pinnate, with 4–6 pairs of **shallowly, bluntly-toothed**, oval, **bright** green, **shining** lfts (**Cc**). Umbels ± stalkless in lf-axils; no bracts; but bracteoles present; fr (**Ca**) **broadly oval**, 1.5 mm long. Mistaken for Watercress (p 124) but not poisonous. Br Isles: Eng, Wales, Ire, c in lowlands; Scot r; Eur: France to Holland, c to S, r to N; in fens, ditches, ponds, springs. Fl 7–8.

D **Lesser Marshwort**, *Apium inundatum*, slender, ± prostrate, hairless per, 10–50 cm long. Lvs pinnate, submerged lvs with deeply **pinnatifid**, **hair-like** lfts, aerial lvs with linear to narrow wedge-shaped three-lobed lfts. Umbels 1–2 cm wide, in lf-axils, on stalks 1–3 cm long; bracts none; bracteoles 3–6, lanceolate, blunt. Fls white, 1 mm wide; fr (**Da**) 2 mm, elliptical, low-ridged. Br Isles, Eur (except NW Scot and mts); f-lc on mud or in water of shallow ponds. Fl 6–8.

E **Marsh Pennywort**, *Hydrocotyle vulgaris*, with no superficial resemblance to Umbellifers, is often put in separate family, Hydrocotylaceae. Hairless prostrate creeping and rooting per, with **circular**, shallow-toothed lvs (rather like those of Wall Pennywort, p 222), 1–5 cm wide, held erect like parasols, on stalks 1–15 cm, attached to lf-centres. Infls (hard to spot and often abs) 2–6 cm tall, with simple **whorls** of 2–5 stalkless pinkish-green fls 1 mm wide, with triangular bracts. Fr (**Ea**) ± circular, flattened, ridged, 2 mm wide. Fls have Umbellifer structure (5 petals, 5 stamens, inferior ovary of 2 carpels). Br Isles, Eur; f-lc in bogs, fens etc. Fl 6–8.

F **Sea-holly**, *Eryngium maritimum*, a beautiful plant. Branched per, 30–60 cm; lvs **waxy-grey** with thick margins, edged with long **spines**; root-lvs long-stalked, palmate-veined, rounded; stem-lvs stalkless. Umbels **simple** (more like teasel heads, p 354, than those of most Umbellifers), oval, 2.5–4.0 cm long, with close-packed fls (8 mm wide) of bright clear blue; bracts of umbels whorled, **oblong**, spiny; bracts of each fl spine-like, three-lobed. Fr (**Fa**) 5 mm long, oblong, covered with hooked bristles. Coasts of Br Isles (except N, E Scot), Eur; f-la on sandy or shingly beaches, dunes. Fl 7–9. ***Fi** *E. viviparum* is like a miniature of F, only 3–12 cm tall; stems produce tiny umbels of few-fld heads in each fork; lvs lanceolate, pinnatifid, spiny; W France; r on sandy coastal flats. Fl 7–8.

G **Field Eryngo**, *E. campestre*, has **pinnate**, stalked root-lvs to 20 cm long, with strap-shaped, spiny, grey-green lfts; stem-lvs shorter, unstalked, with clasping bases. Umbels **1–2 cm long**, oval, with **narrow** spiny bracts, to 3 cm. Fls **mauve-white**, 2–3 mm wide, with individual bracts much longer than fls, spine-like. Fr (**Ga**) smaller than in F, 3 mm long. S Eng vr; Eur: France c; N to N Germany r; dry gslds, banks, dunes, rds. Fl 7–8. **Gi** **Longleaf**, *Falcaria vulgaris*, not v close to

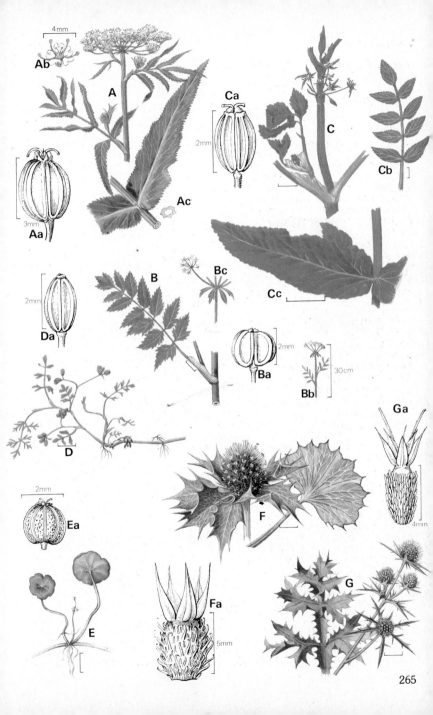

4 mm

Ab

A

Aa

3 mm

Ca

2 mm

C

Cb

Ac

Cc

Da

2 mm

B

Bc

Ba

2 mm

Bb

30 cm

D

Ga

Ea

2 mm

E

Fa

5 mm

F

G

4 mm

◀ G; hairless per to 50 cm. Root-lvs are distinctive feature; once- or twice-trifoliate, long-stalked, with **linear**, **strap-shaped**, pointed, **sharply and finely-toothed**, **curved** lfts up to **30 cm** long, **grey-green**. Stem-lvs shorter, with 3–5 lfts, arranged like spread fingers. Umbels compound, as in Cow Parsley (p 251 A), with many **long** rays and small white fls; bracts, bracteoles present, linear. Eng: Kent, E Anglia introd, r; Eur: France to Denmark native, o-lf; on gsld on calc soils. Fl 7.

▶ **White-fld Umbellifers** continued

*A *Seseli montanum*, slender, branched, hairless per, 50–80 cm tall; stem grey-green, grooved above; root-lvs (**Ab**) on long stalks, oval in outline, 5–10 cm long, twice-pinnate, lfts **linear**, often **forked**, 5–10 mm × 1 mm; stem-lvs once-pinnate, lfts longer. Umbels 2–4 cm wide; **no bracts**, rays downy, bracteoles white-edged, lanceolate; fls white, 2 mm wide; fr (**Aa**) **oblong**, **downy**, each carpel five-angled, **calyx-teeth short**, **persistent**. France, S from R Somme and Laon lf; on calc gsld, rocks. Fl 7–9.

B Moon Carrot, *S. libanotis*, per, is much stouter-stemmed, more downy, and more robust (to 1 m tall) than A, more like D below; stem **solid**, **downy**, **strong-ridged**; remains of old lvs persist at stem-base as tuft of fibres; lvs downy, twice-pinnate, 10–20 cm long; lfts **stalkless**, oval, pinnatifid, with oblong, pointed lobes, **not all in one plane**; some lvs in **opp pairs**. Umbels 5–10 cm wide, terminal, dense, convex; rays many, **downy**; bracts and bracteoles many, narrow. Fls (**Bb**) 1–2 mm, white, with **long calyx-teeth**; fr (**Ba**) **oval**, **downy**, rounded, with strong ridges. Eng: Sussex, Beds to Cambs, vr; Eur: from France f-lc, to Denmark o; on calc gsld, rocks, scrub. Fl 7–8.

C Honewort, *Trinia glauca*, low, bushy, erect, **waxy** grey-green per, 3–20 cm; stem grooved, branched from base. Lvs (**Cb**) 3 times pinnate, lfts narrow-linear, waxy-grey. Dioecious; umbels of male plants 1 cm wide, flat-topped, with 4–7 rays, equal, 5 mm long; umbels of female plants to 3 cm wide, with longer (to 4 cm) unequal rays. Bracts none, bracteoles 2–3. Fls tiny, white; fr (**Ca**) **oval**, 2 mm long, **hairless**, with broad raised ridges. Eng: S Devon, Bristol, N Somerset, r and vl; Eur, not N of R Loire; among limestone rocks in sun. Fl 5–6.

D Wild Carrot, *Daucus carota*, erect, branched, **roughly hairy** bi, to 100 cm, with solid ridged stem; lvs 3 times pinnate, with oval-lanceolate, pinnatifid lfts 5–8 mm long. Umbels 3–7 cm wide, rays many and bristly, bracts **many**, **large**, **lfy**, **pinnatifid**, forming a 'ruff' to umbel below. Fls 2–3 mm, white, but central fl usually **dark red**. Fr (**Da**) 2.5–4.0 mm long, oval, downy, with **4 stout, spiny ridges** on each carpel; umbels concave in fr. Br Isles, Eur, c except in mt and moorland areas; on gslds, cliffs, rds, hbs, especially on calc soils and near sea. Fl 6–8.

Di Sea Carrot, *D. carota*, ssp *gummifer*, has fleshier, blunter lfts, **convex** or flat umbels in fr, spines on fr-ridges **webbed** together. Coasts S Eng, W France.

E Milk-parsley, *Peucedanum palustre*, ± hairless bi, to 150 cm; stems (**Ed**) ridged, hollow; lvs triangular in outline, 2–4 times pinnate, with lfts pinnatifid into oblong-lanceolate lobes **without** spiny tips (**Eb**), 5 mm × 2 mm. Umbels 5–10 cm wide, many-rayed, rays **downy**; **several** bracts and bracteoles, lanceolate. Fls (**Ec**) 2 mm, greenish-white; fr (**Ea**) 4–5 mm long, shortly oval, hairless, much flattened, with broad wings on edges and narrow ridges on faces. Eng: E, S, r (but la in E Anglia); **abs rest of Br Isles**; Eur o-lc; in calc fens. Fl 7–9.

F Cambridge Milk-parsley, *Selinum carvifolia*, v close to E, is tall, ± hairless per, with stems more ridged than in E. Lvs 2–4 times pinnate; lfts have linear-lanceolate, v shortly **spine-tipped** lobes. Umbels of white fls (**Fb**) many-rayed, **without bracts** but with many linear bracteoles; fr (**Fa**) 3–4 mm long, long-oval; 2 side wings, 3 back wings on each carpel, **all thick**, prominent. Cambs vr; Eur N to Denmark o-lf; in fens. Fl 7–10.

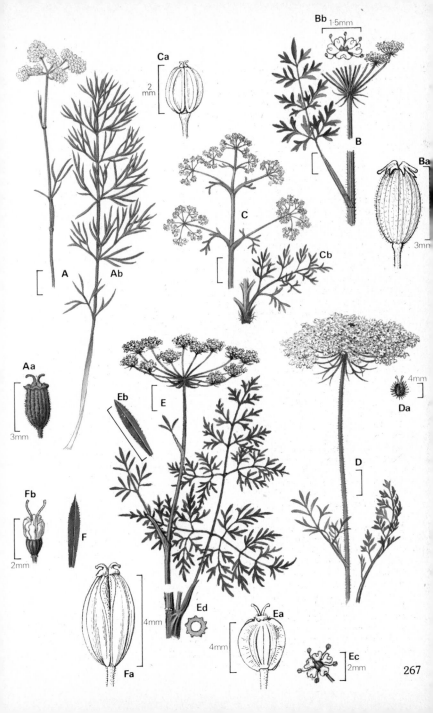

267

DOCK FAMILY

Polygonaceae

Herbs with alt, simple lvs with membrane-like silvery or brown sheathing ochreae. Sepals 3–6, free or joined, small; stamens 6–9; superior ovary ripens into a hard three-angled, one-seeded nut enclosed in the sepals.

Docks (*Rumex*) have erect, much-branched infls, with the 6 greenish sepals in 2 whorls, the 3 outer tiny and narrow, the 3 inner broad, enlarging to enclose the ripe fr. The shape of these inner sepals, and whether or not they bear warts, is a vital feature for identification.

KEY TO DOCKS (*RUMEX*)

1 Lvs halberd-shaped or arrow-shaped, with acid taste – slender plants, usually under 60 cm tall – dioecious.. **2**
  Lvs oblong, lanceolate or round (not arrow- or halberd-shaped), taste not acid – stout plants, usually over 60 cm – not dioecious **3**
2 Lf-lobes spreading out sideways or even forwards – upper lvs not clasping stem ....
  Rumex acetosella (p 272 J)
  Lf-lobes backward-pointing (so lf ± arrow-shaped) – upper lvs clasping stem.................................
  R. acetosa (p 272 I)
3 All 3 inner sepals without warts.. **4**
  One, at least, of 3 inner sepals with a distinct, sometimes coloured wart **6**
4 Fr-stalk without visible joint – by lakes of N Scot, Eur – r .... *R. aquaticus* (p 270 Gi)
  Fr-stalk with an obvious joint.. **5**
5 Lvs round, 20–40 cm wide and long, with cordate base – inner sepals with truncate bases – f in N.. *R. alpinus* (p 270 Ci)
  Lvs oval-lanceolate – inner sepals kidney-shaped – r – only in N of GB.......*R. longifolius* (p 270 Di)
6 Inner sepals long-toothed (teeth 1 mm or more) **7**
  Inner sepals untoothed (or with tiny teeth under 1 mm) **10**
7 Branches spreading nearly at right angles – lvs violin-shaped .... *R. pulcher* (p 270 H)
  Branches erect or at acute angle to stem – lvs not violin-shaped **8**
8 Inner sepals 4–7 mm long, red or brown, coarse-toothed – lvs oval-oblong, their bases cordate......
  R. obtusifolius (p 270 C)
  Inner sepals 2–3 mm long, yellow or golden, with bristle-like teeth – lvs narrow, oblong, tapered into stalk... **9**
9 Inner sepals greenish-yellow in fr, with blunt tips and rigid bristle-like teeth shorter than sepals – fr 2.0–2.5 mm long.. *R. palustris* (p 270 E)
  Inner sepals golden in fr, with pointed tips and fine hairlike teeth, some longer than sepals – fr 1.0–1.5 mm long... *R. maritimus* (p 270 F)
10 Infl of loose distant whorls – inner sepals 4 mm long – all 3 with warts ⅔ length of sepals – lvs grey-green – on rocks by sea in SW of GB... *R. rupestris* (p 270 Bi)
  Infl of dense crowded whorls – inner sepals 4–8 mm long – warts not more than ½ length of sepals.. **11**
  Infl of loose distant whorls – inner sepals to 3 mm only – warts only ½ sepal length **12**
11 Inner sepals triangular with straight bases – lvs lanceolate, not v wavy-edged – v large plant of wet places .... *R. hydrolapathum* (p 270 G)
  Inner sepals oval or round, with cordate bases – lvs oblong-lanceolate, wavy-edged, crisped...........
  R. crispus (p 270 D)
12 Stems straight, erect, branching at acute angle – infls not lfy except at base – one sepal only having large round wart .... *R. sanguineus* (p 270 A)
  Stems wavy, branching widely – infl lfy nearly to top – all 3 inner sepals with large oblong warts......
  R. conglomeratus (p 270 B)

Knotgrasses and **Persicarias** (*Polygonum*) have usually unbranched infls, terminal or in lf-axils, with 5 pink or white sepals, apparently in one whorl, not swelling up around ripe fr.

KEY TO KNOTGRASSES AND PERSICARIAS ETC (*POLYGONUM*)

1 Lvs cordate to arrow-shaped (as in Bindweed, p 294) – stems slender, twining – fls in long racemes in lf-axils... **2**
Lvs not as in Bindweed – stems not twining... **3**

2 Fr-stalks 1–2 mm long – 3 outer sepals bluntly keeled in fr – fr dull black.....................
Polygonum convolvulus (p 274 L)
Fr-stalks to 8 mm long – 3 outer sepals with broad wrinkled wings in fr – fr shiny black ....
P. dumetorum (p 274 M)

3 Plants ± prostrate – lvs narrow elliptical-lanceolate, 1–5 cm long – fls in clusters of 1–6 in lf-axils **4**
Plants ± erect – lvs 5–15 cm long – fls in many-fld spikes, some or all at tops of stems................. **6**

4 Fr smooth, shiny, as long as or longer than calyx.. **5**
Fr dull, rough, ± enclosed in calyx, 1.5–3.0 mm ....*P. aviculare* (p 272 A)

5 Stipules with 4–6 **unbranched** veins, short – fr 4–5 mm, longer than calyx – plant not woody – lvs 1.0–3.5 cm, elliptical-lanceolate ....*P. raii* (p 272 B)
Stipules with 8–12 **branched** veins, extending to base of next lf above – fr 5–6 mm, longer than calyx – plant woody – lvs 2–5 cm, oval-elliptical, edges rolled under .... *P. maritimum* (p 272 C)................ **7**

6 Stems unbranched, erect **8**
Stems with ± spreading branches...

7 Root-lvs with truncate or cordate bases – lf-stalks winged – no bulbils in the infl..............................
P. bistorta (p 274 I)
Root-lvs tapering into unwinged stalks – lower part of infl bearing purple bulbils............................
P. viviparum (p 274 J)

8 Lf-base cordate or round – stamens projecting from fls – often floating in water...............................
P. amphibium (p 274 K)
Lvs narrowed to base – stamens enclosed in calyx – not floating in water....................................... **9**

9 Small dot-like glands present on calyx or on stalk of infl **10**
No dot-like glands present on calyx or on stalk of infl... **11**

10 Infl slender, drooping – many yellow gland-dots on calyx, none on infl-stalks – taste of lvs peppery – fls pinkish-white..*P. hydropiper* (p 272 D)
Infl stout, erect – few glands on calyx, some on infl-stalks – taste of lvs mild – fls greenish-white to pink...*P. lapathifolium* (p 274 G)

11 Infls dense, stout, blunt – fls pink – lvs often dark-blotched .... *P. persicaria* (p 274 F)
Infls slender, pointed, few-fld – lvs not dark-blotched.. **12**

12 Lvs 10–25 mm wide – infl drooping slightly – fr 3–4 mm long.............................*P. mite* (p 272 E)
Lvs 5–8 mm wide – infl erect – fr 2.0–2.5 mm long...*P. minus* (p 274 H)

DOCK FAMILY

Docks

   A Wood Dock, *Rumex sanguineus*, erect per to 100 cm, with branches at an acute angle to stem; lvs oval-lanceolate, their bases rounded, rarely with red veins. Infl much branched, lfy **only at base**; whorls of fls distant. Inner sepals (**Aa**) 3 mm, oblong, untoothed, blunt, **one** only having a round wart 1.5 mm across (the others with none, or minute ones); fr 1.2–1.8 mm long. GB N to mid Scot, Ire, c; Eur c; in wds, hbs, wa. Fl 6–8.

   B Clustered Dock, *R. conglomeratus*, is close to A, except that branches make a wider (30°–90°) angle with the wavy stem; infl **lfy nearly to top**; and **all three** untoothed, blunt, inner sepals (**Ba, Bb**) have **oblong** warts 1.2–1.8 mm long. Fr 1.8–2.0 mm long. Br Isles c (except Scot r-lf); Eur c; on rds, hbs, wa, mds. Fl 7–9. **Bi Shore Dock**, *R. rupestris*, has grey-green, oblong blunt lvs, inner sepals **4 mm long**, oblong, untoothed, blunt, **all three** with **oblong** warts **2.5–3.0 mm long**; branches strictly erect. SW Eng, S Wales, W France r to lf; on rocky shores, dunes. Fl 6–8.

   C Broad-leaved Dock, *R. obtusifolius*, stouter and more robust than A and B, up to 120 cm tall; lower lvs (**Cb**) oval-oblong, blunt, only slightly wavy-edged, to 25 cm long, with **cordate** bases; upper lvs narrower. Infl branched, lfy below, whorls of fls separate. Inner sepals (**Ca**) 5–6 mm long, triangular, at least **one** of them with a **large wart**, edges with 3–5 long, **coarse** teeth. Fr 3 mm. Br Isles, Eur; vc in wa, hbs, rds, field edges. Fl 6–10. **Ci Monk's-rhubarb**, *R. alpinus*, has round, cordate-base lvs, 20–40 cm long and wide; inner sepals untoothed, without warts. N Eng, E Scot, o near houses; Eur r except mts. Fl 7.

   D Curled Dock, *R. crispus*, resembles C in build, but has oblong-lanceolate lvs (**D**), **rounded** or **narrowed** at bases, with strongly **crisped** edges; inner sepals (**Da**) 4–5 mm long, **without** teeth and usually with **warts on all three**. Br Isles, Eur; vc on wa, rds, hbs, ar, shingle beaches by sea. Fl 6–10. **Di Northern Dock**, *R. longifolius*, stout erect per to 120 cm, with wavy **crisped** lvs as in C, though cordate-based; inner sepals **6 mm long**, **kidney-shaped**, **without warts**; fr-stalk jointed. N half GB lc; Eur o-lf; on riversides, wa. Fl 6–7.

   E Marsh Dock, *R. palustris*, erect branched ann or per to 60 cm, with linear-lanceolate pointed lvs; lfy spreading infl-branches. Inner sepals (**Ea**) lanceolate, blunt, 2–3 mm long, all warted, **yellowish** in fr, with each edge bearing 2 or 3 **bristle-like teeth shorter** than sepals; outer sepals curved inwards. SE, E Eng, r-lf; Eur o-lc; on bare muddy gd by lakes and rivers. Fl 6–9.

   F Golden Dock, *R. maritimus*, v like E, but whorls of fls much more crowded, fl-stalks **longer**, **v slender**. Inner sepals (**F**) **triangular**, 2–3 mm long, all warted, golden-brown in fr, with each edge bearing 2 almost hair-like teeth **longer** than sepals; outer sepals curved outwards. Br Isles: S, mid, E Eng, o-lf; Ire vr; Eur o-lc; habitat as for E, but rather more coastal. Fl 6–9.

   G Water Dock, *R. hydrolapathum*, v large erect per, to 200 cm; lanceolate-oval pointed lvs (**Gb**) to 100 cm long; much-branched erect infl has crowded whorls of fls, with the inner sepals (**Ga**) 6–8 mm long, triangular, truncate-based, **each** with a long wart, and a few **short** teeth at base. Fr 4 mm long. Eng f-lc, rarer N and W in Br Isles; Eur f-lc; in shallow water, ditches, riversides, fens. Fl 7–9. **Gi Scottish Dock**, *R. aquaticus*, is like G, but sepals have no warts, and fr-stalks v slender, without joint. Scot; Loch Lomond only; Eur: N to Denmark r; by lake and stream shores. Fl 7–8. **Gii Patience Dock**, *Rumex patientia*, the most f of several large introd Docks, is an erect per to 200 cm, with large oval-lanceolate pointed lvs, with side veins at acute angle to midrib; large fls with inner sepals 8 mm long, oval or rounded, cordate-based, one with a large wart. Eng: wa about London etc (E Eur). Fl 6–7.

   H Fiddle Dock, *R. pulcher*, per, distinct in its branches spreading at up to 90°

◄ from the main stem, and in its violin-shaped lvs (**Hb**), up to 10 cm long, with a 'waist'; whorls of fls distant, inner sepals (**Ha**) all with warts and each sepal-edge bearing 3 or 4 short broad teeth. S, E Eng o-lf; Eur: France lf; on dry sunny gsld, rds on sand or limestone, especially near coast. Fl 6–7.

I Common Sorrel, *R. acetosa* (not to be confused with Wood-sorrel p 176 I), erect hairless per, 30–80 cm tall, slenderer than spp A to H; lvs shiny, arrow-shaped, to 10 cm long, 2–6 times as long as wide, stalked below, stalkless and clasping stem above. Tubular brown fringed stipules above lvs are obvious. Branched infl has loose whorls of small reddish fls (female **Ia**, male **Ib**) with cordate inner sepals without warts; plant dioecious. Br Isles, Eur; vc in gslds, open wds. Fl 5–6. *****Ii *R. thyrsiflorus* is close to I, but lvs up to 12 times as long as wide, and infls much-branched, v dense. Eur: E France o, to Denmark c; on dry gslds, rds. Fl 7–8. **Iii Mountain Sorrel**, *Oxyria digyna*, resembles I in habit, but has fleshy, **kidney-shaped** lvs, 1–3 cm long, infl leafless, and 4 wartless sepals, only the 2 inner enlarging around **flat**, broadly-winged fr. Br Isles: N Wales, Cumbria, Ire r; Scot lc; Eur, mts only; in damp rocky places on mts. Fl 7–8.

J Sheep's Sorrel, *R. acetosella*, appears as much smaller version of I, 10–30 cm tall, with narrower lvs, halberd-shaped, to 4 cm long, their side-lobes spreading or pointing forwards, all lvs stalked. Fls reddish; inner sepals **not enlarging in fr**. Br Isles, Eur; vc on dry acid gsld, hths, shingle beaches, poor ar. Fl 5–8.

Several large alien Docks occur as escapes in wa around ports etc.

► **Knotgrasses, Persicarias**, etc

A Knotgrass, *Polygonum aviculare*, low, prostrate (sometimes erect), hairless ann, forming patches up to 1 m across, usually much less. Lvs elliptical to linear or lanceolate, either ± equal in length (*P. arenastrum*), or shorter on flowering than on main stems (*P. aviculare* proper). Stipules silvery, with fringed edges; veins not clearly seen; infl of 1–6 fls in lf-axils; calyx of 5 sepals, with green bases and white petal-like lobes above. Fr (**Aa**) 1.5–3.0 mm long, three-angled, pointed, brown, not shiny, enclosed in persistent calyx. Br Isles, Eur; vc on wa, ar, seashores, etc. Fl 7–10.

B Ray's Knotgrass, *P. raii*, prostrate like A, has grey-green elliptical-lanceolate lvs (**B**), 1.0–3.0 cm long with slightly turned-back edges; stipules silvery, with 4–6 **unbranched** veins; frs (**Ba**) shiny, three-angled, chestnut brown, 4–5 mm long, **longer** than persistent calyx which has broad white margins. S, W coasts of GB; coasts of Ire; Eur: W coast from Denmark to NW France; o-lf on sand or fine shingle beaches. Fl 7–10.

C Sea Knotgrass, *P. maritimum*, prostrate per, with stem woody at base; lvs 2–5 cm long, waxy, grey-green, oval to elliptical-lanceolate, with edges rolled-back underneath. Frs (**Ca**) chestnut-brown, 5–6 mm long, **longer** than white-edged calyx; silvery stipules (**Cb**) have 8–12 **branched** veins. SW Eng vr; France from Brittany S, o; on coastal sand and shingle beaches. Fl 4–10, according to latitude.

D Water-pepper, *P. hydropiper*, ± erect, ± hairless ann, with branched stem to 70 cm; lvs 5–10 cm, thin, lanceolate, ± stalkless; stipules truncate, hardly fringed; infl slender, pointed, nodding, lfy below; fls (**Da**) pinkish or greenish-white; sepals in fr (**Db**) covered with yellow gland-dots (use lens); infl-stalks without gland-dots. Fr 3 mm long, oval, dark brown, dull, biconvex; plant hot and **peppery** when chewed, unlike other *Polygonum* spp. Br Isles (except N Scot r), Eur c; in damp gd, mds, paths, shallow water. Fl 7–9.

E Tasteless Water-pepper, *P. mite*, is close to D, but infl is slenderer, fewer-fld, more pointed and drooping; lvs 10–25 mm wide; fls (**E**) pink, 3–4 mm long;

A

B

Aa 3mm

Ba 6mm

Ca 5mm

C 2.5cm

Cb

D

Da 3mm

Db 5mm

E 5mm

F

Fb

Fa 3mm

H 3mm

G

Ga 3mm

I

J

K

L

La 5mm

M

Ma 5mm

Mb

273

◀ **no gland-dots**; no hot taste. Fr 3–4 mm long, biconvex, shiny. Br Isles (except Scot), Eur; r in ditches, pond edges. Fl 6–9.

F Redshank, *P. persicaria*, branched, ± erect, ± hairless ann to 70 cm, with reddish stems swollen above the lf-bases; fringed stipules; lanceolate, often **black-blotched** lvs, 5–10 cm long. Infls (**Fb**) stout, blunt, fls pink; no gland-dots. Fr (**Fa**) 3 mm, shiny, biconvex. Br Isles, Eur; c in wa, ar, wet places. Fl 6–10.

G Pale Persicaria, *P. lapathifolium*, larger than F, slightly hairy, with a few gland-dots on calyx and infl-stalks; lvs often black-blotched as in E, but infl stouter; fls (**Ga**) normally greenish-white. Fr 2.5–3.0 mm, biconcave, shiny. Br Isles: S of GB c, Scot o-r; Ire o; Eur c; in wa, ar, wet places. Fl 6–10.

H Small Water-pepper, *P. minus*, resembles F, but lvs only 5–8 mm wide, and infl narrow; fls pink; fr (**H**) 2.0–2.5 mm, oval, shiny. Br Isles (except Scot), Eur; r on bare wet gd, pond edges. Fl 8–9.

I Common Bistort, *P. bistorta*, erect, ± hairless per, 30–100 cm tall; winged, long lf-stalks, broad-oval, blunt root-lvs with ± cordate bases; upper lvs triangular, pointed; stipules fringed. Infl terminal, a stout, dense blunt spike (10–15 mm wide) of pink fls, 4–5 mm across. Br Isles: GB wide-spread, but only c in N Eng, r-o elsewhere; Ire r; Eur, N to S Netherlands o; in mds, rds, often wds. Fl 6–8.

J Alpine Bistort, *P. viviparum*, shorter than I, only 6–30 cm tall; lower lvs linear-lanceolate, **tapering** into **unwinged** stalks, upper lvs stalkless; infl as in I, but slenderer (4–8 mm wide), of white 3–4-mm fls above, purple bulbils replacing fls in lower part. Br Isles: mt areas of N Wales, N Eng, Scot, lf-lc; Ire r; lowland W Eur abs; on mt gslds, moist cliffs. Fl 6–8.

K Amphibious Bistort, *P. amphibium*, hairless or downy branched per, either floating in water or ± erect on dry gd, 30–70 cm long; lvs 5–15 cm, oval to oblong-lanceolate, blunt or pointed, base cordate in floating form, rounded in land form; infl 2–4 cm long, dense, many-fld, terminal; infl-stalk lfless above; fls pink, 2–3 mm long, no gland-dots; stamens 5, protruding; fr 2 mm, biconvex, brown, shiny. Br Isles, Eur; fc in fresh water, wa, banks near water. Fl 7–9.

L Black-bindweed, *P. convolvulus*, twining, scrambling or climbing ann, with stems to 1 m or more; stem angular, mealy; lvs 2–6 cm long, oval-triangular with cordate or truncate bases, v like those of Hedge Bindweed (p 294 B), but mealy below. Fls in long racemes, each fl on 1–2 mm stalk with joint above middle; the 3 outer sepals 5–6 mm long, greenish-grey, with white keels or narrow wings in fr; fr (**La**) 4 mm, dull black, enclosed in sepals. Br Isles (except NW Scot), Eur; c on ar, wa, hbs, wd borders. Fl 7–10.

M Copse-bindweed, *P. dumetorum*, closely resembles L, but may be taller; lvs (**Mb**) as in L; fr-stalks up to 8 mm long, jointed below middle; 3 outer sepals have broad, wrinkled, membranous pinky-white wings (**Ma**). SE Eng r and l; Eur, N to Denmark o; climbing in hbs, open wds. Fl 7–10. **Mi Japanese Knotweed**, *P. cuspidatum* (*Reynoutria japonica*), c gdn escape; tall erect per, with oval-triangular pointed lvs and zigzag reddish stems; fls white, in branched spikes. Several other big *Polygonum* spp are cultivated and often escape.

(*Not illustrated*) **Iceland-purslane**, *Koenigia islandica*, superficially resembles Blinks (*Montia fontana*, Purslane family, p 160), but is in Dock family. Prostrate ann, 1–6 cm long; stems red; lvs opp, rounded-obovate, elliptical, 3–5 mm long, with membranous stipules 1 mm long. Fls in tiny clusters at stem-tips; calyx of 3 pale green, rounded sepals 1 mm long; 3 tiny red-anthered stamens alt with 3 yellow glands; fr three-angled with 2 stigmas. Scot: Skye, Mull; vr on stony moist mt tops (arctic plant). Fl 7–8.

HEATH FAMILY

Ericaceae

Shrubs (and, rarely, trees) with simple, usually narrow leathery, mostly evergreen lvs, without stipules. Fls normally radially symmetrical, with 4 or 5 of each part. Petals joined into a tube; stamens usually twice number of corolla-lobes, joined into an ovary of as many cells as carpels; ovary normally superior, but inferior in **Bilberries** (*Vaccinium*). Style undivided, with cap-like stigma. Anthers open by pores at tip, not by slits. Fr a berry or a capsule. Attractive, distinctive family, mainly low shrubs of acid soils.

KEY TO HEATH FAMILY

DIAPENSIA FAMILY

Diapensiaceae

(*Not illustrated*) **Diapensia**, *Diapensia lapponica*, dwarf cushion-forming evergreen shrub, a few cm tall; lvs oval, blunt, leathery, toothless, 5–10 mm long, tapered to base, in dense rosettes; fls solitary, on stalks 1–3 cm; calyx five-lobed, leathery; corolla white, 1.0–1.5 cm wide, with 5 oval spreading lobes; stamens 5, short, yellow, alt with corolla-lobes; stigma three-lobed; fr a capsule. NW Scot, vr on open rocky mt tops (arctic plant). Fl 5–6. (Close to Heath family, but differs in 5 stamens only, and **three-lobed** stigma.)

Bilberries, Cranberry, Rhododendron, Strawberry-tree

A Bilberry (Whortleberry), *Vaccinium myrtillus*, low hairless deciduous shrub, 20–60 cm; erect four-angled green twigs; lvs alt, oval, **finely-toothed**, flat, **bright green**, 1–3 cm. Fls 1–2 together in lf-axils; corolla globular-urn-shaped, greenish pink, 4–6 mm long, with 5 tiny teeth; **no** calyx-lobes; ovary inferior, ripening to an edible black berry (**Aa**) with a violet bloom. Br Isles (except mid, E Eng) c; Eur: c to N; France, c in W, r in N; on dry acid wds, upland hths, moors. Fl 4–6; fr 7–8.

B Cowberry, *V. vitis-idaea*, has creeping stems from which ± erect branched shoots arise, to 30 cm tall. Twigs **round, downy** at first. Lvs bluntly oval–obovate, **evergreen** and like those of Box (p 228); dark green and glossy above, leathery, with edges **turned down**; pale green and dotted below, ± **untoothed**, 1–3 cm. Fls in short drooping racemes; calyx of 4 short rounded **lobes**; corolla bell-shaped, white or pink-flushed, the 4 lobes bent back half length of tube. Ovary inferior, ripening to an edible **red** berry (**Ba**). Br Isles: GB, SW Eng (vr) through Wales to Scot, c in hills, **abs in lowland S, mid and E Eng**; Ire r and l; Eur: Denmark to Belgium lf; on upland moors, wds, especially pine on acid soils. Fl 6–8.

C Northern Bilberry, *V. uliginosum*, is deciduous and has urn-shaped corollas like A, but twigs **round, brown**; lvs **oval, blunt, untoothed**, blue-green with conspicuous netted veins. Fls 1–4 together in lf-axils, with **short** calyx-lobes; corolla 4 mm, **oval**-urn-shaped, pale pink. Berry (**Ca**) 6 mm, with a blue bloom. Br Isles: mts of N half of Scot f-la; N Eng vr; **abs in S Eng**; **Ire abs**; Eur: Denmark S to Belgium c (France only in mts); high moors, hths, to N. Fl 5–6.

D Cranberry, *V. oxycoccus*, tiny prostrate creeping shrub with threadlike stems, bearing oblong to narrow-elliptical, alt pointed lvs, 4–10 mm long, widely spaced along them; lvs dark green above, waxy grey below, with rolled-under edges. Fls 1–2, drooping, on erect stalks 1.5–3.0 cm; 4 strongly arched-back rosy-pink petals 5–6 mm long; dark stamens project in a column (rather like miniature Cyclamen fls). Fr (**Da**) 6–8 mm, spherical or pear-shaped, red- or brown-spotted, edible. Br Isles, widespread (but vr and l in S, E Eng, N Scot, SW Ire); Eur: Denmark f, rarer to S, vr in lowland France; in acid Sphagnum bogs. Fl 6–8. **Di American Cranberry**, *V. macrocarpon*, sometimes found as escape; has large (6–18 mm) blunt lvs; fls and frs as in D, but ± twice size (N America).

E Rhododendron, *Rhododendron ponticum*, tall, ± hairless evergreen shrub; lvs elliptical, leathery, pointed, dark green, 6–12 cm long; fls conspicuous in rounded heads; corolla widely bell- or funnel-shaped, 5 cm across, dull violet purple, brown-spotted, with 5 long, unequal lobes, and 10 stamens. Ovary superior; fr a dry oblong capsule. Br Isles, now widely introd, especially in S and W of GB and of Ire. W France introd and l; was native further N, at least in Ire in Great Interglacial Period (now native S Eur); in wds, hths, on acid, peaty or sandy soils. Fl 5–6. **Ei Labrador-tea**, *Ledum palustre*, evergreen shrub to 1 m, rather like a small Rhododendron; lvs leathery, dark green above, rusty-downy below, 4 cm long, linear-oblong; fls in umbels, creamy white, petals free to base. Both this (N European) sp and **Eii**, the N American *L. groenlandicum*, with elliptic oblong lvs, midrib only hidden by rusty down below, occur introd in bogs in scattered sites in GB. **Eiii Trailing Azalea**, *Loiseleuria procumbens*, tiny, prostrate mat-forming shrub; lvs **opp**, oblong, 3–8 mm long, with rolled-under edges; fls funnel-shaped, five-lobed, pink, 4–5 mm across, with 5 stamens. Scot; f-lc on high mts.

F Strawberry-tree, *Arbutus unedo*, shrub or small tree to 12 m tall, with reddish-brown bark; lvs 4–10 cm, elliptical, leathery, shiny dark green above, paler below, toothed, pointed at both ends, short-stalked. Fls in panicles, with corolla oval urn-shaped, creamy, five-toothed, 7 mm long; 10 stamens. Fr 1.5–2.0 cm across, globular, dull red, warted. SW Ire, also by Loch Gill near Sligo, r but la; Brittany vr (mainly S Eur); rocky oakwds; also planted. Fl 9–12; frs next 9–12.

277

HEATH FAMILY

Ericaceae

Heather, Heaths, Bearberry, Bog Rosemary (see key, p 280)

A   Heather (Ling), *Calluna vulgaris*, bushy evergreen shrub to 60 cm, with many often tortuous stems. Lvs 1–2 mm, stalkless, adpressed, triangular in shape like tiny hat-pegs, hairless or ± downy, close-set in 4 vertical rows. Fls in dense spikes, each with 4 bracts; calyx 4 mm long, pinky-purple, deeply four-lobed, longer than pink corolla, both persisting in fr; fr a capsule 2.0–2.5 mm long. Br Isles, Eur, widespread, locally dominant; in hths, bogs, upland moors, open wds on acid soils. Fl 7–9.

B   Cross-leaved Heath, *Erica tetralix*, shrub shorter than A (to 30 cm), with ± erect less-branched stems. Twigs downy; lvs **4 in a whorl**, greyish, 2–5 mm long, linear, edges rolled under and nearly meeting below, downy above and also with gland-tipped bristles. Fls in **umbel-like heads**; corolla 6–7 mm long, rose-pink, oval to urn-shaped; sepals 2 mm, both downy and with spreading gland-tipped bristles like those on lvs. Stamens hidden in corolla. Br Isles, Eur f-lc (r in highly-farmed areas); in wet hths, bogs, always on acid soils. Fl 6–9.   **Bi   Mackay's Heath**, *E. mackaiana*, like a denser-branched B, but lvs oblong-lanceolate to elliptical, edges only **slightly** rolled under, showing white underside (as in D below), hairless except for gland-tipped bristles on their edges; heads of fls as in B, but corolla deeper pink; and sepals reddish, not downy but with short straight gland-tipped bristles above. **GB abs**: Ire: Connemara and Donegal r and vl (otherwise only in N Spain); in blanket-bogs. Fl 8–9.

C   Bell Heather, *E. cinerea*, is like B in habit, but quite **hairless**; lvs **3 in a whorl**, 3–6 mm long, linear, dark green, with edges rolled under; fls in short racemes; corolla 5–6 mm long, crimson-purple, oval to urn-shaped; sepals hairless, dark green, stamens hidden in corolla. Br Isles vc except in highly-farmed areas of central Eng, central Ire; Eur: W and central France vc; N France to Netherlands r, mostly near coast; on dry acid hths. Fl 7–9.

D   Dorset Heath, *E. ciliaris*, often to 60 cm; lvs 3 in a whorl, 2–3 mm long, oval, not downy, but with long gland-tipped bristles on edges, (edges slightly turned under, showing white underside). Fls in racemes 5–12 cm long; corolla 8–10 mm long, oblong, urn-shaped, deep pink; sepals downy, with bristles. Eng: Dorset, S Devon, Cornwall, vl but la; Ire, Connemara vr; Eur: W France f-la; on dampish hths. Fl 6–9.

E   Cornish Heath, *E. vagans*, hairless shrub to 80 cm, with long erect branches; lvs 4–5 in a whorl, 7–10 mm long, linear, edges strongly bent back; fls in long dense racemes, lfy at tips; fl-stalks 3–4 times as long as fls; corolla 3–4 mm, widely bell-shaped, pale lilac, pink or white, with deep purple-brown anthers fully protruding. Eng: S Cornwall, lva; Ire: Fermanagh vr but la; Eur: W France from Brittany S vl; on dry hths. Fl 7–8.   **Ei   Irish Heath**, *E. erigena*, is taller than other Heaths (to 2 m); lvs in **whorls of 4**, linear, 5–8 mm long, hairless; fls in long dense racemes, lfy at tips as in E; corolla **5–7 mm**, tubular, dull pink-purple, with reddish anthers protruding halfway. **GB abs**; Ire: Galway and Mayo (SW France); la on bogs and wet hths. Fl 3–5.

F   St Dabeoc's Heath, *Daboecia cantabrica*, heath-like shrub to 50 cm; lvs 5–10 mm, elliptical, pointed, alt, green above, with scattered gland-tipped bristles, white-downy below, edges slightly rolled under. Fls in loose racemes; corolla 8–12 mm, rosy-purple or white, oval, urn-shaped, with 4 teeth; calyx-teeth 4, capsule hairy. **GB abs**; Ire: Galway and Mayo (SW France–Iberia); lc on dry hths, rocks. Fl 7–9.   **Fi   Blue Heath**, *Phyllodoce coerulea*, low erect shrub to 15 cm; lvs blunt, fine-toothed, **linear**, heath-like, green **both** sides; fls five-lobed, drooping, purple, urn-shaped, oval, long-stalked, 7–8 mm long, in terminal heads of 2–6; fl-stalks and calyx reddish, sticky. Central Scot vr on rocky moors in mts. Fl 6–7.

G   Bearberry, *Arctostaphylos uva-ursi*, prostrate, mat-forming, ± hairless evergreen shrub; lvs **(Ga)** obovate, alt, blunt, leathery, dark green above, with

A

B

C

D

E

F

G

Ga

H

I

Ia

◄ conspicuous network of paler veins, paler below, **untoothed**, flat. Fls in short dense clusters; corolla 4–6 mm, globular to urn-shaped, white with pink flush, fr a red shiny berry. GB: N Eng r, Scot vc; Ire to NW r-lf; Eur: Denmark, N Germany lf; on dry acid moors, especially in mts. Fl 5–7. **Gi Alpine Bearberry**, *Arctous alpina*, has similar habit to G, but lvs net-veined, **thin**, **toothed**, **deciduous**; fls white; berry black. NW Scot; vl on mt moors. Fl 8–10.

H Bog Rosemary, *Andromeda polifolia*, low hairless shrub to 20 cm, little branched; lvs 1.5–3.5 cm, elliptical-lanceolate, pointed, glossy grey-green above, edges rolled under, white below. Fls in small umbel-like clusters, long-stalked; corolla rosy-pink or white, globular-urn-shaped, five-toothed; fr a dry capsule. Br Isles: central Wales to mid Scot vl, decreasing to S; central Ire c; Eur: Denmark lf, S to Belgium r, Normandy vr; among Sphagnum in bogs in mt areas. Fl 4–9.

KEY TO HEATHS (*ERICA*) AND LING (*CALLUNA*)

1 Lvs in opp pairs, adpressed upwards to stem, like tiny hat-pegs, 1–2 mm long – calyx coloured
  like corolla, petal-like, deeply four-lobed, enclosing corolla in fl and fr......................*Calluna* (p 278)
  Lvs in whorls, spreading, 2 mm long or more – calyx v small, not petal-like – corolla urn- or bell-
  shaped, conspicuous..*Erica* 2
2 Stamens enclosed wholly inside corolla-tube – lvs 2–5 mm long, rarely more.................................... 3
  Stamens projecting from corolla-tube – lvs hairless, 5–10 mm long 6
3 Lvs and sepals hairless – lvs 3 in a whorl, narrow, dark green ....*E. cinerea* (p 278 C)
  Lvs and sepals edged with bristles, usually with glands on tips... 4
4 Fls in racemes – lvs 3 in a whorl, oval – corollas oblong ....*E. ciliaris* (p 278 D)
  Fls in umbel-like heads – lvs 4 in a whorl, linear or oblong – corolla urn-shaped.............................. 5
5 Lvs grey-downy above, with long gland-tipped bristles – lf-edges curved under nearly to midrib........
                                                  E. tetralix (p 278 B)
  Lvs dark green, hairless above – lf-edges only slightly recurved, leaving white underside showing –
  W Ire, vr..*E. mackaiana* (p 278 Bi)
6 Lvs 4 in a whorl – corolla tubular, ± parallel-sided – anthers only projecting halfway – fl-
  stalks shorter than fls – W Ire – la..*E. erigena* (p 278 Ei)
  Lvs 4–5 in a whorl – corolla widely bell-shaped – anthers fully projecting from it – fl-stalks 3–4
  times as long as fls – Cornwall, N Ire..*E. vagans* (p 278 E)

◄ ## CROWBERRY FAMILY

I Crowberry, *Empetrum nigrum*, much resembles a member of the Heath family, with its linear alt untoothed glossy green lvs, 4–6 mm long, with rolled-back edges; its fls (male, **Ia**), however, have 6 tiny separate pink sepals, and are only 1–2 mm across; plants dioecious, female plant bears black berries 5 mm wide. Br Isles c in upland and mt areas, **abs S and E Eng – E of Exmoor**; Eur: Denmark to Belgium; mts of France; on hths, moors, bogs. Fl 5–6. **Ii** *E. hermaphroditum* differs from I only in **bisexual** fls, young stems **green** (not reddish), lvs **oval-oblong**, 2–3 (not 3–4) times as long as wide. N Wales, N Eng to N Scot; la on high mt moors (Eur mts only).

► ## WINTERGREEN FAMILY

A small family, related to the Heaths, the **Wintergreens** are creeping hairless per herbs with stalked **evergreen** simple lvs all in rosettes; infl erect, ± lfless, bearing racemes of symmetrical fls with 5 tiny sepals, 5 **free**, usually white, petals, 10 free stamens opening by **pores** at ends of the anthers as in Heaths; a superior ovary of 5 joined carpels with a single stout style on top; fr a round capsule. Often superficially like Lily-of-the-valley (p 406). Most grow in vegetable humus, especially in pinewoods.

A Common Wintergreen, *Pyrola minor*, has lvs light green, oval, alt, ± blunt, 2.5–4.0 cm long, on stalks shorter than blades; infl 10–30 cm tall, rather dense; globular, pinkish-white fls (**Aa**) each 6 mm long; styles (**1–2 mm**) **shorter**

than petals, straight; stigma with 5 spreading lobes. Br Isles, widespread but o: Scot, N Eng, f-lc; S Eng vl-lf: Ire r; Eur o (lc to N); in pinewoods, moors, damp rocks, acid dunes. Fl 6–8.

B   Intermediate Wintergreen, *P. media*, taller (15–30 cm) than A; lvs **larger** (3–5 cm-long), almost **round**, shiny **dark green**; fls in looser racemes, and larger (to 10 mm long), but also globular; petals whiter, with **longer** styles (5 mm) **projecting** from fls; stigma with 5 erect lobes. Br Isles: Scot Highlands o-lf; N Eng, Worcs, vr; N Ire r; Eur: Denmark vl; mts only to S; in pinewoods, moors. Fl 6–8.

Bi   Serrated Wintergreen, *Orthilia secunda*, is shorter (3–10 cm) than A and B, differs also in that lvs oval, **pointed, toothed**; fls, in **one-sided racemes**, are greenish-white, 5 mm long, cup-shaped rather than globular, with straight styles **longer** than petals. Br Isles: Scot Highlands o-lf; Ire vr; Eur: Denmark o; in pinewoods, and on damp rock ledges. Fl 7–8.

C   Round-leaved Wintergreen, *P. rotundifolia*, has dark green, shiny rounded lvs as in B, but longer-stalked; infl (10–30 cm) loose, fls (C) white, wide-open, almost **flat**, 12 mm across; **v long style** (8–10 mm) **curves down, then up** at the end. Br Isles: GB scattered and r; mainly Norfolk Broads, Kent, W Coast, Scot Highlands; Ire vr; Eur o-lf; on mt rock ledges, fens, open wds, dune-slacks, usually on **calc** soils. Fl 7–9.   ***Ci   Yellow Wintergreen**, *P. chlorantha*, with **wide-open, greenish** fls and **long, curved** style, and ***Cii   Umbellate Wintergreen**, *Chimaphila umbellata*, with pink fls in a umbel and lvs whorled, occur in pinewoods in Denmark, r.   **Ciii   One-flowered Wintergreen**, *Moneses uniflora*, with **solitary**, drooping, large (15 mm), wide-open fls with straight, long styles, occurs in pinewoods in Scot vr, and Denmark o.

BIRD'S-NEST FAMILY   *Monotropaceae*

D   Yellow Bird's-nest, *Monotropa hypopitys*, erect per herb with yellow stem and scale-like lvs (8–20 cm tall) without any green chlorophyll, lives on decaying organic matter (a saprophyte). Superficially like Bird's-nest Orchid, p 430 (but that is honey-brown, not yellow, and has obvious hanging two-lobed **lips** to the fls). Infl drooping in fl, erect in fr, a raceme. Fls 10–15 mm long on short stalks; 4 or 5 strap-shaped sepals; 4 or 5 equal free petals with ± out-curved tips, all waxy pale yellow and of ± equal length, sometimes hairy within fl; stamens 10 in side fls, 8 in terminal one. Eng, lc in S and E, r to N and in Wales; Scot, Ire, vr; Eur f-lc; in wds, especially of beech or pine, dune hollows. Fl 6–8.

SEA-LAVENDER FAMILY   *Plumbaginaceae*

Per herbs with alt, simple lvs, in basal rosettes only; infl a dense round head (in *Armeria*) or a branched panicle (in *Limonium*). Fls with funnel-shaped, 5–10-ribbed, papery, often coloured calyx, persisting in fr; corolla of 5 petals joined only at base, 5 stamens opp petals, 5 separate styles. Fr a one-seeded capsule.

E   Thrift, *Armeria maritima*, cushion-forming per; woody rootstock bears rosettes of narrow-linear, ± hairless, one-veined lvs, 2–10 cm long. Infl-stalks, 5–30 cm tall, ± downy, bear no lvs but terminal rounded heads (1.5–2.5 cm across) of pink or white fls; a brown, sleeve-like sheath, toothed at lower end, extends 2–3 cm down stem from fl-head. Fls five-petalled, 8 mm across; calyx five-ribbed, hairy. Br Isles, Eur; c all round coasts on cliffs and salt marshes, inland on mt ledges (Br Isles). Fl 4–10. A taller (to 50 cm) form (ssp *elongata*) occurs inland on lowland dry gsld in Lincs vr, and in N Eur.   ***Ei   Jersey Thrift**, *A. plantaginea* (*A. arenaria*), has narrow-**lanceolate** 3–5-veined lvs and spine-like calyx-teeth. Jersey, W France, vl on dunes.

F   Common Sea-lavender, *Limonium vulgare*, per with wdy rootstock, bearing rosettes of ascending, long-stalked, elliptical–lanceolate, 4–12 cm-long lvs, with

pinnate veins and a tiny spine on tips. Infl **rounded** or **flat-topped**, lfless, 8–40 cm tall, branching only above middle, bearing **dense**, arching spikes of fls, gathered in small clusters; each cluster with green bracts, outer one **rounded** on back. Papery, pale lilac, ribbed calyx bears 5 sharp teeth and 5 smaller teeth between. Corolla 8 mm across, with 5 pale purplish-blue petals. Br Isles: coasts of Eng, Wales f, lc in S and E; Scot vr; **Ire abs**; Eur, from Denmark S, lf; in salt-marshes. Fl 7–8.

G Lax-flowered Sea-lavender, *L. humile*, close to F, also has pinnate lf-veins, tall infl, and calyx with small intermediate teeth; but lvs **narrower**, infl divides **below middle** into long erect branches on which fl-clusters are **widely spaced-out**; outer green bracts of clusters have **keeled** backs. GB, more local than A, but o-lc N to S Scot; Ire f; Eur f; in salt-marshes. Fl 7–8.

H Rock Sea-lavender, *L. binervosum*, smaller, usually shorter (8–20 cm) than F and G; lvs shorter (2–5 cm) obovate, with 3 veins, **winged** stalks and **no** pinnate lf-veins. Erect infls branch low down, and fl-clusters more spaced out along branches than in F. Coasts of Eng, Wales lc; S Scot vr; Ire o-lf; Eur: France o-lc; on sea cliffs, shingle drier salt-marshes. Fl 7–9. (Several difficult related spp also occur, described in key below.) **Hi Matter Sea-lavender**, *L. bellidifolium*, low per resembling H in its short (1.5–4.0 cm) obovate lvs with three-veined base and no pinnate veins; but stalks **slender**, lvs **blunt**, and almost **prostrate** infls fork **repeatedly** into many, **mostly fl-less**, branches; fl-clusters only on **uppermost** branches, their **outer** bracts **white**, **papery**. Corollas 5 mm across, pale pink. Eng: Norfolk, Lincs only, vl but lf; NW Eur abs (SW and Mediterranean France only); on dry sandy upper parts of salt-marshes. Fl 7–8. ***Hii Jersey Sea-lavender**, *L. auriculae-ursifolium*, robust plant like F but, like H, has no pinnate veins in lvs; lvs longer (to 10 cm) than in H, broader, spoon-shaped, with **broadly-winged** 5–9-veined stalks. Tall (to 45 cm) infls crowded with fl-clusters as in F but inner fl-cluster bracts have bright **red** papery margins. Jersey, W France; vl rocks by sea. Fl 7–8.

KEY TO SEA-LAVENDERS (*LIMONIUM*)

1 Lf-stalks **long**, **slender** – lvs **pinnately-veined** – in calyx, **5 smaller teeth alt** with 5 larger – tall plant (to 40 cm)..**2**
  Lf-stalks **short** or **winged** – lvs with 1 or more main veins ± parallel below, and **no** pinnate side-veins – calyx with 5 teeth only **3**

2 Stem usually only branched **above middle** – infl a **dense**, round or flat-topped corymb – fl-clusters **crowded** – outer bract of each cluster **rounded** on its back – c................*Limonium vulgare* (p 281 F)
  Stem branched **below middle** – infl **loose** – fl-clusters **spaced out** along ascending, spike-like stems – outer bract of each cluster **ridged** on its back – lf.....................................*L. humile* (p 282 G)

3 Robust plant (to 40 cm) – lvs **broad**, obovate to spoon-shaped, 10 cm or more long, with **5–9** veins below, running down into a broadly-winged stalk – inner bracts of fl-clusters with **bright red** edges – Channel Is, W France only – vl.......................*L. auriculae-ursifolium* (p 282 Hii)
  Smaller plants (to 30 cm) – lvs **narrower**, under 10 cm long, with **1–3** veins only...........................**4**

4 Infl **spreading**, **prostrate**, with much-forked, zigzag, **fl-less branches** below – outer bracts of fl-clusters **wholly chaffy** – E Anglia – vl sandy tidal marshes........ *L. bellidifolium* (p 282 Hi)
  Infl **erect**, with ± **all** branches bearing fl-clusters – outer bracts of fl-clusters green, with only narrow chaffy edges...**5**

5 Infl-stem bearing **v short** side-branches, each bearing **rounded heads of few** (1–3) fl-clusters – lvs one-veined, 30–45 mm long – Pembroke, Donegal only – vr on sea cliffs .... *L. paradoxum*
  Infl-stem bearing **longer** side-branches, each bearing **elongated oblong** spikes of many fl-clusters, in dense rows on upper sides of the branches **6**

6 Spikes of infl **straight**, ± **erect**, – fl-clusters **separated** along branches – bracts of adjacent clusters **not overlapping** – lvs obovate, three-veined – GB, France – lf.......*L. binervosum* (p 282 H)
  Spikes of infl **spreading** or ± **curved outwards** – fl-clusters **v densely set** along branches – bracts of adjacent clusters **overlapping** **7**

7 Lvs narrow-**obovate**, spoon-shaped, **blunt**, tapering into, **three-veined** stalks – infl-spikes **curved outwards** – petals **obovate**, touching – on cliffs at Portland, Dorset .... *L. recurvum*
  Lvs narrow-**lanceolate**, **mucronate**, tapered into **one-veined** stalks – infl-spikes **spreading** at 60°–90° – petals v narrow, **oblong**, separated – vr Pembrokeshire sea cliffs.........*L. transwallianum*

PRIMROSE FAMILY

Primulaceae

Per or ann herbs with lvs either in basal rosettes only, or along the stems; lvs without stipules; fls regular, usually with parts in fives, rarely more; corolla of petals joined into a tube below, wheel-, bell- or funnel-shaped, rarely abs. Stamens attached to corolla-tube and **opp** its lobes. Ovary superior (except in **Brookweed**, *Samolus*) with 1 style; fr a one-celled capsule with many seeds.

KEY TO PRIMROSE FAMILY

1 Lvs all from root – fl-stems lfless 2
　Stem-lvs present 3
2 Corolla-lobes spreading or turned inwards.. *Primula* (p 284–286)
　Corolla-lobes strongly bent back... *Cyclamen* (p 286)
3 Water plant – lvs pinnately-divided, with linear divisions........................... *Hottonia* (p 286)
　Land plant – lvs simple.. 4
4 Lvs alt – calyx-tube adhering to ovary.. 4
　Lvs opp or whorled – calyx-tube free from ovary... *Samolus* (p 286)
5 Lvs in one whorl on unbranched stem – fls white – corolla and calyx usually seven-lobed..................
　　　　　　　　　　　　　　　　　　　　　　　　　　　　　　　　　　　Trientalis (p 288)
　Lvs in several opp pairs (or whorls of 3) along stems 6
6 Fls yellow 6
　Fls pink, red or blue... 7
7 Fls singly in lf-axils or in terminal panicles.. *Lysimachia* (p 286–288)
　Fls in dense racemes in lf-axils.. *Naumburgia* (p 286)
8 Calyx and corolla both present – capsule splitting **across**, its top falling off like a little hat..................
　　　　　　　　　　　　　　　　　　　　　　　　　　　　　　　　　　　Anagallis (p 288)
　Corolla abs – calyx petal-like, **pink** – capsule bursting by 5 slits down sides.................. *Glaux* (p 288)

Primulas, Water-violet, Brookweed, Cyclamen

Most **Primulas** have two types of fl, on separate plants: one kind ('pin-eyed') has pinhead-like styles visible at corolla-mouth, with stamens hidden below in tube; the other ('thrum-eyed') has long stamens visible at corolla-mouth, with short style hidden below.

A   Primrose, *Primula vulgaris*, per herb with rosette of v wrinkled obovate to spoon-shaped lvs, 8–15 cm long, ± unstalked, but narrowed gradually to base, downy beneath, shiny and ± hairless above. Fls upright, wheel- or saucer-shaped, are borne **singly** on woolly lfless stalks 5–12 cm long, arising from lf-rosette. Corolla (**Aa**) 30–40 mm across, pale yellow, with greenish veins, five-lobed, each lobe with shallow notch; thick folds at mouth of corolla-tube nearly close it. Calyx-tube woolly, nearly cylindrical, has 5 triangular narrow teeth. Scent violet-like in hot sunshine. Br Isles c-lvc, r in mts; Eur: France c in W, r in N; Low Countries abs; Denmark r but lf (oceanic sp abs inland in N Eur); in wds, hbs, gslds in W. Fl 3–6.

B   Oxlip, *P. elatior*, per herb with lvs ± **abruptly** narrowing into **long winged stalk**, ± **downy** both sides, **paler green**, **less wrinkled** than in A and C. Fls 10–20 in **umbel**, turned to **one side**, ± **drooping**, on lfless common stalk 10–30 cm tall; corolla (**Ba**) clear pale yellow, 10–15 mm across, **funnel-shaped**, throat of tube **open**, **no folds**; fls peach-scented in hot sun. Calyx and infl-stalk downy, not woolly. Eng: area from W of Cambridge E into Suffolk and N Essex on chky boulder clay, replacing Primrose there, vla (outliers vr in nearby counties); Eur, Denmark S to N and central France (abs W France) c and a; in wds on damp base-rich soils. Fl 3–5.

C   Cowslip, *P. veris*, per herb v like B, but lvs more wrinkled, more gradually tapered to base, 5–15 cm long, downy both sides. Fls apricot-scented, 10–30 in an umbel, spreading, drooping, **not turned** to one side; corolla (**Ca**) apricot-yellow with orange streaks inside, 8–10 mm across, **cup-shaped** with **folds** in throat of

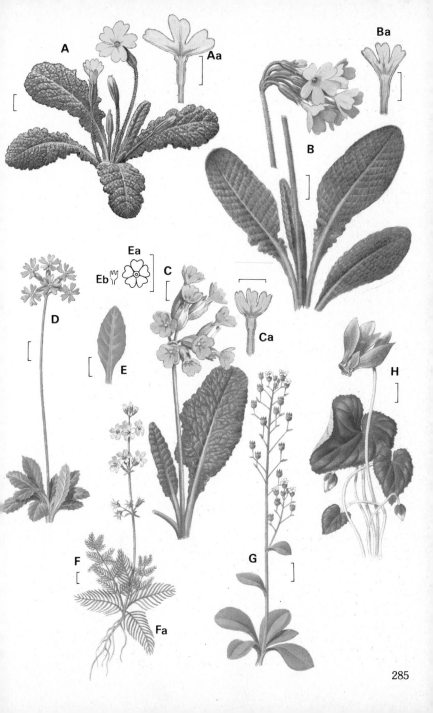

A

Aa

Ba

B

Ea

Eb

C

D

E

Ca

H

F

Fa

G

◀ tube; calyx downy, teeth oval, **blunt**. Br Isles: Eng, Ire f-la; Wales, Scot o-lf (W Scot vr); Eur f-la; in mds, gslds, open wds, on calc or basic soils, decreasing through cultivation. Hybrids of A and C, frequent with parents, resemble B but throat of corolla-tube has folds; lobes have orange streaks within.

D Bird's-eye Primrose, *P. farinosa*, per herb; lvs only 1–5 cm long, obovate, shallow-toothed, **mealy-white** below; infl up to 15 cm tall, stalk mealy; fls 1 cm across, **rosy-violet**, with yellow eye, gaps between petals; calyx (**Da**) mealy, teeth pointed. N Eng, from near Skipton N to Durham and N Cumbria, o-la; **Scot, Ire abs**; Eur: Denmark r, otherwise mts only; on moist mds, open boggy gd on calc soils. Fl 5–6.

E Scottish Primrose, *P. scotica*, v close to D, but lvs **untoothed**, oval, **widest in middle**, and equally mealy below; infl only to 10 cm; fls (**Ea**) on shorter stouter stalks, **purple** with yellow eye; stamens and style of same length on all fls, petals broader, oval, **touching** each other; calyx-teeth (**Eb**) **blunt**. Scot: N coast of Sutherland, Caithness, Orkney, vla; Eur abs (but v similar sp in Norway); in damp mds, clifftops, dunes. Fl 6–9.

F Water-violet, *Hottonia palustris*, has submerged whorls of 2–10 cm long pinnate lvs (**Fa**) with narrow-linear lfts, like a Water-milfoil (p 106), but lfts flattened, and floating stems produce erect ± hairless, lfless infls 20–40 cm tall, with long-stalked, lilac-pink fls in whorls of 3–8 up stems. Corolla 20–25 mm across, with 5 lobes and yellow eye; calyx divided into narrow teeth nearly to base. Fr a globular capsule. Br Isles: E, SE Eng o-lf; Wales vr; **Scot, Ire abs** except as escape. Eur f-lc; in ponds, ditches with basic water. Fl 5–6.

G Brookweed, *Samolus valerandi*, unlike other members of Primrose family, erect hairless per with obovate untoothed lvs short-stalked at base of stem, stalkless and **alt** up infl-stalk. Fls in raceme, long-stalked, with cup-like calyx-tube **fused** to lower half of ovary and bearing triangular teeth; bell-shaped, five-lobed white corolla, 2–3 mm across. Br Isles: Eng, Wales, Ire, SW Scot o-lc in E and near coasts; Eur f-lc especially near coasts; on wet open grassy gd, fens. Fl 6–8.

H Cyclamen, *Cyclamen hederifolium*, ± hairless per; lvs 4–8 cm, on long stalks arising from a large corm, are oval, cordate, five-angled, dark green above with whitish band near edge, purplish below (appearing in 9 after fls). Fls pink (or white), solitary on v long stalks, which coil spirally in fr; 5 strongly bent-back petals 2.5 cm long, arising from short, five-angled corolla-tube. Gdn cultivar, long introd in wds in Kent, Sussex etc (S Eur). Fl 8–9.

▶ **Loosestrifes, Pimpernels, Sea-milkwort, Chickweed Wintergreen**

A Yellow Loosestrife, *Lysimachia vulgaris*, erect downy per, 60–150 cm tall; lvs 5–12 cm, opp or in whorls of 3–4, oval-lanceolate, pointed, ± stalkless, black-dotted; fls in terminal panicles, short-stalked; corolla 15 mm across, bright yellow; calyx-teeth narrow-triangular, with long hairs, orange-edged. Br Isles f-lc (except N Scot vr); Eur f-lc; in fens, riversides, lakesides. Fl 7–8. **Ai Dotted Loosestrife**, *L. punctata*, v like A, but lvs clearly stalked, oval, **not** black-dotted, but hairy-edged; fls to 35 mm across, yellow, with a **purple-brown eye**; calyx-teeth narrower than in A, sticky-hairy, wholly green. GB introd, f in mds, hbs. Fl 7–10. **Aii Tufted Loosestrife**, *Naumburgia* (*Lysimachia*) *thyrsiflora*, is like A in habit, but yellow fls are only 5 mm across, in dense, rounded stalked racemes, 5–10 cm long, in axils of mid stem-lvs only. Lvs blunt, stalkless, hairless, clasping, with many black glands; stamens protrude slightly from fls. Br Isles: N Eng r; central Scot r; Eur lf to N, vr to S; in fens, lakesides. Fl 6–7.

B Yellow Pimpernel, *L. nemorum*, ± prostrate hairless per, to 40 cm long; lvs oval, **pointed**, 2–4 cm long, short-stalked, in opp pairs along stems. Fls solitary in lf-axils, on fine stalks as long as lvs; corolla yellow, wheel-shaped, with 5

287

◀ oval spreading **hairless** lobes; calyx-teeth 5 mm, v narrow. Br Isles, Eur; vc in wds, hbs on less acid soils. Fl 5—9.

C Creeping-Jenny, *L. nummularia*, prostrate, creeping, **rooting** hairless per, rather like B, but lvs **wide-oval** to **almost round**, **blunt**, with gland-dots, 1.5—3.0 cm long; fls (**Ca**) 15—25 mm across, on **stout** stalks shorter than lvs; calyx-teeth 8—10 mm long, **widely oval**, pointed; corolla yellow, **cup-shaped**, lobes **fringed** with tiny hairs. Br Isles: GB N to central Scot, c to S and E, r to N and in SW Eng; Ire o; Eur o-lc; in moist wds, damp mds, hbs. Fl 6—8.

D Scarlet Pimpernel, *Anagallis arvensis*, prostrate to ascending hairless ann; stems, to 30 cm long, four-angled, bear opp pairs of lvs, oval, pointed, stalkless, with black dots below. Fls solitary on slender stalks in lf-axils; narrow, pointed calyx-teeth nearly as long as corolla; corolla 10—15 mm across, flat, wheel-shaped; usually salmon-coloured, sometimes blue or pink; edges of oval lobes with **dense** fringe of tiny hairs; capsule five-veined, opening transversely by a lid. Br Isles c (except N Scot r); Eur c; on dunes, open gslds. Fl 6—8.

E Blue Pimpernel, *A. foemina*, as D, but fls (**E**) always blue, up to 12 mm across, with narrow-oblong petals not overlapping, v few hairs on edges; calyx conceals corolla in bud. S Eng r; Eur o; on ar on chk. Fl 6—8.

F Bog Pimpernel, *A. tenella*, tiny hairless, creeping, rooting per; lvs short-stalked, oval or ± circular, 5 mm long, in pairs along the delicate stems; fls in lf-axils on stalks 10 mm long; calyx-teeth v narrow; corolla to 14 mm across, funnel-shaped, five-lobed, 2—3 times length of calyx, white with fine crimson veins (so appearing pink); fr 3 mm across. Br Isles f-lc, more c in W; Eur, Netherlands S to France: vr and only near coast in N, lf-o to S; in wet mds, less acid bogs, fens. Fl 6—8.

G Sea-milkwort, *Glaux maritima*, creeping and ascending per, 10—30 cm long; stalkless, fleshy, opp, strap-shaped, blunt lvs, 4—12 mm long. Fls (**Ga**) solitary in lf-axils, 5 mm across, with pink five-lobed calyx, no petals, 5 stamens. Br Isles, Eur; vc on coasts, vr inland near salt springs etc; in salt marshes, seaside rocks. Fl 6—8.

H Chaffweed, *Anagallis minima*, amongst smallest flowering plants of Eur, 2—7 cm tall; ± erect hairless ann; lvs 3—5 mm long, stalkless, oval, untoothed, often alt. Fls solitary in lf-axils, 1 mm across, with 5 tiny narrow pointed sepals and a shorter pinkish five-lobed corolla. Frs 1.5 mm across, globular, ± pink-flushed, like tiny apples. Br Isles, widespread but r (except S Eng, W Wales lf); Eur o-lf; on open damp sandy gd on hths, wdland paths etc. Fl 6—7.

I Chickweed Wintergreen, *Trientalis europaea*, slender erect per, 10—20 cm tall; single whorl of hairless obovate lvs, 2—8 cm long, at top of stem, from which arise 1 or 2 long-stalked white starlike fls, 12—18 mm across; corolla usually with 7 oval lobes; fr a globular capsule. Br Isles: Suffolk vr, N Eng r, Scot o-lvc, **Ire abs**; Eur: Denmark to Netherlands f-c; in wds, mostly of pine in Scot, of oak or beech in N Eur. Fl 6—7.

GENTIAN FAMILY

Gentianaceae

Herbs ± hairless, with opp, untoothed, ± stalkless lvs without stipules; infls forked cymes with a fl in each fork (dichasia). Fls regular, with 4, 5 or more lobes, the corolla-lobes twisted round one another in bud. Stamens, on corolla-tube, alt with and same number as lobes. Ovary **superior** (similar-looking Campanulaceae have ovary inferior); 2 carpels, forming a capsule in fr.

KEY TO GENTIAN FAMILY

1 Fls yellow 2
  Fls pink, blue, purple or white 3
2 Fls 6–8-lobed, 10–15 mm across – oval lvs joined round stem in a ring – plant over 15 cm tall ....
                                                                Blackstonia perfoliata (p 292 J)
  Fls 4–5-lobed, 3–5 mm across – linear lvs not joined round stem – plant 3–10 cm tall......................
                                                                 Cicendia filiformis (p 292 I)
3 Corolla pink – style on top of ovary distinct and threadlike, withering in fr.. 4
  Corolla blue, purple or white – style abs, or ovary gradually tapering into short stout style, with 2 stigmas remaining on top of fr 5
4 Minute plant (3–8 cm) – four-lobed corollas only 3 mm across – on damp sandy gd – W France, Guernsey – r ....*Exaculum pusillum* (p 292 Iii)
  Larger plant (to 40 cm tall) – five-lobed corollas, 10–18 mm across.......... *Centaurium* (p 290–292)
5 Corolla blue with small lobes between main lobes – no fringe of white hairs in corolla throat..............
                                                              Gentiana (p 290)
  Corolla purple without any small lobes between main lobes – throat fringed with white hairs ....
                                                            Gentianella (p 290)

KEY TO GENTIANS (*GENTIANA* AND *GENTIANELLA*)

1 Corolla **with tiny lobes** between large lobes, blue, throat **without** fringe of white hairs .. *Gentiana* **2**
  Corolla **without** tiny intermediate lobes, purple-mauve, **throat with fringe of white hairs**
                                                             Gentianella **6**
2 Corolla-**lobes fringed with white hairs along edges** – calyx-tube and corolla-tube four-lobed, corolla to 40 mm across, lobes spreading, oval – **not in Br Isles** .... *Gentiana ciliata* (p 290 Bii)
  Corolla-lobes **not** fringed with hairs... 3
3 Calyx and corolla four-lobed – fls **stalkless**, in a terminal cluster, greenish-blue outside, **shorter** than the upper, oval-lanceolate, lvs – not in Br Isles .... *G. cruciata* (p 290 Ai)
  Calyx and corolla **five-lobed** – fls **stalked**, **longer** than lvs 4
4 Plant with many **basal rosettes** of oval lvs, forming tufts or cushions .... *G. verna* (p 290 B)
  Plant **without** basal rosettes of lvs, lvs on stem only... 5
5 Plant **tall** (15–40 cm) – lvs **narrow-linear**, **blunt**, **1.5–4.0 cm long** – corolla-tube **bell-shaped**, 2.5–4.0 cm long, blue with green stripes down outside .... *G. pneumonanthe* (p 290 A)
  Plant **short** (3–15 cm) – lvs **oval**, **pointed** above, **2–5 mm long** – corolla-tube **cylindrical**, 1.0–1.5 cm long, lobes **spreading**, no green stripes – Scot mts – r........................... *G. nivalis* (p 290 Bi)
6 Calyx four-lobed, **2 outer lobes much broader than 2 inner**, overlapping them ....
                                                  Gentianella campestris (p 290 E)
  Calyx four- or five-lobed, **lobes ± equal**, all narrow.. 7
7 Corolla-tube **23–35 mm long**, twice length of calyx or more – lower lvs **oval** ....
                                                        G. germanica (p 290 D)
  Corolla-tube **13–20 mm long**, **less** than twice length of calyx – lower lvs **lanceolate**.................... 8
8 Fls **cream** inside, **purple-red** outside – N Scot .... *G. septentrionalis* (p 290 Cii)
  Fls **uniform dull purple**.. 9
9 Fls in **May–June** – terminal fl-stalk, together with uppermost internode, **forms half or more** of total height of plant – calyx-teeth adpressed to corolla – S Eng........................ *G. anglica* (p 290 Ci)
  Fls in Aug–Oct 10
10 Terminal fl-stalk plus uppermost internode forms **half or more** of total height of plant – calyx-teeth **spreading** – upper lvs **oval** – in dune hollows – vr S Wales, N France to Denmark.................
                                                        G. uliginosa (p 290 Ciii)
  Uppermost internode plus terminal fl-stalk together **far less** than half height of plant – calyx-teeth **adpressed** – upper lvs lanceolate... *G. amarella* (p 290 C)

Gentians, Centaury, Yellow-wort

A **Marsh Gentian**, *Gentiana pneumonanthe*, erect hairless per, 10–30 cm tall, with blunt linear lvs 2–4 cm × 3–5 mm, not in rosettes at base. Fls 1–7 in a dense terminal group; corolla-tube 2.5–4.0 cm long, bright blue, with 5 green stripes on the outside, narrowing below, its oval lobes ascending (not spreading at 90°). Br Isles: Eng, S (Dorset–Sussex), and E (Norfolk–Yorks) vlf, Lancs – N Wales r; **Scot**, **Ire abs**; Eur o-vla to N; in wet hths, dune slacks. Fl 8–9. ***Ai** **Cross Gentian**, *G. cruciata*, erect, 20–30 mm tall; basal lvs form a tube 10 mm long or more round stem; upper lvs elliptical, over 1 cm wide, longer than fls; fls unstalked, in clusters in lf-axils, dull blue inside trumpet, green-speckled outside; corolla four-lobed, half length of that in A. France o; Belgium r; in gslds. Fl 6–9.

B **Spring Gentian**, *G. verna*, hairless per with dense basal rosettes of oval-elliptical lvs 5–15 mm long. Stems 2–6 cm tall, with few pairs of smaller lvs. Fls solitary, terminal, on erect stems; corolla-tube 1.5–2.5 cm, deep rich blue, cylindrical, its oval lobes spreading out at 90° in a star shape, 1.5–2.0 cm wide. Eng, Teesdale vlf; Ire, Clare, Galway, la; (Eur, mts to S only); on calc gslds, limestone crevices. Fl 4–6. **Bi** **Alpine Gentian**, *G. nivalis*, slender ann native on ledges of mts in Scot; 3–15 cm-tall, ± branched stems; fls only 8 mm across spreading lobes. ***Bii** **Fringed Gentian**, *G. ciliata*, is taller than B, without rosettes of lvs at base; blue corolla has 4 spreading lobes 4–5 cm across, that bear fringes of white bristles on them (not in throat of fl). France o; Belgium r; on dry gslds. Fl 8–10.

C **Autumn Gentian**, *Gentianella amarella*, erect branched bi, 5–30 cm tall; stem-lvs pointed, oval-lanceolate, 1–2 cm long; corolla-tubes purple, 4- or 5-lobed, bell-shaped, 14–20 cm long, with white fringe of hairs in throat and lobes triangular, ± spreading; tube less than twice length of calyx, which has 4 or 5 equal narrow erect lobes. Fls 10 mm across lobes. Br Isles: Eng, Wales c; Scot, Ire lf; Eur: N France to Denmark, r and coastal to S, lf to N; on calc gslds, dunes. Fl 8–9. **Ci** **Early Gentian**, *G. anglica*, only 4–15 cm tall; distance between two uppermost lf pairs is half, or more than half, total height of plant. S Eng r in chk gsld; Eur abs. Fl 5–6. **Cii** *G. septentrionalis* is like C, but fls **cream** inside, **purple-red** outside; **distance between 2 uppermost lf-pairs v short** (1–2 mm). NW Scot only; r-lf on dunes, calc gsld. Fl 7–8. **Ciii** *G. uliginosa* is also like C, but terminal fl **v long-stalked**, together with uppermost internode **forming at least half height of plant**; upper lvs **oval**; calyx-teeth **spreading**, **v unequal**, to 3 mm wide. S Wales vr; Eur: N France, Belgium, vr; Denmark lf; in dune hollows.

D **Chiltern Gentian**, *G. germanica*, is close to C, but lvs broader-based (10 mm across or more) than in C; corolla-tube 25–35 cm long, twice (or more) length of calyx and transversely wrinkled on outside; fls about 20 mm across lobes. Eng, N Hants to Hertford, vlf; Eur: central, N France vc; Belgium, Germany o; on calc gslds. Fl 8–9.

E **Field Gentian**, *G. campestris*, differs from C and D mainly in its calyx (**E**), in which two **wide-oval** acute sepals overlap the two **narrow**-lanceolate inner ones. Corolla as in C, but blue-lilac. Br Isles: N Eng, Scot c; S Eng, Wales r; Ire f; Eur: France o, Denmark lf; on neutral to acid gslds, dunes. Fl 7–10.

F **Common Centaury**, *Centaurium erythraea*, hairless erect ann, 10–40 cm, with basal rosette of obovate lvs over 5 mm wide, and 1 or more stems; lvs oval-elliptical, never parallel-sided. Fls ± unstalked, in ± dense forking cymes on top of stem, not umbel-like; corolla-tube long, lobes flat, oval, spreading, pink; fl 10–12 mm across. Br Isles vc (except NE Scot r); Eur c; in dry gslds, dunes, wd clearings. Fl 6–10. **Fi** **Perennial Centaury**, *C. portense* (*C. scilloides*), creeping per, with round, stalked lvs on creeping stems; fl-stems erect with oblong lvs; fls 16–18 mm across. Pembroke, Cornwall, NW France vr; sea cliffs. Fl 7–8.

cont

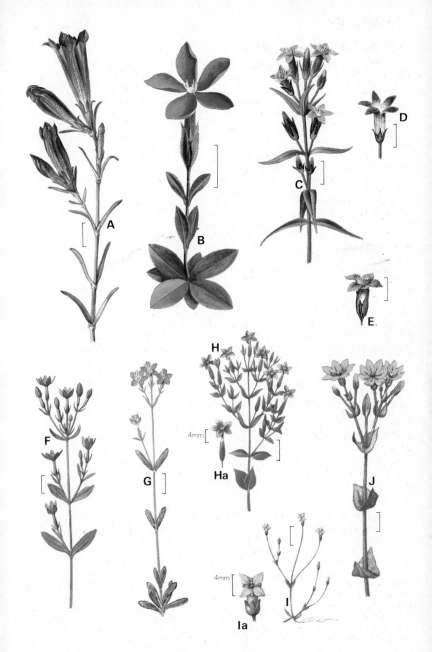

GENTIAN FAMILY

◀ **G   Seaside Centaury**, *C. littorale*, close to F in erect stems, but root-lvs only to 5 mm wide, linear to spoon-shaped; stem-lvs **parallel-sided**, strap-shaped, blunt; fls in **dense** terminal **umbel-like** clusters; corolla 12–14 mm across, **deeper** pink and more concave than in F. Br Isles: N, W coasts of GB lf (Hants vr); Ire vr; Eur, coasts from N France to Denmark lc; on dunes. Fl 7–8.

H   Lesser Centaury, *C. pulchellum*, smaller, slenderer ann than F and G, 3–15 cm, with v open forked branching; fls in the forks and on shoot tips, no basal lf-rosette; lvs all elliptical; fls on 2-mm stalks. Corolla (**Ha**) dark pink, 4–8 mm across, 5- (or 4-) lobed (sometimes reduced to a tiny unbranched one-fld plant). Eng, Wales, o, lc in S; Ire vr; Eur o-lf; on bare, often damp, grassy open gd on calc and acid soils. Fl 6–9.   **Hi   Slender Centaury**, *C. tenuiflorum*, looks like a taller H (10–35 cm tall), but with strictly erect branches and dense infls. S coast Eng vr; Eur, W coast France f; on moist bare gd near sea. Fl 7–9.

I   Yellow Centaury, *Cicendia filiformis*, slender ann, 2–12 cm tall, with simple or few erect rather fleshy pinkish-green branches; wide-spaced pairs of linear lvs 2–6 mm long; fls (**Ia**) yellow, long-stalked, terminal, only open in sun; four-lobed corolla; calyx-tube with 4 short triangular lobes. SW Eng, Wales, r but vlf; SW Ire vl; Eur: W France lc; Belgium to Denmark vr; on damp open sandy gd on hths and in wds (oceanic sp). Fl 8–9.   *****Ii   Guernsey Centaury**, *Exaculum pusillum*, like I, but even smaller (2–6 cm tall); corollas **pink**, four-lobed, 2–3 mm across; calyx deeply four-lobed. W France, Guernsey, r-lf; on moist sandy gd nr coast. Fl 7–9.

J   Yellow-wort, *Blackstonia perfoliata*, erect waxy-grey green ann, 15–40 cm, with basal rosette of obovate lvs; stem-lvs oval-triangular, joined in pairs to form rings round stem. Fls in loose forking cymes; corolla 10–15 mm across, 6–8-lobed, yellow. Br Isles: Eng c; Wales vlc; **Scot abs**; Ire lc; Eur: France to Holland r; on calc gslds, dunes. Fl 6–10.

BOGBEAN FAMILY

These are like Gentian family, but are water plants with alt lvs.

A   Bogbean, *Menyanthes trifoliata*, per with creeping stems, bearing alt, erect long-stalked, trifoliate lvs, with oval untoothed grey-green lfts 3–7 cm long; erect lfless fl-stems, 10–30 cm tall, bearing fl-racemes; corollas five-lobed, star-shaped, pink outside, white within, 15 mm across, conspicuously fringed with stout white hairs; fr (**Aa**) an oval capsule. Br Isles c (except central Eng o); Eur f-lc; in wet bogs, fens, ponds. Fl 5–7.

B   Fringed Water-lily, *Nymphoides peltata*, a floating aquatic, with lvs like small Water-lily lvs (see p 106), round to kidney-shaped, purple below, 3–8 cm across, lower alt, upper in opp pairs; fls few together in lf-axils, long-stalked; corolla 3 cm across, with five fringed **yellow** lobes. SE, E, central Eng o-lf; Eur lf; in ponds, rivers. Fl 6–9.

PERIWINKLE FAMILY

Creeping woody shrubs with opp evergreen oval untoothed lvs, and corollas with 5 spreading lobes, twisted in bud.

C   Lesser Periwinkle, *Vinca minor*, ± prostrate evergreen shrub with hairless, elliptical, shiny dark green short-stalked lvs (**C**) in pairs. Calyx-teeth (**Cb**) lanceolate, hairless. Fls (**Ca**) usually solitary in lf-axils, with corolla of 5 almost flat blue-violet lobes, 25–30 mm across. Br Isles: GB f and probably native in S, rarer and planted to N; Ire r; Eur f-lc; in wds, hbs. Fl 3–5.

D   Greater Periwinkle, *V. major*, v similar to C, but has broader, longer-stalked (1 cm), oval lvs; fls 40–50 mm across; calyx-teeth (**Da**) narrow, hairy. Br Isles f-lc (S Eng r); Eur f-lc; introd in wds, hbs. Fl 4–5.

cont

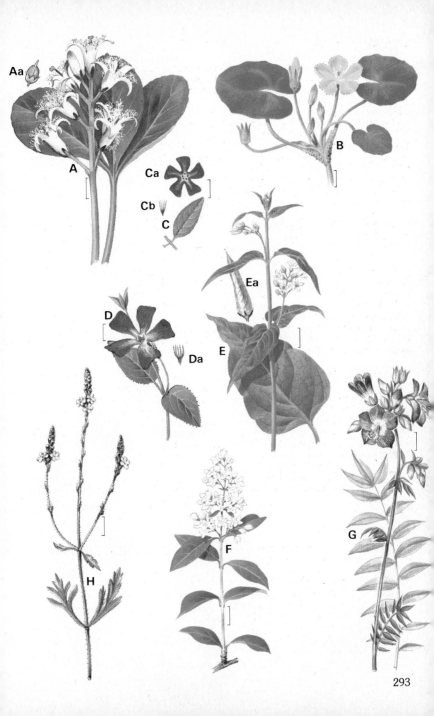

MILKWEED FAMILY

Asclepiadaceae

◀ Differs from Gentian family in its long frs, and seeds with tassels of silky hairs.

*E Vincetoxicum, *Vincetoxicum hirundinaria*, per herb 30–70 cm tall, with narrow to broad cordate, pointed opp lvs, 5–10 cm long; fls in loose clusters in upper lf-axils; corollas five-lobed, star-like, cream or white, 6–10 mm across; pods (**Ea**) to 5 cm long, cigar-shaped, containing silky-plumed seeds. Eur, France to Denmark, f-lc; on gslds, especially on calc soils. Fl 6–9.

OLIVE FAMILY (see also p 238)

Oleaceae

F Wild Privet, *Ligustrum vulgare*, semi-evergreen shrub with opp elliptical-lanceolate lvs, 3–6 cm long (**Garden Privet**, *L. ovalifolium*, the sp usually planted, has oval lvs). Fls in terminal panicles; corolla white, 4–5 mm across, four-lobed, scented, the 2 stamens (number typical of family) projecting from corolla-tube. Fr a black shiny berry, 6–8 mm across. Br Isles c (except N Scot r); in hbs, scrub, gsld, especially on calc soils. Fl 6–7.

PHLOX FAMILY

Polemoniaceae

Herbs with 5 sepals, 5 equal-lobed corollas, 5 stamens and **three**-celled ovary. Fr a capsule.

G Jacob's-ladder, *Polemonium caeruleum*, per herb 30–90 cm, with erect unbranched stem, bearing alt hairless pinnate lvs, lower long-stalked, upper stalkless, 10–40 cm long, with 6–12 pairs of oval-lanceolate lfts. Infl a loose, terminal head; fls 2–3 cm across, drooping; corolla blue or white, with a short tube, and 5 equal spreading lobes; stamens golden, protruding, style long, with 3 stigmas. N Eng r, but vlf from Derby to Northumberland; Eur (mts only); on grassy slopes, rocks, screes on limestone, also gdn escape in wa, hbs. Fl 6–7.

VERBENA FAMILY

Verbenaceae

Very like Labiate Family (see Key to Labiates, p 310) but style **terminal** on fr.

H Vervain, *Verbena officinalis*, erect hairy per herb, 30–60 cm; stems tough, with pairs of opp pinnatifid bristly lvs, 2–7 cm long, of elliptical outline; infls terminal, in uppermost lf-axils, spike-like and lfless, slender, loose, 8–12 cm long. Fls bluish-pink, 4 mm across; corolla-tube twice length of calyx, five-lobed, ± two-lipped; stamens 4; fr with style on top, separating into 4 nutlets. Br Isles: Eng, Wales, c to S, r to N; Ire f in S; Eur f; in gsld, rds, wa, scrub, on dry often calc soils. Fl 6–9.

▶ BINDWEED FAMILY

Convolvulaceae

Mostly climbing plants with alt lvs and no stipules; fls with 5 sepals, corolla trumpet-shaped, five-lobed (or merely five-angled in **Bindweeds**), 5 stamens inside tube of corolla; fr a two-celled capsule. **Dodders** (*Cuscuta*) are climbing parasites.

A Field Bindweed, *Convolvulus arvensis*, creeping and climbing per herb, with ± hairless stems arising from stout fleshy undergd stems (hard to eradicate in gdns); lvs 2–5 cm long, oblong-arrow-shaped, stalked, alt; fls trumpet-shaped, white or pink, 30 mm across, five-angled at mouth; calyx five-lobed, **no epicalyx**. Br Isles vc (except N Scot r); Eur c; in wa, hbs, ar, rds, gsld near sea (a serious weed in gdns). Fl 6–9.

B Hedge Bindweed, *Calystegia sepium*, of similar habit to A, but much larger, climbing to 3 m or more; lvs to **15 cm long** and more **rounded**; fls white (rarely pink), trumpets 3–4 cm across; an **epicalyx** of 2 bracts, longer than calyx-lobes, surrounds calyx. Br Isles vc (except N Scot lf); Eur c; on wa, hbs, scrub, wd borders, fens. Fl 7–9. **Bi Large Bindweed**, *C. sylvatica*, similar, but corolla-trumpet 60–75 mm across; the 2 epicalyx-bracts **strongly inflated**, **overlapping** each other. Br

3mm

295

BINDWEED FAMILY

◀ Isles, Eur; introd in wa, hds, etc. Fl 7–9.

C **Sea Bindweed**, *C. soldanella*, creeping hairless per with ± fleshy, **kidney-shaped** lvs; corolla-trumpets 25–40 mm across, **pink** with **white stripes**; epicalyx-bracts **shorter** than sepals, rounded. Br Isles: coasts of Eng, Wales, SW Scot, Ire; North Sea and Atlantic coasts of Eur; f-lc on sand-dunes. Fl 6–8.

D **Common Dodder**, *Cuscuta epithymum*, parasitic climber without green chlorophyll; threadlike red stems; lvs reduced to small scales; fls in dense clusters, 6–10 mm across, bell-shaped, with projecting stamens, pink five-lobed corollas 3–4 mm across, and 5 scales inside tubes. S Eng f-lc; rest of Br Isles r; **N Scot abs**; parasitic on gorse, heather, clovers etc. Fl 7–9. **Di Greater Dodder**, *C. europaea*, larger, with fl-heads **10–15 mm** across; paler corollas **4–5 mm** across; stamens and styles **enclosed** in corolla-tubes, scales **smaller**, corolla-lobes **blunt**, not pointed. S Eng r; Eur o-lf; parasitic on nettles etc. Fl 8–9.

NIGHTSHADE FAMILY

Herbs and shrubs with alt lvs without stipules, often **poisonous**; fls regular, bell-shaped or wheel-shaped, with 5 sepals; corollas five-lobed, stamens projecting in a column in **Nightshades** and **Potato** (*Solanum*); 5 stamens; fr two- or sometimes four-celled, a berry or capsule.

E **Duke of Argyll's Teaplant**, *Lycium halimifolium*, shrub with arching grey, often spiny, stems to 2.5 m; lanceolate grey-green alt lvs to 6 cm long; fls 1 to 3 in short shoots in lf-axils, brownish to rosy-purple; corollas funnel-shaped, with 5 lobes in a star 1 cm across; fr (**Ea**) a red oval berry. S half of GB introd and f; Ire r; Eur f; in hbs, wa etc. Fl 6–9.

F **Thorn-apple**, *Datura stramonium*, stout ann herb 50–100 cm tall, with alt oval coarsely-toothed lvs to 20 cm long on long stalks; white (rarely purple) trumpet-shaped fls, with long corolla-tubes, and 5 long-pointed corolla-lobes; corollas 6–8 cm across. Fr an oval **spiny** capsule 4–5 cm long. Eng, Wales o-f; Eur f; weed (from SE Eur) most c in hot summers in ar, wa. Fl 7–10.

G **Henbane**, *Hyoscyamus niger*, tall ann or bi with sticky-hairy strong-smelling lvs and stems; lvs oval-oblong, toothed or not, upper clasping, 10–20 cm long, alt up stem. Fls in two rows on a forked cyme, calyx-tube hairy, swollen, with long rigid teeth; corolla funnel-shaped with 5 lobes, not all quite equal, dull yellow with purple veins and eye; fr a large (1–2 cm-long) capsule, opening at top. **Whole plant v poisonous**. Eng, lf in S and E, r in rest of Br Isles. Eur f; on wa, open grassy downs, sandy gd near sea. Fl 6–8.

H **Bittersweet**, *Solanum dulcamara*, downy woody per, scrambling over other plants to 2 m. Lvs alt, stalked, oval, often with two spreading lobes or lfts at base, tip pointed, to 8 cm long. Fls in loose cymes, 1 cm across; corolla with 5 pointed, arched-back, purple lobes, and a conical column of yellow stamens to 8 mm long. Fr (**Ha**) a **red oval** berry, to **1 cm** long. Br Isles: GB, N to Scot c, N Scot, Ire o; Eur c; in wds, hbs, scrub, wa, beaches. Fl 6–9.

I **Black Nightshade**, *Solanum nigrum*, ann, much smaller than H (to 50 cm), with erect or spreading stems; lvs oval, pointed, ± lobed, but **not** with lfts at base as in H; fls similar to H, but 0.5 mm across, **white**. Fr (**Ia**) a **black round** berry, to 8 mm long. Br Isles: Eng, Wales c, Scot, Ire vr; Eur c; on ar, wa. Fl 7–9. **Potato** (*S. tuberosum*) with white fls, and tubers, and **Tomato** (*Lycopersicum esculentum*), with yellow fls, are related plants with similar fl-structure.

J **Deadly Nightshade**, *Atropa belladonna*, tall (to 150 cm) stout, shrubby-looking, per herb; pointed oval lvs, to 20 cm long, narrowed into the stalks, alt or in unequal pairs. Fls 1 or 2 together, in lf-axils and in forks of branches; corollas bell-shaped with ± parallel sides, stalked, 25–30 mm long, drooping, dull brownish-purple or green, with 5 blunt lobes. Fr (**Ja**) a black glossy berry, 15–

NIGHTSHADE FAMILY *Solanaceae*

20 mm across, with the five-lobed calyx persisting below it. **Whole plant v poisonous**. S and E Eng, native and o-lf, elsewhere in Br Isles r; Eur, o to N, lf to S; native in wds, scrub on calc soils, escape in wa near buildings. Fl 8–10. ◀

FIGWORT FAMILY *Scrophulariaceae*

Herbs (in Eur); lvs with no stipules, and often alt above, opp below (or all opp). Fls bisexual; calyx five- or four-lobed; corolla irregular, usually two-lipped, five-lobed (sometimes four-lobed); stamens on corolla-tube, 5, or 4 (or 2 in *Veronica*). Ovary two-celled, with style **on top** of the two lobes; fr a capsule with 2 cells, each several-seeded. (Basic distinction from Labiate family, p 310, is in ovary, which in Labiates consists of 4 rounded lobes with a depression between them, from which style arises; Labiate fr of 4 separating one-seeded **nutlets**, not a many-seeded capsule as in Figwort family.)

KEY TO FIGWORT FAMILY

 1 Stamens 5 – corolla five-lobed, almost regular, lower petal only slightly longer than others – tall plant – lvs alt – fls in long racemes ....*Verbascum* (p 298)
   Stamens 2 or 4.. **2**
 2 Stamens 2 – fls often blue – corolla ± flat, with 4 lobes in unequal cross – lvs opp............................
   ....*Veronica* (key p 302)
   Stamens 4 – fls never bright blue.. **3**
 3 Corolla two-lipped, pouched or spurred below mouth of tube, closed by a two-lobed swelling projecting from lower lip (the 'palate') – Snapdragon-like fls **4**
   Corolla not pouched or spurred, no 'palate' on lower lip.. **8**
 4 Corolla pouched below, but without spur.. *Antirrhinum* (p 302)
   Corolla with a pointed hollow spur projecting from base of lower lip **5**
 5 Fls in terminal racemes or spikes – lower lvs whorled, upper alt................................. *Linaria* (p 300)
   Fls in lf-axils along stem – lvs nearly all alt.. **6**
 6 Lvs linear, strap-shaped – plant erect..*Chaenorhinum minus* (p 300 D)
   Lvs long-stalked, broad, round or arrow-shaped – plant ± creeping... **7**
 7 Lvs pinnately-veined, oval or arrow-shaped..*Kickxia* (p 300–302)
   Lvs palmately-veined, ivy-shaped.. *Cymbalaria muralis* (p 300 C)
 8 Plant small, creeping, rooting at intervals – corollas tiny (under 5 mm), solitary, wheel-shaped, with v short narrow corolla-tubes **9**
   Plant ± erect, lfy, not creeping and rooting – corollas irregular, with long or cup-shaped tubes – fls grouped in infls **10**
 9 Lvs oblong-linear, untoothed – tiny plant of pond edges, on mud – r ....
   ....*Limosella aquatiça* (p 302 J)
   Lvs kidney-shaped, long-stalked, toothed – in moist wds .... *Sibthorpia europaea* (p 302 K)
10 Lvs opp (except bracts sometimes alt in infl)... **11**
   Lvs alt... **17**
11 Calyx clearly five-toothed **12**
   Calyx four-toothed.. **13**
12 Stems square in section – corolla-tube like a small rounded cup, with 2 small (2–3 mm-long), usually red-brown upper lobes, 3 greenish lower lobes ....*Scrophularia* (p 298–300)
   Stems round in section – corolla with tube 10–45 mm long, with 5 large spreading yellow lobes...*Mimulus* (p 302)
13 Calyx-tube inflated, flattened on each side, like a tiny oval purse, narrowed to four-toothed tip – corolla yellow, with 2 violet teeth on upper lip... *Rhinanthus* (p 310)
   Calyx-tube not inflated; but cylindrical or bell-shaped... **14**
14 Upper corolla-lip flattened on each side to form roof-like ridge – mouth of corolla-tube almost closed – lower lvs ± untoothed, or toothed only near their bases ....
   ....*Melampyrum* (p 306–308)
   Upper corolla-lip not flattened at sides – mouth of corolla-tube open – all lvs and bracts toothed along all edges **15**
15 Upper corolla-lip ± erect, two-toothed – lower lip with purple lines .... *Euphrasia* (p 308)
   Upper corolla-lip unlobed, arched forwards **16**

16 Fls purple, over 1 cm long, with oval purple bracts – in mts – r .... *Bartsia alpina* (p 308 Ei)
Fls yellow, over 1 cm long, with lanceolate green bracts .... *Parentucellia viscosa* (p 308 E)
Fls pink, 4–8 mm long, with lanceolate green bracts .... *Odontites verna* (p 308 B)
17 Corolla tubular to bell-shaped, with 5 v short lobes, not clearly two-lipped, much longer than
deeply five-lobed calyx – fls in long one-sided racemes – lvs unlobed, oval-lanceolate ....
.... *Digitalis* (p 300)
Corolla clearly two-lipped, lower lip with 3 spreading lobes, only 2–3 times length of tubular
inflated five-toothed calyx – fls in short racemes – lvs pinnate............................ *Pedicularis* (p 308)

Mulleins, Figworts, Foxgloves

A   Great Mullein, *Verbascum thapsus*, tall (to 2 m) stout white-woolly bi, with
round, usually unbranched stem; broad oval-elliptical alt lvs with winged stalks
running down stem. Infl a dense terminal spike, sometimes with small side spikes
from upper lf-axils. Fls bright yellow, with 5 ± equal spreading lobes, lowest
lobe rather larger; 5 stamens, stalks of **upper 3 only** clothed densely with white or
yellow hairs. Fr an oval capsule. Br Isles, c except N and W Scot r, Ire o; Eur c; in
open wds, dry hbs, wa. Fl 6–8.
B   Dark Mullein, *V. nigrum*, differs from A in angled stem, lvs dark green
above, only thinly downy, lower ones with cordate bases and long stalks, upper
stalkless; also in dense **purple hairs** on stalks of **all** stamens (**Ba**). Corolla yellow,
12–20 mm wide, purple-spotted at base. Br Isles: Eng, Wales o, but lc in S and E;
Scot, Ire casual and r; Eur c; on dry hbs, wa, rds, gsld on calc or sandy soils. Fl 6–9.
C   White Mullein, *V. lychnitis*, has angled stem; lvs short-stalked, dark green,
nearly hairless above, white powdery-downy on undersides. Infl branched like a
candelabrum, side branches almost erect and parallel with main stem; stalks of all
stamens with dense white hairs; fls (**Ca**) usually **white** in Eng, but yellow in
Somerset and often in Eur; Br Isles: Eng r (except SE lc); **Scot, Ire abs**; Eur, France
to N Germany, o-lf; in open wds, scrub, dry banks, on calc soil. Fl 7–8.
D   Moth Mullein, *V. blattaria*, has stem and lvs nearly hairless, but upper part of
stem sticky-hairy; lvs dark shiny green, toothed, wrinkled, lower narrowed to base,
upper cordate at base, stalkless. Fls on stalks longer than calyx, singly in axils of
each bract; stamens all clothed with purple hairs as in B, but fls may be yellow or
white, 20–30 mm wide. Fr a **globular** capsule. Eng, o, possibly introd; Eur N to
Holland o; in wa. Fl 6–9.   **Di   Twiggy Mullein**, *V. virgatum*, is close to D, but
more glandular; fls in clusters of 1–5 in axils of bracts, up infl (not singly) on stalks
shorter than calyx. Eng: native Devon, Cornwall, lf (escape elsewhere o); Eur,
native in France lf; on gsld, wa, hbs. Fl 6–8.
E   Hoary Mullein, *V. pulverulentum*, resembles A, but lvs (**E**) thickly clothed on
both sides with a **mealy** white wool that rubs off easily; upper lvs with **cordate**
bases. Infl branched to form a pyramidal panicle, branches **not** erect as in C, but
more spreading; all stamens equally white-hairy. Eng, E Anglia only, vlf; Eur,
France to Holland, lc; on rds, scrub, gsld on calc soil. Fl 7–8.
F   Common Figwort, *Scrophularia nodosa*, erect per, 40–80 cm, hairless
except for sticky hairs on infl; stem square, but without wings; lvs opp, oval,
pointed, coarsely-toothed but unlobed, short-stalked. Sepals 5, oval, blunt, green,
with scarcely visible white edges; corollas (**Fa**) 1 cm long, green, cup-shaped, with
2 red-brown upper and 3 green lower lobes; stamens 4, plus an upper stamen
without anther (staminode). Br Isles c (except N Scot r); Eur c; in wds, hbs. Fl 6–9.
G   Water Figwort, *S. aquatica* (*S. auriculata*), is close to F, but stems (**Ga**) **four-
winged**; lvs (**G**) **bluntly** tipped, **bluntly** toothed; sepals have **broad** (0.5–1.0 mm)
white borders; staminode rounded as in F. Br Isles: Eng, Wales c; Scot vr; Ire f;
Eur: France to Belgium and W Germany c; in moist wds, marshes, by fresh water.
Fl 6–9.   **Gi   Green Figwort**, *S. umbrosa*, has stems even more broadly winged
than in G, but is quite hairless; lvs pointed as in F, sharply-toothed; bracts in infl

A

Ba

B 5 cm

Ca

C 5 cm

D

E

Fa

F

G

Ga 4 mm

H

I

J

299

◀ longer, lf-like; staminode forked into 2 lobes. Br Isles r, only vlf (SW Eng lf); Eur: E France to Denmark o-lf; in moist wds, by fresh water. Fl 7–9.

H   Balm-leaved Figwort, *S. scorodonia*, has square stem of F, but whole plant **grey-downy**; lvs (**H**) wrinkled, cordate, shortly-pointed, deeply doubly-toothed; bracts lf-like; fls purple; staminode rounded. SW Eng lf; W France la; in scrub on sea cliffs, hbs. Fl 6–8. **Hi   Yellow Figwort**, *S. vernalis*, with yellow fls and pointed green sepals, occurs introd o in GB; Eur: native in Denmark; on wa. Fl 4–6.

I   Foxglove, *Digitalis purpurea*, tall downy bi to 150 cm; unbranched stem; lvs green, oval-lanceolate, softly downy, bluntly-toothed, alt, 15–30 cm, with winged stalks. Fls in long erect raceme, corolla 40–50 mm, tubular to narrow bell-shaped, pink-purple, with dark purple spots on a white ground inside tube; calyx much shorter than corolla, cup-like with pointed lobes. Fr an oval capsule. Br Isles vc (except in the Fens and on chk); Eur: W France c, N and E to Denmark o-r; in wds, mt rocks, on acid soils. Fl 6–8.

***J   Small Yellow Foxglove**, *D. lutea*, slenderer than I, **hairless**, with fine-toothed elliptical lvs; pale **yellow** fls 15–20 mm long, with narrow tubes. Eur: central and N France lc, Belgium r-o; on gsld, open wds, scrub, stony places on calc soils. Fl 6–7.

Toadflaxes, Fluellens etc

Toadflaxes and **Fluellens** have spurred corollas, with their throats closed by a two-lobed swelling on the lower lip, called the **palate**.

A   Common Toadflax, *Linaria vulgaris*, erect grey-green-lvd, ± hairless per, 30–80 cm; lvs 3–8 cm, numerous, ± whorled below, alt above, linear-lanceolate. Fls (**Aa**) in long dense terminal racemes; sepals **oval**, pointed; corollas 15–25 mm long, **yellow** with **orange** palate and long ± **straight** spur. Br Isles: GB c (but NW Scot r); Ire o; Eur c; on gsld, ar, wa, hbs, railways. Fl 7–10. **Ai   Prostrate Toadflax**, *L. supina*, has yellow fls like A, but corollas only 10–15 mm long; stems creeping then ascending, only **5–20 cm** tall; lvs **waxy-grey, blunt**; sepals **linear**, blunt. SW Eng vr; France o-lf; on dunes, wa, on calc soils. Fl 6–9. **Aii   Sand Toadflax**, *L. arenaria*, **sticky-downy** branched ann, 5–15 cm, corollas short-spurred, yellow, only 4–6 mm long, racemes few-fld; lvs 3–10 mm, lanceolate. Eng, N Devon vr; W France f; on dunes. Fl 5–9.

B   Pale Toadflax, *L. repens*, erect per with habit of A, but corollas (**B**) 7–14 mm long, **white** or **lilac**, **striped** with **purple**; spurs **straight**, only ¼ length of rest of corolla. Br Isles: Eng, Wales o-lf; Scot, Ire r; Eur o-lf; on dry calc gslds, hbs. Fl 6–9. **Bi   Purple Toadflax**, *L. purpurea*, is like B, but fls in much denser racemes; corollas **violet, unstriped**, 8 mm long, with **long** (½ rest of corolla) **curved** spur. Br Isles, Eur, o-lc; gdn escape on old walls, wa. Fl 6–8. ***Bii   Jersey Toadflax**, *L. pelisseriana*, only 15–30 cm tall, has violet fls 10–15 mm long, with straight spur ± as long as rest of corolla; fls **few** (10 or less). W and central France; o on hths. Fl 5–7.

C   Ivy-leaved Toadflax, *Cymbalaria muralis*, **creeping** hairless per; lvs **long-stalked, palmate-veined, ivy-shaped, thick, alt**, 2.5 cm long; fls **solitary** in lf-axils; corollas 8–10 mm, lilac or white, with yellow spot on white palate; spur short, curved. Br Isles c (but NW Scot r); Eur c (S Eur); on walls, rocks. Fl 5–9.

D   Small Toadflax, *Chaenorhinum minus*, erect sticky-downy ann, 8–25 cm; lvs alt, linear-oblong, blunt, short-stalked; fls (**Da**) axillary, **long-stalked**; corollas 6–8 mm long, pale purple, spurs short, blunt, curved. GB c (except N, W Scot vr); Ire f; Eur c; on wa, ar, railways. Fl 5–10.

E   Round-leaved Fluellen, *Kickxia spuria*, ± prostrate sticky-hairy ann, 20–50 cm long; lvs oval to ± round, 1–5 cm, long-stalked, hairy; fls in lf-

◀ axils, with **long**, **woolly stalks**; corollas 8–11 mm, **yellow**, upper lips **dark purple**, **spur curved**. S, E Eng c; Wales r; **rest of Br Isles abs**; Eur f-c; on ar, wa especially calc. Fl 7–10.

F Sharp-leaved Fluellen, *K. elatine*, close to E, differs in **triangular**, less hairy, **arrow-shaped**, **pointed** lvs, slenderer habit, **pale** purple upper lips to corollas, **straight** spurs, **hairless** fl-stalks. Br Isles: S, E Eng c; Wales o; S Ire vr; **Scot abs**; Eur c; on ar, wa. Fl 7–10.

G Lesser Snapdragon, *Antirrhinum orontium*, erect ann 20–50 cm, sticky-downy above; lvs 3–5 cm, linear, untoothed; fls in loose lfy racemes; calyx-lobes **linear**, **as long as corollas**; corollas (**Ga**) pink-purple, 10–15 mm, **without** spurs, but pouched below. Br Isles: Eng, Wales f-lc; Ire vr; **Scot abs**; Eur f; on ar on sand. Fl 7–10. **Gi Snapdragon**, *A. majus*, the familiar gdn plant, found on old walls as an escape; lvs lanceolate; corollas **3–4 cm** long, **unspurred**, various colours. calyx-lobes **oval**, **v short**. GB o-lf, Ire r; Eur o-lf; on walls, wa. Fl 7–9.

H Monkey Flower, *Mimulus guttatus*, erect per, creeping, hairless below, 20–50 cm; lvs 2–7 cm, **opp**, oval, toothed, upper clasping. Fls in lfy racemes; calyx and fl-stalks **downy**, calyx tubular, five-toothed; corolla 2.5–4.5 cm, yellow with **small** red spots in throat, strongly two-lipped with three-lobed lower lip much longer than upper, throat nearly closed by palate. Br Isles, Eur; introd (N America) f-lc on streamsides, mds. Fl 7–9. **Hi Blood-drop-emlets**, *M. luteus*, v like H, but calyx and fl-stalks hairless; the scarcely two-lipped corollas have **open** throat and **large** (2–3 mm) red blotches. Scot; introd (S America) o by streams. Fl 6–9.

I Musk, *M. moschatus*, smaller than H, ± **prostrate**, **sticky-hairy** all over; yellow unspotted corolla only 1–2 cm long, 1.0–1.5 cm wide. Br Isles, Eur; introd, o in wet places. Fl 7–8.

J Mudwort, *Limosella aquatica*, low hairless ann, creeping by runners, which produce rosettes of lvs 5–15 mm long, upper with elliptical blades and long stalks, lower linear. Fls (**Ja**) v small, long-stalked, in lf-axils; calyx five-toothed, corolla shorter, star-like, 2–5 mm wide, white or lilac with bell-shaped tube and pointed lobes. Br Isles vr (Scot extinct); Eur r; decreasing everywhere; on mud on pond edges. Fl 6–10.

K Cornish Moneywort, *Sibthorpia europaea*, small creeping and rooting hairy per; lvs alt, long-stalked, kidney-shaped, blunt-toothed, 0.5–2.0 cm wide; short-stalked fls 1–2 mm wide, with almost equally five-lobed spreading corollas; 2 upper lobes yellow, 3 lower pink; stamens 4. Br Isles: Sussex, SW Eng, S Wales vlf; Ire vl; W France lf; by streams, wet gd in wds, avoiding calc soils. Fl 7–10.

Speedwells

Speedwells (*Veronica*) are herbs with opp lvs, flat four-lobed corollas, 4 sepals and 2 protruding stamens; 2 carpels, fr flattened.

KEY TO SPEEDWELLS (*VERONICA*)

1 Fls solitary in axils of bracts like ordinary lvs – plants ± prostrate...**A**

  Fls in racemes, heads or clusters – bracts (upper, at least) much smaller and narrower than the ordinary lvs lower down stems – infl erect.. **2**

2 Infls terminating main stems, not in lf-axils... **B**

  Infls in lf-axils – tips of main stems usually with lvs only .... **C**

FIGWORT FAMILY

A Speedwells with fls solitary in axils of ordinary lvs – plants ± prostrate
1 Lvs with palmate veins, deeply 5–7-lobed, ± ivy-shaped – fls pale lilac – sepals with cordate bases..*Veronica hederifolia* (p 306 F)
  Lvs with pinnate veins, not all arising together from base of lf – fls blue, or blue with white lip **2**
2 Lvs kidney-shaped, v rounded, 5–15 mm wide – fl-stalks several times as long as lvs ....
  ....*V. filiformis* (p 306 E)
  Lvs oval or oblong – fl-stalks usually less than twice as long as lvs...**3**
3 Fr-lobes widely spreading – fls large (8–12 mm wide) – lower petal white...........*V. persica* (p 306 A)
  Fr-lobes ± erect – fls small (4–8 mm wide) **4**
4 Sepals oval, pointed – fr with curled hairs – corolla all blue ....*V. polita* (p 306 B)
  Sepals oblong, blunt – fr with straight hairs only – lower petal white..................*V. agrestis* (p 306 C)

B Speedwells with fls in racemes or heads terminating main stems, not in lf-axils
1 Fls in long, dense lfless, spike-like terminal raceme – lvs elliptical, blunt-toothed, downy – corolla-lobes narrow, deep Oxford blue – r..*V. spicata* (p 304 E)
  Fls in shorter or looser, lfy terminal racemes or heads – lower bracts lf-like, upper narrower............**2**
2 Stem creeping at base, then ascending – lvs scarcely toothed, ± hairless **3**
  Stem erect – lvs strongly toothed or cut, obviously downy – ann **5**
3 Stem woody at base – fls few in a loose head – corolla 10 mm wide, bright blue with a red eye – on mt rocks – vr ....*V. fruticans* (p 304 Cii)
  Stem not woody at base – corolla 7 mm wide or less, white, pale or dull blue...................................**4**
4 Fls white or pale blue, with dark blue lines, in a long raceme – fl-stalks longer than calyx – frs wider than long, ± equalling calyx – style as long as fr – c....................................*V. serpyllifolia* (p 304 C)
  Fls dull blue, in oval head – fl-stalks shorter than calyx – fr longer than wide, far longer than calyx – style v short – on mt rocks – r ....*V. alpina* (p 304 Ci)
5 Lvs deeply 3–7-lobed into segments longer than width of central part of lf – E Eng – r...................**6**
  Lvs oval, merely coarsely-toothed...**7**
6 Lvs stalked – fr broader than long – fl-stalks v short (1 mm)............*V. verna* (p 306 Di)
  Lvs **palmately** 3–7-lobed into segments like radiating fingers – fr as long as wide – fl-stalks 5–8 mm, longer than calyx...*V. triphyllos* (p 306 Dii)
7 Fl-stalks v **short** (1 mm) – upper bracts (4–7 mm) **longer** than fls plus fl-stalks – calyx **longer** than corolla or fr...*V. arvensis* (p 306 D)
  Fl-stalks **long** (5 mm) – upper bracts (3–4 mm) and calyx **both shorter** than fl-stalks – calyx **shorter** than corolla or fr – E Eng – r ....*V. praecox* (p 306 Diii)

C Speedwells with infls (racemes) in lf-axils; tips of main stems usually with lvs only
1 Racemes in opp pairs (ie, in axils of 2 opp lvs) **2**
  Racemes each from axil of only 1 of a pair of opp lvs (v rarely paired) **5**
2 Plant erect – lvs hairy, strongly-toothed – racemes of bright blue fls 10 mm wide – on dry gsld – **Br Isles abs** ....*V. teucrium* (p 304 F)
  Plant ascending – lvs hairless, feebly-toothed – fls 8 mm wide at most – in wet places......................**3**
3 Lvs stalked, blunt, oval – fls deep blue, 7–8 mm wide..................................*V. beccabunga* (p 304 I)
  Lvs stalkless, pointed, lanceolate – fls pale blue or pink, 5–6 mm wide **4**
4 Corolla pale blue – fl-stalks erect in fr ....*V. anagallis-aquatica* (p 304 H)
  Corolla pink – fl-stalks spreading in fr..*V. catenata* (p 304 Hi)
5 Lvs linear-lanceolate, usually hairless (rarely hairy), scarcely toothed – fls white or pale blue – in wet places...*V. scutellata* (p 304 G)
  Lvs oval or oblong – in dry places...**6**
6 Lvs elliptical, usually 1 cm wide or less, with small teeth only – racemes dense – fl-stalks only to 2 cm, shorter than bracts – fls lilac ....*V. officinalis* (p 304 D)
  Lvs oval, mostly over 1.5 cm wide, with coarse teeth – racemes loose – fl-stalks 4 mm or more, longer than bracts...**7**
7 Stem hairy all round – lvs long-stalked – fls lilac, 7 mm wide............................*V. montana* (p 304 B)
  Stem hairy in 2 opp rows only – lvs ± stalkless – fls bright blue, 10 mm wide....................................
  ....*V. chamaedrys* (p 304 A)

FIGWORT FAMILY
Speedwells

A Germander Speedwell, *Veronica chamaedrys*, creeping and ascending hairy per, fl-stems to 20 cm tall; stem (**Aa**) with two **opp rows of long white hairs**, hairless between; lvs 1.0–2.5 cm long, oval-triangular, ± stalkless, blunt, cordate-based, coarsely- and bluntly-toothed, hairy. Racemes in axils of one (or both) of a pair of upper lvs, long-stalked, loose, many-fld; corollas 1 cm wide, bright blue with white eye. Fr shorter than lanceolate calyx-lobes, wider above. Br Isles, Eur; vc in wds, hbs, gsld. Fl 3–7.

B Wood Speedwell, *V. montana*, like A, creeping, hairy; lvs large (2–3 cm long), coarse-toothed; long racemes in lf-axils; but stem (**Ba**) hairy **all round**, lvs have **lf-stalks** 5–15 mm long, and are **pale** green; corollas only 7 mm wide, lilac; fr almost round, longer than oval calyx-lobes. Br Isles c (N Scot r); Eur c; in wds on less acid soils. Fl 4–7.

C Thyme-leaved Speedwell, *V. serpyllifolia*, creeping per, but ± hairless; lvs ± **untoothed**, hairless, 1.0–1.5 cm long; fls in ± erect **terminal** racemes; bracts oblong, longer than fl-stalks. Corollas (**Ca**) white or pale blue with dark blue lines, 5–6 mm wide; fl-stalks longer than calyx; fr broader than long, ± equalling calyx. Alpine forms ± prostrate, with larger (6–7 mm wide) blue fls (ssp *humifusa*). Br Isles, Eur; c on gslds, hths, open wds, wa. Fl 3–10. **Ci Alpine Speedwell**, *V. alpina*, and **Cii Rock Speedwell**, *V. fruticans*, are r plants of Scot mts; see Key (p 302) for details.

D Heath Speedwell, *V. officinalis*, creeping, racemes in lf-axils as in A and B, but is a per herb, with hairy lvs only 1–2 cm, oval, v **shallowly**-toothed; fls in **dense** racemes; fl-stalks only 2 mm (4 mm in A and B), shorter than bract and calyx; corollas (**Da**) only 6 mm wide, pale lilac. Br Isles, Eur; vc in gslds, hths, open wds. Fl 5–8.

E Spiked Speedwell, *V. spicata*, erect downy per, 8–60 cm; lowest lvs oval, stalked, upper lanceolate, unstalked, shallowly-toothed. Infl a lfless, dense, many-fld, terminal spike-like raceme. Fls (**Ea**) v short-stalked, corollas deep Oxford-blue, narrow-lobed; fr rounded. Eng: E Anglia vr (small form to 30 cm only, lvs sparingly-toothed); NW Eng, Bristol, Wales r on rocks (to 60 cm, lvs toothed all round); Eur o-lc; on dry calc gslds, dunes, calc rocks. Fl 7–9.

***F Large Speedwell**, *V. teucrium*, downy per, 10–20 cm tall; stems creeping, then erect. Lvs oblong, strongly but bluntly-toothed, stalkless. Infls long-stalked in **pairs** in axils of 2 opp lvs; lfless racemes to 10 cm long. Corollas (**Fa**) bright blue, 8–10 mm, lobes broader than in E. Eur: France to Denmark, f to S, o to N; on calc gslds, dunes. Fl 6–8.

G Marsh Speedwell, *V. scutellata*, hairless (or rarely downy) per, with **slender** creeping stems, ascending to 30 cm tall. Lvs 2–4 cm, opp, **linear-lanceolate**, pointed, stalkless, clasping, ± untoothed, yellow-green or purplish. Infls open; racemes few-fld in axils of only **one** of a pair of lvs; fl-stalks twice length of the linear bracts; sepals oval; corollas 6–7 mm wide, white, or pale blue with purple lines. Frs flat, wider than long, longer than calyx. Br Isles, Eur; f-lc in bogs, wet mds, ponds. Fl 6–8.

H Blue Water-speedwell, *V. anagallis-aquatica*, more robust than G, with **fleshy**, creeping and ascending stems to 30 cm tall, lvs **oval-lanceolate**, **pointed**, clasping, scarcely-toothed. Infls many-fld racemes in axils of **both** of a pair of lvs. Fl-stalks equalling or **longer** than **linear** bracts; sepals **oval-lanceolate**; corollas (**Ha**) 5–6 mm wide, **pale blue**; frs round, ± inflated, scarcely notched, fr-stalks **erect**. Br Isles, Eur; f-lc in ponds, streams, wet mds. Fl 6–8. **Hi Pink Water-speedwell**, *V. catenata*, differs from H in **pink** corollas, fl-stalks **shorter** than **lanceolate** bracts, sepals **oblong**, fr more notched, fr-stalks **spreading**. Br Isles: Eng, Wales, Ire f-lc; Scot vr; Eur f; in fresh water, mds. Fl 6–8. Hybridizes with H.

I Brooklime, *V. beccabunga*, hairless per, stems creeping and rooting, then

3mm — Ca

3cm

Fa

8mm

Da

6mm

5mm — Ea

Ha

5mm

Ia

7mm

◀ ascending to 30 cm, fleshy; lvs 3–6 cm thick, **oval**, **blunt**, shallow-toothed, **short-stalked**. Infls loose, many-fld racemes in axils of **both** of a pair of lvs; sepals oval, pointed. Corollas (**Ia**) 7–8 mm wide, **blue**; capsule **rounded**. Br Isles, Eur; c in ponds, streams, mds, marshes. Fl 5–9.

▶ **Speedwells** continued, **Cow-wheats**

    A   **Common Field Speedwell**, *Veronica persica*, branched spreading hairy ann, fresh green, 10–30 cm long; lvs 1–3 cm, oval-triangular, coarsely-toothed, short-stalked, hairy underneath. Fls in **lf-axils**, on stalks longer than lvs; calyx-lobes 5–6 mm, oval, hairy, pointed, spreading in fr; corolla (**Ab**) 8–12 mm wide, bright blue, lower lip white; fr (**Aa**) with 2 **spreading**, **sharp-edged** lobes, twice as wide as long, with long hairs. Br Isles, Eur; vc in ar, wa. Fl 1–12.

    B   **Grey Field Speedwell**, *V. polita*, has habit of A, but smaller; lvs grey-green 5–15 mm long; fl-stalks equalling or shorter than lvs; sepals **oval**, **pointed**. Corollas (**B**) 4–8 mm wide, **wholly** bright blue; fr (**Ba**) broader than long, but lobes **erect**, **rounded** (**not** spreading or sharp-edged), with short curled hairs. Br Isles, f-lc in S, r to N; Eur c; on ar. Fl 1–12.

    C   **Green Field Speedwell**, *V. agrestis*, close to B, but sepals **oblong**, blunt; corollas (**C**) 4–8 mm wide, but pale blue with **white** lower lips as in A; fl-stalks **short** as in B; fr (**Ca**) with **erect**, **rounded** lobes as in B, but with **long** hairs (**not** short curled ones). Br Isles, Eur; f-lc in ar. Fl 1–12.   ***Ci**   *V. opaca* has blue fls of B, but sepals **blunt**, **spoon-shaped**; frs with curled hairs as in B. Eur, o in ar.

    D   **Wall Speedwell**, *V. arvensis*, **erect** downy ann, 5–20 cm, ± branched at base. Lvs oval-triangular, coarsely-toothed, to 1.5 cm, upper stalkless; racemes long, terminal, bracts longer than fls, narrow above, grading into ordinary lvs below. Fl-stalks much shorter than calyx; corollas (**Da**) blue, 4–5 mm wide; fr hairy, as long as wide. Br Isles, Eur; vc in ar, dry open gslds, walls. Fl 3–10.   **Di** **Spring Speedwell**, *V. verna*, **Dii** **Fingered Speedwell**, *V. triphyllos*, and **Diii** **Breckland Speedwell**, *V. praecox*, are erect small ann plants related to D, vr on sandy gslds and rds in E Anglian Breckland, o in Eur; see Key (p 302).

    E   **Slender Speedwell**, *V. filiformis*, **creeping**, mat-forming per; lvs stalked, **kidney-shaped**, **rounded**, **pinnate-veined**; fls blue, 8–10 mm wide, with **white** lower lips, stalks 2–3 times length of lvs. Br Isles, f-lc; Eur o; (from Caucasus) in gslds, gdns, wa, churchyards. Fl 4–6.

    F   **Ivy-leaved Speedwell**, *V. hederifolia*, hairy **spreading** ann; lvs stalked, **palmately**-lobed, ivy-shaped, to 1.5 cm long, with large blunt teeth. Fls in lf-axils, stalks shorter than lvs; sepals oval, cordate-based; corollas shorter than calyx, 4–5 mm wide, pale lilac; fr globular, hairless. Br Isles c (but NW Scot r); Eur c; in wds, ar, hbs, wa. Fl 4–5.

    Cow-wheats (*Melampyrum*) are erect ± hairless ann herbs, partially parasitic on other plants; lvs opp, lower ± untoothed; fls in lfy terminal spikes; calyx tubular, four-toothed; corolla two-lipped, upper lip shaped like a roof-ridge, mouth ± closed by arched-up lower lip; fr flattened, with large seeds.

    G   **Common Cow-wheat**, *M. pratense*, variable, ± hairless erect ann, 8–40 cm, branches spreading; lvs 1.5–8.0 cm, ± stalkless, oval to linear-lanceolate, lower untoothed; infl a loose spike, fls in pairs in axils of lf-like, ± toothed bracts, both fls turned to one side. Corolla usually pale **yellow**, 11–17 mm long, **much longer** than calyx; calyx-teeth erect, narrow, long; corolla-mouth ± **closed**, its lower lip **straight**. Br Isles, Eur c-la; in wds, hths, bogs. Fl 5–9.   **Gi**   **Small Cow-wheat**, *M. sylvaticum*, like G, but corolla always **deep** yellow, only 5–8 mm long; tube ± equal to calyx, lower lip **bent down**, corolla-mouth **open**; calyx-teeth **spreading**. GB: Teesdale vr, Scot Highlands r; Eur: N Germany, Denmark o; in hthy pine or birchwds. Fl 6–8.

    H   **Crested Cow-wheat**, *M. cristatum*, ± downy ann, 20–40 cm; differs

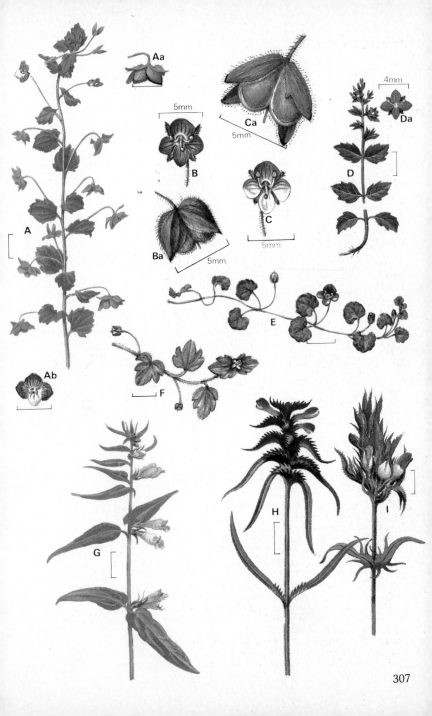

307

◀ from G in its **dense**, **four-angled** fl-spikes, with **arched-back**, **cordate-based** bracts. Bracts, **rosy-purple**, pinnatifid, have 2 mm-long, sharp teeth at bases, but are long-pointed, untoothed, green towards tips. Corollas yellow, purple-flushed, 12–16 mm long. E Eng r-vlf; Eur f-lc; on wd edges on calc soils. Fl 6–9.

I   Field Cow-wheat, *M. arvense*, has fls in dense spikes with coloured bracts as in H, but infls rounded, less dense; bracts **erect**, bright **rosy-red**, pinnatifid **all the way up sides**, with 8 mm-long teeth. Corolla **pink**, 20–24 mm long, with **yellow** throat. S Eng now vr, once c; Eur f-lc; on ar, rds, wa. Fl 6–9.

▶ Eyebrights etc

Eyebrights (*Euphrasia*), are short ± branched ann semi-parasitic herbs; lvs mostly opp, ± oval, deeply-toothed, hairy or hairless, often bronze-tinted, upper often alt; stem with curled white hairs. Fls in lfy spikes; calyx bell-shaped, four-toothed; corolla small, 4–11 mm long, white (more rarely yellow or purple-flushed), two-lipped; upper lip two-toothed, curved forward, lower flatter, three-lobed, with purple lines and a yellow blotch. Some 25 spp recorded in Br Isles, more in Eur. They are difficult to distinguish except by specialists; only the most c sp of the Br Isles and Eur is given here, as an example, plus one v distinct but vl sp.

A   Common Eyebright, *E. nemorosa*, erect, 15–20 cm tall, stem and lvs purplish; lvs oval, hairless above, sharp-toothed, 6–12 mm; bracts oval, pointed, sharp-toothed. Corolla (**Aa**) 5.0–7.5 mm long, white, lower lip longer than upper; fr hairy. Br Isles: Eng, Wales c; Scot, Ire o; Eur f; on gslds, downs, hths, open wds. Fl 7–9.   **Ai   Irish Eyebright**, *E. salisburgensis*, is distinctive: slender, with **v narrow** oblong lvs and bracts, both with few, long teeth; corolla narrow, white; capsule hairless. W Ire lf; on dunes, limestone rocks. Fl 7–8.

B   Red Bartsia, *Odontites verna*, slender, erect, branched downy ann, to 50 cm tall; lvs oblong-lanceolate, few-toothed, unstalked, opp; 1–3 cm long. Infl a long lfy branched raceme with bracts like the lvs; calyx four-toothed, bell-shaped; corollas (**Ba**) 9 mm, pink, two-lipped, upper lip curved forward, ± undivided; lower three-lobed, mid-lobe 4 mm long, throat open, tube equals calyx. Br Isles, Eur; c on ar, wa, gslds, rds. Fl 6–7.

C   Marsh Lousewort, *Pedicularis palustris*, ± hairless ann, to 60 cm tall, with single erect branched stem; lvs 2–6 cm, **alt**, oblong in outline, deeply pinnatifid, lobes toothed; bracts similar. Fls in loose lfy spike; calyx (**Ca**) tubular, ± inflated below, reddish, many-ribbed, with 2 short but lf-like lobes, **downy**; corollas (**Ca**) pink-purple, two-lipped; upper lip arched, flattened on each side, **four-toothed**, lower three-lobed, spreading downwards. Br Isles: N, W of GB, c; SE, central Eng becoming o-r; Ire c; Eur o-lc; in fens, valley bogs, mds. Fl 5–9.

D   Lousewort, *P. sylvatica*, per, shorter than C; **many** stems **spread** from base and then rise to 10–20 cm tall; lvs 2–3 cm; spikes fewer-fld; calyx **stouter**, five-angled, **hairless** (but **downy** in Ire and NW Scot Is), with 4 small lf-like lobes; corollas **pink**, upper lips **two-toothed**. Br Isles, Eur f-c (except in v cultivated areas of mid Eng and Eur); on damp hths, gslds, avoids chky soils. Fl 4–7.

E   Yellow Bartsia, *Parentucellia viscosa*, erect, v sticky, hairy ann, 10–50 cm, ± unbranched; lvs 1.5–4.0 cm long, lanceolate, pointed, opp, stalkless, with few blunt teeth. Fls in long terminal raceme with bracts like the lvs; calyx tubular, ribbed, with 4 spreading teeth; corollas bright **yellow**, 2 cm long, the lower, three-lobed lip **much longer** than upper hooded ± untoothed one. Br Isles: S, W coastal areas of GB N to W Scot, r (but lc in SW); Ire o; W France f (a stray further N); on damp dune-slacks, moist hthy gslds. Fl 6–10.   **Ei   Alpine Bartsia**, *Bartsia alpina*, has the opp unstalked lvs, erect stems, and fl shape of E; but shorter (10–20 cm), quite unbranched; lvs **oval**, blunt-toothed, 1–2 cm long; infls short, with conspicuous **purple bracts**; corollas dull **purple**, 2 cm long, **upper** lip much **longer** than lower. N Eng, Scot Highlands; r in mds, on calc rock ledges in mts. Fl 6–8.

FIGWORT FAMILY

Scrophulariaceae

◄ **F Yellow Rattle**, *Rhinanthus minor*, erect ann, parasitic, ± hairless; stem to 50 cm, black-spotted; opp pairs of stalkless, narrow-lanceolate coarse-toothed lvs. Fls in short lfy spikes; calyx v flattened on each side, inflated and bladder-like in fr, hairless except for margins, four-toothed; corolla yellow, two-lipped; upper lip flattened on each side, with 2 **short** (1 mm) violet teeth, lower three-lobed. Fr flattened; large seeds 'rattle' inside calyx when ripe. Br Isles, Eur; c in gslds, dunes. Fl 5–8. **Fi Greater Yellow Rattle**, *R. serotinus*, more robust, more branched than F, with the violet teeth on upper lip of corolla 2 mm long or more, longer than wide, and tube curved upward (straight in F). GB r and scattered; Eur f; in gslds, dunes. Fl 6–9.

LABIATE FAMILY

Labiatae

A distinctive family of herbs with square stems and opp lvs without stipules; infls in axils of opp pairs of bracts (these often like ordinary lvs), cymose, but so dense as to appear whorled; calyx ± five-toothed, often two-lipped; corolla with a tube, 4- or 5-lobed, usually clearly two-lipped; stamens 4 (or 2 only), fixed to corolla-tube; ovary superior, its 4 lobes ripening in fr to 4 separate one-seeded nutlets, style arising from **hollow** between lobes. Often scented or aromatic when crushed, containing various volatile oils.

This key is based upon characters of lvs, calyx and corolla. Before using it, however, make certain that plant to be named **is** a Labiate, **not** a member of Figwort family with opp lvs and two-lipped fls, eg, Figwort (*Scrophularia*), Speedwell (*Veronica*), or Yellow Rattle (*Rhinanthus*); all these have ovary oval or globular, two-celled, style arising from its **tip** (not from a hollow between 4 lobes) and fr a many seeded **capsule** (not composed of nutlets). Vervain (Verbena family, p 294) is v like a Labiate in its opp lvs, square stem, and fr of 4 nutlets, **but** fls are in **slender spikes**, **not whorled**, and two-lipped corolla has 5 ± **equal**, **spreading** lobes.

KEY TO LABIATE FAMILY

1 Corolla-lobes 4, ± **equal** – corolla 5 mm wide or less... **2**
   Corolla with well-developed lower lip, upper lip abs, or composed of 2 tiny teeth only................. **3**
   Corolla with 2 **unequal**, lobed or toothed lips.. **4**
2 Stamens 2 – lvs pinnatifid, odourless...*Lycopus* (p 312)
   Stamens 4 – lvs shallowly-toothed at most, strongly mint-scented.....................*Mentha* (key p 319)
3 Corolla with a single five-lobed lower lip – corolla-tube hairless inside, with no teeth at top............
      ....*Teucrium* (p 322–324)
   Corolla with three-lobed lower lip – corolla-tube with ring of hairs inside and 2 small teeth at top ....*Ajuga* (p 322)
4 Lower lvs deeply **palmately-lobed** – upper lvs **trilobed** – fls white, in dense whorls spaced out in lf-axils up stem – tall (60–100 cm) downy plant – r..*Leonurus* (p 312)
   Lower lvs **kidney-shaped**, blunt-toothed, on stalks **longer than lf-blades** – fls violet (rarely pink) – creeping and ascending plant...*Glechoma* (p 318)
   Lower lvs oval, oblong or cordate, ± pointed, with pinnate veins.. **5**
5 Calyx tubular, **ten-veined**, equally **ten-toothed** – plant erect, **white-woolly** – stamens hidden in corolla-tube – fls white – not c..*Marrubium* (p 320)
   Calyx with 5 teeth or less.. **6**
6 Stamens obviously **projecting** from fls, spreading out, **longer** than corolla upper lip.................... **7**
   Stamens **shorter** than corolla upper lip, lying beneath it, side by side.................................. **8**
7 Tall (30 cm or more) erect plant – fls in a broad (5–8 cm wide), rounded, **branched** terminal head – lvs oval, **over 1 cm** wide..*Origanum vulgare* (p 318 F)
   Short (usually less than 10 cm tall) creeping and rooting plant – fls in small (1–2 cm wide) heads or short spikes – lvs **small**, **5 mm wide** or less .... *Thymus* (p 312)
8 Calyx of 2 **untoothed** lips, upper with scale on back – erect, narrow-lvd ....*Scutellaria* (p 318)
   Calyx two-lipped, with lips toothed... **9**
   Calyx ± equally five-toothed, **not** clearly two-lipped... **14**

9 Stamens 2, each with anther at end of a **stalk hinged** by its **centre** to main stamen-stalk – upper corolla-lip strongly-arched, hooded, often sickle-shaped...*Salvia* (p 316)
   Stamens 4 – corolla never sickle-shaped **10**
10 Calyx with tube **rounded** above, its upper lip with **3 long narrow** teeth, lower lip with **2 long** teeth.. **11**
   Calyx with tube **v flattened** above, its upper lip with 3 **short** (1 mm) broad-triangular but bristle-pointed teeth, lower lip with 2 long **narrow** teeth.. **13**
   Calyx **bell-shaped**, upper lip with 2–3 tiny blunt irregular teeth, lower with 2 small rounded lobes – erect plant with **v large fls** in lfy racemes – lower corolla-lip 1–2 cm long, white with purple patch – r..*Melittis melissophyllum* (p 314 K)
11 Calyx-tube straight – fls in tall spikes composed of pairs of **loosely**-branched, **stalked** infls in axils of opp pairs of lvs – fls pale, pinkish- or violet-mottled............................. *Calamintha* (p 316–318)
   Calyx-tube curved – fls in **unstalked** clusters in axils of opp pairs of lvs – on calc soils **12**
12 Fls violet, in loose, 3–8-fld whorls – plant creeping and ascending to 10 cm tall – plant not more than 1.5 cm long × 7 mm wide – calyx with a pouch below.............................. *Acinos arvensis* (p 318 E)
   Fls rosy-purple, in **dense, many-fld** whorls – plant **erect**, 15 cm tall or more – lvs at least 2 cm long × 1.5 mm wide; calyx without a pouch below.........................*Clinopodium vulgare* (p 316 A)
13 Calyx-tube strongly flattened above and below, outer edges parallel (so outline from above **rectangular**) – fls in dense oblong heads – lvs **unscented** – corolla-tube straight – c.........................
   ....*Prunella* (p 322)
   Calyx-tube flattened only on upper side, outer edges diverging (so outline **bell-shaped**) – fls in whorls in lf-axils spaced along stems – lvs **lemon-scented** – corolla-tube curved upwards – not c.. *Melissa officinalis* (p 318 Di)
14 Upper corolla-lip **flat** – 2 outer stamens **shorter** than inner 2 – lvs white-woolly **below**, green but downy **above** – stem white-woolly – fls white with purple spots.................*Nepeta cataria* (p 320 H)
   Upper corolla-lip **arched** or **hooded** – 2 outer stamens **longer** than inner 2 .... **15**
15 Calyx **funnel-shaped**, teeth v **short**, broad – plant rough – fls dull purple – harsh smell...................
   .... *Ballota* (p 320)
   Calyx **tubular** or **bell-shaped**, with **long** teeth (2 mm or more long) **16**
16 Lower corolla-lip **forked** at tip, side-lobes **tiny**, ± reduced to teeth or flaps............*Lamium* (p 314)
   Lower corolla-lip **at most notched** at tip, side-lobes well-developed, spreading.......................... **17**
17 Corolla deep yellow – plant with lfy runners...*Galeobdolon* (p 314)
   Corolla purple, pinkish, or creamy yellow – no runners... **18**
18 Calyx-teeth forming **long** (5–7 mm) **spines** – corolla with conical bosses at base of lower lip – upper lip forming **hood flattened** on each side... *Galeopsis* (p 314–316)
   Calyx-teeth long-pointed (3–4 mm), but **not** spinelike – corolla **without** bosses – upper lip arched forward, but **not** flattened on each side to form **hood** **19**
19 Many pairs of lvs up stems, few at bases...*Stachys* (p 320)
   Few pairs of lvs up stems, lvs mostly in basal rosette............................*Betonica officinalis* (p 320 D)

Mint, Thyme etc (see also key, p 319)

Mints (*Mentha*) are aromatic herbs with creeping stems either below or above gd; small, lilac-purple fls have corolla divided into 4 nearly equal lobes, and 4 stamens. Mints are not v easy to name, because various cultivated hybrids have become naturalized in wa, gslds etc.

A   Water Mint, *Mentha aquatica*, downy, erect per herb, 15–60 cm tall; lvs 2–6 × 1.5–4.0 cm, opp, oval, ± hairy, with blunt tips and teeth; infl a terminal rounded **head**, 2 cm long, often with extra whorls below. Calyx-tube hairy; corolla (**Aa**) mauve; stamens projecting from fls; lvs **mint**-scented. Br Isles, Eur; vc in marshes, fens, wet wds, by fresh water. Fl 7–10.

B   Corn Mint, *M. arvensis*, downy prostrate to erect per herb, 10–30 cm tall, 'peppery' scent when bruised; lvs stalked, 2–6 × 1–2 cm, rounded to elliptical, blunt-tipped, teeth ± hairy. Fls in **separated** dense **whorls** in **lf-axils**; calyx (**Ba**) bell-shaped, **v hairy**, with short, **blunt, triangular** teeth; corolla mauve; stamens projecting. Br Isles, Eur; vc in ar, paths in wds, mds. Fl 5–10.   **Bi**   *M. × verticillata* is A × B, c in damp places.   **Bii**   *M. × gentilis* is B × E, r in ditches, wa.   **Biii**   *M. × smithiana* is A × B × E, o in ditches, mds. For differences in calyces, see figures **Bi**, **Bii**, **Biii**. All 3 spp occur in Br Isles and Eur, all fl 7–10.

cont

LABIATE FAMILY

Labiatae

C Horse Mint, *M. longifolia*, erect hairy per herb, 60–90 cm tall; lvs **lanceolate**, stalkless, pointed, 3–8 × 1–3 cm, toothed, green, **hairy** above, **grey-woolly** below, rounded at base. Infls terminal **spikes** 3–10 cm long; narrow bracts longer than fls; calyx and fl-stalks hairy; corolla mauve, hairy, stamens projecting. Br Isles: GB, o-lf in S, r in N; Ire r; Eur o-f; on rds, ditches, wa. Fl 8–9. **Ci Round-leaved Mint**, *M. rotundifolia* (see Key). Br Isles, Eur; o-lf on dunes, rds, wa. Fl 8–9.

D *Mentha × niliaca* is C × Ci. Stout, erect, v hairy per herb, 40–100 cm; lvs **(D)** 3–10 × 2–4 cm, stalkless, **oval** or oblong, **pointed, sharply**-toothed, wrinkled, green, hairy, grey-**woolly** below, bases cordate. Infls terminal **spikes**, 3–8 cm long; bracts narrow, shorter than fls; calyx and fl-stalks hairy; corolla mauve, **hairy**, stamens **enclosed** in corolla. Eng, Wales, Eur; o-lf on rds, ditches, wa. Fl 8–9.

E Spear Mint, *M. spicata*, the usual plant for mint-sauce; erect, ± hairless per herb 30–90 cm; lvs **(E) lanceolate**, pointed, **hairless**; infls in terminal **spikes**, 3–8 cm long; bracts v narrow, longer than fls; calyx **(Ea)** and fl-stalks usually hairless; corolla mauve, **hairless**, stamens **protruding**. Br Isles, Eur; introd o-lf in ditches, rds, wa. Fl 8–9. **Ei** *M. × piperita* (see Key) is A × E. Br Isles, Eur; o in ditches, rds. Fl 7–10.

F Pennyroyal, *M. pulegium*, **prostrate, creeping** downy per herb to 30 cm long; lvs 1–2 cm long × 0.5–1.0 cm wide, oval, short-stalked, finely downy, scented, v blunt-tipped and -toothed; fls in distant whorls in lf-axils; calyx and fl-stalks downy; corolla mauve, hairy outside only. Br Isles; Eng, Wales, vr and decreasing, perhaps now only in S; Ire vr; Eur: France, Belgium r-vlf; on moist bare sandy gd by ponds and on commons. Fl 8–10. **Fi** *M. requienii* is much **smaller** than F; tiny creeping, rooting, mat-forming per herb; stems thread-like; lvs tiny, **round**, ± hairless, **strong**-scented, 3–5 mm long; fls few in each lf-axil, corollas tiny, pale mauve, enclosed in calyx. Eng, Ire; introd r on paths in wds, wet moors. Fl 6–8.

G Gipsywort, *Lycopus europaeus*, erect ± hairy per herb, 30–100 cm tall, with ascending branches. Lvs 5–10 cm, elliptical-lanceolate, short-stalked, **deeply pinnately-lobed**, with pointed tips and lobes. Fls **(G)** in well-spaced dense whorls in lf-axils; calyx bell-shaped, hairy, equally five-spine-toothed; corolla **(Ga)** white, 3 mm or less long and wide, with 4 ± equal lobes, lower lip purple-dotted; stamens only 2, slightly protruding. Br Isles (except NE Eng, E and N Scot r), Eur vc; on stream banks, in ditches, fens. Fl 6–9. **Gi Motherwort**, *Leonurus cardiaca*, also erect downy per, 60–80 cm, fls in whorls in lf-axils; lvs deeply-lobed, lower lvs **palmately**-lobed, with cordate bases, upper lvs deeply trilobed and narrowed into stalks; fls have white, **downy, two-lipped** corollas, 12 mm long. Br Isles introd r; Eur o; on wa, hbs. Fl 7–9.

H Large Thyme, *Thymus pulegioides*, shortly creeping low shrub with ascending fl-shoots to 20 cm, **strongly** thyme-scented. Lvs oval-elliptical, blunt, short-stalked, hairy only at bases, slightly folded upwards, 6–10 mm × 3–6 mm; Fl-stems **(Ha**, cut across) four-angled, **long-hairy on angles**, the 2 broader faces **hairless**, the 2 narrower shortly **downy**; fls in **interrupted spikes** of few-fld whorls; calyx two-lipped, purplish, hairy; corolla **(Hb)** to 5 mm long, two-lipped, rose-purple, stamens **far protruding**. Br Isles: S, E Eng f-lc; Scot, Ire vr; Eur c; on dry calc or hthy gslds, banks. Fl 7–8.

I Wild Thyme, *T. drucei*, close to H, but lower, more mat-forming, far-creeping; only **faintly** thyme-scented; lvs 4–8 mm long, **flat**; fls in dense heads; fl-shoots **(I)** bluntly four-angled, **v hairy** on 2 **opp** faces, ± hairless on other 2. Br Isles vc (except E Anglia o-lf); Eur: France vl, only near W coast; on dry gslds, hths, dunes, rocks. Fl 5–8.

J Breckland Thyme, *T. serpyllum*, close to I, but smaller; fl-stems **(J)** almost round, **equally hairy all round**; lvs erect, shortly oval, blunt; fls in short heads. Eng: Breckland only, vlf; Eur c (but W France r-abs); on sandy hths, gslds. Fl 7–8.

312

cont

Aa

3mm

Ba Bi Bii Biii

A

B

D

Ea

3mm

E

C

F

Ga

3mm

G

Hb

5mm

H

Ha

I

J

K

313

◀ **K Bastard Balm**, *Melittis melissophyllum*, erect hairy-stemmed per, 20–50 cm; lvs 5–8 cm long, oval, stalked, bluntly-toothed. Fls in few-fld whorls in lf-axils; calyx **bell-shaped**, **two-lipped**, upper lip with 2–3 small teeth, lower with 2 **rounded lobes**; corolla **v large**, 2.5–4.0 cm long, cream-coloured or pink; lower lip **to 2 cm long**, with a large rosy-purple blotch. S, W Eng, Wales (from Sussex W), r but vlf; Eur: W, mid, E France lf – S Belgium r; in open wds, hbs, not on chk. Fl 5–7.

▶ **Dead-nettles, Hemp-nettles** etc

Dead-nettles (*Lamium*) have a tubular to bell-shaped calyx, with 5 ± equal, long, **triangular-pointed** teeth; corolla two-lipped, lower lip's 2 side-lobes **v small**, bearing small teeth, mid-lobe divided into **2 large teeth**; fls in dense, separated whorls in lf-axils. **Hemp-nettles** (*Galeopsis*) are like Dead-nettles, but all ann, have 5 **spine-like** ± equal calyx-teeth; corolla has lower lip with 2 narrow side-lobes not **much** shorter than mid-lobe, and 2 cone-shaped **projections** at its base. **Claries** and **Sages** (*Salvia*) have a strongly arched upper corolla-lip and only 2 stamens, the single anther of each on a **hinged** stalk, attached by its centre to the main stamen-stalk.

A Red Dead-nettle, *Lamium purpureum*, ± erect downy ann; stem 10–30 cm, branched from base, ± purplish; lvs and bracts 1–5 cm long, **cordate-oval**, coarse-toothed, all stalked. Infl dense; calyx downy, teeth equalling tube, spreading in fr. Corolla 10–15 mm, pink-purple, tube longer than calyx, with ring of hairs inside. Br Isles, Eur; a on ar, wa, hbs. Fl 3–10.

B Cut-leaved Dead-nettle, *L. hybridum*, close to A, but slenderer; lvs (**B**) and bracts triangular-oval, **truncate** at base, **deeply-toothed** ⅓ **of depth** to midrib; corolla shorter, few or no hairs inside. Br Isles r (but f E Eng); Eur f-lc; on ar, wa. Fl 3–10.

C Henbit Dead-nettle, *L. amplexicaule*, also close to A; downy ann 5–25 cm, branched from base; lower lvs 1.0–2.5 cm, **rounded, blunt**, long-stalked (3–5 cm); base truncate, teeth large but blunt; bracts **stalkless**, ± **clasping** stem in pairs. Calyx-tube with **dense white spreading** hairs, teeth shorter than tube, **erect** in fr; corollas mostly **15 mm**, pink-purple, with **long tube hairless** inside, but also some **v short corollas** enclosed in calyces. Br Isles: S, E of GB c (but Wales, W Scot, o-lf); Ire r; Eur c; on ar, wa. Fl 4–8. **Ci Northern Dead-nettle**, *L. moluccellifolium*, is close to C, but is stouter; has bracts **not** clasping, lower **stalked**; calyx has **adpressed** hairs and long **spreading** teeth in fr. Scot f; Ire o; Eur f; on ar. Fl 5–9.

D White Dead-nettle, *L. album*, erect hairy tufted per, 20–60 cm; lvs and bracts 3–7 cm long, oval, cordate-based, pointed, coarse-toothed and nettle-shaped but **stingless**; fls in dense, well-spaced whorls; corollas (**Da**) 2 cm long, **white**, tiny side-lobes of lower lip with 2–3 small teeth; upper lip long, **hairy**; tube curved backwards in an arch and narrowed suddenly near base. Br Isles: GB vc (except N Scot r); Ire lc in E only; Eur c; on hbs, rds, wa. Fl 5–12. **Di Spotted Dead-nettle**, *L. maculatum*, has habit and size of D, but lvs often bear large white blotches, and fls (same size as in D) **pink-purple**, with only one tooth on side-lobes of lower lip. GB introd o; Eur native, E and N France to Netherlands f-lc; in open wds. Fl 4–10.

E Yellow Archangel, *Galeobdolon luteum* (*Lamiastrum galeobdolon*), ± hairy erect per, 20–60 cm tall, with **long creeping lfy runners**, especially after fl-time. Lvs 4–7 cm long, oval, pointed, rounded at base, stalked, coarsely-toothed. Corolla 2 cm long, **bright yellow** with red-brown streaks; lower lip ± equally three-lobed, mid-lobe **untoothed**. Br Isles: Eng, Wales, N to Yorks c, lf to N; Scot, Ire, vr; Eur c; in wds, hbs, on richer or calc soils. Fl 5–6.

F Red Hemp-nettle, *Galeopsis angustifolia*, erect ± branched downy ann; stem 10–60 cm tall, joints **not** swollen; lvs 1.5–8.0 cm × 0.5–0.8 cm, narrow-

314

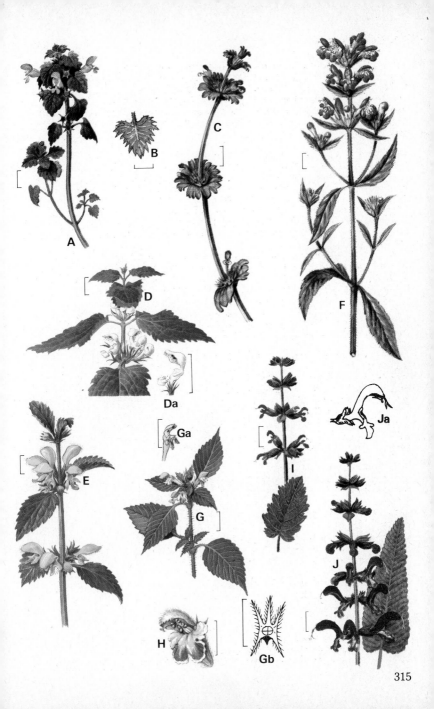

◀ lanceolate, pointed, narrowed to stalk, downy, with **few** small teeth. Calyx hairy, tubular; corolla 1.5–2.5 cm long, rosy-purple, white spots on lip, tube much **longer** than calyx-teeth. Br Isles: Eng lc in S, E, r to W, N; Wales o; Scot, Ire, vr; Eur c to S, r to N; on ar, shingle beaches. Fl 7–10.   **Fi** *G. ladanum*, differs in **oval, strong-toothed** lvs, **1–3 cm wide**; Br Isles vr or now abs; Eur o in ar, wa.   **Fii Downy Hemp-nettle**, *G. segetum*, resembles Fi, except that corollas 2–3 cm long, **pale yellow**, lvs and calyx **velvety-silky-hairy**. Eng vr or extinct; Eur r-o; on ar. Fl 7–8.

G   Common Hemp-nettle, *G. tetrahit*, erect branched ann; stem 10–80 cm, branched, bristly, with sticky hairs, joints swollen; lvs 2.5–10.0 cm long, oval, pointed, coarse-toothed, hairy, narrowed to stalk; calyx (**Gb**) bristly, teeth long, spine-pointed; corolla (**Ga**) 13–20 mm long, pink or white, with purple markings on lower lip; tube ± **equalling** calyx-teeth. Br Isles, Eur; vc on ar, hbs, wds, fens. Fl 7–9.

H   Large-flowered Hemp-nettle, *G. speciosa*, resembles G, but stouter, stem bristly throughout; corollas (**H**) 30 mm long, pale yellow with **large violet spot** on lower lip, tube **twice length** of calyx. Br Isles: GB, c to N, r to S; Ire lc to N, vr to S; Eur f-lc to N; on ar, wa. Fl 7–8.

I   Wild Clary, *Salvia horminoides*, downy, little-branched per, 30–80 cm tall, slightly sage-scented; rosette of root-lvs, each 4–12 cm long, oval-oblong, cordate, blunt, wrinkled, stalked, with **deep, jagged teeth**; stem-lvs few, stalkless above; upper stem-lvs and calyces purplish-blue. Infl of whorled spikes; calyx 7 mm, sticky-downy, two-lipped, with **long white hairs**, upper lip's teeth v short, converging, mid tooth **shorter**; corollas of 2 sizes, larger 7 mm long, violet-blue with 2 white spots on lower lip, upper lip ± arched; smaller corollas ± hidden in calyx, not opening. Br Isles vr (except S, E Eng lc); Eur: W, central France only, lc; on dry gslds, hbs, rds. Fl 5–8.   **Ii   Whorled Clary**, *S. verticillata*, is close to I, but upper calyx-lip has conspicuous straight ± **equal** teeth, and corolla has **hairs** inside; upper lvs stalked. Br Isles, Eur; introd, o on wa. Fl 6–8.

J   Meadow Clary, *S. pratensis*, downy per, 30–100 cm, sage-scented. Root-lvs 7–15 cm long, in a rosette, oval to oblong, blunt, long-stalked, cordate-based, wrinkled, **doubly**-toothed, but **not** deeply-cut as in I; upper lvs stalkless. Calyx 6.5 mm, **without** long white hairs; corollas (**Ja**) of larger fls 15–25 mm long, brilliant blue, upper lip **strongly** arched like a **sickle** and forming a hood; style **long-projecting** (in I style short). Eng: native in S, r, introd N to Lincs vr; Eur: France vc, to Denmark r; on calc gslds. Fl 6–7.

▶ **Calamints etc**

A   Wild Basil, *Clinopodium vulgare*, erect, hairy, weakly-scented per herb, 10–40 cm, little-branched; lvs 2–5 cm, oval, blunt, rounded at base, scarcely-toothed, stalked, v like those of Marjoram (**F**) but veins more impressed; fls in **dense** whorls in lf-axils; calyx tubular, curved, hairy, ± two-lipped, 13-veined, teeth of lower lip longer than of upper; corolla 15–20 mm, bright rosy-purple, two-lipped, hairless within. Br Isles: GB, vc to S and E, o to N, **abs N W** Scot; Ire SE only, vr; Eur, c to S, f to N; on calc scrub, hbs, gslds. Fl 7–9.

B   Common Calamint, *Calamintha ascendens*, erect, tufted hairy per herb, 30–60 cm; lf-stalks green, 1 cm; lvs 2–4 × 1–3 cm, oval, blunt, bases truncate, with adpressed hairs, teeth 5–8 on each side, shallow and blunt; infls in long spikes of distant whorls in lf-axils; whorls (**Ba**) ± **loose**, obviously branched; calyx (**Bb**) 6–8 mm long, tubular, **straight**, five-toothed, hairy on the 13 veins and within throat; calyx-teeth with **long hairs**, 2 teeth of lower lip **curved** up, much **longer** than **spreading** teeth of upper lip; corolla (**Bb, Bc**) 10–15 mm long, pinkish-white, with small purple spots on lower lip. Br Isles: Eng lf to S, r to N; Wales vlf; Ire o to S; **Scot abs**; Eur, France only, o to W and N, c to E; on hbs, wd-borders, scrub on dry or calc soils. Fl 7–9.

cont

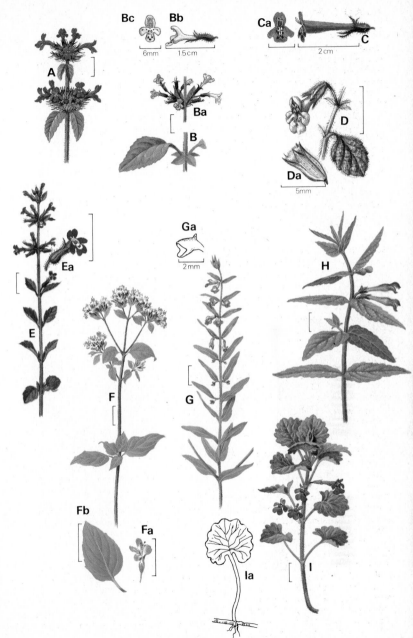

Bc

6mm

Bb

1.5 cm

Ca

C

2 cm

A

Ba

B

D

Da

5mm

Ea

E

Ga

2mm

H

F

G

Fb

Fa

Ia

I

◀

C Wood Calamint, *C. sylvatica*, close to B, but lvs 3.5 to 6.0 cm long; corolla **(C) 15–22 mm long, rosy-pink**, lower lip **(Ca)** 6 mm long × 8 mm wide, side-lobes shallow, purple blotches larger than in B. Eng: Isle of Wight only, vr; Eur: W and central France r (mts of E, S Eur); on hbs, scrub on calc soils. Fl 8–9.

D Lesser Calamint, *C. nepeta*, has tufted habit and height of B, but v aromatic-scented, stems and lvs **grey-downy**; lvs only 1–2 cm long, scarcely-toothed, lf-stalks 5 mm or less; infls looser, more branched than in B; calyx **(Da)** 4–6 mm, **all** teeth ± **straight**, ± of **equal** length, with **v short** hairs; corolla 10–15 mm pale **mauve**, scarcely spotted. Hairs **protrude** from calyx-throat in fr, not confined inside as in B and C. E and S E Eng only, o-lf; Eur: France r to W, f in centre and N; Belgium r; on hbs, rds, dry gslds on sand or gravel. Fl 7–9.

Di Balm, *Melissa officinalis*, erect branched tufted per herb with habit of B, C and D, but lvs **lemon-scented**, **deeply-toothed**, with strongly **impressed** veins; calyx two-lipped, bell-shaped, v hairy upper calyx-lip almost **flat** with 3 v **short, broad, triangular shortly-bristle-pointed** teeth; corolla two-lipped, **white**, 12 mm long, **curved** upwards. Br Isles: S Eng, Wales, S Ire f; Eur o, r to N; introd in hbs, wa. Fl 8–9.

E Basil Thyme, *Acinos arvensis*, creeping and ascending ann, to 15 cm tall; stems hairy; lvs 0.5–1.5 cm, oval-elliptical, ± hairless, shallow-toothed, bases wedge-shaped; infls much shorter than in B, C and D, whorls only 4–6 fld; calyx-tube **(Ea) curved**, with **pouched** base, hairy inside and out, 13-veined; corolla **(Ea)** 7–10 mm, violet with white blotches on lower lip. Br Isles: S, E Eng c, r to N; Wales, Scot, Ire, vr; Eur, c to S, lf N to Denmark; on ar, gslds, rocks on calc soils. Fl 5–9.

F Marjoram, *Origanum vulgare*, erect, tufted, sparsely downy per herb, 30–60 cm; lvs **(Fb)** 1.5–4.5 cm long, oval, stalked, ± untoothed, sweetly-scented. Fls in **dense, rounded**, terminal **panicles**; lower bracts like lvs, upper purple; calyx-tube hairy inside, with 5 short equal teeth; corolla **(Fa)** rose-purple, 6–8 mm, two-lipped, tube longer than calyx, stamens **protruding** from corolla. Br Isles: S of GB c to lva, r to N, **abs N, W Scot**; Ire f; Eur, France c, f-lc to N; on gslds, scrub, hbs on calc soils. Fl 7–9.

G Lesser Skullcap, *Scutellaria minor*, erect ± bushy, hairless per herb, 10–15 cm tall; lvs **1–3 cm** long, oval-lanceolate, cordate-based, pointed, untooth-ed; fls in pairs in lf-axils; calyx **(Ga)** two-lipped, lips **untoothed**, but with small **scale** on back of upper lip; corolla-tube **straight**, 6–10 mm long, 2–4 times length of calyx, two-lipped, **pink**, lower lip purple-spotted. Br Isles: S, W Eng, Wales, f-lc; E, N Eng r; Scot to W, only lc; Ire, S only, lc; Eur: W France c; N France, Belgium r, only near coast; on damp hths, paths in hthy wds. Fl 7–10.

H Skullcap, *S. galericulata*, resembles G in habit, but is taller; lvs 2–5 cm long, **shallow-toothed**; calyx as in G; corolla-tube 10–20 mm, slightly **curved, blue-violet**. Br Isles: GB c (except NE Scot r); Ire o; Eur c; on streamsides, fens, mds, wet wds. Fl 6–9. (The hybrid of G and H, resembling G in lf size, but with fls violet, occurs occasionally, especially with G.) **Hi Spear-leaved Skullcap**, *S. has-tifolia*, differs from H in lvs **arrow-head**-shaped, with spreading **pointed** lobes at bases, toothless above, ± purple beneath; fl-spikes ± **lfless**, with tiny bracts; fls blue-violet, more **curved** than in H. Eng introd, Norfolk only, vr; Eur, central France to Denmark, o-lf; in wds. Fl 6–9.

I Ground Ivy, *Glechoma hederacea*, ± softly hairy creeping and rooting per herb, with ascending lfy fl-stems 10–20 cm tall; lvs **(Ia)** 1–3 cm wide, **kidney-shaped, blunt-tipped** and -toothed, **long-stalked**; fls in 2–4-fld whorls in lf-axils; calyx tubular, ± two-lipped; corollas 15–20 mm, pale violet (or, rarely, pink) with purple spots on hanging, three-lobed lower lip; upper lip flat; tube straight, tapered to base. Br Isles, Eur vc (but NW Scot r); in wds on all except poorest soils, scrub, hbs, gslds. Fl 3–5.

KEY TO MINTS (*MENTHA*) (See also p 311)

1 Small creeping plants – lvs less than 1 cm wide, ± untoothed – calyx-throat hairy, teeth unequal.. **2**
  Larger, ± erect plants – lvs over 1.5 cm wide – calyx-throat hairless, teeth equal **3**
2 Tiny plants – stems creeping, thread-like – lvs rounded, 3–5 mm long – whorls 2–6-fld – o.............
  .... *M. requienii* (p 312 Fi)
  Larger plants – stems ascending, stouter (2 mm thick or more) – lvs oval, 5–15 mm long – whorls many-fld – r...*M. pulegium* (p 312 F)
3 Whorls of fls all in lf-axils, not forming heads, spaced out along stem – stem-tip lfy....................... **4**
  Whorls of fls close-set, forming terminal spikes or heads – stem-tip not lfy................................. **7**
4 Calyx bell-shaped... **5**
  Calyx tube-shaped.. **6**
5 Calyx-tube hairy, teeth triangular, short – stamens protruding from fl – scent peppery – c...............
  .... *M. arvensis* (p 311 B)
  Calyx-tube hairless except for teeth, teeth narrow, twice as long as broad – stamens not protruding – scent minty, aromatic – r ....*M. × gentilis* (p 311 Bii)
6 Calyx-tube hairy – stamens not protruding – scent peppery – c.............. *M. × verticillata* (p 311 Bi)
  Calyx-tube hairless except for teeth – stamens protruding – scent minty-aromatic – lvs ± reddish-purple..*M. × smithiana* (p 311 Biii)
7 Fls in heads ....*M. aquatica* (p 311 A)
  Fls in spikes... **8**
8 Lvs stalked, lanceolate – calyx-tube hairless – peppermint scent – o ....*M. × piperita* (p 312 Ei)
  Lvs ± stalkless **9**
9 Calyx-tube and fl-stalks hairless – lvs ± hairless, lanceolate, smooth – mint-sauce scented –
  f ....*M. spicata* (p 312 E)
  Calyx-tube and fl-stalks hairy – lvs hairy... **10**
10 Lvs lanceolate or narrow-oblong, not wrinkled, ± hairy – o .... *M. longifolia* (p 312 C)
   Lvs broad-oblong, oval, or round, wrinkled, v grey-hairy... **11**
11 Lvs 3–10 cm, bluntly-pointed, sharp-toothed – o-f ....*M. × niliaca* (p 312 D)
   Lvs 2–4 cm, rounded, bluntly-toothed – apple-scented – o....................*M. rotundifolia* (p 312 Ci)

Woundworts (*Stachys*) are rather like Dead-nettles, but have ± long, spike-like infls; calyx bell-shaped, with 5 narrow, equal, pointed but **not** spine-like teeth; corolla with concave (but not helmet-shaped) upper lip, and three-lobed lower lip with mid-lobe **oblong**, **much longer** than side-lobes, **convex**, with a pattern of streaks and dots on it (but **no** conical knobs at its base as in Hemp-nettles).

KEY TO WOUNDWORTS (INCLUDING BETONY, *BETONICA OFFICINALIS*)

1 Lvs mostly in basal **rosette** – stem-lvs **few**, in distant pairs – fls mostly in a dense, short, oblong, red-purple spike ....*Betonica officinalis* (p 320 D)
  Lvs mostly in pairs **up stem** – fls in ± **elongated** whorled spikes **2**
2 Fls creamy-yellow **3**
  Fls pink or purple **4**
3 Tufted per herb – lvs downy, wrinkled, dark-green – calyx-teeth broad, triangular, with hairless tips – **Br Isles abs** ....*Stachys recta* (p 320 Eii)
  Ann herb – lvs hairless – calyx-teeth narrow, hairy...*S. annua* (p 320 Ei)
4 Ann weed of ar, to 20 cm tall – corolla 7 mm long or less, little longer than calyx – fls pink, purple-streaked .... *S. arvensis* (p 320 E)
  Creeping or tufted per or bi herbs, 30–80 cm tall – corolla 12 mm long or more, nearly twice as long as calyx.. **5**
5 Stem and lvs felted with dense white silky hairs – vr .... *S. germanica* (p 320 Ci)
  Stem and lvs green, hairy, but not felted.. **6**
6 Bracts of fls nearly as long as calyx – whorls of fls dense – corollas pinkish-red with yellow eye – calyx-teeth ½ length of tube – plant tufted, no creeping stems – vr.................... *S. alpina* (p 320 C)
  Bracts of fls minute, bristle-like, at most ¼ length of calyx – whorls of fls looser – corollas pink or purple, no yellow eye – calyx-teeth more than **half length of tube** – creeping stems – c............... **7**
7 Lvs lanceolate-oblong, odourless, v short (5 mm)-stalked or stalkless above, bases rounded – fls pink-purple...*S. palustris* (p 320 B)
  Lvs oval, stalks all long (1.5–7.0 cm), cordate-based, with harsh smell; fls beetroot colour with white pattern ....*S. sylvatica* (p 320 A)

LABIATE FAMILY   *Labiatae*

Woundworts, Horehounds etc (see also key, p 319)

A   Hedge Woundwort, *Stachys sylvatica*, harsh-smelling bristly per, with creeping rhizome and erect stems, 30–80 cm; lvs **oval-cordate**, 4–9 cm long, with **stalks 1.5–7.0 cm**; infl a loose terminal spike; fl-bracts minute; calyx (**Aa**) with rigid triangular teeth; fls beetroot-red with white pattern on lip. Br Isles, Eur; vc in wds, hbs. Fl 7–9.

B   Marsh Woundwort, *S. palustris*, odourless bristly per, with creeping rhizome and erect stems, 30–80 cm, lvs **lanceolate or oblong**, 5–12 cm long, **short-stalked** (5 mm) below, **stalkless** above; fls pink-purple with white pattern on lip. Br Isles, Eur; c on streamsides, marshes. Fl 7–9.

C   Limestone Woundwort, *S. alpina*, softly hairy per with tufted stems 40–80 cm, none creeping; lvs **oblong-cordate**, 4–16 cm long, stalks 3–10 cm; infl a long interrupted spike of dense close whorls; fl-bracts linear, ± length of calyx; fls pinkish-red with **yellow eye**. GB: Glos, Denbigh vr; Eur: central, N France to Belgium r-lf; in open wds on calc soil. Fl 6–8. **Ci   Downy Woundwort**, *S. germanica*, per or bi herb, 30–80 cm; differs from other Woundworts in that whole plant **densely felted** with **white silky hairs**; fls in dense terminal spike; corolla 20 mm, pale rose-pink; bracts linear, ± length of calyx. Eng: now Oxon only, vr; Eur: France, Belgium r; on gslds, rds, hbs on calc soils, especially after disturbance. Fl 7–8.

D   Betony, *Betonica officinalis*, sparsely hairy per herb, 10–60 cm; basal **rosette** of long-stalked, oblong, cordate lvs, 3–7 cm long; stem-lvs in few distant pairs, upper sessile; all lvs coarsely-toothed and blunt; infl a short oblong whorled spike, lowest bracts like the lvs; calyx 7–9 mm, with bristle-pointed teeth; corolla 15 mm, red-purple, tube longer than calyx. Eng, Wales c (except E Anglia r); Scot, Ire vr; Eur: France f to Denmark vr; in open wds, hths, gslds on both calc and acid soils. Fl 6–9.

E   Field Woundwort, *Stachys arvensis*, ann with spreading and ascending hairy stems to 20 cm tall; lvs 1.5–3.0 cm, oval, blunt, toothed; infl whorls few-fld; corollas small (6–7 mm long) pale pink, purple-streaked. Br Isles: S of GB f-lc; Scot r; Ire lf; Eur f-lc; on ar on non-calc soils. Fl 4–11. **Ei   Annual Woundwort**, *S. annua*, erect ± hairless ann to 30 cm; lvs blunt, tapered to base; calyx-teeth narrow, hairy; fls creamy-yellow in long spikes. GB vr; Eur, o to S, r to N; on ar. Fl 6–10. ***Eii   Yellow Woundwort**, *S. recta*, also has creamy-yellow fls, but a tufted per herb 30–40 cm tall; lvs **downy, wrinkled, dark green**; calyx-teeth broad, triangular, **hairless**. Eur: France lf to S, E, r to N and in Belgium; on calc gslds, rocks. Fl 6–8.

F   Black Horehound, *Ballota nigra*, roughly hairy per herb, 40–80 cm tall, with **harsh** resinous smell; lvs oval-cordate, stalked, rough, coarse-toothed, 2–5 cm long; infls **spikes** of many-fld whorls in lf-axils; calyx (**Fa**) 1 cm long, **funnel-shaped**, with 10 veins and 5 short, oval, pointed, ± equal teeth; corolla two-lipped, **dull purple**, hairy all over, 12–18 mm long, with short tube and concave upper lip. Br Isles: GB, c N to SE Scot, r N Scot; Ire r; Eur c; on hbs, rds. Fl 6–10.

G   White Horehound, *Marrubium vulgare*, erect per herb 30–60 cm, stem **white-felted**; lvs 1.5–4.0 cm, rounded-oval, **wrinkled**, **blunt-toothed**, white-woolly beneath, grey-downy above, lower stalked; infl in dense whorls in lf-axils up stem; calyx (**Ga**) with **10** small, ± equal, **hooked** teeth; corolla 1.5 cm long, **white**, upper lip flat, two-lobed, hairless. S Eng, S Wales o; rest of Br Isles vr, decreasing; Eur: France o-lf, N to Denmark r; on rds, hbs, gslds, especially near coasts. Fl 6–10.

H   Catmint, *Nepeta cataria*, minty-scented per herb with grey-downy erect stems 40–80 cm; lvs 3–7 cm, oval-cordate, stalked, **coarse-toothed**, grey-woolly below, downy but greener above; infl an oblong head of dense whorls; calyx (**Ha**)

◀ downy, tubular, with 5 straight teeth; corolla 12 mm, two-lipped, tube **curved**, hairless, white with purple dots, upper lip flat, rounded. Eng, Wales, lf in S and E, rest of Br Isles vr; Eur: France f; N to Denmark vr; on hbs, rds on calc soil. Fl 7–9.

▶ ## Selfheals, Bugles, Germanders

Selfheals (*Prunella*) have fls in dense oblong heads, and a purplish calyx flattened above and below. **Bugles** (*Ajuga*) have corollas with three-lobed lower lip; upper lip of 2 unobvious small teeth only. **Germanders** (*Teucrium*) have corollas with five-lobed lower lip, and no upper lip; mid-lobe much larger than others.

A   Selfheal, *Prunella vulgaris*, sparsely downy per herb with creeping runners and erect fl-stems to 20 cm tall; lvs oval, ± untoothed, pointed, bases rounded or wedge-shaped; infl a dense oblong **head**, with hairy, ± purplish bracts; purplish calyx (**Aa**) with 3 teeth of flattened upper lip **v short**, bristle-pointed, the **outer 2 diverging**; lower lip with 2 long narrow teeth; edges of calyx-tube parallel (so outline **rectangular**); corolla 10–14 mm long, violet, rarely white or pink, upper lip v concave. Br Isles, Eur; vc in gslds, wds, wa. Fl 6–10.   **Ai   Cut-leaved Selfheal**, *P. laciniata*, close to A, but fls normally cream, upper lvs pinnate or pinnatifid, v downy; upper calyx-lip teeth **parallel**. Eng: S, SE only, r-o; Eur N to Belgium o-lf; in gslds on calc soils. Fl 6–10. Hybridizes with A where they meet.

*B   Large Selfheal, *P. grandiflora*, is close to A, but much stouter infls have **no lvs** at base; fls **20–25 mm long**, with deep violet corollas and larger purple calyx. Eur: E and S France lc; N to Denmark vr; on gslds, wd borders. Fl 6–9.

C   Bugle, *Ajuga reptans*, ± hairless per herb, with long lfy rooting runners; erect fl-stems 10–30 cm tall, ± hairy on 2 **opp** sides only; root-lvs in a rosette, 4–7 cm long, shiny, obovate, ± untoothed, narrowed into long stalks; stem-lvs in few pairs, shorter, unstalked above; infl a spike of whorls of fls in lf-axils; upper bracts **shorter** than fls, bluish-green; calyx bell-shaped, 5–6 mm, with short teeth; corolla blue (rarely pink or white), lower lip with white streaks. Br Isles, Eur; vc in damp wds, hbs, mds. Fl 4–6.   **Ci   Blue Bugle**, *A. genevensis*, close to C, but has **no runners** above gd, only rhizomes below gd; stem usually hairy all round; root-lvs 5–12 cm long, hairy, **toothed**, withering **before** fls open; fls as in C, but richer blue. Eng: Berks, Cornwall, introd; Eur: France c, to Belgium, W Germany r; on gslds, stony gd on calc soils. Fl 5–7.   **Cii   Pyramidal Bugle**, *A. pyramidalis*, has no runners above gd, and its stem hairy all round as in Ci; but stems tufted, not solitary, oval root-lvs form a dense rosette, infl dense, and its **lfy** bracts hairy and all **much longer** than fls, untoothed and **bright purple**. Br Isles: NW Eng r; N, W Scot o-lf; W Ire vl; Eur, Belgium to Denmark o; calc rocks. Fl 5–7.

D   Ground-pine, *A. chamaepitys*, hairy ann, often branched from base, 5–20 cm tall, with a pine-resin smell when bruised; stem-lvs each divided into 3 narrow, linear, blunt lobes like conifer lvs; fls 2 per whorl, shorter than lvs, corolla **yellow**, lower lip 5–7 mm, red-dotted. SE Eng, o-vlf and decreasing; Eur: France f; Belgium r; on ar, open stony gd on calc soils. Fl 5–9.

E   Wood Sage, *Teucrium scorodonia*, downy erect tufted per herb, 15–60 cm tall; lvs 3–7 cm, oval, cordate-based, wrinkled, blunt-toothed, pointed, stalked; infls loosely-branched lfless spikes; fls (**Ea**) in opp pairs; bracts v small; calyx with uppermost tooth rounded, broader than other teeth; corolla pale greenish-yellow, lip 5–6 mm long, stamens red. Br Isles vc (but E mid Eng, central Ire r); Eur vc to S, o to N; in dry wds, gslds, hths, dunes, not on v calc soils. Fl 7–9.

F   Cut-leaved Germander, *T. botrys*, erect, soft-hairy ann or bi, 10–30 cm; lvs 1.0–2.5 cm, **deeply pinnatifid** into ± lobed blunt segments 1–2 mm wide; fls (**Fa**) in 2–6-fld whorls up stem in lf-axils; calyx tubular, ± equally five-toothed, net-veined, pouched below; corolla **bright pink**, lip 8 mm long. SE Eng,

LABIATE FAMILY   *Labiatae*

◄ SE from Cotswolds, vr; Eur: N to S Belgium f-lc; on ar, open stony gslds on calc soils. Fl 7–9.

G Water Germander, *T. scordium*, softly hairy per with runners, and erect fl-stems to 40 cm; lvs 1–5 cm, oblong, grey-green, **stalkless**, bases rounded, coarse-toothed; side-veins strong. Fls 2–6 together in distant whorls up stem, in axils of lvs much **longer** than fls. Corolla **pink**, lip to 10 mm long. Eng: N Devon, E Anglia, vr; Ire, by R Shannon and in Clare vlf; Eur: France o-lf; N to Denmark r, decreasing; in wet dune-hollows, swamps. Fl 7–10.

H Wall Germander, *T. chamaedrys*, spreading and ascending, ± hairy, tufted per herb, woody at base; fl-stems 10–20 cm tall. Lvs oval, blunt, narrowed to short stalk, shiny dark green, with deep but rounded teeth; infls 5–10 cm, spike-like, upper bracts shorter than fls; calyx with 5 ± equal teeth; corolla deep pinkish-purple, lip 8 mm long. GB: Eng, Sussex coast, probably native in chk gsld, vr; introd, vr on old walls elsewhere; Eur: France f-la; Belgium r; on calc gslds, rocks. Fl 6–9.

*I Mountain Germander, *T. montanum*, spreading dwarf shrub, fl-shoots to 12 cm tall; lvs linear, lanceolate, untoothed, grey-green above, **white** below, edges rolled under; fls in short rounded heads; corolla **cream-yellow**, lip 7 mm long. Eur: France f-la in centre and E, r to W and N; Belgium vr; on calc gslds, rocks. Fl 5–8.

BORAGE FAMILY   *Boraginaceae*

A family of mostly hairy- or bristly-stemmed and -lvd herbs, rarely (*Mertensia*, p 328) hairless, grey-green. Lvs alt, undivided, without stipules; fls in curved or forked cymes. Calyx five-toothed, corolla five-lobed, wheel-, funnel- or bell-shaped, usually regular (with unequal lobes in *Echium*, p 326); stamens 5, attached to corolla-tube; the single style arises from **between** the 4 lobes of the deeply divided ovary (as in Labiate family). Fr of 4 separating one-seeded **nutlets**. The family differs from Labiates in its **alt** (not opp) lvs, the fls in mostly **terminal**, **branched** infls (not in tight whorls in lf-axils) and the usually regular (not two-lipped) corollas. Fls often pink in bud, opening blue; sometimes yellow, purple or white. (Members of Figwort family are not bristly, have two-lipped fls, and fr an oval or rounded capsule with style **on fr-tip**).

KEY TO BORAGE FAMILY

1 Plant **hairless**, waxy-blue or grey-green – N Br Isles, N Eur – r on seashores ....
            Mertensia maritima (p 328 M)
   Plant hairy or bristly **2**
2 Nutlets of fr with **hooked bristles** – calyx-lobes spreading – fls red-purple ..... *Cynoglossum* (p 326)
   Nutlets of fr **without** bristles – calyx-lobes erect, hiding fr... **3**
3 Stamens (some, at least) protruding from corolla **4**
   Stamens all enclosed inside corolla-tube **6**
4 Corolla funnel-shaped, its lobes **unequal**, with definite lip – stamens **spreading** ..... *Echium* (p 326)
   Corolla wheel-shaped, its lobes all **equal**, ± turned back – stamens protruding together in a close column, as in Bittersweet (p 296)... **5**
5 Fls blue – stamens hairless – anthers 8–10 times as long as wide.............................*Borago* (p 330)
   Fls purple – stamens hairy – anthers 2–3 times as long as wide .... *Trachystemon* (p 330)
6 Corolla **tube-like** or **narrow bell-shaped**, hanging down, with 5 **v small** lobes 1–2 mm long..........
            Symphytum (p 328)
   Corolla not tube-like, ± erect, with 5 larger **spreading** lobes forming a funnel or saucer-shape **7**
7 Calyx-lobes **broad, toothed**, enlarging in fr to form a two-lipped, flattened, **wavy-toothed** envelope enclosing fr – prostrate plant – r .... *Asperugo procumbens* (p 326 G)
   Calyx-lobes **narrow**, untoothed, not enlarging in fr... **8**
8 Corolla funnel-shaped, with lengthwise hairy folds in its throat.. **9**
   Corolla wheel-shaped, throat mouth closed by ring of 5 tiny rounded scales ....:......................... **10**

9 Calyx bell-like, divided at most only halfway down into 5 lobes – nutlets brown – lvs usually white-spotted ....*Pulmonaria* (p 330)

Calyx divided nearly to base into 5 v narrow long teeth – nutlets hard, whitish, shiny like porcelain...*Lithospermum* (p 328)

10 Corolla-tube closed by 5 **hairless** flat scales at mouth – fls blue, with **yellow** eye – plant downy or softly hairy **11**

Corolla-tube closed by 5 **hairy** oblong scales at mouth – fls blue or purple, with **white** eye – plant bristly...**12**

11 All lvs stalked, oval-cordate, slightly downy only ....*Omphalodes verna* (p 325 Aiii)

Upper lvs stalkless, oblong, hairy..*Myosotis* (p 325, Key p 330)

12 Lvs oval – corolla-tube straight, shorter than its lobes..*Pentaglottis* (p 326)

Lvs narrow-oblong – corolla-tube curved, as long as its lobes..................................*Anchusa* (p 326)

▶

Forget-me-nots etc

Forget-me-nots (*Myosotis*) form a distinctive group, with ± oblong downy lvs, wheel-shaped blue corollas with yellow eye, the throat closed by hairless, short, transverse scales. To name the spp use the Key on p 330, and the illustrations of spp A–F.

A Water Forget-me-not, *Myosotis scorpioides*, creeping per, with runners, 15–30 cm tall; stem with hairs spreading below, adpressed above and on calyx; lvs oblong, 3–5 times as long as wide; fls (**Aa**) bright blue, 8–10 mm wide; calyx-teeth **short**, triangular, ⅓ **length of calyx-tube**; fr-stalks once or twice length of calyx. Br Isles, Eur; c in marshes, ponds, streamsides. Fl 5–9. **Ai Creeping Forget-me-not**, *M. secunda*, like A in runners and hair arrangement; corollas 6–8 mm wide, with slightly notched lobes; calyx-teeth **long, pointed, half length of calyx-tube**; fr-stalks **3–5 times** length of calyx; **lfy** bracts on lower part of infl. Br Isles, c in N, W, lf in SE, vr in E; W Eur (N Eur); in acid marshes and bogs. Fl 5–8. **Aii Pale Forget-me-not**, *M. brevifolia* (*M. stolonifera*), has fls (5 mm wide) smaller than in A, blunt, **oval** lvs twice as long as wide, hairs adpressed on **whole** stem and calyx, runners from all lower lf-axils with short, **spoon-shaped** lvs. N Eng, S Scot vlf; Eur abs; in wet places in mts. Fl 6–8. **Aiii Blue-eyed-Mary**, *Omphalodes verna*, has fls (10 mm wide) v like those of A, but lvs **broad, rounded, cordate**, pointed at tips, 3–4 cm long × 3 cm wide, on **long** (to 10 cm) **stalks**; infls few-fld, loose; corolla has **white** eye; fr-stalks **bent** down, with **grooved**, hairy margins. GB, Eur; introd (SE Eur) in wds near houses. Fl 3–5.

B Tufted Forget-me-not, *M. caespitosa*, has **no** runners; stem, calyx (**Bb**) with **adpressed hairs** throughout; calyx-teeth **long, pointed**; corollas (**Ba**) **less than 4 mm wide**, with rounded lobes. Br Isles, Eur; c in A's habitats. Fl 5–8. ***Bi Jersey Forget-me-not**, *M. sicula*, differs from B in almost **hairless** calyx with **blunt** teeth, and cup-shaped corolla 2–3 mm wide. Jersey, W France; vl in dune hollows. Fl 4–6.

C Wood Forget-me-not, *M. sylvatica*, downy per, 15–40 cm tall; no rooting runners; hairs on stem **spreading**, on calyx (**Ca**) **stiffly curled** or **hooked**; corollas (**C**) 6–10 mm wide, pale blue, flat; fr-stalks 1½–2 times length of calyx; infl in fr not longer than lfy part of stem; nutlets **brown**. Br Isles: E side of GB lf-la; **W side and in Ire abs**; N Scot r; Eur f-lc; in wds on richer soils, also as escape. Fl 4–8. **Ci Alpine Forget-me-not**, *M. alpestris*, close to C, but usually much shorter; lower lvs **long-stalked**; fr-stalks **as long as** calyx; fls 6–10 mm wide; nutlets **black**; fls fragrant, especially in evening. Teesdale, Scot Highlands vr but la; on calc mt rocks (mts of central Eur). Fl 7–9.

D Field Forget-me-not, *M. arvensis*, close to C, except that corolla (**D**) is only up to 5 mm wide, cup-shaped, with tube **shorter** (not as long or longer) than calyx.

Br Isles, Eur; vc in dry wds, ar, hbs, rds, dunes. Fl 4–9.

E Changing Forget-me-not, *M. discolor*, 8–20 cm tall; stem with hairs **spreading** below, addressed above; long lfless infls exceed lfy part of stem. Tiny fls, 2 mm wide, have curly-haired calyx **longer** than fl-stalk; fls (**Ea**) open **yellow**, then turn blue; corolla-tube **twice length** of calyx; calyx-teeth **erect** in fr. Br Isles, Eur; c in dry open sandy gslds. Fl 5–6.

F Early Forget-me-not, *M. ramosissima*, small slender ann; resembles E in hair patterns and fl-size etc, but is only 2–15 cm tall (rarely more); corollas (**Fa**) **always blue**, tube **shorter** than calyx. In fr calyx-teeth **spreading**, and infl **much** longer than lfy part of stem. GB c (except N, W Scot r); Ire o; Eur c; on dry open gsld, especially on sand. Fl 4–6.   ***Fi** *M. stricta* is close to F, but infl in fr is compact, short, **lfy** below, with fr-stalks adpressed to stem; **curled** hairs on stem and lvs as well as on calyx. Eur f-lc; on sandy gd, especially near coasts. Fl 5–6.

G Madwort, *Asperugo procumbens*, ± creeping bristly ann, 15–60 cm long; stems angled; lvs (**G**) oval-oblong, blunt, 2–7 cm long, lower stalked, upper stalkless, opp or whorled. Fls (**Ga**) 3 mm wide, purple becoming blue, with scaly white eye; calyx, deeply five-lobed at first, in fr (**Gb**) forms **flattened, two-lipped, enlarged envelope** with **veined, triangular, toothed** lobes; nutlets warted. Eng r in wa, ar; Eur o-lf on ar, wa, beaches. Fl 5–7.

H Hound's-tongue, *Cynoglossum officinale*, erect greyish-downy bi, 30–60 cm tall, smelling of **mice**; root-lvs 10–25 cm, stalked, elliptical, pointed; upper lvs stalkless, lanceolate. Infl a long forked cyme; calyx-lobes to 7 mm long, oblong, blunt, **outspread** in fr. Corollas to 1 cm across, widely funnel-shaped, equally five-lobed, dull purplish-red; fr (**Ha**) of 4 flattened oval nutlets, each 5–6 mm wide, covered with **hooked bristles**, and with thick, **raised border**. Br Isles: Eng, Wales, c to E and SE, o to W; Scot, Ire, r and eastern; Eur f-c; on gslds, wd edges on light sandy or calc soils, dunes. Fl 6–8.

I Green Hound's-tongue, *C. germanicum*, differs from H in **glossy dark green** lvs (**I**), almost **hairless above**, fls only 5–6 mm wide, and nutlets (**Ia**) **without thickened border**, but with longer bristles at edge. SE, S, mid Eng, vr; Eur: central, N France, Belgium r; in wds, hbs, on calc soil. Fl 5–7.

J Bugloss, *Anchusa (Lycopsis) arvensis*, erect, v bristly ann, 15–40 cm tall; bristles with bulbous bases; lvs to 15 cm, lanceolate-oblong, wavy-edged, ± blunt, toothed, lower stalked, upper clasping. Infl often forked, elongating, with lfy bracts; calyx-teeth v narrow; corollas (**Ja**) 5–6 cm wide, blue, tube **doubly-bent**, throat closed by 5 **hairy** scales; nutlets 4 mm wide, netted. Br Isles: GB c, but r in mts; Ire f in E; Eur c; on sandy ar, wa, gsld, dunes. Fl 6–9.   **Ji Alkanet**, *Anchusa officinalis*, has lvs oval-lanceolate, bracts **not** wavy-edged; blue-purple fls, to 10 mm wide, with corolla-tubes straight, in **long, curved** cymes. Br Isles o; Eur o-lf; gdn escape in wa, sandy gsld, ar. Fl 6–7.

K Green Alkanet, *Pentaglottis sempervirens*, erect bristly per, 30–60 cm tall; lvs **oval, untoothed**, flat, lower stalked, to 20 cm long. Infls dense, v bristly, long-stalked, each with a lfy bract below it; calyx-teeth v narrow; corollas bright blue, 10 mm wide, wheel-shaped with **short** tube, throat closed by 5 **downy** white scales. Nutlets netted on surfaces. Br Isles (introd): GB f-lc; Ire o; Eur o; in hbs, wa. Fl 4–7.

L Viper's-bugloss, *Echium vulgare*, bristly bi; erect stem to 80 cm, dotted with **red**-based bristles; rosette of stalked, strap-shaped root-lvs to 15 cm long, with strong mid vein but no side veins **apparent**; stem-lvs shorter, stalkless, **rounded** at bases. Fls in **curved** cyme clusters in bract-axils up stem, forming a large panicle; buds pink, resembling clusters of tiny grapes; calyx-teeth narrow, short; corollas (**La**) bright blue, **funnel-shaped** with **unequal** lobes; 5 stamens, 4 of them long and protruding from fl; nutlets rough. Br Isles: GB c to S, E; N Scot r; Ire r, to E only; Eur c; on dry gslds on sand and chk, dunes, cliffs. Fl 6–9.   **Li Purple Viper's-bugloss**, *E. lycopsis*, is similar to L, but **softly** hairy, not bristly; root-lvs **oval**, with

326

Aa

Ba

C

Ca

D

7mm

E

2mm

Ea

A

F

2mm

Fa

B

Bb 5mm

Gb

Ga 3mm

G

H

Ha

K

Ia

I

J

Ja 5mm

L

La

M

◀ side veins **obvious**; stem-lvs with **cordate** bases; corollas red, then **purplish**-blue; only 2 of stamens long-protruding. Cornwall r; Eur, W France o; on ocean cliffs, dunes. Fl 6–8.

M Oysterplant, *Mertensia maritima*, prostrate per herb; stem (30–60 cm) and lvs **blue-grey**, **hairless**, fleshy; lvs oval, lower stalked, uppersides dotted. Infls terminal, branched; fls long- (5–10-mm) stalked; calyx-lobes **oval**; corollas 6 mm wide, bell-shaped, pink, then pale blue, no scales in throat, but with 5 folds. Br Isles: coasts of NW Eng, W and N Scot, N Ire, r (to lf in N); Eur: Denmark N r and vl; on shingly, sandy shores. Fl 6–8.

▶ **Gromwells, Comfreys, Lungworts** etc

A Common Gromwell, *Lithospermum officinale*, erect downy per to 60 cm, with alt lanceolate, **pointed**, **stalkless** lvs to 7 cm long up the stem, their side veins **conspicuous**; infls cymes, in lf-axils and terminal, forming a **V-shaped elongated spray** in fr (**Ac**); calyx (**Aa**) with 5 narrow teeth; corollas creamy-yellow, wheel-shaped, with a short tube, 3–4 mm wide, throat with 5 hairy folds in it; nutlets (**Ab**) oval, 3 mm long, **hard**, **white**, shiny like porcelain. Eng, Wales f-lc in S, E; Scot, Ire r; Eur c; in open wds, scrub, hbs on calc soils. Fl 6–7.

B Field Gromwell, *L. arvense*, erect downy ann to 50 cm, differing from A in little-branched stem, lower lvs **blunt**, **stalked**, with side veins **not** obvious, and upper lvs strap-shaped; nutlets (**Ba**, **Bb**) hard, but conical, **grey-brown**, **warty**. Br Isles r (but S, E Eng f-lc); Eur f; on ar. Fl 5–7.

C Purple Gromwell, *L. purpurocoeruleum*, creeping downy per; erect fl-stems to 60 cm tall; long, arching and rooting, lfy runners up to 90 cm long; lvs stalkless, narrow-lanceolate, dark green and rough above, pointed, to 7 cm long, side veins not obvious. Infls terminal forked lfy cymes; calyx-teeth (**Cb**) to 10 mm, narrow; corollas (**Ca**) red-purple, then bright **deep blue**, 12–15 mm across, funnel-shaped, with white scales in throat, twice length of calyx. Nutlets hard, white, shiny, as in A. SW Eng, Wales r and l; Eur: central France to Luxembourg, Germany, o-lf; in open wds, scrub on calc soils. Fl 4–6.

D Common Comfrey, *Symphytum officinale*, erect bristly per to 1 m tall; stem **strongly winged**; root-lvs stalked, oval-lanceolate, 15–25 cm long, soft-hairy; upper lvs narrower, stalkless, their bases running down stem and clothed with long, down-pointing, tapering hairs. Infl of forked, coiled cymes; calyx-teeth long (4 mm), **pointed**, narrow, twice length of tube; corollas tubular to narrow bell-shaped, 15 mm long, with short (2 mm) triangular bent-back teeth, white or pink; 5 narrow scales inside corolla-tube; nutlets black, shiny. Br Isles: GB, N to mid Scot c; N Scot, Ire o; Eur c; by riversides, in marshes. Fl 5–6. **Di Rough Comfrey**, *S. asperum*, has bristles on stem **hooked**, stem **not winged**; **upper** as well as lower lvs **stalked**, with **swollen-based** bristles; calyx shorter, with **blunt** teeth 2 mm long; corollas shorter, pink, then clear blue. GB, Eur introd (Caucasus); c in wa. Fl 6–7. **Dii Tuberous Comfrey**, *S. tuberosum*, differs from D in tuberous rhizomes, little-branched **unwinged** stems, **mid** lvs of stem longest and stalked; calyx-lobes 3 times length of tube; fls **yellow**. Br Isles: Scot native, c in S and E in wds, hbs; introd on hbs etc in rest of GB, and Ire, r-o; Eur: Germany to France, native o in wds. Fl 5–7. **Diii White Comfrey**, *S. orientale*, smaller than D; stems unwinged; lvs **softly** downy; calyx-teeth only half length of tube; fls always white; nutlets warty brown. SE Br Isles r-lc; Eur o; introd in hbs, wa. Fl 4–5.

E Russian Comfrey, *S. × uplandicum*, hybrid of D and Di, now most c sp; stems v rough, only narrowly ± winged, bristly, upper lvs forming **short** wings only down stem; corollas purplish-blue, variable. Br Isles, Eur; f-c on rds, hbs, wa, wds (unlike D, not usually by water). Fl 6–8.

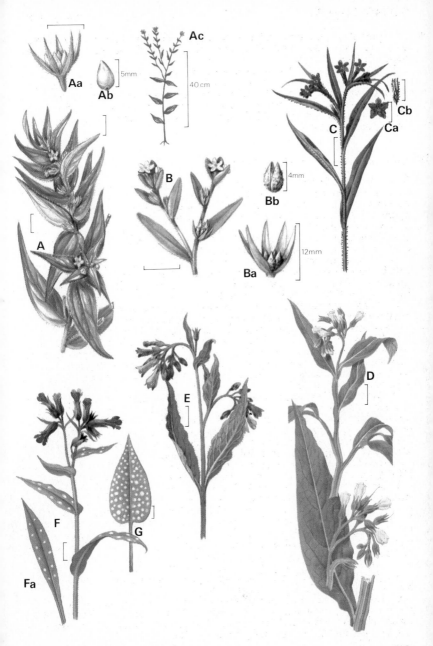

Aa

Ab 5mm

Ac 40 cm

A

B

Ba 12mm

Bb 4mm

C

Ca

Cb

D

E

F

Fa

G

329

◀ **F Narrow-leaved Lungwort**, *Pulmonaria longifolia*, erect downy per, 20–30 cm tall; root-lvs (**Fa**) lanceolate, 10–20 cm, pointed, tapered to bases, white-spotted; stem-lvs broader, clasping. Infls short, in terminal cymes; calyx bell-shaped, teeth half length of tube, narrow; corollas 5–6 mm wide, pink then deep blue, funnel-shaped, with tufts of hairs alt with stamens in throat. Nutlets oval, **flattened**, shiny. Eng: E Dorset, SW Hants, Is of Wight, vlc; Eur, central France to Denmark, o-lc; in wds on clay or loam soils. Fl 4–5.

G Lungwort, *P. officinalis*, has lvs normally white-spotted as in F (but sometimes unspotted in Eur), **oval-cordate**, **pointed**, **long-stalked**; calyx-teeth only ⅓–¼ times length of more cylindrical calyx-tube; corollas 10 mm wide; nutlets oval, **rounded**. GB introd o-r; Eur o-lf especially to N; in wds, hbs, on chk, clay. Fl 4–5. **Gi Borage**, *Borago officinalis*, bristly erect ann to 60 cm tall; lower lvs oval, stalked, upper narrower, wavy-edged, stalkless. Fls in loose branched infls, bright blue, 20–25 mm wide; petals spreading, narrow; stamens hairless, in a purple column as in Bittersweet (p 296). Br Isles, Eur; o introd (S Eur) in wa. Fl 6–8. **Gii Abraham-Isaac-Jacob**, *Trachystemon orientalis*, v similar to Gi, but per, with root-lvs large, **cordate**, **blunt**, **long-stalked**, blades to 30 cm long (10–20 cm in Gi); fls as in Gi, but purple, with **hairy** stamens; anthers only 2–3 times as long as wide (8–10 times in Gi). Eng, Eur; o introd (SE Eur) in wds. Fl 4–5.

KEY TO FORGET-ME-NOTS (*MYOSOTIS*)

1 Hairs on calyx-tube **adpressed** (or almost abs)..**2**
   Hairs (or, at least, some) on calyx-tube **stiff**, **hooked** or **curled** **6**
2 Corollas of the largest fls 5 mm or more wide – corolla-lobes shallow-notched – creeping runners **3**
   Corollas of the largest fls less than 4 mm wide – corolla-lobes rounded – no creeping runners.......**5**
3 Lvs mostly 3–5 times as long as wide – hairs on lower stem spreading – fls bright blue...................**4**
   Lvs rarely over twice as long as wide, oval, blunt – hairs on lower stem adpressed – fls v pale blue, 5 mm wide – runners with short **spoon-shaped** lvs from all lower lf-axils – N Eng, S Scot – in wet places in mts – vlf...*M. brevifolia* (p 325 Aii)
4 Fr-stalks only 1–2 times length of calyx – calyx-teeth **short**, **triangular**, only ⅓ length of calyx-tube – corollas 8–10 mm wide – in wet places..*M. scorpioides* (p 325 A)
   Fr-stalks 3–5 times length of calyx – calyx-teeth **long**, **narrow**, ½ or more length of calyx-tube – corolla 6–8 mm wide – in acid wet places – o ....*M. secunda* (p 325 Ai)
5 Calyx with many adpressed hairs, teeth pointed – corolla flat – in wet places – c ....
   ....*M. caespitosa* (p 325 B)
   Calyx almost hairless, teeth blunt – corolla cup-like – Jersey, W France – **r** .... *M. sicula* (p 325 Bi)
6 Fr-stalks equal to or longer than calyx – tall (8–40 cm) plants – hairs spreading on stem throughout – infl in fr not longer than lfy part of stem **7**
   Fr-stalks shorter than calyx – small (2–15 cm) plants of open dry gd – hairs on stem spreading below, adpressed above – fls only 2 mm wide **9**
7 Corolla not more than 5 mm across, cup-shaped – corolla-tube shorter than calyx – c ....
   ....*M. arvensis* (p 325 D)
   Corolla 6–10 mm across, flat..**8**
8 Fr-stalks equal to calyx – nutlets black – lowest lvs long-stalked – fls fragrant in evening – in mts – vr ....*M. alpestris* (p 325 Ci)
   Fr-stalks 1½–2 times length of calyx – nutlets brown – lowest lvs scarcely stalked – fls unscented – in wds – la ....*M. sylvatica* (p 325 C)
9 Infl compact in fr, lfy below – fr-stalks adpressed to infl-stalk – **Br Isles abs**....... *M. stricta* (p 326 Fi)
   Infl in fr lfless, longer than lfy lower part of stem – fr-stalks spreading out from infl-stalk...............**10**
10 Open corolla yellow, then blue – corolla-tube twice length of calyx – calyx-teeth **erect** in fr ....
   ....*M. discolor* (p 326 E)
   Open corolla always blue – corolla-tube **shorter** than calyx – calyx-teeth **spreading** in fr ....
   ....*M. ramosissima* (p 326 F)

BROOMRAPE FAMILY *Orobanchaceae*

A family of total parasites on roots of various plants; lvs reduced to scales, no chlorophyll; fls in spikes, with two-lipped corollas, as in Figwort family; stamens 4, ovary one-celled (two-celled in Figwort Family), with a single style and two-lobed stigma; fr a capsule with v many tiny seeds; stems and fls usually similarly coloured. **Toothworts** (*Lathraea*) have creeping scaly rhizomes, an equally four-lobed calyx, and a ± tubular corolla with non-spreading, parallel lips. **Broomrapes** (*Orobanche*) have no rhizomes, two-lipped calyx, two-lipped corolla with spreading lips, lower three-lobed, upper ± two-lobed. Broomrapes are not easy to name; important points are: (1) the sp of plant host (2) distribution of hairs and sticky glands on stamen-stalks or filaments (3) colour and degree of separation or joining of the 2 stigma-lobes (4) whether corolla has a straight or curved back. (Most fl 6–7; H, below, fl 5–6.)

*(Not illustrated) **Germander Broomrape**, *Orobanche teucrii*, grows on Germanders (*Teucrium*) in France on chk gslds; like an orange-red D, but fls rich red-brown inside, orange-yellow outside; corollas sharply bent halfway along tube; filaments hairy in lower half, hairs and glands above; stigma-lobes reddish-brown, separated.

BROOMRAPE FAMILY

Orobanchaceae

KEY TO BROOMRAPE FAMILY

(small pictures on right of p 333 show stamens to right and stigmas to left)

1 Parasitic on hazel, elm, other trees – rhizome present – calyx with 4 equal lobes – corolla with lips parallel, not spreading..*Lathraea* **K** below
  Parasitic on herbs, or shrubs of pea family – no rhizome – calyx two-lipped – corolla with spreading upper and lower lips...*Orobanche* **2**
2 Each fl of spike with 3 bracts below it (**apart** from calyx-lobes) – fls dull purplish-blue – 14–40 cm tall – on yarrow – S Eng, W France N to Denmark – r...............**Yarrow Broomrape**, *O. purpurea* **J**
  Each fl of spike has single bract only...**3**
3 Stigma-lobes yellow...**4**
  Stigma-lobes purple, red, or brown (not yellow)...**6**
4 Robust plants, 50–80 cm – corollas long, 18–25 mm, yellowish **5**
  Smaller plants, 10–40 cm – corollas short, 10–20 mm, cream, veined with purple – filaments (**Ib**) ± hairless below, with glands above – stigma-lobes (**Ia**) partly joined – on ivy – S Eng, Wales, Ire, o-lc – Eur N to Belgium o-lc .... **Ivy Broomrape**, *O. hederae* **I**
5 Upper corolla-lip untoothed – filaments (**Fb**), hairless below, attached at base of corolla-tube, few glands above – stigmas (**Fa**) with lobes yellow, separate – on broom and gorse – Eng, Ire, Eur, r and decreasing everywhere .... **Greater Broomrape**, *O. rapum-genistae* **F**
  Upper corolla-lip (**Ec**) finely-toothed; stamens hairy below, attached halfway up corolla-tube, with glands throughout (**Eb**) – stigmas (**Ea**) yellow, with lobes touching – on Greater Knapweed – S, E Eng, f-lc – France f-lc – on calc soils .... **Knapweed Broomrape**, *O. elatior* **E**
6 Stem and corolla purplish-red – corolla 15–20 mm long – filaments (**Db**) ± hairy below, with glands above – stigma-lobes touching, reddish (**Da**) – plant 8–25 cm tall – on thyme – Cornwall, W Scot, Ire r – Eur: France, Belgium o – on rocky slopes especially by sea ....
                                                          Thyme Broomrape, *O. alba* **D**
  Stem and corolla not purplish-red, but yellow, brown, purplish or cream – not on thyme or other member of labiate family...**7**
7 Corolla large, 20–30 mm long, tube bell-shaped, back curved – lobes of lower lip ± equal, crisped, toothed, pink or creamy yellow – deliciously clove-scented – filaments (**Hb**) hairy below, with glands above – stigma-lobes (**Ha**) well separated, purple – plant 15–40 cm tall – on bedstraw – Kent coast – r and l – Eur: France, Belgium lf – on dunes, chk gsld.................................
                                         Bedstraw Broomrape, *O. caryophyllacea* **H**
  Corolla smaller, 10–20 mm long, not strongly scented **8**
8 Stem purple, 10–50 cm – calyx shorter than corolla-tube – lower corolla-lip with mid-lobe biggest, kidney-shaped, yellow veined with purple – stamens (**Cb**) hairy below, hairless above – stigma-lobes (**Ca**) partially joined, purple – on carrot, less often sea holly – S coast Eng, W France r – by sea .... **Carrot Broomrape**, *O. maritima* **C**
  Stem yellow to white, sometimes purple-flushed – calyx equalling corolla-tube – lower lip of corolla with 3 equal lobes...**9**
9 Corolla 10–18 mm, yellowish, purple-veined, its back arched in smooth curve, upper lip notched, lower lip rounded – stem 10–50 cm, yellowish, ± purple-flushed – stamens (**Ab**) ± hairless except at base – stigma-lobes (**Aa**) separated, purple – on pea family, especially on crops of clovers, rarely on hawkbits – S half Br Isles vc – in N r-abs – Eur N to Belgium c................
                                          Common Broomrape, *O. minor* **A**
  Corolla 15–22 mm, its back sharply curved at base, straight above..**10**
10 Corolla with pale glands, upper lip unnotched, lower lip squarish – stem and corollas ivory to creamy yellow – filaments (**Bb**) v hairy below, ± hairless above – stigma-lobes (**Ba**) just touching, purple – on Hawkweed Oxtongue – S Eng, especially S coast vr – Eur N to Denmark r...........
                                          Oxtongue Broomrape, *O. picridis* **B**
  Corolla with dark purplish glands – stem yellow to purple – corollas yellow with purple margins, upper lip notched, lower lip squarish – stamens (**Gb**) attached near base of corolla-tube, with a few hairs and a few glands above – stigma-lobes (**Ga**) touching, dark purple – on thistles – Yorks vr – Eur N to Denmark r – in gslds .... **Thistle Broomrape**, *O. reticulata* **G**

K **Toothwort**, *Lathraea squamaria*, has stout stem, white or pale pink, 8–30 cm; fls in one-sided spike with scaly bracts; calyx sticky-hairy, tubular below, yellowish-white; corolla pink, nearly tubular, little longer than calyx. Parasitic mostly on hazel and elm. GB N to mid Scot o-lf; E Ire r; Eur f-lc; in wds on richer or calc soils. Fl 4–5.

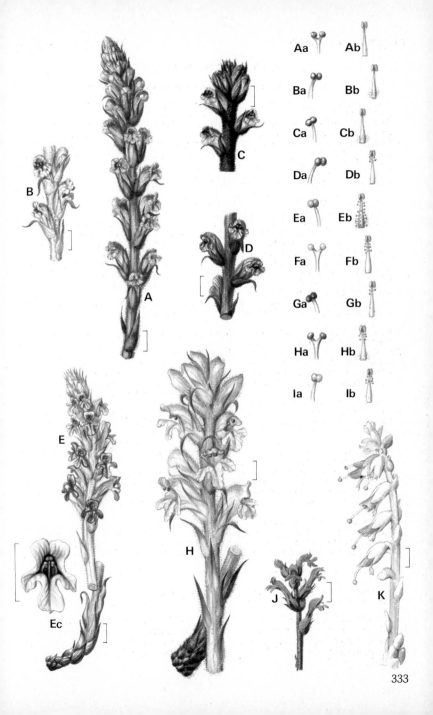

BUTTERWORT FAMILY

Lentibulariaceae

Butterworts, Bladderworts

A small family of per insect-catching herbs of fresh water or wet places, related to Figwort family. Calyx five-lobed, corolla two-lipped, spurred, five-lobed; stamens 2, attached to corolla; carpels 2, forming one-celled fr-capsule with many tiny seeds. They over-winter either as rootless buds, or as lf-rosettes (**C**). **Butterworts** (*Pinguicula*) have undivided lvs in basal rosettes; fls solitary on long erect lfless stalks; sticky glands all over the lf-surfaces trap insects, whose soft parts are then digested. **Bladderworts** (*Utricularia*) are rootless aquatic plants with long, lfy floating stems. Lvs deeply divided into v narrow green segments, of which some or all bear tiny bladders that trap small animals by a vacuum mechanism and digest their soft parts for nitrogen compounds. Fls in short racemes on erect lfless stems, rising above water; corollas yellow, two-lipped, spurred, with a **palate**; in structure v like those of Toadflax (*Linaria*, p 300).

A   Common Butterwort, *Pinguicula vulgaris*, with rosette of spreading oval-oblong, ± pointed yellow-green lvs, 2–8 cm long, resembling a yellowish starfish. Fl-stalks 5–15 cm tall; calyx two-lipped; lobes blunt, oval. Corolla **violet**, 10–15 mm long × 12 mm wide, with white patch in throat; lower lip lobes **well-separated**, **flat**, longer than broad; spur 4–7 mm long, back-pointing, **tapered to a point**. Br Isles: uplands of Wales, N Eng, Scot, c; mid, S Eng r; Ire f-c; Eur r-o to S, more f in Denmark; in (especially calc) bogs, fens, on wet rocks, decreasing in lowlands. Fl 5–7.

B   Large-flowered Butterwort, *P. grandiflora*, close to A, but fl-stalks 8–20 cm tall; corollas (**B**) violet, 15–20 mm long × 25–30 mm wide; lower lip lobes ± **overlapping**, **wavy**, broader than long; white throat patch **longer**, more **purple-streaked**; spur 10 mm or more long. SW Ire lc; Cornwall introd (mts of SW Eur); in bogs, wet rocks. Fl 5–7.

C   Pale Butterwort, *P. lusitanica*, has lvs of rosette 1–2 cm long, **olive**, with **purple veins**, oblong, blunt. Fl-stalks only 3–10 cm tall; corollas **lilac-pink**, 5–8 mm wide, with **yellow** throat, lobes of upper lip **rounded**, 2–3 mm long; spur **cylindrical**, **blunt**, 2–4 mm long, bent **downwards**. Br Isles: Eng, Hants to Cornwall, lf-lc; S Wales vr; W, N Scot f-lc; Ire lf; Eur, W France o-lf; in Sphagnum bogs, wet hths. Fl 6–10.

D   Common Bladderwort, *Utricularia vulgaris*, has floating stems, to 40 cm long, bearing **pinnately**-divided lvs (**Da**) 2.0–2.5 cm long, oval; green; threadlike lf-segments bear groups of bristles and oval bladders to 3 mm long. Infl 10–20 cm tall, 2–8-fld; corollas 12–18 mm long, bright yellow; upper lip only **as long as** palate of lower lip; margins of lower lip turned down ± vertically; spur conical. Br Isles, Eur; o-lf in still, often peaty and calc fresh water. Fl 7–8.

E   Greater Bladderwort, *U. neglecta*, **v close** to D, but differs in corolla-lips; lower lip (**E**) **flat**, spreading out ± **horizontally**, upper lip **twice length** of lower lip's palate. Br Isles: less c than D: Eng, S Scot, Ire o (but E Anglia lf); Eur o; habitat as for D. Fl 7–8.

F   Lesser Bladderwort, *U. minor*, smaller (7–20 cm long) slenderer plant than D and E; lvs, only 3–6 mm long, **palmately-divided** into **thread-like** untoothed segments bearing **bladders** 2 mm long. Shoots buried in the peaty substratum have fewer lvs, many bladders. Infl 4–15 cm tall, 2–6-fld; corollas 6–8 mm long, **pale yellow**, with short **blunt** spurs. Br Isles o but lc; Eur o-lf; in peaty bog pools. Fl 6–9.

G   Intermediate Bladderwort, *U. intermedia*, is near to F in size, but with two distinct types of shoots; some horizontal, 10–25 cm long, bearing palmately-divided lvs (**G**), 3–6 mm long, with segments **flat**, **toothed**, 1–2 mm wide, and **no** bladders; others, descending into the peat substrata, have no lvs, but **bear bladders** 3 mm long. Fls r; infl 9–16 cm tall, 2–4-fld; corollas 8–12 mm long, **bright yellow** with reddish lines; spurs **conical**. Br Isles: Eng, in Norfolk, Dorset,

335

BUTTERWORT FAMILY *Lentibulariaceae*

◀ New Forest vr; Wales vr; N Eng, Scot, Ire o-lf; Eur: France to Denmark r, but lf to N; in peaty pools in bogs, fens. Fl 7–9.

▶ **PLANTAIN FAMILY** *Plantaginaceae*

Herbs with lvs usually all in basal rosettes; infls in heads or spikes on long lfless stalks; fls tiny, with the chaffy calyx and corolla both four-lobed, 4 long conspicuous stamens, and 2–4-celled ovary forming a capsule in fr. **Plantains** (*Plantago*) are land plants with no runners and bisexual fls; **Shoreweed** (*Littorella*) is ± aquatic, on sandy lake-shores, with stolons, and male and female fls on separate stalks.

A Ribwort Plantain, *Plantago lanceolata*, rosette-forming per herb; lfless, silky-hairy fl-stems 10–40 cm; lvs all basal, lanceolate or oval-lanceolate, spreading or erect, scarcely-toothed, with 3–5 strong, ± parallel veins, narrowed to short stalk; infl-stalk deeply **furrowed**; oblong infl of many small fls, each with a tiny pointed bract; fls 4 mm, calyx green, corolla brownish, its 4 bent-back lobes with brown midribs; stamens long, white. Br Isles, Eur; va on gslds, wa, rds. Fl 4–10.

B Greater Plantain, *P. major*, differs from A in ± hairless, **broad-oval** to **elliptical**, many-veined lvs (**B**), all **abruptly** narrowed into **stalks as long as lvs**; infl-stalk **unfurrowed**, 10–15 cm, about as long as lvs; corolla-lobes dirty-white, with no brown midribs; stamens short, yellow. Br Isles, Eur; va on ar, wa, rds, especially trodden places. Fl 6–10.

C Hoary Plantain, *P. media*, differs from B in **greyish-downy**, 5–9 veined elliptical or diamond-shaped lvs, gradually narrowed into **short** stalks, mostly forming **flat rosette** on gd; unfurrowed infl-stalks bear oblong spikes, 2–6 cm long, of **scented** fls; corollas white, stamens **pinkish** with **purple** stalks. Pollinated by insects (unlike other Plantains, which are wind-pollinated). Br Isles r or vl (but Eng f-lc); Eur c; on calc gslds. Fl 5–8.

D Sea Plantain, *P. maritima*, ± hairless per herb with wdy base; lvs 5–20 cm long, ± erect, **fleshy**, 3–5-veined, ± untoothed, **narrow-linear**; infl-spike 2–6 cm long, on a long erect unfurrowed stalk; Fls (**Da**) 3 mm long, corollas brown with darker midribs; stamens pale yellow. Br Isles: coasts o; mts of N Wales, N Eng, Scot, lc; inland limestone areas of W Ire; Eur c; on salt marshes, wet mt cliffs. Fl 6–8.

E Buck's-horn Plantain, *P. coronopus*, usually downy bi herb; flat rosette of deeply **pinnatifid** lvs, 2–6 cm long, segments linear, one-veined, often again deeply-lobed (but lvs sometimes narrow-linear, unlobed, merely toothed; sometimes erect). Bracts of fl-spike with usually long, spreading points; corolla brownish, stamens yellow. Br Isles, Eur; c near coasts (also inland in S, E Eng, f-lc); on rocks, sea-cliffs, dry sandy or gravelly gslds near sea, on commons inland. Fl 5–7. **Ei Branched Plantain**, *P. indica*, is unlike other Plantains in erect **branched** stems bearing **along them opp**, narrow-linear lvs to 10 cm long; and in long-stalked infls in lf-axils; fl-heads egg-shaped, 1 cm long. Br Isles introd (S Eur) r; Eur o-vlf; on wa, dunes. Fl 7–8.

F Shoreweed, *Littorella uniflora*, hairless turf-forming per herb of shallow water or lake shores; creeping and rooting runners form rosettes or erect tufts of linear lvs; lvs, 2–10 cm long, flat one side, rounded on other (thus half-cylindrical in shape), spongy inside, not pointed, have sheathing bases. Male fls (**F**) solitary on stalks 5–8 cm long, have 4 small scale-like sepals, 4 tiny whitish petals, and 4 long-stalked (1–2 cm) stamens; female fls (**Fa**) almost stalkless, 1–3 at base of male fl-stalk, with style 1 cm long. Br Isles widespread; Scot, N Eng, Wales, Ire lc; S, mid Eng r-vlf; Eur r-lf, France to Netherlands o, Denmark lc; submerged (to 4 m deep) in shallow non-calc lakes, and exposed on their sandy or gravelly shores as water falls in summer. Fl 6–8.

336 *cont*

A

B

C

Da

3mm

D

E

Fa

F

G

Ga

8mm

H

337

LOBELIA FAMILY   *Lobeliaceae*

◀ Herbs (in Eur) with alt simple lvs without stipules; fls irregular, corolla ± two-lipped, of 5 lobes joined below; calyx-teeth 5; stamens 5; ovary inferior, with 2 cells and two-lobed stigma; fr a capsule. Close to Bellflower family, but with irregular fls.

G Heath Lobelia, *Lobelia urens*, ± hairless erect per herb, 20–60 cm tall, with bitter taste; stems angled, lfy; lvs **obovate** below, linear-oblong above, toothed, shiny dark green, scarcely stalked; fls in a loose branched raceme; bracts linear, ± equalling calyx; calyx-teeth **(Ga)** long, v narrow, spreading; corolla 10–15 mm long, **bluish-purple**, with 2 narrow lobes to upper lip, 3 narrow teeth on lower lip. S, SW Eng, r but vlf; France, W and S from Normandy and Paris area f-lc; on grassy hths, open hthy wds. Fl 8–9.

H Water Lobelia, *L. dortmanna*, hairless erect per, 20–60 cm, with rooting runners; rosettes of submerged, **linear**, blunt, untoothed, arched back, fleshy lvs 2–4 cm long. Infl-stem, emerging from water, lfless except for small scales, bears a few-fld raceme of drooping fls with stalks to 1 cm long, and blunt bracts much shorter than fl-stalks; calyx-teeth oval, blunt, short, erect; corolla 15–20 mm, **pale lilac-mauve**. Br Isles: Wales, NW Eng, Ire, lf; W, N Scot, c; Eur: Netherlands, Denmark, lf; on stony bottoms of shallow lakes of non-calc fresh water, especially in mts, also in dune lakes in Eur. Fl 7–8.

BELLFLOWER FAMILY   *Campanulaceae*

A family of herbs with **alt**, **undivided** lvs without stipules; fls either small, in dense heads or spikes, or large, showy, ± bell-shaped in loose infls; calyx five-lobed, lobes green, not spinous; corolla **regular**, with 5 **equal lobes**; 5 stamens alt with corolla-lobes; ovary **inferior**, 3–5-celled, with 3–5 stigmas; fr a capsule. **Bellflowers** can be confused with Gentians (p 290), but latter have ovary **superior** and lvs **opp**. **Rampions** and **Sheep's-bit** can be confused with Scabiouses (in Teasel family, p 354), but in latter lvs **opp**, calyx has 5 long obvious **spine-like** teeth, and an outer cup-like **epicalyx** encloses each fl.

KEY TO BELLFLOWER FAMILY

1 Fls small, narrow (under 5 mm wide) with linear petals, in dense heads or spikes............................ 2
   Fls at least 7 mm wide, mostly much more, bell- or wheel-shaped, solitary, or in open spikes or panicles... 3
2 Plants hairless – fl-buds curved – petals at first joined together at their tips – stigma-lobes v narrow .... *Phyteuma* (p 340)
   Plants hairy – fl-buds straight – petals never joined at tips – stigma-lobes short, stout ....
                                                                                                                            Jasione (p 342)
3 Ovary and fr cylindrical – corolla-tube v short, lobes ± flat, forming a wheel shape – ann plant of chalky ar... *Legousia* (p 340)
   Ovary and fr oval or globular – corolla with bell- or funnel-shaped tube – creeping or tufted plants of gslds, wds, hbs, etc... 4
4 Plant small, creeping – stems thread-like – all lvs tiny (1 cm wide), rounded, ivy-shaped, long-stalked – fls 1–2 together, on long stalks, bell-shaped, 6–10 mm long × 7 mm wide...........................
                                                                                       Wahlenbergia hederacea (p 340 H)
   Plant ± erect – fl-stems bearing spikes or panicles of fls – upper lvs stalkless, always smaller than lower .... *Campanula* (key below)

KEY TO BELLFLOWERS (*CAMPANULA*)

1 Epicalyx of broadly cordate, bent-back lobes present between the 5 calyx-teeth – lvs oval-lanceolate, toothed – corolla large (4–5 cm long), inflated-bell-shaped – stigmas 5 – robust, bristly plant – S Eng, Eur – introd in wa, on railway banks – o .... *C. medium*
   No epicalyx present – calyx of 5 lobes only – stigmas 3 2
2 Lvs on middle of stem oval (length 2–4 times breadth) 3
   Lvs on middle of stem linear, lanceolate, or narrow-oblong.. 6

3 Fls in dense terminal heads, often extra fls down stem – all fls erect, stalkless – corolla hairless, purplish blue – root-lvs stalked, downy, cordate-oval..*C. glomerata* (p 339 D)
Fls in loose spikes, racemes, or panicles – all fls with their own stalks – corolla-lobes ± hairy..**4**

4 Calyx-teeth **spreading** or bent back in fl – fls (in a ± lfless narrow raceme) drooping to one side, corolla only 20–30 mm long, funnel-shaped, lobes equalling tube – plants 30–60 cm – Br Isles introd r – Eur o – on gsld, hbs, wa – fl 7–9...*C. rapunculoides*
Calyx-teeth **erect** in fl – fls erect or spreading, 30–50 mm long, bell-shaped, lobes shorter than tube – plant 50–100 cm tall..**5**

5 Plant softly downy – stem bluntly-angled – root-lvs tapering into stalk, stem-lvs stalkless – fls in an unbranched lfy raceme – corolla 40–50 mm long..*C. latifolia* (p 339 B)
Plant bristly-hairy – stem sharply-angled – root-lvs cordate-based, not tapering into stalk, stem-lvs stalked – fls in loose clusters in a branched lfy panicle – corolla 30–40 mm long.................................
....*C. trachelium* (p 339 A)

6 Calyx with **spreading, lanceolate** lobes (3 mm wide at base) – infl a tall, loose **raceme**, fls 1–2 together – stem-lvs hairless, linear-lanceolate (to 10 cm long) with small distant teeth – corolla widely cup-shaped with v short lobes – GB introd r, Eur o-lf – fl 6–9...........................*C. persicifolia*
Calyx with **erect linear** lobes (not over 1 mm wide at base) – infl with **spreading** branches.............**7**

7 Plant ± hairless, smooth – root-lvs long-stalked, rounded-cordate, about 1 cm wide – lower stem-lvs stalked – fls drooping on hair-like stalks, bell-shaped, lobes v short.......................................
....*C. rotundifolia* (p 339 C)
Plant rough to touch – root-lvs oblong-ovate, narrowed to short stalks – all stem-lvs stalkless – fls erect, corolla funnel- or widely bell-shaped, lobes widely spreading **8**

8 Root-lvs gradually **narrowed to base, running down stalk** – infl with several long, spreading branches – fl-stalks with **bracts** on **middle** – corolla to **40 mm wide**, with spreading lobes as long as tube, purple ....*C. patula* (p 340 E)
Root-lvs suddenly **narrowed to stalk** – infl **narrow**, fls clustered below – fl-stalks with bracts at **base** – corolla **10–15 mm wide**, lobes half as long as tube, pale mauve – GB introd r and scattered, Eur N to Netherlands o-lc – on hbs, wa – fl 5–8...*C. rapunculus*

A   Nettle-leaved Bellflower, *Campanula trachelium*, erect robust bristly-hairy ▶ per herb, 50–100 cm tall, with sharply angled stem; root-lvs long-stalked, oval-triangular, **cordate-based**, blades to 10 cm long; stem-lvs short-stalked, oval, pointed, all lvs **coarsely** sharp-toothed; infl a lfy **panicle** with fls in groups of 1–4 on branches; fls with stalks to 1 cm, spreading or erect; calyx-teeth erect, 1 cm long, pointed-triangular; corolla **30–40 cm long**, bell-shaped, pale purplish-blue, with short lobes, hairy outside. Fr globular. Br Isles: Eng, Wales, N to R Humber, c to S, o to N; SW Eng, **Scot abs**; Ire SE only, vr; Eur: c to S, lc N to Denmark; in wds, hbs, on calc soils. Fl 7–9.
B   Giant Bellflower, *C. latifolia*, ± downy per herb, 50–100 cm tall; differs from A in **bluntly**-angled stem, root-lvs **(B) tapering** into stalks, 10–20 cm long, long-pointed, **less deeply-toothed** than in A; stem-lvs stalkless; infl a lfy **raceme**, rarely branched; fl-stalks 2 cm; corolla **40–50 mm long**, paler than in A, often white; fr oval. Br Isles: GB from S mid Eng to Ross-shire, r to S, lc in N Eng, o-lf in Scot; **Ire abs**; Eur: France only in mts to E; NW Germany, Denmark o-lf; in wds, hbs on calc or richer soils. Fl 7–8.
C   Harebell, *C. rotundifolia*, slender, erect hairless per herb, 15–40 cm tall, stems shortly creeping then ascending; root-lvs 1 cm wide, **rounded, cordate-based**, long-stalked; stem-lvs narrow-linear, lower stalked, upper stalkless; fls few in a loose panicle, **drooping** on long thread-like stalks; calyx-teeth spreading, bristle-like; corolla 15 mm long, bell-shaped, with short oval lobes, pale blue. Fr globular. Br Isles: GB c (but r SW Eng); Ire, c in N, o in S; Eur c; on dry gslds, hths, hbs, dunes. Fl 7–9.
D   Clustered Bellflower, *C. glomerata*, erect, closely downy per herb, 3–30 cm; root-lvs long-stalked, oval, blunt, **cordate-based, downy**, with small blunt

teeth; upper stem-lvs stalkless, clasping, oval-lanceolate; fls in a **dense terminal head**, often with extra fls lower down stem, all erect, **stalkless**; calyx-teeth narrow-triangular, pointed; corolla 15–20 mm long, narrow-bell-shaped, rich purplish blue, hairless, lobes ± equalling tube; style not protruding from corolla. Br Isles: S, E Eng, f-lc, o-lf to N; E Scot r; **Ire abs**; Eur: central, E France, f-lc; N to Denmark o; on calc gslds. Fl 6–10. ***Di** *C. cervicaria* is like D, but has lower lvs lanceolate, **narrowed** into stalk, **blunt** oval sepals, pale blue fls, and **protruding** style. Eur, central France to Denmark; r in wds. Fl 7–8.

E Spreading Bellflower, *C. patula*, slender erect per herb, 20–60 cm tall, stems and lvs rough; root-lvs 4 cm, obovate, blunt, feebly-toothed, running down into short stalk; stem-lvs stalkless, small, narrow, pointed; infl **much branched**, v open, spreading; fls erect, on slender 2–5-cm stalks, each with a little bract in the middle; calyx-teeth 1 cm, bristle-like; corolla (**E**) funnel- or widely bell-shaped, lobes spreading, oval, pointed, as long as the tube, bright **rosy-purple**. GB: S, W midland Eng, E Wales, r and scattered; **abs rest of Br Isles**; Eur, France to Denmark, r-o in lowlands; on riverbanks, hbs, rds. Fl 7–9.

F Venus's-looking-glass, *Legousia hybrida*, erect or sprawling bristly ann, with stems 5–20 cm; lvs oblong, wavy-edged, stalkless, 1–3 cm long; fls erect, in loose terminal clusters; calyx-teeth 5, oblong-lanceolate, half length of **cylindrical** ovary; corolla **wheel-shaped**, mauve to dull purple, five-lobed, 5–10 mm across, only opening in sunshine, lobes only half length of calyx-teeth; fr a three-angled linear-oblong capsule 15–25 mm long, opening by pores below calyx. S, E, mid Eng, f-lc; **abs rest of Br Isles**; Eur: France f-lc; Belgium, Netherlands, W Germany r; on ar on calc soils. Fl 5–8.

G Large Venus's-looking-glass, *L. speculum-veneris*, differs from F in more spreading habit; **linear** calyx-teeth **equal** length of ovary; corolla, **red-purple**, to 20 mm across, with broader lobes **equalling** calyx-teeth, stays **open** in dull weather. Eng introd vr; Eur: France, Belgium f-lc; Netherlands, W Germany r; on ar on calc soils. Fl 5–7.

H Ivy-leaved Bellflower, *Wahlenbergia hederacea*, delicate, **creeping**, patch-forming, hairless per herb; with stems to 20 cm, weak, **thread-like**; lvs all long-stalked, alt, rounded, palmately-lobed, rather **ivy-shaped**, pale green, 5–12 mm long and wide, bases ± cordate; fls on fine stalks 1–4 cm long, in lf-axils, erect or inclined; calyx-teeth narrow, 2–3 mm long, longer than ovary; corolla (**Ha**) bell-shaped with 5 short lobes, **pale sky-blue**, 6–10 mm long × 5–8 mm wide. S Eng, Kent to Cornwall o-lf; Wales f; NW Eng, W Scot r; S Ire r; Eur: France from Normandy S and W, f-lc; Belgium, Netherlands, NW Germany vr; on moist hthy tracks in wds, boggy moorland rivulets. Fl 7–8.

I Spiked Rampion, *Phyteuma spicatum*, erect hairless per herb, 30–80 cm tall; lower lvs long-stalked, cordate-based, oval, blunt-toothed and -tipped, 3–7 cm long; upper lvs narrower, stalkless. Infl a dense **spike** 3–8 cm long; fls with calyx-teeth narrow, spreading in fr, corollas creamy-yellow, 1 cm long, curved in bud, their narrow lobes at first **joined at tips**; stigmas slender; frs in a dense cylindrical **spike**. Eng: E Sussex only, vl; Eur: central and E France to Denmark, f to S, o to N; in open wds, hbs. Fl 5–7. ***Ii** *P. nigrum* has **blue** fls in **spikes**, and **broader** oval-cordate, ± **untoothed** stem-lvs; NE France, Belgium, W Germany, o; in wds on calc soils. Fl 5–6.

J Round-headed Rampion, *P. tenerum*, slender erect hairless per herb, 8–40 cm tall; lvs as in I, but root-lvs less cordate, more oblong, all stem-lvs stalkless, linear-lanceolate, few; infl a dense **rounded head** 1.0–2.5 cm wide, of deep **Oxford-blue** fls. S Eng, Sussex to Wilts only, f-lva; Eur, NW, central France, vl; on calc gslds. Fl 7–8. ***Ji** *P. orbiculare*, close to J, but has **broad oval**-lanceolate (not narrow-lanceolate) bracts below head, **longer** than the outer fls. Eur, central and E France o-lf; on calc gslds. Fl 6–7.

BELLFLOWER FAMILY
Campanulaceae

K Sheep's-bit, *Jasione montana*, erect or sprawling **downy** bi herb, 5–30 cm tall, with rosette of short-stalked, **strap-shaped**, **wavy-edged**, weakly-toothed root-lvs to 5 cm long, stem lvs shorter, stalkless; fls in dense rounded **heads** 10–30 mm across; corollas 5 mm long, **pale sky-blue**, their narrow lobes **not** joined at tip, and 2 **stout** stigmas on tip of style. Br Isles: GB, f-lc to W, o-r to E, **abs N Scot**; Ire lc; Eur f-lc, especially near coasts, from W France to Denmark; on cliffs, dry gslds, hths, dunes, on acid sandy or stony soils. Fl 5–8.

▶ ## HONEYSUCKLE FAMILY
Caprifoliaceae

Elders, Honeysuckles etc

Shrubs, or more rarely herbs, with **opp** lvs; fls in heads or umbels; ovaries **inferior**; petals joined into a five-lobed corolla-tube; 5 stamens; 2–5 carpels; fr **fleshy** (in Eur and Br Isles), except in Twinflower. **Elders** (*Sambucus*) have pinnate lvs; in other genera lvs undivided. In **Guelder-rose** and **Wayfaring-tree** (*Viburnum*) fls are in umbel-like cymes; in **Honeysuckles** (*Lonicera*) they are in whorls, heads, or pairs in lf-axils, trumpet-shaped and two-lipped. **Twinflower** (*Linnaea borealis*, not illustrated) is a tiny creeping shrub with lvs 5–10 mm long, with bell-shaped pink fls 8 mm long, hanging in pairs on erect stalks 3–7 cm tall; fr a dry nutlet; r in mossy pine forests in NE Scot, and in Denmark, The Netherlands, N Germany. Fl 6–8.

A Elder, *Sambucus nigra*, shrub or small tree, to 10 m tall, producing erect straight suckers from base; bark deeply-furrowed and corky. Lvs opp, pinnate; lfts 3–9 cm long, oval or elliptical, toothed, ± hairless; infl umbel-like, flat-topped, much-branched, 10–20 cm across; corolla 5 mm across, creamy, five-lobed; stamens 5, creamy; stigmas 3–5; fr (**Aa**) a black edible berry-like drupe 6–8 mm wide. Br Isles c; in wds, scrub, wa (disliked by rabbits so common near their colonies). Fl 6–7; fr 8–9, edible.

B Dwarf Elder, *S. ebulus*, robust hairless per **herb**, 60–120 cm tall; stems stout, erect, grooved; lvs as in A, but strong-smelling and with lfts 5–15 cm long, narrower and more sharply-toothed, stipules at base of lvs oval, **conspicuous** (tiny or abs in A); infl similar, but 7–10 cm across; fls (**Ba**) often pink-tinged outside; stamens **purple**; fr black, **poisonous**. Br Isles introd, o (but Scot vr); Eur, f to S, r to N; on rds, wa. Fl 7–8; fr 8–9.

C Red-berried Elder, *S. racemosa*, hairless shrub to 4 m; lvs and fls as in A, but infls **oval panicles** (**not flat-topped**), and frs (**Ca**) bright **red**, 5 mm wide. GB introd: Eng vr, E Scot lf; Eur, native f-lc in mts, introd but o-lf elsewhere; in wds. Fl 4–5; fr 6–7.

D Guelder-rose, *Viburnum opulus*, deciduous shrub 2–4 m tall, with grey hairless angled twigs, and **scaly** buds; opp **palmately-lobed** lvs, 5–8 cm long, lobes sharply-toothed, dark green, hairless above, ± downy below; infls flat umbel-like heads, inner fls fertile, 6 mm across, outer fls sterile (no stamens or stigmas), 15–20 mm across, all fls white; fr (**Da**) 8 mm long, globular, shiny red. Br Isles c (but N Scot r-o); Eur c; in wds, scrub, hds, especially on damper soils. Fl 6–7; fr 9–10 (**poisonous**).

E Wayfaring-tree, *V. lantana*, deciduous shrub 2–6 m tall, with pale brown downy rounded twigs, and buds **without** enclosing scales; opp, undivided, oval, wrinkled pointed finely-toothed lvs, 5–10 cm long, sparsely downy above, densely grey-downy below. Infls flat umbel-like heads, 6–10 cm across, but fls **all alike**, fertile, 5–6 mm wide, creamy. Fr (**Ea**) 8 mm long, oval, flattened, first red, then black. S Eng: c to W to S Devon and N and E to Cambridge, S Lincs and Worcs; introd and vr to N and W and in rest of Br Isles; Eur, N to S Belgium only, c; in scrub, hds, wds on calc soils. Fl 5–6; fr 7–10 (**poisonous**).

cont

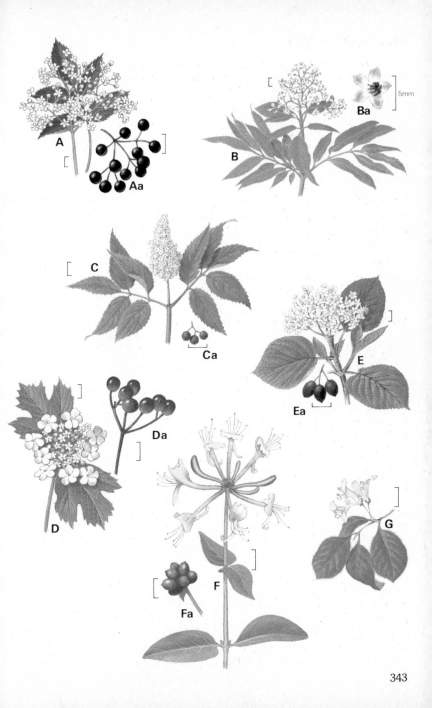

A

Aa

B

Ba

5mm

C

Ca

D

Da

E

Ea

F

Fa

G

◀ **F Honeysuckle**, *Lonicera periclymenum*, twining shrub, climbing trees etc, to 6 m, and then flowering, also carpeting gd in dry wds (but then without fls); lvs opp, 3–7 cm long, oval to elliptical, grey-green, ± downy or not, **untoothed**, pointed, the lower short-stalked; fls in whorled terminal **heads**, 5–6 cm across, stalkless, with **tiny** bracts; corollas 4–5 cm long, trumpet-shaped and two-lipped, upper lip four-toothed, curved up, lower untoothed, curved down, creamy-yellow within, yellow to purplish-pink outside, v fragrant; style and the 5 stamens all long-protruding. Fr (**Fa**) a red globular berry. Br Isles, Eur; vc in wds, hds, scrub, rocks, mostly on acid soils. Fl 6–9; fr 8–9 (**poisonous**). **Fi Perfoliate Honeysuckle**, *L. caprifolium*, twining shrub close to F, but lvs and the **large** bracts to fl-heads are **joined in pairs** round stems. GB introd r; Eur: NE France, Germany, o (introd rest of Eur); in wds, hds. Fl 5–6.

G Fly Honeysuckle, *L. xylosteum*, erect bushy **non-climbing** shrub, 1–3 m tall; twigs **downy**; lvs opp, grey-green, downy, oval, stalked, pointed, 3–6 cm long; fls in **pairs** on a shared stalk in upper lf-axils; corollas as in F, but only 1–2 cm long, yellow, **downy**; berries red. Eng: Sussex only, vr native in wds on chk; Eur, from central and N France to Denmark f-lc; in wds, scrub. Fl 5–6.

VALERIAN FAMILY

Valerianaceae

A family of herbs with **opp** lvs, no stipules; infls **head-** or **umbel-like cymes** of **small** fls, sometimes dioecious; calyx **small**, like a rim on top of ovary, toothed or not; corolla funnel-shaped, sometimes with a spur, and with 5 blunt lobes; stamens 3 or 1; ovary **inferior**, **three-celled** (but only 1 cell producing a seed); fr a **nutlet**. **Valerians** (*Valeriana*) are erect pers with pinnate lvs, corolla-tubes swollen below, 3 stamens, and a feathery pappus on top of fr, as in Dandelion (p 388), but much smaller; **Spur-valerians** (*Centranthus*) are tall herbs with unlobed lvs, spurred corollas, 1 stamen per fl, and a pappus; **Cornsalads** (*Valerianella*) are small anns with forked branches, tiny mauve fls in heads, 3 stamens and no pappus.

KEY TO CORNSALADS (*VALERIANELLA*)

(References are to illustrations on p 347)

1 Calyx above fr **minute**, scarcely visible.. **2**
   Calyx above fr **larger**, obvious.. **3**
2 Fr **flattened** on 2 sides (and so elliptical in cross-section), 2.5 mm long × 2 mm wide, almost round in side view – cell with seed inside has **swollen corky wall** ....*V. locusta* (p 347 D)
   Fr (**E**) almost square in cross-section, oblong in side view, 2.0 mm long × 0.75 mm wide – cell with seed inside has thin (not swollen, not corky) wall – on old walls, rocks – Eng o-lf to S; **Scot abs**; Ire vr; Eur N to Netherlands o-lf – fl 4–6..*V. carinata* (p 347 E)
3 Fr **hairy**, oblong, 1.2 mm long × 0.9 mm wide – calyx above fr as wide as fr and as long, with 5–6 unequal **net-veined** teeth – S Eng, Eur, introd and r – on old walls, wa (S Eur) – fl 6–7 ..*V. eriocarpa*
   Fr **hairless**, calyx-teeth unveined... **4**
4 Fr (**G**) **broadly** egg-shaped, not flattened, 2.0 mm long × 1.5 mm wide – calyx above fr **small**, only third width of fr – calyx-teeth all short – S Eng, S Ire, r, decreasing – Eur r-o – on ar on calc soil – fl 6–7 ....*V. rimosa* (p 347 G)
   Fr (**F**) **narrow**-egg-shaped, **flat** on **one side**, 2 mm long × 1 mm wide – calyx on top **larger**, **half width** of fr, with one much longer tooth – Eng f-vlc in S and E, rest of Br Isles r – Eur f-lc – on ar on calc soil – fl 6–7.. *V. dentata* (p 347 F)

VALERIAN FAMILY *Valerianaceae*

A **Common Valerian**, *Valeriana officinalis*, erect per herb, 30–120 cm tall, stem hairy below; **all lvs** opp, pinnate, to 20 cm long, lower long-stalked, upper stalkless; lfts lanceolate, ± bluntly-toothed, ± hairless, side veins conspicuous; infl a terminal umbel-like head, 5–12 cm wide; corollas (**Aa**) funnel-shaped, pinkish-white, five-lobed, tube swollen at base; stamens 3, protruding; fr (**Ab**) 4 mm long, oblong, with a white feathery pappus. Br Isles, Eur; c in fens, riversides, wet wds, also as a smaller form in dry calc gslds and scrub. Fl 6–8.

B **Marsh Valerian**, *V. dioica*, erect dioecious herb, 15–30 cm tall, with creeping runners at base; root-lvs long-stalked, blades oval-elliptical, blunt, **undivided**, 2–3 cm long; stem-lvs ± stalkless, **pinnatifid**. Infls in terminal heads; on male plants 4 cm across with fls 5 mm wide; on female plants only 1–2 cm across, with florets (**Ba**) 2 mm wide; all fls pinkish. Frs as in A, but smaller. Br Isles: GB N to central Scot f-lc; **N Scot**, **Ire abs**; Eur f-lc; in fens, wet mds. Fl 5–6.

C **Red Valerian**, *Centranthus ruber*, erect per herb, 30–80 cm tall; lvs **grey-green**, opp, oval-lanceolate, **undivided**, untoothed, 5–10 cm long, lower stalked; infls terminal panicles; corollas (**Ca**) 5 mm wide, deep pink, scarlet, or white, with slender tube 8–10 mm long bearing a pointed **spur** 3–4 mm long; stamen 1 only, protruding; fr with a pappus. Br Isles, Eur, introd, but o-la (**abs N Scot**, Denmark); on old walls, cliffs, rocks, wa. Fl 6–8.

D **Cornsalad**, *Valerianella locusta*, slender, ± hairless ann, 7–30 cm tall, with repeatedly forked branches, much more compact in dry places (**Db**); lvs blunt, ± untoothed, lower spoon-shaped, upper oblong. Fls in dense terminal heads, 1–2 cm across; corollas (**Dc**) pale mauve, 1–2 mm across, five-lobed; stamens 3; fr (**Da**) a nutlet 2.5 mm long × 2.0 mm wide, without a pappus, with a corky bulge on the cell with the seed in it. Br Isles f-lc (except N Scot r); Eur f-lc; on dunes, sandy gslds, ar, banks, rocks. Fl 4–6.

This is the commonest Cornsalad; others (**E–G**) are of v similar appearance, but differ in their frs; use key p 345 to separate them from D.

MOSCHATEL FAMILY *Adoxaceae*

H **Moschatel**, *Adoxa moschatellina*, erect hairless per herb, 5–12 cm tall, with creeping scaly rhizomes. Not closely related to other flowering plants, so in a family on its own. Root-lvs long-stalked, twice-trifoliate, lfts 5–10 mm long, with 2–3 blunt lobes, each tipped with a **tiny spine**; lvs on fl-stem 2 only, opp, short-stalked, smaller, trifoliate; all lvs **fleshy**, **pale green**. Infl a long-stalked head of 5 fls; 4 face outwards at right angles (like faces of a clock-tower) and have three-lobed calyx, five-lobed corolla, 10 stamens; fifth fl faces upwards, with two-lobed calyx, four-lobed corolla, 8 stamens; all fls pale yellow-green with golden stamens and inferior ovaries. Fr green, fleshy, drooping. Br Isles: GB N to mid Scot f-lvc; N Scot r; Ire, N only, vr; Eur c; in wds on richer soils, mt ledges. Fl 4–5.

Aa

3 mm

Ab

Ba

3 mm

A

B

C

Ca

D

Da

2 mm

Db

Dc

E

2 mm

F

2 mm

G

2 mm

H

347

BEDSTRAW FAMILY   *Rubiaceae*

Herbs (rarely woody below) with lvs apparently in **whorls** of 4–12 along the four-angled stems (technically, lvs are in opp pairs, with lf-like stipules making up the rest of each whorl). Fls small, in clusters, terminal or in lf-axils; calyx small or abs; corolla 4–5-lobed; stamens 4–5, alt with corolla-lobes; inferior ovary of 2 rounded cells; fr of 2 nutlets, or a berry. Many members of the family lacking whorled lvs (eg, Coffee plant, *Coffea*) exist in the Tropics, but not in Eur.

KEY TO BEDSTRAW FAMILY (SPP IN BR ISLES AND EUR)

1 Scrambling woody evergreens to 120 cm long – lvs elliptical, **rigid**, **leathery**, **dark green**, one-veined, prickly on their edges, 2–6 cm long, 4–6 in a whorl (resembling tiny holly lvs) – corollas yellow-green, five-lobed – fr a black berry...*Rubia peregrina* (p 352 A)
Non-evergreen herbs – corollas four- (or three-) lobed – fr 2 dry nutlets.......................... **2**
2 Fls with **distinct** 4–6-toothed **calyx** – corollas mauve-pink, funnel-shaped – fls in small dense heads with a ruff of bracts below each head................................*Sherardia arvensis* (p 352 C)
Fls with calyx abs, or reduced to a small rim on ovary top... **3**
3 Corolla **funnel-shaped**, with tube as long as, or longer than, the 4 lobes.................................... **4**
Corolla **wheel-shaped**, with v short tube and 4 ± flat lobes .... (most *Galium* spp, see key below)
4 Plant **prostrate** to ascending – infls loose, few-fld – fls with corollas white inside, pinkish outside – lvs linear, 4–6 per whorl, **ascending** at an angle – frs warted.........*Asperula cynanchica* (p 352 D)
Plant **erect** – fls white, in terminal umbel-like heads – lvs in **spreading** whorls up stems............... **5**
5 Plant 15–30 cm tall – lvs **elliptical-lanceolate**, 6–8 per whorl – corolla four-lobed – frs covered with hooked bristles – c..*Galium odoratum* (p 352 B)
Plant 30–70 cm tall – lvs narrow-linear, 4 per whorl above, 6 per whorl below – corolla often three-lobed – frs quite smooth – r – Br Isles abs.....................................*Asperula tinctoria* (p 352 Bi)

KEY TO BEDSTRAWS (SPP OF *GALIUM* WITH FLAT, WHEEL-SHAPED, FOUR-LOBED COROLLAS)

1 Fls yellow – fr smooth.. **2**
Fls white, cream or greenish – fr wrinkled, warted or bristly.. **3**
2 Lvs linear, mucronate, one-veined, hairless, at least 10 times as long as wide, 8–12 in a whorl ....
                                                                                                     Galium verum (p 350 J)
Lvs oval-elliptical, blunt, three-veined, hairy, not more than 3 times as long as wide, 4 in a whorl...*G. cruciata* (p 350 I)
3 Lvs **three-veined**, elliptical-lanceolate, blunt, widest at or **below** middle, rarely more than 5 times as long as wide, 4 to a whorl – fls white – fr with hooked bristles......................*G. boreale* (p 350 G)
Lvs **one-veined**, mostly widest **above** middle, 10 times as long as wide, 4–8 per whorl **4**
4 Lvs blunt or slightly pointed, never mucronate at tips – in wet places... **5**
Lvs mucronate at tips **6**
5 Lvs linear-lanceolate to broad-lanceolate, 1–3 cm long – tiny **backward-pointing** prickles on lf-edges – panicle of fls loosely pyramidal with wide-spreading branches – fls 3.0–4.5 mm across ....
                                                                                                    G. palustre (p 350 E)
Lvs narrow-linear, 0.5–1.0 cm long – tiny **forward-pointing** prickles on lf-edges – panicle of fls V-shaped, with ascending branches – fls 2.5 mm across – in SW – r...................*G. debile* (p 350 F)
6 Stems v rough with backward-pointing prickles on angles.. **7**
Stems ± smooth on the angles.. **11**
7 Lvs with **forward-pointing** prickles on edges, only 3–10 mm long – fls 0.5 mm across, reddish outside, whitish inside – fr 1 mm long, warted, hairless – in dry places – r....*G. parisiense* (p 349 Bi)
Lvs with **backward-pointing** prickles on edges – fls 1–3 mm across, white or greenish (not reddish)... **8**
8 Frs hairless, but ± wrinkled and warted – fls white or cream... **9**
Frs covered with hooked bristles – fls greenish-white.. **10**
9 Fls white, 2.5–3.0 mm across – frs 1 mm long, wrinkled, not warted – fr-stalks **straight** – erect plant of wet places – f...*G. uliginosum* (p 349 D)
Fls cream, 1.0–1.5 mm across – frs 3–4 mm long, v warted – fr-stalks **strongly arched down** – sprawling plant of dry ar – vr ....*G. tricornutum* (p 350 Hii)

10 Fls 2 mm across – fr 4–6 mm long, purplish when ripe, its hooked bristles with swollen bases –
robust plant – often scrambling in hds – vc..*G. aparine* (p 350 H)
   Fls 1 mm across – fr 1.5–3.0 mm long, blackish when ripe, its hooked bristles without swollen
bases – smaller plant – on ar – r...*G. spurium* (p 350 Hi)
11 Lvs of fl-shoots lanceolate-obovate, not more than 5 times as long as wide – prickles on lf-edges
forward-pointing or abs – c **12**
   Lvs of fl-shoots linear to narrow-lanceolate, more than 5 times as long as wide – prickles on lf-
edges **backward-pointing** **14**
12 Plant robust – lvs 8–25 mm long – fls in large terminal panicles – frs wrinkled (**not warted**) **13**
   Plant slender, more creeping – lvs 5–10 mm long – fls in small clusters on stem-tips and in lf-axils
   – corolla-lobes not long-pointed – frs with pointed **warts** – in hthy places........*G. saxatile* (p 349 B)
13 Lvs bright green, tips pointed – stem solid, four-angled – fl-stalks firm, spreading – petals with
long points – fls not drooping in bud – vc ....*G. mollugo* (p 349 A)
   Lvs grey-green, blunter – stem hollow, rounded below – fl-stalks hair-like, drooping in bud – Br
Isles abs, Eur r..*G. sylvaticum* (p 349 Ai)
14 Plant ± creeping – short ascending fl-stems with close-set lf-whorls – frs with pointed
warts ....*G. sterneri* (p 349 Ci)
   Plant ± erect – lf-whorls distant – frs with low dome-shaped warts...............*G. pumilum* (p 349 C)

Bedstraws

    A **Hedge Bedstraw**, *Galium mollugo*, robust per herb; stems sprawling to erect
and scrambling, to 100 cm long, downy or not, four-angled, smooth, solid; lvs 8–
25 mm long, 6–8 per whorl, lanceolate-obovate, one-veined, mucronate, prickles
(**Aa**) on edges **forward**-pointing. Infls are large loose terminal panicles; corollas
(**Ab**) white, 3–4 mm across, with sharp points to lobes; fr (**Ac**) hairless, wrinkled,
1–2 mm long. Br Isles: Eng vc; Wales, Scot, Ire, r-o; Eur, vc to S, o to N; in hbs,
scrub, open wds on richer soils. Fl 6–9. *Ai* *G. sylvaticum* has robust habit
similar to that of A, but stems **hollow**, **round** below; lvs blunter, edges without
prickles, **grey-green**; fl-stalks **hairlike**, **drooping** in bud. Eur: E France; W
Germany; S Belgium; r-lf in mt wds. Fl 6–8.
    B **Heath Bedstraw**, *G. saxatile*, mat-forming per herb, with ascending fl-
shoots 10–20 cm tall; stems (**Bc**) hairless, four-angled, smooth, v branched; lvs 7–
10 mm long, 6–8 per whorl, lanceolate and broadest above middle on fl-shoots,
obovate on prostrate stems, all mucronate and one-veined, with prickles (**Ba**) on
edges **forward**-pointing. Infls open lfy cylindrical panicles; corollas white, 3 mm
across, lobed (not sharp-pointed); fr (**Bb**) 1.5–2.0 mm long, hairless, with pointed
warts. Br Isles c (except E mid Eng r-o); Eur c; on hths, gslds, wds on acid soils. Fl
6–8. **Bi** **Wall Bedstraw**, *G. parisiense*, sprawling slender herb with stems 10–
20 cm long, rough on the 4 angles, with small **down-pointing** prickles; **narrow** lvs
only 3–10 mm long, with **forward-pointing** prickles as in B; fls in small open
clusters in lf-axils, forming a narrow panicle; corollas only 2 mm across, reddish
outside, whitish within; fr 1 mm long, warted, hairless. Br Isles E, SE Eng only, r;
Eur, central and W France o-lf; on old walls, sandy gsld. Fl 6–7.
    C **Slender Bedstraw**, *G. pumilum*, slender ± erect herb, 20–30 cm tall,
with ± smooth four-angled stem; lvs (**C**) linear-lanceolate, 14–18 mm long,
with mucronate tips and a few **backward**-pointing prickles on edges, in distant
whorls of 5–7. Fls cream, 3 mm across, in a long open terminal panicle; fr (**Ca**)
1.5 mm long, hairless, with **dome-shaped** warts. Br Isles, S half Eng only, r-o; Eur,
central and N France to Denmark, f-lc; on calc gslds, rocks. Fl 6–7. **Ci** **Limestone Bedstraw**, *G. sterneri*, is close to C, but of more compact, mat-forming habit,
with shorter (10–20 cm) ascending fl-shoots; crowded whorls of mucronate lvs with
more, **backward-pointing**, prickles; fr 1.3 mm, hairless, with **pointed** warts. Br
Isles, hill areas of N Eng, Wales, Scot, Ire, lf; Eur, Denmark only, lc; on calc gslds,
rocks. Fl 6–7.
    D **Fen Bedstraw**, *G. uliginosum*, slender herb with ascending weak stems 10–
50 cm long, **v rough** on the 4 angles, with **backward-pointing** prickles (**Db**); lvs

one-veined, linear-lanceolate, wider above, **mucronate**, also with **backward-pointing** prickles (**Da**) on their edges, 6–8 per whorl; panicle narrow; corollas white, 2.5–3.0 mm across; fr 1 mm long, hairless, wrinkled. Br Isles: GB f-lc (except **N Scot abs**); S Ire o: Eur f-lc; in calc fens. Fl 6–8.

E   Common Marsh-bedstraw, *G. palustre*, variable slender or robust herb with creeping stems and also erect fl-stems to 100 cm tall, four-angled, hairless, smooth or rough; lvs (**Ea**) to 3.5 cm long, one-veined, obovate-lanceolate, ± blunt, (but **never** with mucronate tip like D), 4, 5 or 6 in a whorl; prickles on lf-edges **backward**-pointing. Fls 3.0–4.5 mm across, white; fr wrinkled, hairless, 1–2 mm long, in **pyramidal**, **wide-spreading** panicles. Br Isles, Eur; vc in marshes, fens, ditches, ponds. Fl 6–8.

F   Slender Marsh-bedstraw, *G. debile*, is smaller, slenderer and more prostrate than E; stems (**Fc**) smooth or slightly rough, lvs only 0.5–1.0 cm long, 4–6 per whorl, linear, one-veined, **never mucronate**, with prickles on edges **forward-pointing** (**Fa**); fls 2.5 mm across, in **V-shaped** panicles with **ascending** branches; fr (**Fb**) 1 mm long, hairless, warted. Br Isles: New Forest vlf, S Devon, Yorks, vr; W Ire vr; Eur, W France only, r: in damp hollows in gsld and around ponds on acid soils. Fl 6–7.

G   Northern Bedstraw, *G. boreale*, erect herb 20–40 cm tall, with rigid smooth four-angled lf-bearing stems; lvs (**G**) **elliptical-lanceolate**, **three-veined**, **blunt**, widest **at** or **below** middle, rarely over 5 times as long as wide, in whorls of 4; fls white, 4 mm across, in lfy pyramidal terminal panicles; fr 2.5 mm long, with many **hooked bristles**. Br Isles: N Eng lf; Scot f-lc; Wales vr; W Ire o; Eur: mts of France and S Belgium lf; Denmark f-lc; in mt mds, wds, mt ledges, rocks, dunes. Fl 7–8.

H   Cleavers, *G. aparine*, sprawling or ascending ann herb, often climbing over other plants to 100 cm long; four-angled stems (**Hb**) v rough, with large **backward-pointing** prickles; lvs 12–50 mm long, 6–8 to a whorl, linear-lanceolate or elliptical, mucronate, one-veined, ± bristly, edges with **backward**-pointing prickles. Fls in 2–5-fld axillary cymes, whitish-green, 2 mm across; fr (**Ha**) 4–6 mm long, purplish when ripe, covered with **hooked bristles** with **swollen** bases. Br Isles, Eur; vc on hbs, stony slopes, ar, wa, beaches, moist wds, etc. Fl 6–8.

Hi   False Cleavers, *G. spurium*, is close to H, but ± prostrate; fls 1 mm across; fr only 1.5–3.0 mm long, **blackish** when ripe, bases of its hooked bristles **not swollen**. S half of Eng vr; Eur, France to Denmark, f-lc; on ar. Fl 7.

Hii   Corn Cleavers, *G. tricornutum*, in appearance like H and Hi, has similar prickly stems, but frs hairless, 3–4 mm long, v warted; fr-stalks **strongly arched downwards**; fls cream, 1.0–1.5 mm across. S, E Eng, now vr, decreasing; Eur, N to Netherlands now r; on ar on calc soils. Fl 6–9.

I   Crosswort, *G. cruciata* (*Cruciata laevipes*), per herb with spreading, then erect hairy stems 15–60 cm tall; lvs to 2.5 cm long, **4 in a whorl**, oval-elliptical, **three-veined**, v **hairy**, yellow-green. Fls in dense axillary clusters **shorter** than lvs, 2–3 mm across, clear **yellow**, **honey-scented**; fr 1.5 mm long, hairless, smooth, black when ripe. Br Isles: GB c (but r near W coast); **N**, **W Scot**, **Ire abs**; Eur, vc to S, r in Netherlands, only introd in Denmark: in open wds, scrub, gslds, rds, hbs. Fl 5–6.

J   Lady's Bedstraw, *G. verum*, per herb with creeping stems at base and fl-stems ± erect, ± four-angled, ± hairless, 15–60 cm tall; lvs **linear**, mucronate, 6–25 mm × 0.5–2.0 mm, one-veined, dark green above with margins rolled back, 8–12 to a whorl. Panicles lfy, terminal; corollas 2–3 mm across, **golden-yellow**, with pointed lobes; fr 1.5 mm long, hairless, smooth, black when ripe. Hybridizes with A to produce plants with pale yellow fls. Br Isles, Eur; vc in gslds, hbs, dunes. Fl 7–8.

BEDSTRAW FAMILY

Madders, Woodruff, Squinancywort

A Wild Madder, *Rubia peregrina*, evergreen per, woody below, with scrambling hairless four-angled stems, prickly on angles, to 200 cm long; lvs 4–6 in a whorl, rigid, leathery, dark green, elliptical-lanceolate, one-veined, shiny, 2–6 cm long, with curved prickles on edges and on midrib below, rather like tiny holly lvs. Fls (**Aa**) in spreading cymes in lf-axils; corollas 5 mm across, yellow-green, the 5 lobes long-pointed; fr a black berry, 4–6 mm across. Br Isles: S and SW Eng, Wales, f-la near coast (but r E to Kent and inland); S Ire r but lf; Eur, France only, S and W from Normandy; on scrub, bushy cliffs, wds, rocks, hds, especially near sea. Fl 6–8.

B Woodruff, *Galium odoratum*, erect per, 15–30 cm tall, vanilla-scented when bruised, stems unbranched, four-angled, only hairy below the distant, spreading whorls of 6–8 elliptical-lanceolate, pointed, hairless lvs, that have forward-pointing prickles on edges. Fls in umbel-like heads; corollas (**Ba**) 4–6 mm long, white, **funnel-shaped**, four-lobed halfway; fr (**Bb**) 2–3 mm long, rough with hooked bristles. Br Isles: GB c (but E Anglia o, N Scot r); Ire o-f; Eur c (but o to SW in France); in wds on calc or richer soils. Fl 5–6. ***Bi Dyer's Woodruff**, *Asperula tinctoria*, looks like B, but 30–70 cm tall; lvs **narrow-linear**, 4 to a whorl above, 6 to a whorl below; corolla often three-lobed only; frs **smooth**. Central and E France to Denmark r-o; in open wds. Fl 6–8.

C Field Madder, *Sherardia arvensis*, hairless ± prostrate ann with stems 10–30 cm long; lvs 4 to a whorl below, 5–6 to a whorl above, elliptical, pointed, 5–20 mm long, with backward-pointing prickles on edges. Fls 4–8 together in dense terminal heads, each head with a ruff of bracts below it; sepals 4–6, green, enlarging in fr; corollas mauve-pink, funnel-shaped, 2–3 mm across, 4–5 mm long, with long tube; fr dry, 4 mm long, with sepals persisting on top, bristly. Br Isles: GB f (c in S and E, r to N); Ire f; Eur c; on ar, wa. Fl 5–10.

D Squinancywort, *Asperula cynanchica*, per hairless prostrate herb, with branched four-angled ascending shoots 5–20 cm long; lowest lvs elliptical, others linear, 4 to a whorl, 6–20 mm long, often **unequal** and at **acute angle** to stems; infls few-fld, long-stalked clusters; corollas funnel-shaped, 6 mm long × 3–4 mm wide, white within, pink outside, four-lobed; fr 3 mm long, warted. Br Isles: S, SE Eng, S Wales f-lc, rest of Eng N to Yorks and Westmorland r; **Scot abs**; Ire vlf in W; Eur: France, S Belgium, f-lc, abs to N; on calc gslds, dunes. Fl 6–7.

GLOBULARIA FAMILY

A family **abs in Br Isles** but with several spp in Eur.

*E Globularia, *Globularia vulgaris*, hairless per herb, with basal rosette of obovate, short-stalked lvs, untoothed or three-notched at tips, and erect unbranched stems 5–20 cm tall with shorter, alt, stalkless lanceolate stem-lvs. Fl-heads, dense, rounded, **scabious-like**, terminate stems and are 1.5–2.0 cm across; each has a whorl of short lfy bracts at its base and scales between the stalkless florets. Calyx-tubes have 5 persistent teeth; corolla-tubes pale blue, 6–8 mm long, with 2 lips, upper small, two-toothed, lower longer, three-toothed; 4 stamens, a long style; ovary **superior** (unlike Scabious or Sheep's-bit); fr a tiny one-seeded nutlet. Eur: central and E France N to Somme valley; S Belgium; W Germany; o-lc on calc gslds, rocks. Fl 4–7.

Aa

Ba 5mm

Bb 3mm

5mm

A

B

C

D

E

A family of herbs with erect stems, **opp** lvs, and fls in dense **heads** seated on a common receptacle-disc, with calyx-like whorl of bracts below each head. Fls small, often asymmetrical; each fl surrounded by a tubular **epicalyx**. Calyx tubular, cup-like, or divided into 4–8 long bristle-like teeth; corolla tubular, 4–5-lobed, lobes ± equal or else fl ± two-lipped; stamens **long-protruding**, separate, 2 or 4; style long; stigma simple or two-lobed; **ovary inferior**; fr an achene. V like Daisy family, Compositae, but differs clearly in the long-protruding free stamens (in Compositae joined in a tube and not, or little-protruding), in the persistent epicalyx round each fl (and, later, fr), and in the long calyx-teeth. Scabiouses can be confused with Rampions (*Phyteuma*) and Sheep's-bit (*Jasione*) in Bellflower family (p 338), but in the latter stamens do **not** protrude from the fls, calyx-teeth are short, and there is no epicalyx cup. See key p 356.

Teasels, Scabiouses

 A Teasel, *Dipsacus fullonum*, stout bi herb, in first year producing a lf-rosette of short-stalked, oblong-lanceolate lvs, with swollen-based prickles; stem to 2 m, **hairless**, **v prickly**, branched, arises in second year with opp, 10–15 cm-long narrow lanceolate lvs (**joined into a cup** at base of each pair) with few teeth and prickles only on underside of midribs. Fl-heads 3–8 cm long, **egg-shaped**, erect; bracts below head linear, rigid, spiny, 5–9 cm long; bracts among florets linear, spiny, **longer** than pink-purple corollas 5–7 mm long. Br Isles: Eng, Wales, c; SE Scot, Ire r; **N**, **W Scot abs**; Eur c; in open wds, stream banks, rds, gslds, especially on clay soils. Fl 7–8.
 B Small Teasel, *D. pilosus*, erect bristly bi herb to 120 cm, much slenderer than A, with angled **weakly**-prickly branched stems; root-lvs oval, **hairy**, **long-stalked**, prickly **only** on midrib below; stem-lvs oval-elliptical, ± toothed, hairy (**not** prickly, **not** joined round stem). Fl-heads **globular**, 2.0–2.5 cm wide, on weak prickly stalks; bracts below head hairy, narrow-triangular, spine-tipped, **shorter** than fl-head; bracts among florets obovate, hairy, spine-tipped; corollas 6–9 mm, white or pinkish. Br Isles: Eng, Wales, o-lf; **Scot**, **Ire**, **abs**; Eur o-lf; in damp open wds, by streams, hbs. Fl 7–8.
 C Small Scabious, *Scabiosa columbaria*, slender erect per, 15–70 cm; rosette-lvs long-stalked, obovate, toothed, or ± pinnatifid with large end lft; stem-lvs pinnate, ± downy, upper ones stalkless, with **linear** lobes; fl-heads 2–3 cm wide, on long downy stalks; bracts of head linear, shorter than florets; outer florets much larger than central ones; 5 long, blackish, bristle-like calyx-teeth; corollas blue-violet with 5 unequal lobes. Br Isles: Eng, Wales, f-lc; Scot vr; **Ire abs**; Eur, c to S, o to N; on calc gslds. Fl 7–9. ***Ci** *S. canescens* has grey-downy **untoothed** lanceolate root-lvs, pale lilac, scented fls, **purple** anthers. Denmark to E France; r in dry gslds. Fl 7–9.
 D Field Scabious, *Knautia arvensis*, a **stouter**, more **roughly-hairy** version of C; root-lvs larger, roughly-hairy, usually **unlobed**, but often blunt-toothed; stem-lvs deeply pinnatifid, with **coarse** hairy segments and **elliptical** end-lft; fl-heads 3–4 cm wide, stalks **stout** (2–3 mm); bracts of head oval; calyx-teeth 8; corollas blue-violet with 4 unequal lobes; epicalyx four-angled. Br Isles c (but N, W Scot r); Eur c; on dry gslds, hbs, rds. Fl 7–9.
 E Devil's-bit Scabious, *Succisa pratensis*, differs from C and D in its **undivided**, opp, obovate-lanceolate, ± hairy, ± untoothed lvs; stem-lvs narrower than root-lvs, otherwise v similar. Fl-heads 1.5–2.5 cm wide, outer florets (unlike those in C and D) **no larger than inner**; calyx with 5 bristle-teeth; bracts among florets lfy, **longer** than calyx-teeth; corollas mauve to dark purplish-blue, with 4 ± **equal lobes**. Br Isles, Eur; vc in gslds, mds, fens, damp wds, on acid and calc soils. Fl 6–10.

TEASEL FAMILY

Dipsaceae

KEY TO TEASEL FAMILY

1 Stems spiny – long spiny bracts below fl-heads, shorter spine-tipped bracts among narrow florets.. *Dipsacus* (p 354)
  Stems hairy but not spiny – bracts of fl-heads and florets not spine-tipped – corollas broad-lobed... **2**
2 Stem-lvs pinnatifid – outer florets of head larger than central ones – corollas all unequally 4- or 5-lobed.. **3**
  Stem-lvs untoothed or only feebly so – all florets equal in size – corollas all equally four-lobed...........
  .... *Succisa* (p 354)
3 Florets attached to a dome-shaped recptacle-disc – no bracts among florets – calyx with 8 long bristle-teeth – epicalyx four-angled .... *Knautia* (p 354)
  Florets attached to a conical receptacle – bracts among florets – calyx with 5 long bristle-teeth – epicalyx a cylindrical funnel.. *Scabiosa* (p 354)

DAISY FAMILY

Compositae

The world's largest family of flowering plants, with more than 14,000 spp, and in evolution one of the most advanced. In Br Isles and Eur herbs (many shrubs elsewhere); no stipules to lvs; small fls (florets) in dense heads, the florets seated unstalked on a flat or rounded disc (the **receptacle**) on the end of a stem. The disc is surrounded by a calyx-like series of bracts of varied form, in one or more rows, called the **involucre**. Individual florets may, or may not, have undivided scale-like bracts between them, attached to the receptacle-disc; in different spp florets may have both stamens and ovary together, stamens only, ovary only, or may be sterile. Ovary, when present, is always **inferior**. Petals are always joined into a corolla-tube with (normally) 5 teeth or lobes; corolla is of 2 main types, either **tubular** and ± regular, tipped with 5 small ± equal teeth, or **strap-shaped**, composed of a long petal-like strip extending out to one side of the floret with 5 (or 3) small teeth at its tip. The 5 stamens are joined into a tiny tube attached to the inside of the corolla-tube; the single style is forked into 2 stigmas above; ovary produces a single seed. Calyx may consist of: (1) a parachute-like **pappus** of one or more rows of simple or pinnate-feathered hairs, for wind dispersal of the small achene-like frs; (2) small scales sometimes joined in a cup; or (3) calyx may be abs.

The Daisy family is close to the Teasel family (Dipsaceae) in its dense heads of florets on a disc, but the latter have stamens all **separate**, **long-stalked**, distinctly **protruding** from florets, bristle-like calyx-teeth, and an epicalyx to each floret (abs in Compositae). Compositae may also be confused with Sheep's-bit and Rampions in the Bellflower family, but in these latter stamens are separately stalked and short, and calyx has 5 narrow green teeth. Valerians (*Valeriana*) also have a pappus, but their stamens are 3 in number (5 in Compositae).

Within the Daisy family itself important distinguishing features are: (1) florets tubular, or strap-shaped, or of both shapes: (2) arrangement, length and shape of the bracts surrounding fl-heads; (3) presence or absence of pappus on frs, and whether its hairs, if present, are simple or feathered; (4) shape of fl-heads; (5) presence or absence of scale-like bracts among florets.

KEY TO DAISY FAMILY

(Note: go directly to section F for all Compositae not agreeing with headings of Keys A–E, especially for Compositae with tiny heads, that are not obviously daisy-, dandelion- or thistle-like)

1 Florets of fl-heads **all** strap-shaped (as in a dandelion), all either yellow or blue – stems with milky latex.. **A**
  At least central florets of fl-heads tubular, regular – stems without milky latex............................. **2**
2 Heads with florets all tubular – no strap-shaped florets visible **3**
  Heads with at least **some** strap-shaped outer florets (perhaps v short, erect), as well as tubular inner florets (as in a daisy) **5**

3 Florets in **thistle-like heads**, either with florets projecting, ± like a shaving brush, well beyond the elongated cup of spiny or scale-like bracts (or, if florets not projecting, bracts hooked or spine-tipped)..**E**
  Florets **not** in thistle-like heads, but either in button-like discs or in narrow, few-fld heads, variously grouped or clustered **4**
4 Florets in well-separated, button-like, rounded or flattish heads – heads broader than deep, with many (20–60) densely-packed yellow florets...**D**
  Florets in heads longer than broad, with few (5–20) florets – heads themselves often clustered in heads, panicles or racemes...**F**
5 Ray-florets yellow, like the disc-florets...**B**
  Ray-florets white, blue, or purple – disc-florets yellow (sometimes white or greenish-grey)............**C**

A Dandelion-like Compositae, with florets of fl-heads all strap-shaped, either yellow, blue or purple; stems with milky latex
1 Fls blue, purple or mauve..**2**
  Fls yellow or orange **5**
2 Fls bright blue – heads 2.5–4.0 cm across – pappus of scales only (not of hairs)................................
                                                                                   Cichorium intybus (p 390 D)
  Fls pale blue, purple or mauve – pappus of hairs **3**
3 Achenes narrowed into a beak above...**4**
  Achenes not narrowed into a beak – lvs with large terminal lobe, small side-lobes............................
                                                                                   Cicerbita alpina (p 392 Ii)
4 Lvs narrow, grass-like – pappus feathery – bracts round fl-heads in one row, all equal........................
                                                                                   Tragopogon porrifolius (p 390 Bii)
  Lvs pinnatifid, terminal lobe narrow – pappus of unbranched hairs – bracts round fl-heads overlapping in several unequal rows...*Lactuca perennis* (p 392 I)
                                                                                                             6
5 Pappus abs on frs **7**
  Pappus of hairs on frs ....
6 Stem much branched, lfy – fl-head-stalks slender..............................*Lapsana communis* (p 394 G)
  Stem little branched, lfless – fl-head-stalks much swollen at tips ....*Arnoseris minima* (p 394 Bi)
7 Pappus with at least its inner hairs feathery..**8**
  Pappus wholly of unbranched hairs..**13**
8 Stem-lvs tiny or abs – lvs nearly all in basal rosette **9**
  Stem-lvs large, conspicuous (at least below)..**10**
9 Lanceolate chaffy scales present between florets on receptacle-disc........*Hypochoeris* (p 392–394)
  No scales between florets on receptacle-disc ....*Leontodon* (p 394)
10 Stem and lvs bristly – stem-lvs oblong – outer bracts of fl-heads ± spreading in a ruff, different from adpressed inner ones – pappus soft..*(Picris)* **11**
   Stem and lvs ± woolly when young, ± hairless when mature – stem-lvs all narrow – bracts of fl-heads all similar, adpressed to head – pappus with many rays, rigid **12**
11 Outer ruff of fl-head bracts widely cordate – bristles on lvs with white swollen bases – achenes with long (6 mm or more) beaks...*Picris echioides* (p 396 H)
   Outer ruff of fl-head bracts narrow, lanceolate, spreading – bristles on lvs without swollen bases – achenes with short (1–2 mm) beaks...*Picris hieracioides* (p 396 G)
12 Bracts of fl-heads long, **narrow**, in a **single, equal** row – stem-lvs grass-like, sheathing, 10 cm or more – root-lvs similar, but longer...*Tragopogon pratensis* (p 390 B)
   Bracts of fl-heads **oval-oblong**, in **many overlapping** rows – stem-lvs flatter – root-lvs elliptical-lanceolate, stalked...*Scorzonera humilis* (p 390 C)
13 Lvs all in a basal rosette – infl-stem hollow, lfless, with 1 fl-head......*Taraxacum officinale* (p 388 A)
   Stems lfy, at least on creeping runners – infl-stem solid or hollow...**14**
14 Achenes ± cylindrical, not flattened..**15**
   Achenes strongly flattened, lens-shaped in cross-section..**17**
15 Plants with lfy runners at base – stem-lvs abs or few – rosette-lvs unlobed, untoothed – achenes unbeaked, toothed at tips, below brownish brittle pappus.....................................*Pilosella* (p 398)
   Plants with no runners at base – stem-lvs usually numerous – rosette-lvs and stem-lvs ± toothed or lobed – achenes not toothed at tips...**16**
16 Involucre-bracts many, overlapping, **unequal** – frs never beaked – pappus brownish, brittle...........
                                                                                   Hieracium (p 398)
   Involucre-bracts in one inner row of longer **equal** ones (also some shorter outer ± spreading bracts) – frs sometimes beaked – pappus white, soft ....*Crepis* (p 395–396)

357

17 Achenes with no beak, not narrowed upwards – stems stout, hollow – fl-heads 1.5 cm wide or more, with many florets, in loose umbels...*Sonchus* (p 400)
Achenes beaked – stems slender, ± solid – fl-heads under 1 cm wide, with only 5–12 florets, in panicles or racemes... **18**

18 Side-branches of infl spreading at 90° to main stem – florets only 5 per fl-head – bracts around fl-heads in an inner row of equal long ones, plus outer row of v short bracts ....
Mycelis muralis (p 390 E)
Side-branches of infl ascending at acute angle to main stem – florets more than 5 per fl-head – bracts around fl-heads in many unequal overlapping ranks ....*Lactuca* (p 390–392)

B **Compositae with yellow tubular disc-florets in centre of head, and yellow strap-shaped ray-florets round edge of head; latter may be v short, or erect (rather than spreading and daisy-like)**

1 Stem-lvs (mostly) opp **2**
Stem-lvs (mostly) alt, or all lvs from base of stem only **3**

2 Heads not more than 3 cm across (including rays) – fr crowned by 2–4 persistent barbed spines – no basal lf-rosette...*Bidens* (p 370)
Heads 4 cm across or more – fr with a pappus of simple hairs in one row – basal lf-rosette present – not in Br Isles..*Arnica montana* (p 364 E)
Heads 5 cm across, or much more – fr with 1–4 narrow scales on top, that soon fall off – no basal lf-rosette – plant 50–100 cm tall...*Helianthus rigidus* (p 364 Ei)

3 Heads solitary, terminal, on unbranched scaly lfless stems (in early spring) – lvs all basal, long-stalked, cordate, toothed (appearing later) – pappus of white hairs .... *Tussilago farfara* (p 372 A)
Heads not solitary, not on unbranched lfless stems.. **4**

4 Heads **many**, 5–10 mm across, arranged in elongated racemes or panicles – lvs ± stalkless, simple – pappus of white hairs. ....*Solidago virgaurea* (p 366 G)
Heads not in elongated racemes or panicles **5**

5 Fr without hairy pappus **6**
Fr with pappus of hairs **7**

6 Lvs grey-green, hairless, toothed or pinnately-lobed, with broad segments – no scales between disc-florets..*Chrysanthemum segetum* (p 370 D)
Lvs bright green, hairy below, deeply twice-pinnatifid into narrow segments – scales present between disc-florets ....*Anthemis tinctoria* (p 374 Bii)

7 Involucre-bracts in 1 (or 2) rows, all bracts of **equal** length, erect – also a few small bracts at involucre-base.. **8**
Involucre-bracts in several **overlapping** rows, outer bracts progressively shorter.............................. **9**

8 Fl-heads not over 3.5 cm across, in loose, umbel-like infls – involucre-bracts in **1** equal row – also a few small bracts at involucre-base...*Senecio* (p 362–364)
Fl-heads 4 cm or more across, few per fl-stem, long-stalked, not in a loose, umbel-like infl – involucre-bracts in 2 equal rows ....*Doronicum pardalianches* (p 364 F)

9 Fr with a row of small scales on top, surrounding base of hairy pappus....................*Pulicaria* (p 366)
Fr with no scales surrounding pappus-base ....*Inula* (p 366–368)

C **Compositae with daisy-like heads, disc-florets yellow or whitish, but ray-florets white, purple, or bluish (not yellow)**

1 Lvs opp – heads under 1 cm across – ray-florets white, v short, only 4 or 5 – erect ann plants of wa, ar...*Galinsoga* (p 370)
Lvs alt, or all in a basal rosette **2**

2 Frs with a hairy pappus.. **3**
Frs without a hairy pappus **5**

3 Ray-florets v short, narrow, erect or ascending at an angle **4**
Ray-florets broad, spreading, their length at least equal to width of fl-head disc – lvs hairless...........
Aster (p 368)

4 Fl-heads 12–18 mm across, in a loose umbel – ray-florets purple, ascending – plant hairy...............
Erigeron acer (p 368 G)
Fl-heads 3–5 mm across, many, in a long panicle – ray-florets whitish, erect, v short – plant ± hairless..*Conyza canadensis* (p 368 H)
Fl-heads 10–15 mm across, vanilla-scented, appearing late winter, spreading on long stalks in a spike-like raceme – ray-florets pale lilac, erect, short – lvs long-stalked, kidney-shaped, 10–20 cm wide..*Petasites fragrans* (p 372 C)

5 Fl-heads solitary on lfless unbranched stalks – lvs all in a basal rosette, undivided, obovate to spoon-shaped ....*Bellis perennis* (p 370 I)
   Fl-heads on lfy, ± branched stalks – lvs not all in a basal rosette.. **6**

6 Disc-florets whitish or greenish-white (never bright yellow) – ray-florets white or pink – fl-heads small (4–15 mm across), in umbel-like heads...*Achillea* (p 372)
   Disc-florets yellow – ray-florets always white – fl-heads larger (15–50 mm across) **7**

7 Lvs coarsely-toothed, or pinnatifid with broad segments at least 3–4 mm wide ....
   ....*Chrysanthemum* (p 369–370)
   Lvs twice pinnatifid into narrow (1 mm wide) linear or hairlike segments....................................... **8**

8 Scales present between disc-florets on receptacle-disc **9**
   No scales between disc-florets **10**

9 Ann plants of wa, ar – tubes of disc-florets flattened, winged below – achenes cylindrical, ribbed both sides..*Anthemis* (p 374)
   Creeping per plant of gslds, hths – tubes of disc-florets not flattened, not winged below – achenes flattened, smooth ....*Chamaemelum nobile* (p 374 D)

10 Fl-head receptacle solid, slightly dome-shaped – ray-florets always spreading – achenes with 2 black spots near apex – plant ± unscented........................*Tripleurospermum maritimum* (p 374 A)
    Fl-head receptacle hollow, conical – ray-florets soon bending downwards – achenes without black spots near apex – plant strongly aromatic...................................*Matricaria recutita* (p 374 Ai)

D **Compositae with yellow disc-florets in button-like rounded or flattish heads; heads not more than twice as long as broad, with many (20–60) densely packed florets (resembling daisy-heads with the ray-florets missing); bracts to heads not spiny**

1 Stem-lvs in opp pairs – fr crowned with 2–4 stiff barbed spines – no hairy pappus ... *Bidens* (p 370)
   Stem-lvs alt **2**

2 Lvs simple, toothed or untoothed... **6**
   Lvs pinnately lobed or divided **3**

3 Lvs hairless .... *Aster linosyris* (p 368 E), and rayless forms of *A. tripolium* (p 368 F)
   Lvs hairy **4**

4 Lvs white-woolly – no pappus on fr – on beaches – vr......................................*Otanthus maritimus* (p 366 H)
   Lvs hairy, but not white-woolly – hairy pappus on fr **5**

5 Fl-heads to 1 cm across, in irregular umbel-like infls – ray-florets abs or v short, disc-florets dark yellow – lvs oval-oblong, downy (like foxglove lvs) ....*Inula conyza* (p 366 C)
   Fl-heads 3–5 mm across, many in a long panicle – disc-florets pale yellow – minute white erect ray-florets often present, but not always easy to see – lvs linear-lanceolate, hairy.................................
   ....*Conyza canadensis* (p 368 H)

6 Hairy pappus present – bracts of involucre in one row..*Senecio vulgaris* (p 362 F)
   No hairy pappus... **7**

7 Disc-florets with corolla-**tube white**, but with 4 **yellow** lobes – fl-heads solitary, dome-shaped – plant aromatic – r ....*Cotula coronopifolia* (p 374 Ci)
   Disc-florets with five-lobed corollas **wholly yellowish** **8**

8 Lvs 2–3 times pinnately-divided into **hairlike** segments – fl-heads conical, greenish-yellow, pineapple-scented, terminating lfy branches ....*Matricaria matricarioides* (p 374 C)
   Lvs once-pinnately-divided into flat, lanceolate, toothed segments – fl-heads flat-topped, many, in umbel-like flat-topped corymbs...*Chrysanthemum vulgare* (p 369 C)

E **Compositae with thistle-like fl-heads (either with florets projecting in a shaving brush-like tuft from the involucre cup of bracts, or, if florets shorter, fl-head has hook-tipped or spiny bracts)**

1 Florets yellow... **2**
   Florets purple, red, blue or white... **4**

2 Lvs and outer bracts of fl-head spiny, thistle-like – inner bracts of fl-head chaffy, yellow, spreading in fr..*Carlina vulgaris* (p 388 D)
   Lvs with hairs or fine bristles on margins, but without strong spines... **3**

3 Upper stem-lvs oval, clasping, hairs only on edges – stem unwinged – bracts of fl-heads ending in a single v short slender spine ....*Cirsium oleraceum* (p 381 C)
   Upper stem-lvs lanceolate, running down stem as wings – bracts of fl-heads ending in a stout palmately-branched spine, 10–20 mm long...*Centaurea solstitialis* (p 386 Ci)

4 Florets **blue**, radiating outwards in **all** directions, in **spherical** fl-head 4–6 cm wide – each floret with whorl of outer bristle-like bracts, and inner pinnate bracts – lvs spine-tipped – tall thistle-like plant...*Echinops sphaerocelphalus* (p 386 F)

Florets not (or only shortly) projecting beyond bracts – bracts of fl-head involucre narrow, rigid, spreading, hook-tipped – head in fr forming a round burr that sticks to clothes or hair......................
....*Arctium* (p 386)

Florets projecting thistle-like in a tuft well beyond fl-head bract – bracts of fl-head broader, erect, not hook-tipped **5**

5 Bracts of fl-head involucre each formed of 2 segments, the lower pale or greenish, the upper brown, black or silvery, chaffy or spiny – **pappus (if present) not longer than achenes** ....
....*Centaurea* (p 385–386)

Bracts of fl-head not composed of 2 separate segments – pappus always longer than achenes **6**

6 Lvs and fl-heads quite devoid of spines or prickles **7**

Lvs spiny, or at least fringed with fine prickles...**(Thistles) 8**

7 Pappus feathered – lvs unlobed, but ± toothed, white-cottony below – fl-heads few, in a dense terminal cluster – on mts – r-lf ....*Saussurea alpina* (p 388 Bi)

Pappus simple – lower lvs pinnatifid, upper lvs ± unlobed but fine-toothed, hairless below – fl-heads in a v open terminal cluster...*Serratula tinctoria* (p 388 B)

8 Pappus of feathered hairs..**9**

Pappus of simple hairs..*Cirsium* (p 381–382)

9 Lvs hairless, shiny dark green, with strong milk-white veins above – stems without spiny wings ......
....*Silybum marianum* (p 388 A)

Lvs ± hairy, without strong white veins above – stems with spiny wings.....................................**10**

10 Both sides of lvs, and the winged stem wholly whitish-grey with cottony hairs – achenes four-angled...*Onopordon acanthium* (p 388 C)

Upper sides of lvs green, not cottony – lower sides of lvs and stem ± cottony – achenes rounded..*Carduus* (p 382–384)

F **Compositae with tubular florets only; florets rarely bright yellow, 5–40 together in narrow elongated fl-heads, not daisy-, dandelion- or thistle-like**

1 Stem-lvs opp, palmately-lobed, with 3–5 elliptical segments, or else simple, oval-lanceolate – fl-heads small, tassel-like, of 5–6 pinkish-purple florets, grouped into large terminal panicles or corymbs – robust plant to 120 cm tall ....*Eupatorium cannabinum* (p 372 F)

Lvs large, all from root, long-stalked, cordate or kidney-shaped – infl-stalk with alt scale-like lvs only..**2**

Stem-lvs well-developed, alt – root-lvs (if present) ± similar to stem-lvs..**3**

2 Fl-heads gathered into racemes on stout lfless but scale-bearing stalks, produced in winter or spring – root-lvs large (10 cm or more wide), cordate, often appearing later than infls – florets pink or white ....*Petasites* (p 372)

Fl-heads solitary, terminal, on slender lfless but scale-bearing stalks – root-lvs kidney-shaped, small (to 4 cm wide), appearing with infls – florets purple – on mts of Scot – vr.................................
....*Homogyne alpina* (p 372 Ai)

3 Lvs twice pinnately-divided – fl-heads v small (2–4 mm wide), bell-shaped or oval, grouped into long, usually much-branched panicles...*Artemisia* (p 376)

Lvs undivided, narrow, strap-shaped or obovate, ± woolly – fl-heads ± woolly **4**

4 Long lfy runners arising from basal rosette of obovate lvs, green above and white below – fl-heads woolly, in an umbel-like head – plants dioecious – male fl-heads with spreading white chaffy tips to bracts – female fl-heads with erect pointed pink-tipped bracts – per plant....................
....*Antennaria dioica* (p 370 G)

Plants without long lfy runners at base..**5**

5 Fl-heads grouped into dense rounded or egg-shaped clusters in forks of repeatedly branching stems, along stem branches and at branch tips – outer bracts of fl-heads woolly, inner bracts chaffy – lvs strap-shaped, untoothed, woolly – woolly ann plants with no lf-rosette at fl-time.............
....*Filago* (p 378)

Fl-heads either in spike-like racemes or in terminal looser umbel-like clusters surrounded by lvs (not in tight clusters as in *Filago*) – all bracts of fl-heads chaffy **6**

6 Bracts of involucre golden yellow, petal-like, curved back in fr – not in Br Isles.................................
....*Helichrysum* (p 378–380)

Bracts of involucre greyish, often dark-tipped, or straw-coloured, ± erect, or spreading, but not curved back in fr...*Gnaphalium* (p 380)

Ragworts and **Groundsels** (*Senecio*) are a genus of ± cottony-hairy herbs (in Eur), with alt lvs and fl-heads in loose or dense umbel-like infls; bracts of fl-heads in **one** long **equal** row, with mostly a few **short** outer bracts at base of head. Disc- and ray-florets all yellow (latter sometimes abs); achenes cylindrical, ribbed, not beaked; pappus white, of simple hairs only; no scales between florets.

KEY TO *SENECIO* SPP

1 At least some lvs deeply pinnatifid **2**
  All lvs unlobed, oval-lanceolate **10**
2 Lvs thickly white-felted below – ray-florets spreading ....*S. cineraria* (p 362 E)
  Lvs ± hairless (or merely cottony or downy) below **3**
3 Ray-florets v short (5 mm or less) or abs **4**
  Ray-florets long, spreading, conspicuous **6**
4 Heads, when young, stalkless, in dense clusters, later stalked – ray-florets usually abs ....
                                                                                        S. vulgaris (p 362 F)
  Heads always stalked, in loose umbel-like clusters – ray-florets present, short, erect or recurved... **5**
5 Stems and lvs v sticky-hairy – about 20 bracts per fl-head, the outermost 2 or 3 at least ⅓ as long
  as others – heads 10–12 mm long × 8 mm wide – achenes hairless ....*S. viscosus* (p 362 H)
  Stems and lvs ± cottony, not sticky – about 13 bracts per fl-head, the outermost v short,
  scale-like – heads 7–9 mm long × 5 mm wide – achenes downy .... *S. sylvaticus* (p 362 G)
6 Fl-heads in dense umbel-like corymbs on erect stems... **7**
  Fl-heads in loose, spreading long-branched infls **9**
7 Side-lobes of lvs short, oval, with crisped edges, v cottony – Br Isles abs .... *S. vernalis* (p 362 Fi)
  Side-lobes of lvs long, narrow, not crisped, not v hairy above... **8**
8 Fls golden-yellow – lvs bright green, ± hairless below – end-lobes of lower stem-lvs and
  root-lvs broad, blunt – outer bracts of heads v short (¼ length of inner ones)...................................
                                                                                        S. jacobaea (p 362 A)
  Fls pale clear yellow – lvs grey-green, cottony, especially below – end-lobes of all lvs v narrow,
  pointed – outer bracts of heads ½ length of inner, longer ones.....................*S. erucifolius* (p 362 C)
9 Stem-lvs with large oval terminal lobe – root-lvs elliptical, often without side-lobes – fl-heads
  golden, 2.5–3.0 cm wide – bracts without black tips – in wet places ....*S. aquaticus* (p 362 B)
  Stem-lvs with all lobes narrow – fl-heads clear yellow, 1.5–2.0 cm wide – bracts of heads **all**
  black-tipped – on wa, walls, rds...*S. squalidus* (p 362 D)
10 Involucre with some short outer bracts forming a cup round the long equal inner ones – lvs sharp-
   toothed, hairless above **11**
   Involucre with no short outer bracts, bracts **all** long and equal – lvs scarcely toothed, cottony
   both sides.. **13**
11 Lvs **elliptical**-lanceolate, **stalked**, **fine-toothed**, **spreading** – long, narrow fl-heads only 1.5–
   2.5 cm across, in a loose corymb – tall wdland plant – not in Br Isles ....*S. fuchsii* (p 364 A)
   Lvs **narrow**-lanceolate, **stalkless**, **sharply-toothed**, erect – tall marsh plant................................ **12**
12 Lvs v **cottony** below, shiny, **hairless above** – fl-heads 3–4 cm wide, each with 10–20 ray-florets,
   in a dense corymb – vr ....*S. paludosus* (p 364 B)
   Lvs **hairless both sides** – fl-heads 2–3 cm wide, each with 6–8 ray-florets, in a dense corymb –
   r ....*S. fluviatilis* (p 364 Bi)
13 Fl-heads in corymbs **both** on tip of main stem **and** on side branches – lvs woolly, lanceolate,
   pointed – marsh plant – vr ....*S. palustris* (p 364 Di)
   Fl-heads in a **simple** terminal umbel – lvs v cottony, oval to elliptical or obovate, **blunt** – in dry
   gslds.. **14**
14 Basal lvs in a rosette flat on gd, short-stalked, round-oval, 3–6 cm long – fl-heads 1–10 –
   involucre 5–8 mm long – bracts with tuft of hairs on tip – fls orange-yellow – plant 10–30 cm
   tall...*S. integrifolius* (p 364 C)
   Basal lvs ± erect, long-stalked, obovate to spoon-shaped, 10–20 cm long – fl-heads 12–20
   – involucre 8–12 mm long – bracts without tuft of hairs on tip – fls clear yellow – plant 30–
   100 cm tall – not in Br Isles...*S. helenitis* (p 364 D)

Ragworts, Groundsels (see also key p 361)

   A   Common Ragwort, *Senecio jacobaea*, erect bi, 30–100 cm; stems furrowed, ± hairless, lfy; basal rosette-lvs pinnatifid, with large oval terminal
lobes, stem-lvs 1–2 times pinnatifid, with short, blunt, toothed terminal lobes, all
green, ± cottony below. Fl-heads in a branched terminal umbel-like corymb;
heads 15–25 mm across, bright yellow; outer bracts less than ¼ length of the long
equal ones; ray-florets spreading, 5–8 mm long, their achenes (**Aa**) hairless, with
simple pappus; disc-floret achenes hairy. Br Isles, Eur; vc on neglected gslds, rds,
wa, dunes. Fl 6–10.
   B   Marsh Ragwort, *S. aquaticus*, differs from A in elliptical-oval undivided
root-lvs, stem-lvs with **large**, **oval** end-lobes, and in the **spreading, loosely-
branched** infls, larger **golden**-yellow fl-heads 25–30 mm across; achenes all
hairless. Br Isles, Eur; c in mds, marshes. Fl 7–8.
   C   Hoary Ragwort, *S. erucifolius*, has erect habit and umbel-like infls of A, but
stem and lvs **grey-green** with cottony hairs, especially on lf-undersides; all lvs (**Cb**)
have both side- and end-lobes **narrow, pointed**, with curved-back margins; fl-
heads (**Ca**) 15–20 mm across, their outer bracts half length of the long inner equal
ones; florets all **pale** clear yellow, achenes all hairy. Br Isles: Eng, Wales, c in
lowlands; **Scot abs**; E Ire only, r; Eur, France c, to Denmark r; on gslds on clay or
calc soils. Fl 7–9.
   D   Oxford Ragwort, *S. squalidus*, usually ann, more spreading and bushy than
A–C; lvs almost hairless, 1–2 times pinnatifid, with **all** lobes narrow, pointed; fl-
heads 16–20 mm across, bright yellow, with all bracts conspicuously **black-tipped**;
all achenes hairy. Br Isles: Eng, Wales f-la; Scot, Ire vr; Eur, France o-lf; introd (S
Italy) increasing, on wa, railways, walls, rds. Fl 5–12.
   E   Silver Ragwort, *S. cineraria*, low shrub, 30–60 cm; lvs twice-pinnatifid,
white-felted below, green on uppersides; fl-heads in umbel-like corymbs, 8–
12 mm across, bright yellow; bracts woolly; achenes hairless. Br Isles: Eng, S coast,
r but lc; Ire vr; Eur: France o; introd (Mediterranean) on sea cliffs, beaches, wa.
Fl 6–8.
   F   Groundsel, *S. vulgaris*, ann weed, with weak erect stems to 40 cm; lvs
± cottony, pinnatifid, with short, oval-oblong, blunt lobes, upper lvs clasping,
lower stalked; short outer bracts black-tipped, inner narrow, 8–10 mm; ray-florets
usually abs; achenes hairy. Br Isles, Eur; a on ar, wa. Fl 1–12.   **Fi   S. vernalis*
resembles F in habit, but is taller (15–40 cm), **much woollier**, with more outer
bracts; side-lobes of leaves v short; fl-heads golden-yellow with **spreading** ray-
florets; achenes hairy. Denmark to Netherlands f-lc; on dunes, sandy gslds, rds.
Fl 5–6.
   G   Heath Groundsel, *S. sylvaticus*, taller (30–70 cm) plant than F; lvs
pinnatifid, longer-lobed than in F, cottony at first, but later hairless; infl much looser
than in F, with long-stalked heads; fl-heads (8 × 5 mm) more conical, with **v short**
outer bracts, and ± **sticky-hairy** long inner bracts **not** black-tipped. Ray-
florets present but v short, recurved, achenes green, hairy. Br Isles, Eur; f-lc on
open wds, hths, gslds on acid sandy soils. Fl 7–9.
   H   Sticky Groundsel, *S. viscosus*, v close to G in habit, lf-form and fl-heads,
but **v sticky-hairy** all over stem, lvs and involucres. Fl-heads (**H**) **longer, wider** (12
× 8 mm) than in G (9 × 5 mm), with more long, equal bracts; short outer bracts
nearly **half length** of inner. Ray-florets as in G, but longer; achenes **hairless**. Br
Isles: GB f-lc (**NW Scot abs**); Ire vr; Eur f-lc; on beaches, wa, railways. Fl 7–9.

Aa 5mm

A

B

C

Ca

Cb

D

E

F

G

H

Ragworts, Fleaworts, Leopard's-bane, Goldenrod, Cottonweed etc

*A Alpine Ragwort, *Senecio fuchsii*, erect per to 1 m, ± hairless; lower lvs large, **elliptical-lanceolate, stalked**; upper lvs ± stalkless, all **fine-toothed**; infl in loose umbel-like corymb; fl-heads (15–25 mm wide) much longer than wide; outer bracts few, spreading, inner 8–9; ray-florets only 4 or 5, deep yellow. Eur: E France N to NW Germany o-lf; in open wds mostly in mt areas. Fl 7–9.

B Fen Ragwort, *S. paludosus*, tall per (to 200 cm); stems and **undersides of lvs cottony**; lvs (**B**) shiny, narrow-lanceolate, sharp-toothed, erect, stalkless, **hairless above**; fl-heads 3–4 cm wide, bright yellow, each with 10–20 ray-florets in a dense erect compound umbel-like corymb. Eng, E Anglia vr in the fens; Eur, France to Netherlands, now vr; in fens. Fl 7–8. **Bi Broad-leaved Ragwort**, *S. fluviatilis*, close to B, but lvs **hairless both sides**; fl-heads 2–3 cm wide, with 6–8 ray-florets only. Br Isles introd, r-lf; E France to Netherlands o; in fens, by streamsides. Fl 7–9.

C Field Fleawort, *S. integrifolius*, erect per, 7–30 cm tall; stem and lvs all ± cottony, especially above; rosette-lvs ± **untoothed, round-oval, short-stalked, flat on gd**, 3–5 cm long; stem-lvs few, lanceolate, stalkless, ± clasping. Fl-heads 1–10, orange-yellow, 1.5–2.5 cm across; involucre 5–8 mm long, bracts with **tuft of hairs** at tip; receptacle surface rough; pappus of disc-florets **equalling** corollas; achenes hairy. Plants of Pennine and Anglesey colonies are taller (to 60 cm) stouter, fleshier, but resemble C rather than D in details of fls. GB: S, E Eng, o-lf (Westmorland, Anglesey vr); Eur: Denmark, N Jutland only, r; in short turf in calc gslds. Fl 5–6.

*D *S. helenitis* is close to C, usually taller (to 100 cm), but in exposed coastal sites (ssp *candidus*) may be only 30 cm; rosette-lvs **erect, long-stalked**, 10–20 cm long, ± **obovate,** ± **bluntly-toothed**; fl-heads, 12–20 in well-grown plants, are paler, wider (2.5–3.0 cm); involucre bracts 8–12 mm long with **no tuft of hairs** at tip; surface of receptacle smooth, wartless, pappus only **half length** of that in C. Eur, N France, S Belgium, o-lf; on calc gslds, damp wds, mds. Fl 5–6. ***Di-Marsh Fleawort**, *S. palustris*, tall (to 100 cm) erect woolly per, with furrowed lfy stems; lvs broad-lanceolate, pointed, ± untoothed, woolly; fl-heads pale yellow, 2–3 cm across, infls v dense and umbel-like, on main stem **and on branches**. Bracts of heads all equal, woolly; ray-florets about 20; achenes hairless. Br Isles, N France extinct; Belgium to Denmark, r; in fens. Fl 6–7.

*E Arnica, *Arnica montana*, downy erect per, 30–40 cm tall; rosette-lvs with **strong ± parallel** main veins, oval-lanceolate, pointed, 5–8 cm long, v short-stalked; stem-lvs **opp**, narrow-lanceolate, few; fl-heads few, **solitary**, 4–8 cm across, orange-yellow, long-rayed; bracts of fl-heads lanceolate, in equal rows; no scales between florets; achenes hairless, pappus of simple hairs. Eur: E France to Denmark, o-lf; on mds, hths, gslds. Fl 6–8. **Ei Perennial Sunflower**, *Helianthus rigidus*, has large long-stalked daisy-like heads as in E, but 6–10 cm across, with clear-yellow rays and **brown** disc-florets; plant is tall (50–200 cm), erect, with opp lvs up stem to 10 cm long; lvs ± stalkless, untoothed, v rough, with 3 main veins; pappus of 2 scales only. Br Isles, Eur; introd (N America), o in wa. Fl 8–10.

F Leopard's-bane, *Doronicum pardalianches*, erect per, 30–90 cm tall, with hairy stems and all lvs; rosette-lvs long-stalked, **broadly cordate**, untoothed; stem-lvs stalked below, upper clasping, all **cordate**, pale green, thin, hairy, ± untoothed. Fl-heads terminal on stem and branches, 4–6 cm across, bright yellow; bracts on saucer-shaped involucre in 2–3 equal rows. Achenes black, pappus simple. GB introd: Eng, Wales o-lf, E Scot f-lc; Eur, E France to Denmark, native but often introd; in wds, hbs. Fl 5–7.

cont

Ga

3mm

365

◄   **G   Goldenrod**, *Solidago virgaurea*, per herb with erect little-branched lfy stems 5–70 cm tall; root-lvs obovate, 2–10 cm long, short-stalked, ± hairless, weak-toothed; stem-lvs narrower, pointed, ± untoothed. Fl-heads in a **raceme** or **panicle**, each 6–10 mm across, with yellow ray- and disc-florets; bracts narrow, unequal, many, overlapping, rough-edged. Achenes (**Ga**) brown, downy; pappus of white hairs. Br Isles, Eur; c in dry wds, gslds, cliffs, dunes. Fl 7–9.   **Gi   Canadian Goldenrod**, *S. canadensis*, much taller plant (60–200 cm) than G, with downy stems and strap-shaped lvs; infl with long, dense side-branches forming a **pyramidal** panicle 10–15 cm wide; fl-heads only 5 mm across, rayflorets v short. Br Isles, Eur, f-lc; introd (N America) in wa, on railways. Fl 8–10.

H   Cottonweed, *Otanthus maritimus*, a striking plant; erect tufted per, with stems and lvs all densely **white-woolly**, lvs oblong-lanceolate, shallow-toothed, 2–3 cm long; fl-heads in a dense umbel-like corymb, each 6–9 mm across; tubeflorets bright yellow; **ray-florets abs**; involucre of many overlapping woolly bracts. Achenes hairless, pappus abs. SE Ire, vr but lva; France from Cherbourg peninsula W and S, o-la; on sandy, shingly seashores. Fl 8–9.

▶ **Fleabanes, Ploughman's-spikenard, Golden Samphire, Asters** etc
Fleabanes (*Pulicaria*) have alt downy lanceolate lvs; both ray- and disc-florets yellow; bracts to fl-heads in **overlapping** rows; achenes hairy, with a **simple** hairy pappus and also a row of **scales** on top. *Inula* is close to *Pulicaria*, but there is no row of scales on top of achene around pappus.

A   Common Fleabane, *Pulicaria dysenterica*, erect hairy branched per herb with runners, 20–60 cm; lvs alt, downy, oblong, ± untoothed, 3–8 cm long, upper lvs **cordate**-based, clasping. Fl-heads 1.5–3.0 cm across, in a loose corymb; ray-florets **twice as long** as disc-florets, all florets golden-yellow; bracts of head narrow, pointed, sticky-hairy; achenes (**Aa**) hairy, pappus surrounded by a scaly cup. Br Isles: Eng, Wales, c in lowlands; Scot, S only, r; Ire f; Eur: France c; N to Denmark o-lf; in mds, rds, ditch-sides, on clay or wet soils. Fl 8–9.

B   Small Fleabane, *P. vulgaris*, erect ± sticky-hairy branched ann, 8–40 cm; stem-lvs as in A, but rounded- **not** cordate-based, 2.5–4.0 cm long; flheads (**Ba**) many, only 1 cm across, outer bracts **spreading**; ray-florets **short**, ± equal to length of disc-florets, erect, all florets **pale** yellow. Achenes as in A, but scales on top are **separate**, **not** forming a cup. S Eng, decreasing; Wilts to Sussex only, vr (but New Forest f-lc); Eur: France vr; Belgium to Denmark probably extinct; on open, well-grazed hollows or tracks on commons, pond edges ± flooded in winter, ± dry in summer. Fl 8–10.

C   Ploughman's-spikenard, *Inula conyza*, bi or per herb, erect, downy, 20–80 cm; lower lvs foxglove-like, oval-oblong, stalked, pointed, toothed, downy; upper narrower, ± stalkless. Fl-heads 1 cm across, many, in an umbel-like corymb; outer bracts green, downy, spreading; inner chaffy, ± purplish; rayflorets **v short, or abs**; all florets dark yellow. Achenes (**Ca**) dark-brown, hairy, with pappus of simple rosy hairs, but **no scales** around it. Br Isles: Eng, Wales only, f-lc; Eur: France c; Belgium r-lf, N to Denmark vr; on gsld, scrub, rocks on calc soils. Fl 7–9.

D   Golden Samphire, *Inula crithmoides*, fleshy tufted erect per herb 15–80 cm; lvs many up stems, alt, **linear**, **fleshy**, hairless, stalkless, three-toothed at tip or untoothed, 2.5–6.0 cm long, ± clustered above in lf-axils. Fl-heads few, 2.5 cm across, in a loose umbel-like corymb; bracts to heads hairless, erect; rayflorets many, golden, **twice as long as longest bracts**; disc-florets orange; achenes downy, pappus white. Br Isles: S Eng, Wales, S Ire only, o-lf on coast; Eur, W France only, o-lf; on upper drier salt-marshes, shingle banks, sea cliffs. Fl 7–9.   **Di   Elecampane**, *I. helenium*, differs from D and from most other yellowrayed daisy-like Compositae in its stout stems 60–150 cm tall; in its v large lvs, the

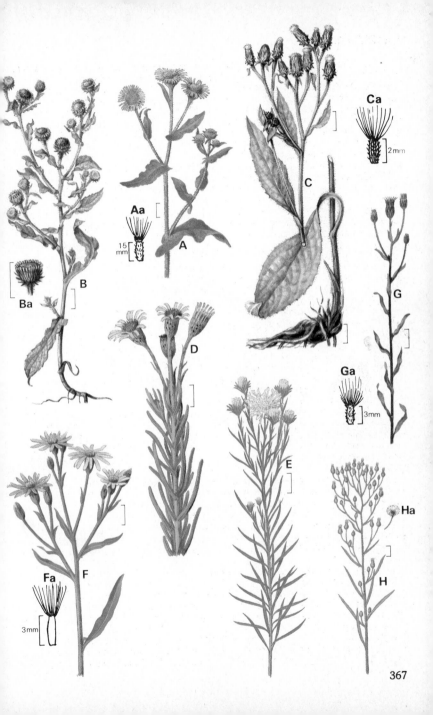

Aa

15
mm

Ba

B

Ca

2mm

C

Ga

3mm

G

D

Fa

3mm

F

E

Ha

H

◀ basal lvs elliptical, long-stalked, 25–40 cm long, the stem-lvs stalkless, clasping, oval-cordate, all ± hairless above, woolly below; and in its **v large** fl-heads, 6–8 cm across, with many narrow rays; in its stout cup-like involucres with hairy overlapping oval spreading bracts; achenes are hairless, pappus reddish. Br Isles, Eur: introd on wa, rds. Fl 7–8. **Dii Irish Fleabane**, *I. salicina*, is close to D in habit and fl-head size; erect per 25–50 cm tall; stem-lvs, many, alt, **elliptical-lanceolate**, pointed, 3–7 cm long, are firm but **not fleshy**, ± untoothed, hairless above but fine-**bristly** on edges and veins below. Fl-heads 2.5–3.0 cm across, 1–5 in a loose head as in D, ray- and disc-florets yellow; outer bracts of fl-heads **hairless**, lanceolate; achenes hairless. Ire, by Lough Derg, r-vlf; Eur, E France to Denmark, o-lc; in fens, by stony lake shores. Fl 7–8. ***Diii** *I. britannica* is close to Dii, but lvs **narrow**-lanceolate, softly **hairy**; bracts **linear**, **hairy**. E France to Denmark, r-lf; in wet mds. Fl 7–8.

E Goldilocks Aster, *Aster* (*Crinitaria*) *linosyris*, slender erect hairless per herb, 10–40 cm tall; stems bear many alt, narrow-linear, pointed lvs 2–5 cm long, untoothed but rough-edged; fl-heads in a dense umbel-like corymb, each head 12–18 mm across, its bracts v **narrow**, many, **overlapping**, outer spreading, inner addressed; **no ray-florets**; disc-florets bright yellow, longer than bracts, in a brush-like tuft. Achenes downy; pappus reddish, simple. GB: W Eng, Wales, vr (5 places only, on coasts); Eur: France, S Belgium, vr; limestone rocks, cliffs. Fl 8–9.

F Sea Aster, *Aster tripolium*, is closer to a fleshy-lvd Michaelmas Daisy than to E. Erect branched hairless per, 15–100 cm; lvs 7–12 cm long, **fleshy**, ± untoothed; basal lvs stalked, obovate; upper lvs linear-oblong. Fl-heads in loose umbel-like corymbs, 8–20 mm across, involucre bracts **blunt**, addressed, overlapping, chaffy-tipped; ray-florets long and spreading, **mauve** or white, or **abs** (var *discoideus*); disc-florets yellow. Achenes (**Fa**) brown, hairy, with brownish simple pappus. Br Isles, Eur; c all around coasts, estuaries on salt-marshes, sea cliffs, rarely inland by salt springs. Fl 7–10. **Michaelmas Daisies** (*Aster* spp) resemble F in blue, reddish (or white) ray-florets and yellow disc-florets, but lvs thin, not fleshy, involucre-bracts long and pointed. Many spp (from N America) are grown in gdns and occur as escapes in wa, etc in Br Isles and Eur. ***Fi** *A. amellus* is similar to F in its blunt, round-tipped involucre-bracts and blue ray-florets, but it is shorter (20–40 cm); lvs are **hairy** (**not fleshy**); involucre-bracts **spreading** (**not** addressed to fl-heads). Eur: E France, NW to Laon, r; W Germany o-lf; calc rocks. Fl 8–10.

Erigeron is close to *Aster*, but fl-head bracts are **equal**, and ray-florets are **narrow** and **numerous**.

G Blue Fleabane, *Erigeron acer*, resembles a shorter, narrow-lvd version of C with purple ray-florets, but bracts to fl-head are **equal** and not overlapping. Erect hairy ann or bi, 8–40 cm tall, with many alt linear-lanceolate, untoothed clasping stem-lvs and basal rosette of stalked, obovate-lanceolate lvs. Fl-heads 12–18 mm across, in a loose panicle; ray-florets pale purple, narrow, erect, many, little longer than yellow disc-florets. Achenes (**Ga**) yellow, hairy, pappus long, reddish-white. Br Isles: Eng, Wales, c to E, f to W; Scot, Ire r; Eur: France to Denmark c; on calc gslds, hbs, wa. Fl 7–8. **Gi Alpine Fleabane**, *E. borealis*, close to G, but **short** (7–20 cm), unbranched; lvs and stem much hairier; fl-heads only 1–3, 20 mm wide, with purple ray-florets **much longer** than disc-florets. Scot, Perthshire to Aberdeenshire, vr; on calc mt rock-ledges. Fl 7–8.

H Canadian Fleabane, *Conyza canadensis*, ann, 8–80 cm tall, resembles a narrow-lvd, slender, less hairy version of G, with many more, much smaller (3–5 mm across) fl-heads in long panicles: ray-florets erect, narrow, **v short**, **whitish**; disc-florets yellow; achenes (**Ha**) downy, pale yellow with simple **yellowish** pappus. SE Eng c; rest of Eng, Wales o; **Scot, Ire abs**; Eur f-lc; on wa, rds, dunes. Fl 6–10.

Oxeye Daisy, Tansy, Bur-marigolds, Daisy etc ▶

Chrysanthemum are herbs with alt lvs with segments **not** hairlike; bracts of involucre unequal, **overlapping**; no scales on receptacle; achenes **without** pappus of hairs. **Bur-marigolds** (*Bidens*) have **opp** lvs; fl-heads usually **without** ray-florets; pappus of a few barbed **spines** only; bracts of heads in 2 rows, outer row spreading, lf-like, in a ruff, inner oval, erect; scales among the florets.

   A   Oxeye Daisy, *Chrysanthemum leucanthemum* (*Leucanthemum vulgare*), erect, slightly hairy little-branched per herb, 20–70 cm tall; basal rosette of long-stalked, ± spoon-shaped, toothed lvs (**Aa**), and stalkless, clasping, oblong, alt, deeply-toothed stem-lvs, all dark green. Fl-heads long-stalked, daisy-like, 2.5–5.0 cm across, ray-florets **white**, disc-florets **yellow**; bracts oblong, overlapping, purple-edged. Achenes (**Ab**) hairless, ribbed, without a pappus. Br Isles, Eur; vc in gslds, mds, rds, on fertile soils. Fl 5–9.

   B   Feverfew, *C. parthenium* (*Tanacetum parthenium*), erect, downy, strongly **aromatic** per herb, 25–60 cm, much branched above; lvs oval in outline, **pinnate** with toothed segments, the lower long-stalked; fl-heads in a loose, ± flat-topped umbel-like corymb; heads 12–20 mm across, with **short, broad, white** rays, **yellow** discs; bracts to heads overlapping, oblong, **downy**, with **pale** chaffy edges. Achenes without pappus, ribbed, hairless. Br Isles: GB c (except NE Scot r); Ire f; Eur c; introd (SE Eur) everywhere; on hbs, wa, rds, walls. Fl 7–9.

   C   Tansy, *Chrysanthemum* (*Tanacetum*) *vulgare*, erect **strong-smelling** hairless per herb, 30–100 cm; lvs, 15–25 cm long, up the stems, are alt, pinnate, their lfts deeply pinnatifid. Fl-heads in a dense umbel-like corymb 7–15 cm across, each head 7–12 mm across, yellow, button-like, **without** ray-florets; overlapping **hairless** bracts with pale chaffy edges; achenes (**Ca**) ribbed, hairless, without a pappus, but with a toothed **cup** on top. Br Isles: GB c; Ire f; Eur c; on rds, hbs, wa, riverbanks. Fl 7–10.

cont

D Corn Marigold, *C. segetum*, ± erect hairless ann, 20–50 cm; lvs grey-green, ± fleshy, deeply-toothed, oblong; fl-heads large (3.5–6.5 cm), solitary, with both **disc** and rays **golden-yellow**; bracts of heads overlapping, with broad pale brown chaffy margins; achenes **cylindrical**, hairless, without pappus. Br Isles, Eur; f-lc introd (Mediterranean) on ar on acid or sandy soils. Fl 6–10. **Di Garden Marigold**, *Calendula officinalis*, also has large (4–5 cm across) heads, but with both rays and disc **orange**; lvs downy, oblong-obovate ± untoothed; achenes **boat-shaped**, without pappus. Br Isles, Eur; c garden escape. ***Dii Field Marigold**, *C. arvensis*, f weed of European vineyards, is like Di, but fl-heads only 1–2 cm across; lvs narrower, toothed; inner achenes curved into **rings**.

E Nodding Bur-marigold, *Bidens cernua*, erect ann, 8–60 cm; lvs **opp**, **undivided**, lanceolate, pointed, coarsely-toothed, stalkless, ± **hairy**; fl-heads few, long-stalked, **drooping**, 15–25 mm across, button-like, dull yellow, usually **without** ray-florets (rarely with few, golden-yellow, broad rays, 12 mm long). Achenes (**Ea**) straight-sided, flattened, with **4** barbed spines on top. Br Isles: Eng, Wales, o-lc to S, o to N; Scot vr; Ire o; Eur c; by muddy pond edges, on grassy commons, where water stands in winter but not in summer. Fl 7–10.

F Trifid Bur-marigold, *B. tripartita*, is close to E, but **hairless** or downy only; lvs (**F**) **trifoliate**, with toothed, lanceolate lobes and short winged stalks; fl-heads ± **erect**; ray-florets v rarely present. Achenes (**Fa**) **obovate**, 7–8 mm long, v flattened, with only **2** barbed spines (rarely extra shorter ones) on top. Br Isles: Eng, Wales, f-lc to S, o to N; Scot vr, Ire o; Eur c; habitats as for E. Fl 7–10.

G Mountain Everlasting, *Antennaria dioica*, per herb with creeping woody stem that produces lfy rooting runners, and erect unbranched, lfy white-woolly fl-shoots 5–20 cm tall; rosette- and runner-lvs obovate to **spoon**-shaped, blunt, mucronate, stem-lvs erect, narrow, pointed; all lvs alt, **green** above, **white**-woolly below. Fl-heads white-woolly, in a close terminal umbel; dioecious; female heads 12 mm across, with their woolly bracts narrow, pointed, **erect**, with **pink** chaffy tips; male heads 6 mm across, with bracts obovate, **blunt**, **spreading** like ray-florets, usually **white**-tipped; florets all tubular, pink; achenes with slender white pappus, male fls (**Ga**) with few pappus hairs, club-shaped above like **butterfly antennae**. Br Isles: S, E Eng vr; Wales, N Eng o-lf; Scot f, vc in N; Ire o-lc; Eur: NE France, Belgium, Netherlands, r; N Germany, Denmark, f-lc; on hths, dry gslds, mt ledges. Fl 6–7.

H Gallant Soldier, *Galinsoga parviflora*, erect hairless ann, 10–70 cm tall; lvs **opp**, oval, pointed, stalked, few-toothed; forked cymose infls with a fl-head in each fork; fl-heads 3–5 mm across, bracts few, oval; ray-florets usually only 5, 1 mm long × 1 mm wide, white; disc-florets yellow; achenes (**Ha**) black, bristly, three-angled, oval, with a pappus of 8–20 silvery lanceolate **scales** without bristle-tips. Eng o, but lc in SE; rest of GB r; **Ire abs**; Eur o-lf; on wa, ar. Fl 5–10. **Hi Shaggy Soldier**, *G. ciliata*, v like H, but clothed with spreading **hairs**; usually 4 narrower ray-florets; pappus-scales of achenes shorter, tapering into **bristle**-tips. Eng o, but lc in SE; rest of GB vr; **Ire abs**; Eur o-lf; in wa. Fl 5–10.

I Daisy, *Bellis perennis*, per herb with short-stalked, obovate, blunt-tipped, blunt-toothed downy lvs 2–4 cm long, **all in a basal rosette**. Fl-stems 3–12 cm tall, **lfless**, hairy, each with 1 fl-head 16–25 mm across; bracts many, green, blunt, hairy, oblong; ray-florets many, white, spreading; disc-florets yellow; achenes (**Ia**) obovate, pale, flattened, downy, pappus **abs**; receptacle beneath achenes **conical**. Br Isles, Eur; a in short gslds, mds. Fl 3–10.

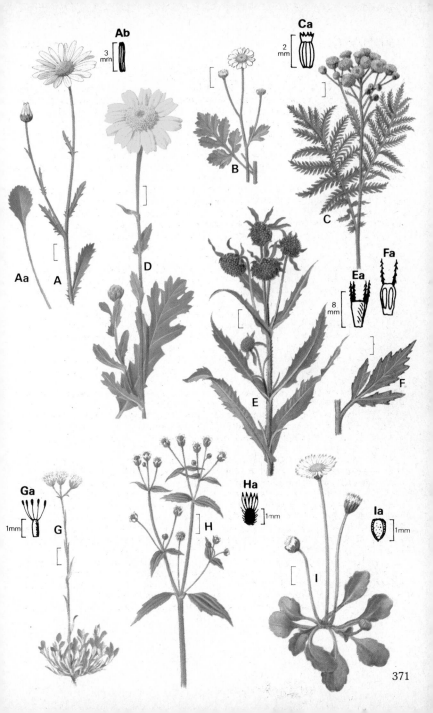

Colt's-foot, Butterburs, Yarrows, Hemp-agrimony

A Colt's-foot, *Tussilago farfara*, per herb with stout scaly runners, and solitary fl-heads on erect scaly lfless stems 5–15 cm tall; fl-heads 15–35 mm across, rays and disc florets yellow, bracts of head many, ± purplish, narrow, in **one** equal row forming a long narrow cup, with a few broader outer ones; fl-stem in fr lengthens to about 30 cm; achenes hairless, pale, pappus of long simple white hairs. Lvs appearing **after** fls, long-stalked, rounded-triangular, cordate-based, 10–20 cm across, downy above, white-felted below, with small sharp teeth. Br Isles, Eur; vc on wa, ar, on pits, cliffs, landslips, on clay, dunes, scree etc. Fl 3–4. **Ai Purple Colt's-foot**, *Homogyne alpina*, creeping per; like A in lfless scaly fl-stems with solitary fl-heads; but **kidney-shaped** glossy dark green lvs, purple below, 4 cm wide, appear with fls. Stems bearing heads are 10–30 cm tall in fl; fl-heads of purple **tubular** florets only. Scot: Glen Clova, vr (mts of central and N Eur); on moist open places in mts. Fl 6–9.

B Butterbur, *Petasites hybridus*, per herb with stout rhizomes, producing fl-heads in **stout**-stalked racemes, 10–40 cm tall, in spring; fl-stems have green lanceolate scales only; plants ± dioecious; fl-heads reddish-pink, male 7–12 mm long, all florets **tubular**; female fl-heads shorter (3–6 mm long), florets narrower. Root-lvs (**Ba**), appearing after fls, long-stalked, rounded, distantly-toothed, deeply cordate, 10 cm wide at first, but becoming huge (60 cm across or more) in summer, green above, grey-downy below. Pappus white. Br Isles f-lc (except **N Scot abs**); Eur f-lc; on wet mds, rds, streamsides, wet copses; male plants general, but female plants lc only in N Eng, parts of Eur. Fl 3–5. **Bi** *P. japonicus* has **creamy** fls in **branched** flattish panicles, with broad, dense pale green bract-scales on their stalks, appearing like cauliflowers from afar; lvs v large (to 1 m across), rounded-cordate. Introd (N Japan) o in Eng, Eur. **Bii** *P. albus* also has **white** fl-heads, but smaller (to 30 cm wide) rounded-cordate lvs, **white**-woolly beneath. N of GB, N Ire, introd o; Denmark, Germany o-lf; in moist wds. ***Biii** *P. spurius* has triangular-spearhead-shaped lvs, white-woolly below, and white or pale yellow fl-heads. Denmark, N Germany; r on dunes etc.

C Winter Heliotrope, *P. fragrans*, **slenderer** plant than B, with 10–25 cm-tall racemes of few, **lilac**, **vanilla-scented** fl-heads with short erect **rays** to outer florets; lvs, **appearing with** fls (in winter), are **rounded**, kidney- to heart-shaped, 10–20 cm wide, evenly-toothed, **green both sides**. Br Isles f-lc (except Scot r-o); Eur: France, Belgium, o; introd (SW Eur) on wa, banks, rds, streamsides. Fl 12–3.

D Yarrow, *Achillea millefolium*, erect tufted downy per, 8–40 cm tall, strongly-scented, with runners; lvs lanceolate in outline, 5–15 cm long, 2–3 times pinnate into short narrow **linear** segments, lower lvs stalked, upper stalkless, shorter. Fl-heads (**Da**) many, 4–6 mm across, in dense terminal umbel-like corymbs; involucre oval, of many overlapping oblong, blunt, keeled bracts with chaffy edges; ray-florets usually 5, three-toothed at tip, as long as **wide**, white or pink; disc-florets **dirty white** or **creamy**. Achenes (**Db**) flattened, hairless, **without** pappus. Br Isles, Eur; vc in mds, gslds, rds, hbs. Fl 6–8.

E Sneezewort, *A. ptarmica*, erect tufted per herb, 20–60 cm, little-branched, hairy on upper parts; lvs **unlobed**, linear-lanceolate, 1.5–6.0 cm long, ± hairless, **finely** and sharply toothed; fl-heads larger, fewer than in D, 12–18 mm across; ray-florets (4 mm) longer than in D, oval, white; disc-florets greenish white. Br Isles, Eur, f-lc but r in chky or v cultivated areas; on wet mds, hthy gslds, scrub, on acid soils. Fl 7–8.

F Hemp-agrimony, *Eupatorium cannabinum*, tall downy per to 120 cm; root-lvs obovate, stem-lvs ± stalkless, trifoliate, each of 3 (or 5) elliptical-lanceolate toothed lfts 5–10 cm long; all lvs **opp**. Fl-heads v small (and superficially more Valerian- than Composite-like) with only 5–6 reddish-pink tubular florets

Da

5mm

Db

1·5mm

Fa

2mm

A

D

E

B

C

Ba

F

2cm

◀ and 8–10 oblong purple-tipped bracts, but grouped into large, rounded, much-branched panicles to 15 cm across; achenes (**Fa**) black, angled with white simple pappus-hairs. Br Isles, c to S, r-o N Scot; Eur c; in fens, marshes, wet wds. Fl 7–9.

▶ **Mayweeds, Chamomiles, Mugworts, Wormwoods**

Mayweeds, and **Chamomiles** (*Tripleurospermum*, *Matricaria*, *Anthemis*, *Chamaemelum*) have daisy-like fl-heads with disc-florets yellow and ray-florets (mostly) white (or abs); alt lvs are 2 or more times **pinnate** into almost **hairlike** segments. *Tripleurospermum* and *Matricaria* have **no scales** among disc-florets; in *Anthemis* and *Chamaemelum* each disc-floret has a **chaffy lanceolate scale** at its base (best seen by rubbing off some disc-florets from receptacle).

   A   Scentless Mayweed, *Tripleurospermum maritimum*, ann or per herb 10–50 cm tall, erect or sprawling, ± **scentless**; lvs alt, hairless, 2–3 times pinnate into narrow segments (thread-like, fine-pointed in inland ssp *inodorum*, blunt, cylindrical, ± fleshy in seaside ssp *maritimum*). Fl-heads in loose infls, 2.0–4.5 cm across, with many spreading white ray-florets and yellow disc-florets; involucres cup-like, of blunt, oblong, overlapping bracts with brown chaffy edges; achenes (**Aa**) top-shaped, flattened, with 2 **black spots** near top and no pappus, but a narrow rim on top; no scales among disc-florets; receptacle **solid**, **dome-shaped**. Br Isles, Eur, c; ssp *inodorum* in ar, wa; ssp *maritimum* on sandy or shingly shores, rocks, by sea. Fl 7–9.   **Ai   Scented Mayweed**, *Matricaria recutita*, v near to A but pleasantly **aromatic**; receptacle of fl-head **hollow**, **conical**; achenes have **no** black spots (oil-glands) near top; ray-florets soon bend back. Br Isles: Eng, Wales, f-lc; Scot, Ire, r; Eur f-lc; on ar, wa, on sandy soils. Fl 6–7.

   B   Stinking Chamomile, *Anthemis cotula*, looks v like A, is also ± hairless, but has unpleasant smell, and narrow **scales** occur on the conical receptacle among **inner** disc-florets (**B**); achenes ribbed, **warty**, no pappus. Br Isles, f-lc to S, r to N; Eur f-lc; on ar, wa, especially on clay. Fl 7–9.   **Bi   Corn Chamomile**, *A. arvensis*, resembles B in most points, but **downy** or woolly, **not** hairless; **aromatic**, **not** nasty-scented; scales on receptacle **lanceolate**-mucronate, **not** linear; ray-florets have styles (abs in B's rays); achenes strong-ribbed, but **not** warty. Br Isles: Eng f; rest of GB r; **Ire abs**; Eur f-lc; on ar on calc soils. Fl 6–7.   **Bii   Yellow Chamomile**, *A. tinctoria*, is distinctive in its fl-heads 2.5–4.0 cm across, both ray- and disc-florets **yellow**; structure and lvs as in Bi, but looks more like Corn Marigold (p 370 D). GB, introd in wa, r; Eur r-o; on ar, rds, wa. Fl 7–8.

   C   Pineappleweed, *Matricaria matricarioides*, erect ann with habit and fine lf-segments of A, and without scales between disc-florets, but **lacks** ray-florets, has **conical**, **hollow** receptacles to fl-heads, greenish-yellow disc-florets, and smells strongly of **pineapples** when crushed. Br Isles, Eur; vc (E Asia ?) on wa, trackways, rds, ar. Fl 5–11.   **Ci   Buttonweed**, *Cotula coronopifolia*, short **aromatic** hairless ann, creeping and ascending, 8–15 cm tall; lvs alt, linear-pinnatifid, but with lobes **flat**, **not hairlike**, bases **sheathing** stem; fl-heads yellow, **button-like**, 6–10 mm across, single on long stalks; bracts of heads blunt, chaffy-edged, in 2 rows; disc-florets with **white** tubes and **4 yellow** corolla-lobes; pappus abs. Eng, Eur, r-lf; introd (S Africa) on wa, dunes. Fl 7–10.

   D   Chamomile, *Chamaemelum nobile*, **creeping** downy **per** herb, strongly chamomile-scented; stems 10–30 cm long; lvs 1.5–5.0 cm, 2–3 times pinnate, with short linear ± hairy segments; fl-heads 18–25 mm across, solitary on short erect stems; ray-florets white, spreading; disc-florets (**Da**) yellow, with oblong blunt **scale** at base of each, and bases of corolla-tubes **swelling** to cover top of achenes in a hood (use lens); receptacle conical; bracts of fl-head blunt, overlapping, chaffy-edged. S Eng, S Wales, lf; **N Eng**, **Scot**, **abs**; Ire r (lc in SW); Eur: W France f; N France, Belgium, vr; on sandy gsld on commons. Fl 6–8.

cont

A

Aa

3mm

B

3mm

Ea

4mm

E

Ga

4mm

G

Fa

3mm

F

C

D

Da

3mm

H

◀ **Mugworts** and **Wormwoods** (*Artemisia*), a genus of tall herbs that superficially look more like Docks or Goosefoots than Composites; lvs alt, **pinnatifid**; long, much-branched **panicles** of tiny fl-heads, each with rather few **tubular** florets only (see Key to *Artemisia*, below). Involucre globular or bell-shaped, of many hairy, chaffy-edged, overlapping bracts; florets yellowish or reddish; pappus abs. **Cudweeds** (*Gnaphalium, Filago*) have similar tiny ± woolly fl-heads, but lvs are **simple**, strap-shaped.

E Mugwort, *Artemisia vulgaris*, erect tufted ± downy, aromatic per, 60–120 cm tall; grooved, reddish stems with **large** white pith inside. Lvs 5–8 cm long, dark green, hairless above, white-cottony below, twice-pinnatifid; lower lvs stalked, upper unstalked, clasping and less divided, with lanceolate-oblong pointed segments, 3–6 mm wide; only **main** veins translucent. Infls of erect racemes in a lfy panicle; fl-heads (**Ea**) 3–4 mm long × 2–3 mm wide, oval, erect; their bracts lanceolate, woolly, chaffy-margined; florets all tubular, red-brown; achenes hairless. Br Isles vc (except Scots mts r); Eur vc; on wa, rds, hbs, scrub. Fl 7–9. **Ei Chinese Mugwort**, *A. verlotorum*, close to E, but stems **downy** (**not** tufted), on creeping rhizomes, and pith **narrow**; **all** lf-veins translucent; infl-branches, v lfy, **arching** outwards, do not produce fls till late autumn (if then). SE Eng; introd (China) lf in wa. Fl 10–12.

F Wormwood, *A. absinthium*, erect, v aromatic per, 30–90 cm tall; differs from E in its **blunt** lf-segments, **silky-hairy both** sides; fl-heads cup-shaped, 3–4 mm wide, drooping, with blunt silky-hairy bracts and yellow florets. Br Isles: Eng, Wales, f-lc; Scot, Ire, r; Eur f; on wa, rds, hbs. Fl 7–8. **Fi Hoary Mugwort**, *A. stellerana*, differs from F in that it is **not** aromatic; **whole** plant **densely** white-felted; fl-heads **bell-shaped**, longer than broad, 5–9 mm wide. Eng, Ire, Eur; introd, r but lf. Fl 7–9. **Fii Norwegian Mugwort**, *A. norvegica*, small aromatic alpine per herb, 3–6 cm tall, **v unlike** other Mugworts. Basal lvs 2 cm long, stalked, palmately-lobed, with 3–5 toothed wedge-shaped lobes; stem-lvs pinnate, stalkless; all lvs silky white. Fl-heads only 1–3, 12 mm across, nodding on erect stems; bracts with green midribs and broad dark brown chaffy edges. Scot, mts of W Ross, vr (Norway); in alpine moss-hth. Fl 7–9.

G Field Wormwood, *A. campestris*, scentless, ± hairless ascending per, with shoots 20–60 cm long, woody below. Lower lvs 2–3 times pinnate, stalked, upper lvs stalkless, undivided; all with segments linear, pointed, to 1 mm wide, becoming hairless. Panicles loose, erect; fl-heads (**Ga**) oval, 3 mm wide; bracts oval, hairless, green with chaffy edges; florets yellow or red. Eng: E Anglian Breckland only, vr; Eur: E France to Denmark o-lc; on sandy grassy hths. Fl 8–9.

H Sea Wormwood, *A. maritima*, strongly aromatic per, with spreading to erect fl-stems 20–50 cm long, and also separate lf-rosettes. Lvs 2–5 cm, twice-pinnate, segments linear, blunt, 1 mm wide; lower stalked, upper not; all **white**-woolly both sides. Fl-heads many, 1–2 mm wide, oval, in panicles, side-branches and heads usually drooping, sometimes erect; bracts of heads oblong, downy, chaffy-edged; florets yellow or reddish. Br Isles: GB, coasts N to E Scot, f-lc in SE, o to N; Ire r; Eur: coasts from W France to Denmark, f-lc; drier salt marshes, sea walls. Fl 8–9.

KEY TO MUGWORTS AND WORMWOODS (*ARTEMISIA*)

1 Plant only 3–6 cm tall – fl-heads **only 1–3**, nodding, **12 mm wide** – lvs silky-white, ± pinnately-lobed into narrow 3–5-toothed, wedge-shaped segments – Scot mts – vr ....
                                             A. norvegica (p 376 Fii)
   Plant over 20 cm tall – **many small** fl-heads in **long panicles**...**2**
2 Terminal lf-lobes **narrow-linear** or hair-like, **1 mm** wide or less **3**
   Terminal lf-lobes **flat**, linear-lanceolate, **2 mm** wide or more...**4**
3 Plants unscented, ± hairless or slightly silky – on hths – r............................ *A. campestris* (p 376 G)
   Plants strongly scented – lvs white-woolly below – in salt marshes – lc .... *A. maritima* (p 376 H)

4 Lf-lobes ± **hairless above, white-woolly below** – fl-heads narrow-oval..................................... **5**
  Lf-lobes whitish-hairy **both** sides – fl-heads bell-shaped.. **6**
5 Plant tufted – stems ± **hairless** – **only the larger** lf-veins translucent – infl-branches all erect
  – fls in summer – vc...*A. vulgaris* (p 376 E)
  Plant with stems borne singly, on long runners – stems **downy** – **all** veins of lvs translucent – infl-
  branches v lfy, arching outwards – fls not before late autumn, if at all – on wa – r ....
  ....*A. verlotorum* (p 376 Ei)
6 Plant v aromatic, grey-green, not white-felted, silky white hairs all over – fl-heads 3–5 mm
  wide × 2–4 mm long – cup-shaped – f ....*A. absinthum* (p 376 F)
  Plant not aromatic, densely **white-felted** all over – fl-heads 5–7 mm wide × 6–10 mm long, bell-
  shaped – r ....*A. stellerana* (p 376 Fi)

KEY TO CUDWEEDS AND IMMORTELLES (*FILAGO, GNAPHALIUM, HELICHRYSUM*) ▶

1 Fl-heads in dense, globular or oval clusters, in lf-axils, stem-forks and branch-tips – outer bracts
  of heads woolly, inner chaffy...*(Filago)* **3**
  Fl-heads in spikes, racemes, or purely terminal dense or umbel-like clusters............................... **2**
2 Bracts of fl-head involucres **bright yellow**, blunt, **spreading** star-wise **in fr** like the petals of a
  yellow fl – fl-heads bright yellow, in v loose umbels – **not in Br Isles**...................... *(Helichrysum)* **8**
  Bracts of fl-head involucres **never bright yellow**, narrow, only **slightly** spreading **in fr** and then
  not petal-like – fl-heads brownish to pale yellow, in spikes, or in dense umbel-like clusters – all
  bracts of heads chaffy-tipped..*(Gnaphalium)* **9**
3 Clusters of fl-heads globular, 8–40 heads per cluster – bracts bristle-pointed, erect in fr............... **4**
  Clusters of fl-heads narrow, ± oval, 2–7 heads per cluster – bracts not bristle-pointed,
  spreading star-wise in fr... **6**
4 Lvs wavy-edged, without mucronate points at tips – clusters of fl-heads longer than the lvs at their
  bases – 20–40 fl-heads per cluster .... *Filago germanica* (p 378 A)
  Lvs ± flat-edged, with mucronate points at tips – clusters of fl-heads shorter than the lvs at
  their bases – 8–20 heads per cluster... **5**
5 Each fl-head cluster with 3–5 lvs at its base – outer bracts of each fl-head with **yellow, outward-
  curved**, bristle-points – plants branched from base, spreading, **white**-woolly – r ....
  ....*F. spathulata* (p 378 B)
  Each fl-head cluster with 1–2 lvs at its base – outer bracts of each fl-head with **bright red-tipped,
  erect** bristle-points – plants erect, branched only above, **yellowish**-woolly – r ....
  ....*F. apiculata* (p 378 C)
6 Lvs narrow-linear, upper far longer than fl-head clusters just above them – r.....*F. gallica* (p 378 Di)
  Lvs lanceolate, upper shorter than fl-head clusters just above them.. **7**
7 Branches long, erect, ± equal, apparently forking – outer bracts of the five-angled fl-heads
  woolly in lower half, chaffy, hairless and blunt in upper half ....*F. minima* (p 378 D)
  Branches all short, along the sides of a single erect **unforked** main stem – outer bracts of the
  eight-angled fl-heads woolly right to their pointed tips – **not in Br Isles**.........*F. arvensis* (p 378 Dii)
8 Lvs flat, lower lvs elliptical – fl-heads cylindrical – N Eur only ...... *Helichrysum arenarium* (p 378 E)
  Lvs with edges rolled under, lower lvs parallel-sided – fl-heads broad, cup-shaped – W France
  only...*H. stoechas* (p 380 Ei)
9 Ann plants with fl-heads in dense terminal clusters – bracts of fl-heads without dark edges – lvs
  woolly on both sides... **10**
  Tufted or creeping pers with fl-heads in spikes or racemes – bracts of fl-heads with chaffy dark
  brown edges.. **11**
10 Lvs narrow-oblong, ± pointed – terminal clusters of fl-heads surrounded by long lvs
  simulating petals – bracts of fl-heads dark-tipped – fls brownish-yellow with pale stigmas – short
  branched plant to 15 cm – c ....*Gnaphalium uliginosum* (p 380 F)
  Lower lvs broadly oblong and blunt, upper clasping, pointed – terminal clusters of fl-heads
  without petal-like lvs around them – bracts of fl-heads wholly pale yellow – fls yellow with red
  stigmas – erect little-branched plant to 40 cm ....*G. luteoalbum* (p 380 Fi)
11 Short (under 12 cm) v tufted plant with 1–7 fl-heads in short compact terminal spikes – lvs woolly
  both sides – on Scot mts – f ....*G. supinum* (p 380 Gii)
  Taller (12–60 cm) erect plants with fl-heads in elongated spikes.. **12**
12 Lvs linear-lanceolate, one-veined, hairless on undersides, woolly below – lvs progressively
  shorter above – infl over half length of whole plant stem ....*G. sylvaticum* (p 380 G)
  Lvs lanceolate, three-veined, woolly both sides – lvs all ± equal in length – infl only quarter
  length of whole plant stem – Scot mts – r...*G. norvegicum* (p 380 Gi)

Compositae

Cudweeds, Immortelles

Cudweeds (*Filago* and *Gnaphalium*) and **Immortelles** (*Helichrysum*) are ± woolly all over, with narrow strap-shaped untoothed lvs. Fl-heads small, few-fld, of tubular florets only, and frs with a hairy pappus, bear no superficial resemblance to Daisies, Dandelions or Thistles. In *Filago* fl-heads are gathered into dense stalkless globular, oval and conical clusters in lf-axils, stem-forks, and at branch-tips, always with lvs at base of each cluster; involucres have **outer** bracts **woolly** grey-green, **inner** bracts **chaffy**, ± straw-coloured; fl-head receptacles conical, **scaly-edged** under the florets. In *Gnaphalium* fl-heads, separately stalked, are in spikes, racemes, panicles or terminal umbel-like clusters; **bracts all chaffy-edged**, receptacles flat, **without** scales at edges. *Helichrysum* are v like *Gnaphalium*, but florets and fl-head bracts are brightly coloured, blunt, and spread star-wise like fl-petals in fr. See key, p 377.

    A **Common Cudweed**, *Filago germanica* (*F. vulgaris*), erect ann, 50–30 cm, stems and lvs v woolly, stems ± branched at base, then forking into 2–3 branches below terminal fl-head clusters. Lvs erect, 1–2 cm long, strap-shaped, wavy, blunt-tipped; fl-heads in dense globular clusters of 20–40 together in branch-forks and terminating branches; lvs below clusters shorter than clusters; bracts of fl-heads linear, five-rowed, **straight**, keeled, the outer woolly, the inner **yellow**-bristle-pointed, **erect**. Br Isles: GB lf (but decreasing) to S, r to N; Ire r; Eur f-lc; on sandy gslds, ar, wa, rds, on dry ± acid soils. Fl 7–8.
    B **Broad-leaved Cudweed**, *F. spathulata* (*F. pyramidata*), white-woolly **spreading** ann, close to A, but branched from base, stems 6–30 cm long, lvs mucronate, obovate; fl-heads 8–15 per cluster, clusters terminal and **along** stems, the 3–5 lvs at each cluster base are longer than cluster; outer fl-head bracts have **yellow**, **outward-curving** bristle-points. S Eng r (**rest of Br Isles abs**); Eur: France to S Belgium o-lf; on ar on calc soils. Fl 7–8.
    C **Red-tipped Cudweed**, *F. apiculata* (*F. lutescens*), also close to A, but with erect **yellow**-woolly stems, **mucronate** non-wavy lvs; fl-heads 10–20 per cluster (C) with 1–2 overtopping lvs; fl-head bracts with **bright-red-tipped**, **erect** bristle-points. SE Eng r (**rest of Br Isles abs**); France to Denmark r-o; sandy ar. Fl 7–8.
    D **Small Cudweed**, *F. minima*, slender erect grey-woolly ann 5–15 cm tall, with ± erect branches above middle; lvs 5–10 mm long, linear-**lanceolate**; five-angled fl-heads 3 mm long, in oval clusters of 3–6, at tips and in forks of stems, **longer** than lvs at their bases; bracts of fl-heads (**Da**) woolly-based with hairless chaffy **blunt** yellowish tips, spreading star-wise in fr. GB f-lc (**but NW Scot abs**); Ire r; Eur f-lc; on sandy gslds, wa, railways, hths. Fl 6–9. **Di** **Narrow-leaved Cudweed**, *F. gallica*, close to D, but all lvs **narrow-linear**, 8–20 mm long; fl-heads, 4 mm long, are in clusters of 2–6 in forks and at stem tips, and are **much exceeded** by lvs at their bases; bracts of fl-heads with sharp tips. Eng, Essex, possibly extinct; Eur, France to Netherlands, r-o; on gravelly gslds, wa. Fl 7–9. ***Dii** *F. arvensis*, ann, is nearer to D, 10–40 cm tall, with **erect unforked** stems bearing v **short side-branches**; fl-heads 4–5 mm long, in clusters **exceeded** by lvs at their bases; fl-heads **eight-angled**, bracts woolly right up to their **pointed** tips. Eur, E. France to Denmark, r-lf; on ar, wa. Fl 7–9.
    *E **Immortelle**, *Helichrysum arenarium*, erect white-woolly ann, 20–40 cm tall; lvs **flat**, lower elliptical, upper linear, woolly both sides; fl-heads (in a loose branched umbel-like corymb) 3–4 mm wide, with bright **golden-yellow** florets and **golden-yellow** blunt bracts (**Ea**) that spread in fr like a fl's petals, making heads then to 1 cm wide. Eur: E France to Denmark o-lc; on sandy gslds, hths. Fl 7–

◄ 8.   ***Ei**   *H. stoechas* is close to E, but lvs **all linear**, with **rolled-under** edges. W
France o-lc; on dunes near sea. Fl 5–7.

   F   Marsh Cudweed, *Gnaphalium uliginosum*, v woolly ann 4–20 cm tall,
much-branched from base; lvs woolly both sides, 1–5 cm long, narrow-oblong,
narrowed to base, ± pointed; fl-heads 3–4 mm long, in dense **terminal**
clusters of 3–10 surrounded by **long lvs** simulating **petals**; fl-head bracts woolly,
pale below, with **dark** chaffy hairless **tips**; florets **brownish**-yellow; stigmas **pale**.
Br Isles, Eur; vc on damp ar, gslds, commons, paths, on acid soils. Fl 7–
9.   **Fi   Jersey Cudweed**, *G. luteoalbum*, taller than F (8–10 cm), little-branched
above; lower lvs broad-oblong, blunt; upper lvs clasping, pointed, wavy, all lvs
woolly both sides; fl-heads 4–5 mm long, in dense terminal **lfless** clusters of 4–12;
bracts elliptical, chaffy, shiny, pale yellow; florets **bright yellow**; stigmas **red**. Eng:
Norfolk vr; Eur: W France (including Channel Is) to N Guernsey, o-la; on sandy
hths, dunes. Fl 6–8.

   G   Heath Cudweed, *G. sylvaticum*, per herb with short lfy runners and erect
unbranched lfy fl-shoots 8–60 cm tall; rosette and lower stem-lvs stalked,
lanceolate, pointed, 2–8 cm long, upper lvs progressively shorter and narrower,
stalkless; all lvs one-veined, **hairless** above, **white-woolly** below. Infl a long spike,
sometimes with short side-branches forming over half height of plant; fl-heads (**Ga**)
6 mm long, separate or in open clusters; bracts of fl-heads with green centre and
broad chaffy **dark brown** edges; florets pale brown; achenes (**Gb**) hairy, pappus-
hairs reddish. Br Isles: GB f-lc (especially SE Eng, Scot); Ire o; Eur f-lc; in open wds,
hths, gslds on acid soils. Fl 7–9.   **Gi   Highland Cudweed**, *G. norvegicum*, has
habit of G, but only 8–30 cm tall; lvs three-veined, all ± **equal** in length, v
woolly **both sides**; spike short, ± compact, only quarter height of plant. Scot,
central and N Highlands r; on acidic mt rocks. Fl 7–8.   **Gii   Dwarf Cudweed**, *G.
supinum*, dwarf tufted per with unbranched ± erect woolly fl-stems 2–12 cm
tall; lvs lanceolate below, linear and pointed above, 0.5–1.5 cm long, woolly **both
sides**; fl-heads 1–7 in a short, ± compact terminal spike; bracts elliptical with
woolly greenish central stripe and **broad**, **brown**, **chaffy** margins. Scot Highlands f-
lc; on mt rocks, mt hths (alpine). Fl 7–8.

Plume-thistles, Thistles

Plume-thistles (*Cirsium*) differ from other Thistle genera (*Carduus*, *Silybum*,
Onopordon) in having a pappus of **feathered** hairs to their achenes (in the other
genera, the pappus is of simple, unbranched hairs). Most Thistles are v spiny, but
some only have short, soft prickles on their lf-edges.

KEY TO PLUME-THISTLES (*CIRSIUM*)

1 Fl-heads yellow – plant tall, scarcely spiny, with large oval bract-like lvs below fl-heads – **not in Br
   Isles**...
   .... *Cirsium oleraceum* (p 381 C)
   Fl-heads red-purple, mauve, or white.. **2**
2 Plant consisting of a spreading **rosette** of wavy- and spiny-edged, pinnatifid lvs, with, at its center, l
   ± unstalked fl-head (rarely 2–3, and rarely stalked to 10 cm)............................. *C. acaulon* (p 382 F)
   Plants with tall, lfy stems.. **3**
3 Lf-edges with only soft short **prickles** (not sharply spiny) – bracts of fl-heads **never** strongly spine-
   tipped – fl-heads **only 1–3** on each rounded cottony stem.. **4**
   Lf-edges with strong sharp **spines** – bracts of fl-heads sometimes strongly **spine**-tipped – fl-heads
   many, on each much-branched, round or winged stem **6**
4 Lvs deeply twice pinnatifid, green both sides, only slightly cottony beneath – no creeping runners
   – r .... *C. tuberosum* (p 382 Hi)
   Lvs elliptical-lanceolate, ± toothed, but at most shallowly-lobed, green above, white-
   cottony beneath – creeping runners present.. **5**

5 Lvs thickly **white-felted** below, hairless above, over 4 cm wide – upper lvs with broad cordate **clasping** bases – fl-heads **large** (3.5–5.0 cm long × 3–5 cm wide)........*C. heterophyllum* (p 382 G)
  Lvs only white-cottony (**not** felted) below, **hairy** above, under 3 cm wide – upper lvs **narrowed** to bases, scarcely clasping – fl-heads **smaller** (2.5–3.0 cm long × 2.0–2.5 cm wide) ....
  ....*C. dissectum* (p 382 H)
6 Stems with spiny wings or flanges.. 7
  Stems round, without spiny wings 8
7 Lvs shiny, without prickles on upper surface, ± purple-flushed – stem-wings continuous – fl-heads in crowded clusters, each head 1.5–2.0 cm long × 1.0–1.5 cm wide – outer bracts purplish, with erect, only shortly-pointed tips...*C. palustre* (p 381 D)
  Lvs dull, with hairs and prickles on upper surface, not purple-flushed – stem-wings interrupted – fl-heads few, in loose clusters, each head 3–5 cm long × 2–4 cm wide – outer bracts green, with ·long, arched-back spine-tips...*C. vulgare* (p 381 A)
8 Stout plant – lvs deeply pinnatifid, prickly-hairy above, the lobes tipped with stout long spines – involucres globular, to 4 cm long × 4–7 cm wide – bracts thickly webbed with white cotton – florets red-purple...*C. eriophorum* (p 381 B)
  Slender plant – lvs shallow-pinnatifid, ± hairless and shiny above, lobes tipped with slender short spines – fl-heads with oval involucres, 1.5–2.5 cm long × 1 cm wide – bracts purplish, ± hairless – florets mauve or white... *C. arvense* (p 381 E)

  A Spear Thistle, *Cirsium vulgare*, erect bi 30–150 cm, branched above; stems cottony, with interrupted spiny **wings**; root-lvs 15–30 cm long, short-stalked, deeply pinnatifid, wavy-edged and toothed, lobes and teeth with long **stout spines**; stem-lvs stalkless, smaller, with long terminal lobes; all lvs prickly-hairy above, not shiny. Fl-heads few, in loose clusters or solitary; heads 3–5 cm long × 2–3 cm wide, ± **cottony**, outer bracts green, with long, **arched-back yellow** spine-tips; florets pink-purple. Pappus of fr (**Aa**) feathered. Br Isles, Eur; vc on wa, rds, gslds, open wds. Fl 7–10.

  B Woolly Thistle, *C. eriophorum*, stout erect bi 60–150 cm, branched above; stems v cottony, round, unwinged, not prickly; root-lvs to 60 cm long, short-stalked, deeply pinnatifid into narrow lanceolate two-lobed segments tipped with strong stout spines, one lobe arched up, one down, making lf three-dimensional; stem-lvs similar, but stalkless; all lvs prickly-hairy and green above, white cottony below. Fl-heads solitary, **v large**; involucres 5 cm long × 4–7 cm wide, bracts spine-tipped (with a purple wing just below tip in Br Isles – not usually present in Eur), **thickly cobwebbed with white wool**; florets red-purple. Mid, S, E Eng, N to Durham, f-lc: SE Eng, S Wales, r; **rest of Br Isles abs**; Eur: France to Netherlands, f to S, r to N; on calc gsld, scrub, rds. Fl 7–9.

  ***C Cabbage Thistle**, *C. oleraceum*, per herb 50–120 cm tall, little-branched, stems furrowed, unwinged, ± hairless; root-lvs to 40 cm long, elliptical in outline, stalked, unlobed to deeply pinnatifid; upper lvs ± unlobed, clasping with **cordate** bases, pointed; all lvs edged with **stiff bristles**, toothed, **not spiny**, pale green, ± hairless; fl-heads 2.5–4.0 cm long, oval, erect, clustered, overtopped by oval yellowish upper lvs; bracts narrow-lanceolate, erect, outer spine-tipped; florets **yellow**. **Br Isles abs** (except as r introd in E Scot); Eur: N and E France to Denmark, c to S, f to N; in fens, ditches, wet wds. Fl 7–9.

  D Marsh Thistle, *C. palustre*, erect bi, with continuously **spiny-winged** hairy stem 30–150 cm, branched above; lvs ± deeply pinnatifid, with wavy spine-tipped and -edged lobes; lvs shiny, but hairy above, dark green and often **purple-flushed**, like stem; root-lvs lanceolate, stalked, less deeply lobed. Fl-heads in crowded clusters, each head 1.5–2.0 cm long × 1.0–1.5 cm wide; outer bracts purplish, with erect, shortly-pointed tips; florets dark red-purple or sometimes white. Br Isles, Eur; vc in marshes, mds, damp gslds, open wds, hbs. Fl 7–9.

  E Creeping Thistle, *C. arvense*, creeping per herb with erect, branched, spineless, furrowed, **unwinged** fl-shoots 30–90 cm tall, ± hairless. Lvs oblong-lanceolate, ± pinnatifid, with strong slender spines on their wavy and toothed edges; upperside ± **hairless**, grey-green, ± cottony beneath; lower lvs stalked, upper clasping stem. Fl-heads in open clusters, 1.5–2.5 cm long × 1 cm wide; involucre-bracts purplish, ± hairless, oval, with spreading spine-tips; florets **mauve** or white. Br Isles, Eur; va in gslds, rds, wa, ar (where a serious weed). Fl 7–9.

F Dwarf Thistle, *C. acaulon*, per herb with spreading rosette of deeply pinnatifid, wavy-edged, stoutly spine-edged lvs 10–15 cm long, ± hairless above, ± hairy beneath. Fl-heads usually 1, sometimes 2–3, **stalkless** from centre of rosette (rarely stalked to 10 cm or more), 3–4 cm long, oval; florets bright red-purple. S, E Eng, N to Yorks, S Wales, f-lc; **rest of Br Isles abs**; Eur: France to Denmark, c to S, f to N; on short calc gslds. Fl 6–9.

G Melancholy Thistle, *C. heterophyllum*, erect **spineless** per herb with runners, 45–120 cm tall; stems grooved, ± unbranched, cottony, unwinged. Root-lvs 20–40 cm long, 4–8 cm wide, elliptical-lanceolate, stalked, with fine soft-prickly (but hardly **spine-like**) teeth; upper lvs unstalked with **cordate clasping** bases, prickly-edged, mostly **unlobed**; all lvs **green**, **hairless** above, thickly **white-felted** below. Fl-heads **solitary** (or rarely 2–3), 3.5–5.0 cm long × 3–5 cm wide; involucre oval, with oval short-pointed bracts, purple-tipped, adpressed. Florets red-purple. Br Isles: N Wales, N Eng to N Scot, f-lc; **S Eng, S Wales abs**; Ire vr; Eur: Denmark lf; in upland mds, gslds, rds, open wds. Fl 7–8.

H Meadow Thistle, *C. dissectum*, erect per herb with runners, 15–50 cm tall, resembling a slender version of G in its round grooved unwinged cottony stem and elliptical-lanceolate, scarcely-lobed, spineless lvs; but lvs narrower (under 3 cm wide) and white-**cottony**, (**not felted**) beneath, **green** and **hairy** above, narrowed to bases and scarcely clasping; lf-edges wavy-toothed with soft prickles. Fl-heads solitary, sometimes 2–3 on long branches, 2.5–3.0 cm long × 2.0–2.5 cm wide; bracts of heads lanceolate, adpressed, outer shortly spine-tipped, cottony, purplish; florets dark red-purple. S Eng, S Wales, N to Yorks, o-lc, **abs to N**; Ire c; Eur: W France to Netherlands and NW Germany, lc to SW, r to N and near coast; in fens and less acid peat bogs. Fl 6–8. **Hi Tuberous Thistle**, *C. tuberosum*, close to H in fl-heads and cottony wingless stem, but **no runners**, tuberous roots, and lvs mostly deeply twice **pinnatifid**, green **both sides**, only **slightly** cottony below, edges bristly but scarcely spiny. Eng: Wilts r; Cambs vr; Glamorgan vr; Eur: France r; in calc gslds. Fl 6–7.

Carduus has stems always ± **spinous-winged**; lvs spine-edged, green above, ± cottony beneath; and pappus of fr is of **simple** hairs.

I Welted Thistle, *Carduus acanthoides* (*C. crispus*), erect v branched bi 30–120 cm tall, with narrow, **wavy**, **spinous-edged wings** ± continuous along stems. Lvs pinnatifid, with lobes, each itself three-lobed, oval, spinous, dull green, cottony below; lower lvs elliptical in outline, stalked, upper narrower, running down stem, more deeply cut. Fl-heads 3 cm long × 2 cm wide, many, in clusters of 3–5; involucre oval, ± cottony, bracts v narrow, ± spreading, **weakly** spine-tipped, ± purplish; florets **two-lipped**, red-purple. Achenes (**Ia**) with **simple** pappus. GB c (except N, W Scot r); Ire o; Eur: France to Denmark, c to S, f to N; in open wds, scrub, hbs, wa, mostly on ± calc soils. Fl 6–8. **Ii Slender Thistle**, *C. tenuiflorus*, bi, 15–100 cm tall; close to I, but more erect and narrowly branched; spinous stem-wings **broader** (to 5 mm); stems and lvs more greyish-cottony; fl-heads **narrower**, oblong-cylindrical, 1.5 cm long × 0.8 cm wide, in **dense** terminal clusters; bracts oval-lanceolate, hairless, tipped with **outward-curved** spines; florets **paler**, pink, in a **narrower** brush, **equally** five-lobed. Br Isles: GB, f-lc near coasts in S, r-o inland and in N Scot; Ire

◀ o-lf; Eur: W, N France, f near coast; N to Netherlands r near coast; on dry banks, wa, beaches, rds, especially near sea. Fl 6–8.

J   Musk Thistle, *C. nutans*, bi, 20–100 cm tall; stem erect, cottony, branched above, with spinous wings interrupted and abs for some way below fl-heads. Lower lvs wavy-edged, upper deeply pinnatifid with lobed spine-tipped segments; all lvs shiny but ± hairy above, woolly on veins below. Fl-heads rounded, **large** (4–6 cm across), well-separated on long stalks, **drooping**, with involucre of long, bent-back, lanceolate, spine-tipped, **purple-red** bracts; florets in a red-purple brush much narrower than involucre, v fragrant, tubes **two-lipped**. Br Isles: GB, N to R Forth f-lc, N, W Scot vr; Ire vr; Eur: France c, to Denmark vr; on calc gslds, wa, rds. Fl 5–8.

Knapweeds and **Star-thistles** (*Centaurea*) have **non-spiny** but ± bristly lvs and thistle-like fl-heads, with distinctive **involucre-bracts**. These each consist of two segments: the lower is green or pale; the upper, called the **appendage**, is **either** flat, pale to blackish-brown, **chaffy**-textured, its margins shortly-toothed or fringed with long, branched, bristle-like teeth, **or** consists of one or more stout, woody, pale yellow **spines**. In some, fl-heads are surrounded with a crown-like circlet of enlarged, sterile, trumpet-shaped outer tube-florets, each with several corolla-lobes 5–10 mm long. Achenes have either a short hairy pappus or none.

KEY TO *CENTAUREA*

1 Appendages of bracts each bearing one or more yellowish **spine** **2**
  Appendages of bracts **chaffy**, spineless, ± toothed, silvery to dark brown.. **4**
2 Appendages curved back, palmately-branched into **equal** spines – fls pinkish – r..
                                                        Centaurea aspera (p 386 Ci)
  Appendages with one **long straight** spreading spine, and **shorter** ones at its base........................... **3**
3 Florets purple-pink – lateral spines pinnate – r...*C. calcitrapa* (p 386 C)
  Florets **yellow** – lateral spines palmate – r..*C. solstitialis* (p 386 Cii)
4 Outer florets enlarged, **bright blue**, inner purple... **5**
  All florets **red-purple** or pink **6**
5 Fl-heads 2–4 cm wide – upper lvs **linear**-lanceolate – ann plant of ar................*C. cyanus* (p 386 D)
  Fl-heads 6–8 cm wide – upper lvs **oblong**-lanceolate – per plant – r ....*C. montana* (p 386 Di)
6 Brown appendages **horseshoe**-shaped at base, deeply-toothed round edges, **enclosing** tip of **green** lower part of bracts – lvs deeply pinnatifid – outer florets enlarged.........*C. scabiosa* (p 385 B)
  Brown appendages **not** horseshoe-shaped at base, **not** enclosing tip of green lower part of bracts.. **7**
7 Involucres 5–6 mm wide – bract appendages small (under 5 mm wide), pale brown, deeply-toothed – stem-lvs **pinnatifid** into narrow lobes – r ....*C. paniculata* (p 386 Bi)
  Involucres 10 mm wide or more – bract appendages larger, 8 mm or more wide – stem-lvs **untoothed** or only shallowly-toothed.. **8**
8 Appendages **pale brown**, with at most only **short** shallow teeth – r......................*C. jacea* (p 385 Ai)
  Appendages **dark brown**, fringed with **long, branched, bristle-like** teeth ....*C. nigra* (p 385 A)

Knapweeds, Star-thistles, Burdocks, Globe-thistle, Cornflower

A Black Knapweed, *Centaurea nigra*, erect rough-hairy per 15–60 cm tall, stems grooved, branched above; lower lvs stalked, upper stalkless, all ± unlobed, or at least never deeply pinnatifid, oblong to linear-lanceolate. Fl-heads 2–4 cm across, terminal, solitary; involucre globose; appendages of bracts (**Ab**) brown, ± triangular, fringed with long, branched, **bristle-like** teeth; lower parts of bracts oblong, pale. Florets red-purple, outer enlarged into a crown-like whorl in few local populations only. Achenes (**Aa**) hairy, with pappus of v short bristly hairs. Br Isles, Eur; vc on gslds, rds, wa. Fl 7–9. (Variable and often divided into: ssp *nemoralis*, downy, with slender stems not swollen below fl-heads, lvs narrow-lanceolate, fls pink-purple, bract-appendages light brown with fringe-teeth **longer** than undivided part; c on chk, sand in S Eng, France; and ssp *nigra*, bristly, with stouter stems swollen below fl-heads, lvs oblong, lanceolate, ± toothed, fls dark-purple, bract-appendages dark brown with teeth **equalling** undivided part; c on clay soils, especially in N of GB and N Eur.) **Ai Brown Knapweed**, *C. jacea*, differs from A in **pale** brown bract-appendages, only **shallowly-toothed** or even **untoothed**; pappus abs. SE Eng r, introd, mostly found as hybrids with A; Eur f-lc; on gslds, wa. Fl 8–9.

B Greater Knapweed, *C. scabiosa*, erect downy per 30–80 cm tall, stems grooved, branched above; rosette-lvs stalked, 10–25 cm, upper stalkless, stouter, all ± **deeply pinnatifid**, lobes ± toothed. Fl-heads 3–6 cm across, terminal, solitary, ± **always** with enlarged outer florets, florets all **bright**

cont

purple-red; involucre globose, bracts with oval **green** lower parts and dark brown **horseshoe**-shaped appendages, **enclosing** tip of green part and fringed with bristle-like teeth. Achenes (**Ba**) with pappus as long as achene. Br Isles: Eng, Wales, f-lvc; Scot r but lf; mid-Ire lf; Eur, vc to S, lf to N; on gslds, rds, hbs, scrub on calc soils. Fl 6–8.   ***Bi   Jersey Knapweed**, *C. paniculata*, resembles B in pinnatifid lvs and enlarged purple outer florets; but is bi, and small pale brown fringed bract-appendages scarcely enclose more than tips of lower parts of bracts; involucre only 5–6 mm wide, oblong. GB vr, not seen recently; Jersey r-lva; introd (W Mediterranean) on dry gsld. Fl 7–8.

  C   Red Star-thistle, *C. calcitrapa*, bushy bi, with hairless, ascending or erect, grooved stems 15–60 cm tall, branching below fl-heads; lower (**Ca**) lvs deeply pinnatifid, lobes narrow, upper ± unlobed, stalkless, all lvs hairy, bristle-toothed. Fl-heads 1–3 cm across, purplish-pink; involucre oval, hairless, 1 cm wide, bract-appendages (**Ca**) each with a **stout yellow spine** to 2.5 cm long, and shorter **pinnate** side-spines at base. Eng, probably native near S coast, Thames estuary, r-lf; introd elsewhere vr; Eur: France, S Belgium, o-lc; N to Denmark introd r; on dry calc gslds, wa. Fl 7–9.   **Ci   Rough Star-thistle**, *C. aspera*, also pink-fld, differs from C mainly in the bract appendages (**Ci**) with 3–5 **palmately arranged**, ± **equal**, **arched-back** spines. S Wales introd; Channel Is, SW France, o-la: on dunes, wa. Fl 7–9.   **Cii   Yellow Star-thistle**, *C. solstitialis*, differs from C in **yellow** fls and **palmately** arranged, spiny bract-appendages (**Cii**) with middle spine only 1–2 cm long (**twice** length of side-spines). S Eng, Eur; introd (S Eur) r-o on ar (especially in lucerne fields). Fl 7–9.

  D   Cornflower, *C. cyanus*, cottony ann with erect branches 20–50 cm tall; lower lvs stalked, pinnatifid, 10–20 cm, upper stalkless, linear-lanceolate. Fl-heads 1.5–3.0 cm across, solitary, long-stalked; outer florets enlarged into trumpets, bright blue, inner red-purple. Involucre-bracts with green, **dark-margined centre**, and **silvery**, **jagged-toothed** edges. Br Isles, formerly f-lvc, now r to vr; Eur, f-lc; on ar, wa. Fl 6–8.   **Di   Perennial Cornflower**, *C. montana*, resembles D in enlarged blue outer florets; but **per**, stouter; **oblong-lanceolate** lvs **run down stem**; fl-heads 6–8 cm across. GB, NW Eur, introd, o in wa; E France, S Belgium, native, r; in wds. Fl 6–8.

Burdocks (*Arctium*) are robust, downy, branched herbs; lvs large oval-cordate, non-spiny; fl-heads oval-globose, with red-purple florets; involucre-bracts many, overlapping, narrow, with long spreading **hooked** tips, forming burrs in fr that attach to clothes etc; pappus of rough hairs.

  E   Lesser Burdock, *Arctium minus*, 60–130 cm tall; stems furrowed, ± woolly; lf-stalks hollow, lvs longer than wide, to 40 cm long; fl-heads 1.5–3.0 cm wide, **oval** in bud, ± **narrowed at top** in fr, **short-stalked**, in **racemes**; corollas usually **longer** than the 10–13 mm bracts (**Ea**). Br Isles, Eur; vc in open wds, scrub, hbs, rds, wa. Fl 7–9.   **Ei   Greater Burdock**, *A. lappa*, differs in: basal lf-stalks **solid**; lvs as wide as long; fl-heads 3–4 cm wide, **long-stalked**, in a **flat-topped** corymb, **globular** in bud, **wide open** in fr; corollas ± **equalling** inner bracts. S half Eng, S Wales, f-lc; Eur c: in wds, rds, hbs on clay soils. Fl 7–9. (Other spp are sometimes recognized, but may be hybrid forms and are not universally accepted.)

  F   Globe-thistle, *Echinops sphaerocephalus*, tall (50–200 cm) thistle-like per herb; lvs oval-oblong, pinnatifid, green and sticky-hairy above, white-woolly below, ends of lvs and their lobes strongly spine-tipped. Fl-heads **globular**, 4–6 cm wide; actually composed of **many**, **one-fld** fl-heads attached to and radiating from a central point, each with an outer involucre of bristle-like bracts and an inner one of fringed scales; florets tubular, pale blue; achenes (**Fa**) with a cup of partly fused hairs on top. Eng, Eur; introd (central, S Eur) o on wa, scrub. Fl 6–9.

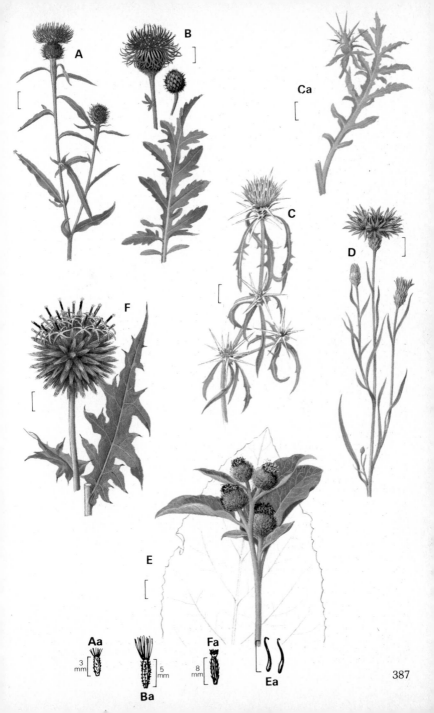

A

B

Ca

C

D

F

E

Aa

3
mm

Ba

5
mm

Fa

8
mm

Ea

387

Milk Thistle, Saw-wort, Cotton Thistle, Carline Thistle

A Milk Thistle, *Silybum marianum*, erect ann or bi, 40–100 cm; stem grooved, ± branched, unwinged, ± cottony; lvs oblong-lanceolate, wavy-lobed or pinnatifid, spiny-edged, hairless, shiny green, and netted with conspicuous **milk-white veins** above; lower lvs narrowed to base, upper clasping. Fl-heads 4–5 cm long × 4 cm wide, solitary, long-stalked, florets red purple. Bracts hairless, with oval bases and long, **triangular**, **spine-edged** appendages, each tipped with a **stout yellow spine**. Achenes (**Aa**) blackish, obovate, with **simple**, long white pappus surrounded by a yellow basal ring. SE Eng, possibly native near sea, r-lf; r and introd rest of Br Isles; Eur: France o-lf; introd and r N to Denmark; on dry banks near coasts, wa. Fl 6–8.

B Saw-wort, *Serratula tinctoria*, spineless, hairless per herb, with wiry, branched, erect, grooved stems, 20–80 cm tall. Lvs 12–20 cm, hairless, edges finely **bristle-toothed**, vary from ± undivided, lanceolate, to deeply **pinnatifid** with narrow lobes; lower stalked, upper not. Fl-heads 1.5–2.0 cm long in loose lfy infls, florets red-purple, involucre **narrow-oblong** with bracts adpressed, oval, pointed, purplish, **not spiny**. Achenes (**Ba**) with **simple** yellowish pappus. Br Isles: Eng, Wales, S Scot, f-lc; **N Scot abs**; Ire vr; Eur: France o-lc; N to Denmark r; on hths, calc gslds, fens, open hthy wds. Fl 7–9. **Bi Alpine Saw-wort**, *Saussurea alpina*, spineless, erect, thistle-like per, 7–40 cm tall, near to B; but stem **cottony**, lvs **undivided** but ± toothed, oval to lanceolate, ± hairless on uppersides, **white-cottony** beneath; lower lvs stalked. Fl-heads 1.5–2.0 cm long, narrow as in B, but in a **dense terminal** cluster, unstalked; florets purple; bracts oval, blunt, **hairy**. Achenes brown, 4 mm, pappus **feathered**. Br Isles: mts of Scot f; of NW Eng, Wales, Ire, vr (Eur, mts only); on ± calc alpine cliffs. Fl 7–9.

C Cotton Thistle, *Onopordum acanthium*, erect robust bi, 45–150 cm; stem **white-cottony**, **continuously** and **broadly spinous-winged**, branched above; lvs, oblong, stalkless, wavy-lobed, are edged with **strong spines**, v white-cottony both sides, running down into stem-wings. Fl-heads solitary, involucre globose, 3–5 cm wide, bracts green, lanceolate, cottony, ending in strong ± spreading yellow spines; florets purplish-pink. Achenes (**Ca**) wrinkled, grey-brown, pappus **simple**, long, pale reddish. Br Isles: GB, f in E and S, r to N; Ire vr; Eur: France f; N to Denmark o; on dry banks, rds, wa. Fl 7–9.

D Carline Thistle, *Carlina vulgaris*, erect **spiny** bi, 10–60 cm, ± cottony and ± purple-flushed; lvs oblong-lanceolate, wavy-lobed, cottony below, fringed with weak spines, clasping stem. Fl-heads solitary or clustered, conical in bud, opening to 3–4 cm wide in fl and fr; outer bracts spine-edged, lanceolate, green, cottony; inner **straw-yellow**, linear, **spreading** like ray-florets in fr; florets brownish-**yellow**. Achenes (**Da**) with rusty hairs and long, **feathered** pappus. Br Isles (except N Scot vr), Eur, f-lc; on calc gslds. Fl 7–10.

► **Dandelion and other Compositae with fl-heads of strap-shaped florets** (see p 391)
►

A Dandelion, *Taraxacum officinale* agg, comprises some hundreds of closely similar 'microspecies', too complex to separate here. In general, a per herb with tap-root and **basal rosette** of lanceolate-obovate, sparsely hairy, ± sharply-lobed and -toothed lvs; fl-heads 2–6 cm across, solitary on **lfless**, **hollow**, **unbranched** stems, several per plant; **milky latex abundant**, florets bright yellow; no scales among florets; involucre-bracts in 2 erect inner rows, and an outer row of shorter ones that may be adpressed to head, or spreading, or arched back. Achenes ribbed, beaked, with white pappus of simple hairs. Br Isles, Eur; va in mds, gslds, rds, wa, dunes, mt rocks. Fl 3–10.

cont

Ba

5 mm

Aa

6 mm

A

B

Ca

5 mm

C

D

Da

3 mm

B Goat's-beard, *Tragopogon pratensis* agg, erect bi with milky latex, 30–100 cm tall, little-branched, ± woolly when young, later hairless. Lower lvs 10–30 cm long, linear-lanceolate, keeled lengthwise, grass-like, grey-green, long-pointed, untoothed, hairless, with white midrib, wider and sheathing at base; upper lvs shorter, erect. Fl-heads to 5 cm wide, solitary, long-stalked, only opening in **morning sunshine**, otherwise closed (**Ba**). Bracts of heads **equal**, 8 or more, lanceolate, pointed, ± hairless, **in one row**. Achenes (**Bb**) rough, long-beaked, pappus with main rays almost woody and radiating, interwoven across like a spider's web with fine white side-hairs. In ssp *pratensis* (illustrated, B) florets are **bright yellow**, **equalling bracts**, 23–28 mm long × 3–5 mm wide, **widest near middle**; bracts have **red-brown** borders 1 mm wide; achenes 15–20 mm long. GB: S, E Eng only, r-lf; Eur c; on rds, gslds, wa. Fl 5–7. **Bi** ssp *minor* is commoner in Br Isles; florets **pale yellow**, **shorter** than involucre-bracts, 15–18 mm long × 2–3 mm wide, **widest near tip**. Bracts have brown borders 0.5 mm wide; achenes (as in **Bb**) 10–12 mm long. Br Isles: GB o (except N, W Scot, and mts, vr); Ire o; Eur, f to SW, o to N; on rds, gslds, wa. Fl 5–7. **Bii Salsify**, *T. porrifolius*, closely resembles B, but stems **v swollen** just below fl-heads, and florets mauve-**purple**, ± equalling the bracts; achenes 4 mm long only. S, E Eng, mostly by lower Thames, introd (Mediterranean) o-lf; rest of Br Isles vr; Eur r-o. Fl 5–7.

C Viper's-grass, *Scorzonera humilis*, slender erect per rather like B in habit, but only 7–50 cm, usually unbranched, more persistently cottony in lf-axils; root-lvs **elliptical**-lanceolate, **flat** at tips, sheathing at base, untoothed as in B; stem-lvs narrow, **flat**, **short**, but ± clasping at bases. Fl-heads 2.5 cm wide, solitary, florets deep yellow, involucre-bracts woolly-based, 2.0–2.5 cm long, **oval**-lanceolate, **unequal**, **overlapping**, often **orange-flushed**. Achenes (**Ca**) smooth-ribbed, **beakless**, pappus as in B. Eng: Dorset, Warwick, vr; **rest of Br Isles abs**; Eur f-lc; in moist mds. Fl 5–7. ***Ci** *Podospermum laciniatum* is like C in yellow fls, overlapping bracts to heads, and pappus; but lvs **deeply pinnatifid** into **linear** lobes, and **beakless** achenes have **long**, **swollen stalks**. Eur: E France, Belgium, W Germany, r; in dry gslds. Fl 6–8.

D Chicory, *Cichorium intybus*, per herb with erect, tough, grooved ± hairy, stiff-branched stems 30–100 cm; basal lvs stalked, lanceolate, unlobed, pointed, clasping with pointed basal lobes. Fl-heads 2.5–4.0 cm wide, on thick stalks, in clusters in lf-axils; florets **bright blue**; 2 rows bracts, inner bracts longer, erect, outer row shorter, ± spreading. Achenes (**Da**) angled, **without pappus**, but with **toothed scales** on top. Eng c: rest of Br Isles r-lf; Eur, lc to S, f to N; on rds, gslds, banks, on ± calc soils. Fl 7–10.

E Wall Lettuce, *Mycelis muralis*, erect hairless per herb 25–100 cm; lower lvs **lyre-shaped**, pinnatifid, stalk winged, lobes triangular, end-lobes larger and three-lobed; upper lvs stalkless, smaller, less lobed, clasping with **arrow-shaped** bases; all lvs **thin**, ± **reddish-tinged**. Fl-heads small, 1 cm wide or less, florets yellow, usually only 5, in an **open** panicle with **branches at 90°** to main stem; involucre narrow, inner bracts **erect**, linear, **equal**, outer **v short**, spreading, all blunt. Achenes (**Ea**) short-beaked, spindle-shaped, black, pappus of simple white hairs, the inner longer than outer. Br Isles: Eng, Wales, f-lc; Ire o; Eur c; in wds (especially beech) on calc soils, walls, calc rocks. Fl 6–9.

F Prickly Lettuce, *Lactuca serriola*, erect ± hairless bi 30–120 cm; stems often reddish, much milky latex. Lvs (**Fb**) **erect**, oblong-lanceolate, often pinnatifid (especially lower lvs), all waxy grey-green, **thick**, with fine **spines** along edges and on undersides of **whitish** veins, clasping stem with spreading **arrow-shaped** basal lobes. Infl a loose panicle with branches at **acute angle** to main stem; fl-heads 11–13 mm wide, with 7–12 yellow florets; involucre narrow, 8–12 mm long, bracts **unequal**, erect, overlapping, lanceolate, grey, **purple**-tipped. Achenes (**Fa**) olive-grey, **bristly** at tips, **beaked**, pappus white, of **equal** simple hairs. Wales, Eng, f-la

◀ to S and E, vr to N; **rest of Br Isles abs**; Eur f-lc, increasing; on wa, railways, rds. Fl 7–9.

G   Great Lettuce, *L. virosa*, bi, close to F, but **taller** (to 200 cm), stouter, stem and lvs more **purple-flushed**; lvs less divided, more **spreading**, basal clasping-lobes **rounded**, adpressed to stem; ripe achenes (**G**) **purple-black**, **without** bristles at tip; pappus as in F. Br Isles: Eng, f-lc to SE, E; rest of GB r-vr; **Ire abs**; Eur: France o; Belgium r; on wa, rds, railways. Fl 7–9.

H   Least Lettuce, *L. saligna*, ann, much slenderer than F and G, 30–70 cm tall; stems-lvs ± **vertical**, **linear**-lanceolate, wavy-edged, ± untoothed; bases clasping, arrow-shaped; lower lvs pinnatifid with narrow lobes, or unlobed; midribs broad, **white**; all lvs grey-green, hairless. Fl-heads in axils of arrow-shaped bracts, in a narrow, spike-like raceme or panicle. Bracts of **narrow**-cylindrical involucre erect, **linear**, blunt, greenish with **white** edges; florets few, pale yellow, little longer than the involucre. Achenes **pale**, 3–4 mm, long-beaked; pappus white, simple. SE Eng, mostly near coast, r and decreasing; **rest of Br Isles abs**; Eur: N to Netherlands and W Germany, o to SW, r to N; on dry banks near sea and estuaries. Fl 7–8.

*I   Blue Lettuce, *L. perennis*, erect hairless per, 30–60 cm, with pinnatifid grey-green lvs clasping stem; all lf-lobes narrow, pointed. Fl-heads **30–40 mm** wide, **bluish-purple**, long-stalked, in axils of arrow-shaped bracts in a **loose** infl; involucre-bracts overlapping, unequal. Achenes as in F. Eur: France f-lc; Belgium to W Germany r; on rds, dry gslds, wa. Fl 5–8.   **Ii   Alpine Sow-thistle**, *Cicerbita alpina*, erect bristly per, 50–200 cm; stem with **dense red sticky hairs** above, little-branched; lower lvs lyre-shaped, pinnatifid, with large, triangular-pointed end-lobes; upper smaller, less lobed, with cordate clasping bases; all lvs **hairless**, grey-green. Fl-heads in a close **short** panicle 7 cm wide × 10 cm long, at top of tall stem, each head 20 mm wide, florets **pale-violet-blue**; involucre sticky-hairy, bracts in 2 unequal rows, purplish. Achenes beakless, pappus white, of simple hairs. E Scot vr (Eur, mts only, c); on moist mt rocks. Fl 7–9.   **Iii   Blue Sow-thistle**, *C. macrophylla*, differs from I in **pale blue** fl-heads 30 mm wide; plant much more spreading and loosely, bushy-branched; lvs with cordate end-lobes and only 1 pair side-lobes, clasping stem, **all** sticky-hairy. Br Isles, Eur, introd o; on wa, rds. Fl 7–9.   **Iiii**   *C. plumieri* is like Iii, but smaller (to 100 cm), **wholly hairless**; lvs lyre-shaped, pinnatifid; fl-heads **clear blue** in loose infl. Br Isles, Eur, introd o; in wa, rds. Fl 7–9.

▶ Cat's-ears, Hawkbits, Nipplewort

Cat's-ears (*Hypochoeris*) and **Hawkbits** (*Leontodon*) have basal lf-rosettes, **lfless** infl-stems, unbranched or little-branched, and **feathered** pappus to frs. **Cat's-ears** have narrow **chaffy scales** on receptacle between the strap-shaped florets (as in **Aa**); **Hawkbits** have **no** scales between the florets (as in **Ea**). **Nipplewort** has tall, lfy, **much-branched** infl-stems, and frs with **no pappus**.

A   Common Cat's-ear, *Hypochoeris radicata*, per herb with basal rosette of oblong-lanceolate, bristly, wavy-toothed lvs, 5–12 cm long. Fl-stems, 20–40 cm, ± hairless, simple or branched 1 or 2 times only, are ± lfless but have a few scale-like dark-tipped bracts along them, and **enlarge** towards fl-heads. Fl-heads 2–4 cm across, florets bright yellow, outer greyish beneath. Involucre, narrow bell-shaped, suddenly narrowed to stalk, is of many unequal erect overlapping purple-tipped bracts, hairless except for bristles on midribs. Receptacle with scales among florets, visible when florets pulled off (**Aa**). Achenes (**Ab**) rough, beaked, with both feathered and simple pappus-hairs. Br Isles, Eur; vc in mds, gslds, rds, dunes, not usually on v calc soils. Fl 6–9.

B   Smooth Cat's-ear, *H. glabra*, 10–20 cm tall, smaller than A; lvs shorter,

393

◀ ± **hairless**, glossy ± red-tinged; **florets scarcely longer than** purple-tipped **involucre-bracts**, their yellow straps only **twice as long as wide**, only spreading **in sunshine**. Achenes (**Ba**) 4–5 mm, as in A. Br Isles: Eng, Wales, lf to E, r to W; Scot, Ire, vr; Eur, f to SW, o to N; on sandy gslds, ar, hths, dunes. Fl 6–9. **Bi Lamb's Succory**, *Arnoseris minima*, resembles B in height, hairlessness, basal rosette, lfless little-branched stems and short florets; but infl-stems **hollow**, **extremely swollen** upwards to fl-heads, root-lvs more coarsely-toothed, and achenes **without pappus**. S, E Eng, now vr; **rest of Br Isles abs**; Eur: France to Denmark o-lf; on sandy ar. Fl 6–8. *Bii *Lagoseris sancta* is ± hairless ann looking similar to B, with basal rosettes and lfless infl-stems; but fl-heads, 1–2 cm across, have longer ray-florets; no pappus. Eur: France to Germany, o-la and increasing; on ar. Fl 4–6.

C Spotted Cat's-ear, *H. maculata*, per herb with bristly-hairy lvs 7–15 cm long, all in a basal rosette as in A, but blotched with **dark purple spots** and with red midribs, wavy-toothed. Infl-stems **bristly**, unbranched or once-branched, **hardly** enlarged upwards, with few or no scale-like bracts. Fl-heads 3–5 cm across, florets **lemon-yellow**, much longer than v hairy unequal blackish-green, lanceolate involucre-bracts. Achenes (**Ca**) wrinkled, short-beaked; pappus **wholly** of feathered hairs. E, NW Eng, Cornwall, N Wales, vr; **rest of Br Isles abs**; Eur: France, Belgium, o-r, scattered; Denmark lf; on gslds, grassy sea cliffs, on calc soils and on serpentine rock. Fl 6–8.

D Rough Hawkbit, *Leontodon hispidus*, **v hairy** per herb, with basal rosette of lanceolate coarse wavy-toothed lvs, narrowed to base; infl-stems **lfless**, **unbranched**, 10–40 cm, **v hairy throughout**, hairs forked (**Da**, use lens); fl-heads 2.5–4.0 cm across, involucre narrowing **suddenly** into stalk; florets golden-yellow, far longer than **hairy unequal** involucre-bracts. Achenes (**Db**) unbeaked, **dirty-white** pappus of **both** feathered and simple hairs; **no scales** among florets. Br Isles: GB c (except N Scot vr); Ire f to S, **abs to N**; Eur c; on calc gslds, mds, fens. Fl 6–9.

E Autumn Hawkbit, *L. autumnalis*, differs from D in being ± hairless (or with few, **unforked** hairs), lvs **deeply pinnatifid**, fl-stems (to 40 cm) **branched** 2 or 3 times, involucre **long-tapered** into stalk. Achenes (**Eb**) ribbed, with white pappus of feathered hairs only. Receptacle (**Ea**) without scales, as in D and F. Br Isles, Eur; vc in mds, gslds, rds, not usually on v calc soils. Fl 6–10.

F Lesser Hawkbit, *L. taraxacoides*, resembles D in wavy-toothed rosette-lvs, bristly with forked hairs, and solitary fl-heads on unbranched lfless infl-stalks; but infl-stalks shorter (8–20 cm), **bristly** below, **hairless** above; involucre-bracts, **hairless** except for few bristles on midribs, in one inner longer **equal** row with a **few** overlapping outer ones. Fl-heads 2.0–2.5 cm across. Inner achenes (**Fa**) 5 mm, v short-beaked, pappus of **both** feathered **and** simple hairs; outer achenes scaly-topped, **without** pappus. Br Isles c (except N Scot vr); Eur: France to Denmark o; on dunes, dry sandy or calc gslds. Fl 6–9.

G Nipplewort, *Lapsana communis*, erect **lfy-stemmed** ann, **much-branched** and hairless above, hairy below. Root-lvs lyre-shaped, pinnatifid with large, oval, toothed end-lobes; upper lvs oval to diamond-shaped, with few large teeth; all lvs **thin**, ± hairy. Fl-heads 1.0–1.5 cm wide, in a loose panicle; only 8–15 florets, pale yellow, short; involucre an oval **cup** of one row of narrow equal bracts and few tiny outer ones. Achenes (**Ga**) ribbed, **without beak or pappus**. Br Isles, Eur, vc (except mt areas); on hbs, wds, rds, walls, wa. Fl 7–9.

Hawk's-beards, Oxtongues

Hawk's-beards (*Crepis*) are erect, branched, usually v **lfy-stemmed** (except Fi p 396); florets all yellow, strap-shaped, inner involucre-bracts in **one erect**, **equal** row, outer **shorter**, spreading (but ± adpressed in C and E); achenes cylindrical, with **simple**, **white** (except in E) soft pappus. **Oxtongues** (*Picris*) are also erect, branched, lfy-stemmed, with similar (inner erect, outer spreading) involucre-bracts; but plants v **bristly**, achenes **curved**, ribbed, wrinkled, and pappus of **feathered** hairs.

KEY TO HAWK'S-BEARDS (*CREPIS*)

1 Stem lfless, except for small lfy bracts at bases of infl-branches – outer fl-head bracts adpressed – **not in Br Isles** – E France to Denmark – r ....*Crepis praemorsa* (p 396 Fi)
   Stem lfy.. **2**
2 Lvs pinnatifid **6**
   Lvs toothed but unlobed, elliptical-lanceolate **4**
3 Frs beaked – lvs roughly hairy.. **5**
   Frs unbeaked – lvs hairy or not... **5**
4 Fl-heads **drooping** in bud – plant smelling of **prussic acid** – outer achenes short-beaked, inner long-beaked – r... *C. foetida* (p 395 B)
   Fl-heads erect in bud – plant not smelling of prussic acid – all achenes long-beaked – c ....*C. vesicaria* (p 395 A)
5 Plant tall (40–100 cm), bristly-**hairy** – outer fl-head bracts spreading................*C. biennis* (p 396 D)
   Plant shorter (20–60 cm), ± **hairless**, with shiny lvs – outer fl-head bracts adpressed to heads ....*C. capillaris* (p 396 C)
6 Stem-lvs **linear**, hairless, edges **rolled under**, clasping with arrow-shaped bases – **not in Br Isles** – on sandy ar ....*C. tectorum* (p 396 Di)
   Stem-lvs **elliptical** or **oblong**, hairless, **strongly-toothed**, clasping with **arrow-shaped** bases – pappus **dirty white**, **brittle**..*C. paludosa* (p 396 E)
   Stem-lvs oblong, ± **hairy**, scarcely-toothed, clasping with **cordate** bases – pappus **pure white**, **soft** – r..*C. mollis* (p 396 F)

  A **Beaked Hawk's-beard**, *Crepis vesicaria*, ± erect, **downy**, branched ▶ bi, 15–70 cm tall, stem furrowed, bristly, ± purple-flushed below; lower lvs lyre-shaped, ± deeply pinnatifid, terminal lobes ± diamond-shaped; upper less lobed, clasping, all downy. Fl-heads **erect** in bud, 15–25 mm across, long-stalked, gathered into loose corymbs; involucres 8–12 mm long, cylindrical, downy, outer bracts **spreading** in a ruff; florets golden-yellow, outer **orangey-red-striped** outside. Achenes **all** long (5 mm)-beaked (**Aa**). Br Isles: Eng, Wales, c to S and E, r to N; **Scot abs**; Ire o; Eur c; on gslds, banks, rds, wa. Fl 5–7.
  B **Stinking Hawk's-beard**, *C. foetida*, like A downy with beaked achenes; but unlike A **smells of prussic acid** (bitter almonds) when bruised, is shorter (10–40 cm), more branching from base, has stalked rosette-lvs v **hairy**, with large triangular end-lobes, and fl-heads droop in bud. Inner involucre-bracts each **wrap round** an outer achene; outer achenes **short-beaked**, the inner ones **long-beaked** (to 10 mm). Eng: Kent (and Sussex ?) now vr; Eur: France, Belgium, r; on shingle beaches, wa. Fl 6–8.

cont

C Smooth Hawk's-beard, *C. capillaris*, ± **hairless**, **glossy-lvd** ann or per, ± branched from base; basal lvs 5–15 cm, lyre-shaped, pinnatifid with narrow ± toothed lobes; upper lvs lanceolate, pointed, stalkless, clasping, bases arrow-shaped, all lvs ± shiny and hairless. Fl-heads 10–13 mm across, **erect** in bud, slender-stalked, in loose corymbs. Involucre **flask-shaped**, 5–8 mm long, **all** bracts adpressed, **hairless** on inner faces, downy and ± bristly on outer. Achenes (**Ca**) curved, **beakless**, pappus white. Br Isles, Eur, vc except in mts; on gslds, wa, hths, walls, rds, hbs. Fl 6–9.

D Rough Hawk's-beard, *C. biennis*, more rough-hairy, more erect, taller (to 120 cm) than A; stem-lvs clasping, but **not** arrow-shaped at bases. Fl-heads in a loose corymb, 20–35 mm across, with inner involucre-bracts **dark-hairy** outside, **downy inside**, outer **spreading** in a ruff; florets clear **pale** yellow (not red-striped outside); achenes (**Da**) **unbeaked**, pappus white. SE Eng: Kent, Surrey, Herts, f-lc and native; rest of Br Isles r-o, probably introd; Eur, c to S, lf to N; on gslds, scrub, hbs, rds, mostly on calc soils. Fl 6–7. ***Di** C. tectorum* is slender ann or bi, 20–40 cm, with grey-downy stem; stem-lvs **linear**, **edges rolled under**, **unlobed above**, ± **hairless**, with clasping **arrow-shaped** bases. Involucre hairy, not sticky, bracts **downy** on **inner** sides, outer bracts spreading; achenes beakless, pappus **white**, **soft**. Eur f-lc; on sandy ar. Fl 6–7.

E Marsh Hawk's-beard, *C. paludosa*, erect ± hairless per 30–90 cm tall, branched above only; lower lvs elliptical-lanceolate with **short** winged stalks, upper lvs clasping with long, **back-pointed basal lobes** forming **arrow-shape**; all lvs shiny, thin, sparsely wavy-toothed, hairless. Fl-heads few in a loose corymb, 15–25 mm across, erect; florets golden yellow, involucre-bracts woolly with **black sticky-tipped hairs**, outer shorter, **adpressed**. Achenes (**Ea**) beakless, pappus of **brittle**, **brownish** hairs. Br Isles: Wales and N Eng to N Scot f-lc; **S Eng abs**; Ire o-lf; Eur: E France, Belgium, to Denmark, o-lf to N, only on mts and r to S; in moist mds, damp wds on richer soils, in hilly or mt areas. Fl 7–9.

F Northern Hawk's-beard, *C. mollis*, rather like E, but stem-lvs clasping with **rounded** bases (**F**), wavy-toothed or untoothed, ± hairless; root-lvs lanceolate, **blunt**, narrowed into **long** winged stalks; fl-heads 20–30 mm across, as in E but less **hairy**; achenes unbeaked, pappus **white**, **soft**. N Eng, Scot, r-o; **rest of Br Isles abs**; Eur, mts to E only, r; in moist wds, by streams in mts. Fl 7–8. ***Fi** C. praemorsa* is related to F; but rosette-lvs scarcely toothed; downy stem, 15–40 cm, ± lfless except for bracts, and bears few, pale yellow heads in a short terminal **raceme**. Achenes **unbeaked**, pappus **white**, **soft**. Eur: E France, Denmark, N Germany, r, decreasing; in fens, mds, gslds. Fl 6.

G Hawkweed Oxtongue, *Picris hieracioides*, erect bi or per with stout **bristly** furrowed stem 15–70 cm, branched above; lower lvs 10–20 cm, lanceolate, blunt, **short-stalked**, upper narrower, clasping at base, all wavy with shallow teeth, bristly. Fl-heads 20–30 mm across, in a loose umbel-like corymb; involucre oval, inner bracts **narrow**, equal, erect, outer shorter, **spreading**, bristly on midribs; florets bright yellow. Achenes (**Ga**) spindle-shaped, curved, v **short-beaked**, wrinkled, pappus creamy, of **feathered** hairs. Eng and Wales, c to SE, o to N and W; **Scot abs**; Ire vr; Eur, c to S, r to N; on gslds, scrub, cliffs, rds, wa, on calc soils. Fl 7–10.

H Bristly Oxtongue, *P. echioides*, of habit similar to G, but more thickly covered with **bristles** with **swollen**, **whitish bases**; stem-lvs lanceolate, with clasping **cordate** bases; 3–5 outer involucre-bracts are sepal-like, **broadly cordate**, 7–10 mm wide; inner narrower; all v bristly. Achene beaks as long as achenes (**Ha**). Br Isles: Eng, Wales, f-lc, mostly in S and E; Scot, Ire, vr; Eur: France c, to Denmark (r and mostly near coast); in hbs, mds, gslds, banks on clay soils or chk. Fl 6–10.

DAISY FAMILY   *Compositae*

Hawkweeds, Sow-thistles

Hawkweeds (*Hieracium*) form a large genus (over 400 'microspecies' described for
Br Isles alone) of great difficulty. Because they reproduce non-sexually, the ovules
forming seeds without pollination, many v similar, self-reproducing (but not cross-
breeding) forms occur. These cannot be considered in detail here, but an example
is given of each of 3 of the 7 or 8 main groups of microspecies. They are all erect,
± lfy-stemmed pers **without** runners; all have yellow strap-shaped florets
only; fl-heads with overlapping, **unequal** rows of bracts; and achenes (**Ac**) 2.5–
4.5 mm, cylindrical, ribbed, beakless, with a **ring** on top, and pappus of **simple,
brittle, brownish, unequal** hairs. (For further details, see P. D. Sell and C. West,
'Account of *Hieracium*', in *Flora Europaea* vol 5, ed by T. G. Tutin, 1980.) **Mouse-
ear Hawkweeds**, *Pilosella* (formerly in the genus *Hieracium*), are shorter plants;
lvs all (or **mostly**) in a **basal rosette**, usually with **lfy runners**; achenes only 1.5–
2.0 mm long, and with 10 **teeth** at their tips; all pappus hairs of ± **equal**
length. **Sow-thistles** (*Sonchus*) are tall, robust; stems, **stout, hollow**, containing
abundant milky latex in canals, bear lvs ± deeply pinnatifid with clasping
bases; fl-heads in umbels; florets strap-shaped, yellow; achenes **unbeaked,
flattened**, ribbed, with a pappus of white, **simple** hairs.

A *Hieracium perpropinquum* is most c member of the *Sabauda* group; plant
50–100 cm tall; no basal rosette; stem-lvs (**Ab**) many, crowded; lower lvs **stalked**,
toothed, oval-lanceolate; upper short, stalkless with **broad** rounded bases not
clasping stems; bracts of involucre olive (or blackish)-green; stems v hairy with
white, bulbous-based hairs, bracts white-hairy with sticky (but not star-shaped)
hairs; fl-heads several (**Aa**), 20–30 mm across. Br Isles: Eng, Wales, c; Scot, Ire, o-
lf; Eur f; in open wds, hbs, rocks, on acid or sandy soils. Fl 8–10.

B *H. umbellatum* is most c member of the *Umbellata* group, which differs from
A in that **all** the many crowded lvs are **stalkless**, narrow or **linear-lanceolate**, with
rolled-back edges; fl-heads are in an **umbel-like** corymb (not a **looser** panicle as in
A); involucre-bracts **hairless**, blunt, with arched-back tips; styles **yellow** (not **dark**
as in A). Br Isles, Eur; c in open wds, hbs, rocks, hths, gslds, on various dry soils. Fl
6–10.

C *H. exotericum* is most c member of the *Glandulosa* group; these are 20–
60 cm tall, with a well-developed **basal rosette** (**Ca**) of **stalked**, toothed, oval-
oblong lvs with rounded or cordate bases; stem-lvs **few** or **none**; lvs and stem
± hairy, grass- or yellow-green; infl an umbel-like corymb with sticky glands
on the involucre-bracts of the fl-heads; achenes black. Related microspecies may
have **purple-blotched** lvs, but can be distinguished from Spotted Cat's-ear (p 394
C) by the **simple** pappus of **brown** hairs (feathered, white, in Cat's-ears). S Eng,
Wales, f-lvc; rest of Br Isles r; Eur f-lc; in wds (especially beechwds on calc soils),
rds, banks, rocks. Fl 6–8.

D **Mouse-ear Hawkweed**, *Pilosella officinarum* (*Hieracium pilosella* of CTW),
per herb with **long, lfy, runners**; basal rosettes of obovate ± blunt untoothed
lvs, 3–8 cm long, stalked, **white-felted** below, **green** but with scattered **stiff long
white hairs** above; infl-stems, 5–30 cm tall, lfless, unbranched, bear **solitary**
heads 15–25 mm wide of **pale** yellow florets (**Da**); involucres oval, with narrow
bracts that have both sticky, black-based, and also white hairs; florets **red-striped**
beneath, styles yellow, achenes purple-black. Br Isles, Eur; vc in gslds, hths, banks,
rocks, walls. Fl 5–8.

E **Orange Hawkweed**, *Pilosella* (*Hieracium*) *aurantiacum*, differs from D in
having a **few stem-lvs** as well as basal rosette, in height usually **over 20 cm**, and
plant (but not lvs) **densely long-hairy**; several fl-heads of **brick-red florets** in a
close-umbellate cluster. Br Isles, Eur; introd (central Eur), f-lc in wa, banks, rds,
railway banks. Fl 6–7.

Ac

A

Aa

Ab

Ca

8 cm

C

E

B

Ga

G

Da

D

Fa

2.5 cm

F

3 cm

Fb

H

I

399

DAISY FAMILY

Compositae

◀   **F   Marsh Sow-thistle**, *Sonchus palustris*, tall robust per 90–300 cm tall, with
stout **hollow** angled stem (**Fb**), hairless below, sticky-hairy above. Basal lvs
lanceolate-oblong, with deeply clasping **arrow**-shaped bases, and pinnatifid with
few narrow side-lobes and large lanceolate end-lobes, edges and teeth finely
spine-tipped; upper lvs **lanceolate**, untoothed, with long-pointed clasping basal
lobes; all lvs wavy, grey-green, ± hairless. Fl-heads in large open umbel-like
corymbs, each head **30–40 mm** across; all stalks and bracts densely covered with
blackish-green sticky hairs; involucres **oval**, 12–15 mm long, florets **pale** clear
yellow, 25 mm long (**Fa**); achenes **yellow**, 4 mm long, ten-ribbed. Pappus white, of
simple hairs. Eng: E Anglia lf-la; Kent (R Medway etc), Hants, r but la; **rest of Br
Isles abs**; Eur: N, E France to Denmark, o-lf; in reed-swamps by tidal rivers,
ditches, fens. Fl 7–9.

G   Perennial Sow-thistle, *S. arvensis*, per herb 60–150 cm tall; stem much as
in F; stem-lf bases **rounded**, clasping; all lvs ± pinnatifid, with side-lobes
broader, shorter than in F, **shiny green**, edged with fine spines. Fl-heads **40–
50 mm** across, florets **deep** yellow; branches in infl (**less** branched, looser, less
umbel-like than in F) and involucres all covered with **yellow** sticky gland-tipped
hairs (**Ga**). Involucres **bell-shaped**, 13–20 mm long. Achenes dark **brown**, 3.0–
3.5 mm long, ten-ribbed. Br Isles, Eur; vc on ar, wa, hbs, fens. Fl 7–10.

H   Smooth Sow-thistle, *S. oleraceus*, erect ann 20–150 cm tall; stout **hairless**
stems; lvs, hairless except when young, with **pointed spreading** basal lobes, grey-
green, pinnatifid into **broad**-triangular, toothed, but **non**-spiny lobes. Fl-heads,
20–25 mm across, in a loose umbel; florets **pale** yellow, involucre short (10–
15 mm), usually hairless, **not** sticky. Achenes 3 mm, yellow, **wrinkled**, six-**ribbed**.
Br Isles, Eur; vc on ar, wa, hbs, open wds. Fl 6–10.

I   Prickly Sow-thistle, *S. asper*, ann, close to H; lvs (**I**) less pinnatifid, lobes
narrow, but **deeply doubly-toothed**, **crisped**, **spinous** on edges like thistle lvs;
basal clasping lobes **rounded**, **adpressed** to stem. Fl-heads as in H, but florets **deep
golden** yellow; achenes yellow, 2.5 mm long, **smooth**, six-ribbed. Br Isles, Eur; c
on ar, wa, open wds, hbs. Fl 6–10.

MESEMBRYANTHEMUM FAMILY

Aizoaceae

(*Not illustrated*) **Hottentot Fig**, *Carpobrotus edulis*, creeping per, with angled
± woody stems below, and narrow-linear, opp, **fleshy** curved lvs, 7–10 cm
long, triangular in cross-section, toothed on the back. Fl-stalks 3 cm, v swollen
below fls; fls to 5 cm wide, solitary, superficially like large **Daisies** (but **single** fls,
not **heads** of fls); calyx-tube with 5 lfy lobes; petals **v many**, linear, purplish-pink or
yellow; stamens many; fr fleshy, rather fig-like, edible. Sea cliffs of SW Eng, Ire, W
France, vla, introd (S Africa). Other members of the family also occur on SW Eng
coast.

MONOCOTYLEDONS

WATER-PLANTAIN FAMILY   *Alismataceae*

A family of **aquatic** herbs which is the counterpart, in the **Monocotyledons**, of the Buttercup family in the **Dicotyledons**. Lvs untoothed, parallel-veined; fls have 3 sepals, 3 petals, as in most Monocotyledons, but the carpels, **numerous, free** from one another, in whorls or heads, ripen into **achenes** v like those of Buttercups; sepals **green**, unlike the petals; stamens 6 (or more); carpels **superior**.

KEY TO WATER-PLANTAIN FAMILY

1 Aerial lvs **arrow-shaped** (in the native sp) – fls **20 mm or more across** – fls in several, usually simple, successive whorls up erect infl – **separate** male fls with **many** stamens – female fls with carpels in a **dense round head** .... *Sagittaria* (p 402 D)
   Aerial (and floating) lvs **not arrow-shaped** – fls only to 15 mm across – all fls bisexual, with 6 stamens and 6 to many carpels **2**
2 Fls usually **solitary**, long-stalked, arising from horizontal floating stems .... *Luronium* (p 402 Ci)
   Fls in **erect, whorled infls** **3**
3 Lvs **cordate-based** – ripe carpels 6 (–10), 12 mm long, **long-beaked**, in a **spreading, star-like** whorl .... *Damasonium* (p 401 Bii)
   Lvs **narrowed to, or rounded at,** base – ripe carpels many, 1–2 mm long, **without** long beaks **4**
4 Infl either a simple **umbel** or of 2 successive **simple** whorls – carpels oval, **pointed,** in a crowded **head** .... *Baldellia* (p 401 C)
   Infl of **several** successive whorls, which are **themselves whorled-branched** – carpels **flattened, blunt,** style attached to one side, in a **single whorl** .... *Alisma* (p 401 A, B)

A   Common Water-plantain, *Alisma plantago-aquatica,* erect hairless per, 20– ▶
100 cm; lvs long-stalked, 8–20 cm long, ± erect, oval, pointed, rounded at base; infl of several tiers of whorled branches which again branch in whorls; fls to 1 cm across, sepals 3, blunt, green, petals 3, rounded, pinkish, stamens 6; carpels many in a flat **single** whorl (**Aa**); each carpel (**Ab**) **blunt, flattened**-oval, long with **long straight** style **arising from near base**. Br Isles, Eur, c (except N Scot r); on mud in and by fresh waters. Fl 6–8.
   B   Narrow-leaved Water-plantain, *A. lanceolatum,* differs from A only in its **narrow**-lanceolate lvs, **tapered** to stalk (**B**), and in its carpels (**Ba**) with style **short** and ± straight, arising from **side** of carpel near **top**. Br Isles: Eng, Wales, o-lf; Scot vr; Ire r; Eur, France to Denmark, o-lf; habitat as for A. Fl 6–8.   **Bi   Ribbon-leaved Water-plantain,** *A. gramineum,* **shorter** (15–30 cm) than A and B; lvs **linear, ribbon-like,** ± submerged; styles **coiled like springs**. Eng, S Lincs, Worcs, vr; Eur: France to Denmark, r; in ponds etc. Fl 6–8.   **Bii   Starfruit,** *Damasonium alisma,* low ann, 5–20 cm tall, with blunt **cordate-based** ± **floating lvs,** 3–5 cm long, in a basal rosette; infl of a few superimposed whorls of white fls 6 mm across; carpels 6(–10), **12 mm long, long-beaked,** ± two-seeded, in a **spreading star-like** whorl. SE Eng, now vr, decreased; W France r; in or beside shallow sandy or gravelly-bedded ponds, where animals (especially geese) graze. Fl 6–8.
   C   Lesser Water-plantain, *Baldellia ranunculoides,* erect per 5–20 cm tall, like a small version of A or B, but with infl either a simple **umbel** or of 2 successive simple whorls; lvs 2–4 cm long, mostly basal, **linear-lanceolate,** pointed, tapered into long stalks; fls (**Ca**) 15 mm wide, pale pink; carpels many, in a **crowded head** (**Cb**), oval, with **pointed** tips. Br Isles: GB, o-lf to S; N Scot vr; Ire o-lf; Eur: France to Denmark o-lc; in fens, ponds, ditches, usually on calc peat. Fl 6–8.   **Ci   Float-**

ing **Water-plantain**, *Luronium natans*, has **horizontal**, floating or submerged stems, bearing **blunt elliptical** floating lvs 1.0–2.5 cm long, on long stalks, and linear submerged lvs to 10 cm long × 2 mm wide; fls usually **solitary**, long-stalked, arising from lf-axils, 12–15 mm wide, white with **yellow spots** at bases of their 3 petals; carpels in a crowded head as in C. Mid and E Eng, Wales, r-lf, but increasing; **abs rest of Br Isles**; Eur: W, central France, r-o; Belgium to Denmark r; in lakes and canals in acid water. Fl 7–8.

D Arrowhead, *Sagittaria sagittifolia*, erect hairless per, over-wintering by detached submerged buds; submerged lvs **linear**, translucent (**Da**), floating lvs **oval**-lanceolate, aerial lvs ± erect, long-stalked, **arrow-shaped**, 5–20 cm long; infl a simple erect whorled raceme, 30–80 cm tall, fls 2 cm or more across, 3–5 per whorl; lower fls **female** with many carpels in a **dense head**; upper fls **male**, larger and longer-stalked, with **many stamens**; all petals white with **purple spot** at base. Br Isles: Eng f-lc; Wales vr; **Scot abs**; Ire o-lf; Eur, France f-lc to Denmark o-lf; on muddy substrates in still or slow-moving fresh waters. Fl 7–8. **Di Canadian Arrowhead**, *S. rigida*, like D erect, with white fls 2 cm across, but aerial lvs **oval**, as in A, infl **shorter** than lvs, whorled fls have **v short** stalks (male) or **none** (female), and petals have **no** purple spot. Eng, Exeter in R Exe, vl introd (N America). Fl 7–8.

FLOWERING-RUSH FAMILY *Butomaceae*

The Flowering-rush family differs from the Water-plantain family in the carpels, which are oblong and form **many-seeded follicles** in fr, opening at tips to release seeds.

E Flowering-rush, *Butomus umbellatus*, hairless erect per to 150 cm, with **linear**, pointed, three-angled, twisted lvs ± as long as fl-stems, all from base; infl-stems round, with terminal **umbel** of many, unequally- and long-stalked fls; fls (**Ea**) 2.5–3.0 cm across; 3 sepals smaller than 3 petals, but **all** rosy-pink; stamens 6–9; carpels 6–9, **free** except at base, dark red, oblong, to 7 mm long, each **many-seeded**, style on top. Br Isles: Eng f-lc; Wales, Scot, vr; Ire r; Eur, N to Denmark, f-lc; in still and slow moving fresh water on muddy substrates. Fl 7–9.

FROGBIT FAMILY (see also p 444) *Hydrocharitaceae*

A family of **aquatic** plants related to the two foregoing; fls with 3 sepals, 3 petals, but **ovary inferior**, **one-celled**, producing several seeds; fls 1–3 together, in bud enclosed in a **spathe** of 1 or 2 bracts; fls unisexual. (See also Canadian Waterweed etc, p 444 H.)

F Frogbit, *Hydrocharis morsus-ranae*, floating herb with long runners, over-wintering by detached buds in mud; lvs 3 cm across, floating, **rounded-kidney-shaped**, long-stalked, with large chaffy basal stipules; fls long-stalked, 2 cm across, arising from water; petals 3, **crinkly**, white, with yellow spot at base; sepals green, smaller; male fls 2–3 together in a spathe of 2 bracts, female solitary. Br Isles: Eng o-lc; Wales vr; **Scot abs**; Ire o; Eur f-lc; over mud or peat substrates in ponds, ditches, fens. Fl 7–8.

G Water-soldier, *Stratiotes aloides*, aquatic herb with runners, ± submerged, but rising partly out of water to flower; lvs in a large ascending **crown-like** rosette, 15–40 cm long, rigid, lanceolate, pointed, **spine-edged** like aloe lvs, but **translucent**, many-veined, **brownish-green**; in GB female plants only; fls erect, solitary, on stalks 5–8 cm long, with 2 large bracts below fl; fls 3–4 cm across, three-petalled, white; male fls (S Eur) 2–3 together, each with 12 stamens. Eng o, but lf in E; r introd rest of Br Isles; Eur o, but lf; in ponds, ditches, fens. Fl 6–8.

2mm

A

B Ba

Ca Cb

C

Aa

Ab
2mm

Da

D

E

Ea

G

F

A large family of herbs with bulbs or tubers and a few shrubs, of diverse form, but all with 6 equal, similar perianth segments (May Lily has fl-parts in fours), in some joined into a tube, in others separate; 6 stamens, a three-celled **superior** ovary, forming in fr either a dry capsule or a berry. In **Orchid**, **Daffodil** and **Iris** families, **ovary is inferior**; **Daffodil** family have **6 stamens** per fl, **Iris** family **only 3 stamens**. In **Orchid** family, one petal is enlarged, v different from rest of perianth segments, and forms a **lip to fl**, usually on the **lower side**; there is usually only one, stalkless, anther. **All** families named above have **parallel-veined**, **unlobed**, **untoothed** lvs, like most Monocotyledons.

KEY TO LILY FAMILY

1 Much-branched **low shrub** – true lvs **reduced to tiny chaffy scales** – **oval, tough, evergreen, spine-tipped cladodes** (flattened lf-like stems) in **axils** of the scale-lvs, bear fls on their upper sides – berry red..*Ruscus* (p 406)
   Much-branched **herb** – true lvs reduced to tiny chaffy scales – **bright green, needle-shaped cladodes** in axils of scale-lvs – fls in axils of scale-lvs on normal stems – berry red...........................
   ....*Asparagus* (p 406)
   Herbs with aerial stems **unbranched**, or branched only in infls – true lvs present, either linear, grass-like or ± oval, **parallel-veined**, at base of, and/or up the stems...**2**
2 Infl a terminal **umbel**...**3**
   Infl a terminal **raceme**...**4**
   Infl a **branched panicle**..**12**
   Fls **solitary** on stem-tips...**13**
   Fls in **clusters** of 1–3 in **axils** of elliptical or lanceolate lvs up lfy stem – perianth **tubular** or **bell-shaped**, six-lobed – fr a berry..*Polygonatum* (p 405–406)
3 Fls **many** per umbel (**sometimes** partly or wholly replaced by small **bulbils**) – **papery spathe** enclosing infl in bud, splitting into 1 or more **bracts** in fl – plants with **garlic** or **onion** smell when bruised...*Allium* (see key p 413)
   Fls **few** (2–5) per umbel, always yellow, **never** mixed with bulbils – 1–3 lf-like **green** bracts at base of, but **not** enclosing infl – no garlic smell when bruised...
   ....*Gagea lutea* (p 412 E, key to *Gagea* spp p 412)
4 Lvs linear, all **flattened** and **folded in one plane**, **edgeways-on to stem** (as in a gdn Iris) – lvs mostly, but not all, basal – in bogs...**5**
   Lvs variously shaped, **broadside**-on to stem, **not** all flattened in one plane...................................**6**
5 Fls **creamy** – stamens hairless – styles 3.. *Tofieldia* (p 408)
   Fls **yellow** – stamens orange-woolly – style 1 ....*Narthecium* (p 412)
6 Fl-stem **lfy**...**7**
   Fl-stem **lfless** (but sometimes with scales) – lvs all from root...**8**
7 Lvs **cordate**-based, alt, 2–3 only – infl a dense raceme only 2–5 cm long – fls **small**, white, 2–5 mm wide, with **4 free** perianth segments only................................... *Maianthemum* (p 406)
   Lvs elliptical-lanceolate, **not** cordate-based, **whorled** or alt, **many** – infl a **loose** raceme 20–30 cm long – fls **large**, various colours, 30 mm wide or more, with **6 free** perianth segments, often arched back... *Lilium* (p 410)
8 Lvs **oval-lanceolate**, in pairs, **stalked** – rootstock **creeping** – perianth white, cup-like, six-lobed – fr a red berry...*Convallaria* (p 406)
   Lvs **linear** or **grass-like**, **stalkless** – rootstock a bulb..**9**
9 Perianth-tube **inflated** in middle, **narrowed** to mouth, its lobes v short...................*Muscari* (p 408)
   Perianth **not** inflated, not narrowed to mouth, its 6 segments **free almost to base**.......................**10**
10 Fls **white** – the 6 free perianth segments each with a **green central stripe** on the **outside**...............
   ....*Ornithogalum* (p 410)
   Fls blue or purplish (rarely white) – perianth segments **never** with a green stripe on outside **11**
11 Infls with **no bracts** (or **one** only) below each fl – perianth segments **8 mm or less** long, **free** to base, forming an open **cup**- or **star**-shape...*Scilla* (p 412)
   Infls with **2 bracts** below each fl – perianth segments **10 mm or more** long, **joined** at base, forming a **bell**-shape..*Endymion* (p 410)
12 Fls white inside, **purplish-pink** outside, 15–20 mm across – perianth segments **5–7-veined** – stamen stalks **white-woolly** – infl an **umbel-like** panicle ....*Simethis* (p 408)
   Fls **wholly white**, 25–50 mm across – perianth segments three-veined – stamen stalks **hairless** – infl with long, **spike-like** branches – **not in Br Isles**..*Anthericum* (p 408)

13 Fl-stalk erect, **lfless**, **pink**, arising **directly from ground** in **September**, no lvs at base – thick lvs, as in gdn hyacinth, produced in spring .... *Colchicum* (p 408)
Fl-stalk bearing lvs.. **14**
14 Fls **drooping**, bell-shaped, 3–5 cm long, **chequered pink and purplish** or sometimes pure white, with 6 free segments, with a shiny nectary at base of each inside – lvs **linear** .... *Fritillaria* (p 406)
Fls **erect**, **yellow** (or other colours), bell-shaped, 3–5 cm long, **no nectaries** – lvs **lanceolate**.........
Tulipa (p 406 Ai)
Fls erect, **white**, cup-shaped, 1–2 cm long, **nectary present** – lvs almost thread-like – **Wales** – vr .... *Lloydia* (p 410 Gi)
Fls erect, yellow, star-shaped, 1–2 cm long, **nectary abs** – lvs thread-like – **not in Br Isles**..............
Gagea bohemica (see key p 412)

YAM FAMILY   *Dioscoreaceae*

A mostly tropical family of creeping or twining and climbing monocotyledonous herbs with tuberous rhizomes and **cordate**, **net-veined** lvs; fls small, in racemes, **dioecious**, with **3 sepals and 3 petals all alike** and joined in a tube below; ovary **inferior**, 6 stamens in male fls. Fr (in Br Isles and Eur) a berry.
   A   Black Bryony, *Tamus communis*, climbing herb, twining clockwise, without ▶ tendrils; lvs **cordate**, pointed, 3–10 cm × 2.5–10.0 cm, hairless, long-stalked, v **glossy** dark green, with **palmate main veins** and **netted side-veins** (unlike most Monocotyledons except Herb-Paris (**B**), and Arum family (p 418). Fls in racemes in lf-axils, male stalked, female ± stalkless, 4–5 mm across, bell-shaped, the 6 perianth lobes narrow, yellow-green; frs (**Aa**) red **poisonous** berries. (White Bryony, *Bryonia dioica*, p 228, quite unrelated, is also a dioecious, climbing herb, **but** with palmately-**lobed** lvs, **tendrils**, and **five**-petalled fls; frs also red berries.) Eng, Wales, c (except in mt areas) N to S Lakeland and Durham; **rest of Br Isles abs** (except Lough Gill, Ire, introd); Eur: France c; W Germany, Belgium, r; in open wds, scrub, hbs, on richer or calc soils. Fl 5–7.

HERB-PARIS FAMILY   *Trilliaceae*

A family of monocotyledonous herbs with **net-veined** lvs in **one** whorl on top of erect stem below the solitary fl.
   B   Herb-Paris, *Paris quadrifolia*, erect hairless per herb with naked stems 15–40 cm tall, topped by a parasol-like **whorl** of usually 4 (sometimes 3, 5 or more) obovate to diamond-shaped, **net-veined** pointed lvs 6–12 cm long, tapered to bases. Fl in centre of lf-whorl, **solitary**, long-stalked, with 4 (rarely more) green lanceolate sepals 2.5–3.5 cm long, 4 narrower green petals, 8 long narrow stamens, and a superior 4(or 5)-celled purple ovary. Fr a black berry. Br Isles: Eng f-lc (**Devon, Cornwall abs**); Wales, E, S only, r; Scot, S, E only, r; **Ire abs**; Eur: France vc; N to Denmark o-lf; in damp wds on calc soils. Fl 5–7.

LILY FAMILY (see key, p 404)   *Liliaceae*

Solomon's-seals, Lily-of-the-valley etc

Solomon's-seals (*Polygonatum*) have lfy stems bearing alt or whorled, **parallel-veined** lvs with tubular or bell-shaped whitish fls, in clusters in lf-axils.
   C   Common Solomon's-seal, *Polygonatum multiflorum*, hairless per herb 30–80 cm tall, with **cylindrical (Ca) arching** stems; lvs alt, 5–12 cm long, untoothed, oval-elliptical, pointed, stalkless, ± spreading on each side of stem; fls in stalked clusters of 2–4 in lf-axils, pendulous; perianth 9–15 mm, tubular, six-toothed, **narrowed** in middle, greenish-white; stamen-stalks **downy**; fr a **blue-black** berry. S Eng, NW Eng, S Wales, native, lf-lc; introd and r rest of Br Isles; Eur: France vc; N to Denmark o-lf; in dry wds on calc or sandy soils. Fl 5–6. The hybrid

C × D is the usual garden plant, sometimes escaping.

D   Angular Solomon's-seal, *P. odoratum*, like A, but shorter (15–30 cm), with fls longer (18–22 mm), **not** narrowed in middle but **narrow bell-shaped, fragrant**; stamen-stalks **hairless**; stem (**D**) **angled** in cross-section. Eng, Cotswolds, S Pennines, NW Yorks, S Westmorland, r but vlf; Wales vr; **Scot, Ire, abs**; Eur: France r and scattered; Belgium to Denmark o-lf; in wds on limestone and on calc sands. Fl 6–7.

E   Whorled Solomon's-seal, *P. verticillatum*, **erect** per herb 30–80 cm, with ± angled stem and **linear-lanceolate** lvs in **whorls** of 3–6, 5–12 cm long; fls 1–4 per cluster, pendulous; perianth 6–8 mm long, **narrowed** in middle as in C; stamen-stalks **rough**; fr a **red berry** (unlike that of C and D). Scot, Perthshire vr; **rest of Br Isles abs**; Eur: hills of NE France, Belgium, W Germany, r-lf; Denmark o-lf; in mt wds (and fen wds in Denmark). Fl 6–7.

F   Lily-of-the-valley, *Convallaria majalis*, hairless per with creeping rhizomes; lvs **long-stalked**, in pairs from rhizomes, **oval-elliptical**, untoothed, parallel-veined, 8–20 cm long × 3–5 cm wide; infl-stalks **lfless**, 10–20 cm tall, with fls in **one-sided racemes**; fls **white**, 5–8 mm long, **globose**, six-toothed, v fragrant; fr a red berry. Br Isles: Eng f-la; Wales, Scot, vr; Ire vr, introd only; Eur, France to Denmark f-lvc; in wds on calc or sandy soils. Fl 5–6.

G   May Lily, *Maianthemum bifolium*, erect per, 8–20 cm tall, hairless except on upper stem; lvs deeply **cordate**-based, oval, pointed, root-lvs long-stalked, stem-lvs 2, alt, v short-stalked, all 3–6 cm long; fls in a **dense** raceme 2–5 cm long, each 2–5 mm across, unscented, white, with **4 free** perianth segments; fr a red berry. E Eng: Norfolk, Lincs, Yorks, Northumberland, vr but la; **rest of Br Isles abs**; Eur: N, E France to Denmark, f-lc; in dry wds on acid sandy soils. Fl 5–6.

H   Butcher's-broom, *Ruscus aculeatus*, erect hairless, much-branched dioecious evergreen shrub 25–100 cm tall, with creeping rhizomes; lvs reduced to small chaffy scales; lf-like **cladodes** (flattened stems) in their axils are **oval, tough, evergreen, spine-tipped**, 1–4 cm long; fls, 1–2 on upper sides of cladodes in axils of tiny bracts, are 5 mm across, six-petalled, greenish-white; fr a red berry 1 cm wide. Br Isles: S Eng, S Wales, native f-lc; N to central Scot, Ire, introd r; Eur: W, N France, o-lc; Belgium introd, r; in dry wds. Fl 1–4, fr 10–5.

I   Wild Asparagus, *Asparagus officinalis*, per hairless herb, either erect to 100 cm, or with procumbent stems, also creeping underground stem. Stems stout, ann, much-branched; lvs tiny chaffy whitish scales, with clusters of green needle-shaped lf-like **cladodes** (really modified stems) in axils of some. Fls 1–2 together on stalks in axils of some scale-lvs on larger stems (**Ia**), 3–6 mm long, with bell-shaped greenish-yellow six-lobed perianth; male and female fls separate; male larger, stamens 6. Fr a red berry. **Erect** form in Eng, Wales, Eur, o-la in wa, dunes; often an escape, but probably native on some dune areas; **procumbent** form (ssp *prostratus*) native on grassy sea cliffs, SW Eng, S Wales, SE Ire, r and vl; W France lf. Fl 6–9.

▶
▶ Fritillary, Grape Hyacinths, Meadow Saffron, Martagon Lily etc (see p 409)

A   Fritillary, *Fritillaria meleagris*, erect hairless herb 20–40 cm, with few narrow-linear alt stem-lvs; fls **solitary** (rarely 2), **drooping**; perianth segments 6, 3–5 cm long, oblong, forming a parallel-sided cup **chequered pink** and **brownish-purple** (rarely all white), with a glistening **nectary** at base of each segment inside; stigmas 3, long, narrow; capsule globose, three-angled. GB: S central Eng, E Anglia, r but la, decreasing; Eur: W, N France, r-la; Belgium, Denmark, Netherlands, W Germany, r (often introd to N); in mds, especially those flooded in winter. Fl 4–5. **Ai   Wild Tulip**, *Tulipa sylvestris*, differs from A in its **erect**,

407

yellow fls; **no nectaries** on base of pointed perianth segments inside; lvs linear-**lanceolate**, to 12 mm wide; stigmas 3, v short. GB, introd N to SE Scot, r-o; Eur, introd (S Eur) r-o; in mds, parks. Fl 4–5.

*B *Anthericum ramosum* is an erect hairless per 40–60 cm tall; lvs linear, grass-like, all basal; stem much-branched, forming a v loose panicle of white star-like fls (**Ba**) 20–25 mm across; 6 elliptical perianth segments; 6 yellow anthers with slender, **hairless** stalks; fl-bracts 5 mm long; fr an oval capsule. Eur: central, N, NE France, W Germany, o-lc; Belgium, Denmark, r; on dry calc gslds, rds, Fl 6–7. ***Bi   St Bernard's Lily**, *A. liliago*, v close to B, but **little-branched**, and fls **30–50 mm across**, in elongated racemes; fl-bracts **10 mm** long. Eur: central, NE France, Belgium, W Germany, r; Denmark vr; on dry calc gslds. Fl 5–7 ***Bii   White Asphodel**, *Asphodelus albus*, like Bi, but much **stouter-stemmed**; 60–120 cm tall, with fls 4–6 cm across in a long, ± dense raceme; perianth segments white, lanceolate, with brown midrib; anther-stalks **broad** and **hairy below**, **arching inwards** above ovary. W France lf; on hths, rocky gd. Fl 4–5.

C   Kerry Lily, *Simethis planifolia*, erect hairless per herb 15–45 cm tall; lvs linear, **grey-green**, grass-like, all from base, as long as infl, ± curved; infl a loose panicle of fls (**Ca**) each 20 mm across, with short bracts; 6 perianth segments, **white inside**, **pink outside**; 6 stamens, **white-woolly**-stalked; style undivided; capsule globose. Ire, Kerry r but lf; W, central France, o-lc; hths, rocky gd. Fl 5–7.

D   Scottish Asphodel, *Tofieldia pusilla*, erect hairless per herb 5–20 cm tall; lvs mostly basal, **all flattened in one plane**, **edgeways on** to stem (like a miniature gdn Iris). Infl a **short**, **dense** raceme; fls with short (1 mm) stalks, short **three-lobed** bracts, and 6 **blunt**, oblong greenish-cream perianth segments 2 mm long; styles 3; capsule short, oval. GB: Teesdale r but lf; Scot Highlands f-lc (Eur only in high mts); in springy mt bogs on basic soils. Fl 6–8.

Grape Hyacinths (*Muscari*) have racemes of blue or purple fls with **inflated** perianth-tubes, **narrowed** to their six-toothed mouths.

E   Grape Hyacinth, *Muscari atlanticum*, erect hairless per herb 10–25 cm tall, arising from a bulb; lvs linear, half-cylindrical, grooved on inner sides, 15–30 cm long × **1–3 mm wide**, all basal; fls in a **dense cylindrical** terminal raceme 2–3 cm long, **plum-scented**; **dark blue** perianth-tubes 3–5 mm long, **oval**, inflated, with 6 white teeth at the narrow mouth; upper fls smaller, paler, sterile. Capsule globular. Eng: E Anglia, Oxford, r; Eur: W, central France, f-lc; N to Belgium, W Germany, r-o; also introd widely; on dry calc gslds. Fl 4–5.   ***Ei   Small Grape Hyacinth**, *M. botryodes*, close to E, but lvs 3–7 mm wide, keeled, **widened** to blunt tips, more rigid; fls **unscented**, **pale blue-violet**, **globular**, in looser, more **conical**, heads. W, central France, W Germany, o; Belgium r; introd N to Denmark and rarely in GB; on calc gslds. Fl 4–5.

F   Tassel Hyacinth, *M. comosum*, taller (20–50 cm); lvs **6–15 mm wide**; **long, loose infl** of long (1–2 cm)-stalked fls, lower fls brown, fertile, **oblong**, spreading, upper fls sterile, **purple**, in an **erect tassel**. Eng, Wales, introd r; Eur: W, N France, o; N to Denmark introd, r: on dunes, wa. Fl 4–7.

G   Meadow Saffron, *Colchicum autumnale*, hairless herb with underground corm producing erect fls arising directly from gd **in autumn**, **without lvs**; apparent **white** stalk of fl, 5–20 cm tall, is actually its perianth-tube, bearing at its tip 6 oblong **rosy-pink** perianth segments 3.0–4.5 cm long, resembling a Crocus fl, but with 6 stamens (Crocuses have only 3 stamens). Styles 3, v long, separate up tube from below gd level. Lvs, oblong-lanceolate, 12–30 cm long × 1.5–4.0 cm wide, thick, glossy-green (like lvs of a **gdn Hyacinth**), are produced **in spring** with frs from **previous** year's fls; capsule oval, 3–5 cm long, on short stalk with lvs below. Eng, E Wales, c in a belt from N Dorset N to Salop and E to Oxfordshire; r-o elsewhere; **rest of Br Isles abs**; Eur: W France to Denmark, f-la to S and E, introd N

A

Ba

B

1.5 cm

4 cm

C

Ca

D

E

G

F

H

409

◀ of Belgium; in mds, damp wds on clayey soils. Fl 8–10, fr 4–6. **Gi Snowdon Lily**, *Lloydia serotina*, erect hairless herb 5–15 cm tall, with a small bulb in gd; lvs linear, almost **thread-like**, basal 15–25 cm long, stem-lvs few, much shorter; fls **solitary**, erect, bell-shaped, perianth segments 6, oblong, 1 cm long, **white** with **purple veins**, pointed, **crocus-like**. Fr a three-angled capsule. N Wales, Snowdon range, vr (mts of central Eur); on mt ledges on basic rocks. Fl 5.

H Martagon Lily, *Lilium martagon*, erect, robust per herb to 100 cm; stem rough; lvs oval-lanceolate, 5–15 cm long, in **whorls** of 5–10 up stem, uppermost alt; fls in a raceme, each 4–5 cm across, with 6 oblong, **strongly curved-back**, **red-purple** perianth segments with darker spots. Anthers red, long-stalked. S Eng, Kent to Wye Valley, r, scattered but la, possibly native; introd r elsewhere in GB; Eur: mts of France f, lf in lowlands; introd N to Denmark o; in wds on calc soils. Fl 6–7. **Hi Pyrenean Lily**, *L. pyrenaicum*, (from S Eur mts), naturalized in N Devon; lvs **alt**, fls **yellow**, black-dotted. Fl 5–7.

▶ **Bluebells, Stars-of-Bethlehem, Bog Asphodel, Squills**

Bluebells (*Endymion*) grow from undergd bulbs; all lvs basal; racemes of blue, bell-shaped fls each with 2 bracts and 6 perianth segments **joined at the base**. **Stars-of-Bethlehem** (*Ornithogalum*) have racemes of **white** fls; green stripe down back of each of 6 perianth segments; stamens with broad flattened hairless stalks. **Yellow Stars-of-Bethlehem** (*Gagea*) have erect **yellow** fls with a green stripe down back of each perianth segment; fls in **umbels**, with a spathe of lf-like bracts **below umbel**. The only sp in GB is E (below); for others that occur in Eur see key on p 412. **Squills** (*Scilla*), bulbous plants, are close to Bluebells, but with no bracts or 1 only in each fl; perianth is **wide open**, cup- or saucer-(not bell-) shaped, its segments **separate** to base.

A Bluebell (Hyacinth in Scot), *Endymion non-scriptus* (*Hyacinthoides non-scriptus* is latest name), hairless herb 20–50 cm tall; lvs linear, all basal, glossy-green with hooded tips, 20–40 cm × 1–2 cm; infl a one-sided raceme of **drooping** fls, each with **2 blue bracts** at base. Fls sky-blue (or white), **cylindrical-bell-shaped**; 6 perianth segments, **parallel** below, **arched back** at tips, are joined at **base** and bear filaments of **cream** anthers; capsule oval, 15 mm long. Br Isles, vc except high mts, fens; **Orkney, Shetland, abs**; Eur: W, N, central France, vc (but abs E of Rheims); Belgium f to W, r to NE and in W Netherlands; rest of Eur abs; in wds, hbs, gslds, sea cliffs in W. Fl 4–6. **Ai Spanish Bluebell**, *E. hispanicus*, similar, but lvs **broader** (1.0–3.5 cm); fls **erect**, **widely bell-shaped**, perianth segment tips **not** arched back; anthers **blue**. Br Isles, France, o introd (SW Eur); in wa, wds. Fl 4–6.

B Spiked Star-of-Bethlehem, *Ornithogalum pyrenaicum*, erect hairless per with **stout** stem 50–100 cm tall; lvs, linear, grey-green, all basal, 30–60 cm × 3–12 mm, wither before fls open; raceme **dense**, many-fld; bracts of fls whitish, short; perianth segments 6–10 mm long, separate, narrow, **spreading starwise**, greenish-**cream** with green stripes, filaments lanceolate, **narrowed** to anther; capsule oval, 8 mm long. Eng: E Somerset to Wilts and Berks, f-la; Bedford, r but lf; r introd elsewhere in Eng; Eur: SW, central, E France to W Germany, f-la; N, NW France, Belgium, r; in wds, hbs, on calc or clay soils. Fl 6–7.

C Common Star-of-Bethlehem, *O. umbellatum*, has lvs **shorter** (15–30 cm), **narrower** (6 mm) than in B, with white stripes down midrib. Fls in a short, **umbel-like** raceme, lower fls on long ascending stalks, nearly **level** with upper ones; fls **erect**, **cup-shaped**, **larger** than in B; perianth segments 1.5–2.0 cm long, **white**, with **conspicuous** green stripe on back; capsule **obovate**, six-angled; bracts **2–3 cm long**. Br Isles: GB o-lc, probably native in E Anglia, otherwise introd; **Ire abs**;

6mm

◄ Eur, f-lc to S, o-lf introd to N; in dry gslds, hbs, wa. Fl 4–6. **Ci Drooping Star-of-Bethlehem**, *O. nutans*, like B has fls in long racemes, but **all turn to one side**; separate fls as in C, but **larger**, **drooping**; perianth segments 2–3 cm long, **bell-shaped**, with green stripe on back v broad, white edges narrow. Filaments v broad, **two-toothed at tips**, **anther in the notch**; capsule **pendulous**. Mid, E Eng, introd r-lf; Eur, central, E France to Denmark, introd (S Eur) o-lf; in wa, gslds. Fl 4–5.

D Bog Asphodel, *Narthecium ossifragum*, creeping hairless per with erect fl-stems 10–40 cm tall; lvs mostly basal, ± curved, 5–20 cm long, **all flattened in one plane** as in gdn Iris; stem-lvs shorter, sheathing. Infl an erect raceme; bracts of fls 5–10 mm, equalling fl-stalks; fls **star-like**, with 6 **bright yellow** lanceolate perianth segments 6–8 mm long; 6 **orange-red** anthers, filaments **orange-woolly** (**Da**); capsules elliptical, 12 mm long, turning orange like rest of plant in fr. Br Isles, uplands of W, N, f-lvc, hth areas of S Eng f; **S mid**, **E Eng** (except Norfolk vlf); ± **abs**; Eur: W France f-lc; N to Denmark o-lf, vr to E away from coasts; in wet hths, sphagnum bogs. Fl 7–8.

E Yellow Star-of-Bethlehem, *Gagea lutea*, almost hairless, 8–25 cm tall, arising from a bulb; the **solitary** linear basal lf, 15–40 × 5–12 mm, is like those of A, but hooded tip ± **curled over** like a **crozier**, with **3–5 ridges on back**. Fls **golden-yellow** inside, **star-like** when fresh, fading **pale** yellow and partially closing up to show green stripe down outside of each of 6 narrow oblong perianth segments that are 10–15 mm long. Br Isles: GB: from central S Eng and E Anglia to E Scot, o but vla; **SE, SW Eng, Wales, N Scot, Ire, abs**; Eur: France to Denmark, r to S, f-lc to N; in wds on basic soils. Fl 3–4. (See *Gagea* Key below.)

F Autumn Squill, *Scilla autumnalis*, ± hairless per 4–20 cm tall; lvs all basal, narrow-linear, 4–15 cm long × 1–2 cm, with fls; infl a dense erect 4–20-fld raceme. Fls stalked, **without bracts**; 6 spreading oblong **dull purple** perianth segments 4–6 mm long; anthers **purple**. S Eng, Cornwall to Essex, r; Eur: W, N France, c to W, o to N; on dunes, sea cliffs, dry gravelly gsld inland. Fl 7–9.

G Spring Squill, *S. verna*, close to F, but fl **in spring** and linear curly lvs appear **before** fls: infl a 2–12-fld raceme, dense, round-topped, 5–15 cm tall. Fls each with 1 **bluish-purple bract** longer than fl-stalk; perianth segments obovate, **pale violet-blue**, 5–8 mm long; anthers **violet-blue**. GB: W coast from S Devon N to Hebrides, and in Shetland, f-la; NE Scot, Northumb, N, E, Ire, lf; Eur: W France la; in short gsld on rocky sea cliffs. Fl 4–5. ***Gi*** *S. bifolia* is near G, but with usually only 2 lvs, both on stem, and broader (5–6 mm) than in F and G: fls **bright** blue, with **no** bracts (as in F). Eur: France, Belgium, r. Fl 3–4.

KEY TO W EUR SPP OF YELLOW STARS-OF-BETHLEHEM (*GAGEA*)

1 Stem with **single** root-lf.. 2
  Stem with **2 or more** root-lvs.. 4
2 Lvs **2–12 mm wide, keeled on back** – perianth segments blunt 3
  Lvs **1–2 mm wide, without keel** – perianth segments pointed – France r, N to Denmark lf – in wds, mds.. *G. minima*
3 Stem and fl-stalks **hairless** – lvs **5–12 mm wide, tips hooded**, curled – stigma 1, green....................
                                                                                                              G. lutea (p 412 E)
  Stem **downy** – lvs **2–6 mm wide, tips flat**, rounded – stigmas 3, yellow – France to Denmark, r – on open wds, gslds.. *G. pratensis*
4 Stem, fl-stalks and bracts **downy**... 5
  Stem, fl-stalks and bracts **hairless** – fls few – **1 large, broad and spathe-like** bract below umbel – E France, Belgium, r – Denmark lf – in wds .... *G. spathacea*
5 Fls many – fl-stem with **2 opp** bracts at base of umbel – perianth segments lanceolate, pointed – France to Denmark r – on ar, gslds.. *G. arvensis*
  Fls usually solitary, rarely 2 – 2 thread-like, long basal lvs and 3–4 narrow alt stem-lvs – perianth segments obovate, blunt – W, central France, r – in wds.. *G. bohemica*

LILY FAMILY   *Liliaceae*

Garlics, Leeks, Onions (*Allium*), erect per herbs arising from bulbs; **onion smell** when bruised. Fls in terminal **umbels**, a **spathe** of one or more papery or greenish **bracts** below umbel; **bulbils** mixed with fls in some spp; perianth segments and stamens 6 each, ovary **superior**. Key below covers many more spp than illustrated on p 415.

KEY TO GARLICS, LEEKS, ONIONS ETC (*ALLIUM*)

1 Lvs **elliptical, long-stalked** – fls white ....*Allium ursinum* (p 414 A)
  Lvs **narrow, grass-like** or ± **cylindrical, stalkless**...**2**
2 Infl-stalk **three-angled** **3**
  Infl-stalked **round**...**4**
3 Infl **without** bulbils among the **white** fls – lvs 2–5, dark green....................*A. triquetrum* (p 414 D)
  Infl with **many** bulbils among the **white** fls – If l, bright green – Br Isles, Eur, introd, o in wa ....
                                                             A. paradoxum (p 414 Di)
  Infl **without** bulbils, fls **rose-pink** – E France, Germany – on calc rocks.......................*A. senescens*
4 Lvs **flat, solid** – bulbils usually present in infl **5**
  Lvs **round** or **half-cylindrical, hollow** – bulbils present or not..**10**
5 Robust plants 60–200 cm tall – stems **stout** – lvs 12–35 mm wide – spathe of one bract only,
  longer than umbel – umbel **7–10 cm** across..**6**
  Slender plants 30–80 cm tall – stems **thin** – lvs 4–15 mm wide – spathe of 1–4 bracts – umbel
  5–6 cm across...**8**
6 Umbel globular, many-fld, with no or with few small bulbils **7**
  Umbel irregular, few-fld, with many large bulbils......................................*A. babingtonii* (p 414 Ci)
7 Spathe **green**, persistent – fls white – **anthers red**, long-protruding – garden escape, (Leek), o ....
                                                                   A. porrum
  Spathe **chaffy**, soon falling off – fls pale purple or whitish – **anthers yellow**, slightly protruding.......
                                                     A. ampeloprasum (p 414 C)
8 Spathe of **1 long-pointed bract**, soon falling – fls **whitish** – lvs smooth – stamens not protruding
  from perianth – escape (Garden Garlic), o...*A. sativum*
  Spathe of **2 long-pointed** bracts **much longer than umbel** – fls **pink** – stamens **long-protruding**
  – introd, established in Br Isles, o – Eur native – in wds, on river banks ....*A. carinatum*
  As above, but fls **whitish** – stamens **not** protruding.........................*A. oleraceum* var *complanatum*
  Spathe of 2 or more **short** bracts – stamens **not** protruding..**9**
9 Lvs with **keel** on back, **rough-edged** – perianth segments 5–8 mm, red-purple ....
                                                          A. scorodoprasum (p 414 Bii)
  Lvs **without keel, smooth-edged** – perianth segments 10–12 mm, bright pink – Br Isles, Eur,
  introd, o in wa – native SW France..*A. roseum*
10 Stem **inflated** – fls whitish, v many, bulbils none..**11**
  Stem cylindrical in cross-section, **not inflated** **12**
11 Stem v swollen **below** middle – lvs **half-circular** in section – fls greenish-white, perianth
  segments 4–5 mm long – garden escape (Onion) o ....*A. cepa*
  Stem swollen **above** middle – lvs **circular** in section – fls yellowish-white, perianth segments 6–
  8 mm long – garden escape (Welsh Onion) o ....*A. fistulosum*
12 Umbels **without** bulbils among fls – spathe of 2 short bracts...**13**
  Umbels **with** bulbils (or of bulbils **only**) **14**
13 Plant 15–40 cm tall – lvs **cylindric**, grey-green, 10–25 cm × 1–3 mm – perianth segments 7–
  12 mm long, **spreading**, pale pink-purple – fl-stalks shorter than fls – stamens **not protruding**
  from fls – fl-head dome-shaped.................................,....................................*A. schoenoprasum* (p 414 E)
  Lvs **half-cylindric**, grooved, green, 20–60 cm × 1–2 mm – perianth segments red-purple, 5 mm
  long, **erect** – fl-stalks ± equalling fls – stamens **protruding** – fl-head globular – r ....
                                                          A. sphaerocephalon (p 414 Ei)
14 Spathe of **1 bract no longer** than fls, soon falling – **stamens protruding** – filaments of stamens
  broad, divided into 3 teeth, anther on the shorter middle tooth .... *A. vineale* (p 414 B)
  Spathe of **2** lf-like pointed **bracts**, much longer than fls – stamens **not protruding** – filaments of
  stamens undivided, slender – lvs sometimes ± flattened, but hollow below ....
                                                         A. oleraceum (p 414 Bi)

Garlics, Leeks, Onions

A Ramsons, *Allium ursinum*, has 2–3 lvs, **elliptical-oval**, 10–25 cm × 4–7 cm, bright green, pointed, on **long stalk** twisted through 180°; stem 10–45 cm tall, weakly three-angled; spathe of 2 papery bracts shorter than fls: umbel 6–20 fld, ± flat-topped, **bulbils abs**; perianth segments **white**, 8–10 mm long, lanceolate; stamens with short, narrow stalks. Br Isles, c (except NE Scot, Ire, o); Eur, N to Denmark c; in moist wds, hbs, especially on calc or richer soils. Fl 4–6.
B Wild Onion, *A. vineale*, has lvs **half-cylindric**, grooved above, **hollow**, smooth, 20–60 cm × 2 mm; stem 30–80 cm tall, round; spathe of 1 papery bract no longer than fls; umbel has oval, green-purple **bulbils** usually mixed with fls, sometimes bulbils only (var *compactum*), rarely fls only; fl-stalks 1–2 cm long, fls with pink or greenish-white oblong perianth segments 5 mm long; stamens **protruding**, filaments of inner 3 three-toothed, with anther on tip of middle tooth which is only half as long as the others. Br Isles: GB, c to S, r to N; Ire r; Eur f-lvc; on dunes, rds, ar. Fl 6–7. **Bi Field Garlic**, *A. oleraceum*, differs from B in its spathe of **2 v long-pointed** lf-like **bracts**, **much longer** than umbel of bulbils and fls; fls long-stalked; stamens not protruding from perianth, their stalks untoothed. Br Isles: GB, mid, N Eng, f (elsewhere r); **Ire abs**; Eur: France to Denmark f; on dry gslds. Fl 7–8. **Bii Sand Leek**, *A. scorodoprasum*, rather like B, but lvs **flat**, **solid**, linear, keeled **rough-edged**, spathe of **2** bracts **shorter** than umbel; few **reddish-purple** fls, with stamens as in B, but **enclosed** in perianth; purple bulbils. GB: N Eng to central Scot **ohly**, o; Eur o-lf; dry gslds, rds. Fl 5–8.
C Wild Leek, *A. ampeloprasum*, tall (60–200 cm) **robust** per herb with **stout** cylindrical stem; lvs **flat**, but **keeled**, 15–60 cm × 12–35 mm, rough-edged, waxy grey-green. Spathe of **1** papery bract, falling as fls open; umbels 7–10 cm across, globose, many-fld, bulbils none or few; perianth (**Ca**) bell-shaped, pale purple, 6–8 mm long; stamens slightly protruding; style (**Cb**) protruding. GB: Cornwall, Somerset, S Wales, vr; W France r; on dunes, hbs, rocky gd near sea. Fl 7–8. **Ci Babington's Leek**, *A. babingtonii*, resembles C, but umbels **irregular**, with **many** short-stalked **large bulbils** and **few** fls, some of these in clusters in stalked secondary umbels. Br Isles: Cornwall, NW Ire; Eur: SW France; vr but lf on rocks and dunes near sea. Fl 7–8.
D Three-cornered Leek, *A. triquetrum*, has **linear**, **flat to keeled** lvs 12–20 cm × 5–10 mm, and erect strongly **three-angled stem** 20–50 cm tall; spathe of 2 narrow papery bracts **shorter** than fls; umbel of **drooping** long-stalked fls, **no bulbils**; perianth segments, 12–18 mm long, **white** with **green** stripe outside, form a bell longer than stamens. GB: Cornwall, N Devon, introd lvc; rest of Br Isles vr; **Scot abs**; Eur: W France introd (S Eur) vlf; on wa, hbs, rds, scrub. Fl 4–6. **Di Few-flowered Leek**, *A. paradoxum*, differs from D in having only **1** brighter green lf, and **few fls**, but **many bulbils**, per umbel. GB: Eng r; central Scot lf; Eur: W France o (Caucasus). Fl 4–5.
E Chives, *A. schoenoprasum*, tufted per herb with **cylindrical hollow** lvs all from base, 10–25 cm × 1–3 mm; stem 15–40 cm, **cylindrical**, with **dense** umbel of pale purplish-pink fls and **no bulbils**; perianth segments 7–12 mm, spreading, **longer** than stamens, rather **thin and papery**; spathe of **2 short bracts**. GB: Cornwall, Wales, Wye Valley, N Eng, r; **rest of Br Isles abs** (except as gdn escape r); Eur: introd (mts of central Eur f) in lowlands o, but vr native in SW France, Germany, Denmark (Bornholm); on rocky calc gslds. Fl 6–7. **Ei Round-headed Leek**, *A. sphaerocephalon*, taller (30–80 cm), with lvs **half**-cylindrical, hollow, but **grooved** on upper side; umbel dense, ± **spherical**. 2.0–2.5 cm across, with spathe of 2 short bracts; fls many, bulbils **abs** as in E; perianth segments **5 mm long**, **red-purple**; stamens **protruding** from perianth. Eng: Avon Gorge near Bristol only, vr; Eur: W France lc; central France, W Germany, Belgium, r; on limestone rocks, coastal dunes. Fl 6–8.

cont

A

B

Ca

C

Cb

6mm

6cm

D

E

G

I

F

H

415

DAFFODIL FAMILY

Amaryllidaceae

◄ Bulbous herbs, close to Lily family, but ovary always **inferior**; fls (or fl-clusters) in bud enclosed in a **spathe**; perianth segments 6, stamens 6, style single, ovary three-celled. In *Narcissus* perianth consists of 6 segments around a central **trumpet**.

F   Wild Daffodil, *Narcissus pseudonarcissus*, hairless per herb with flat, linear, erect grey-green lvs 12–35 cm × 5–12 mm, and **solitary** fls, turned to one side, on ± flattened stalks 20–35 cm tall; fls 5–6 cm wide, with outer whorl of **6 pale yellow** perianth segments and inner **trumpet-shaped** tube 25–30 mm long, **golden yellow** with many small blunt lobes at its mouth; capsule obovate, 12–25 mm long. Eng, Wales, scattered but f-la especially in W and S; **Scot, Ire, abs**; Eur: France f-la; Belgium, W Germany, r, not E of Rhine; introd N to Denmark; in wds, old gslds, on clay and loam soils. Fl 3–4.   **Fi   Tenby Daffodil**, *N. obvallaris*, has ± erect fls, **both** trumpet **and** outer perianth segments **deep yellow**, and trumpet **expanding** to mouth, with **spreading** edges. Wales: Pembroke, vla; Eur abs; in mds. Fl 4.   **Fii   Poet's Narcissus**, *N. poeticus*, **sweet-scented**; outer whorl of perianth segments 5.5–7.0 cm wide, **white**, ± **flat**; trumpet **v short** (3 mm long), yellow, with **crisped red edge**. GB, Eur, introd (S Eur) o; in parks, wds. Fl 4–5.   **Fiii   Primrose-peerless**, *N.* × *biflorus*, of hybrid origin, has fls as Fii in size and shape, but outer perianth segments **creamy-yellow**, trumpet short, **deep yellow**, and fls **2 together**. Eng, Wales, S Ire, W France, introd o; in parks, mds. Fl 4–5. Many gdn Daffodil varieties, often hybrids and usually with larger fls, occur as escapes.

G   Snowdrop, *Galanthus nivalis*, small bulbous herb 15–25 cm tall; lvs keeled, grey-green, linear, 4 mm wide, all basal; fls **solitary**, **drooping**; narrow oblong spathe notched into 2 lobes, green with broad chaffy edges; the 3 outer perianth segments 14–17 mm long, obovate, blunt, pure white; the 3 inner half as long, deeply-notched, with **green spot near tip**; capsule oval. GB f but mostly introd (perhaps native in Welsh Borders); Eur: France to Netherlands f, but often introd to N; in damp wds. Fl 1–3.

H   Summer Snowflake, *Leucojum aestivum*, **taller** (30–60 cm), **stouter** than G; with **3–7 fls** in a loose **umbel**; spathe **undivided**, 4–5 cm long, green; perianth segments all **alike and equal**, obovate, white with a green spot near tip, 14–18 mm long; capsule pear-shaped; lvs **bright** green, 30–50 cm × 10–15 mm. Eng: mid-Thames Valley lf-vla; rest of S Eng r; S Ire r but la; **rest of Br Isles abs**; Eur: central France lf; in swamps, wet mds, willow wds by both fresh and tidal rivers. Fl 4–5.   **Hi   Spring Snowflake**, *L. vernum*, has perianth segments all alike and equal as in H, but they are **larger** (20–25 mm long), fls are usually **solitary**, and the spathe **bilobed** at tip. Eng: W Dorset, Somerset, vr, possibly native; Eur: N, E France, Belgium, o-lf; in wds, scrub, hbs. Fl 2–4.

IRIS FAMILY

Iridaceae

Resembles Daffodil family in fls having **inferior** ovary; but only **3 stamens**, and perianth segments joined into a tube below; style **three-lobed**.

I   Blue-eyed-grass, *Sisyrinchium bermudiana*, hairless erect per herb with short rhizome; lvs linear, 1–3 mm wide, all basal; **flattened, winged** stem; fls 2–4 in a loose raceme with 2–3 **lf-like** bracts below; perianth segments 7 mm long, blue, obovate, with **mucronate** points; stamens joined below; capsule globular. W Ire, Kerry to Donegal, o-lf; Eur abs (closely related spp in N America); on marshy mds, lake shores. Fl 7–8.

▶

Irises, Gladiolus, Sand Crocus

Iris (*Iris*) fls are of distinctive form. The three outer perianth segments (**falls**) arch outwards and downwards; the three inner ones (**standards**) are ± erect and stalked. The three stamens arise from bases of the falls, the three strap-shaped, **petal-like**, style-branches arch outward over each stamen; a flap at each style-branch tip prevents self-pollination. Stems grow erect from stout creeping rhizomes; lvs, both basal and up stems, are hairless, sword-shaped, and **flattened in one plane**. Frs are three-angled capsules.

A   Yellow Iris, *Iris pseudacorus*, per herb with erect stems 40–150 cm, arising from a stout rhizome; lvs sword-shaped, ± equalling infl, 15–25 mm wide; infl ± branched, with fls 2–3 in each papery-tipped spathe; fls 8–10 cm across, bright **yellow**; falls oval to oblong, **unbearded**, veins purple; standards spoon-shaped, v short (2 cm); styles yellow; seeds brown. Br Isles, Eur; vc in fens, marshes, wet wds, by and in fresh water. Fl 5–7.

B   Stinking Iris, *I. foetidissima*, per **tufted** herb with erect stems 30–80 cm, and clumps of sword-shaped **evergreen** lvs ± equalling infl, 10–20 mm wide, smelling of **fresh meat** when crushed (hence local name of Roast-beef plant, more accurate than official name); fls in infls arranged as in A, but 6–8 cm across, falls obovate-lanceolate, **unbearded**, **dull grey-purple** at margins, **brownish-yellow** to centre, veins purple; standards spoon-shaped, brown-yellow, shorter (3–4 cm) than falls. Styles coloured as standards; capsule (**Ba**) club-shaped, 4–5 cm long, splitting into 3 segments when ripe to expose **orange-red** seeds. Br Isles: Eng and Wales only, c in S, r to N, **abs N of line Chester-Lincoln**; Eur: W, central France, N to Normandy only, f-lc; in wds, hbs, scrub, on sea cliffs and inland, mainly on calc soils. Fl 5–7.   **Bi   Blue Iris**, *I. spuria*, per herb 20–60 cm tall; lvs, **linear**, shorter than infl, smell **unpleasant** when crushed; fls 5 cm across, 1–3 in each spathe, falls with **long, narrow, yellow-keeled** stalks and **cordate**, pale **blue-violet** darker-veined unbearded tips, styles violet, standards **erect**, elliptical, violet, shorter than falls. Capsule with **long point** at tip. Eng: Lincs, Dorset, vr; Eur: W France to Denmark r-lf; in marshes near sea, calc gslds. Fl 6.   **Bii   Garden Iris**, *I. germanica*, has fls of various colours (wild form purple); falls **yellow-bearded** above, standards **erect**, **longer** than falls, **incurved**, oval: fls 10 cm or more wide; lvs 5 cm wide, grey-green; gdn escape, o-lf in various colour varieties in Br Isles, Eur (SE Eur); on walls, wa. Fl 5–6.

C   Wild Gladiolus, *Gladiolus illyricus*, slender erect hairless per herb 40–90 cm, growing from a corm; lvs at base and up stem, to 30 cm long × 1 cm wide, tapered to tips, all **flattened in one plane**, grey-green; fls in a long one-sided raceme, each fl with a spathe of 2 green, purple-tipped bracts; perianth segments 2.5–3.0 cm long, obovate, long-stalked, **v unequal**, the 3 lower narrower and pointing down to form a **lip**, 3 upper broader, forming a loose **hood** to fl, bright **crimson-purple** with paler streaks. Capsule obovate, three-angled; anthers only **half length** of their filaments; 3 stigmas **suddenly swollen** towards tips. Br Isles, New Forest only, lf-vla; Eur: W France r; under bracken on hths and in open wds on acid loamy soils. Fl 6–7 (brief).   **Ci   G. segetum**, also purple-fld, differs from C in having anthers **as long as** filaments, stigmas **widened gradually** to tips, and uppermost perianth segment **longer**, and **twice width of**, those on either side of it (not ± equal to them). S Eng introd (S Eur), but r; W France o; on wa, ar. Other Gladioli occur as escapes.   **Cii   Montbretia**, *Crocosmia* × *crocosmiiflora*, hybrid of gdn origin frequently found introd in S Eng, W France (and especially in W Ire in wild places); like C, but **densely** tufted and has runners; fls 2.0–5.0 cm across, deep orange, funnel-shaped.

D   Sand Crocus, *Romulea columnae*, small crocus-like herb growing from a corm; basal rosette of wiry, curly lvs 5–10 cm long × 1–2 mm wide, and 1 (to 3) fls on an erect stem 3–5 cm tall. Fls **star-shaped**, only open in sun, 7–10 mm wide;

perianth segments **all alike**, **purplish-white inside** with darker veins and yellow spot at base, **greenish outside**, pointed; stamens 3. Eng: Dawlish, S Devon, vr but lf; Eur: France from Cherbourg W and SW, lc; in short turf on sea cliffs, dunes. Fl 4. Crocuses (*Crocus* spp). from S Eur etc, introd o-la in Eng and Eur, have erect showy cup- or funnel-shaped fls to 5 cm long; long pale stalks are in fact perianth-tubes arising from gd; lvs narrow, green with white midrib; **stamens 3**, **ovary inferior**. **Di Autumn Crocus**, *Crocus nudiflorus*, can be confused with Meadow Saffron (p 408 G), as fls appear in 9–10, **lvs in spring only**, but Meadow Saffron has **6** stamens and is **pink**-fld (**not** purple as in Di). **Dii Spring Crocus**, *C. purpureus* (*C. albiflorus*) has **purple fls** in **spring**, appearing with the lvs.

ARUM FAMILY (see also p 422) *Araceae*

This family has tiny fls crowded into a dense, spiked infl (the **spadix**). In *Arum*, spadix is **enclosed** in a large sheathing bract (the **spathe**), the whole resembling a large one-petalled fl with the naked, club-shaped spadix tip visible above the rolled-up cup-like lower part of the spathe. Fls have **no** perianths and are **unisexual**; lower part of spathe contains, at **base** of spadix, whorls of **female** fls (with tiny yellow ovaries and long bristle-like stigmas), then above them the **male** fls (with tiny short red-brown stamens), finally a ring of **sterile** bristle-like fls which close the cup's **top**. Small flies, attracted by the meaty scent, push down past sterile fls to enter cup, are at first trapped, and, if carrying pollen from another fl, pollinate the female fls. Later, the flies pick up pollen released by the male fls, and, when the sterile fls wither, escape and may pollinate another plant. In *Arum*, lvs are **triangular** to arrow-shaped, and (rare in Monocotyledons) **long-stalked**, **net-veined**. Frs are red berries in a dense spike. *Acorus* (p 422 F) has no spathe, spadix is borne on **side** of stem, and fls each have 6 tiny **perianth segments**, 6 stamens **and** an ovary; lvs, **linear**, sword-like, smell of tangerines when crushed.

 E Lords-and-Ladies (or **Cuckoo-pint**), *Arum maculatum*, erect hairless per, 30–50 cm tall, from a tuber. Lvs arrow-shaped to triangular, 7–20 cm long, net-veined, ± wrinkled, thin, v shiny bright green, often purple-spotted, on **long stalks**, appearing Feb–March. Spathe with cup-shaped, rolled-up, basal part, and cowl-shaped, **erect**, **pointed** upper part 15–25 cm long, pale yellow-green, **purple-edged**, sometimes purple-spotted. Spadix 7–12 cm long, upper part cylindrical club-shaped, 3–4 cm long, naked, **chocolate-purple**, rarely yellow; lower part (with fl-spike) hidden in cup. Frs (**Ea**) red berries 5 mm wide, in a dense spike 3–5 cm long. Br Isles: Eng, Wales, vc; S half Scot, Ire, f; **N Scot abs**; Eur vc; in wds, hbs, mostly on calc or richer soils. Fl 4–5, fr 7–8.

 F Large Lords-and-Ladies, *A. italicum* ssp *neglectum*, close to E, but some lvs appear in **autumn**, and are blunter, **thicker**, more **leathery-textured**, **never wrinkled or spotted**; midribs of the **triangular spring** lvs ± **paler** yellow-green (not dark green); upper part of spadix **always bright yellow**; **spathe** up to **40 cm** long, wholly yellow-green, **3 times as long** as whole of **spadix** (only twice as long in E); tip of spathe **bends forward** and **hangs down** over spadix when mature; frs scarlet berries 10 mm wide, in a spike to 14 cm long. S Eng, S Wales: Cornwall to Sussex o-vlf; Kent, Glamorgan, vr; Eur: W France, only NE to W Normandy; in wds, scrub near sea, but in Hants, W Sussex, to 42 km (*c.* 26 m) inland on moist calc screes at foot of steep wds on chk. Fl 6, fr 8–9. **Fi Italian Lords-and -Ladies**, *A. italicum* spp *italicum* has **broad-triangular dark green** lvs with **cream-white** veins. S Eng, France introd (S Eur) o. **Fii Bog Arum**, *Calla palustris*, aquatic plant with unspotted **cordate**-oval pointed lvs 5–10 cm long, long-stalked. Spathe white inside, **flat**, **not enclosing** the stout spadix which is covered in tiny greenish fls **to tip**. Eng: introd r-la in ponds etc; Eur: E France to Denmark, r-lf in swamps. Fl 6–7.

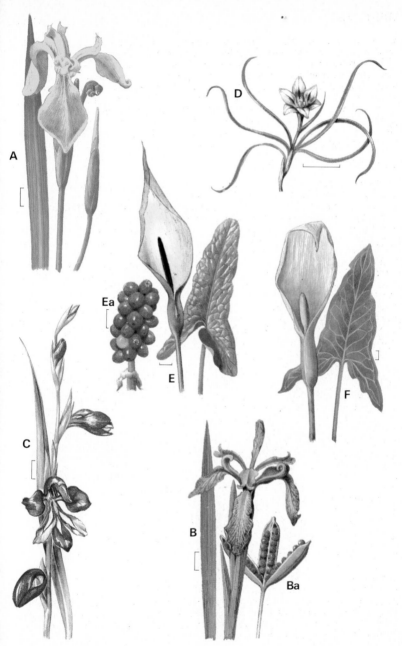

419

BUR-REED FAMILY   *Sparganiaceae*

Per aquatic herbs with creeping rhizomes, simple or branched stems, and linear lvs **broadside-on** to stems; fls tiny, in unisexual **globular heads**, the female heads at base of infl or its branches, the male heads above; perianth of 3–6 chaffy spoon-shaped scales; female fls have one-celled stalkless ovary with elongated style at its tip, male 3 or more stamens. Fruiting-heads are globular and spiky; fr a nut.

KEY TO BUR-REEDS (*SPARGANIUM*)

1 Infl **branched**, **each branch** with male heads above, female below – perianth segments black-tipped.. (*Sparganium erectum*, p 420 A) 2
  Infl **unbranched**, male heads above, female below on stem – perianth segments wholly pale 3
2 Fr with an obvious 'shoulder' [p 421 **Aa**), upper part dark, **flattened**, 4–6 mm wide at shoulder ....
                                                                              S. erectum var *erectum*
  Fr with an obvious 'shoulder', upper part dark, but **domed and wrinkled** below style, 2.5–4.5 mm wide at shoulder.. *S. erectum* var *microcarpum*
  Fr **ellipsoidal**, tapered evenly into style, no 'shoulder', 7–9 mm long × 2.0–3.5 mm wide................
                                                                              S. erectum var *neglectum*
  Fr ± **spherical**, tapered into style, 5–8 mm long × 4–7 mm wide .... *S. erectum* var *oocarpum*
3 Stem-lvs **keeled** at base, triangular in cross-section – male heads 3 or more.... *S. emersum* (p 420 B)
  Stem-lvs **flat** – male heads 1, or 2 close together... 4
4 Lf-like bract below lowest female head 10–60 cm, twice length or more of whole infl – male heads usually 2.. *S. angustifolium* (p 420 D)
  Lf-like bract below lowest female head 1–8 cm, no longer than whole infl – male head usually 1 ....
                                                                              S. minimum (p 420 C)

  A   Branched Bur-reed, *Sparganium erectum*, erect **branched** hairless per 50–150 cm; stem-lvs **keeled** at base, broadside on to stems, all erect. Perianth segments (**Aa**) 6, black-tipped. For varieties see key above: all are f in S Eng; var *microcarpum* is c in most of Br Isles but vr in NW Scot; all are c in Eur except var *oocarpum*, not know yet in Denmark but f in France; in still and moving fresh water. Fl 6–8.
  B   Unbranched Bur-reed, *S. emersum* (*S. simplex*), erect plant 20–60 cm tall, v like B, but smaller and with **both** erect, **keeled** stem-lvs and **flat**, ribbon-like basal **floating**-lvs; infl an **unbranched** raceme, male heads 3 or more, perianth segments wholly pale (**Ba**); fr (**Ba**) elliptical, narrowed into style. Br Isles (except NW Scot r), Eur f-lc; in still and moving fresh water, especially on mud substrates. Fl 6–7.
  C   Least Bur-reed, *S. minimum*, small floating plant with stems 6–80 cm long; **all lvs flat**, unkeeled, 2–6 mm wide, hardly inflated at bases; infl emerging from water, **unbranched**, with 1 male fl-head and 2–3 ± **stalkless** female heads, all under 1.5 mm wide; bract of lowest female fl-head **no longer** than whole infl. Fr (**Ca**) **obovate**, 3.5–4.5 mm long (excluding style on top). Br Isles: N half of GB, Ire, f-lc; S Eng, Wales, vr; Eur, r to S, lf to N; in peaty fen and bog pools, ditches. Fl 6–7.
  D   Floating Bur-reed, *S. angustifolium*, close to C, but the flat lvs are **longer**, with sheathing bases **inflated** (**D**); unbranched infl has usually 2 male fl-heads and 2–4 female ones; bract of lowest female fl-head is **twice or more** length of whole infl; fr (**Da**) **elliptical** in outline, 7–8 mm long (including style). Br Isles: N, NW Scot, f-lc; NW Eng, N Wales, Ire, r-vlf; **S, E Eng, abs** (except New Forest vr); Eur: mts of E France r; Denmark, N Germany, lf; in peaty lakes, pools. Fl 8–9.

REEDMACE FAMILY   *Typhaceae*

Reedmaces (*Typha*) are tall erect stout-stemmed herbs, growing from rhizomes in shallow water or mud; lvs mostly basal, linear, flat, grey-green, on **two opp sides** of stem, with sheathing bases; infl a **cylindrical spike** of densely packed tiny fls; its **lower** part **stout**, **brown**, of many female fls each with a one-celled stalked ovary

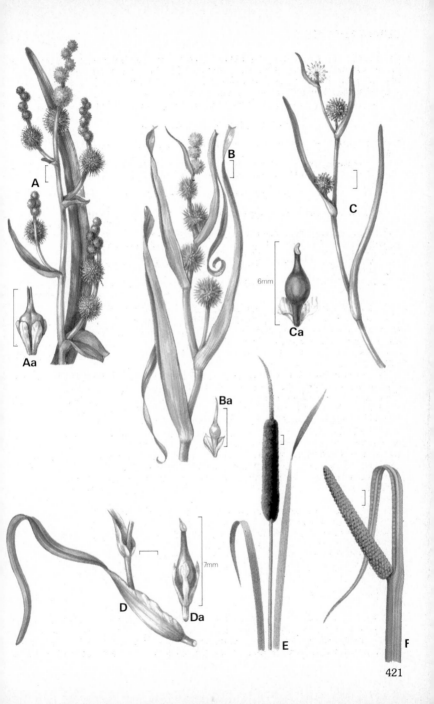

A

Aa

B

Ba

C

6mm

Ca

D

Da

7mm

E

F

REEDMACE FAMILY   *Typhaceae*

◀ surrounded by densely-packed brown hairs; its **upper** part **narrow, yellow**, of many male fls each with 2–5 stamens.

E   Common Reedmace (often wrongly called Bullrush), *Typha latifolia*, 1.5–2.5 m tall; lvs **10–20 mm wide**; infl with **no** gap between male and female parts of spike; female part of spike **3–4 cm wide**; **no** bracts to female fls. Br Isles: Eng c; Wales, S, E Scot, o-lf; **N Scot abs**; Ire f; Eur c; in reed swamps on mud or silt in still or slow-moving fresh water. Fl 6–7.   **Ei   Lesser Reedmace**, *T. angustifolia*, as tall as E, but slenderer; lvs **only 4–5 mm** wide, curved on the backs; **a gap** 2–9 cm long between male and female parts of spike; female part of spike **1.5–2.0 cm wide**; female fls have tiny **bracts**. Br Isles: Eng f-lc; Wales, S Scot, Ire, r; **N Scot abs**; Eur c; in reed swamps, often on more peaty soils than E, and more c in ditches near sea. Fl 6–7.

ARUM FAMILY (see also p 418)   *Araceae*

F   Sweet-flag, *Acorus calamus*, stout hairless erect per herb to 1 m tall; lvs bright green, sword-shaped, narrowed to tips, 1–2 cm wide, with thick midrib, and wavy, often **crinkled** edges, smelling strongly of **tangerines** or **dried oranges** when crushed. Infl, borne **laterally** at angle of 45° on the flattened winged stem, is a stout cigar-shaped spike, tapering to blunt tip to 8 cm long; stem **continues** as a long lfy point above spike. Fls densely packed, **each** with 6 tiny **yellowish-green** perianth segments, 6 stamens, and a 2–3-celled ovary; **no spathe** or bract to infl. Br Isles: E, central, SE Eng, o-lc; Wales, Scot, Ire, vr; Eur o-lf; introd (S Asia) by 1557, never fruits in Eur; in shallow fresh water of ponds, rivers, ditches. Fl 5–7.

ORCHID FAMILY   *Orchidaceae*

One of the largest and most distinctive families of flowering plants, with perhaps 30,000 spp; in tropics many are **epiphytes**, growing on trees, but in Eur all grow in the ground. Per herbs, with rhizomes or tuberous roots, and erect fl-stems; lvs undivided, untoothed, parallel-veined. Some orchids are **saprophytes**, ie, plants without, or with v little green **chlorophyll**, which, with lvs either **abs** or **reduced** to scales, feed on vegetable humus in the soil through the partnership of a fungus whose filaments penetrate their roots. Fls, in spikes or racemes, have perianth segments in 2 whorls: the **outer** of 3 sepals, ± alike, and usually coloured; the **inner** of 3 petals, but with one v different from the others, forming a **lip** to the fl, called the **labellum**. This is usually on lower side of fl, but sometimes on upper, or pointing upwards; it may be much lobed, sometimes furry, insect-like, sometimes pouch-like, often of different colours from rest of fl. Ovary **inferior**, in effect forming part of fl-stalk. Except in **Lady's-slipper**, (with 2 anthers) there is only 1 stalkless anther at back of fl, which forms two stalked, or stalkless, pollen-masses called **pollinia**. These normally have sticky bases which can adhere to heads of insects visiting fls. Below the anther and above the concave, stalkless stigma a projection, called the beak or **rostellum**, normally prevents self-pollination – but in some spp beak is abs and fls can pollinate themselves if not visited by insects. Insects are attracted to the fls by colour, scent, shape, or by **nectar** often secreted in the hollow **spur** developed in many spp at rear of labellum. There is evidence that male bees, wasps etc may mistake the bizarre insect-like labella of some orchids for females of their own species, and attempt copulation, so removing pollen from the fl and carrying it to another, effecting fertilization of the ovules. Fls of some spp are so specialized in shape, size and attractiveness, that only one sp (or few) of flying insect are able to extract nectar from their spurs and so cross-pollinate them. After fertilization the ovary ripens into a one-celled capsule containing a large number of minute, sawdust-like seeds, which can be wind-dispersed for long distances, and may account for the unexpected appearance of orchid colonies in totally new places.

Many orchids are v rare; **none** should ever be picked, still less dug up, only photographed or painted in the field. Some only produce fl-stems (or even lvs) at intervals, so may incorrectly be supposed to have disappeared from a locality. Many are found only in chky soils, but some in bogs, fens, on acid hths and moors, or in the deep peaty humus of pine or beech wds. They cannot easily be confused with other monocotyledonous plants with parallel-veined lvs, because in Eur they are the only Monocotyledons with inferior ovaries and irregular fls with a definite lip, except *Gladiolus*, in which lip formed of 3 (not 1) perianth segments. The non-green **saprophytic** orchids, however, can be confused with **either** parasitic Broomrapes (p 332), or with Yellow Bird's-nest (p 281 D). The former have a superior ovary, a **tubular** corolla, all in one piece, with lip formed of 3 corolla-lobes and only 2 lobes arching over it, and 4 long-stalked stamens. The latter, rather like Bird's-nest Orchid (p 430 A), has, however, **regular** fls and corolla-tube divided into 4 or 5 **equal** lobes and **no lip**. Some members of Labiate and Figwort families have rather orchid-like fls with elaborate lips, but these can be distinguished by their **superior** ovaries, their usually **broad**, **net-veined** lvs, **long-stalked stamens** and **long styles**.

KEY TO ORCHID FAMILY

1 Fls **v large**, solitary or only 2 on stem – lip **pouch**-shaped, 3 cm or more long, **hollow, yellow** – other perianth segments **4–6 cm long** – vr...................................*Cypripedium calceolus* (p 428 H)
   Fls in **spikes** or **racemes**, rarely 1 alone – lip **not** pouch-shaped, not hollow – other perianth segments **not over 2 cm long**.. **2**

2 Plants without green lvs (though stem and fls **may** be greenish) – lvs reduced to small scales up stem.. **3**
   Plants with well-developed **green lvs** at base of, or up stem **5**

3 Lip three-lobed, mid-lobe cordate, pink, on **upper** side of fl, spurred – other perianth segments banana-flesh-coloured – vr ....*Epipogium aphyllum* (p 430 B)
   Lip pointing downwards, on **lower** side of fl **4**

4 Plant wholly **violet-purple** – lip **spurred**, cordate, 15 mm long – other perianth segments wide-spreading – fls to 40 mm wide – **not in Br Isles** ....*Limodorum abortivum* (p 432 D)
   Plant **wholly honey-brown** – lip **unspurred**, two-lobed, to 10 mm long – other perianth segments forming a **hood** – fls to 10 mm wide..*Neottia nidus-avis* (p 430 A)
   Plant with **yellow-green** stem – lip **unspurred, three-lobed**, to 4 mm long, **white**, side-lobes v small – other perianth segments forming a loose hood, yellow-green – fls to 6 mm wide..................
                                                                                            Corallorhiza trifida (p 432 C)

5 Fls with **spur** or **pouch** extending back (or down) from rear of lip.. **6**
   Fls **without** spur or pouch at back of lip... **13**

6 Tall (30–50 cm) plant with mid-lobes of lips 3–6 cm long, coiled in bud like watch-springs, ribbon-like, twisted in fl – fls in long spikes, smelling of billy-goats ....
                                                                                            Himantoglossum hircinum (p 438 F)
   Lips of fls under 2 cm long, not coiled or twisted.. **7**

7 Lip long **strap-shaped, unlobed**, to 15 mm long, greenish-white – spur 15–30 mm long – fls sweetly-scented – stem with only 2 oval-elliptical lvs at base but sometimes v small upper lvs on stem also..*Platanthera* (p 436–438)
   Lip **toothed** or **lobed, not** long strap-shaped... **8**

8 Spur **v short** (2 mm or less), **blunt, pouch-like** – lip short (6 mm or less), unspotted, except sometimes at its base – fl-spikes dense, perianth segments forming a close hood to fl.................... **9**
   Spur **conical** or **cylindrical**, usually over 5 mm long (if **under** 2 mm, lip white, three-lobed, bearing red spots on lobes)... **10**

9 Fls yellow-green to reddish-brown – lip **rectangular** in outline, **hanging down**, with 3 v short teeth at tip .... *Coeloglossum viride* (p 438 E)
Fls greenish (or pinkish-white) – lip pointing **forward**, with 2 side-lobes **shorter** than **three-toothed** mid-lobe, pink or whitish, sometimes purple-spotted at **base** of lip only – Ire, Is of Man – r .... *Neotinea intacta* (p 438 G)
Fls **creamy-white** – lip with 3 ± **equal** lobes, **curved downward** ....
.... *Pseudorchis albida* (p 438 D)

10 Spur **12 mm long or more**, cylindrical, **v slender** – lip ± **equally** three-lobed, fls wholly pink or reddish, unspotted (as are lvs) **11**
Spur **under 10 mm long**, conical, **stout** – lip variously lobed but **never equally** three-lobed, fls either spotted or lined with darker markings, or lip with a whitish patch on a darker ground **12**

11 Lip divided **nearly to base** into 3 ± equal lobes, and with 2 ± erect **ridges** running out onto its base – fl smell **foxy** – lvs **grey-green**, arranged **spirally** up stem – fl-spike **short, blunt** .... *Anacamptis pyramidalis* (p 434 I)
Lip only divided **less than halfway** into 3 ± equal lobes (or outer lobes longer), and with **no ridges** – fls **v fragrant** – lvs **shiny bright green**, arranged in **2 opp ranks** on lower part of stem – fl-spike **long, cylindrical** .... *Gymnadenia* (p 436)

12 Fl-spike in bud emerging from gd **wrapped round** with spathe-like lvs – bracts of fls **narrow** (1–2 mm wide), **short, membrane-like** – lvs arranged **spirally** around base and up stem.....................
.... *Orchis* (p 433–434)
Fl-spike in bud emerging from gd **naked** – bracts of fls **broad** (3–5 mm wide), **long, like small lvs** – lvs in **2 ± opp ranks** at base of, and up stem.................................... *Dactylorhiza* (p 442–443)

13 Plants with 2 ± **equal** lvs in an **opp** pair at base of, or above base of stem – **no** (or only 1–2 tiny) stem-lvs above this pair.. **14**
Plants with lvs all **alt, never** in equal opp pairs.. **15**

14 Plants with the opp pair of lvs spreading at a **wide** angle from a point on the stem **several cm above gd** – lips of fls long, **forked**, on **lower** side of fl.. *Listera* (p 432)
Plants with the opp pair of lvs spreading at an **angle up to 45°** from **base of stem** – lips of fls **unlobed**, on **upper** side of scentless fl – in fens – r .... *Liparis loeselii* (p 432 G)
Plants with the opp pair of lvs spreading ± **flat on gd from base of stem** – 1 or 2 smaller alt stem-lvs usually present – lips of fls v short, **three-lobed**, on **lower** side of **honey-scented** fl ....
.... *Herminium monorchis* (p 436 A)

15 Plants with at least **some** lvs arising at (or beside) **base** of stem, often in a rosette........................ **16**
Plants with **no lvs** arising from base of stem, stem ± scaly, but **lfless** at base, largest lvs **well above** stem-base – lips on **lower sides** of fls.. **19**

16 Tiny plant (usually under 12 cm) – 3–5 blunt **obovate** lvs **under 1 cm** long, **one above the other** at **base** of stem – fls green, measure 7 mm or less across vertically, flat-faced, lips on **uppersides** – in sphagnum bog pools – r ....*Hammarbya paludosa* (p 432 H)
Taller plants (usually over 12 cm) – lvs, all **over 3 cm long**, at base of (or in a rosette adjacent to base of) stem – lips on **lower sides** of fls.. **17**

17 Lips of fls **velvety-brown**, convex on upper side, **insect-like**, with a ± complex pattern of lines and patches of different colours – fls **few** (2–6, rarely more) in a v **loose** spike ....
.... *Ophrys* (p 440)
Lips of fls **hominoid**, with 2 arms and 2 legs, hanging down from lower side of fl, **hairless**, yellowish, often brownish-edged – the other perianth segments forming a close green (often red-edged) helmet – fls **many**, in a **dense** spike .... *Aceras anthropophorum* (p 434 H)
Lips of fls small, **undivided**, forward-pointing, (**not** insect or man-shaped) – fls whitish, **downy**, small, in 1 or more **spirally**-twisted rows, the fl-stalks together resembling a **plait of green hair** ......
.... **18**

18 Plant with **obvious creeping runners** – lvs **stalked**, oval, their **cross-veins conspicuous** between main parallel veins – lips of fls with **untoothed** edges, spout-shaped – in pinewds – vl.....................
.... *Goodyera repens* (p 430 G)
Plant **without** creeping runners – **lvs stalkless**, oval-lanceolate, cross-veins **not** obvious – lips of fls with **frilled** edges, **curved** downwards .... *Spiranthes* (p 430)

19 Fls **large** (2 cm or more long), **white** (rarely **rosy-red**), **not** opening widely, **held erect** or ascending – ovaries **twisted** – **few** (3–15) fls per spike – lip formed of an inner and an outer joint (but inner joint **not** forming a cup)..*Cephalanthera* (p 428)
Fls **smaller** (under 1 cm long), **greenish** to **brick-red**, ± wide open, **held horizontal** or drooping – ovaries **not** twisted – **many** (10–100) fls per spike – lip of 2 joints, but inner joint forming a **cup**, outer triangular and ± **bent downwards**.............................. *Epipactis* (p 426–428)

ORCHID FAMILY   *Orchidaceae*

Helleborines (*Epipactis*), **Lady's-slipper** (*Cypripedium*)

Epipactis spp have no basal rosette-lvs, only stem-lvs, of which those on mid-stem are larger than those above and below. Fls are usually many (sometimes only few), in long dense spikes. Each fl has 3 pointed outer perianth segments and 2 inner ones, which are usually all ± alike, and wide-spreading in most spp (**not** spreading in F), and a lip on the lower side of each fl. The lip is jointed into 2 parts, an inner, usually ± cup-shaped **hypochile** usually containing glistening nectar, and an outer, triangular or cordate **epichile**, which is often turned downwards in a flap. The ovary below fl is straight, not twisted, and pear-shaped in fr; the two **pollinia** are **unstalked**, and lie side-by-side on top of the **beak**, but in D, E, F, and Fi there is **no** beak in the mature fl, so the pollen-masses can fall on to the hollow **stigma** below and effect self-pollination. In A, B, C, Ci, and G, the projecting beak **persists** below the anther, preventing self-pollination, so that these spp are dependent on wasps (or, in G, on bees) for cross-pollination. Some spp are v difficult to name, so use the key below.

KEY TO HELLEBORINES (*EPIPACTIS*)

1 Fen and marsh plant – fls brownish-grey outside, purplish-red within – lip-epichile **large** (to 10 mm long × 7 mm wide), **white, frilly-edged, blunt-tipped**, with **yellow** spot at base, **flexibly** hinged to lip-hypochile .... *E. palustris* (p 428 G)
  Wdland, scrub and rock-crevice plants – fls green-purplish outside and within – lip-epichile **smaller** (5 mm wide or less), greenish-reddish, edges **untoothed, never frilly**, tip **pointed** (but sometimes curved under), **never** yellow-spotted, fixed ± **rigidly** to lip-hypochile 2

2 Lvs **v small, narrow, not over 20 mm long × 6 mm wide** – beak present – **not in Br Isles** ....
                                                                                        E. microphylla (p 426 Ci)
  Lvs larger, some at least 4 cm long × 2 cm wide 3

3 Fls wholly **brick- to purple-red** – lip-epichile wider than long, with **wrinkled, red** swellings near base – stem **reddish** above but with **dense whitish down** – ovary v **downy** –beak present.................
                                                                                        E. atrorubens (p 426 B)
  Fls greenish or yellowish to purplish-flushed only – lip-epichile with **no** (or only **smooth**) swellings near base – stem hairless or **slightly** downy, **not** reddish above – ovary ± **hairless**........................ 4

4 Lvs **spirally** arranged up stem 5
  Lvs in 2 **opp ranks** (but **not** in opp **pairs**) up stem.. 7

5 Fls with **no beak** below anther – small **slender** plant, under 60 cm tall – infl **loose**, 4–20-fld – perianth segments green, **incurved** – lvs broad-**lanceolate**, pointed, **weakly-veined**.....................
                                                                                        E. muelleri (p 428 Fi)
  Fls with **well-developed beak** below anther – **robust** plants (to 80 cm) – infl **dense** :30–100 fld) – perianth segments **widely**-spreading – lvs **strong**-veined 6

6 Stems **clustered** – lvs **oval-lanceolate** to lanceolate, **ascending** at an acute angle, **grey-green** above, **purple-flushed** below and on stem – hypochile-cup of lip **violet-mottled** – perianth segments **whitish-green**, lip-epichile **pinkish-white**....................................*E. purpurata* (p 426 C)
  Stems **single** or up to 3 together – lower lvs **broad-oval**, ± **horizontally spreading**, upper narrower, all **dull green both sides** – hypochile-cup dark red or green, **not** mottled – perianth segments **green** or **purplish**, lip-epichile often **purple**...................................*E. helleborine* (p 426 A)

7 Lvs oval-lanceolate, to **10 cm long, yellowish-green**, with **strong**, ± pleated veins – stem ± hairless – fls ± **horizontal** – lip-hypochile **cup**-like.. 8
  Lvs oval-elliptical, to **6 cm long, fresh** green, with **v weak** veins – stem downy – fls **drooping, not** opening fully – lip-hypochile **almost flat**..*E. phyllanthes* (p 426 F)

8 Fls **widely open**, lip-epichile forming a **long**, ± **flat, narrow-triangular** point, greenish-**yellow** – in wds on calc soils ....*E. leptochila* (p 426 D)
  Fls **not** opening widely, lip-epichile **broad**-triangular, tip **curved under**, greenish-**white** with a ± pink streak – in dune hollows ....*E. dunensis* (p 426 E)

ORCHID FAMILY
Orchidaceae

Helleborines, Lady's-slipper

A Broad-leaved Helleborine, *Epipactis helleborine*, robust erect per, 25–80 cm, with only 1–3 stems arising together; stem ± downy above; no lf-rosette at base, lowest lvs are no more than sheathing **scales**; largest lvs on mid-stem 5–17 cm long × 2.5–10.0 cm wide, **broad-oval**, ± **horizontally** spreading, upper smaller and narrower, all strongly veined, **dull green** both sides, spirally arranged up stem. Infl dense raceme 7–30 cm long with 30–100 **wide-open** fls, held **horizontal** or ± inclined; bracts narrow, lowest longer than fls; outer perianth segments (**Aa**) 1 cm long, oval-lanceolate, green-purplish; lip-hypochile **cup-shaped**, dark red or green within, **not mottled**; epichile (**Aa**) cordate, **broader than long**, green to purple, tip turned **under**, swellings on lip **smooth**; beak **well-developed**; ovary drooping in fr, ± hairless. Br Isles: GB, N to mid Scot f-lc; NW Scot r; Ire o-lf; Eur: France, Germany, f-lc; Belgium to Denmark, o-lf; in wds, dune hollows. Fl 7–9.

B Dark Red Helleborine, *E. atrorubens*, shorter than A (only 15–40 cm); stem **reddish** above, but with **dense white down**; lvs in two opp ranks, largest oval-elliptical, pointed, ± reddish-tinged, more folded than in A; raceme dense, 8–20-fld, fls (**Ba**) **wholly red-purple** or **brick-red**, less wide-open than in A; hypochile cup **red-spotted** within; epichile with tip turned under, swellings on lip **wrinkled**, **bright red**; beak well-developed; ovary drooping in fr, **v downy**, **purplish**. Br Isles: N Eng, N Wales, NW Scot, W Ire, r-lf; in wds, rocks, screes, on limestone; Eur: central, N France, o-lf; Germany, Belgium, Denmark, r-vr; on chk downs, open wds on limestone. Fl 5–8.

C Violet Helleborine, *E. purpurata*, robust like A, but many **stems clustered** together; lvs (**C**) in spiral up stem as in A, but **narrower** (oval-lanceolate), **ascending** at an angle, **grey-green** above, ± **purple-flushed** below (and on stem), **strong-veined**; fls (**Ca**) wide-open, horizontal, in dense racemes; outer perianth segments **greenish-white**, lanceolate; hypochile-cup **violet-mottled** within; epichile cordate, **dull whitish**, with **purple streak** in centre; lip swellings smooth; ovary rough, ± hairy, horizontal in fr; beak well-developed; bracts longer, purplish. Eng: SE, S central, lf-lc; Eur: N France to Denmark, r-lf; in wds (mostly beech) on clay, often over chk. Fl 8. *Ci **Small-leaved Helleborine**, *E.* *microphylla*, has fls as in A, but paler, with beak present; lvs **v small**, **narrow**, **under 20 mm long** × 6 mm wide. E France, Belgium, Germany; r in mt wds. Fl 6–8.

D Narrow-lipped Helleborine, *E. leptochila*, tall like A, but slenderer; stem ± hairless; lvs in 2 **opp ranks**, oval-lanceolate, 10 cm long, **yellow-green**, **strong-veined**; fls (**D**) **wide open**, horizontal, **greenish-yellow**, lip-epichile forming a long, **straight**, **narrow-triangular** point; hypochile with a cup; beak scarcely developed. Eng: Kent to Chilterns and Cotswolds, r but lf; Eur: France (Normandy), W Germany, Belgium, Denmark, vr; in beechwds on calc soils. Fl 6–7.

E Dune Helleborine, *E. dunensis*, close to D in colour, lvs, and lack of beak to fls; but fls (**E**) **less open**, lip-epichile **broad-triangular** with tip **curved under**, greenish-white, ± pink-tinged. **GB**: Lancs, Northumberland, Anglesey, r-lf; reported NW coast Eur; in dune hollows, dune pinewds. Fl 6–7.

F Green-flowered Helleborine, *E. phyllanthes*, slender plant 20–40 cm; stem downy; lvs in 2 **opp ranks**, **fresh green**, oval-elliptical, **weakly-veined**, to 6 cm long. Fls (**Fa**) **drooping**, **rarely widely open**, **yellow-green**, lip-hypochile with cup scarcely hollowed, epichile **flat**, longer than broad, **greenish**, **without swellings**; **beak abs**; v variable; fls in some forms never open. Br Isles: Eng, Wales, N to Barrow-in-Furness, r, but lf in S Eng and on Lancs coast; Ire vr; Eur: Germany, Denmark, r: in beechwds on calc soils, dune hollows etc. Fl 7–9. *E. confusa* (in Denmark, N Germany), scarcely distinct from F, is slenderer, with fls pink-lipped,

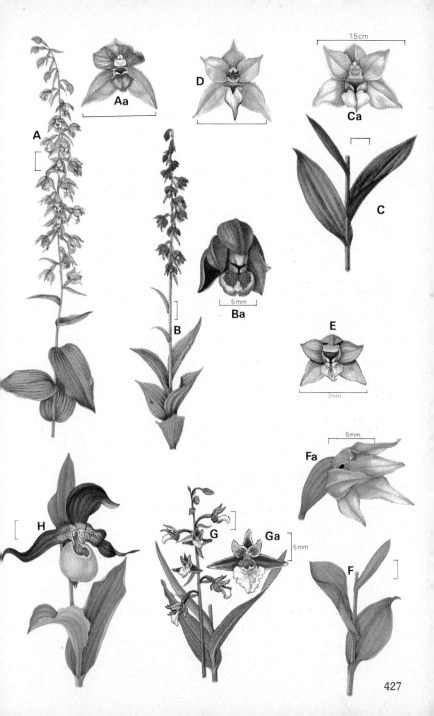

A

Aa

D

1.5 cm

Ca

B

Ba

5 mm

C

E

7mm

Fa

5mm

H

G

Ga

5 mm

F

427

◀ more open. *Fi **Mueller's Helleborine**, *E. muelleri*, resembles F in its short, broad-lanceolate **weakly-veined** lvs; but lvs **spiral** up stem, hypochile has a **cup, reddish** within, epichile **broader than long, whitish**; beak abs as in F. France, N, NW Belgium, Holland, vr; in wds, scrub on calc soils. Fl 7–8.

G Marsh Helleborine, *E. palustris*, per herb 15–50 cm, with runners; stem downy above; lvs oblong-oval to lanceolate, upper ascending at an angle to 15 cm long, concave above and folded, veins strong and pleated; infl 7–15 cm, with 7–14 fls in a **loose** raceme; bracts lanceolate, not longer than fls; fls (**Ga**) wide open, to 15 mm wide, horizontal in fl, drooping in bud; perianth segments **brownish-grey, downy** outside, **purplish-red** within; lip-epichile to 10 mm long, cordate-oval, blunt, white, **frilly-edged**, with a **yellow spot at base**, hypochile joined to it by narrow **hinge**, its cup white with **red** veins; beak well-developed. Br Isles: Eng, Wales, Ire, o-lf (lc in Norfolk); Scot, E only, vr; Eur f-lc; in calc fens, calc dune-hollows. Fl 7–8.

H Lady's-slipper, *Cypripedium calceolus*, a striking plant; per herb, 15–40 cm, erect, ± downy; lvs oval-oblong, sheathing, pointed, fresh green, strongly pleated-veined. Fls usually 1 (rarely 2) per stem; bract large, lf-like; perianth segments **maroon**, 6–9 cm long, elliptical-lanceolate, the 2 lower outer ones conjoined; lip 3–5 cm long, obovate, bright golden-yellow, **hollow**, like a pouch or blunt slipper, red-spotted inside; column in centre of fl spotted, **without** an anther on top as in most orchids, but with **2 anthers** below it, one on each side; ovary downy. Eng: W Yorks vvr; Eur: E France, Denmark vr (much decreased); in wds on limestones. Fl 5–6.

▶ **White and Red Helleborines, Lady's-tresses**

White and Red Helleborines (*Cephalanthera*) resemble *Epipactis* in both absence of basal or rosette-lvs, and jointing of fl-lips into 2 segments (though this is less obvious in *Cephalanthera*); but fls much **larger** (2 cm or more long), ± oval, **rarely** widely open, white or rosy-red; ovary **twisted**. **Lady's-tresses** (*Spiranthes*) have small, **downy**, whitish fls in dense, **spirally twisted** spikes, not widely open, with lvs at base of and up stem; lip **frilly-edged**, curved down. **Creeping Lady's-tresses** (*Goodyera*) differs in having **runners**, oval rosette-lvs with conspicuous **cross-veins** between main veins and **untoothed spout-like** lips to fls.

A White Helleborine, *Cephalanthera damasonium*, erect hairless per herb, 15–50 cm tall; angled stem bears brownish sheathing scales below and oval to elliptical-lanceolate lvs 5–10 cm long above, held at an angle of c. 45° to stem, **never** drooping at tips and **not** exceeding the fl-spike. Infl of 3–12 fls, each with a **lf-like bract longer than** the lower fls; fls (**Aa**) **creamy**, 2.0–2.5 cm long, ± **erect**, elliptical, **scarcely opening**; lip with orange blotch on hypochile and a curved, blunt-toothed cordate epichile with orange ridges along it (best seen by easing fl open with a pencil). Ovary hairless, ± erect; perianth segments **blunt**. Eng, calc areas of SE, S central Eng, N to Hereford and Cambridge, f-lc; **rest of Br Isles abs**; Eur: N, E France, f-lc; N to Denmark r; in beechwds on calc soils. Fl 6–7.

B Narrow-leaved Helleborine, *C. longifolia*, like A, but 15–40 cm tall; stem, less angled, bears whitish sheathing scales below, and **long, linear, lanceolate lvs** above, often folded lengthwise, with **drooping tips**, upper often **longer** than fl-spike. Fls (**Ba**) in a **closer** spike, **much longer** than their bracts, **pure white**, 2 cm long, opening more than in A to show smaller orange spot at lip-base; outer perianth segments **pointed**; ovary held at 45° to stem. Br Isles, wide-scattered but r N to Ross, lf in E Hants only; Ire r; Eur: E, N France, o-lf; N to Denmark r; in beechwds on calc soils, also oakwds on more acid soils. Fl 5–6, earlier than A.

C Red Helleborine, *C. rubra*, resembles B in its narrow lvs, but these are

429

◄ shorter, **without** long drooping tips; bracts shorter than the **rosy red**, ± wide-opening fls (**Ca**); ovary and upper stem sticky-hairy above; whole plant slightly purple-flushed. Eng: Cotswolds, Chilterns, vr; Eur: E France to Denmark vr (mts of C Eur c); in beechwds on calc soils. Fl 6–7.

D   Autumn Lady's-tresses, *Spiranthes spiralis*, short (7–20 cm) erect per herb; round stem bears only **bract-like**, **green** scale-lvs; plant unusual in that **lf-rosette** does **not encircle** stem-base, but arises adjacent to it and has **oval**, **blue-green** lvs 2.5–3.0 cm long. Infl a long (3–10 cm), dense, **spirally-twisted** spike of 7–20 small (4–5 mm long) hardly open, white fls (**Da**) with **coconut-scent**; bracts equal downy ovaries; perianth segments blunt-lanceolate, downy; lip with **green** centre, **frilled** white edge, curved down. Br Isles: GB, N to Morecambe Bay, f-lc to S, r to N; Ire, S half only, o-lf; Eur: France to Denmark, f-lc to S, vr to N; on dry calc or sandy gslds, dunes. Fl 8–9.

E   Irish Lady's-tresses, *S. romanzoffiana*, **stouter** than D, 12–25 cm tall; lvs ± erect, **lanceolate-linear**, in a rosette **around** stem-base; upper stem-lvs small, bract-like, sheathing; infl **short** (2.5–5.0 cm long), **broad** (2 cm wide), **oblong**; fls in **3 spirally-twisted rows**. Fls (**Ea**) larger (8–11 mm long) cream, hawthorn-scented, lowest bract longer than its fl; lip cream with green veins; ovary sticky-hairy, spreading. Br Isles: S Devon vr; W Scot (Coll, Colonsay, Barra, W coast Highlands) vr; W, N Ire, r-vlf; Eur abs (N America c); in moist mds, bogs cut away for peat. Fl 7–8.

F   Summer Lady's-tresses, *S. aestivalis*, v like a **taller** (10–40 cm) version of D, with similar ·but longer (7–12 cm) fl-spike; but **linear-lanceolate** lvs **borne up infl-stem**, **bright green**, **shiny**, lower lvs to 12 cm long, upper shorter, fls (**Fa**) as in D, but slightly larger, pure white, night-scented. Br Isles: New Forest only (now ? extinct); Eur: W, N France to Belgium and W Germany; vr in wet hths, sphagnum bogs. Fl 7–8.

G   Creeping Lady's-tresses, *Goodyera repens*, looks rather like F, but with **creeping runners** ending in rosettes of **broad-stalked**, oval, **evergreen** lvs with **conspicuous cross-veins** between the main parallel ones (unlike D-F); upper stem-lvs bract-like. Stem 10–25 cm tall, with narrow infl of **cream** fls (**Ga**) as in D and F but hardly opening; perianth segments blunt-oval, sticky-hairy; lip short, narrow, **untoothed**, arched. Eng: Norfolk, Cumberland, r; Scot, lf-lc in E and NE, r in W; Eur: W, N France, Netherlands to Denmark, r-vlf; in ancient Scots pinewds, and (to S, E) in **new** pine plantations (mts of Eur). Fl 7–8.

► **Non-green Saprophytic Orchids, Twayblades, Fen and Bog Orchids**

A   Bird's-nest Orchid, *Neottia nidus-avis*, **entirely honey-coloured** erect saprophyte 20–40 cm tall, with brownish sheathing scales (no green lvs) up the stout stem; infl a raceme, 5–20 cm long, loose below; bracts of fls short, chaffy; fls (**Aa**) with perianth segments forming a loose hood; lip 12 mm long, unspurred, hanging down, divided halfway into 2 oblong, blunt **diverging** lobes. Capsule 12 mm, erect. Br Isles: SE, S and central Eng, f-lc; N to Inverness o-lf; Ire o; Eur: France f-lc; N to Denmark o-lf; in wds, especially beech, in deep lf-litter. Fl 5–7.

B   Ghost Orchid, *Epipogium aphyllum*, erect saprophyte 10–20 cm tall; stem, ± translucent, pale yellowish, **pink-tinged**, bears a few sheathing brownish scales only, no lvs. Fls 1–4; in a v loose spike, each fl about 2 cm across, pendulous, with a bract equal to the slender stalk; perianth segments linear, pale yellow, down-pointed, blunt; lip pointing **upwards**, cordate; ground colour **white**, with **crimson ridges** along it; 2 short side-lobes present; spur 8 mm × 4 mm, **blunt**, upturned, yellowish tinged with red. Eng: Chilterns vr; formerly in Hereford and Salop; Eur: mts of E France, S Belgium, Denmark, vr; in beechwds in deep lf-litter, v erratic in its appearances. Fl 7–9.

430   *cont*

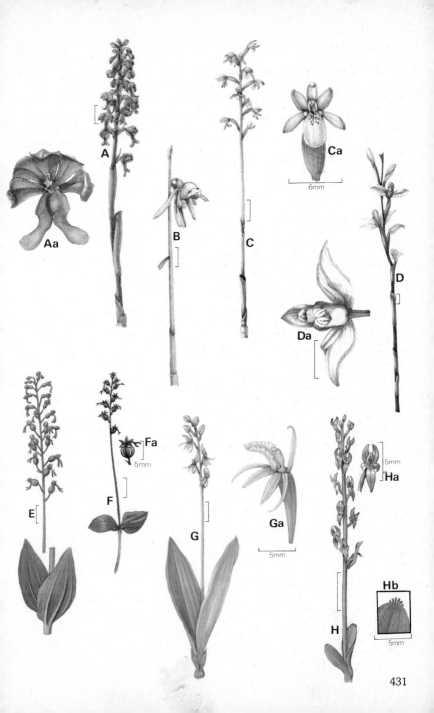

Aa

A

B

C

Ca

6mm

Da

D

E

F

Fa

5mm

G

Ga

5mm

H

Ha

5mm

Hb

5mm

431

◀   **C** **Coralroot Orchid**, *Corallorhiza trifida*, erect, saprophytic herb 7–25 cm tall; **yellow-green**, hairless stem bears long, brownish **sheathing** scales; raceme of 4–12 fls with tiny bracts; fls (**Ca**) with **yellow-green** perianth segments, strap-shaped, curved down; lip 5 mm long, on **lower** side of fl, unspurred, oblong with 2 tiny basal side-lobes, white with crimson spots. GB: N Eng vr; E Scot r; Eur: mts of E France, S Belgium, Denmark, vr; in acid boggy wds, dune slacks. Fl 5–7.

*D **Violet Bird's-nest Orchid**, *Limodorum abortivum*, tall (30–50 cm), wholly ± violet-coloured saprophytic herb, violet scales sheathing stem; infl a loose spike; fls (**Da**) have **spurred**, cordate lip 1.0–1.5 cm long, and spreading whitish to pinkish-purple perianth segments to 2 cm long; lip on lower side of fl (to **right** in **Da**), yellowish with violet streak; spur long, slender. Eur: central, E, NE France, r-o; Belgium vr; in wdlands in deep lf-litter. Fl 6–7.

E **Common Twayblade**, *Listera ovata*, erect herb, 20–60 cm; stem green, hairless below, downy above; an opp pair of broad **ovate-elliptical**, unstalked, **strongly-ribbed**, horizontally spreading or ± ascending lvs, 5–15 cm long, on stem **below** its middle but **several cm** above gd level; only a few tiny bract-like lvs above them. Fls many, in a loose raceme, 7–25 cm long; each fl green, with perianth segments forming a hood; lip 10–15 mm long, **yellow-green**, hanging down, forked almost halfway; **spur abs**; capsule ± globular. Br Isles, Eur, c except in high mt areas; in wds, mds, gslds, dunes on basic soils. Fl 6–7.

F **Lesser Twayblade**, *L. cordata*, much smaller than E; slender **reddish** stem, only 6–20 cm tall, bears below mid-stem an opp pair of stalkless oval-**triangular** to **cordate** lvs, 1–2 cm long, dark green and **shiny** above, pale green below. Some stems bear lvs only; others a loose raceme, 1.5–6.0 cm long, of 6–12 tiny brownish fls (**Fa**); uppermost perianth segments oval, forming a hood; others narrow, forward-pointing, green outside, **reddish** within, 1.5–2.0 mm long; lip **reddish**, hanging down, 3.5–4.0 mm long, v narrow, forked halfway; **spur abs**; capsule globular. Br Isles: S Eng, Exmoor only, vr; N Eng and N Wales to N Scot, r to S, f-lc to N; Ire r; Eur: mts of E France; Denmark, N Germany, r; in pinewds, shaded bogs, hth moors on peaty soils. Fl 6–8.

G **Fen Orchid**, *Liparis loeselii*, hairless herb; erect angled stem, 6–20 cm tall, arises from green scaly bulb among wet moss. Lvs normally only **1 opp pair**, arising from **base** of stem, oblong, elliptical, pointed, shiny, **greasy**-looking, yellowish-green, 2.5–8.0 cm long; fls 2–10, in a loose raceme 2–10 cm long; lower bracts as long as fls. Fls (**Ga**) yellow-green, perianth segments **linear-lanceolate**, 5–8 mm long, spreading, **incurved**; lip on **upper** side of fl, often vertical, **obovate, furrowed**, with **wavy** edges, 5–7 mm long; **spur abs**; capsule erect, narrowed to tip. GB: E Anglia, now vr, but still vlf; S Wales, N Devon, r-la (as small form with oval lvs, in dune slacks); Eur: central, N, E France, r but vlc; Belgium, Netherlands, Denmark, vr; in calc mossy fens, moist dune slacks. Fl 6–7.

H **Bog Orchid**, *Hammarbya paludosa*, tiny plant 3–12 cm tall; erect hairless stem arises from a tiny bulb among moss; lvs 3–5, one above the other at stem base, only 0.5–1.0 cm long, oval, concave, rounded at tip and with a fringe of tiny green bulbils (**Hb**) from which new plants grow. Raceme 1.5–6.0 cm long, spike-like, of small flat-faced green fls (**Ha**), 7 mm from top to bottom, greenish-yellow, with narrow spreading perianth segments; lip pointed, short, on **upper** side of fl; **spur abs**. Br Isles: Eng, Wales, vr (now extinct central Eng, but New Forest – Dorset vlf); Scot Highlands o-lf; Ire vr; Eur: W, E France, Belgium, Netherlands, vr; N Germany, Denmark, r-vlf; in sphagnum, around pools in valley bogs with some flow of water. Fl 7–9.

ORCHID FAMILY

Genus *Orchis*; also Man, Pyramidal, and Fragrant Orchids ▶

In *Orchis*, fl-spike is **wrapped round** by sheathing lvs in bud; bracts of fls v narrow, **shorter** than fls, **membranous** (not lf-like); lvs arranged in a spiral from basal rosette up stem; fl-lips 3- to 5-lobed, on lower side of fl, not jointed into two parts, but with a stoutish **spur no longer** than lip at rear; 1 erect stalkless anther rises above beak of fl; this anther has, enclosed in a pouch, 2 stalked pollen-masses that give the appearance of 2 'eyes', the beak resembles a 'nose', and the hollow below beak leading to stigma and spur resembles a 'mouth', forming a tiny 'face' within the helmet of the fl; the lip is either divided into 'arms' and 'legs', or resembles a 'skirt', so the whole fl from front resembles a human figure. The tubers are egg-shaped. See key p 438.

Marsh and **Spotted Orchids** (*Dactylorhiza*) are similar in some ways; use the key p 438 to identify spp. The tubers are lobed like fingers of a hand; but **never** dig up plants to see this feature; use the key instead! Hybrids are frequent between *Dactylorhiza* spp; these make naming v difficult at times.

A   **Early-purple Orchid**, *Orchis mascula*, erect hairless herb 20–40 cm tall; lvs shiny dark green, oblong, 5–10 cm long × 2–3 cm wide, usually with dark purple **blotches**, arranged **lengthwise** (blotches **transverse** on lvs in Spotted Orchids, p 442 E, F); lvs in a basal rosette and sheathing up stem, spirally arranged. Stem solid, fleshy; infl a loose raceme 5–15 cm long; fls bright purple-crimson, tom-cat-scented, especially at night; 2 outer sepals **erect** or **spreading**, rear sepal and 2 petals forming a loose helmet; lip 8–12 mm long × 8–10 mm wide, ± equally, bluntly and shallowly three-lobed, central lobe longest, notched, sides of lip ± folded back; lip with paler, purple-dotted, central patch; spur stout, ± curved up, as long as ovary; bracts narrow, purplish. Br Isles, Eur; f-lc in wds, gslds on ± base-rich soils. Fl 4–6. **Ai   **Pale-flowered Orchid**, *O. pallens*, differs from A in **yellow fls**, **elder-flower scent**, lvs always **unspotted**, spur shorter than ovary. Eur: E France, Germany, Belgium, vr: in mt wds and gslds. Fl 4–6.

*B   *O. palustris* has fls (**Ba**) v like those of A, with 2 outer sepals spreading, but mid-lobe of lip **narrow**, **tooth-like**, equalling or longer than side-lobes; lvs **narrow-lanceolate**, **unspotted**, **folded** lengthwise, 7–20 cm long × 1–2 cm wide, in 2 opp ranks up the taller, slenderer stem (to 60 cm); spike looser, long. Eur: N France, Belgium, Germany, v-lf: in wet mds, fens. Fl 5–6.   **Bi   **Loose-flowered Orchid**, *O. laxiflora*, v like B, differs only in lip, which has mid-lobe **much shorter** than side-lobes, or **abs**. W France to Netherlands, Channel Is, lf; in wet mds. Fl 4–6.

C   **Lady Orchid**, *O. purpurea*, one of the most beautiful European plants. Stem stout, erect, 25–45 cm tall; lvs to 15 cm long × 5 cm wide, oval-oblong, ± blunt-pointed, mostly in a basal rosette, upper lanceolate and sheathing stem, all glossy green, **unspotted**. Fl-spike 5–15 cm long, dense, conical at first then cylindrical; fls sweetly vanilla-scented, the 3 sepals forming a close **oval**, **blunt** helmet v heavily flecked with dark brownish-purple on a green background, but v variable from pale green (in albino plants) to blackish-purple; petals within helmet narrow. Lip 10–18 mm long, hanging below helmet, white or ± rose-flushed, with 2 'arm'-like side-lobes 2–3 mm wide, and a broad (5 mm wide) central 'body' divided into 2 short **broad**, **blunt**, slightly diverging 'legs' with a tiny tooth between them, the whole lip sprinkled with **tiny tufts of crimson hairs** (rarely wholly white). Spur curved down, cylindrical, blunt, half length of ovary; bracts v tiny (whole fl resembles an early Victorian woman in wide spotted dress and poke-bonnet, hence the name). Eng: Kent f-lc; rest of SE Eng vr and sporadic only; **rest of Br Isles abs**; Eur: France c-la (except Brittany abs); Belgium, W Germany, Denmark, r; in open wds, scrub, gslds on calc soil. Fl 5–6.

D   **Monkey Orchid**, *O. simia*, has lvs and habit of C, but shorter (15–30 cm), slenderer. In fls (**D**) 3 **long-pointed whitish-grey** sepals form a helmet **nearly as long as lip**, dotted and streaked with pink especially within; lip with narrow white (2 mm wide) 'body' (with tufts of crimson hairs as in C), v narrow (1 mm wide), long, curved crimson 'arms' and 'legs' with a short 'tail' between 'legs'; spur as in C. Eng, Kent, Oxford, SE Yorks, vr; Eur: central France lf; N to Belgium vr; on calc gslds, open wds. Fl 5–6.

   E   Military Orchid, *O. militaris*, close to C in lvs and habit, but usually less tall; fls (**E**) with helmet of **long-pointed** sepals as in D, but ash-grey, only ± flushed pink or violet; lip nearer to C's, with 'body' **3 mm wide**, white, with tufts of crimson hairs, 'arms' as in D but shorter; 'legs' **much broader** (2–3 mm) than in D, crimson, **blunt**, **diverging widely**, with v short blunt 'tail'; spur as in C and D. Eng: Bucks, Suffolk, vr; Eur: central, N, E France, f-la; N to S Holland r; on calc gslds, scrub. Fl 5–6.   **Ei   Three-toothed Orchid**, *O. tridentata*, combines the habit, and **pale**, **pointed** helmet as long as lip, of D and E, with the **broader**, pinker, crimson-spotted lip of C, with broad pale 'arms' and 'legs' and tiny central tooth; helmet pink with purple veins. Eur: E France, Belgium, vr; on calc gslds. Fl 5–6.

   F   Burnt Orchid, *O. ustulata*, small erect herb **5–15 cm** tall (more in mts of Eur); lvs 2.5–6.0 cm long × 0.5–1.0 cm wide, pointed, mostly in a rosette; spike short (2–3 cm), **dense**; fls (**Fa**) with helmet of **blunt**, **oval** sepals only **2–3 mm long**, blackish-purple in bud and when young (so tip of spike appears scorched), paler in older fls; lip 4–5 mm long, white with **few**, **flat**, red dots, lobed into short, blunt 'arms' and 'legs' (resembling a tiny clown's suit); scent as of stewed cherries; spur v short. Eng: S, SE, o-lf; N to Cumberland vr; Eur: N, mid, E France, o-lf; N to Belgium and Denmark vr; on calc gslds with short turf. Fl 5–6 (some populations 7–8).

   G   Green-winged Orchid, *O. morio*, erect herb 10–30 cm tall; lvs **unspotted**, glossy-green, elliptical-lanceolate, 3–9 cm long × 1–2 cm wide, upper sheathing stem as in other *Orchis* spp, lower in a rosette; spike 2.5–6.0 cm long, rather loose, bracts narrow, purplish. Fls (**Ga**) much as in A, but unscented, with **all 3** sepals in a **close**, **blunt**, **oval** helmet, rich deep **purple-veined** with **strong green stripes**; lip broader than long, the sides ± folded back, **deep purple** with a pale crimson-dotted central patch, and bluntly three-lobed as in A; spur stout, nearly as long as ovary (fls vary to pink or white). Eng, Wales, o-lf (decreasing through ploughing of old gslds); Scot vr; **Ire abs**; Eur: France c; N to Denmark o-r; in gslds, mds, on calc or heavy clay soils. Fl 5–6.   ***Gi   Bug Orchid**, *O. coriophora*, resembles G in its close helmet of sepals and unspotted lvs; but lvs **narrow**-lanceolate, **erect**, **adpressed** to stem, fl-spike **narrow**, **dense**, helmets pale pinkish, and lip **narrow**, usually dark red-purple, bluntly three-lobed with mid-lobe **much longer** than side-lobes, and fls smell v unpleasant. W, central, E France, Belgium, Germany r; in mds. Fl 4–6.

   H   Man Orchid, *Aceras anthropophorum*, erect per 20–40 cm; lvs in a basal rosette and up stem, 6–10 cm long, oblong-lanceolate, glossy grey-green, unspotted, pointed, with a few **transverse wrinkles** on upper side of mid-lf. Fl-spike 8–15 cm long, many-fld; fls (**Ha**) with close oval hood 5–6 mm long of yellowish-green sepals, often with a narrow red-brown edge; lip hanging down, 10–12 mm long, yellow, often red or chocolate-edged, **narrow**, with 2 narrow 'arms' and 'legs' but **no** 'tail'; **spur abs**; plant has vanilla smell when bruised. Eng: Kent and Hants N to Chilterns and S Lincs, f-lc in SE, vr to N; **rest of Br Isles abs**; Eur: France f-lc to S, vr to N and in Belgium; on calc gslds, scrub, open wds. Fl 5–6.

   I   Pyramidal Orchid, *Anacamptis pyramidalis*, erect hairless herb 20–30 cm; lvs grey-green, unspotted, lanceolate, pointed, spirally arranged, in a rosette and up stem. Fls in a dense, **short** (2–5 cm) **dome-shaped** to conical spike, **wholly** rich pinkish-red, foxy-scented; 2 outer sepals lanceolate, spreading; upper sepal and 2 petals forming a small helmet; lip 5–6 mm long, as broad as long, **deeply** three-

A

B

Ba

C

D

E

F

Fa |6mm

G

Ga

H

Ha

I

J

Ja

K

◀ lobed nearly to base, lobes oblong, ± equal, side-lobes spreading; 2 ± erect **ridges** run out onto lip from its base; spur 12 mm long, ± straight, ± thread-like, pointed, longer than ovary; the two pollen-masses attached to a **common** base, thus always removed together by insects (in *Orchis* spp they can be removed separately). Br Isles: GB, f-lc in S Eng, o-lf N to central Scot and Hebrides; Ire f-lc; Eur: central France o; N to Denmark vr; on calc gslds, dunes. Fl 6–8.

J Fragrant Orchid, *Gymnadenia conopsea*, resembles I in its pink long-spurred fls, but taller (to 40 cm), with **glossy green, unspotted**, oblong-lanceolate **strongly keeled** lvs, 6–15 cm long × 1–3 cm wide, in **2 dense ranks** up **opp sides** of stem. Fl-spike **cylindrical**, 6–15 cm long, **dense**, with green bracts ± equalling fls; fls (**Ja**) rosy-pink, unspotted, 8–12 mm wide, **sweet-scented**, but with an **acid** or **rancid** overtone; lateral sepals narrow, with rolled-under edges, **pointed**, spreading but **curving down** at a **slight angle**; upper sepal and 2 petals forming a little helmet; lip broader than long, near to that of I, but **without** erect ridges on it, three-lobed about **half-way**; spur narrow-cylindrical, to 20 mm long, twice length of ovary, **curved**, pointed. Br Isles lf-lc; Eur: France f-lc; N to Belgium and W Germany o-lf; on dry calc gslds. (The plants of hill pastures on more acid soils in N and W of GB are slenderer, with lips **longer than wide** and only slightly three-lobed; they are carnation-scented like K and may be a distinct sp.) Fl 6–7. ***Ji** *G. odoratissima* is near to J, but shorter, with smaller, strongly **vanilla- to chocolate-scented** fls with spurs **no longer than ovaries**. Eur: E, central, NW France, Belgium, W Germany, r-lf; on calc gslds. Fl 6–7.

K Marsh Fragrant Orchid, *G. densiflora* (*G. conopsea* var *densiflora*), appears to be a distinct sp; often taller and stouter than J, but key differences are: fls **deep** pink; lip **much broader than long**, with 'shoulders' to the side-lobes; side sepals ± **square-tipped, straight, horizontally** spreading; spur only a **little** longer than ovary; sweet **carnation**-scent; and fl **later**. Eng, Wales, o but lf; Eur: France f-lc; Belgium to Denmark r; in calc fens, also sometimes on dry calc gslds. Fl 7–8.

▶ ## Musk, Butterfly, Lizard, Small White, Frog, and Dense-flowered Orchids

A Musk Orchid, *Herminium monorchis*, small erect orchid 5–15 cm tall; normally only 2, ± oblong, pointed yellow-green unspotted basal lvs and sometimes 1–2 tiny, bract-like stem-lvs. Fl-spike 2–6 cm long, narrow, dense, cylindrical, many-fld. Fls (**Aa**) **greenish-yellow**, with strong **honey-scent**, 3–4 mm wide, bracts shorter than fls; sepals pointed, forming a **loose** hood; lip 3 mm long, **deeply** three-lobed, mid-lobe longer and blunter than side-lobes, **spur abs**. SE Eng only, from Somerset and Kent to Cotswolds and Chilterns, r, but lc on N and S Downs; S Wales vr; **abs rest of Br Isles**; Eur: N, central, E France, f-lc; N to Denmark r, mostly near coasts; on short calc gslds (in Eur also fens and dune hollows). Fl 6–7.

B Greater Butterfly Orchid, *Platanthera chlorantha*, erect hairless orchid 30–40 cm tall; 2 ± opp, unspotted, elliptical-oblong **blunt** lvs, 10–15 cm long, rise at an angle from near base of stem. Spike 5–20 cm long, loose, conical at first, then cylindrical, with fls (**Ba**) 18–25 mm wide, with long lfy bracts, on long, ± horizontal stalks, v sweetly-scented; side sepals oval-lanceolate, pointed, spreading horizontally; other perianth segments forming a short hood, all **greenish-tinged creamy**; lip **undivided**, strap-shaped, blunt, pointing down, green to greenish-cream, 10–15 mm long; **spur v long** (20–30 mm × 1 mm), curved downwards and forwards; **pollinia** long (3–4 mm), 4 mm apart at base, **converging above** with tips **close together**. Br Isles f-lc; Eur: France c; N to Denmark lf; in wds, scrub, on basic clays and calc soils. Fl 6–7.

cont

◀ **C Lesser Butterfly Orchid**, *P. bifolia*, close to B, but rather smaller; lvs often shorter (5–8 cm), more oval, especially in bog plants (but more like B in wds); spike narrower in proportion to length; fls (**C**) **narrower** (11–18 mm wide), with less greenish tinge, lip only **6–10 mm** long and proportionately **broader**; **pollinia 2 mm long, vertical, parallel, close together** (**C**); Br Isles, Eur; o-lf in open wds on basic or calc soils, mds, fens, acid bogs. Fl 6–7.

D Small White Orchid, *Pseudorchis* (*Leucorchis*) *albida*, small (10–20 cm), slender, erect orchid, with oblong-lanceolate unspotted lvs 2.5–8.0 cm long up the stem, uppermost v narrow and short; spike 3–6 cm, **narrow**, v **dense**, **cylindrical**, of tiny greenish-**creamy** fls (**Da**) 2.0–2.5 mm long × 5 mm wide, with vanilla scent; perianth segments forming a short flat hood, lip 3–4 mm long, three-lobed, curved down, triangular mid-lobe only slightly longer than side-lobes; spur v short (2–3 mm), bluntly conical, curved down. Br Isles: Wales, and N Eng to S Scot, r; N Scot f-lc; S, mid Eng, vr, possibly extinct; Ire o; Eur: E France, Belgium, Denmark, vr; in mds, gslds in hill or mt areas. Fl 6–7. (Note: green body in **Da** is ovary.)

E Frog Orchid, *Coeloglossum viride*, short erect orchid, 4–20 cm tall, with basal rosette of blunt oval hairless unspotted lvs, and narrow short lvs up stem; spike short (1.5–7.0 cm long), loose-fld, with green bracts, of which lower are as long as the fls; fls (**Ea**) **greenish** to **brown-purple**, with a close helmet of sepals with darker edges not unlike that of Man Orchid (p 434 H), 3–5 mm long; lip hanging down, 4–6 mm long × 2–3 mm wide, **oblong, green-yellow** or brownish, with edge often chocolate, shortly three-toothed at **tip**; spur 2 mm long, bluntly conical, stout and pale. Br Isles, widespread, but r (except in central S Eng lf on chk, and lc in N Eng and N Scot); Eur: N, E France to Denmark, r; on calc gslds to S, hill-pastures, dunes, mt rock-ledges to N. Fl 6–8.

F Lizard Orchid, *Himantoglossum hircinum*, a striking plant, 30–100 cm tall, with stout erect hairless stem; root-lvs oblong-elliptical, in a rosette, 10–20 cm long, withered by time fls open; upper lvs narrower, pointed, clasping, all unspotted, grey-green. Spike 10–30 cm long, many-fld, with lower bracts equal to fls. Fls (**Fa**) with perianth segments forming a close blunt helmet 5–6 mm long, greenish-grey outside, purple-streaked within; lip to **5 cm long**, at first coiled like a **watch-spring**, then **ribbon-like** and **spirally twisted**; three-lobed, mid-lobe v long, narrow, tip notched, side-lobes less than half as long, lobes pale olive-brown, body of lip whitish, spotted with clusters of purple hairs; fls strongly **billy-goat** scented, more tadpole than lizard-shaped; spur blunt, 4 mm long. Br Isles: Eng, S only, vr, but vlf in a few places; **Wales, Scot, Ire, abs**; Eur: central France c; N to Netherlands r; on calc gslds, scrub, dunes. Fl 6–7.

G Dense-flowered Orchid, *Neotinea intacta*, a short (10–30 cm) erect orchid with rosette of oblong basal lvs, **often** with **small brown spots**; upper lvs smaller, clasping. Spike 3–8 cm long, **v dense**, cylindrical. Fls (**Ga**) with helmet 4 mm long, greenish-white or pink; lip pink or white, 4–5 mm long, with 2 narrow pointed side-lobes, and **longer, broader, notched** mid-lobe, often purple-spotted at base; spur 2 mm, blunt, curved. Br Isles: **GB abs**; central, W Ire vlf; Isle of Man vr; abs from Eur (SW France and Mediterranean region); on rocky gslds on limestone, calc dunes. Fl 4–6.

KEY TO *ORCHIS* AND *DACTYLORHIZA*

1 Bracts **shorter** than fls, **narrow, membranous** (1–2 mm wide) – fl-spike **wrapped** round with sheathing lvs in bud .... (*Orchis*) **2**
Bracts **as long**, or **longer** than, fls, **broad** (2–6 mm wide), **lf-like** – fl-spike **never** enclosed in sheathing lvs in bud...(*Dactylorhiza*) **10**

ORCHIS

2 All perianth segments (except lip) forming a **helmet** to fl – spur curved **down**.............................. **3**
Two of outer perianth segments **erect** or **spreading** – spur ± curved **up** **7**

3 Lip **shallowly** three-lobed, mid-lobe **no longer** than side-lobes, notched at tip – perianth segments of helmet with **lengthwise green and purple stripes** .... *O. morio* (p 434 G)
  Lip deeply three-lobed, the **much longer** central lobe divided again into **2 lobes** (often with a tooth between them), so producing 2 'arms' and 2 'legs' like a **human figure** – perianth segments of helmet **without** lengthwise green and purple stripes.. **4**
4 Outer perianth segments of helmet **oval, shortly**-pointed, much **darker** than lip **5**
  Outer perianth segments of helmet **oval-lanceolate, long-pointed, paler** than lip........................ **6**
5 Plant only 8–15 cm – lip only 4–6 mm long, narrow, **white** with a few **flat red** spots – 'legs' ± parallel (suggesting a tiny clown's figure) – helmet **blackish-purple** in bud, paler purple in open fl... *O. ustulata* (p 434 F)
  Plant 25–45 cm – lip 12–18 mm long, broad, **rosy**, with many spots formed of **tufts of crimson** hairs – 'legs' spreading (but ± variable in shape and colour) – helmet dark **reddish-purple-flecked** on a green ground.. *O. purpurea* (p 433 C)
6 All 4 'arms' and 'legs' of lip **v narrow, long**, curved, red, 1 mm wide – 'body' white – helmet **white** with ± **pink flush** and **streaks** ....*O. simia* (p 433 D)
  'Arms' of lip narrow but shorter and **broader** (1.5 mm wide), 'legs' red, **broader** (2–3 mm) and shorter, blunt, **out-turned** – 'body' white red-spotted – helmet **ash-grey** outside, pink-streaked **inside**.. *O. militaris* (p 434 E)
  'Arms' of lip 2 mm wide, 'legs' broad, hardly separated – 'body' red or pink-flecked on white – helmet white, purple-streaked – **not in Br Isles**.. *O. tridentata* (p 434 Ei)
7 Fls yellow, elder-flower scented – lvs oblong, unspotted – **not in Br Isles** .... *O. pallens* (p 433 Ai)
  Fls purple, not elder-flower scented.. **8**
8 Lvs elliptical-**oblong**, normally **purple-blotched**, 2–4 cm wide – fls **tom-cat-scented** at night – lip three-lobed, mid-lobe longest, blunt – spur equalling ovary....................... *O. mascula* (p 433 A)
  Lvs **linear-lanceolate, unspotted**, 1–2 cm wide – fls **unscented** – lip two-lobed or with narrow, tooth-like mid-lobe – spur shorter than ovary... **9**
9 Lip clearly three-lobed, mid-lobe equalling or longer than side-lobes – **not in Br Isles**.....................
                                                                 O. palustris (p 433 B)
  Lip scarcely three-lobed, mid-lobe abs or minute – **not in Br Isles** .... *O. laxiflora* (p 433 Bi)

DACTYLORHIZA (for sspp see also individual descriptions, p 442–443)
10 Stem **solid** – lvs ± always with transverse blotches – bracts 2–3 mm **wide, no longer** than fls.. **11**
  Stem **hollow** (can be felt by compressing – do **not** pick or cut) – lvs spotted or not – **bracts 3–6 mm wide, longer** than fls **12**
11 Lip trident-shaped, with 3 **deep,** ± **equal** oblong lobes, mid-lobe usually longest ....
                                                                D. fuchsii (p 442 E)
  Lip skirt-shaped, with 3 **v shallow** lobes, mid-lobe **narrower** and **shorter** than rounded, toothed side-lobes.. *D. maculata* (p 442 F)
12 Stem-hollow large – lvs erect, keeled, **hooded** at tips, normally unspotted – lip-edges **folded back at sides**, perianth segments **arched back** (so fls appear **v narrow**) – lips with 2 oblong dotted areas on each side of centre, each surrounded by a dark U-shaped line................................
                                                                 D. incarnata (p 442 H)
  Stem-hollow small – lvs ± spreading, **scarcely hooded** – lips **flat** or concave – perianth segments **spreading** (so fls appear **broad**) **13**
13 Lvs few (3–5), **narrow** (to 1.5 cm wide only), keeled, with tiny (1 mm) spots near tip, or none – fls few (8–10) – lip three-lobed, mid-lobe much longer than side-lobes – fls red-purple, **heavily crimson-streaked** ....*D. traunsteineri* (p 442 J)
  Lvs **many** (5–8), **broad** (over 2 cm) – fls **many** in dense spikes... **14**
14 Lip **shield-** or **diamond**-shaped, **unlobed**, under 9 mm wide, **deep** purple with heavy crimson streaks all over – lvs short, flattish, with large (3 mm) spots near tip, or none ....
                                                              D. purpurella (p 442 I)
  Lip **not** shield- or diamond-shaped, ± **three-lobed, over** 9 mm wide... **15**
15 Lvs normally **unspotted** (sometimes with ring-spots), widest **below** middle – fls **pale** pink-purple to rosy-purple – light crimson **dots** and **speckles** confined to centre of **v shallowly** three-lobed, flat or **concave** lip, which is broader than long, with **v short**, blunt mid-lobe ....
                                                                 D. praetermissa (p 442 G)
  Lvs **heavily spotted**, widest **at middle** – fls **deep** purple – **heavy** pattern of crimson **blotches** and **streaks** mostly towards **sides** of strongly **three-lobed**, v broad, ± flat lip......................................
                                                                 D. majalis (p 443 K)

ORCHID FAMILY *Orchidaceae*

Bee, Spider and Fly Orchids (*Ophrys*); **Spotted and Marsh Orchids** (*Dactylorhiza*)

Ophrys has fl's lip **velvety**, **insect-like**, often with a complex pattern of markings; **spur abs**. For **Spotted Orchids** and **Marsh Orchids** (*Dactylorhiza*), see key on p 438. **Spotted Orchids** may **sometimes** have unspotted lvs, but stems always **solid**; **Marsh Orchids** may, or may **not**, have spotted lvs, but stems **hollow** and usually stout (check by gently compressing stem between finger and thumb – do **not** pick or cut).

A Bee Orchid, *Ophrys apifera*, erect orchid, 10–40 cm tall; lvs grey-green, elliptical-oblong, pointed, in a basal rosette and up the hairless stem. Fls (**Aa**) 2–10, large (to 3 cm across), spaced out up stem; sepals 12–15 mm × 5–7 mm, **rosypink** or whitish with ± green mid-vein, pointed, oblong-elliptical, spreading; 2 upper petals much shorter, downy, **greenish**, **square-ended** (or reddish and ± pointed in E Kent and parts of France); lip 10–15 mm long × 8–10 mm wide, **bee-like**, rich brown, furry, convex, blunt-tipped, with two narrow short pointed side-lobes; lip bears a **U- or W-shaped pale** brown loop bordered within and without with a pale yellow line; within the U or W is a reddish-orange U-shaped patch; lip ends in a long narrow tooth, but this is curved up underneath, so not visible from above; base of lip has 2 eye-like glossy bosses. Anther large, green, shaped like a duck's head; pollinia **long-stalked**, falling forwards on their stalks onto stigma to cause self-pollination if not removed by insects; **spur abs**. Br Isles: Eng f-lc, especially in S and E; Wales, Ire, r-o; **Scot abs**; Eur: France f-lc; Belgium, W Germany, r; on calc gslds, dunes, also disturbed gd, quarries etc. Fl 6–7. **Ai Wasp Orchid**, *O. apifera* var *trollii*, looks v different from A in its **longpointed**, ± **straight**, yellow lip, with usually **no** U or W pattern, but with **scattered brown blotches** on it. Anther as in A. Eng: Cotswold area r; ± similar forms occur, but only sporadically, in other parts of S Eng and Eur.

B Late Spider Orchid, *O. fuciflora*, differs from A only in the fls (**B**), in which sepals are much as in A, but the 2 upper petals **broad-triangular**, **pink**, downy, **blunt-pointed**; lip **larger** (15–20 mm long × 12–15 mm wide), often **widening** towards the tip, usually with a more complex pattern than in A, often like an H with side-lobes, but sometimes ± as in A; tip of lip, however, **always** has a **cordate**, **forward-pointing green appendage**. Anther short, pollinia short-stalked, never falling forward. Br Isles: E Kent only vr; Eur: central, N, E France, lf; Belgium vr; on calc gslds. Fl 6–7, earlier than A, but hybridizes with it.

C Fly Orchid, *O. insectifera*, usually much taller (20–60 cm), slenderer than A, B or D, fls more widely-spaced up stem. Fls (**C**) have **narrower** lip (15 mm × 4–5 mm) with 2 arm-like side-lobes and a deeply notched mid-lobe; lip **sides** turned-down but lip, purple-red to blackish-purple, velvety, with a broad, **oblong shiny blue patch** in the centre, is **straight**, **not convex**, at tip as in A, B and D and has no appendage. Sepals **green** as in D, but only 6–12 mm long; upper petals, **blackish-purple**, velvety, **thread-like**, resemble an insect's antennae. Whole lip resembles a fly sitting on a green fl. Anther short; lvs narrower, greener than in A and D. Br Isles: Eng o-lf in S, r N to Kendal; N Wales, Ire, r; **Scot abs**; Eur: France f-lc; Belgium r; Denmark vvr; in open wds, scrub, gsld on calc soils. Fl 5–6.

D Early Spider Orchid, *O. sphegodes*, differs from A in its fls (**Da**) with pale **yellow-green** sepals, **narrower** than in A (4–5 mm); in **brownish-yellow strapshaped** upper petals **not much shorter** than the sepals; and in furry oval convex lip **without** any appendage, **dark purplish-brown** when fresh (but fading to garden-spider colour when older) with a glossy blue π-shaped mark on it. Anther short like B; side-lobes of lip sometimes well-developed, but often abs. Br Isles: S Eng only, Dorset to Kent, r-vlc, mostly near sea; Eur: central France c; to N France and Belgium r (S Eur vc); on calc gslds in short turf. Fl 4–5 (or early 6).

cont

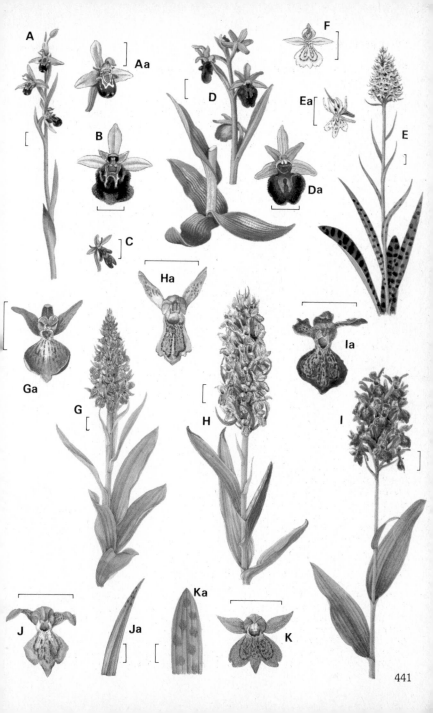

441

◀ **E Common Spotted Orchid**, *Dactylorhiza fuchsii*, usually slender, 15–40 cm tall, stem **solid**; rosette-lvs broad-elliptical, blunt, grey-green, with many **transversely** elongated purple spots (sometimes unspotted, especially in white-fld plants); stem-lvs narrow-lanceolate, pointed, merging in size into the lfy bracts of fls above. Fl-spike conical, then cylindrical, to 10 cm long; fls (**Ea**) **pale** pink, with purple streaks and spots (sometimes all pure white); outer sepals **spreading**, upper sepal and 2 petals forming a loose hood; lip 6–8 mm long, with three ± **equal**, **pointed**, well-separated lobes, mid-lobe **slightly** longer than side-lobes; spur 5–8 mm, conical. Br Isles, Eur; vc in wds, scrub, gslds on calc or ± basic soils. Fl 6–8.

F Heath Spotted Orchid, *D. maculata*, differs from E in lvs **all** lanceolate, pointed, with ± **circular** purple spots; but mainly in the fls (**F**), which have lip **broad**, **triangular** (with the apex at top), v shallowly three-lobed, mid-lobe **much** narrower and usually **shorter** than the **broad**, toothed side-lobes; lip markings often more **streak-** or **loop-like** and **less dot-like**. Br Isles, Eur, f-lc except in calc or v cultivated districts; in hths, bogs, acid gslds. Fl 6–8.

G Southern Marsh Orchid, *D. praetermissa*, erect orchid, 20–60 cm tall, with stout **hollow** stem; lvs normally unspotted (ring-spotted in var *pardalina*), 10–20 cm long, widest **below** middle, broad-lanceolate, pointed, in two ± **opp ranks** up stem, **not** sheathing stem, slightly hooded at tip, but hardly keeled lengthwise. Fl-spike dense, conical, 5–10 cm long, the broad (5 mm) lfy bracts **longer** than fls; fls (**Ga**) **pale** pink-purple to rosy-purple, with **spreading** outer sepals, lip ± flat or concave, 9–14 mm wide, broader than long, three-lobed but with side-lobes **v shallow**, mid-lobe short and blunt, pattern of **light** crimson dots and speckles confined to lip centre; spur v **stout**, conical, ± curved. Br Isles: Eng, Wales, c to S, r to N; **Scot**, **Ire**, **abs**; Eur: W, N France to Netherlands and W Germany, c to S, o to N; in fens, wet mds on ± calc soils. Fl 6–8.

H Early Marsh Orchid, *D. incarnata*, differs from G as follows: stem-hollow larger (hence more compressible); lvs more **erect**, yellow-green, strongly **keeled**, normally unspotted, tapering to narrow **hooded** tip; fl-spike **narrower** (to 4 cm wide) more cylindrical, **denser**, lower bracts to 3 mm wide, **much** longer than fls. Fls (**Ha**) with outer perianth segments ± **erect**, and sides of lip **strongly bent back** in vertical plane, so making fls **v narrow** from front view; lip narrow (5 mm wide) oblong, weakly three-lobed at tip, with a pattern of 2 long **U-shaped purple loops** enclosing purple-dotted **patches**; fls normally flesh-tinted. Br Isles, widespread but only o-lf; Eur: France o-lc; N to Denmark o-f; in calc fens and wet mds. Fl 5–7. Species v variable: ssp *cruenta*, with lvs spotted both sides and fls pale purple, only in Ire, r; ssp *coccinea*, with brick-red fls, vlc in dune hollows in W of GB and Ire; ssp *pulchella*, like D but with fls purple, f-lc in acid bogs of Br Isles; ssp *ochroleuca*, with cream or yellow fls without lip markings, o in fens of E Anglia, Wales, Eur; ssp *gemmana*, over 40 cm tall, having lip over 9 mm wide with dots but no lines, r in fens of Norfolk and W Ire.

I Northern Marsh Orchid, *D. purpurella*, replaces G in N of Br Isles and in N Eur; shorter (10–25 cm) than G; stem with **v narrow hollow** in centre, lvs short, **flat** (5–10 cm long), with **large** (3 mm wide) **spots** near tip, or unspotted. Fl-spike **short**, **broad** (5–6 cm long × 3–4 cm), dense; fls (**Ia**) with stout spur, **spreading** outer sepals, lip **shield-** or **diamond-shaped**, **unlobed**, under 9 mm wide, **deep rich purple** with **heavy crimson streaks** all over. Br Isles: N Wales and N Eng to N Scot, r to S, c to N; S Eng, Hants only, vr; N Ire o-lf; Eur: N Germany, Denmark, vr; in fens, wet mds. Fl 6–7.

J Narrow-leaved Marsh Orchid, *D. traunsteineri*, differs from E in being shorter (15–20 cm tall); stem **slender**, only slightly hollow; lvs (**Ja**) few (3–5), **v narrow** (1.0–1.5 cm wide), keeled, **linear-lanceolate** with slightly hooded tip,

ORCHID FAMILY

usually with tiny purple spots (1 mm wide) or bars near tip; fl-spike **short**, **loose**, few-fld. Fls (**J**) red-purple, a little darker than in G (but less dark than in I); side sepals ± spreading; lip 8–10 mm wide, narrowed to base, ± diamond-shaped, flat, but **three-lobed**, the mid-lobe usually **much longer than** side-lobes, marked with a **strong** pattern of dark crimson lines and dots; spur straight, **slender**. Br Isles: central S, E, N Eng, N Wales, r-lf; Ire o-lf; **Scot abs**; Eur: N France to Denmark r-vlf; in calc fens, dune slacks. Fl 5–6.

K Broad-leaved Marsh Orchid, *D. majalis* ssp *majalis*, resembles G in robust habit (to 60 cm tall), but differs in the more spreading **broad-lanceolate** to oblong lvs (**Ka**), **broadest in middle** and flat-tipped, **heavily transversely purple-blotched** or ring-spotted; fl-spike **dense**, 5–10 cm long, oblong; fls (**K**) deep magenta to pink-purple, side sepals spreading; lip **v broad** (10–12 mm wide), ± flat, **strongly three-lobed**, with broad, rounded ± notched side-lobes and narrower, pointed mid-lobe **longer** than side ones; upper part of lip with **strong** pattern of crimson loops and dots. Eur: central France to Denmark, o to SW, vc to E and N; in fens, wet mds. Fl 5–7. **Ki** ssp *occidentalis*, only ssp in Br Isles, is much shorter (10–25 cm), with **shorter** (4–5 cm) spike, **darker** purple fls, and mid-lobe of lip blunt, narrower than in K, and much shorter than side ones; lip pattern less intense. Lvs sometimes without spots. NW Scot, Hebrides, r; W Ire f-lc; in fens, mds, dune-hollows. Fl 5–6.

WATER-STARWORT FAMILY

Water-Starworts (*Callitriche*) are herbs of fresh water (or creeping over mud) with slender stems and opp pairs of untoothed, linear or oval lvs without stipules; in many spp upper pairs of lvs are close-set to form a floating terminal rosette. Fls, tiny, male and female separate but on same plant, lack perianths; male of one stamen, female of an oval, flattened four-lobed ovary with 2 styles. Fr 1–2 mm long, the 4 lobes **winged** in some spp. Spp are not easy to name because lvs vary in form according to whether fls are floating, submerged, or on mud: in still or flowing water: also because fls are often abs. The key p 450 includes all, except the rarest, spp of Br Isles and Eur, and uses both lf and fr characters.

A Common Water-starwort, *Callitriche stagnalis*, has all lvs (**Aa**) ± oval, stalked, lf-rosettes usually present; lower lvs v similar to upper, never linear; roots arise from bases of lf-pairs; frs (**Ab**) 1.6–2.0 mm long, the lobes with conspicuous **keels**. Br Isles, Eur; c in ponds, streams, ditches, on wet mud in paths etc. Fl 5–9.

B Intermediate Water-starwort, *C. intermedia* (*C. hamulata*), is distinctive in **lower** lvs (**Ba**) **linear**, 15–25 mm long × 0.5–1.0 mm wide, with deeply notched, expanded, **spanner-shaped** tips; upper submerged lvs (and any floating lvs) may be **spoon-shaped** or elliptical, or else **all** lvs may be linear and parallel-sided. Frs 1.25 mm long, lobes ± keeled as in A. Br Isles, Eur; c in lakes, streams, ditches etc. Fl 4–9.

DUCKWEED FAMILY

Tiny floating plants that form green carpets on the surface of fresh water. No obvious division into stem and lvs, but with merely a rounded or elliptical thallus. In *Lemna*, roots are present, hanging down from thallus; in *Wolffia*, roots abs. Fls, minute, hard to see and rarely produced in most spp, consist of tiny male fls with 1–2 stamens, and female fls with minute ovary, borne in a pocket on thallus edge or upper surface. See key p 450.   *cont*

DUCKWEED FAMILY

Lemnaceae

C **Common Duckweed**, *Lemna minor*, plants flat both sides, 1.5–4.0 mm across, each with a **single** v long root hanging down into water. Br Isles, Eur; vc in fresh, still or slow-moving water. Fl 6–7.

D **Greater Duckweed**, *L. polyrhiza*, plants flat both sides as in C, 5–8 mm across, often purple below, each with **several** long roots. Br Isles: Eng f-lc; Ire o-lf; Wales, Scot, vr; Eur: France f, N to Denmark o; in still fresh water. Fl 7 (vr).

E **Fat Duckweed**, *L. gibba*, plants green and convex above, white, spongy and v swollen below (**Ea**), each with **one** long root; (**Ea** also shows a plant forming a daughter thallus by budding). Br Isles: Eng f-lc; Wales, Ire, r; **Scot abs**; Eur: France f; N to Denmark o; in still water. Fl 6–7 (r).

F **Rootless Duckweed**, *Wolffia arrhiza*, plants like tiny ovoid or ellipsoid grains of green sand, 0.5–1.0 mm long, **without roots**; no fls in Br Isles or Eur. Br Isles, S Eng only, r-lf; Eur: France to Holland and N Germany, r; in still fresh water.

G **Ivy-leaved Duckweed**, *Lemna trisulca*, differs from other Duckweeds in its **elliptical-lanceolate**, **translucent thalli**, which taper when mature into **stalks** at the base, and are usually joined up at right angles into branched colonies, the terminal triplets of thalli looking ± like tiny ivy lvs. Br Isles: Eng c; Ire o-lf; Wales, S half Scot only, r; Eur c; slightly submerged in still fresh or brackish water. Fl 5–7. **Gi** **Water Fern**, *Azolla filiculoides*, resembles a Duckweed in habit and habitat, but has tiny oval **lvs** 2–3 mm long closely overlapping along short **branched stems**, and turns **red** in later summer; it is, in fact, a fern. S Eng o-lf, Ire vr; Eur: France o-lf; introd (N America) in fresh water.

FROGBIT FAMILY (see also p 402)

Hydrocharitaceae

Submerged Waterweed members

H **Canadian Waterweed**, *Elodea canadensis*, submerged per aquatic herb with oblong ± blunt, dark green translucent lvs 10 mm long × 3–4 mm wide, in whorls of 3 (rarely 4) along stems, lvs bearing minute untoothed green scales on upper sides near base. Dioecious: male plant vr in Br Isles and Eur, female plant usual; female fls (to right of **H**) 5 mm across, **floating** at surface on v long thread-like stalks, greenish-purple, with 3 sepals and 3 petals, 3 styles and **inferior** ovary; fl-stalk with **two-toothed** tubular **sheath** 1–2 cm long surrounding its base. Br Isles, Eur; introd (N America), f-lc in still or slow-moving fresh water. Fl 5–10. Several other similar-looking plants are now naturalized in Br Isles and Eur, mostly thrown out from aquaria etc; see key to these on p 80.

PIPEWORT FAMILY

Eriocaulaceae

I **Pipewort**, *Eriocaulon septangulare* (*E. aquaticum*), slender aquatic herb; creeping rootstock produces at intervals erect to spreading tufts of linear, submerged translucent basal lvs 5–10 cm long, flattened at sides, tapered to fine points, and with internal cross-partitions. Fl-stems arising from lf-rosettes, lfless, **erect**, **6–8 (usually 7)-angled** (**Ib**), 20–60 cm tall, twisted, bearing button-like heads 0.5–2.0 cm across, of tiny close-packed fls at tips, each head with tiny grey bracts around it in a tightly adpressed whorl. Fls (**Ia**) 4 mm long, with 2 grey sepals with hairy tips, 2 whitish black-tipped petals, 2–4 stamens and stigmas; infls resemble whitish-headed knitting-needles. Br Isles: Scot, only in Skye, Coll, W Argyll, vla; Ire, Donegal to Cork near W Coast, vla; Eur abs (only closely related spp are in N America); in shallow lakes and pools of acid water on peaty substrates, avoids limestones. Fl 7–9.

cont

◀ Marsh or aquatic herbs with **linear**, sheathing, mostly basal lvs; fls **small**, **greenish**, in **erect spikes** or **racemes**; fl-parts in threes, but carpels either **3 or 6**, joined into a **superior** ovary; fr a capsule. **Arrowgrasses** (*Triglochin*) have long narrow racemes of many fls, with 6 carpels; **Rannoch-rush** (*Scheuchzeria*) has short racemes of few, long-stalked fls with 3 carpels joined only at their bases.

J Marsh Arrowgrass, *Triglochin palustris*, slender erect per herb 15–40 cm tall; pleasant aromatic smell when bruised. Lvs linear, 10–20 cm long, rounded on lower side, deeply **grooved** on upper; raceme many-fld. Fls (**Ja**) with 6 green, ± purple-edged perianth segments 2 mm long; style short, white-woolly; raceme elongating in fr; frs (**Jb**) **club-shaped**, 10 mm long × 2 mm wide near tip, adpressed to stem, opening **from below** when ripe into 3 valves pointed at base to form **arrow-shape** (**Jc**). Br Isles, Eur, f-lc, especially to N, except in v cultivated regions; in fens, calc mds, calc springs. Fl 6–8.

K Sea Arrowgrass, *T. maritima*, like J, but stouter, with half-cylindrical **fleshy** lvs **not** furrowed above, not v aromatic; raceme denser, and more like that of Sea Plantain (p 336); fls (**Ka**) **fleshier**; frs (**Kb**) **oval** when ripe, 4–5 mm long × 2 mm wide, the opening valves **not** forming arrow-shape, but falling off completely. Br Isles, Eur, vc on coasts, vr inland; in salt marshes, mostly near sea. Fl 7–9.

L Rannoch-rush, *Scheuchzeria palustris*, erect per herb 10–20 cm tall; creeping rhizome clothed with papery, straw-coloured remains of old lf-bases, swollen at joints; lvs present up stem, alt, linear, ± flat, to 20 cm long, some overtopping fls; lf-tips blunt, with **conspicuous pore** at tip (**L**); infl **short**, **v loose**, of few (3–8) fls on long stalks each in axil of a long lf-like green bract with **inflated sheathing base**. Fls yellow-green, 4 mm across, with 6 narrow perianth segments, 6 stamens, and (usually) 3 carpels joined only at base and in ripe fr oval, 4–5 mm long, glossy, pointed. Br Isles: Scot, Rannoch Moor only, vlf; Eng extinct; Ire probably extinct; Eur: Belgium to Denmark, now vr, decreasing through drainage (mt bogs of central France, central Eur); in pools and wet hollows of ancient undisturbed sphagnum bogs. Fl 6–8.

For key to water plants with ± linear, quill-like lvs in rosettes, see p 81.

▶ **PONDWEED FAMILY** *Potamogetonaceae*

Fresh water floating or submerged aquatic herbs with opp or alt lvs in 2 opp ranks; infls stalked **spikes** in lf-axils. Fls small, each with 4 perianth segments, 4 stamens, and 4 separate carpels ripening to small nutlets, 4 or less per fl, membranous scales (stipules) usually present in axils of lvs, which may be free, or joined to lf-base on its lower part. Some members of this family are not easy to identify, particularly those with narrow lvs, and also the hybrids which occur between several of the spp and may multiply vegetatively and become v abundant locally. In the key on pp 451–452 it has not been possible to include any hybrids.

Pondweeds (*Potamogeton*); and other submerged aquatic plants with long, narrow lvs

A Broad-leaved Pondweed, *Potamogeton natans*, submerged and floating aquatic herb, stems cylindrical, little branched, 1–2 m long or more; floating lvs dark green, leathery, **opaque**, **oval** to **elliptical-lanceolate**, 10–30 cm long, pointed at tips, rounded at base, and with a discoloured **flexible joint** just below top of the long lf-stalk; submerged lvs narrow-linear, to 30 cm or more; stipules 5–15 cm long. Fl-spikes dense, cylindrical, 3–8 cm long, stout-stalked, emerging from water; frs (**Aa**) 4–5 mm long × 3 mm wide, olive, obovoid, ± flattened, both

447

◀ margins convex; beak short, straight. Br Isles, Eur; c in still and slow moving fresh water. Fl 5–9.

B Bog Pondweed, *P. polygonifolius*, close to A in habit and lvs, but with lvs often reddish-brown, **all** lvs **stalked**, with lanceolate-**oval blades**; floating lvs leathery, 6–10 cm long, either tapered into stalk or cordate-based, but **without any** discoloured flexible **joint** at stalk-top; stipules 2–4 cm; submerged lvs with **translucent** blades. Fl-spikes dense, as in A but smaller; fls (**Bb**) with 4 perianth segments, 5 mm across; frs (**Ba**) only 2.0–2.5 mm long × 1.5 mm wide, reddish, beak tiny. Br Isles c (but mid, E Eng, and v cultivated regions, o-lf only; Eur f-lc; in shallow peaty acid water, bog pools. Fl 5–10.

C Fen Pondweed, *P. coloratus*, also near to A, but all lf-stalks **shorter** than blades, which are **thin**, **translucent**, olive to reddish-brown, **tapered** into stalks, with a fine network of **cross-** and parallel-veins; like B has **no joint** or hinge at top of lf-stalk. Floating lvs oval-elliptical, 5–10 cm long, submerged lvs narrow; frs (**Ca**) 1.5–2.0 mm long × 1 mm wide, green, ovoid, flattened, inner edge ± straight, beak v short. Br Isles: GB, N to Edinburgh, and in Hebrides, r (but lf E Anglia to E Yorks); Ire o-lf; Eur: N to Denmark o-lf; in calcareous peaty ditches, fens. Fl 6–7.

D Shining Pondweed, *P. lucens*, **wholly submerged** aquatic herb; lvs all **similar**, **translucent** green, **wavy**, **shiny**, **oblong-lanceolate**, 10–20 cm long × 2.5–6.0 cm wide, edges **minutely-toothed**; lf-stalks **v short or abs**; stipules 3–8 cm, blunt, keeled; infl-stalks thickened above; frs (**Da**) 3.5 mm × 2.2 mm long, olive-green, ovoid, not flattened, inner edge ± straight, beak v short. Br Isles: S, mid, E Eng, f-lc; rest of GB o-r; Ire o; Eur f-lc; in still and slow-moving fresh, especially calc, water. Fl 6–9.

E Perfoliate Pondweed, *P. perfoliatus*, distinct in its **stalkless**, ± oval, **translucent** dark green lvs, all **submerged**, 2–8 cm long, ± **completely clasping** stem-bases; frs (**Ea**) 3.0–4.0 mm long × 2.5–3.0 mm wide, olive-green, ovoid, swollen, inner side concave near base, hardly keeled. Br Isles widespread and f, to lc in S and E Eng; Eur f-lc; in still or flowing fresh water. Fl 6–9.

F Curled Pondweed, *P. crispus*, submerged aquatic, distinct in its **four-angled**, furrowed stems, and translucent **dark green**, **stalkless**, toothed linear-oblong lvs with **blunt** tips and strongly **waved** or **crisped** margins, 3–5 main veins only, the outer near the margins, **no** fainter intermediate veins present. Infls loose, stalks slender; frs (**Fa**) 2–5 mm long (without the long curved beak), olive, oval, flattened, with outer edge keeled, **toothed**. Br Isles, Eur, c (except in mts); in still and flowing fresh water. Fl 5–10.

G Small Pondweed, *P. berchtoldii*, **slender** submerged aquatic herb; lvs **narrow-linear**, flat, 2.5–5.0 cm long × 0.5–2.0 mm wide, stalkless, rounded but **mucronate** at tip; lvs always with **3** longitudinal veins **only**, outer veins **meeting** midrib nearly at **right angles** half to 1 lf-width from tip. Frs 2.0–2.5 mm long × 1.5 mm wide, dark olive, obovoid, tapered to tip, not flattened, short-beaked. Br Isles, Eur; f-lc in still and slow-moving fresh water. Fl 6–9.

H Fennel Pondweed, *P. pectinatus*, submerged aquatic, distinctive in its many long **narrow-linear** lvs, 5–20 cm long × 0.3–2.0 mm wide, each lf composed of **2 slender parallel tubes**; stipules join lf-base to form a long, tubular, but **wholly open** sheath round stem above and below lf-base. Infls open, v loose, on long, slender stalks; frs (**Ha**) 3–5 mm long × 2–4 mm wide, olive-brown, obovoid, flattened, beak short, curved. Br Isles: GB, N to mid Scot, o; N Scot, Ire, o; Eur c; in still and flowing fresh water, especially in lowlands and near coasts (only sp of *Potamogeton* c in brackish ditches near sea). Fl 5–9.

I Opposite-leaved Pondweed, *Groenlandia densa*, submerged aquatic with **all** lvs in **opp** pairs (in *Potamogeton* lvs **alt**, except sometimes those with infls in axils);

PONDWEED FAMILY   *Potamogetonaceae*

lvs **without** stipules (except those with infls in axils), oval-triangular to lanceolate, green-olive, **unstalked**, minutely-toothed on edges, often lengthwise folded, **densely-set**. Fls in tiny, few-fld **heads**, (not spikes); frs (**Ia**) 3 mm long × 2 mm wide, olive, shortly oval, flattened, both edges keeled and convex; beak v short, central on fr-tip. Br Isles: Eng f-lc; Scot, Wales, vr; Ire o; Eur: France c; N to Denmark r-o; in running or still fresh water. Fl 5–9. ◀

NAIAD FAMILY   *Najadaceae*

J Slender Naiad, *Najas flexilis*, slender submerged aquatic herb with smooth stems to 30 cm long; lvs (**Jb**) linear, **minutely-toothed**, 20–25 mm long × 0.5–1.0 mm wide, in **opp** pairs or whorls of 3, translucent, pointed, with few-haired sheathing bases; fls 1–3 together in lf-axils: male with a tiny sheath, two-lipped perianth and 1 stamen; female fls naked with three stigmas forming a narrow oval fr (**Ja**) 4–6 mm long including beak and stigmas. Br Isles: NW Eng, W Scot, Hebrides, vr; W Ire r; Eur: N Germany, Denmark, vr; in lakes of acid water. Fl 7–9. **Ji Holly-leaved Naiad**, *N. marina*, has broader, **strongly spinous** lvs, and a few teeth on the stiff, brittle stems. Lf-sheaths hairless; plant dioecious; frs **twice** as long as in J. Eng: Norfolk Broads only, r but lf; Eur: France to Denmark r; in lakes. Fl 7–8.

HORNED PONDWEED FAMILY   *Zannichelliaceae*

K Horned Pondweed, *Zannichellia palustris*, submerged aquatic with much branched slender shoots to 50 cm long; lvs opp, linear, 1.5–5.0 cm long × 0.5–2.0 mm wide, flat or sometimes hairlike, fine-pointed, translucent, with few parallel veins (rather like those of the narrow-lvd *Potamogeton* spp and like them with stipules, but with tiny fls in ± **unstalked clusters** in lf-axils, usually 1 male fl of 1 stamen and 2–6 female together in a tiny cup-shaped sheath). Frs (**Ka**) distinctive, 2–6 together, green, 2–3 mm long, oblong, usually short-stalked, often with toothed edge, beak to 2 mm long. Br Isles: Eng, lc to E and S, o-lf to W; Scot, Wales, Ire, r-o; Eur lf-lc; in still or slow moving fresh brackish water. Fl 5–8.

TASSELWEED FAMILY   *Ruppiaceae*

L Beaked Tasselweed, *Ruppia maritima*, looks like K, but lvs longer (to 10 cm), only 0.5 mm wide, more bristle-like and less flattened than in K, may be **alt** or **opp**. Fls in small umbel-like heads of 3–5, on a common stalk to 5 cm long, **not more** than **twice length** of **individual** fl- or fr-stalks; each fl with 2 stamens and several carpels; fr (**La**) ovoid, v asymmetrical, beak to **one side**. Br Isles, o to N, W, and in Ire, lc in S, E, Eng; Eur f-lc; in brackish ditches near sea. Fl 7–9. **Li Spiral Tasselweed**, *R. spiralis*, close to L, but common stalk of infl is **10 cm or more**, **much longer** than individual fl- or fr-stalks, and usually **coiled** in a spiral in fr; frs ovoid, but **nearly symmetrical**, beak ± **central**.

EELGRASS FAMILY   *Zosteraceae*

M Narrow-leaved Eelgrass, *Zostera angustifolia*, submerged herbaceous flowering plant, growing in the sea; lvs linear, ribbon-like, 15–30 cm long × 2–3 mm wide, 1–3-veined, notched at tips, bases sheathing. Fls in **spikes** on one side of a flattened axis, ± enclosed inside lf-sheaths; fls of two sexes separate but

EELGRASS FAMILY *Zosteraceae*

◄ male and female fls alt within spikes, without bracts or perianth; style equals stigma; seeds 2.5–3.0 mm long, ribbed. Br Isles, scattered around coasts N to Orkney, r but vlc on S, E coasts; Eur: Denmark r; on muddy seashores, mud-flats. Fl 7–12. **Mi Common Eelgrass**, *Z. marina*, similar to M, but much **larger**, lvs **20–50 cm** (or more) long × 5–10 mm broad, with **3 or more** veins, rounded with **mucronate** tips; fl-stems much branched as in M; stigma twice length of style; seeds 3.0–3.5 mm long, ribbed. Br Isles, lf around most of coast, but decreased; E coast lva; Eur f-lc; in sea from spring tide low water down to a vertical depth of 4 m, on sand or mud. Fl 6–9. **Mii Dwarf Eelgrass**, *Z. noltii*, has fl-stems **unbranched (unlike** M, Mi); lvs one-veined only, **6–12 cm long**, under **1 mm wide**, with notched tips, only one vein and lf-sheaths **open** (**not closed** as in M and Mi); seeds 2 mm long, smooth. Br Isles, r-lf round coasts; Eur: N to Denmark o-lc. Fl 6–10.

WATER-STARWORT FAMILY *Callitrichaceae*

KEY TO WATER-STARWORTS (*CALLITRICHE*)

1 Lower lvs ± **parallel-sided, linear,** ± **notched** at tips.. **2**
  Lower lvs **never** parallel-sided and linear, but **elliptical-oval, not** notched or scarcely so – uppermost lvs (or floating rosettes) ± circular in outline, smooth, stalked – frs with their 4 lobes all **broadly** winged ....*C. stagnalis* (p 443 A)

2 All **lower** lvs (at least) with **deeply**-notched, **expanded, spanner-shaped** tips – frs 1.4 mm wide, with **narrow** wings to lobes – styles bent back, pressed to sides of frs............ *C. intermedia* (p 443 B)
  Lower lvs ± parallel-sided, but with only shallow-notched (**never** expanded, spanner-shaped) tips – styles erect.. **3**

3 Upper lvs forming **floating rosettes**, oval, spoon- or diamond-shaped, lower lvs narrower – lvs **not** translucent.. **4**
  Upper and lower lvs **all** alike, ± parallel-sided, linear, translucent and submerged.......................... **6**

4 Rosette-lvs ± **diamond-shaped, strongly-veined** above – frs 1.5 mm long, with blunt, **unwinged** lobes – S Eng N to Yorks o-lf – Ire o – France to Netherlands o-f – in peaty or calc fresh water – fl 5–9..*C. obtusangula*
  Rosette-lvs rounded, **weak-veined** above – frs **winged**, 1.4–1.8 mm long **5**

5 Frs **brownish**, lobes **narrow-winged all round** – Br Isles o-lf – France to Denmark f – in still water – fl 4–10 ....*C. platycarpa*
  Frs **blackish**, lobes narrow-winged (**at tip only**) – Eur o ....*C. palustris*

6 Lvs dark **blue**-green, most **under** 1 cm long, tips **square-cut, scarcely** notched – fr vr – Kent, Somerset, Notts, vr – Eur N to Belgium r – in still and flowing fresh water........................*C. truncata*
  Lvs **pale** to **yellow**-green, most **over** 1 cm long, tapered to **distinctly**-notched tips – frs ± circular, broadly winged – styles spreading – GB N from Staffs lf – Ire lf – France to Denmark r – in ± peaty still or slow fresh water – fl 5–9 ....*C. hermaphroditica*

DUCKWEED FAMILY *Lemnaceae*

KEY TO DUCKWEED FAMILY

1 Plant thallus ovoid or globular, rootless, only 0.5–1.0 mm wide...................*Wolffia arrhiza* (p 444 F)
  Plant thallus ± flattened above, with **roots**, over 1.5 mm wide ....(*Lemna*) **2**

2 Plants floating just **below** surface of water, **translucent, elliptical, stalked**, several plants **attached together** ± in a branched cluster...*Lemna trisulca* (p 444 G)
  Plants floating **on** surface of water, **opaque, round** or **oval, unstalked**, separate except when v young... **3**

3 Each thallus with **several** roots, flat, 5–8 mm wide...*L. polyrhiza* (p 444 D)
  Each thallus with **one root only**.. **4**

4 Thallus ± flat above and below, 1.5–4.0 mm wide ....*L. minor* (p 444 C)
  Thallus convex above, v swollen and spongy below, 3–5 mm wide.......................*L. gibba* (p 444 E)

KEY TO PONDWEED FAMILY

This key is based mainly on lf and stem characters. Points to look at carefully include: **lf-shape**, **toothing** and **texture**; **vein pattern**, **spacing**, and **number**; whether or not stipules are **fused** to lf-base; whether or not they form a **tube** below; also fr-shape. It is essential to float out pieces of the **narrow-lvd** spp in clean water, and then spread them out on white paper or card for examination with a lens. All spp found in Br Isles and Eur are included, many more than those illustrated and fully described on pp 446–448. Hybrids occur to complicate matters; in particular *Potomageton* × *nitens* (*P. gramineus* × *perfoliatus*), *P.* × *zizii* (*P. gramineus* × *lucens*) and *P.* × *salicifolius* (*P. lucens* × *perfoliatus*) are scattered through Br Isles and Eur, and show features **intermediate** between their parents; plants that do not 'key-out' may well be hybrids, which are sterile (except *P.* × *zizii*, sometimes with frs) and **may** occur in the absence of one or both parents.

1 All lvs in **opp** pairs – stipules **abs** (except on those lvs in whose axils fl-spikes occur) ....
    Groenlandia densa (p 448 I)
    All lvs **alt** and with **stipules** (except that lvs in whose axils fl-spikes occur may be in **opp** pairs).......
    (*Potamogeton*) **2**
2 **Upper** lvs (at least) **broad** (10 mm wide or more), **lanceolate, elliptical** or **oval**...........................**3**
    All lvs under 6 mm wide, **narrow-linear**, parallel-sided, grass-like or thread-like **15**
3 **Floating** (or aerial) lvs **present**, always stalked...**4**
    Floating lvs **abs** – **all** lvs submerged, **thin, translucent**..**10**
4 Floating lvs **thin, translucent** – stalks shorter than blades (frs not over 1.75 mm long, green).........
    P. coloratus (p 448 C)
    Floating lvs **leathery, opaque**...**5**
5 **Floating** lvs with a flexible hinge-like **joint** where stalk joins blade – **submerged** lvs **linear**, opaque, with no expanded blade – fr 4–5 mm long...*P. natans* (p 446 A)
    Floating lvs with **no** hinge-like joint where stalk joins blade – **submerged** lvs (if present) with obvious translucent blade..**6**
6 Stems **flattened** – floating lvs oblong-elliptical – submerged lvs **linear**, stalkless, ribbon-like, under 8 mm wide, with a wide band of **air-containing tissue** bordering midribs – native Outer Hebrides, r in lakes – introd W Yorks, r in River Calder and nearby canals ....*P. epihydrus*
    Stems **cylindrical** – submerged lvs **broader**, **not** linear, usually over 8 mm wide, without air-tissue...**7**
7 Submerged lvs elliptical-lanceolate, 10–16 cm × 3.5–5.0 cm, translucent, with v conspicuous **network** of **cross-veins** between main veins – floating lvs broader, leathery – all lvs long-stalked – fr 3.5–4.0 mm long – S Eng (in Bristol Avon, Dorset Stour, Upper Thames, Loddon and Blackwater etc) vlf – France o..*P. nodosus*
    Submerged lvs (if present) translucent, but **not** with conspicuous cross-veins, or all lvs floating or aerial..**8**
8 **All** lvs clearly **stalked**, all (or nearly all) **floating** or **aerial**, similar, leathery, elliptical-oval – frs 2.0–2.5 mm long – usually in shallow acid peaty water or among sphagnum ....
    P. polygonifolius (p 448 B)
    Submerged lvs **present**, all (or nearly all) of these **stalkless** **9**
9 Submerged lvs **blunt** or **round-tipped**, **untoothed**, 1–2 cm wide – floating lvs with stalks **shorter** than blades, ± reddish – fr 3 mm long × 2 mm wide, long-beaked – Br Isles, Eur, o-lf – in rivers (avoids chlk) ....*P. alpinus*
    Submerged lvs **pointed**, **v finely-toothed** (use lens), 0.5–1.0 cm wide – floating lvs (if present) with stalks usually **longer** than blades – Br Isles o (lf to N, not in extreme S Eng) – Eur, o to S, f to N – in acid peaty lakes..*P. gramineus**
10 Lvs linear-oblong, stalkless, 4–9 cm long × 1.0–1.5 cm wide, with **strong-toothed**, **v undulat-ing** margins – stem **flattened, four-angled** – fr with beak as long as its body.....*P. crispus* (p 448 F)
    Lvs oval-lanceolate, **untoothed** (at least to naked eye), margins **never** strongly undulating – stem ± **cylindrical**, not four-angled **11**
11 Lvs blunt, **clasping stem** with their cordate bases...**12**
    Lvs **not** clasping stem at bases..**13**
12 Lvs **hooded** at tip, half clasping stem at base, untoothed – stipules large (0.5–6.0 cm long), oval, persisting – GB from Thames Valley N, r but lf – Ire r-o – Eur o-f (lf to N) – in lakes, canals etc.........
    P. praelongus
    Lvs **flat** (**not** hooded) at tip, ± completely clasping stem at base, v finely-toothed (use lens) – stipules small, (to 3 mm long) concave on outer side, soon falling............*P. perfoliatus* (p 448 E)†
13 Lvs short-stalked, oblong-elliptical, 10–20 cm long, somewhat wavy.................*P. lucens* (p 448 D)
    Lvs stalkless **14**

14 Lvs **blunt, untoothed**, 1–2 cm wide.....................*P. alpinus* (form without floating lvs, see 9 above)
   Lvs **pointed**, minutely-**toothed**, 0.5–1.0 cm wide..
                          P. gramineus (form without floating lvs, see 9 above)
15 Lvs v narrow, **thread-like**, composed of 2 **hollow tubes**, one each side of midrib – stipules **fused**
   to lf-base, forming a basal **sheath** to lf.. **16**
   Lvs **flat, grass-like, not tubular** – stipules **free, not** fused to lf-base, but ± sheathing
   stem.. **17**
16 Lf-sheaths **open** down one side, **not** forming a closed tube – lf-tips **pointed** – frs 3–5 mm long –
   c..*P. pectinatus* (p 448 H)
   Lf-sheaths forming a **closed tube** below (at least on younger lvs) – lf-tips **rounded** – frs 2.0–
   2.75 mm long – Anglesey r – Scot o-lf – Ire o – Eur, r to S, f to N – in lakes, especially near
   coasts...*P. filiformis*
17 Lvs with 3 or 5 **main** parallel veins and **many faint vein-like streaks** between them – stems
   strongly **flattened**... **18**
   Lvs with 3 or 5 **main** veins and **no** faint vein-like streaks between them – stems **cylindrical**, or v
   slightly flattened.. **19**
18 Lvs with **5** main veins – lf-tips **rounded**, but **mucronate** – lvs 10–20 cm long × 3–4 mm wide –
   mid, E Eng, f-lc – E Scot vr – Eur f – in lakes, ponds etc...*P. compressus*
   Lvs with **3** main veins – lf-tips **finely tapered** to a point – lvs 5–13 mm long × 2–4 mm wide –
   SE, E Eng, r – Eur o – in calc water..*P. acutifolius*
19 Lvs normally five-veined, 2–3 mm wide, blunt, mucronate – 2 outer veins on each side of lf **close
   together near margin** – stipules forming a closed tubular sheath – Eng N to Yorks f – rest of Br
   Isles r – Eur o-lf – on mud-bottomed lakes, ditches...*P. friesii*
   Lvs with 3, 1, or 5 veins – if 5 veins, veins equally spaced.. **20**
20 Lvs 2–4 mm wide, **v blunt**, with 3 or 5 veins – stipules forming an open sheath – Br Isles, Eur, o-
   lc – in ponds, streams..*P. obtusifolius*
   Lvs under 2 mm wide.. **21**
21 Stipules forming a **closed tubular** sheath below... **22**
   Stipules forming an **open** sheath (with overlapping edges) to stem below.................................. **23**
22 Lvs tapered to a fine point – stipules tubular only at base – Shetland, Uist, r – Denmark r – in
   lakes...*P. rutilus*
   Lvs parallel-sided, blunt-tipped but mucronate – stipules tubular for ²/₃ of their length – GB N to
   Angus f – N Scot, Ire, r – Eur f – in ponds, streams etc...*P. pusillus*
23 Lvs not over 1 mm wide, bristle-like but flattened, tapered to a fine point – midrib thick, 2 side-
   veins v indistinct – no air-spaces in lf – Eng o-lf – Wales, Scot, vr – **Ire abs** – Eur r – in ponds,
   ditches .... *P. trichoides*
   Lvs 1–2 mm wide, strap-shaped, parallel-sided, blunt-tipped but mucronate – 2 side-veins
   distinct, meeting midrib at almost 90° – air-spaces border midrib below – Br Isles f-lc – Eur c – in
   ponds, streams etc ....*P. berchtoldii* (p 448 G)

Note:* *P.* × *zizii* (*P. gramineus* × *lucens*) is like *P. gramineus*, but has lvs 2–3 cm (not 0.5–1.0 cm)
wide, and has long stipules (2–5 cm, not 1–2 cm as in *P. gramineus*).
† *P.* × *nitens* (*P. gramineus* × *perfoliatus*) is like *P. perfoliatus*, but lvs are lanceolate rather than
oval, and stipules are 1–2 cm long and do not fall off.

RUSHES, SEDGES, GRASSES   *Juncaceae, Cyperaceae, Gramineae*

Although there is not space in this book fully to describe these families, the features
used in identifying them are outlined below, while on pp 455–460 a selection is
illustrated and described. For further information, see *The Observer's Book of
Grasses, Sedges & Rushes*, Frederick Warne, London, revised edition by Francis
Rose, 1974; *Grasses*, by C.E. Hubbard, Penguin Books, Harmondsworth, 1954
(not now available from publisher); *British Sedges*, by A.C. Jermy and T.G. Tutin,
Botanical Society of the British Isles, London, 1968; and *Flora of the British Isles*,

RUSHES, SEDGES, GRASSES   *Juncaceae, Cyperaceae, Gramineae*

by A.R. Clapham, T.G. Tutin and E.F. Warburg, Cambridge University Press, 2nd edition, 1962. **Rushes, Sedges** and **Grasses** form a v important part of the world's vegetation. They are Monocotyledons, with narrow, grass-like or cylindrical lvs; fls small, usually clustered, individually inconspicuous, with perianth either abs or reduced to chaffy scales. All wind-pollinated, they have therefore, in the course of evolution, developed fls unattractive to insects.

Rushes (Family Juncaceae), slender herbs with small clustered wind-pollinated fls, are often confused with Grasses and Sedges, but in fact their individual fls (**1**) are similar in essentials to those of Lilies and Tulips, with 6 perianth segments, 6 (or, rarely, only 3) stamens, and a superior ovary with 3 stigmas. Rushes, however, differ from the Lily family in their perianth segments, which are inconspicuous, chaffy, brown or pale (conspicuous, white or coloured, petal-like in Lily family). Frs are tiny capsules which open to release seeds. In **true Rushes** (*Juncus*) lvs are **hairless**, usually **cylindrical**; and each capsule contains **many tiny seeds**. In **Wood-rushes** (*Luzula*) lvs are **hairy**, ± flat or folded grass-like, but with sheathing base v short; each capsule contains only **3** seeds.   Three examples of the Rush family are illustrated, and a few others described, on pp 455–457.

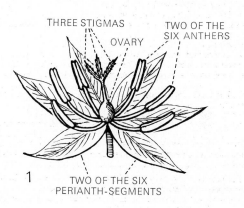

THREE STIGMAS
OVARY
TWO OF THE SIX ANTHERS
1
TWO OF THE SIX PERIANTH-SEGMENTS

Sedges (Family Cyperaceae) are grass-like plants, but stems are **solid, unjointed**, often ± triangular in cross-section, at least below; lvs in 3 vertical ranks up the stem (lvs sometimes reduced to scales in some genera). Each lf has 3 distinct parts: the **blade**; the **sheath**, a hollow cylinder below the blade, surrounding the stem, either totally encircling it or open down one side; and the **ligule**, a small flap attached to upperside of blade where it joins sheath. Fls are tiny, individually inconspicuous, and grouped into small spike-like clusters called **spikelets**. Each fl arises in axil of a chaffy scale called the **glume**; perianth is either quite abs or reduced to a few bristles, which, however, in the **Cotton Sedges** (*Eriophorum*, p 456 D, Di) become a long white cottony tuft in fr. In most genera (except *Carex* and *Kobresia*) fls are bisexual, with 3 stamens and a tiny ovary (bearing 2 or 3 stigmas), which forms a little one-seeded nutlet-like fr. In **true Sedges** (*Carex*), fls are of separate sexes and are either grouped into separate, catkin-like male and female spikelets, as in *Carex sylvatica* (p 456 F), or in mixed spikelets, usually with

453

female fls (**3**) at base of spikelet and male fls (**2**) at tip, as in *Carex otrubae* (p 456 G). In a few there is a simple terminal spike only, either with female fls below and male above as in **Flea Sedge** (*C. pulicaris*) or with male and female fls on separate plants, as in **Dioecious Sedge** (*C. dioica*). In *Carex* female fls each have a tubular sheath developed round and enclosing the nut, called the **utricle** or 'fruit', the shape of which is the **most important character** in identifying the different species.

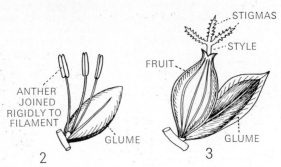

In **Grasses** (Family Gramineae) stems are **hollow**, with ± swollen joints or **nodes**; lvs, in **2** vertical ranks along the stems (3 ranks in Sedges), are otherwise as in Sedges. Fls are individually tiny and inconspicuous, without any obvious perianth, subtended by glumes and grouped into spikelets. Infl consists of either a loose, obviously branched panicle of spikelets, as in **Red Fescue** (p 458 A), and in B, C, D and G on p 458; or of a raceme of spikelets, as in **Sea Couch** (p 458 F); or else of a dense spike-like panicle, as in **Crested Dog's-tail** (p 458 E) or **Marsh Foxtail** (p 460 H). In every case infl is composed of units called **spikelets**. A typical spikelet (of *Avena*, the **Oat**) is illustrated here (**4**). At the base of each spikelet there are two bract-like chaffy scales (in Grasses called glumes), the **upper** and the **lower** glume. Each spikelet above the glumes contains either one fl (as in **Creeping Bent**, *Agrostis stolonifera*, p 458 G), 2 (or, rarely, 3) fls as in the **Oat Grasses**, or a number of fls arranged in two opp but alternating ranks, as in **Red Fescue** (p 458 A), **Sweet-grass** (p 458 B) or **Sea Couch** (p 458 F). Each fl of a grass (**5**) has two scales at its base, the lower one, called the **lemma**, usually opaque and

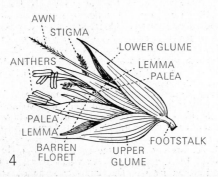

green, and the upper, called the **palea**, delicate, transparent and silvery. The fls normally have 3 stamens (only 2 in *Anthoxanthum odoratum*, key p 461), with anthers attached to the long filaments by **flexible** joints (in Sedges, anther is **rigidly** fixed to a **stiff** filament), and an ovary with two long, feathery stigmas. In some Grasses, a long bristle (the **awn**) arises from the lemma, in **Oat** (**4**) from low down on the outside, in **Red Fescue** (p 458 A) from the lemma's tip. The florets open briefly due to the swelling of two small bodies called **lodicules** (**6**) inside the fl; when pollinated they close again.

For key to all the commoner Grasses see p 460.

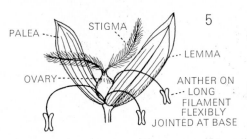

PALEA · · · STIGMA · · · 5 · · · LEMMA · · · OVARY · · · ANTHER ON · · LONG FILAMENT FLEXIBLY JOINTED AT BASE

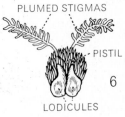

PLUMED STIGMAS · · · PISTIL · · · 6 · · · LODICULES

RUSH FAMILY   *Juncaceae* ▶

A   Common Rush, *Juncus conglomeratus*, erect, tufted per, 30–100 cm; stems, stiff, **strongly-ridged**, 2–3 mm thick, contain white spongy pith; lvs reduced to pointed sheathing scales at stem-base. Infl, apparently from **side of stem** some way below tip, is a densely-branched, rounded brown head; perianth segments (**Aa**) narrow, pointed, 2.0–2.5 mm long; fr ovoid, with a mucronate point in the concave tip. Br Isles, Eur; c in wet mds, bogs, wet wds. Fl 5–7.   **Ai   Soft Rush**, *J. effusus*, differs in **smooth**, **scarcely-ridged** stem, infl which may be **loose** or dense; and fr **without** a mucronate point in the concave tip. Br Isles, Eur; c in similar habitats. Fl 6–8.   **Aii   Hard Rush**, *J. inflexus*, has stems slenderer (1–2 mm thick) than in A, **grey**-green, strongly ridged; lateral infl a **loose** cluster of fls; frs dark brown, narrow, 4 mm long. Br Isles vc (except N and W Scot r-abs); Eur c; in damp mds, mostly on clay soils. Fl 6–8.   **Aiii   Heath Rush**, *J. squarrosus*, has tough wiry lvs in a spreading basal **rosette**, 8–15 cm long, **bent horizontally** above their sheathing bases, grooved on upper side; infl **terminal** on stem; frs obovoid, 4–6 mm long. Br Isles, Eur; f-lc in hths, moors, bogs. Fl 6–7.

B   Jointed Rush, *J. articulatus*, erect or ascending per to 80 cm tall; lvs, up stem, long, narrow-cylindrical, pointed, have internal **cross**-partitions, visible if lf opened with the thumbnail. Infl **terminal**, much-branched, loose; perianth segments pointed, dark brown; frs **ovoid**, **shiny dark brown**, 5 mm long, pointed at tips. Br Isles, Eur; c in wet mds, fens. Fl 6–9.   **Bi   Sharp-flowered Rush**, *J. acutiflorus*, is near B but more erect; infl denser, shorter, main branches spreading at nearly 90° (less than 90° in B); perianth segments pointed; frs **tapered** to long points, **elliptical**, red-brown. Br Isles, Eur; c in wet acid mds, moors, bogs. Fl 7–

9. **Bii Blunt-flowered Rush**, *J. subnodulosus*, differs from B and Bi in lvs having **both vertical and cross-partitions** inside, and in perianth segments and frs **pale** brown, **blunt**. Br Isles o-lf (E Anglia la, Scot vr); Eur f-lc; in calc fens, wet mds. Fl 7–9.

C Great Wood-rush, *Luzula sylvatica*, tufted per, 30–80 cm tall; lvs many, broad, glossy, ± fringed with long whitish hairs, 6–20 mm wide, in tussocks and up stem; infl much-branched, spreading, **terminal**, with **dark brown** fls in **clusters**; perianth segments 3.0–3.5 mm long, lanceolate, equalling pointed oval fr. Br Isles c (except mid and E Eng o); Eur f-lc; in oakwds on acid soils. Fl 5–
6. **Ci Hairy Wood-rush**, *L. pilosa*, much slenderer, shorter (15–30 cm) than C; lvs only 3–4 mm wide; infl loose, with unequal, stiff, spreading and bent back v slender branches 2–3 cm long, each with **only 1 or 2** fls at tip; frs ovoid-conical, blunt. GB c; Ire o; Eur c; in dry wds, hbs. Fl 4–6.   **Cii Field Wood-rush**, *L. campestris*, only 8–20 cm tall; fls in a loose panicle of dense brown stalked **clusters**; stamens yellow, conspicuous. Br Isles, Eur; vc in gslds. Fl 3–6.

SEDGE FAMILY *Cyperaceae*

D Hare's-tail Cotton Sedge, *Eriophorum vaginatum*, tussock-forming per; lvs from base, long (10–20 cm), bristle-like (to 1 mm wide), three-angled; stems, smooth, slender, 30–50 cm tall, round below, three-angled above, bear pale **inflated sheaths** with v short lf-blades. Infls of a **single** oval spikelet at each stem-tip, 2 cm long in fl, 3 cm in fr; **each** fl (**Da**) with silvery-black glume, 3 golden stamens and an ovary with 3 stigmas; in fr the bristles around the heads elongate to form a **pure white hares-tail-like tuft**. Br Isles, vc in N and W, r in SE, E, mid Eng; Eur, vr to S, f-lc to N; in acid sphagnum bogs, peaty moors, wet hths. Fl 4–
5. **Di Common Cotton Sedge**, *E. angustifolium*, differs from D in its creeping rhizomes, **broader** (3–6 mm) **channelled** lvs with three-angled ± purplish points, and in infls each of **several** white-haired spikelets at top of each fl-stem. Br Isles, Eur, c except in v cultivated areas; in bog pools, acid fens. Fl 6–7.

E Sea Club-rush, *Scirpus maritimus*, tall (30–100 cm) erect herb with **three-angled** stems bearing keeled lvs 10 mm wide, and infls of ± branched clusters of dark brown, oval spikelets 10–20 mm long at stem-tips, with several long, lfy bracts below infl. Fls have each 3 yellow stamens **and** 3 white stigmas. Coasts of Br Isles, Eur; f-lc on tidal river banks, brackish ponds and ditches. Fl 7–
8. **Ei Bulrush**, *S.* (*Schoenoplectus*) *lacustris*, has ± **lfless**, **cylindrical** stems, 1–3 m tall; infl as in E, but red-brown and apparently lateral on stem. Br Isles, Eur; f-lc in freshwater rivers, lakes. Fl 6–7.

F Wood Sedge, *Carex sylvatica*, erect tufted per, 20–60 cm tall, with many fresh green keeled lvs, 3–6 mm wide, from the base; stems, slender, bear spaced along them 3–4 drooping, cylindrical, long-stalked spikelets of female fls, each with a lfy bract, and also a single, terminal spikelet of male fls. Female fls have pale brown, oval, pointed glumes, and ellipsoidal, **long-beaked**, green frs (**Fa**); male fls have a narrow pale brown glume and 3 yellow stamens. Br Isles, Eur, c (except N Scot r); in wds on less acid soils. Fl 5–7, fr 7–9.

G False Fox Sedge, *C. otrubae*, erect tufted per, 60–90 cm tall; lvs from base and up stem, 4–10 mm wide, with **rough** edges; infl a **dense** cylindrical panicle of unstalked 1-cm-long spikelets, each with a long bract. In **each spikelet lower fls** are female (**Ga**), forming oval, greenish frs 5–6 mm long, turning brown when ripe, tapered to a shortly forked beak, convex outside, flat within; **upper** fls are male, with 3 stamens only. Glumes subtending fls oval, pointed, with translucent brownish margins and green midrib. Br Isles c (except N Scot r-abs); Eur f-lc; in ditches, marshes, by riversides. Fl 6–7; fr 7–9.

A Red Fescue, *Festuca rubra*, a tufted grass 10–70 cm tall, hairy or not, with runners producing new plants; root-lvs bristle-like, grooved above, 10–30 cm long; stem-lvs **flat**, 0.5–3.0 mm wide, with **closed** sheaths (see picture p 62). Infl a pyramidal panicle, 3–15 cm long, of many stalked spikelets (**Aa**) 7–14 mm, each with 4–8 florets; glumes lanceolate; lemmas lanceolate, with short **awns** at their tips. Br Isles, Eur; vc in gslds, hbs, mds, dunes etc. Fl 5–7.   **Ai Sheep's Fescue**, *F. ovina*, smaller (10–30 cm tall), tufted, without runners; lvs shorter (5–12 cm long), **all** bristle-like with **open** sheaths (see picture p 62); spikelets only 3–7 mm long. Br Isles, Eur; c in dry gslds. Fl 5–6.

B Floating Sweet-grass, *Glyceria fluitans*, erect or ascending hairless grass 25–90 cm long, with creeping, rooting stems, often floating; lvs flat, pointed, rough, 5–6 mm wide, with smooth sheaths; ligule to 15 mm long, silvery, jagged. Panicle usually unbranched, with ± cigar-shaped grey-green spikelets 15–30 mm long, of **many** florets; glumes and lemmas one-veined, membrane-like; lemmas 7–9, **blunt**, awnless. Br Isles, Eur; c in still or slow moving fresh water and on mud. Fl 5–8.

C Annual Meadow-grass, *Poa annua*, tufted ann grass 5–30 cm tall, sometimes creeping; lvs flat, blunt, keeled, smooth, narrowed to tip, often **wrinkled** transversely near base; sheaths **smooth**, flattened; ligule 2–3 mm long, **blunt**. Infl with spreading branches like a little fir tree, 1–4 branches arising in a whorl; spikelets 3–5 mm long, lanceolate, with 3–5 florets closely packed; lemmas oval, five-veined, with translucent edges and no awns. Br Isles, Eur, va everywhere. Fl 1–12.   **Ci Rough Meadow-grass**, *P. trivialis*, per, taller, erect (20–60 cm); has similar whorled spreading panicles of spikelets with 2–4 florets, but ligules to 8 mm **long**, **pointed**; lf-sheaths **rough**. Br Isles, Eur; va in mds, wds, wa etc. Fl 6–7.

D Yellow Oat-grass, *Trisetum flavescens*, erect per grass 20–50 cm, with runners; lvs flat, downy above; ligules v short, truncate; panicle oblong with spreading branches in whorls; spikelets **yellowish**, each with 2–4 florets; lemmas lanceolate, shiny, with a **long awn** arising from **back** of each. Br Isles (except N Scot r), Eur c; in mds, gslds. Fl 5–6.

E Crested Dog's-tail, *Cynosurus cristatus*, erect hairless wiry tufted per grass, 15–70 cm tall; flat smooth lvs, 2 mm wide, and smooth sheaths; panicle erect, ± oblong, dense, spike-like, spikelets several on each branch, **all turned** to one side of spike; upper spikelet of each cluster fertile, with a few fls; lower spikelets sterile, with narrow rigid empty lemmas. Lemmas of fertile fls ± cylindrical, shortly awned, downy. Br Isles, Eur; c in gslds, mds. Fl 6–8.

F Sea Couch, *Agropyron pungens*, tufted, tough, **grey-green** hairless per grass, 30–90 cm tall, with creeping rhizomes; lvs inrolled, v stiff, rough on the strongly-ridged upper sides, pointed, 10–20 cm long. Infl a spike of many spikelets in two alt ranks close-set up each side of stem; each spikelet fan-shaped, **broadside-on** to stem, with 2 glumes at base shorter than the florets; lemmas lanceolate, blunt, v shortly awned, 4–6-veined. Br Isles: coasts of Eng and Wales N to Cumberland c; Ire o; Eur: N to S Denmark f; in salt marshes on banks near sea and estuaries. Fl 7–9.   **Fi Common Couch**, *A. repens*, is fresh green, not grey-green; lvs **flat**, only **weakly**-ridged above, with scattered long hairs. Br Isles, Eur; vc in gslds, ar, wa, rds etc. Fl 6–9.   **Fii Perennial Rye-grass**, *Lolium perenne*, differs from Fi in being softer; spikelets alt up the stem as in F and Fi, but **edgeways** on, each with only one (outer) glume. Br Isles, Eur; vc in gslds, mds, wa. Fl 5–8.

G Creeping Bent, *Agrostis stolonifera*, per grass with creeping lfy **runners**; lvs flat, rough, linear-**lanceolate**, 2–5 mm wide, with ligules to **5 mm long**, rounded and jagged at tips; infls with spreading whorled branches as in C, but spikelets only 1.5–3.0 mm long, each containing only **one** fl; glumes and lemma lanceolate-oval, pointed, awnless, grey-green to pale brown. Br Isles, Eur: vc in mds, gslds, wa.   Fl

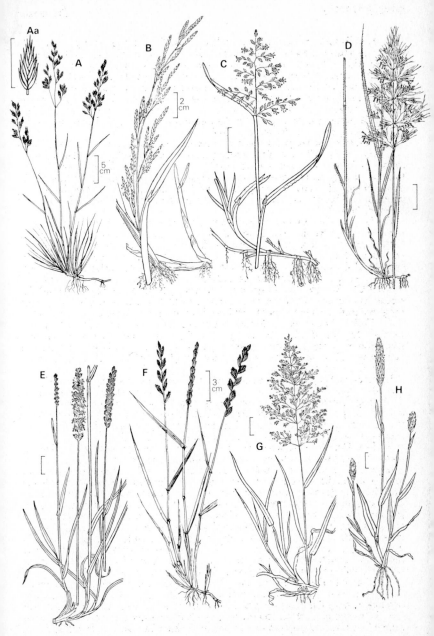

◀ 7–8. **Gi Common Bent**, *A. tenuis*, is tufted, **without** lfy runners but with underground rhizomes; ligules of lvs on sterile shoots **v short** (not over 1 mm long), broader than long; panicle open in fr (closed up in fr in G). Br Isles, Eur; c in dry acid gslds. Fl 6–8.

H Marsh Foxtail, *Alopecurus geniculatus*, creeping and rooting per grass 15–40 cm tall, with the erect fl-stems bending upwards abruptly from the gd; lvs linear-lanceolate, rough above, with inflated sheaths and ligules 5 mm long. Infl cylindrical, foxtail-like, blunt, 2–4 cm long, with densely packed ± stalkless one-fld spikelets 2–3 mm long; glumes silky-hairy, lanceolate, **blunt**; lemmas truncate, with **awns** ± twice their length. Br Isles, Eur; f-lc in wet mds, pond edges. Fl 6–7. **Hi Meadow Foxtail**, *A. pratensis*, **erect**, **tufted** per grass without runners, 30–90 cm tall; infl 4–8 cm long; spikelets have both glumes and lemmas pointed, awns twice length of lemmas. Br Isles, Eur; c in mds, gslds, Fl 4–6. **Hii Cat's-tail**, *Phleum bertolonii*, resembles Hi, but spikelets have each **2 ± equal**, **awned**, bristly-edged glumes, and the lemma of the single floret in each spikelet has **no** awn. Br Isles, Eur; c in gslds. Fl 7.

KEY TO THE COMMONER BRITISH GRASSES

1 Basal lvs bristle-like, not easily flattened **2**
  Basal lvs flat, or, if bristle-like when dry, can be flattened easily with thumbnail **8**
2 Scales of florets with silvery translucent margins **3**
  Scales of florets opaque, greenish, purple or brown **5**
3 Plants ann, small (under 15 cm tall), slender – on dry open sandy gd **4**
  Plants per, robustly tufted – on hths, in dry wdlands on sandy soil ....*Deschampsia flexuosa*
4 Lf-sheaths rough, panicle open .... *Aira caryophyllea*
  Lf-sheaths smooth, panicle close – on dry open sandy gd ....*Aira praecox*
5 Lvs bent back at 90° to whitish sheaths – panicle narrow, one-sided, with purple narrow pointed
  lemmas – on moors, hths .... *Nardus stricta*
  Lvs not at 90° to sheath **6**
6 Ligules to 4 mm, acute – awn from low on back of lemma – glumes greenish to brownish – on dry
  hths.. *Agrostis setacea*
  Ligules v short or abs – if awned, awns on **tips** of green lemmas.............................. **7**
7 Runners present – stem-lvs flat when fresh – spikelets 8–14 mm long – on hbs, downs, mds etc......
  .... *Festuca rubra* (p 458 A)
  Runners abs – stem-lvs always tightly rolled – spikelets 4–7 mm long, lemmas awned – on chk
  downs .... *Festuca ovina* (p 458 Ai)
  Runners abs – stem-lvs always tightly rolled – spikelets 3–6 mm long, lemmas unawned – on
  grassy hths .... *Festuca tenuifolia*
8 Ligule a fringe of hairs only **9**
  Ligule a membraneous flap **10**
9 Tall reed (1–2 m) – c in marshes, swamps .... *Phragmites communis*
  Tussocky grass (30–50 cm) – lvs long, flat, grey-green, – on damp hthlds ....*Molinia coerulea*
  Small grass (15–23 cm) – few swollen oval silvery spikelets, 3–5 mm long – on dry hths..................
  .... *Sieglingia decumbens*
10 Panicle densely spike-like.. **11**
  Panicle loose, ± obviously branched **16**
  Panicle with sessile or v short-stalked spikelets arranged alt up it on each side, singly or in groups
  of 2 or 3 .... **45**
11 Spikelets each only one-fld **12**
  Spikelets each with 2 or more fertile fls **14**
12 Spikelet **stalks** bear long stiff bristles – ann grass of waste gd .... *Setaria* spp
  Spikelet **stalks** without long stiff bristles **13**

13 Lemmas within spikelets awned, glumes not awned – panicle soft – in mds.................................
Alopecurus pratensis (p 460 Hi)
Lemmas awnless, glumes sharp-pointed – panicle stiff – on drier mds, downs.................................
Phleum bertolonii (p 460 Hii)
Lemmas and glumes awnless – panicle v long (7–15 cm), grey green – lvs inrolled, to 40 cm long
– on seaside sand-dunes ....*Ammophila arenaria*
14 Lemmas short-awned at tip – panicle with spikelets all turned to one side – on dry gslds.................
Cynosurus cristatus (p 458 E)
Lemmas awned on back – panicle oblong, not one-sided – lvs smelling of vanilla when bruised –
c in all dry gslds ....*Anthoxanthum odoratum*
Lemmas awnless...**15**
15 Ligule short – lvs keeled, hairless – panicle silvery – anthers blue – on limestone in N of GB............
Sesleria coerulea
Ligule short – lvs narrow, hairy – panicle silvery – anthers yellow – on chk downs, sand dunes..........
Koeleria gracilis
Ligule long – lvs wide, reed-like – panicle grey-green – in marshy places ....*Phalaris arundinacea*
16 Spikelets one-fld **17**
Spikelets 2 – to many-fld..**23**
17 Stiff salt-marsh grass – several spikelets arranged like fingers of a hand.............*Spartina townsendii*
Tall, reed-like grass – tufts of white hairs at base of lemmas – in damp open wds.........................
Calamagrostis epigeios
Grass not reed-like – not tufts of hairs in spikelets...**18**
18 Infl loose, glumes egg-shaped, large, shining purple-brown – in dry wds.................*Melica uniflora*
Infl whorled...**19**
19 Lemmas with silky straight awns over 5 mm long ....*Apera spica-venti*
Lemmas with awns short or abs..**20**
20 Glumes brown, only half as long as green lemma – lvs keeled – in water or swamps ....
Catabrosa aquatica
Glumes as long as lemma – lvs flat – grass not aquatic..**21**
21 Tall grass, 40–80 cm high – florets shining, whitish – lvs wide (10–15 mm), greyish, strap-shaped
– in dry wds...*Milium effusum*
Shorter grass – florets purplish, brown or green – lvs narrower, lanceolate............ (*Agrostis* spp) **22**
22 Ligules long, acute – awns shortly projecting from spikelets – in bogs, damp acid wds, hths.............
Agrostis canina
Ligules long, blunt – awns abs – in gslds, moist mds.........................*Agrostis stolonifera* (p 458 G)
Ligules v short, truncate or abs – no awns visible – in acid gslds, hths.......*Agrostis tenuis* (p 460 Gi)
23 Spikelets 2–3-fld, short, wide – awns usually arising from **backs** of lemmas...............................**24**
Spikelets 3– to many-fld, ovoid or elongated – awns, if present, from *tips* of lemmas **29**
24 Spikelets 10–30 mm – awns 12–60 mm, usually abruptly bent...**25**
Spikelets 2–11 mm – awns to 17 mm..**26**
25 Spikelets erect – lvs downy – per of chk downs ....*Helictotrichon pubescens*
Spikelets erect – lvs greyish, hairless – per of chk downs ....*H. pratense*
Spikelets drooping – ann weeds of cultivated gd ....*Avena* spp
26 Florets 2, upper bisexual, awned or not, lower male, awned – tall grass with whorled panicle – on
mds, rdsides..*Arrhenatherum elatius*
Florets 2 or 3, lowest one bisexual..**27**
27 Glumes hairy, not shining – lower lemma awnless – in mds......................................*Holcus lanatus*
Glumes hairless, shining – lower lemma awned..**28**
28 Awn from middle of lemma – florets yellow – lemmas pointed – on mds,
downs ....*Trisetum flavescens* (p 458 D)
Awn from near base of lemma – florets silvery brown – lemmas blunt – lvs 3–4 mm wide, rough
when rubbed downwards, many-grooved – in moist wds, wet mds............*Deschampsia caespitosa*
29 Lemmas keeled, compressed laterally..**30**
Lemmas rounded at least on back below..**35**
30 Spikelets in dense clusters on long stiff unwhorled panicle branches – lemmas short-awned at tip
– lvs rigidly keeled – in mds, pastures..*Dactylis glomerata*
Spikelets in loose whorled panicles – lemmas unawned .... (*Poa*) **31**
31 Ligule long – stems tufted – no creeping rhizomes..**32**
Ligule short – creeping rhizomes present...**33**

32 Blade shining below – lvs stiff, unwrinkled, sheath rough – per of mds, wds..*Poa trivialis* (p 458 Ci)
Blade dull below – lvs flaccid, wrinkled in places, sheath smooth – ann of cultivated gd and wa ....
Poa annua (p 458 C)
33 Stem flattened, ribbon-like – on dry gd, wall tops..*Poa compressa*
Stem round.. **34**
34 Blades hooded at tip, 2–4 mm wide – spikelets 4–6 mm – in gslds etc........................*Poa pratensis*
Blades fine-pointed, narrow, 1–2 mm – spikelets 2–3 mm – in shady places.............*Poa nemoralis*
35 Lemmas blunt, awnless.. **36**
Lemmas pointed, awned or not at tip **39**
36 Spikelets short, plump, nodding, v long-stalked – on mds, downs .... *Briza media*
Spikelets elongated, narrow, erect or spreading **37**
37 Lemmas seven-veined – spikelets 15–30 mm long – sheaths tubular – in or by fresh water..............
Glyceria spp
Lemmas five-veined – spikelets to 12 mm long.. **38**
38 Rigid grass, 5–10 cm tall, with spiky infl branches – ann of dry gd .... *Catapodium rigidum*
Tufted, not so rigid grasses, with runners – in salt-marshes or brackish mud – usually per ....
Puccinellia spp
39 Glumes v unequal – lemmas v long, narrow, tapering into long awns – ann plants .... *Vulpia* spp
Glumes ± equal – lemmas oval-oblong, awned or not – per or ann plants **40**
40 Awns tapering from the lemma apex, or lemma merely pointed ....(*Festuca* spp) **41**
Awns in a little notch at lemma apex .... (*Bromus* spp) **42**
41 Lvs to 6 mm wide, no auricles – lemmas pointed but not awned – in mds.............*Festuca pratensis*
Lvs to 20 mm wide, with purple claw-like auricles – lemmas long-awned – in wds on basic soils.......
Festuca gigantea
42 Lf-sheaths with stiff white bristles – tall grass of wds...*Bromus ramosus*
Lf-sheaths without stiff bristles – not in wds **43**
43 Spikelets ovoid, conical, swollen – on mds, rds .... *Bromus mollis*
Spikelets compressed, elongated, long-awned **44**
44 Spikelets on stalks 5–10 cm long, drooping – blades 2–7 mm wide, softly hairy – ann grass of dry
places..*Bromus sterilis*
Spikelets on shorter stalks, to 5 cm long, erect – blades 2–3 mm wide, stiffly hairy on margins –
per grass of chk gslds...*Bromus erectus*
45 Alt spikelets borne singly up stem.. **46**
Alt spikelets in clusters up the stem **48**
46 Spikelets edge-on to stem – on mds, downs etc....................................*Lolium perenne* (p 458 Fii)
Spikelets broadside-on to stem **47**
47 Spikelets stalkless, ± fan-shaped .... *Agropyron* spp
Spikelets shortly-stalked, long, conical or cylindrical.....................................*Brachypodium* spp **49**
48 Spikelets in pairs, large and greyish – on **sand-dunes only**....................................*Elymus arenarius*
Spikelets in triplets, bristly and barley-like ....(*Hordeum* spp) **50**
49 Lvs soft, downy, yellow-green – spikelets drooping – awns as long as lemmas – in wds, scrub ....
Brachypodium sylvaticum
Lvs rigid, ± hairless, green to orange-green – spikelets erect – awns shorter than lemmas –
on calc gslds .... *Brachypodium pinnatum*
50 Uppermost lf-sheath inflated – in mds ....*Hordeum secalinum*
Uppermost lf-sheath not inflated – on rds, dry places ....*Hordeum murinum*

INDEX TO KEYS

INDEX

This index gives scientific but not English family names. Both scientific and English names of species are included, the former under generic headings; the few scientific synonyms given are set in brackets. English plant names are normally listed under the last word of the name, but readers should also look under the first or middle word, eg, to find Purple Viper's-bugloss look up 'Viper's'. In a few cases, where popular names suggest that a plant belongs to a different genus from the one it is actually in (eg, 'Bermuda Buttercup'), the English name may be indexed under both component words.